CULTURE IN NAZI GERMANY

OTHER BOOKS BY MICHAEL H. KATER

*Das "Ahnenerbe" der SS, 1935–1945: Ein Beitrag zur Kulturpolitik des
Dritten Reiches* (1974)

*Studentenschaft und Rechtsradikalismus in Deutschland, 1918–1933:
Eine sozialgeschichtliche Studie zur Bildungskrise in der Weimarer Republik* (1975)

The Nazi Party: A Social Profile of Members and Leaders, 1919–1945 (1983)

Doctors under Hitler (1989)

Different Drummers: Jazz in the Culture of Nazi Germany (1992)

The Twisted Muse: Musicians and their Music in the Third Reich (1997)

Composers of the Nazi Era: Eight Portraits (2000)

Hitler Youth (2004)

Never Sang for Hitler: The Life and Times of Lotte Lehmann, 1888–1976 (2008)

Weimar: From Enlightenment to the Present (2014)

Culture in Nazi Germany

Michael H. Kater

YALE UNIVERSITY PRESS
NEW HAVEN AND LONDON

For information about this and other Yale University Press publications, please contact:
U.S. Office: sales.press@yale.edu   yalebooks.com
Europe Office: sales@yaleup.co.uk   yalebooks.co.uk

Set in Adobe Caslon Pro by IDSUK (DataConnection) Ltd
Printed in Great Britain by Gomer Press Ltd, Llandysul, Ceredigion, Wales

Library of Congress Control Number: 2018967785

ISBN 978-0-300-21141-2

A catalogue record for this book is available from the British Library.

10 9 8 7 6 5 4 3 2 1

For Georgia

Contents

CONTENTS

Illustrations

1. Wassily Kandinsky, *On White II* (1923). © Centre Pompidou, MNAM-CCI, Dist. RMN-Grand Palais / Image Centre Pompidou, MNAM-CCI.
2. A watercolor painting allegedly by Adolf Hitler. Adrian Sherratt / Alamy Stock Photo.
3. A portrait of composer Carl Orff (1920). Lebrecht Music & Arts / Alamy Stock Photo.
4. A portrait of actress Hansi Burg (1926). Ullstein bild Dtl. / Getty Images.
5. Carola Neher, Rudolf Forster, and Valeska Gert on the set of the film *The Threepenny Opera* (1931). Glasshouse Images / Alamy Stock Photo.
6. Nazi Party officials at a gymnastic exhibition in Stuttgart (1933). Everett Collection Historical / Alamy Stock Photo.
7. A charcoal drawing of Adolf Hitler by H. Oloffs. Universal History Archive / Getty Images.
8. A photograph of Bertolt Brecht (1930s). Chronicle / Alamy Stock Photo.
9. Hubert Lanzinger, *The Standard Bearer* (1934).
10. The front page of Nuremberg Gauleiter Julius Streicher's anti-Semitic weekly *Der Stürmer*. Special issue (May 1, 1934). PRISMA ARCHIVO / Alamy Stock Photo.
11. A reproduction of Arnold Schoenberg, *Self Portrait* (1935). SPUTNIK / Alamy Stock Photo.

12. Adolf Hitler, Willy Liebel, and Albert Speer at the Nuremberg Reich Party rally site (*c.* 1936). ImageBROKER / Alamy Stock Photo.

13. Marlene Dietrich and Erich Maria Remarque in Paris (1937). Everett Collection Historical / Alamy Stock Photo.

14. The cover of the exhibition guide to the Nazi "Degenerate Art" show in Munich (July 1937). Author's archive.

15. The cover of the exhibition guide to the Nazis' "Degenerate Music" show in Düsseldorf (May 1938). Author's archive.

16. A page from the exhibition guide to the Nazis' "Degenerate Music" show in Düsseldorf (May 1938). Author's archive.

17. Elk Eber, *Thus was the SA* (1938). The Picture Art Collection / Alamy Stock Photo.

18. A poster for the German film *Wunschkonzert*, starring Ilse Werner (1940). Ullstein bild Dtl. / Getty Images.

19. Ferdinand Marian in the Nazi propaganda film *Jud Süss* (1940). Photo 12 / Alamy Stock Photo.

20. The cover for Ernst Hiemer, *The Mongrel and Other Thought-Provoking Tales* (1940). Author's archive.

21. A painting of Erwin Rommel by Wolfgang Willrich (1940–1). Ullstein bild Dtl. / Getty Images.

22. A photograph of a Luftwaffe correspondent handing his film reels to a motorcyclist (*c.* 1941). INTERFOTO / Alamy Stock Photo.

23. A photograph of Gerhart Hauptmann being modeled by Arno Breker, October 26, 1942. The Print Collector / Alamy Stock Photo.

24. Franz Eichhorst, *The Memory of Stalingrad* (1943). History and Art Collection / Alamy Stock Photo.

25. Hans Albers in the film *Baron Münchhausen* (1943). World History Archive / Alamy Stock Photo.

26. Nobel laureate Thomas Mann making an anti-Nazi broadcast in Los Angeles (1943). Pictorial Press Ltd / Alamy Stock Photo.

27. A portrait of film actress Margot Hielscher (1950s). INTERFOTO / Alamy Stock Photo.

28. Gustaf Gründgens as Mephisto in Goethe's drama *Faust II* (1959). Dpa picture alliance / Alamy Stock Photo.

29. A portrait of composer Werner Egk (May 1981). Keystone Pictures USA / Alamy Stock Photo.

30. A portrait of author Ernst Jünger (1986). INTERFOTO / Alamy Stock Photo.

Abbreviations

AEG	Allgemeine Elektrizitätsgesellschaft
ARD	Arbeitsgemeinschaft der öffentlich-rechtlichen Rundfunkanstalten der Bundesrepublik Deutschland (=First Channel, Public Television, Germany)
BBC	British Broadcasting Corporation
BMW	Bayerische Motoren-Werke
BZ	*Berliner Zeitung*
CBE	Commander of the Most Excellent Order of the British Empire
CBS	Columbia Broadcasting System
CDU	Christlich Demokratische Union Deutschlands (German Christian Democratic Union)
CSR	Czechoslovak Republic
DAF	Deutsche Arbeitsfront (German Labor Front)
DAZ	*Deutsche Allgemeine Zeitung*
DDP	Deutsche Demokratische Partei (German Democratic Party)
DNB	Deutsches Nachrichtenbüro (German News Bureau)
DNVP	Deutschnationale Volkspartei (German National People's Party)
DSt	Deutsche Studentenschaft (German Student Union)

DTU	Deutsches Tanz- und Unterhaltungsorchester (German Dance and Entertainment Orchestra)
FDP	Freie Demokratische Partei Deutschlands (German Free Democratic Party)
FZ	*Frankfurter Zeitung*
Gestapo	Geheime Staatspolizei (secret police)
HJ	Hitlerjugend (Hitler Youth)
KdF	Kraft durch Freude (Strength through Joy)
KdF-Wagen	Kraft-durch-Freude-Wagen (=Volkswagen)
KfdK	Kampfbund für deutsche Kultur (Combat League for German Culture)
KPD	Kommunistische Partei Deutschlands (German Communist Party)
MGM	Metro-Goldwyn-Mayer
NEP	New Economic Policy
NR	*Neue Rundschau*
NS	Nationalsozialistisch (Nazi)
NSBO	Nationalsozialistische Betriebszellenorganisation (National Socialist Shop Organization)
NSDAP	Nationalsozialistische Deutsche Arbeiterpartei (Nazi Party)
NSDStB	Nationalsozialistischer Deutscher Studentenbund (National Socialist German Students' League)
NSKG	Nationalsozialistische Kulturgemeinde (National Socialist Cultural Community)
OMGUS	Office of Military Government of the United States for Germany
OSS	Office of Strategic Services
PEN	Poets, Essayists, Novelists (=PEN International)
PK	Propaganda-Kompanie
PNF	Partito Nazionale Fascista (National Fascist Party)
POW	Prisoner of war
Promi	Reichsministerium für Volksaufklärung und Propaganda (Reich Propaganda Ministry)
RAD	Reichsarbeitsdienst (Reich Labor Service)
RKK	Reichskulturkammer (Reich Culture Chamber)

RMK	Reichsmusikkammer (Reich Music Chamber)
RRG	Reichs-Rundfunk-Gesellschaft (Reich Broadcasting Corporation)
RSK	Reichsschrifttumskammer (Reich Literature Chamber)
SA	Sturm-Abteilungen (storm troopers)
SD	Sicherheitsdienst (security service of the SS)
SPD	Sozialdemokratische Partei Deutschlands (German Social-Democratic Party)
SRP	Sozialistische Reichspartei Deutschlands (German Socialist Reich Party)
SS	Schutzstaffel (protection squadron)
UCLA	University of California at Los Angeles
U.S.S.R.	Union of Soviet Socialist Republics
VB	*Völkischer Beobachter*
VDA	Verband Deutscher Architekten

Preface

Revolutions are never reduced to the purely political;
from there they affect all other functions of human existence.
Neither the economy or culture, nor the sciences
and the arts remain untouched by them.

Joseph Goebbels, November 1933[1]

THIS BOOK PRESENTS the story of culture in the Third Reich. In particular it examines how various branches of culture were utilized to control the masses and, after 1938, dedicated to the Nazi purpose of European if not world subjugation. But it also looks at how the workings of totalitarianism impacted the arts and artists themselves.

The relationship between culture and tyranny is complex – and whether or not culture is even possible in a dictatorship remains a ripe question. If the aesthetic, formal, and ethical power of culture thrives on contradiction to prevailing social and political norms, or even the exposition of unresolved tensions, then it will arguably always fail under tyranny. The Nazis nipped aesthetic pluralism in the bud when Hitler came to power in early 1933. Nor did the arts and letters ever attain sovereign originality under the dictator. Nonetheless there was a concerted effort to create a National Socialist aesthetic – an effort which links to the Nazis' increasingly pervasive control over German life, and their war aims. So although we already know in broader terms that culture was pressed into totalitarian uses by Nazi agencies, led by the Propaganda Ministry, looking at how this was achieved in more detail, how a new Nazi culture was constructed (and what was eliminated), as well as how this all fitted into a wider agenda of annihilation of the Jews, other Nazi-nonconformist groups, and coveted territorial dominance, should reveal much about the nature and inner workings of the Third Reich. Such is this book's undertaking.

The book's first contention is that in order for a new Nazi type of culture to take hold, the preceding forms first had to be wiped out. This mainly affected the artistic and intellectual achievements most hated by the Nazis, those of the Weimar Republic, whose aesthetic and political hallmark was Modernism. The police controls Hitler used to carry out purges in political and social contexts were also used against Modernist art forms and their creators. We shall see the various other mechanisms the Nazis used to stamp out Modernism and what they put in its place. We shall also see how far the Modernists were able to withstand this assault and when, if at all, they had to concede defeat.

Chapter 2 will look at how, once a new Nazi type of culture was in place, it fitted into a totalitarian pattern of governance in the pre-war years. The cultural forms of music, film, radio, the press, the visual arts and architecture, live theater and literature, supplied the content that Propaganda Minister Joseph Goebbels, above all others of Hitler's cronies, needed in order to intimidate or encourage the masses, and ultimately control them under his and Hitler's tyrannical regime. Goebbels ingeniously organized these art forms in a conveniently pliable system of, eventually, six culture chambers as early as the fall of 1933, which he personally oversaw and could manipulate. How these different elements of culture were utilized politically and socially will be examined, as well as how effectively such control was exercised and what happened to the cultural media and their creators in the process.

Chapters 3 and 4 will look at Jews in the Nazi cultural establishment, and how the uses of culture shifted when Germany was at war. We know today that at the dawn of World War II one of Hitler's main aims had already been well realized: the exclusion of the Jews from the German völkisch community. What we know less about, however, is the significance of the Jews in the formation of Weimar culture, and how those Jews were dealt with after January 1933. It will be shown to what extent Nazi culture, such as it was, was used to move forward the total elimination of the Jews. As should become clearer in this book, anti-Semitism was expressed through the Nazi arts, and the historian today can point to many human tragedies in the retracing of that course. The war itself further defined the arts in Germany, new and of older vintage, squarely in terms of service to the recently constructed totalitarian polity, with a dedicated martial purpose after 1938. We shall see what specific qualities in the arts were employed to render culture serviceable in this fashion, and how this affected the artists themselves. We shall also see how far the wartime uses of culture had a bearing on the final outcome of the conflict for the regime's leadership and its subjects.

It is already well known that after 1933, part of German culture, traditionalist and Modernist, was carried on in countries other than Germany, where anti-Nazi émigrés attempted to take root. Chapter 5 will look at these efforts as well as the lines of continuity that existed from German-defined art to émigré art, with the outbreak of World War II as a possible caesura. Many refugees have described how the lives and work of artists and men and women of letters changed in emigration substantially. The unusual case of Nobel laureate Thomas Mann, who continued with his work as an émigré in almost exactly the same manner as he had done before his exodus, therefore deserves special attention. It remains to be seen why, if Mann had withstood the trauma of exile and continued to write so prolifically, he was not welcomed back to Germany after the war, as well as why he himself did not wish to return to a society that had once included him as its member.

Chapter 6 will consider the ways in which the creative class after 1945 attempted to revive true culture in a Germany emancipating itself from the Nazi past. It will be shown how such a resurrection was hampered and delayed by surviving functionaries of the Nazi cultural establishment, who tried to sabotage fresh initiatives embedded in a new democracy, and by political turncoats who usually were more of a hindrance than a help.

This book is not only the story of culture in Nazi Germany, however incomplete it may necessarily have to be, but also a new history of the Third Reich from 1933 to 1945, told from the vantage point of culture, its protagonists and detractors. It builds on earlier studies of culture in Germany

I have published in the past, some with an emphasis on music. A strong catalyst for writing this book was my participation in the pioneering Miller Symposium on the arts in the Third Reich, organized by Francis R. Nicosia and Jonathan Huener at the University of Vermont in the spring of 2004.[2] Those scholars must be commended even now for having asked fresh questions and encouraging the symposium's participants to look further and perhaps find some answers.

A prior, single-volume history of culture under the Nazis does not exist bar a few exceptions.[3] An early milestone in the field is Joseph Wulf's five volumes, each of which looks at a different aspect of culture in the Third Reich. But Wulf's work consists of edited selections of printed primary sources, mostly newspaper and journal pieces, rather than overarching analysis. There are also other important, sometimes even pioneering, partial studies. Outstanding interpretations of film in the Third Reich have been contributed by Eric Rentschler, David Hull, and David Welch, lately also by Bill Niven, and of the press by Bernd Sösemann; literature has been expertly analyzed by Ralf Schnell and music by Fred K. Prieberg, Erik Levi, and Pamela M. Potter.[4] In the visual arts, the writings of Jonathan Petropoulos have long been pace-setting, and both he and Potter have in more recent times provided important monographs that come close to a more global treatment of the arts under Hitler, each in its own fashion.[5]

Some of the work for this book goes back to a time when I began enjoying the active support (as I still do now) of York University's research funding connected to my research chair, as well as the support of four major granting agencies. First was a Guggenheim Fellowship in the 1970s. Next to the rescue came the Canada Council Killam Foundation (Ottawa), which granted me a Senior Killam Fellowship twice, to relieve me of teaching for a total of four years. Third, the Social Sciences and Humanities Research Council of Canada (SSHRC) in Ottawa supported me many times over the decades, financing research in the field, and finally the Alexander von Humboldt-Stiftung in Bonn awarded me a Konrad-Adenauer Research Prize for field work in the 1990s and beyond. To all these institutions, without whose help this book could not have been written, I once again extend my heartfelt thanks. The most recent research in Canada was enabled by the inter-library-loan offices of York University, where I had the good fortune of being assisted by four skilled librarians, Gladys Fung, Mary

Lehane, Samantha McWilliams, and Sandra Snell. As they have done before, they helped me again not only in their capacity as librarians, but as research assistants who secured and processed sources for me even when I thought they could never be obtained.

Friends like William E. Seidelman, Herman Schornstein, and Kevin Cook, as well as, especially, my wife Barbara and I, had countless discussions about problem areas and confrontational situations that may have paralleled some in our present day, as global politics seems to be moving in the direction of authoritarianism once again – a political climate in which violations against what should always be autonomous, inviolable, culture, with all its manifestations, occur all too easily. Not least with these thoughts in mind, parts of my manuscript received a careful screening by sage colleagues, Peter Loewenberg, Hans R. Vaget, and Claudio Duran, who read one chapter each with constructive feedback, for which they deserve my gratitude. Alex Ross read the whole manuscript, and his subsequent constructive suggestions are much appreciated. Much credit finally must go to Heather McCallum, Marika Lysandrou, Rachael Lonsdale, and Clarissa Sutherland of Yale University Press. Heather was always at my side offering generous but firm guidelines, and Marika, Rachael, and Clarissa expertly helped turn the manuscript into print. Should there be any mistakes in this book, I alone am accountable for them.

CHAPTER ONE

◆ ◆ ◆

Deconstructing Modernism

A FTER THEIR ASSUMPTION of political power on January 30, 1933, the National Socialists systematically set out to destroy Modernism in the arts throughout Germany, to make room for their own kind of culture, but they had made plans to do this several years before. They wished German culture to be related to the core values of their ideology, representational not abstract, clear and clean aesthetics and not crooked corners, inspired by what they perceived as the virtues of the Nordic race, extolling the natural beauty of the countryside against the ugliness of industrial cities, exuding the strength and confidence of a racially pure Germanic people in opposition to alien and specifically Jewish influences. Most of this culture should be created anew; whatever was useful from the past might be skillfully integrated, provided ancestral traditions were considered in support of the rising generation.

The Modernism that had first to be demolished had characterized the culture of the Weimar Republic, from 1918 to 1933, although numerically the creators of modern art had been in the minority, compared with conventional artists. Their often daring efforts had come about, not least, as a form of reaction to the horrors of World War I, as this war was attributed squarely to the *ancien régime* of Kaiser Wilhelm II and its philistine elites, and they were paralleled, in the political realm, by the formation of a democratic republic. In that sense, both the new politics and culture were experimental. But some of

1

the Modernist arts, such as Expressionism in painting and, in music, the mature operas of Richard Strauss such as *Elektra* and *Salome*, reached back before the time of the Great War; moreover, by no means were all Modernists republican or politically left-wing.[1] By the same token, there were conventional artists who believed in a new, democratic form of government.

After the armistice of November 1918, writes Peter Gay, "all artists, or nearly all, were seized with the quasi-religious fervor to make all things new."[2] They wanted to try bold experiments with new forms and contents, of artistic objects, of artistic processes. They congregated in the Novembergruppe – Bertolt Brecht, Kurt Weill, Alban Berg, Paul Hindemith, and Walter Gropius – and in December 1918 proclaimed: "The future of art and the seriousness of this hour forces us revolutionaries of the spirit (Expressionists, Cubists, Futurists) toward unity and close cooperation."[3]

What followed was the artistic regime of the Bauhaus movement shortly after the establishment of the political republic in 1918, a movement that was to put its cultural stamp on the Weimar era. The Bauhaus masters under Gropius focused on new design and painting, first in the town of Weimar by early 1919 and after 1925 in Dessau, where architecture became a core subject. In Dessau itself a signature building was erected, with its clean rectilinear form and flat roof textbook-like in the Gropius mold.[4] Still, in late summer of 1923, the Bauhaus had assembled representatives of virtually every important artistic discipline freshly conceived for an exhibition in Weimar. Standing for music and critical journalism was Hans Heinz Stuckenschmidt, who was a follower of dodecaphony, or twelve-tone music, evolving at that time with Arnold Schoenberg as its pioneer. In Weimar, Stuckenschmidt took part in a "Musical Cabaret," for which he had written an avant-garde score inspired by Dada, that seemingly inchoate new movement, which dressed in sensual nonsense works of the visual, literary, and sound arts. Hermann Scherchen contributed, the most progressive conductor of the Weimar era next to Otto Klemperer, and Hindemith premiered his recently composed *Marienleben* song cycle, marked by the composer's new predilection for polyphony. Ernst Krenek put in an appearance, whose jagged jazz opera *Jonny spielt auf* (*Jonny Plays*) would be the hit on German operatic stages in 1927.[5]

The Bauhaus had its own jazz band, and jazz was becoming the rage in Germany, even with – for this country – a typically over-pronounced drumbeat reminiscent of marching bands, after its prior introduction from the United States into England and France. In the 1920s, jazz was played by German combos in the large cities, chiefly Berlin, in dedicated clubs such as the Rio Rita or Moka Efti, but also in huge emporiums such as Scala and Wintergarten that Adolf Hitler and his propaganda expert Joseph Goebbels sometimes patronized because of operettas featured there, and in cabarets, where stars and starlets of film and operetta, like the young Trude Hesterberg, performed. Jazz also appeared in film, even the first meaningful German talkie *The Blue Angel* with Marlene Dietrich in 1930, a coy violin student in Weimar when the Bauhaus had started there. For this film the jazz pianist Friedrich Hollaender, later of Hollywood fame, had written the music.[6]

Filmmakers as such were not at the 1923 Weimar exhibition, but several of the Bauhaus artists were interested in movie-making or photography, such as the painter and designer László Moholy-Nagy, whose new techniques included placing objects directly onto unexposed film. Three feature films were to stand out in the republic and gain eternal fame as avant-garde works of high art: *Das Cabinet des Dr. Caligari* (1920), *Metropolis* (1927), and *Mädchen in Uniform* (1931). *Dr. Caligari* showed angular background scenery, oblique walls with borders and ceilings askew. The characters were shifty, morally good or bad or, simultaneously, both: the viewer was confused. Horror was pervasive. Fritz Lang's *Metropolis* repeated the play on good or bad, with an evil robot called Maria imitating a physically and morally beauteous maiden, also called Maria. In *Mädchen in Uniform* lesbian love shone through the plot, exemplifying the republic's greater tolerance in sexuality, but also the authoritarianism exercised in private schools, a not so veiled criticism of hierarchical structures implanted in the past that had refused to go away.[7]

Among the painters at the 1923 exhibition were the Bauhaus's own Wassily Kandinsky and Paul Klee. Kandinsky had developed abstract painting around 1910 and in Weimar created, among many others, an oil on canvas entitled *Auf Weiss II* (*On White II*), in 1923: two black sharp spikes crossing each other, against an abstract of yellow and reddish triangles, a black circle, and other geometric shapes, all on an off-white backcloth. Klee painted somewhat less geometrically and also less abstractly but often in miniature; his *Angler* of 1921 is finely chiseled; he is standing on a thin board above the water, elegantly handling his fishing line, against a back-drop of gentle blues and whites.[8]

An early expert on theater at the Bauhaus was Lothar Schreyer (a poly-math who also had a doctorate in law from Heidelberg University, painted, wrote prose, and edited an arts journal). He designed and staged a *Mondspiel*, a "Moon Play," which was performed in Weimar in the early 1920s to, alas, little acclaim; later, the Bauhaus painter Oskar Schlemmer's *Triadisches Ballett* was more successful. Outside of Weimar, Max Reinhardt was still instru-mental in Berlin, although his fame as a theater director had reached its first peak already before the Great War, and now he excelled most particularly as a teacher. As dramaturgs, Leopold Jessner and Erwin Piscator were his most illustrious colleagues, both of them dedicated socialists who saw eye to eye with the Marxist playwright Bertolt Brecht on the need for the theatrical arts to serve the masses, and thus society.[9] A pace-setting actor just growing into maturity in the mid-1920s was Gustaf Gründgens, who, an androgynous bisexual, was briefly married to Erika Mann, the bisexual daughter of the Nobel laureate Thomas Mann. She helped him in the performance of cabaret, but at that time Gründgens too clamored for revolutionary theater, as he bril-liantly starred as Goethe's Mephistopheles from *Faust*, yet also in roles created by the new dramatists of Expressionism: Frank Wedekind, Carl Sternheim, and Georg Kaiser. Reinhardt would call Gründgens to Berlin in 1928.[10]

Several of the multitalented masters at the Bauhaus composed poetry and prose. The most prolific major writers in the Weimar Republic were Gerhart Hauptmann and Thomas Mann, but neither of them was a member of the Weimar *Sturm und Drang*, as they were intellectually and aestheti-cally more beholden to the pre-war era. More typically representing the new Weimar dynamics were Brecht with his socialist concerns and Alfred Döblin, a Berlin Jewish physician ministering to the city's poor with a deep understanding of and compassion for the socially downtrodden. In his novel *Berlin Alexanderplatz* of 1929 the lead character, Franz Biberkopf, emerges from prison determined to go straight, but through his surroundings becomes embroiled in new complications that distract him. Döblin's book clearly illustrated the need for social change and individual compassion. But it also warned about ascendant Nazism.[11]

Social change was not really something the Nazis were interested in during the 1920s, to say nothing of the attendant political risks. Moreover, a cultural agenda for them was virtually non-existent in the early half of the decade. They were too busy establishing themselves politically and were interrupted in their political progress by the Nazi Party's tightly circum-scribed area of influence (with a presence merely in Bavaria), Hitler's November 1923 Munich putsch and his detention in Landsberg prison until Christmas 1924. After his release, Hitler was too busy organizing new outposts all over Germany and winning popular support, a process that was many times hampered by German states forbidding him to speak publicly.

This began to change in 1927, when at the national Party convention in Nuremberg in late August, Hitler announced a few opaque guidelines for what he viewed as cultural renewal.[12] They were not to be mistaken for a blueprint for a "culture state," or the intention to regard politics as "the highest form of culture," as has recently been claimed.[13] Indeed, future developments before and after 1933 do not bear this out; culture was to be subordinated, was to serve propaganda; in that context, "politics as a form of culture" amounts to a meaningless metaphor. Nonetheless, Alfred Rosenberg, Hitler's early Munich paladin who had established himself as the official ideologue of the movement, was not slow to take up the cue and found a Kampfbund für deutsche Kultur (KfdK), or combat league for German culture. It was supported mainly by politically right-leaning cultural elites such as the Munich publisher Hugo Bruckmann and his wife Elsa, and Winifred Wagner (the composer's daughter-in-law) in Bayreuth. As such it received an official charter and called for more founding members in May 1928. In a manifesto by Rosenberg, followers were asked to fight in an all-out effort against contemporary literature and the liberal content of the largely city-based (Jewish) press, such as the *Frankfurter Zeitung*. Implicitly, modern music, architecture, the visual arts, and other sub-disciplines of Expressionism were attacked.[14] Following this, local cells of the Kampfbund were founded, like the one in the Goethe town of Weimar under the völkisch theater expert Hans Severus Ziegler. In Weimar, Ziegler set the tone by delivering an inaugural address, identifying one of the chief enemies of National Socialism, international Communism. His lecture was entitled "Bolshevism threatens German Culture."[15]

Defamatory work against Weimar republican accomplishments by active members of the Kampfbund began in earnest in 1929. By this time, much characteristic avant-garde art of the republic had become discernible, such as the satirical paintings by George Grosz and Otto Dix, Gropius's Dessau Bauhaus, Weill and Brecht's *Threepenny Opera*, and the Weintraub Syncopators' jazz dazzlings in Berlin. Rosenberg himself lectured in April, identifying a "trend toward greater sensuality in art," which he regarded as a threat to German culture.[16] One of the most pernicious spokesmen for his league would now be Gropius's rival, the architect Paul Schultze-Naumburg, who advocated traditional architecture, houses with gables instead of flat roofs, and expansive, ornamental, and comfortable old-style interior designs, such as were found in first-class ocean liners. He became the Nazis' earliest champion of a völkisch art, traveling much on the speaker's circuit. In 1932 he published a booklet, comparing Modernist paintings to the random pictures by patients in German insane asylums. In Munich that year the architect organized a public exhibition dominated by a similar theme.[17] Additionally, the right-wing poet Hans Friedrich Blunck gave a lecture in front of university students in the spring of 1932, in which he castigated the vulgarized eroticism inherent in Weimar art and mannerist modern music.[18] At the end of the republic, the Nazis had drawn up blacklists with the names of actors whom they considered Marxist or Jewish, to be sent to stage directors and film companies for boycotts to be launched. Fritz Kortner, Heinrich George, and Gründgens were among the names.[19] At the beginning of the Hitler regime, right-wing authors, among them Rosenberg's stooge Walter Stang, summarized the attempts of their Weimar-era fight against what they regarded as the excrescences of the republican avant-garde: "jazzband, Nigger song and Negro art," in addition to "erotics of an alien race" and "Bolshevist agitation."[20]

When in January 1930 the Nazis wrested control of the government of Thuringia, based in the town of Weimar, after a popular regional vote, Hitler managed to have one of his confidants, the jurist Wilhelm Frick, installed as the leading minister of the new cabinet. Well programmed, Frick embarked on a veritable purge of the Thuringian cultural establishment. Not least because of those cultural raids, apart from other changes, political and economic, that the Nazis implemented in Weimar, this was their first experiment in manipulative democracy, since they considered themselves, correctly, as the victors in a constitutionally legal election process. But such nominal correctness rendered them not less, but more dangerous, because they could do much evil under the guise of legality. For the Modernist culture of the storied Goethe town, this spelled nothing less than demolition. As Ziegler had had a hand in drawing up ordinances for change, he became the new chief of Weimar's national theater. Now forbidden were the staging of modern plays, the performance of atonal music or jazz, visiting cabarets or risqué circus acts. As Schultze-Naumburg was taking over as head of what remained of the Bauhaus, Schlemmer's frescoes that had been created in the school were deleted, and seventy Expressionist paintings, including works by Klee and Kandinsky, were removed from exhibits in the ducal museum. All scheduled films were censored, especially those with merely a touch of eroticism.[21]

Disruptive and destructive activities by increasingly radicalized adherents of the National Socialist German Workers' Party (NSDAP), which was picking up steam amidst rising unemployment in the late 1920s, pleased no one on the outside of that movement, especially if they had looked favorably on certain manifestations of Modernism such as films by Lang or intelligent comment in a liberal-bourgeois newspaper. Rather than engaging in nihilist destruction, the Nazi culture brokers would have been more successful had they managed to introduce new artistic and other cultural forms persuasively in line with their ideology, undeniably original, and easily consumable. But in this they failed early, as they would fail again later: hence the early hallmarks of indigenous Nazi culture were a low level of output and poor quality. There was, for example, no film made celebrating Nazi street-fighter heroes by a Nazi-leaning film company, and very few novels by the end of the republic managed to describe the Party's rise to strength in the past few years.[22] Instead, the Nazis were forced to resort to products of culture long tried and true, declare them unjustly neglected and now to be embraced with fervor. Hence for pliable material they were looking to German conventional art mostly of the nineteenth century, to the homely, traditionalist and feel-good architecture of the kind Schultze-Naumburg was promoting, and to novels depicting World War I idols. If little of that could be declared National Socialist in character outright, the Nazis were still able to claim that every new political movement needed precursors and that in their case the inherent purpose of such earlier art ultimately was to lead to specifically Nazi creations. And indeed, most of the artworks the Nazis eventually produced were syncretic, derivative of an earlier, representational and reactionary, culture.

For its followers, most of whom, at the beginning, came from Germany's conservative educated classes, the Kampfbund proceeded to sponsor a conventional cultural program, in gradual steps. The league's journal, *Deutsche Kultur-Wacht*, presented its readers with "a combination of serious cultural feature stories and *völkisch* treatises."[23] Demanding "racial rejuvenation" of art by way of a return to völkisch sources, Schultze-Naumburg organized art shows of nineteenth-century painters Wilhelm Leibl, Franz Defregger, and Hans Thoma, but also works of the German Renaissance.[24] The combat league became especially busy in the support of Nazi-minded musicians, who for one reason or another were opposed to the new Modernism. For example, the violinist Gustav Havemann, who had been playing Schoenberg and Hindemith with his vaunted Havemann Quartet, experienced a conversion to National Socialism in 1932; it was then that he assumed the conductorship of the Kampfbund's own orchestra and from there on continued to serve the Nazi cultural agenda well by performing only traditional works.[25] Other musicians who were now lifted into the Nazi Olympus were composers Max Trapp and Paul Graener, minor figures in the German world of music but influential as teachers at the academy of music and the Stern Conservatory in Berlin.[26]

Always closely watched by the directors of the combat league, if not Hitler and Goebbels themselves, artistic activities unfolded on the rightist fringe of German political life, stretching from film to art criticism, but inevitably beholden to Germany's traditionalist cultural past. Hence the South Tyrolean Luis Trenker, a veteran World War I officer and ski instructor with nature-boy charm, made films at the turn of the 1920s about nature's beauty in the Alps, when he was not meeting for trysts with a young mountain-obsessed actress named Leni Riefenstahl. His movies appealed to patriotic sentiments among Germans, through images of rootedness in valley pastures and conquest of native mountain peaks, especially by conjuring up the unity, across the Alps, between Bavarians, Austrian Tyroleans and their German-speaking cousins in Italian Alto Adige.[27] Here, as later, there was a strong patriotic, even chauvinistic subtext. Toward the end of the republic, more kitschy agrarian-based novels were published than ever before about Germany as the home of simple yet trusty peasants.[28] Schultze-Naumburg risked more daring analyses between Modernist works of art and staid German classics such as the static Bamberg Horseman, an authoritarian icon, and Blunck extolled traditional German folk dance and German folk song, hoping for a broader renaissance of a Teutonic tribal value system to be galvanized into endurable form by a government under Hitler.[29]

A PURGE OF THE WEIMAR ERA

At the end of February 1933 the actor Hans Otto was given notice that he would be dismissed from the Prussian State Theater in Berlin. After more than 100 appearances in the 1932–3 season, Otto performed for the last time as Kaiser in Goethe's *Faust* at the end of May. He refused offers from the Vienna and Zurich theaters, because he did not wish to give in to oppressive Nazis. Instead, he went underground, until in mid-November he was arrested by Nazi storm troopers (SA) in a small café on Viktoria-Luise-Platz. In SA and Gestapo headquarters, he was beaten until unconscious, then thrown from the building onto the street. He died in a Berlin hospital on November 23.[30]

The young, handsome, and hugely popular Hans Otto was a typical representative of the Weimar culture the Nazis wanted to destroy. He had starred in classical plays as much as in Weimar-era pieces, such as dramas by Wedekind or Strindberg. But he was also a Communist functionary. Jan Petersen, too, was a Communist, and a journalist working out of Berlin. Lucky enough not to be caught by the Nazi regime, he wrote a book detailing Berlin proletarian life during the last phase of the Weimar Republic, in which the Nazis were not spared. Having baked the manuscript pages into a cake, he disguised himself as a ski tourist, this way smuggling them across the border with Czechoslovakia during Christmas 1934. As the book could be published abroad, Petersen himself escaped to Britain, via Switzerland, in the mid-1930s.[31]

Another Communist actor, thirty-two-year-old Wolfgang Langhoff from Düsseldorf, spent most of 1933 in the concentration camps Papenburg-Börgermoor and Lichtenburg. In Papenburg he wrote the words for the swamp-soldier song, which, with its defiant refrain, would be proudly adopted by many future inmates: "We are the moor soldiers/Marching with our spades into the moors." Released early in 1934, Langhoff fled to Switzerland, where he, the young man "with the knocked-out teeth," as Thomas Mann noted, met with the writer's family in a transitory refuge.[32]

Other, formerly well-known Weimar-era artists made it out of the Third Reich more easily, as they were not on the political left. The conductor Erich Kleiber, for example, originally an Austrian and especially fond of music by Alban Berg, was impelled to leave the Reich in 1935. Kleiber's anti-Nazi cachet was ambiguous. Previously, along with Wilhelm Furtwängler, he had aided Hermann Göring as a member of a Nazi film censorship board. During the Röhm Purge of June–July 1934, Kleiber was heard to express his hope, among a close circle of friends on the island of Sylt, that Hitler, the "savior of Germany," had not been harmed. But as one of the avant-garde conductors of the Weimar Republic, Kleiber eventually had to make his home in Argentina.[33]

And then there were the suicides. Ernst Ludwig Kirchner, the painter born in 1880, had been influenced by Kandinsky and French neo-Impressionists. In 1905 he had co-founded the Dresden avant-garde movement Die Brücke, along with Erich Heckel and Karl Schmidt-Rottluff. The year 1911 found him in Berlin, where he indulged in street scenes, varieté and circus themes. Animated by the company he kept, especially prostitutes, he became addicted to morphine and eventually was drinking one liter of absinthe a day. Having volunteered in World War I, he suffered a nervous breakdown. He retired to a Davos sanatorium during the war, and after his release in 1917 he stayed in Switzerland. But the main market for his work remained in Germany, and Kirchner considered himself a German patriot. That the Nazis, upon their ascent to power, could not abide his paintings but dismissed them as degenerate, puzzled and annoyed him. "We founded Die Brücke to encourage truly German art, made in Germany, and now it's supposed to be un-German," was his complaint, but the Nazis included his works in their "Degenerate Art" exhibition in July 1937 and stripped him of his fellowship in the Prussian Academy of Arts. Living in a farmhouse near Davos, yet despairing on account of his substance addictions, the Nazis' rejection, and what he saw as political turmoil in Germany after the Anschluss of Austria, Kirchner shot himself near his house in June 1938.[34]

After January 1933, Kirchner and his progressive artist consorts, irrespective of their political leanings, were viewed by most National Socialist politicians as proponents of a culture that had to be eradicated. More strongly even than in the last half of the Weimar Republic, those politicians associated the Modernist cultural currents that had burst forth after World War I with the German defeat, the prominence of Jews as creators or managers, left-wing or anarchic politics, and an aesthetic distortion of content and form. Twisted sexuality, derelict behavior, atonality, "Nigger jazz," perverse dance routines, pimps and whores, images of cripples and beggars – all were manifestations of "asphalt culture," touted as Dada, Cubism, Expressionism, or *l'art pour l'art*, charged their Nazi critics. This flotsam was the product of the big city rather than values organically linked to the countryside. Culture in Germany had become tainted by foreign influences and hence been rendered un-German. The individual had been more important than the community, a national community defined by its members' purity of blood. "Sick people and the demented do not belong on a stage," ranted Propaganda Minister Goebbels; Expressionism had to be fought because it attracted "the shrill, the unharmonic and the ill" – in the words of the art reviewer Karl Hans Bühner.[35]

Many measures taken by the Nazis against art and artists were spontaneously enforced by state-sanctioned paramilitary bands such as the storm trooper SA, the SS, or the army veterans' association Stahlhelm, particularly early on in the regime. But other measures were based on legislation, such as the Reichstag Fire Decree of February 28, 1933, and the Enabling Act of March 23. Both had roots in Article 48, the emergency law of the Weimar Republic, which was technically still in place.[36] Special legislation regarding culture was also passed, such as the Schriftleitergesetz of October 4, 1933, an editors' set of strangulating codes for regulating the press.[37] But the singularly most flexible and potentially most lethal piece of legislation for the new censors turned out to be the Law for the Reconstitution of the Civil Service, proclaimed on April 7, 1933. Its paragraph 4 stated that persons of dubious political persuasion who would not unequivocally back the new state could be dismissed from the state bureaucracy, with only three months' pay. Paragraph 3 targeted Jews in the same manner, and paragraph 2 decreed that officials lacking the correct "aptitude" must be let go.[38] This law was immediately meant to eliminate civil servants with all their traditional rights of tenure, including pensions, and hence it was well suited to marginalize suspect artists employed by state institutions at all levels, be they municipal, regional, or national. Into this category fell opera singers, for instance at the Prussian State Opera in Berlin, or actors at the municipal theaters in Hamburg and Düsseldorf. But beyond the civil service, the law also came to be broadly used by non-government institutions, such as teachers' associations or physicians' leagues. In the realm of culture, therefore, any band of Nazis with an anti-Modernist bent was liable to refer to it in attempts to terminate unwanted colleagues.

In addition, expulsion from the Prussian Academy of Arts in Berlin, which had been a token of republican culture, was meant to signal shame for all its members, affecting all artistic disciplines. An early victim was Heinrich Mann, the head of the academy's writers' section, who was dismissed by President Max von Schillings on February 15.[39] A composer, von Schillings's colleague Arnold Schoenberg, who had taught at the academy since 1925, followed in March, after Schillings had declared that "the Jewish influence at the academy must be eliminated." Schoenberg and his small family had fled to Paris by May 17.[40] Also during May, the Jewish honorary academy president, Max Liebermann, declared his resignation from that post and his definitive retreat from the school. In a statement of justification, published by the press, Germany's foremost Impressionist painter maintained that he had devoted his entire life to German art and that "art had as little to do with politics as had lineage."[41] By that time, in a process that would last for months and even years, Jewish, left-wing, or pronouncedly Modernist artists were either being dismissed outright or pressured, like the sculptor Ernst Barlach, to resign on their own volition.[42] Only one of them protested in the course of her resignation. The esteemed novelist Ricarda Huch, politically more to the right of center but cherishing tolerance, let Schillings know that she rebuked "several of the measures by the new government," including the current demand that academy fellows sign a declaration of loyalty to the regime. Huch was correct in assuming that her protest translated into an instant severance from the institution, as she retreated to her private home.[43]

Turning to individual artistic disciplines, from the German stage alone, not counting the film industry, 10 percent of all pre-1933 personnel were ousted during the first months of the Reich, and one-third of all directors, many of those Jews. In Munich, the entrepreneurial theater Intendant Otto Falckenberg, who had favored works by Brecht and other Modernists, was briefly incarcerated by the secret police, but then released.[44] Falckenberg had notoriously championed the genres that were now taboo: the Naturalism at the turn of the last century and, subsequently, Expressionism, which began before World War I. Dramas in those genres featured the psychology of individuals in their interpersonal, often conflicted, relations, rather than positivist dynamism in racially defined communal settings, preferred by the Nazis. Authors from the Naturalist school, whose works were now officially shunned (constituting almost one-half of the Weimar repertoire), included Hermann Sudermann, Arthur Schnitzler, Frank Wedekind, Walter Hasenclever, Ernst Toller, and Carl Zuckmayer.[45] Georg Kaiser, the most prolific Expressionist dramatist of the 1920s, was having his latest play *Der Silbersee* (*The Silver Lake*), a quasi-socialist object lesson, premiered simultaneously at three theaters in the Reich in late February 1933. In Magdeburg, to a score by Weill, the Communist Ernst Busch was singing and playing the leading role. Stahlhelm and NSDAP functionaries declared the performance forbidden, causing its untimely cancellation. Similar interruptions occurred in Erfurt and in Leipzig, where the Jewish composer Gustav Brecher had contributed the soundscape. Brecher later had to flee, killing himself in Belgian Ostend in 1940.[46]

Many German actors of the stage also played in films; indeed, similar prohibitions would affect the movie scene too. Hence actors who had been featured in typically Weimar-era films lost their jobs. One of these was the formerly much-beloved Hertha Thiele, who had played in the left-wing, Expressionist classic *Kuhle Wampe* (*Who Owns the World?*, 1932), co-written by Brecht and co-starring Busch. After she had refused to impersonate Erna Jänicke, the girlfriend of Nazi hero Horst Wessel, who had been murdered by the Red Front in 1930, she lost her certification as a German actress and eventually left for Switzerland. Apart from *Kuhle Wampe*, many other films produced during the Weimar Republic were proscribed, because of unacceptable themes or styles, or because leading actors were Jewish. The half-Jewish director Fritz Lang's *Das Testament des Dr. Mabuse* (1933), for instance, appeared as too Expressionist, quite apart from the murky racial pedigree of Lang himself. Several special laws aiming for prohibition were passed after January 1933, the most important being the one of February 16, 1934, when an all-inclusive censorship decree was promulgated.[47]

In a culture setting where, on a scale of one to ten, Richard Wagner occupied a ten and jazz and atonal music a one, much German traditional music was able to survive under the Nazis, while most modern works were cast aside. Characteristically, the Nazis condemned truly atonal compositions such as those by Schoenberg and his pupil Alban Berg, but in addition they made the convenient mistake of conflating atonality with any form of cacophony, which for them included not only jazz but also modern if not yet dodecaphonic pieces, for instance those by Hindemith or Hermann Reutter.

Of Reutter, Goebbels said as late as January 1938 that he would oppose his candidacy, as an "atonalist," for a position at Frankfurt's conservatory, for which Reich Education Minister Bernhard Rust had earmarked him. (Here the conflict between two Nazi ministers was typical of the heterogeneity of Third Reich gubernatorial structures; in the culture domain, Goebbels usually won out: a strange constellation of competencies in Hitler's model of government, which will deserve another, closer, look in Chapter 2.)[48] As far as Berg was concerned, his opera *Wozzeck* was rejected for its atonality; beyond that, its social message, reflecting post-World War I humanitarian impulses, was disdained by the Nazis. So was Berg's opera *Lulu*, featuring a harlot, over the Berlin premiere of which the Modernist Erich Kleiber, not originally anti-Nazi, was impelled to leave Germany. Under this pressure other musicians also left, while some, after having been fired from an opera stage or symphony orchestra pit, tried to make do in other jobs. Among the former were Hindemith and Vladimir Vogel, a Modernist but not atonalist, yet branded as such; Berg, always an "Aryan" Vienna resident, died there on Christmas Eve 1935 after a lethal bee-sting infection.[49]

One last Weimar-style performance of opera took place at the Berlin Staatsoper on February 12, 1933, after having been rehearsed months before. Its avant-garde creators were Jürgen Fehling, the stage director, and Otto Klemperer, the conductor; Oskar Strnad was the stage designer. This partially surreal interpretation of Wagner's *Tannhäuser* was meant as an anti-Bayreuth demonstration, opposing a style that Wagner's dowdy son Siegfried had still championed and traditionalist-leaning Nazis favored. Klemperer and Strnad were Jewish, and both of them left the Reich – Klemperer for the United States and Strnad for his native Austria, where he died in 1935. Fehling, however, remained in Berlin, entering into a tenuous relationship with the regime.[50]

As before, much music was transmitted over the broadcasting system, the structure of which was now changed and its contents modified. Radio had been an instrument of propaganda the Nazis had not fully realized before January 1933, for two reasons. First, Hitler had limited opportunities for public speaking after his Landsberg imprisonment in 1924; as such it was a privilege extended to him depending on the presence or absence of censorship exercised by individual German states. This was not conducive to broadcasting. Second, the idea of radio was intimately connected to the era of the Weimar Republic during which it was created, making propaganda mavens of the Nazi Party like Goebbels suspicious and wary.[51]

That changed after the Nazis' rise to power. In a speech on August 18, 1933, Goebbels suggested to his followers that radio was a superb instrument of political control and henceforth was to be neatly accommodated to the Nazi Führer principle. In its current shape it had to be cleansed of the effect of abuses by its former staff, such as corruption, a sinecurial infestation, and bloated salaries – quite apart from any changes to its thematic content.[52] The purge of Weimar radio personnel now getting under way targeted leading broadcast officials, among them the Intendanten of almost all local stations of the former nationwide Reichs-Rundfunk-Gesellschaft (RRG). Several of them, after losing their positions, were put on trial, as was the founder of German broadcasting Hans Bredow; some committed suicide.[53] Ernst Hardt, the chief of Westdeutscher Rundfunk in Cologne, had had prior experience as Intendant of the Nationaltheater Weimar and, like many of the others, was a staunch Social Democrat. Although his Cologne imprisonment lasted only a few days, he emerged from it impoverished, seeking refuge with his married daughter in Berlin.[54]

Parallel to the purging of radio personnel, Goebbels, who officially oversaw all aspects of broadcasting following his appointment to the propaganda portfolio by Hitler in March 1933, initiated changes to the programming. As a first step, elements of modernity, such as "Nigger jazz," were scheduled for elimination. Music by Jewish or even half-Jewish composers fell into this category, as did some foreign compositions. By contrast, music by "German composers" was supposed to be stressed. In this context, Beethoven's works were regarded as a strong antidote to "the sport of dissonance, the incest of harmony and the chaos of form."[55]

A combination of spontaneous paramilitary enforcement and statutory regulation also caused changes in the situation of the press. First targeted were the left-oriented newspapers, such as the Social Democratic *Vorwärts* and the Communist Party's *Rote Fahne*. An emergency law of February 4, 1933, added a legalistic veneer to sudden outbreaks of violence, so that by March all leftist broadsheets had been effectively stopped.[56] Subsequently, many middle-of-the-road bourgeois papers also became victims of the regime in short order, as did confessional ones. If they were not forbidden outright, they were amalgamated or repossessed. And so, where there had been over 3,000 newspapers in Germany by January 1933, there were only some 2,000 four years later. In many cases, apart from the firing or incarceration of old newspaper personnel, buildings and other assets were confiscated or acquired by Party businesses for nominal sums. As for the staff, beyond the emergency decrees of spring and early summer, on October 4 the new editors' law (Schriftleitergesetz) was promulgated, whose paragraph 5 outlined criteria for sackings. Besides non-"Aryan" lineage, those deficiencies of journalists were mentioned that were apt to prevent a "spiritual guidance for the public." Such perceived shortcomings would provide ideological or – in the case of culture – aesthetic reasons for dismissal.[57]

A few case histories reveal the proportions of institutional upheaval and human suffering. The SA stormed the headquarters of the Social Democratic *Münchener Post*, wreaked havoc in the halls, and arrested those not able to flee. The Catholic weekly *Der gerade Weg*, also in Munich, with a history of pre-1933 opposition to the Nazis, was overrun and Franz Gerlich, its chief editor, manhandled on the spot; he was later murdered in Dachau. The high-bourgeois *Frankfurter Zeitung* meanwhile, a mainstay of liberal-conservative opinion in the Weimar Republic and famous for its feuilleton section, was visited by policemen as early as March 31, 1933, who arrested some of the editors. The result was that the (at that time still Jewish) owners were cowed into submission, and the paper was remodeled into a showpiece Nazi medium. And the *Neue Badische Landeszeitung* in Mannheim was prohibited on March 1, 1934, presumably after it had been discredited as anti-regime by a Nazi insider. Its chief editor Heinrich Rumpf tried to work in a lending library for a while, but then committed suicide.[58]

Different conditions than for radio and the press obtained for other arts, because here creators were individually more independent. In architecture, for example, only architects employed by institutions could be dismissed, from the bureaucracy, teaching, and state or regime-beholden firms. Self-employed ones relied on their order books for income and could stay in Germany, unless harm could come to them as Jews or political leftists. As far as architectural style was concerned, as yet no Nazi consensus appeared to evolve, and therefore no systematic discrimination, on that account.

Nevertheless, there is no question that after January 1933 the Weimar-republican architectural Bauhaus style, initiated by Bauhaus founder Walter Gropius in Dessau, was out of favor. Gropius and other associates of the vaunted Ring architects, such as Ludwig Mies van der Rohe, were officially marginalized. "The so-called New Objectivity constructed smooth façades and empty walls," explained the culture bureaucrat Otto von Kursell in 1933.[59] As part of that movement, the Bauhaus was accused of preferring a flat roof over a peaked one such as traditional German houses possessed, which was judged technically awkward and aesthetically unpleasant; Bauhaus style tended to emphasize horizontal lines instead of Gothic, vertical ones. Rather than German, it was "Bolshevist" art and fully in keeping with Weimar's "asphalt culture."[60] By and large, Nazi ideologues wanted to return to the historicist traditions of pre-war architecture, with emphasis on a rural rather than urban character.[61]

Not least in order to purge unwanted colleagues, including several of the Ring such as Gropius's friend Erich Mendelsohn, the Verband Deutscher Architekten (VDA), the republican near-monopoly association of German architects, was infiltrated by a Nazi group close to former architect Alfred Rosenberg and, later in 1933, was integrated into Goebbels's newly founded Reichskulturkammer (RKK, Reich Culture Chamber).[62] In April 1933 the Berlin remnants of the original Weimar Bauhaus fell victim to Nazi censors; the school was closed after decisive action by the chief Party ideologue Rosenberg, a pompous obscurantist. Bauhaus-influenced architects lost their positions: Ernst Wichert at the Frankfurt School of Arts and Crafts, Hans Scharoun and Adolf Rading, "designers of some of the most radical housing developments built during the Weimar Republic," both at Breslau's Academy of Arts. Hans Poelzig was driven from an architectural school in Berlin, and Robert Vorhoelzer from the Technische Hochschule in Munich. But most lesser disciples of the Bauhaus were retained in state-administrative or teaching positions, as they were able to adapt themselves to the regime's own requirements. Heavily marked by the Bauhaus aura, both Gropius and his successor Mies van der Rohe tried to get by as self-employed consultants. They offered their services to exhibitions sponsored by the regime, Gropius even designing swastika-flagged sites for an event in 1934, "clearly pandering to the Nazi regime." Later that year, however, he had found it too difficult financially and decided to move to Britain, hoping for better times. But even after he had arrived at Harvard University in 1937 he insisted that he was not there as an immigrant, but for "serving German culture." Mies van der Rohe, after similar disappointing experiences in

Germany, followed Gropius to the United States in 1938, while their mentor Peter Behrens remained in the service of the Third Reich.[63]

For the Nazis, painting and sculpture constituted a much more contentious issue than architecture, for the latter always served practical purposes, no matter the design. Avant-garde pictorial art of the post-World War I era was placed in disrepute by critics believing in Rosenberg or Goebbels, whose remarks were made to concur with judgments that Hitler himself (who had failed the exam for the Vienna Academy of Arts) had made as early as the mid-1920s, in *Mein Kampf.* Here he had spoken of "Cubism and Dadaism," to be subsumed under "the Bolshevism of art." When in key public speeches from 1933 to 1937 Hitler repeated those phrases almost verbatim in reference to modern art, he never bothered to qualify them, such as demonstrating that he knew the difference between the various new art forms – Dadaism or Cubism, Impressionism or Expressionism. Inevitably and simplistically, he linked all such movements to degeneracy, to a sick corporeal and mental state, and to Jews.[64] Hence Rosenberg's sycophant Robert Scholz charged in 1933 that Karl Hofer, Klee, and their friends were involved with Expressionism and Cubism, and thus had brought "the poison of artistic nihilism" to Germany. Wolfgang Willrich in 1934 reproduced examples of Emil Nolde's and Barlach's work, which were supposed to demonstrate their path to "degeneracy, on to distortion and smuttiness."[65] From their often unintelligible scribblings it is clear that these Nazi censors hated modern art's color schemes, not reflecting nature, and shapes or forms, non-representational or abstract.

Based on such ideology, Nazi authorities embarked on a two-pronged, mutually complementary policy: removing unwanted *objets d'art* from public view and showcasing them, in especially arranged exhibitions, for all Germans to see and reject. In June 1933, Hitler himself received a group of anti-Modernists, including the chief Bauhaus enemy, the architect Schultze-Naumburg, and ordered 500 avant-garde paintings to be removed from the Kronprinzen-Palais, Germany's national gallery in Berlin, based on photos they had showed him. In October 1936 he acted again to order the Kronprinzen-Palais's doors shut for good. Next to Hitler's actions, regional galleries were closed or thinned out chiefly by followers of Rosenberg. In Munich, the Bavarian Minister of the Interior and Gauleiter Adolf Wagner snatched pictures from an exhibition of Berlin artists in 1935. In

Essen, the new director of the Folkwang Museum, Klaus Graf von Baudissin, withdrew works by Kandinsky, a native of Russia, whom Baudissin called "uprooted" in the process. Concomitantly, exhibitions designed as horror shows were organized, starting with Mannheim in 1933 – a project that then traveled to Munich and Erlangen. Mannheim was followed by Karlsruhe, Stuttgart, Chemnitz, and especially the art metropolis Dresden. Here Hitler was so impressed with what he considered degenerate art that he ordered the exhibition to travel throughout Germany. Institutionally supportive of these early activities was Rosenberg's Kampfbund für deutsche Kultur, aided by a fanatically Nazi art society, the Deutscher Kunst-Verein (German Art Society), under the leadership of the obscure painter Bettina Feistel-Rohmeder.[66]

Dismissals from the German art world began immediately after the Nazi takeover and lasted for years. One of the first to go was the republic's aesthetic mentor, Reichskunstwart Edwin Redslob, who had presided over the format of state funerals as much as over the design of coins and stamps. Museum and gallery directors were dismissed, such as Gustav F. Hartlaub from the post in Mannheim, or Carl Georg Heise from the Hamburg Museum. From their teaching positions, Karl Hofer was removed in Berlin, Willi Baumeister in Frankfurt, and the Bauhaus sculptor Gerhard Marcks in Halle. The early Bauhaus's Paul Klee was forced to leave Düsseldorf's Academy of Arts, moving back to his native Switzerland in late 1933.[67]

Several of Klee's colleagues did not have such an easy way out of the Nazi dilemma and sought, in fact, to re-engage themselves after their initial dismissal. Their cases deserve scrutiny. Otto Dix was an Expressionist who had crossed over to Neue Sachlichkeit (New Objectivity), an extension of Expressionism but also a reaction, in that its protagonists turned to a sharply focused verisimilitude, as in a detailed photograph – in contrast to the exaggerated shapes and colors of the preceding genre.[68] Extreme realism and social criticism were hallmarks of Neue Sachlichkeit, and therefore Dix's brothel scenes were castigated by prurient Nazi fanatics as "vulgarities of the lowest taste." The Saxon government released Dix from his Dresden academy post on April 8, 1933, in line with the new civil service order. He moved to his brother-in-law's castle near Lake Constance, acutely short of money, endured exclusion from all exhibitions in 1934 and, apart from minor local appointments, had to lie low until 1945.[69] Max Beckmann too lost his professorship, at the Frankfurt Städelschule early in 1933, attempted basic survival in Berlin and later, during July 1937, when hundreds of his paintings were featured at Munich's "Degenerate Art" exhibition, fled to Amsterdam, and from there to New York. In 1935 the Nazi critic Carl Linfert, who happened to dislike the fanatic Rosenberg, had tried to save Beckmann's skin by attempting to dissociate him publicly from Expressionism – an unpersuasive attempt, even from today's perspective.[70] The painter Oskar Schlemmer tried everything under the sun to reverse his dismissal from the Bauhaus, now in Berlin, in April 1933. Penurious and eager for adaptation, he insisted in a letter to Goebbels that he belonged to "the type of artist which National Socialism needs." To Baudissin he wrote, pleading in Bauhaus aesthetic terms: "Is National Socialism not a form idea? After all, a whole Reich is supposed to be formed, newly formed!" And he saw a place for himself in this novel, productive process.[71]

In addition to all these actions, the Nazis stopped the influence of Weimar-era books through censorship of existing ones, manuscript publication indictments, and a spectacular nationwide book-burning. Modernist writers who had teaching appointments at universities or schools were few and far between; less prominent ones were able to adjust by changing their scripts. The extreme treatment of a few famous freewheeling authors was to serve as a general threat to anybody not toeing the line. Thomas Mann, for instance, who was abroad on a speaking tour when the Nazis came to power in January 1933 and would not return to Germany until after World War II, was shown to have lost his Reich citizenship in December 1936, along with his Bonn University honorary doctorate. His older brother Heinrich had fled to France already in February 1933, conspicuously losing his citizenship in August of that year.[72]

Nazi literary critics eyed for extermination works by Communists and Social Democrats or by Confessional (Lutheran) Christians, volumes on women's emancipation, pacifism, sexuality, and trivia. Non-fiction broadly included all literature of the Weimar avant-garde, as well as Jewish and certain international authors' books, such as those by the French Communist Henri Barbusse and the American social critic Upton Sinclair. There were blacklists by various Party and government agencies, some drawn up long before January 1933. On the basis of those, renowned publishers such as Deutsche Verlags-Anstalt, Rowohlt, and Propyläen were told to halt production and distribution of books in the styles of what the Nazis regarded as Naturalism, Expressionism, Dadaism, and New Objectivity. Public and lending libraries had to give up a good proportion of their stock. Already in December 1933 over 1,000 titles had been prohibited or cashiered; this number would climb higher in the years that followed.[73]

Public and university libraries were explicitly targeted by the book burnings of May 1933. Evidently instigated by Goebbels himself, who was backed by Hitler, they took place at most German universities. On the basis of the already extant blacklists and aided by representatives of the KfdK and criminal police, members of a Nazi student association (DSt) selected indexed titles by authors already declared off limits. The search extended to school libraries and was also supposed to motivate individuals to relieve private collections of their dross. After weeks of preparation, the burnings took place, well coordinated, on May 10; various NSDAP and Party affiliate members, such as SA and SS, put in appearances. Adorned in academic robes, university faculty assisted students – Professor Ernst Bertram in Cologne, Professor Hans Naumann in Bonn, and Rector Leo von Zumbusch in Munich. In Frankfurt the books were dragged to the burn site on a manure cart drawn by oxen, in Mannheim horses towed an execution wagon. Thus in Würzburg, at least 280 books were destroyed; this would have been the standard in other university towns. In Göttingen a portrait of Lenin crowned the book pile; the Weimar-republican flag was draped to defile others.[74]

In Berlin the auto-da-fé's choreography demanded the presence of Propaganda Minister Goebbels himself. From an open car, he delivered a speech honoring the event's all-encompassing motto, "Against the un-German Spirit," at Kaiser-Franz-Josef-Platz between the Staatsoper and Friedrich-Wilhelm-Universität. He riled against Jewish intellectualism and the materialism of November 1918 and urged the students to toss into flames "the spiritual scum" of years past. The works of Sigmund Freud, Karl Marx, Heinrich Mann, Carl von Ossietzky, Erich Maria Remarque, and other preeminent authors as far back as the nineteenth century, were then thrown onto the pyre, each with a denunciation.[75]

NEW NAZI CONTROLS

Purging the cultural establishment of vestiges of the Weimar-republican cultural era was one thing, but keeping the realm clean of future malformations was another. Inasmuch as the Nazis had been using the existing laws of the republic immediately after they came to power in January 1933 and persisted in exploiting them for the fortification of a tightening dictatorship, this was ideally applicable in the cultural realm. Hence the Nazis carried on basing new laws on old ones, but they also created some novel laws specifically tailored to their needs and not grounded in the Weimar legislative system.

One of the first laws thus promulgated was the Reichsfilmgesetz of July 14, 1933, designed to commence organizational and thematic control of the German film industry, which was in disarray. Under it, a provisional Filmkammer (Chamber of Film) was installed, incorporating anyone involved in film production.[76] It stipulated that any new film script had to be handed to the authorities for prior authorization and that directors and actors be vetted. One film that fell victim to these procedures was *Horst Wessel*, which was forbidden on October 9 of that year, on the day of its scheduled premiere in Berlin. The film, designed as a paean to the Nazi martyr Wessel, a Berlin storm-trooper leader murdered by Communists in January 1930, was judged "to do neither justice to Horst Wessel, whose heroic figure it belittles through inadequate representation, nor the National Socialist movement, on which the state now rests." After it had been returned for re-editing and many cuts, the film was reissued under the title *Hans Westmar*, finally approved by the censors and first shown on December 13.[77]

On February 16, 1934 the Reichsfilmgesetz film decree was passed. This allowed not only for a cleansing of the Weimar film canon, but also amplified the prerogative of the Nazi censors. To ensure an ideologically sound film review, the office of a Reichsfilmdramaturg was created, which now would oversee the business of proper script examination as well as the sanctioning of a finished picture. Not least because it turned out to work in a cumbersome and time-consuming fashion, Goebbels himself acquired a direct privilege of supervision over the Reichsfilmdramaturg from Hitler himself, in June of 1935. Supervision was enhanced even more after the Nazi regime began nationalizing the German film industry in 1936. In a roundabout manner, Third Reich films could be pulled from distribution if they violated National Socialist or artistic sensibilities – two elastic categories indeed.[78] It is not known exactly how many new German films were censored and then given a green light; the film scholar Gerd Albrecht lists thirteen films for 1933, fourteen for 1937, and twenty-three for 1941.[79]

Also new was the editorial legislation of October 4, 1933, the Schriftleitergesetz, used to purge the Weimar press. In view of future publications, editors' qualifications had to guarantee obedience to strict Nazi content standards. "It is incumbent on editors," stated paragraph 13, "to deal with objects to be treated truthfully, and to judge them to the best of their knowledge." Between the lines, it was clear that "truthful" was based on Nazi norms and the best of an editor's knowledge could work against him if it ran counter to Nazi interests.[80] The law reduced individual freedoms of independent writers to the point of subservience, making editors and journalists subject to the demands of political masters such as Goebbels. To facilitate controls, each contribution in a newspaper now had to be identifiable by author; anonymity was disallowed.[81] Nazi press experts lauded this. Professor Emil Dovifat, from the University of Berlin, demanded that from now on the will of the highest leadership be fused with public opinion, so that the latter echoed the former, and a single unit be forged, "for the sake of the nation." To this Guido Enderis from *The New York Times* objected, as he summed up the changes negatively: "Journalism as a free profession becomes a thing of the past in the Third Reich and in its place there is created a sort of personal union between the individual newspaper worker and the State, with the profession hedged in by stringent rules and regulations."[82]

Strengthening press controls further, a stop was put to analytical criticism on November 6, 1936. Analysis and criticism, of course, had been tokens of the intellectual world in the Weimar Republic. The new blanket measure, affecting mostly newspaper feuilletons (features) but also broadcasting, was decreed by Goebbels in his capacity as Propaganda Minister.[83] It meant that from now on only qualified Nazi authors were permitted comments about books, films, theater productions, *objets d'art*, or any other cultural medium. Because all of these, after January 1933, had to be motivated by a National Socialist spirit, there was, by definition, nothing for the writer to criticize. Henceforth an author, to be renamed "Kunstbetrachter" from "Kunstkritiker" – art observer from art critic – was to merely describe approvingly his or her preordained subjects rather than dissect them analytically, lest this be seen as criticism of the regime. This signaled that future creators who were long on Party ideology, even though they were short on skills, were welcome to step forward, at the expense of true talent.[84] The SS broadsheet *Das Schwarze Korps* characterized the workings of the new decree as ideal in a situation where "one views a work of art as a totality, meaning one does not abuse one's expert knowledge through analysis."[85] Rudolf Kircher, chief correspondent of the formerly renowned *Frankfurter Zeitung*, applauded this when he remarked that an author henceforth had to place himself "in the service of a conscious cultural policy, which is meant as a decisive part of National Socialism's work in the state and on the state."[86]

As for actual books, authors were cautioned not to place themselves on the existing blacklists, whose criteria were constantly expanded, and new ones issued. Apart from Goebbels and his tentacles, the criminal police also possessed the means to search and confiscate even private libraries, should this be warranted. Henceforth warned by previous examples, authors practiced self-censorship before handing in a manuscript to the boards to be examined, registered, and approved.[87] In this area, as Goebbels and the Reich Interior Ministry's police forces were increasingly collaborating, Rosenberg, always vying with Goebbels for control, again sought a piece of the action. Having instituted an Amt für Schrifttumspflege, an office for publishers' control, by June 1934 within the Party, he craved power over authors and publishers, only to remain impotent in the end. For just as his Kampfbund für deutsche Kultur was reduced to insignificance by 1935, in the face of Goebbels's growing powers, Rosenberg's censorship office was also eclipsed by his rivals, and thereafter effective only in the more limited realm of the Party.[88]

Yet another new law of the regime was passed, on the instigation of Goebbels, on May 5, 1934, regulating the stage. This law placed all affairs of theater, opera, and operetta squarely under the jurisdiction of the Propaganda Minister. (Exempt were the Prussian state stages, as well as the state orchestras, of Berlin, Kassel, and Wiesbaden, which remained under the Minister President of Prussia, in the person of Göring.) Paragraphs 3 and 4 of the new law governed supervision over the proprietors and directors of German stages, whether governmental or private, while paragraph 5 determined which (new) pieces of tragedy, comedy, or opera were suitable to be performed.[89] As an executive under these new orders, a Reichsdramaturg was to be appointed, with powers of acceptance or rejection. These functions were fulfilled throughout the Third Reich by Rainer Schlösser, a World War I veteran and doctor in German letters (until his capture by the Red Army and eventual execution in 1945). Schlösser would receive and process proposals for all theaters, exercising judgment of the kind that soon caused writers for the stage, composers, and librettists to resort to self-censorship, pre-empting any indictments, just as in the case of book publishers.[90]

It has already been observed how, through the existence of Goebbels's Propaganda Ministry (Promi), many facets of the administration of culture could be channeled, and how legislative action could be authorized and sustained. Yet another such administrative bracket was designed to further standardization and streamlining, this time on the personnel side. On September 22, 1933 the Propaganda Ministry was charged with the central coordination of artists, writers, and journalists in job-specific Kammern, or "chambers," after the establishment of the Reichskulturkammer (RKK). In their completed form, the individual genre chambers constituted a horizontal order in accordance with the corporatist principle characteristic of fascist regimes, after the initiation of such (Syndicalist) chambers by Benito Mussolini in the early 1920s, originally conceived to avoid industrial class struggle. Six chambers were created, one each for writers, journalists, radio workers, theater artists, musicians, and visual artists (the provisional Film Chamber of July 14 was later integrated, with the Press Chamber eventually removed).[91] In the judgment of historian Alan Steinweis, the conjoining of two parties of interest here promised advantages for both. "Signaling the regime's readiness to reward loyalty to the state with opportunities for material gain and latitude for professional autonomy, Goebbels succeeded in winning the cooperation of conservative (or apolitical) non-Nazis; these artists believed that a chamber system consisting of self-regulating corporations would help promote professional agendas that had remained unfulfilled during the economically troubled Weimar years."[92] In future, as membership in those chambers became compulsory, "Aryan" Germans, with Jews progressively filtered out, could elect to collaborate with the regime artistically according to the ever-amplified guidelines. If they transgressed, as did the novelist Jochen Klepper within the Reich Schrifttumskammer (RSK, Reich Writers' Chamber), they could face variably tight supervision or a writer's ban leading to exclusion, which Klepper incrementally suffered. Klepper, actually a right-wing patriot, had committed the capital crime of staying loyal to his Jewish wife, one of whose daughters from a first marriage was scheduled for deportation to the East at the height of World War II. The entire family of three committed suicide before the SS could knock on their door, in December 1942.[93]

A telling example of the Reich Culture Chamber's key role in music is provided by the Hindemith affair. Hindemith had Jewish relations, had played with prominent Jewish musicians such as the cellist Emanuel Feuermann in the past, and had himself written music that bordered on the avant-garde. This had turned Hitler against him, and Rosenberg's cohorts were determined to destroy him. On the other hand, Hindemith himself was intrigued by the possibility of exciting new ventures in the incipient Third Reich, and sympathizers close to Goebbels wanted him in the role of a nationalist innovator, notwithstanding his Modernist leanings. In February 1934, therefore, he was invited to join the Reich Music Chamber's (RMK) leadership council, as part of the overall Reich Culture Chamber (RKK) structure; what eased his decision to accept was that Richard Strauss already acted as the RMK's president, and conductor Wilhelm Furtwängler as Strauss's deputy. In March 1934, Hindemith presented a symphonic version of his opera-in-progress, *Mathis der Maler*, under Furtwängler's baton, in Berlin. It was well received, even in Nazi circles. Yet Rosenberg and Hitler continued their opposition, especially to a planned premiere of the composer's forthcoming opera. To aid Hindemith, Furtwängler published an article in his favor, trying to excuse his earlier, more pronounced, exploits in the avant-garde and characterizing him as apolitical. Objecting to such interference, Goebbels, as president of the overarching RKK, now turned openly against both Furtwängler and Hindemith, who then resigned from the Berlin Hochschule für Musik. Like Hindemith, Furtwängler lost his RMK post, temporarily falling out with the Nazi regime. Without official ties to the RKK, the future of both musicians in the Third Reich looked uncertain.[94]

Apart from the RKK, the Nazi regime also used professional associations to keep artists in lock step. One such organization was the Reichsverband der Deutschen Presse, the Reich association of the German press, which exercised job-specific jurisdiction over all its compulsory members working in the newspaper sector. The quasi-legal basis for this had been the Nazi Schriftleitergesetz of October 1933. Within this jurisdiction any journalist could be hauled before a professional tribunal for whatever might be deemed a transgression against the Nazi code of aesthetics, or of politics. As a local history from Franconia in 1936 demonstrates, suspected journalists could be placed at the whim of capricious superiors for months on end.[95]

And then there was continuous surveillance in some areas of cultural activity, implicitly, in film production, and again, explicitly, in the press and radio, with the latter two deemed so eminently political as shapers of public opinion. In broadcasting, programming was constantly reshaped on a weekly, if not daily basis.[96] For the press, Goebbels had regular meetings scheduled in Berlin, which representatives of Germany's main newspapers had to attend. Goebbels's lieutenants issued press directives that had to be followed by newspaper editors to the letter, and had to be kept secret. For instance, in December 1935 they were instructed not to mention butter in the preparation of Christmas cakes, lest a false sense of agricultural plenitude arose. That December also, the readers' attention was to be directed to a collection of speeches Minister Goebbels had just published. In September 1936 the sixtieth birthday of Nazi composer Georg Vollerthun was not to be announced, because of a pending charge of homosexuality against him. This and all other pieces of information were classified, subject to the threat of heavy penalties if released. When Walter Schwerdtfeger, a young journalist, was found to have passed on such instructions to foreign colleagues for several months, he was tried in 1935 and sentenced to a long term in penitentiary.[97]

The governance of the Third Reich, including the administration of its culture, took place through the application of fixed laws, several of them newly minted, and arbitrary decision-making, undertaken by senior and the most senior leaders. This led to an admixture of multiple executive orders and private judgment by State and Party grandees. In culture, the superimposition of arbitrary, personal rule over written law was chronic throughout the Third Reich, affecting the freedom of artists as much as the quality of their work. At times, such a work's very existence depended on the whim of a self-appointed censor, but also on a micro-managing Hitler.

Sometimes these censors, arrogating power unto themselves, could be relatively minor potentates. Alfred Rosenberg, with his drab personality, was merely a Reichsleiter in the Party. As such, he usually succumbed to functionaries who, next to their Party positions, also held office in governments of state, at Reich or regional levels, as did Göring as Prussian Minister President and Minister of Aviation and Goebbels as Reich Propaganda Minister. (In addition, Göring occupied the Party post of Reich Hunt Master and Goebbels that of Berlin Gauleiter.) But using whatever Party instruments he had,

Rosenberg managed every now and then to outdo even Goebbels as a controller, such as when he caused Rudolf Wagner-Régeny's opera *Die Bürger von Calais*, under Herbert von Karajan's musical direction, to be removed from the program of the Staatsoper in Berlin, even under Göring's sponsorship. The reason had been a libretto by Weimar-era Caspar Neher, which featured among the Calais citizens "a downtrodden group of people desperately brokering for peace," as well as Neher's bleak stage design. In January 1939 both were ill forebodings in an atmosphere where Nazi Germany was preparing for war. In addition, while the libretto had been based on a work by Georg Kaiser, the music was reminiscent of Weill's.[98] Next to a Reichsleiter, a Party department head, such as Rosenberg, a Gauleiter – Party district leader – could also interfere. This happened when Gauleiter Adolf Wagner of Munich – after messing with the city's art – forbade a performance of Schiller's drama *Maria Stuart* on Good Friday 1940, on the abstruse logic that a Catholic-tendentious piece would offend all Protestants. "The National Socialist state is disinterested in church matters of both confessions." The real reason was, however, that Wagner, guided by his personal sense of taste, wished to remove Schiller's classic from the playlists altogether. In this case, the Gauleiter had successfully overridden Goebbels's Reichsdramaturg, Rainer Schlösser.[99]

In his Prussian fiefdom, Göring usually had more power than Rosenberg and could rival even Goebbels as Gauleiter of the capital. When in 1939 a Berlin stage production of Shakespeare's *Richard II* scheduled for the Vienna Reich Theater Week was declined by Goebbels's Promi, Göring protested successfully. It had been the creation of his protégés at the Staatstheater, Gustaf Gründgens and Jürgen Fehling, and Göring's wife, the former actress Emmy Sonnemann, stood behind it; Gründgens was to play the main protagonist. Goebbels did not demur.[100] In another instance, also in 1939, Werner Egk's opera *Peer Gynt* was denounced by Göring to Hitler, possibly because the Minister President saw himself made fun of in the character of a fat stage troll (but probably also because he did not like the jazz-like dazzle). Yet Hitler, who had been enthralled by the music, dismissed his complaint, personally taking care that Egk became a favored artist, and even a department head in Goebbels's Music Chamber.[101]

In June 1933, Hitler had accorded to Goebbels's Propaganda Ministry supervisory powers – in excess of the minister's regular privileges – excised from other ministries, such as certain art supervision from the Foreign Ministry, and press and radio prerogatives from that of the Interior Ministry.[102] Thus fortified, and over and above fixed clauses if need be, Goebbels could oversee culture production in any shape or form as he saw fit, whenever the spirit moved him. Usually, he concentrated on film reviews; he possessed studios both in his offices and two residences. In the course of this, he also discussed film outlines with directors and actors, as he did with Jenny Jugo in March 1935, regarding a *Pygmalion* project. Sometimes he went to great lengths to delay a film for which he desired substantial improvements, as in the case of *Land der Liebe* (*Land of Love*), which remained in limbo from April 1937 until it was finally approved in June. How many films Goebbels vetted personally – beyond any other routine controls – is not exactly known; experts estimate approximately two-thirds until 1942–3, and thereafter less than half. Yet even this is an astonishing amount, given the minister's many other burdens.[103]

Hitler, too, with studios both at the Reichskanzlei and his private get-away, the Berchtesgaden Berghof, was interested in scrutinizing cinema. He often viewed pictures with Goebbels, more typically with a coterie in private.[104] He decided to proscribe films such as *Weisse Sklaven* (*White Slaves*, 1936) starring Camilla Horn, because it touched on Bolshevism,[105] and *Das Leben kann so schön sein* (*Life Could Be So Beautiful*, 1938). Here Hitler had the government's social policy in his mind: *Life Could Be So Beautiful* was the story of a newly married couple trying against all odds to make a decent living. The young hero was running up and down stairs peddling insurance, while his pregnant wife, helping financially with work at home, could not come to grips with life in their single, shabby apartment room. The message of this movie, that an indigent young couple can hardly afford to bring a child into their sad existence, was not lost on Hitler, who flew into a rage and forbade it. For a people professing lack of Lebensraum it was demographically impossible to conjure a scenario in which babies were not wanted.[106]

However, as far as films were concerned, the most acute interest shown by Hitler was in the weekly newsreels. These embodied for him what film was all about: an ideal instrument for political control. He regularly commented on newsreels to Goebbels, and had some severely cut or modified. More so than in the case of feature films, Hitler was liable to override any decisions Goebbels had already made on them. Even long before the war broke out Hitler was adamant that newsreels display the heroic – rows of military men.[107] This was a sure sign that Hitler knew many years ahead of time where his politics were to lead, to aggressive war in the course of which much of the art he was now in control of would also change.

THE QUARREL OVER EXPRESSIONISM

Gottfried Benn, the son of an East Elbian clergyman, took his leave from the military and began practicing pathology in Berlin in 1912, at the age of twenty-six. It was then that he published his first work, a thin volume of poems entitled *Morgue*, Benn's impressions from his autopsies. Beneath the front cover of a violin-playing skeleton and a reclining nude girl, the fourth poem began: "Bedded on a pillow of dark blood there lay the blonde neck of a white woman/The sun created havoc with her hair, licking its way up her brilliant legs/. . . A Nigger beside her, his eyes and forehead ripped by a horseshoe's iron/Was sticking two toes of his dirty left foot into her small white ear."[108] Purporting to examine "the banality of human existence and its physical decline," with its novel, direct, language this booklet became part of the Expressionist literary canon at the time. A follow-up volume, *Söhne (Sons)*, was dedicated to the Jewish writer Else Lasker-Schüler, with whom Benn was romantically involved.

During World War I, Benn re-entered the army to serve as a field physician in Brussels, where he authored the so-called *Rönne* novels. The protagonist Rönne was Benn himself, obsessed with sexuality. In 1917 he became a dermatologist in Berlin, publishing *Gehirne (Brains)*, a collection of prose, and poems under the heading *Fleisch (Flesh)*; they appear nihilistic, showing a disdain for humankind, as his reaction to the cruelties of war. This work then paralleled the paintings of Grosz and Dix, equally cynical reactions to the Great War and its excrescences beyond the armistice of November 1918. Benn supplied the text for the secular oratorio *Das Unaufhörliche (The Never-Ending)* by Hindemith – he of the New Objectivity – which, after its premiere in 1931, was generally deemed nihilistic. In 1932, Benn was elected a fellow of the Prussian Academy of Arts and, unlike Ricarda Huch and others, he remained a fellow after the Nazi rise to power in January 1933, advancing to become provisional head of the poetry section in February.[109]

As he explained in a radio address in the spring of 1933, Benn had been disillusioned with the Weimar Republic because of a degeneration of democracy and a corrupt liberal intelligentsia more interested in Ascona real estate than staying at home and working the soil by hand. By contrast, the youths currently supporting the new Reich were vitalist, vanguards of a new biological race, a "master race" of the type Nietzsche had once forecast. They shunned the intellectuality of the city and instead chose the organic order of the land. These were protectors of the white race, defending their priorities against lower species such as black colonial troops who had roamed Germany earlier in the service of the occupying French. Such a new form of rule was already being supported by the lower classes, rendering Communists and Socialists of old superfluous. Hitler's populist, direct democracy deserved support, as did the new state he was in the process of constructing.[110]

In November, Benn published an article, "Affirmation of Expressionism," in which he rued the regime's critical stance toward that art form, emphasizing that he still believed in it. He elucidated that Expressionism was a European movement chiefly covering the years 1910 to 1925, with Spaniards such as Pablo Picasso adhering to it, as well as Frenchmen such as Georges Braque, Romanians like Constantin Brancusi and Russians like Wassily Kandinsky. In Germany, Hindemith was its representative, said Benn, and in Italy, Gian Francesco Malipiero and Filippo Tommaso Marinetti, the originator of Futurism, which Mussolini had adopted as an element of Fascism. In a more distant past, Nietzsche, Hölderlin, and Goethe had served as precursors, as had, not least, Richard Wagner. Benn invested Expressionism with political significance for the new National Socialist epoch by assigning to it an "anti-liberal function of the spirit," and he hastened to add that the art form in and by itself did nothing to alienate the German people. After World War I a philosophy of destructionism had taken hold, declared Benn, and Expressionism had come forth to oppose it, as a "formal absolutism excluding every chaos."[111]

As a self-professed fascist as well as defender of an art form he knew most leading Nazis rejected, Benn had tried to square the circle – an exercise that was to count heavily against him. His fearless mention of the European universality of Expressionism as well as the names of non-"Aryans" as its proponents, such as Sigmund Freud and Marcel Proust, caused widespread hostility. He was accused of being a Jew – a charge against which he found it acutely necessary to defend himself publicly.

He also published follow-up articles, singing the praises of the new regime, particularly in racist-eugenic terms, which, as a physician, he thought legitimate. But when in 1936 an anthology of his earlier poems, reaching back to 1911, appeared in print, the SS's *Das Schwarze Korps* embarked on a massive attack, labeling his literary output "deviant obscenities." Officially out of favor, Benn withdrew to the army, again practicing his trusted profession as a physician, within its ranks. He was to lose his membership in the Reich Schrifttumskammer in March 1938.[112] And thus, one prominent attempt to salvage Expressionism for the Nazi regime by a Nazi had come to a pathetic end.[113] This attempt did not stand in isolation.

Among the artists of the German avant-garde after World War I, the sculptor Ernst Barlach and painter Emil Nolde, next to Benn, stood out as veritable giants. Like Benn eventually, to the Nazis they appeared as emblematic of modernity in the arts and potentially liable for prosecution. Yet they followed different paths from one another, as they did from Benn, and came through the Third Reich in different ways.

Barlach was born in 1870 in a small Holstein town, the son of a country doctor. He studied in Hamburg and Dresden, then Paris in the mid-1890s. On a trip to Tsarist Russia in 1906 he developed a decisive talent for registering human expressions that was to characterize his style of modeling people. A year later he became a member of the Berlin Secession, as did many of Germany's modern visual artists. He never married, but in 1906 had a son with a seamstress well below his social station. In 1907 he also began writing, mostly stage plays. In 1910 he moved to Güstrow, a small town in the north-east region of Mecklenburg. And here he developed what would make him excel as an Expressionist painter and sculptor: reduction of his human torsos to a minimal size, in relation to the hands and face, through which he aimed to show his subjects' inner constitution. On Barlach's humans, faces and hands tended to look exaggerated. Barlach served briefly in Sonderburg near Denmark during the war and thereafter re-emphasized, in his art, the biblical motifs on which he had already been working. In 1919 he became a member of the Prussian Academy of Arts, the eminent Jewish culture broker Paul Cassirer serving as his main agent, both for his graphic works and dramas. A recipient of the Kleist prize for literature in 1924, as a sculptor Barlach began accepting commissions for anti-war monuments after 1926. He produced important works until 1933, among them the soon famous honor monument in Magdeburg Cathedral and sculptures in Kiel from 1928, which were attacked by nationalist fanatics even then.[114]

After January 1933, Rosenberg loyalists attacked Barlach because his "solitary, ruminating individuals, introspective even in a group, contradicted every National Socialist ideal of German men and women, who find themselves by serving country and Führer."[115] Since he was losing his current Jewish agent Alfred Flechtheim, whose Düsseldorf gallery was forced to surrender to the Nazis in March, Barlach was selling less; contracts were not honored and he was being owed money. Soon he found himself in financial difficulties, with taxes in arrears and debts on a mortgage. Like Benn, he had to contend with accusations that he was Jewish but, unlike Benn, saw himself unable to do anything about it in public. He was aware that unorthodox radicals from the National Socialist German Students' League (NSDStB) were in his favor, but realistically did not attach significance to that.[116]

In February 1934, Mecklenburg's Gauleiter Heinrich Hildebrandt denounced Barlach in a speech. "Barlach may be an artist, but he is foreign to the German essence. It is incumbent on the artists' estate to comprehend German man in his simple genuine form, as God has created him." And he continued: "German man does not know of the peasant as a person stretched out lazily on the soil, but as a hard and self-confident man willing to overcome all vicissitudes, who cuts a swath with a brutal fist, indeed with a sword in his hand."[117] With only a few Nazis still willing to defend him in print and Rosenberg as vociferous as ever, Barlach's health was deteriorating by the month.[118] Hoping for some relief from the authorities, he joined other intellectuals and artists in signing a declaration of loyalty to Hitler in the summer. Half-convinced, he wrote in September to a friend that he would counsel all young people to join the Nazi Party, for "the best blood, the best qualities of character are merely good enough for it."[119] By March 1935, Barlach the dramatist was out of favor.[120]

In 1936 his old admirer Joseph Goebbels turned openly against him after Rosenberg appeared to have won the Expressionism struggle ideologically. When in March the Bavarian political police forbade a book of the artist's drawings and confiscated 3,149 already published copies in the Munich warehouse of Barlach's publisher Reinhard Piper, Barlach wrote to Goebbels asking him to intervene: "The artistic value or non-value of my works exists beyond the decisions thought necessary by the political police." Goebbels did nothing, but commented in his diary, most likely lying to himself: "This is not art any more. This is destruction, incompetent fake. Horrible! This poison must not enter the people."[121]

In the following months, after works of his had been confiscated in ongoing exhibitions, Barlach was working less, selling less, becoming increasingly unwell in his isolated house in Güstrow, befriended only by his lover Marga Böhmer and, occasionally, her former husband, the Nazi-inclined art dealer Bernhard Böhmer (who actually tried to help him out with the authorities as best he could). Although he had to suffer loss of sales and the proscription of any shows, a formal indictment of Barlach's profession as an artist was never uttered, however afraid of it he was. He became embittered, loath even to receive any visitors. The removal by the Nazis of his important Magdeburg memorial gave rise to cries for the dismantling of other of his statues. In 1937 alone, 317 of his monuments were impounded. The German public was encouraged to show its contempt for his works at the "Degenerate Art" exhibition in July. Forlorn, Ernst Barlach died on October 24, 1938, at the age of sixty-eight.[122]

Much like Barlach, Emil Nolde has been canonized after 1945 as a martyr of National Socialism. But whereas Barlach had always been indifferent to the politics of the Third Reich (as he had been to that of the Empire and the Weimar Republic), Nolde, like Benn, was a Nazi early on, irrespective of the difficulties he encountered with the regime. It was therefore not appropriate to depict him as Max Ludwig Nansen, the intrepid resistance fighter in the Schleswig village of Rugbüll, as Siegfried Lenz did in 1968 in his novel *Deutschstunde* (*German Lesson*), with other German authors following suit. Not least, the venal Nolde's own autobiographies have smoothed the path for such distortions.[123]

Nolde's path in the Third Reich turned out to be one between acclamation and defeat, with defeat stealthily winning the upper hand. He was born Hans Emil Hansen in Nolde, Schleswig, the son of peasants, in 1867. Of Danish-German lineage, he was part of an ethnic minority that opted for life in the German Reich even under foreign citizenship. He became a carver and draftsman and in 1892 began creating watercolors of mountain motifs in Switzerland. In 1899, Franz von Stuck turned down his application to the Munich Academy of Arts, eight years before Adolf Hitler would be refused by the academy in Vienna. But Nolde did visit the private Académie Julian in Paris, which taught painting in the staid academic style opposed to the new Impressionism. In 1901 he became a member of the Berlin Secession, a junction with Modernism, and two years later his paintings turned out to be very bright and intensive. During an exhibition in Dresden in 1906, Emil Nolde, as he now called himself, got to know artists of Die Brücke, which influenced his painterly style decisively yet again: expressive paintwork, simple pronounced shapes, with the emphasis on form. In 1911 the Berlin Secession repudiated Nolde's pictures, now more imbued with biblical motifs, which led to a controversy with Germany's leading Impressionist, the Jewish Max Liebermann, and Nolde's eventual exclusion from that movement. This quarrel with Liebermann, the head of the Secession at that time, as well as with the art dealer Paul Cassirer, most certainly was the source of Nolde's subsequent hatred of Jews, as well as his definitive rejection of Impressionism, which he declared to be French and degenerate. Such sentiments help to explain why Nolde became a follower of the xenophobic, anti-Semitic Nazis as early as 1920. Residing, after 1925, in the North Frisian hamlet of Seebüll, Nolde was elected a fellow of the Prussian Academy of Arts in 1931. He greeted the political victory of the National Socialists two years later with enthusiasm.[124]

At the beginning of the new regime Goebbels attempted to appoint this representative of what many regarded as "Nordic Expressionism" to the head of a Berlin art academy. But Hitler had found a Nolde painting on Goebbels's premises and told him to remove it. With his traditionalist beliefs in art, the Führer hated Nolde because of his concentration on New Testament themes and "the violent distortions and colors in his work."[125] At all events, when interviewed for the new position in the Propaganda Ministry, Nolde consented to a new ordering of the German art world, denouncing his old compatriot of Die Brücke and fellow candidate for the job, the "Aryan" Max Pechstein, as a Jew.[126] In the following months and years, in all probability aware of Hitler's opposition and Goebbels's wavering, Nolde fought hard for his recognition in the Nazi movement. He still had backers from its early days, one being Erna Hanfstaengl of the influential Hanfstaengl art-publishing family, who had shielded Hitler right after the fatal Beer Hall Putsch. At her private art gallery on Munich's Karlsplatz, Hanfstaengl now made a point of exhibiting several Nolde paintings, "because we are here in the focus of the Nazis and theoretically all official Nazis have to pass by here." She also planted several Nolde watercolors in her brother Ernst ("Putzi") Hanfstaengl's Munich apartment, so that Hitler, a personal friend of Putzi's, would see them there.[127] In November 1933, Erna Hanfstaengl prevailed upon her close friend Marga Himmler to get her husband Heinrich to invite Nolde to a banquet commemorating the 1923 November putsch; Captain Ernst Röhm, leader of the SA and an ox of a man, came to be seated next to him. Reflecting on this event, Nolde wrote shortly thereafter: "The Führer is great and noble in his aspirations and a genius man of action. He is still being surrounded by a swarm of dark figures in an artificially created cultural fog. It seems as if the sun will break through here and dispel this fog in the near future."[128]

However, if Nolde had thought of himself in this connection he was to be disappointed. Even though, like Barlach, he still had his admirers in the Nazi camp (and like Barlach signed the declaration of loyalty to Hitler in 1934), forces influenced by Rosenberg and no doubt riveted to Hitler were turning increasingly against him.[129] In Theodor Fritsch's influential *Handbook of the Jewish Question* of 1935, Nolde was lumped together with Jewish painters, as he had been as guilty as they were of championing Expressionism, having tested aesthetic limits even more than they had.[130] Rosenberg's follower, the painter and critic Wolfgang Willrich, wrote in 1937 that even if Nolde was politically acceptable, "his work and his imagination are sick," totally in line with artistic Bolshevism.[131] At this time Nolde was asked to leave the Prussian Academy of Arts; only after his strong protests in which he flaunted his Party membership was he, for the time being, allowed to stay. Nevertheless, by the time of the "Degenerate Art" exhibition in July, 1,052 works by Nolde had been confiscated from public displays, more than that of any other artist.[132]

Although Nolde was given several of the boycotted paintings back as time went on, his overall situation did not improve. In August 1941 he was expelled from Goebbels's Reich Art Chamber, and three months later came a formal order forbidding him to paint or sell any paintings.[133] Yet, however much the artist himself may have dramatized this injustice after World War II, he was in fact not prevented from painting in private, barring any sales. This he did, in the isolation of his northern village, after a 1942 meeting with Gauleiter Baldur von Schirach in Vienna, brokered by the admiring film star Mathias Wieman, had proved fruitless. As late as 1944, Nolde's Danish wife Ada was writing letters to high-level individuals in the Party and in government, citing Nolde's patriotism no less than his Party membership: "His followers, young and old, are all waiting for the day when the state will give him the recognition he is currently denied for some sad reason."[134]

In the early Third Reich, Nolde, just like Benn, stood firmly in the camp of a number of National Socialists who championed Expressionism, thinking it would perfectly exemplify the new fascist spirit. To this group belonged university students, artists, intellectuals, and also politicians. Joseph Goebbels, as a young man with intellect and taste, had shown pro-Modernist leanings. Although he took issue with leading Expressionists such as Georg Kaiser, his own play, *Der Wanderer* of 1927, which exulted in a prophecy of the Third Reich, bore elements of Expressionism, as the critics noted at the time. Helmut Heiber, Goebbels's first serious biographer, detected "Expressionist love lyrics" in the young man's novel *Michael*, written between 1923 and 1929. And although in music, as his diaries show, Goebbels adhered to traditional forms as in the works of Beethoven, Richard Strauss, and – less so – Wagner, in the visual arts he admired the works of Ernst Barlach and Emil Nolde.[135]

Expressionism in the Third Reich can be explained in three ways: a reaction against pre-existing art forms; the inability of the Nazis to create something ideologically apposite in the immediate term; and, in principle, the indifference of art, even in the late, conflicted, Weimar Republic, to politics. That is to say: the creators of modern art in the Weimar era were not necessarily left wing, even though many of them were; they could also be politically neutral (as was Barlach), or on the conservative to extreme right (as were Benn and Nolde).[136]

The institutional struggle between Rosenberg and Goebbels served as a political background, against which the fate of Expressionism was decided. On June 29, 1933, National Socialist student leaders in Berlin, only weeks after they had burned books, staged a public event at Berlin University under the heading "Youth is Fighting for German Art." Almost certainly, they had been influenced by an article in mid-March in the Berlin newspaper *Deutsche Allgemeine Zeitung*, intellectual in content and decidedly hostile to Rosenberg, authored by Bruno E. Werner. He was a thirty-six-year-old doctor of philosophy from Leipzig, on the political right, but an early admirer of the

Bauhaus. Werner argued that "the new art" had been pioneering the national revolution in that it had fought against the liberal nineteenth century and the French model of Impressionism as early as twenty-five years before. At that time, painters of the art movements Die Brücke and Der Blaue Reiter, notably Nolde, Barlach, Pechstein and Franz Marc, Klee and Lionel Feininger, had been in the vanguard.[137] Rosenberg countered this with an article in *Völkischer Beobachter*, maintaining that even though Nolde and Barlach possessed talent, especially Nolde's artwork was "negroid, bereft of piety, raw and without true inner power of form," and some of Barlach's "half-idiotic."[138] But on June 29 Berlin university students organized in the Nazi Student League (NSDStB), allied with Goebbels's Promi, picked up their cue from Werner and advanced their own arguments, contra Rosenberg, on behalf of Nolde, Barlach, and other Expressionists.[139] In Peter Paret's able summation, "they believed in the mythic power of German blood, in the essential bond between the German people and the German artist who served the race, whose work expressed in spirit, if not necessarily in form or thematically, the Nordic, Aryan values that had sustained Germans through centuries of delusions and betrayals and that were now infused with political power and given new life by Hitler." Anti-Semitism was enlisted, for Jews had introduced Impressionism to Germany, argued the students, and Expressionism was an antidote to it.[140]

In the fall the controversy escalated. Hans Weidemann, head of the Berlin student group and a painter in his own right, founded a new journal with the title *Kunst der Nation* (*Art of the Nation*), which aimed to further "Nordic Expressionism" by featuring in its pages works by Nolde, Barlach, Käthe Kollwitz, and others. Encouraged, the pro-avant-garde director Alois Schardt opened a show of Expressionist paintings at the Berlin Kronprinzenpalast gallery in October, with an introductory lecture attempting to draw parallels between Expressionist exuberance and Germanic art of the Bronze Age. A month later, Benn's "Affirmation of Expressionism" appeared in print. But on the other side Hitler had, at the Reich Party rally in September, been chastising all modern art as a "Cubist-Dadaist cult of primitivism." Schardt lost his post at the national gallery a few weeks later and eventually fled to the United States; the future of the new journal was uncertain.[141]

In 1934 the demise of the students' pro-Expressionist cause accelerated. Early in the year a book by the Nazi art critic Kurt Karl Eberlein appeared,

What is German in German Art?, in which he asserted that currently the German battle was being waged "against the un-German, the foreign, the blood-alien, against the Romanic, French, Slavic-Russian, against everything non-national, antinational, international in German art." He then questioned whether "it is very easy to argue that the German element is manifestly recognizable in these 'Expressionist' pictures." Eberlein was only meekly rejected by the art historian Wilhelm Pinder, a National Socialist but internationally respected authority, who stated that his comments amounted to "a destructive judgment on the Expressionists," without elaborating.[142] And even though other moderately progressive art critics such as Winfried Wendland and Hans Weigert came forth in defense of the embattled art form, the latter holding that "the heritage of the best Expressionism" might be worth treasuring, their statements were timid, and they were writing under the shadow of Rosenberg.[143]

The position of the chief Party ideologue had been strengthened on January 24, 1934 by Hitler, who had appointed Rosenberg "plenipotentiary for the supervision of the spiritual and ideological schooling of the NSDAP."[144] Although this was merely a Party post, not a government one, Rosenberg himself arrogated powerful prerogatives to himself with reaches into all facets of public life and, as far as culture was concerned, assuming something like equilibrium with the offices of Goebbels and of Göring. And so he struck out again, charging that the students were being seduced by Jewish art dealers into drawing a line "from Grünewald via Caspar David Friedrich to – Nolde and consorts," with the aim of summoning up the Expressionists' "subhumanity."[145] The Röhm Putsch at the end of June strengthened Rosenberg's position as Hitler, in September, reiterated his resolve to purge "these charlatans."[146]

In 1935 the authorities cashiered *Kunst der Nation*. Otto Andreas Schreiber and Fritz Hippler, co-conspirators of Weidemann, had already been expelled from the NSDStB and were now seeking positions in Goebbels's ever expanding operations. In the face of Hitler's own traditionalist aesthetic predilections and opposed by an ambitious Rosenberg, Goebbels's more progressive efforts were being attenuated. His executive powers, however, were growing by virtue of an expanded bureaucracy: his Propaganda Ministry, the Reich Culture Chamber with its variegated subchambers (although nominally part of the ministry), simply overwhelmed

Rosenberg's new office, whose KfdK was fading into oblivion. Its successor organization the NSKG (Nationalsozialistische Kulturgemeinde) became powerless, as it drifted into the orbit of Robert Ley's Labor Front (DAF), the overarching National Socialist organization created to replace the independent trade unions after Hitler became Chancellor.[147] In a speech in Weimar during May, Goebbels showed himself of two minds: he spoke against ambitious reactionaries, which could have buoyed the avant-garde, but he also railed against "cultural-Bolshevist attempts scheming to use National Socialism" to attain public recognition, which would have encouraged traditionalists.[148]

After further polemics in the following months, in which the anti-Modernist forces showed more strength,[149] Hitler himself made the final decision during the opening of the "Grosse Deutsche Kunstausstellung" ("Great German Art Exhibition") on July 18, 1937, sounding the death knell for the avant-garde. Hitler said: "Until the National Socialist assumption of power there existed in Germany a so-called 'modern' art, meaning almost every year a new one, as the term implies. National Socialist Germany, however, wants a 'German art,' and this is destined to be an eternal one, just as all creative values of a people."[150]

However, as the protagonists of Expressionism were fighting for survival, this allegedly subversive art was still manifesting itself in several ways up to and even beyond 1937. Still in 1933 and with the encouragement of Goebbels, Schreiber fled under the wings of Ley, who was ideologically more indifferent than either Goebbels or Rosenberg. He was in the process of building up his offices for "Strength-through-Joy," and there Schreiber established a department of visual art. It was to show the works of Expressionists such as Pechstein, Marc, and Schmitt-Rottluff in factories throughout the land for the next ten years, until defeat at the battle of Stalingrad (1942–3) changed all the rules.[151]

Also in 1933, at least two pronouncedly pro-Nazi works of art still bore the stamp of Expressionism. One was the stage play *Schlageter* by Hanns Johst, which had its premiere in Berlin on April 20, the birthday of the Führer. Admittedly, Johst was a well-known Expressionist himself, from the days of World War I when he knew and admired Gottfried Benn; he conceived the prose of this drama as the republic was petering out. The Modernist touch showed especially toward the end of the play, as the German nationalist martyr, accused saboteur Albert Leo Schlageter, faces the French execution squad and exclaims: "One last word! One wish! Command! Germany!!! Awake! Break into Flames!! Burn! Burn monstrously!!"[152]

Moreover, ironically, the most Nazi of films, *Hitlerjunge Quex* (*Hitler Youth Quex*), which celebrated the martyr's death of Herbert Norkus after he was murdered by Berlin Communist youths in January 1932, showed itself indebted to Weimar-era film. An observant viewer could not escape allusions to *Kuhle Wampe* (*Who Owns the World?*, 1932), *Die Dreigroschenoper* (*The Threepenny Opera*, 1931), and *Mutter Krausens Fahrt ins Glück* (*Mother Krause's Trip to Happiness*, 1929) – all highlights of Expressionist cinema.[153] All spectacular, peculiarly Nazi Thingspiele, plays that flourished between 1933 and 1936, also bore a resemblance to Expressionist and workers' drama, a factor that helped spell their doom.[154]

In 1937, when Hitler personally caused a sea change in the German art world, the very building in which he announced it, the new, monumentalist, and neo-classicist Munich Haus der Deutschen Kunst (House of German Art), featured a flat roof and plain, functional construction, thus reminding viewers of the Bauhaus. "The museum's blocky masses and flat surfaces," notes historian Barbara Miller Lane, "free of all ornament save minimal base and cornice projections, and the horizontal orientations of the building, proclaimed its debt to the radicals of the twenties." And the show that Hitler subsequently opened, the "Great German Art" exhibition, itself contained *objets d'art* influenced by the modern art style the Führer was now denouncing.[155] Also in 1937 the quarter-Jewish Jürgen Fehling directed Shakespeare's *Richard III* at Berlin's Prussian State Theater. An admirer of Barlach and himself a product of the Expressionist school, Fehling had asked his protagonist Werner Krauss, as the tyrant, to insinuate himself into the character of Joseph Goebbels – shadowy, ominously quiet, and with limping foot. The scenery onstage was bleak and economical, adorned with little but the occasional Bauhaus-like steel-tube furniture.[156] Fehling was walking a tightrope, but for the moment he survived critique.

EXHIBITIONS OF DEGENERATE ART AND MUSIC

At the "Degenerate Art" exhibition, which opened in Munich on July 19, 1937, Nolde was represented by over fifty of his artworks. Of Kirchner's works, thirty-two were shown, after more than six hundred of his paintings had been confiscated from public museums. Barlach was represented by his bronze cast *The Reunion* and the prohibited book of drawings, shown in a glass case with other forbidden items, and labeled *Kulturschänder* (*Defilers of Culture*). As Barlach complained, a few leaves had been cut from the volume and displayed separately – unfairly, he thought, because they did not represent the entire book.[157]

Behind this exhibition was Joseph Goebbels, who had been realizing for some time that Rosenberg was outsmarting him in the presence of Hitler with his arch-reactionary, anti-Modernist ideas, even though the minister enjoyed the advantages of organization. In art, Hitler agreed with those ideas – however much he may have despised the empty self-importance of Rosenberg. So in order to safeguard any position of strength, Goebbels had at least to be seen as being in accord with such a cultural course, while at the same time putting his own, much sharper, administrative instruments to action. Hence, during the first half of 1937, he seized the initiative again, prevailing upon Hitler to authorize him to stage an exhibition of "degenerate art," on the model of the earlier punitive exhibitions at Karlsruhe, Stuttgart, and Nuremberg. Goebbels conceived this venture as a convenient political manoeuvre that would effectively freeze out Rosenberg. Once mandated, he used Hitler's authorization on June 30 to delegate Professor Adolf Ziegler, the current president of the Reich Art Chamber in the RKK, and safely within the Promi, to collect the required artifacts.[158]

As Ziegler acknowledged subsequently in his Munich opening speech, such collecting was a mammoth job, for in order to accomplish it, he had to visit "nearly all German museums."[159] To aid him, Ziegler had assembled a five-member committee, which included, besides himself, the ambitious Count Baudissin from the Essen Folkwang Museum and the venomous art writer Wolfgang Willrich, author of the treatise "Purging the Art Temple." Allegedly under instructions from Hitler, the committee looked to confiscate works created after 1910, which was the year Kandinsky had presented the first-ever abstract painting, as well as the founding date of Herwarth Walden's pace-setting Expressionist journal *Der Sturm*.[160] The principal museums called upon (with the reluctant acquiescence of the Education Minister Bernhard Rust, under whose jurisdiction they fell) were those in Frankfurt, Dresden, Düsseldorf, and Berlin. Approximately 5,000 paintings were culled as well as 12,000 prints; in the end upwards of 500 works of art were chosen for display, by altogether 112 condemnable artists. Broadly speaking, the style categories were Expressionism, Verism, Dadaism – the main areas of Modernist art, allowing for possible overlaps. Of storied movements, Die Brücke and Der Blaue Reiter were signally affected. Leading German artists such as Kirchner, Pechstein, and Beckmann were instant victims, but Ziegler also focused on the works of foreigners such as Picasso, Henri Matisse, Edvard Munch, and Marc Chagall, seeking to smear those painters' names.[161]

After Hitler and Goebbels had privately viewed the exhibits three days prior, the "Degenerate Art" exhibition opened in Munich, at the archaeological institute, on Monday, July 19. The entire German press, including the formerly bourgeois papers now under the restrictions of the critics' guidelines from November 1936, waxed lyrical. "Trainloads of dirt" had been emptied into the museum's halls, wrote the once venerable *Deutsche Allgemeine Zeitung*, "magazines and basements have opened up to disgorge their refuse," shrilled the *Münsterischer Anzeiger*.[162] The National Socialist organ *National-Zeitung* of Essen, Graf Baudissin's haunt, ironically was in keeping with original Expressionist intentions when it stated that Expressionist colors literally screamed at the visitors, "instilling horror into us, with the wackiness of the lines, with the decadence of expression."[163] The Nazi organizers had done their best to present the paintings in a most disadvantageous fashion, by hanging them obliquely from the walls and too close together, in primitive wooden frames and sometimes touching the floor.[164] Nolde himself complained about "the unfavorable light" and "red tags with spiteful slogans."[165] In some cases, perfidiously, the purchase price paid by a public institution for a work with taxpayers' money was indicated – many thousands of marks to shock the viewers. What was left unsaid was that these had been inflation-era amounts from the early 1920s when 10,000 marks would not even have bought a loaf of bread.[166]

By all accounts the Munich show was popular.[167] Before it was sent on the road it had been seen, in the vast number of cases approvingly, by over two million men and women, free of charge – those under legal age were barred.[168] Originally scheduled to run until the end of September, it was extended to the end of November.[169] The effect of such defamatory displays on the artists concerned naturally was disastrous, even if some of them, such as the heirs of the sculptor Wilhelm Lehmbruck, received their exhibits back some time later.[170] By the end of 1943, Karl Hofer was still mourning the loss of sixty of his paintings in his Berlin atelier alone.[171]

As the exhibition was sent on its way throughout Germany, it was introduced by a brochure guide authored by one Fritz Kaiser of Munich, on the authority of Goebbels's offices.[172] This explained in some detail the criteria by which the exposition "groups" had been assembled. Group one concerned itself with form and color – the accentuation of which had been central to Expressionist art. Here Kaiser deplored the culprits' "motif selection" and "contempt of every craftsmanlike expertise."[173] In group two Kaiser pretended Modernist artists like Nolde and Barlach had violated religious sensitivities – a ludicrous argument in a totalitarian state simultaneously fighting the two Christian Churches.[174] With group three Kaiser endeavored to demonstrate the "political background" of the exhibition: "artistic anarchy" had dominated those creators, with a Bolshevist "class struggle" as its goal.[175] As if all avant-garde artists in the republic had been on the political extreme left! Pacifist tendencies were singled out in group four, as crippled war veterans of the type Dix and Grosz had been painting were shown.[176] Group five presented artists' works as emblems of bordellos: "for them humankind consists of whores and pimps." Here intersections with the Marxist group were unmistakable.[177] Groups six and seven shone light on the significance of race, especially as it was tied to issues of eugenics: the spiritual ideal of Modernist art had been "the idiot, the cretin, and the paralytic." Likewise, images of "Negroes and South Sea islanders" in the manner of Gauguin were condemned.[178] Stopping at group eight, the viewer had arrived at the problem of the Jews as exemplified by the canvases of Jewish artists such as Otto Freundlich and Ludwig Meidner, depicted on page 21.[179] (One drawback of the organizers in their hasty planning of the exhibition had been the scarceness of German Jews in their capacity as visual artists; hence the planners' resolve to include foreigners like Chagall – when it came to art and Jews, merely the proverbial Jewish art dealer could serve as bogeyman. Max Liebermann, who had died in 1935, was spared, perhaps because he had simply been too famous.) Group nine, finally, attacked the concept of abstraction in the form of "isms," using works by the former Bauhaus associate Johannes Molzahn and the Dadaist Kurt Schwitters.[180] The booklet then continued with a partial reprint of Hitler's speech at the opening of the

House of German Art, hours before the "Degenerate Art" exhibition.[181] At the end was a comparison between two Modernist graphics with the drawing of an insane-asylum inmate, obviously based on Schultze-Naumburg's examples from 1932. Which of the three was a dilettante's work, went the riddle. "The upper right one! But the other two were once described as magisterial graphics authored by Kokoschka."[182]

That there were "groups" denouncing Jews and Marxists was hardly surprising for contemporaries. But the emphasis on the sick, more particularly the mentally ill, was a relatively novel twist in this German culture, even though Schultze-Naumburg and Hitler himself had publicly harped on the nexus between Modernist art and insanity for some time. Adolf Ziegler emphasized this point in his opening address, and the newspapers duly elaborated on it, the *Hamburger Tageblatt* excoriating "pathological phenomena and horror."[183] Indeed, halfway through 1937 regime leaders were already preparing the case for what they were to call "euthanasia," the forced mercy-killing of patients in insane asylums, which the people would have to get used to. Even then, they were sterilizing the so-called Rhineland bastards, children of unwanted unions between German girls and what were considered colored French colonial soldiers – occupation troops in western Germany after World War I.[184] One scholar who realized this connection well was Professor Carl Schneider of Heidelberg University, the director of its mental-illness care facilities, who in 1939, as the "Degenerate Art" exhibition was viewed in several German cities, would write a lecture on the subject of degenerate art and madness, holding that "degenerate art must be a truly sick art." Schneider was about to assist the regime in its "euthanasia" policies, and years after that committed suicide in an American military prison.[185]

The "Degenerate Art" exhibition migrated from Munich to Berlin, from there to Leipzig, Düsseldorf, Salzburg, Hamburg, and even smaller places like Weimar. In Berlin, artworks by Heidelberg asylum patients were included, for pictorial comparisons to evoke the onlookers' derision; in Düsseldorf it was surmised that by mid-July 1938 some 100,000 Germans had seen the exhibits. Even in small-town Stettin by early 1939, 75,000 visitors had been counted.[186] By 1941, when the show was stopped in its path because of the war, several more municipalities had been covered; all told, visitors by then were in the hundreds of thousands. Apart from its punitive function, the show served as a deterrent: never again should decadent art corrupt healthy German culture.[187]

Toward that general aim, the string of legislative actions enabling boycott and seizure was continued. Even in August 1937, Göring, as Minister President of Prussia, authorized Bernhard Rust to search all museums for remnants of unwanted art; "eradication" was to follow, in the Prussian realm.[188] For the entire Reich, Goebbels by January 1938 was working on a more comprehensive law enabling authorities to confiscate, without compensation, all artwork considered devious, from private individuals as well as public institutions. With the Führer's backing this was promulgated on May 31.[189] Three years later Ziegler redoubled his efforts to act against those "who produce works of decadent art or who distribute them in a capacity as artist or as broker."[190]

What happened to all the confiscated canvases, graphics, and sculptures? They were sold mostly abroad, often for the benefit of regime leaders such as Göring or Hitler himself, and more often than not for bargain-basement prices by Swiss art dealers with less than altruistic motives. In any case, they brought in welcome foreign exchange. Göring, who came from an upper-middle-class home with requisite tastes of Bildung, is said to have kept many items for his private enjoyment, selling others for personal profit that he did not like. Articles that could not be got rid of, however, were destroyed by burning, just as the books had burned a few years before. In the end, what the Nazis viewed as a winning situation for the Reich turned out to be, by all accounts, a deplorable loss for the civilized world.[191]

The "Degenerate Art" exhibition thereafter served as a role model. In May and June 1938 an exhibition of so-called degenerate music was staged in Düsseldorf, the town of Robert Schumann, whose occasional suspicion of Jews the Nazis liked to exploit for propaganda reasons.[192] It was modeled on the Munich exhibition of nearly a year before. Under Goebbels's sponsorship, it was organized by two men who worked for or were close to him: Hans Severus Ziegler and Heinz Drewes. Ziegler had already acted on behalf of Nazi cultural politics as the new Intendant of the Weimar national theater in Thuringia after January 1930. Born in 1893 in Thuringian Eisenach, this son of a banker with international connections spent time in Cambridge as well as German schools and attained his doctorate in German literature. (Ironically, Ziegler was related, through his mother, to the New

York Schirmer music company that was publishing, after his forced emigration from Germany, much of the work of Schoenberg – whom Ziegler never tired of berating.) For the Nazi minister Wilhelm Frick he drafted the text against "Negro culture," which would become notorious because it foreshadowed restrictions on a larger scale, three years hence in the Third Reich. After Hitler's coming to power in Berlin, Ziegler advanced to the post of commissar for Thuringian theaters. In 1935 he was temporarily suspended, as the authorities investigated charges of homosexuality against him, from which, nonetheless, he was able to extricate himself. But as he emerged from those clouds, he tried to compensate for this by intensifying his efforts as an administrator of culture, now leaning heavily on Goebbels. In 1937 the Promi Minister appointed him a member of his Reich culture senate.[193]

In early 1938, Ziegler teamed up with conductor Heinz Drewes, another Thuringian well on his way to high achievements in the Nazi cultural establishment. Although Drewes had been born in western Germany, he had become Kapellmeister in Altenburg, a post he owed to Ziegler, ten years his senior, and where in 1930 he had also founded a KfdK chapter. In 1937, Drewes, now Generalintendant in Altenburg, was appointed by Goebbels to head the newly founded music section in the Propaganda Ministry, at arm's length from the RMK, charged with screening compositions for elements "harmful to the German nation."[194]

In the spring of 1938, Drewes organized the Reich Music Festival (Reichsmusiktage) in Düsseldorf as a project of the Promi and, motivated by his high personal ambition and rabid ideological fervor, it is not surprising to find Ziegler superimposing an exhibition of degenerate music on that event. Goebbels had not exactly asked for that, but had not prohibited it either, so he allowed it to happen without fanfare.[195] Ziegler's own ideological training had been rigorous and his views on music were fanatically fixed. An author of several treatises on culture in the past, he advanced the cause of völkisch art in a speech in Danzig, in February 1937, characterizing it as the quintessential antidote to Modernism. German folk songs were the epitome of "simplicity and elementary greatness in art." They would defeat "all intellectual constructivism" and remove "the last vestiges of cultural Bolshevism, which are particularly discernible in the area of music and the visual arts." Tonal or not tonal were "the be-or-not-to-be of German music and a question of one's weltanschauung." The union of melody, harmony, and rhythm was the essential, archetypal element of music, as it rang out in the folk song and spoke of "the German soul." The problems posed by Hindemith, Igor Stravinsky, and that entire movement had to be solved, once and for all. Hence "a parallel exhibition to the Munich exhibition of 'degenerate art,' of all musical and opera experiments of the last three decades, exemplified by recordings of every kind, would open the eyes and ears to the infernal, bolshevistic attempts to destroy the inner balance, the feelings, and the senses of German man."[196]

The official main event in Düsseldorf was the Reich Music Festival, opened there on May 22 and running until May 29. The opening speech was delivered by the composer Paul Graener, one of the vice-presidents of the Reich Music Chamber. Since this was to be a showcase of not only tolerated but expressly desired music in the Third Reich, Graener's own new work *Feierliche Stunde* (*Festive Hour*) was featured by Düsseldorf's Generalmusikdirektor Hugo Balzer, as a prime example. Yet if neither the composer nor the conductor was first-rate, they were both an expression of the specific quality of contemporary music in the new Reich. Objectively, the entire slate of offerings in the program was mediocre, apart from mainstays such as Beethoven, Richard Strauss, and Pfitzner, and peripheral activities threatened to dominate the music. Military marches were played, marching music was provided by the Reich Labor Service (RAD), mixed in with samples from the Nazi Reich symphony orchestra. There was a music camp staffed by the Nazi student league and morning music from the Hitler Youth (Hitlerjugend, HJ). There were open choirs alternating with chamber-music offerings and the premiere of the *Ostmark Overture* by Otto Blesch, a composer hitherto unknown. (Yet, oddly, there was also the premiere of *Violin Music* by the Dresden choir director Boris Blacher. Influenced by Milhaud, Satie, and Stravinsky, Blacher had written music with unconventional rhythms and in a jazz style. Being a quarter Jewish, Blacher was still permitted to be active in the Reich under the 1935 Race Laws.) Outright political activities on the side included an honor march by the participants to the Schlageter monument on May 26 at 3:30 in the morning – Schlageter had been shot by the French in the nearby Golzheim heath.[197] Goebbels closed the exhibition himself with yet another political statement, reminding listeners that music was the most German of the arts, if almost eliminated by international Jewry. Only in the last few years had National Socialism wreaked a change, in that it had "swept away the pathological symptoms of musical, Jewish, intellectualism."[198]

Apart from a peripheral musicological convention, at which "the problem of music and race" was explored, Ziegler's music exposition, open to the public on May 24, provided some welcome diversion from the drab offerings of Goebbels's main festival.[199] The chief attraction to many must have been that he had arranged for listening booths to be available to visitors. Once inside, one pushed a button to hear the music of a defamed composer, be it Weill, Schoenberg, or Krenek, and pushing several buttons, up to eight simultaneously, produced the cacophony Nazis said was typical of atonal sound. In reality, having pushed for Mozart, Beethoven, and Wagner, their combined sound would not have been dissimilar.[200]

As the Nazi music critic Karl Laux remembered after World War II, the exhibits consisted of "portraits, theoretical treatises, examples of written music and libretti, posters and stage props for music-drama works."[201] Wall placards announced "principal perspectives of the new German music policy."[202] The posters displayed the portraits of banned composers, usually with a disparaging caption. Under a painting of Tsarist Russian aristocrat Stravinsky, for instance, his racial pedigree was questioned; caricatures of the heads of Jewish operetta composers Leo Fall and Oscar Straus were shown.[203] There was a photographic image of twelve-tone composer Anton Webern, said to have outdone even his "animal trainer" Schoenberg in the way he put notes to paper. Webern was included regardless of the fact that after the Anschluss of Austria, this resident of Vienna had sent his daughter to the local Hitler Youth, where she had met and married an Austrian storm trooper.[204] Ziegler also played havoc with scriptures. Schoenberg's *Harmonielehre* (*Lessons in Harmony*) of 1910 was condemned as the wellspring of dodecaphony, when in fact he had developed twelve-tone serialism only after its publication.[205] Hindemith's much more recent *Unterweisung im Tonsatz* (*Instructions in Composition*) was said to have had a similarly noxious function.[206] On a poster, Schoenberg's portrait, a photograph of the artist from 1924, was underwritten by a slogan, allegedly by a Jewish music critic: Schoenberg, a master of hysteria, creator of an "army of cramps." Hindemith was shown in a photograph with his wife, "a daughter of the Jewish Frankfurt opera conductor Ludwig Rottenberg," but it was suppressed that her mother was not Jewish. More convincingly conveyed was the impression which had motivated Ziegler in the first place, namely that degenerate music and degenerate art were but two sides of the same coin: Paul Klee's *Musikalische Komödie* (*Musical Comedy*) was hanging on one wall while, even more plausible, Karl Hofer's *Jazzband* was on another.[207]

The success of the music exhibition, which closed prematurely on June 14, was not anything comparable to the Munich art show of a year before, even though Ziegler had issued a carefully designed guide.[208] In it, he reproduced his speech from the opening, interspersed with some of the more prominent images featured at the exhibition, such as Schoenberg's portrait, but also, for example, a picture of Kurt Weill and one each of Ernst Toch and Franz Schreker – all prominent, and mostly Jewish, Modernists. In his article, Ziegler repeated the main themes of his earlier prose, hammering home that Jews in German culture had to be eliminated and that "art Bolshevism" was the exemplification of musical derangement. Ziegler had secured some professional advice from his Weimar musician cronies and now proceeded to pose as an expert musicologist when he stated that the quality of the music in an opera could be judged according to the nature of its libretto – an obvious attack on *The Threepenny Opera* and its authors Weill and Brecht, fixed in a notorious exhibit. He then moved on to a definition of music in terms of an organic law inherent in the triad. "The secret of all discovery ultimately lies in simplicity: if the greatest masters of music have been creative through a realization of tonality and the obviously Germanic element of the triad, then we have the right to brand those as dilettantes and charlatans who dismiss those elementary musical laws, trying instead to improve or enlarge on them using whatever tonal combinations, with the true aim of devaluing them." He then ranted, more specifically, against the "atonality" of Schoenberg, contrasting it with "the purity of the German genius Beethoven." Moving on, he indicted "the degeneration resulting from the intrusion of brutal jazz rhythms and jazz sounds into the Germanic music world." One could not treat the great tonal development of a thousand years as an error, he concluded, instead one had to regard the masterpieces of that formidable period, including recent decades, as the crowning of the occidental spirit. Therefore, "whoever wishes to rearrange the borders of the sound combinations permanently dissolves our Aryan tone order."[209]

After its less than enthusiastic reception in Düsseldorf the music show was put on ice, traveling to Weimar, Ziegler's home turf, only in the spring of 1939, where in the state museum it was combined with the "Degenerate Art" exhibition. Ziegler arranged for a performance of Franz Lehár's operetta *Land des Lächelns* (*Land of Smiles*), as proof of the degeneracy of this operetta in particular and as an overall theme, not being aware that Hitler was a connoisseur of all of Lehár's works. (At the time, its Jewish librettist Fritz Löhner-Beda was wasting away in nearby Buchenwald concentration camp, soon to be murdered.) Such dilettantish improvisation may have had something to do with the fact that Ziegler was unable to make a permanent exhibit out of it, but in May the show moved on to Vienna. The war prevented further exhibitions.[210]

Goebbels's Reich Music Festival was not yet doomed to oblivion, it was newly scheduled for years ahead. Whatever the quality of the original – still in 1938 German musicians of all stripes felt inspired enough to send in new proposals. For the 1939 event, they applied with 1,121 scores, among them 36 operas, 431 symphonies, works for choir and instrumental accompaniment, in addition to any number of chamber-music pieces.[211] Were these applicants all mediocre? They were of course not Jewish and had not assayed works in the dodecaphonic or jazz idioms. In that sense, the exhibition of degenerate music must have borne some fruit. Apart from such narrow uses, in the wider cultural realm it has gone on record for having put the very final stop to any debate in the Reich involving Modernism.

Both the art and the music exhibition stand for institutionalized attempts by the National Socialist regime to eradicate Modernism, insofar as its proponents had managed to integrate themselves into the Third Reich. Because of Hitler's speech in July 1937, declaring an end to what he defined as aesthetic aberrations, Modernism may be said to have come to an official end at that time, in the month of the "Degenerate Art" exhibition, with the music exhibition serving as a reaffirmation, even though certain manifestations of the movement continued on in isolation and often under cover – because no humanly motivated trend can be so suddenly extinguished, even in the most repressive dictatorship.[212]

The elimination of aesthetic value systems as hallmarks of the Weimar Republic was aimed against shapes and forms, colors and sounds, experimental initiative, liberty, and tolerance – all ingredients of an open, inclusive society in the republic, as opposed to the strictures designed to serve the closed, exclusive community of the fascists, with narrow, prejudiced tastes.

Immediately, one can detect parallels between the political progress of the Nazis and the growth of their anti-Modernist trends: as they grew in power after the general elections of September 1930, they intensified their campaign against republican Modernists, to the detriment of the latter. No holds were barred after Hitler's rise to power in January 1933, when arbitrary street violence generated by SA storm troopers combined with questionable legislative powers to accelerate the damaging dynamics. Hence the Law for the Reconstitution of the Civil Service of April 7, 1933, was used early on in the regime to immobilize, even remove many Modernist artists and their creations, such as master painters in art academies and their works. Complementarily, new statutes were established to introduce censorship, with resultant self-censorship, such as Goebbels's prohibition of art criticism in November 1936. Two years later he had decided on a law facilitating the confiscation of art from individuals and corporations without compensation. Also in 1938, Ernst Barlach died of a broken heart. By that time, the Third Reich as a political construct had reached its pinnacle of success, possessed of absolute power to destroy any obstacle in its chosen path of racial consolidation and external aggression. This was the year when the regime showed itself – so far – at its most devastating, as exactly two weeks after Barlach's death it burned down Jewish synagogues, harmed Jewish men and women, and threw thousands of them into concentration camps, killing hundreds. Whereas in 1933 about 4,000 inmates, Jews and non-Jews, had been held in German camps, that number had climbed to 54,000 by the end of 1938.[213] Jews of course had been, not coincidentally, highly instrumental in the rise of Modernism in pre-Nazi times.

In the process of demolition and the subsequent imposition of replacement constructs, yet to be discussed, the Nazi leaders frequently followed seemingly contradictory courses that today raise questions. For example, how is one to understand the sympathy extended to Expressionists like Barlach by students belonging to one group of Nazi-organized students in 1933, when during the same year students who belonged to another group organized, nationwide, the burning of undesirable books?[214] Both groups were totally Nazified, and yet, whereas one of them demonstrated sympathies for Modernism, the other one was hostile. Arguably, there were members in both who, at one time, showed pro-Modernist understanding, and, at another time, condemned the movement. Also puzzling is the relationship between Nazi lieutenants in their attitude to Modernism, for or against, with one faction of them winning out over another, as Rosenberg's cohorts did over Goebbels's, a former Expressionist sympathizer, in the quarrel over Hindemith, and then again in the final decision on the future of Modernism in the Third Reich by 1937. Was the intellectual Goebbels, in everyday dealings with Rosenberg from 1925 to 1938, not always much stronger than the witless Party philosopher? Upon closer observation, one discovers that in both cases involving Rosenberg, it was Hitler himself who gave the ultimate nod – not to Goebbels but to his rival. This suggests peculiarities in the leadership pattern of the Third Reich, the intricacies of which must be subjected to further scrutiny.

CHAPTER TWO

◆ ◆ ◆

Pre-War Nazi Culture

EFORE DETERMINING THE essence of Nazi culture in pre-war
Germany, a few issues concerning the nature of the Third Reich
must be settled. For one, the gubernatorial structures within which
the Nazis made changes in the German cultural landscape, either by
revoking old aesthetic standards or by establishing new ones, should be
more clearly defined. Further, it would be instructive to know about Hitler's
own role, exactly how interested he was in cultural affairs, and how instrumental in imposing any change.

International debates concerning the texture of the Third Reich and
Hitler's place in it, begun some fifty years ago and currently still relevant,
provide a thought-provoking background. In the 1960s, Karl Dietrich
Bracher established that the Third Reich was an authoritarian system, with
Party and State as instruments of "totalitarian rule," and Hitler linking the
two in a position of "omnipotence." "National Socialist doctrine," wrote
Bracher, "captured the culture and values of German society."[1] This theory
of monocracy was bolstered by Eberhard Jäckel, who spoke of the centrality
of Hitler in the government of the Third Reich, because its political realization had ultimately occurred as the logical consequence of two strong,
personal impulses, both during and following 1919: Hitler's need to conquer
living space for the Volksgenossen (after a necessary revocation of the Treaty
of Versailles) and his quest to physically eliminate the Jews.[2]

Against such monolithic views, Hans Mommsen by the 1970s was well into developing a rather more differentiating thesis, arguing against the central position of Hitler in the hallways of power and stressing social, economic, and psychological factors in the dictatorship's development, even the element of chance. Having, in the mid-1960s, already called Hitler "a weak dictator," he argued in the early 1980s on behalf of multiple structures, where the State rivaled the Party, offices in both sought to overwhelm one another, and officials multiplied their efforts in attempts to cancel each other out.[3] Mommsen presented images of competing Führer and sub-Führer structures with no clear hierarchical markings, patterns of deficient coordination and situations of indecision, in which Hitler almost always failed to exercise his supremo prerogatives. There existed a "polycracy of portfolios," held Mommsen, producing governmental chaos, with Hitler thriving on top, as he usually withheld final decision-making – a system begetting itself over and over again, until it surpassed a point of cumulative radicalization, ad infinitum. If ever Hitler interfered in governmental or administrative procedures, wrote Mommsen, as a rule it was to apply a brake, although he did encourage initiatives and then watch the unfolding of potential chaos. Such chaos he would tolerate, even incite, as long as his own position was not threatened.[4] Where, in such a necessarily self-destructive process could "political energy" be generated and preserved, asked Manfred Funke, himself a student of Bracher, energy that was fundamentally necessary to propel the nation.[5]

In more recent times Ian Kershaw has found a synthesis between the "intentionalist" school of Bracher and Jäckel and the "functionalist" school of Mommsen. Based on earlier research focusing on what he called the "Hitler Myth," he arrived at a formula according to which key National Socialist personages in the hierarchy of State or Party under Hitler geared their work such as to make it appear that everyone, no matter their real agenda, was "working towards the Führer." In a 1987 book Kershaw had explained the myth around the Führer, as a functional element in government, likening it to an aura in which Hitler was rendered "aloof from the selfish sectional interests and material concerns" so characteristic of officials from Party and State, already identified by Mommsen. This aura, whose construction was mostly due to the machinations of Goebbels as part of his propaganda efforts, lasted well into the war, with radical dynamics. Within this Hitler, far from being a "weak dictator," by about 1935 was recognized by his universe as the strongman who had repaired the economy, controlled the unruly SA, safeguarded hallowed traditions treasured by the two Christian Churches, defended German rights in foreign policy, and demonstrated military leadership. And not least, he had shown himself resistant against perceived threats by Communists and Jews. Hence within the German population, if corruption and administrative malfeasance were observed at the hands of the State and Party bureaucracy, these were often dismissed as something Hitler at the top would not have ordained, had he known about them. Hitler's putative strength, reasoned Kershaw, was accepted by his subjects in the face of relative weakness by his underlings, in situations where many ordinary Germans thought that, theoretically, a personal appeal to the Führer, bypassing governmental channels, was possible. Such an interpretation of Nazi rule, therefore, portrayed a strong dictator, at least in the minds of a plurality whom Goebbels had persuaded to believe in the "Hitler Myth." Hitler showed additional strength by aiding and abetting the myth constructed around him. "In his portrayed public image, Hitler was able to offer a positive role in the Third Reich, transcending sectional interests and grievances through the overriding ideal of national unity, made possible through his necessary aloofness from the 'conflict sphere' of daily politics, separating him from the more unpopular aspects of Nazism."[6]

Kershaw's magisterial two-volume biography of Hitler of the late 1990s specified the "Führer Myth" and its workings still further. The choreography of government in Hitler's Führer state obliged the actors Mommsen and his predecessors had recognized, government and Party officials as well as Hitler, to interact according to a once-tried and indefinitely repeated pattern. Kershaw explains: "Hitler's personalized form of rule invited radical initiatives from below and offered such initiatives backing, so long as they were in line with his broadly defined goals. This promoted ferocious competition at all levels of the regime, among competing agencies, and among individuals within those agencies. In the Darwinist jungle of the Third Reich, the way to power and advancement was through anticipating the 'Führer will', and, without waiting for directives, taking initiatives to promote what were presumed to be Hitler's aims and wishes." In such a personalized system of governance geared teleologically to Hitler, the one who had the most guaranteed and the most direct access to the Führer would succeed most with his goals.[7] Any imagined private initiative by ordinary Volksgenossen, such as denouncing someone to the Gestapo for personal reasons, apart from all manner of official acts, could also be taken, regardless of motive, as individually "working towards the Führer."[8] Such activities would help propel "an unstoppable radicalization which saw the gradual emergence in concrete shape of policy objectives embodied in the 'mission' of the Führer."[9] (Such radicalization manifested itself during the war in several extremes, the velocity of the early *Blitzsiege*, the ferocity of the eastern campaign as determined by the Nazis, Hitler's erratic moves at the helm of the military, the abject brutality in the treatment of Soviet POWs, accelerated terror within the judicial and concentration camp systems, and, most of all, the persecution of the Jews.) Kershaw's synthesis was complete: while he allowed for the environment, and players underneath the top of the regime, he had restored Hitler as the fount of action, the focus of the dramatic narrative about the Third Reich. Ultimately, as Volker Ullrich, one of Hitler's more recent biographers has again emphasized, the Führer claimed "the solitary right" to decide on "fundamental issues," never mind routine matters.[10]

With Kershaw's model in mind, the question of Hitler's agency may be reopened for scenarios where the culture of the Third Reich was affected. Before it can be answered, it is, first, necessary to establish criteria for judging Hitler as a cultural persona, and, second, to ascertain what cultural achievements the Nazi regime was able to generate on its own, at least for the pre-war period. Hitler has been called a genius, by devotees and some historians over time. It may be asked whether this would apply to his earlier role as an artist and his later preoccupation with art, with culture, as it came to be witnessed in the Third Reich.

If Hitler possessed genius, it expressed itself solely in politics. The key to this was his intuitive relationship with people, whose emotions he mastered to the point of absolute control. "Hitler was blessed with instinct, he sniffed out people like a dog," Otto Strasser, his associate of the late 1920s, told me in the spring of 1974, a few months before his death.[11] Goebbels, who had worked closely with Otto and his brother Gregor Strasser since their initial meetings with Hitler after the Landsberg hiatus, indeed had been their subordinate, appears to have agreed on the intuitive capabilities of the Führer, as his diaries evince. Hitler's "great gift was for politics alone," asserts Ullrich. "In his ability to instantaneously analyze and exploit situations, he was far superior not only to his rivals within the NSDAP but also to the politicians from Germany's mainstream parties. There is no other way to explain why he emerged victorious in all of the crises within the Nazi Party leading up to 1933."[12]

Apart from that extraordinary talent for politics, Hitler was endowed with other gifts, albeit not nearly to the same extent. A considerably over-average intelligence supported Hitler's truly impressive memory, but only in areas of knowledge and of culture he chose to cultivate (as he chose to tolerate only satraps who were clearly "working towards the Führer"). Very fond of music, Hitler recalled in early summer 1939 how "on June 29, 1932, in the concert hall of the Bayerischer Hof" in Munich he had listened to aspiring bass-baritone Hans Hotter singing the two Hans Sachs arias from Wagner's *Die Meistersinger*.[13] Instances where Hitler remembered minute details about military hardware or automobiles were legion; since World War I, he was constantly stocking up on his knowledge of the military and, always favoring Mercedes (and later anything proposed by Ferdinand Porsche), was a car fanatic besides.[14] For modern times, this was not so special; Kaiser Wilhelm II had struck his contemporaries in similar fashion, in particular regarding anything from the military, specifically the navy. Still, Hitler was acquainted with the basics of Carl von Clausewitz's mili-tary-political theory, details of which he could recite by heart, although they were hardly applicable to a twentieth-century military strategy.[15]

Finer points of learning and scholarship escaped Hitler; taking a cue from his own failed formal education, he hated teachers and university professors (which may explain, a seeming paradox, why he later created many professors of his own, ultimately showing disdain for those minions). Although as an autodidact he could choose what field to become well versed in, economics was not one of them, even if he spouted half-truths about it for the length of his political career.[16] The Harvard-educated Ernst Hanfstaengl (after 1919 a Nazi, friend of Hitler, businessman, and amateur pianist) discovered a remarkable library in Hitler's first humble Munich flat, containing books on history, geography, and some philosophy, such as Schopenhauer. Much of this was later duplicated in Hitler's comfortable prison cell in Landsberg. In history, unsurprisingly, the German past, apart from Greek and Roman antiquity, interested Hitler the most, in particular, the biography of Prussia's Frederick the Great. For his racist education he could draw from the works of Houston Stewart Chamberlain, Paul de Lagarde, and Hans F. K. Günther. The *belles lettres* were not represented in his Munich bedroom, but he was familiar with some contemporary plays such as Wedekind's and Ibsen's (the latter's undoubtedly because Hitler's sometime mentor Dietrich Eckart had translated *Peer Gynt*). On his prose and fiction shelves were detective stories and light literature, folksy and satirical stories of the kind the Bavarian Ludwig Thoma wrote, and – since his youth – the contrived stories of the American Wild West by the Saxon author Karl May.[17]

Hitler adored actors, and one of his favorite pastimes was film. He appreciated many of the film highlights from conservative Ufa productions controlled by the magnate Alfred Hugenberg and had favorites among German film stars such as Henny Porten; but he also came to love certain American movies and, along with Goebbels, was a great fan of Greta Garbo. During the Third Reich and until the outbreak of war, he regularly viewed films privately and often enough for propaganda purposes, as the preceding chapter showed. Eventually, many German movie stars were able to call Hitler their friend.[18] Less frequently found in theaters than in cinemas, Hitler still liked the stage; apart from the acting he observed during performances of his favorite operettas he also watched several of his favorite movie actors, such as Emil Jannings, in impressive drama and comedy performances on stages throughout Germany: Munich, Berlin, Weimar. Acting was important to him, and was one of the arts he mastered to an appreciable degree; for political purposes, addressing the masses in the Weimar Republic and also during the first half of the Third Reich, he practiced postures and gestures in front of a mirror as well as working on his oratorical skills.[19]

Hitler's love of music was nourished mostly by the sounds of Wagner, which he had experienced during his youth in Linz and Vienna, and nurtured later in Munich and forever after. As he demonstrated to Hanfstaengl already in 1919–20 in Munich, he was able to hum or whistle from memory arias from *Die Meistersinger*, *Lohengrin*, and (like Thomas Mann, who preferred doodling on the piano) *Tristan und Isolde*. On the lighter side, and consonant with his originally humble milieu, the Führer's favorite march was always the *Badenweiler*, and cherished musical stage works were all operettas, especially Franz Lehár's *The Merry Widow* and Johann Strauss's *Die Fledermaus*. (Hitler protected Lehár throughout the regime despite his Jewish wife.)[20] During the Third Reich, his preferred lead tenor Danilo from *The Merry Widow* was the beloved Dutch singer and all-time heart-throb Johannes Heesters. Later in life, Hitler appeared to appreciate Anton Bruckner (most certainly he overemphasized this affection, because of their mutual home town of Linz), but never the composers Goebbels tried to foist upon him: Schubert, Brahms, or Mozart, and not even the heroic Beethoven.[21] All told, Hitler had "little real interest in or understanding of music."[22]

If Hitler loved Wagner, it was not least because that composer offered to the dictator, through his "Gesamtkunstwerk," a combination of features he appreciated as a skill set in a demagogic career: action-drama that suited his penchant for pathos and then ideology, a stage from which to sing, act, or declaim to the masses, and scenery suited to impress with color and with shape. The visual effects of scenery were tied to Hitler's very own twin predilections: painting and architecture. His often-proclaimed self-belief as an artist derived from the low-level painting activity he practiced in Vienna during his indigent years and then in Munich, until he joined the Bavarian Army in the First World War. Having been twice rejected by the Vienna Academy of Arts as a student, his skills in painting were never more than dilettantish. Anyone, including Hitler himself, intent on tying a cult of genius to such endeavors would be misinterpreting the facts.[23] The same holds true for architecture: Hitler's interest therein derived from sketches he had made of buildings in Vienna or, eventually, during the war at the Western Front, in Belgium or in France; later Hitler broadened this to include interior design. Hitler's sometime remarks, especially during World War II, that he wished nothing else for himself than to return to the life of an artist, were self-delusional and intended to impress followers within a fabricated genius cult.[24]

There is no question that Hitler's artistic output, whatever his skill level, could not even vaguely be connected to the new schools of Modernism developing in Austria and Germany in his years of early adulthood. As the Viennese and Berlin Secessions and their avant-garde outflows left him untouched, Hitler remained mired in the tastes of the late Romanticism practiced by academic painters of both countries: Adolph von Menzel, Hans Makart, Anselm Feuerbach, Carl Spitzweg, Arnold Böcklin, and Eduard von Grützner, and their ilk. In architecture, he admired neoclassical works by Karl Friedrich Schinkel and Gottfried Semper, trying to emulate them in ever novel sketches. After 1933, Hitler favored and actively supported artists who painted in succession to those masters.[25] Yet, considering visual art, music, the stage, and cinema, what did Hitler's personal interest in these sectors, his overall middle-brow taste, mean for the shaping of culture as a whole in the Third Reich?

THE PROPAGANDA MINISTRY AND CULTURE

One morning late in October 1938 the Viennese poet Josef Weinheber rose from among 250 of his compatriots assembled in the landmark Elephant hotel in Weimar. Fortified by two bottles of wine he stepped up to the lectern at the front of the hall and gave what contemporaries experienced as a rousing speech in honor of Friedrich Hölderlin, the Romantic poet and a particular favorite of the Nazis. It was in the aftermath of Germany's annexation of Austria, and Weinheber and his friends were buoyed by pride and gratitude when in the evening they returned from Weimar's classical treasures to listen to Dr. Goebbels, who delivered the concluding address to what had been politically arranged as a German poets' meeting, the first of several to follow. As Goebbels spoke Weinheber, encouraged by more bottles of wine, interrupted the minister enthusiastically, time and again shouting "Heil Hitler!," thus seriously encumbering the flow of Goebbels's speech. Knowing how fond Weinheber was of Hitler and he of him, two towering SS men eventually approached him gently, persuading him to retire to his room upstairs. Goebbels was able to make his points unbroken; Weinheber, an acute alcoholic, years later committed suicide during the Red Army's approach to Vienna.[26]

The presence of prominent writers from the new Ostmark and the soon-to-be-occupied Sudetenland was crucial for Goebbels, in order to illustrate the significance of Nazi politics in general, and the prerogative of such politics over poetry in particular. All culture, insinuated Goebbels, had to be subservient to the state in times of national alert, it had to play an integral part in the state's totalitarian fabric. German writers had to be reminded of this, as had all other artists in the Reich. It was clear that this was not the first time Goebbels was issuing such demands, but knowing that the Reich was on an expansionist course and facing what was an unusually receptive audience, the minister seized the occasion to remobilize the intellectuals and artists of the realm.[27]

The timely reminder was issued in Goebbels's capacity as Minister of People's Enlightenment and Propaganda. The pairing of those two terms to serve as one functional heading for the ministry had not occurred as a result of an idle whim but was a carefully considered move: guidance of the people to be administered by messages created and manipulated in accordance with the requirements of the day, and exclusively in the interests of the regime leaders. The concept was originally traceable to Hitler's *Mein Kampf*, and it was he who had issued the decree anointing Goebbels, in March of 1933. At the end of June, Hitler elaborated that Goebbels was responsible for "all duties relating to the spiritual influence of the nation, to the promoting of the state, culture and the economy."[28] From this Goebbels deduced a mandate to define culture as an instrument of propaganda, looking upon it as a life-giving elixir of the racially cast Volksgemeinschaft and, successively, as an expression of that people's community. "The essence of propaganda," maintained Goebbels, "invariably has to be simplicity, as well as repetition." Within that framework, the contents of propaganda were to rely on truths, half-truths, and outright lies, as would befit Nazi politics. The interdependence of culture, propaganda, and politics was constantly emphasized by Goebbels – counting from the time of his appointment – and paid continuous lip service by his employees, parroted by officials in every bureaucratic nook and cranny of the Reich.[29] An important part of this effort was bolstering the already existing "Hitler Myth," starting with popular-cultural events, including films, and reaching the sometimes absurd heights of state-sponsored hymnic scripture.[30]

There could be no such thing as art for art's sake; in the Nazi cosmos, art was tendentious. As the "standard bearer of national culture," as Goebbels called it, art could assume many forms and cast the artist in various roles, and it served several purposes for the state.[31] The first use was, not surprisingly, to influence popular attitudes toward the regime, with the aim of achieving total acquiescence with its policies. As George L. Mosse has written, "in the Third Reich the central task of culture was the dissemination of the Nazi world view."[32] This required, for example, racial norms to be adopted, such as the images of blond, blue-eyed "Aryans" in paintings. Anyone who refused to be conditioned in this way was to be marked as a deviant, either to be brought into line or removed from the Volksgemeinschaft. Another use of culture, high or low, was entertainment, to keep the people satisfied, diverting their attention from problems in the community, such as joblessness early in the regime or the dearth of potatoes and shoe leather at the height of the war. There was, therefore, not one cultural genre in the Third Reich, not a single product of cultural creativity, which, however seemingly innocent, was not of political value, barring Nazi censorship. Yet a third use was to impress foreign governments, which would cede credit to the Berlin regime as a world advocate of civilization, such as when Hitler decided to continue favoring Richard Strauss after 1935, although he had given cause for being blacklisted. During the war, impressing foreign governments took second place to brainwashing chosen groups in occupied territories, such as the Flemish in Belgium who had to be reminded of a common Germanic heritage.[33] Keeping just these three uses of art for the regime in mind, it was right to claim, after the war, that generators of culture had legitimized and transfigured Nazi rule through their complicity in art, and it was wrong to deny this, as did the prominent actor Bernhard Minetti, a chief beneficiary of film and stage roles during the Nazi era.[34]

Not every art form was viewed as adaptable to the Third Reich's requirements in the same way, or with equal efficacy. Film was envisaged as one of the most pliable. It would be comparatively easy to project Nazi conformist images onto celluloid and invent Nazi legends as a storyline. Hence Goebbels proclaimed the medium of film to be a primary "leadership tool of the state" early in the regime and argued for political ideas that had to assume aesthetic forms. Such ideas could surface in moving pictures of the historical kind, detailing, for example, the struggle of Nazis with Communists in the streets of German cities during the end of the Weimar Republic. Other films could teach about the ideals of a healthy, eugenically well-rounded family, for "the family is the nucleus of the state." Seemingly harmless entertainment movies such as comedies would provide members of the Volksgemeinschaft a "rest before the struggles" of daily life, enabling them to carry on as bona fide members of the racial community.[35]

Next to film, and related to it, the German stage was serviceable. It had to be transformed to emphasize political objectives, so that a new "political consciousness at the theater" would arise – according to the celebrated playwright Hanns Johst. Theater must help develop the German Man, "a man of National Socialist views and attitudes." He must pattern himself on the

Germanics of the Edda saga, whose practices were regarded as exemplary. From these must arise a new awareness of race, of the cultic, the heroic and, in particular, an awareness of the function of sacrifice by individuals for the community, as themes of tragedy in newly to be conceived drama. Sacrificing individuality not least would have to show itself in a defeat of the actors' star system of yesteryear. The overall aim of new theater was to show the communal "struggle for the great questions of German existence."[36]

The race motif surfaced again as a model for the visual arts. Painters had to present racially perfect Germanic Man to allow the German people to appreciate the benefits of eugenics. Beyond that, pictures could raise expectations toward desirable goals, such as a love of nature, the soil, and even eastern settlement. Territorial customs and national legends were appropriate subject matter, so that "lovers of history and of völkisch life would benefit."[37] The chief purpose of architecture, a closely related art form, would be to show the monumental inherent in the Nazi idea of state, yet another variation on the heroic theme.[38]

The uses of a contemporary literature were seen much like those for the visual arts, in that books could generate exemplary conceptualizations and devise exemplars of racially correct behavior. A Völkischer Realismus, or Heroic Realism, would take the place of Expressionism and Naturalism of decades gone by, would ground itself in blood and soil and in the Germanic past. German existentialist issues would form the core of many novels and short stories about love of countryside and settlement, family values as embodied in Germanic Woman – the eternal avatar of virtue, modesty, industry, and protector of the blood, with her readiness to assist the combat-ready and protective male.[39] One method to revisit here was that of the historic novel, as it told about the Vikings of prehistoric times, of Arminius who defeated the Romans, of Widukind who dared Charlemagne, the Peasant Wars, Henry the Lion, Baron vom Stein, and the German inventors and scholars, yet also of the patriotic war and the grave betrayal of 1918.[40]

And how would music contribute to the political culture of the next thousand years? Music is "always in the world," observes *The New Yorker* critic Alex Ross, "neither guilty nor innocent, subject to the ever-changing human landscape in which it moves."[41] Would this suggest political neutrality? Clearly, music's structure demonstrated the least capacity for ideological communication, unless one thought of the libretto for an opera or the lyrics for a song. Only in that respect could composers and poets conjoin their efforts. So on the whole, the claim of Alfred Rosenberg's lieutenant Friedrich Herzog sounded hollow, when he demanded "a music that is characterized by the expressive powers of the National Socialist idea. As a revolutionary music it will serve progress, as a national music it will be novel, and as a socialist music it will enter the heart of every völkisch comrade, irrespective of age, status, or gender, and it will be understood."[42] Goebbels himself showed more caution when he refrained from assigning a patriotic duty to music, demanding only that a monopoly of *German* music in the world be reaffirmed.[43] Music could, however, bend emotions, and as such it had an embellishing value, for instance at political gatherings or on radio.[44]

Indeed, radio and the press, considered as cultural modes, allowed for the most direct transfer of political messages to the people, among all the related media. To the extent that after January 1933 the Nazi leaders looked upon themselves as revolutionaries, they professed an affinity for broadcasting as revolutionary action *par excellence*. To the extent that they thought of themselves as modern, radio was their innovation of choice. Radio was regarded as the ultimate instrument of ideological indoctrination and control. This would occur via speeches and other, non-musical, programming. Current-event reportage and radio plays were excellent ploys. Like film, music could entertain and steel Hitler's subjects for the battles ahead; so could appropriately tailored word content, for instance quiz, humor, and variety shows, let alone sports reporting. More than the serious drama and opera, which reached the upper social strata, more than film, with its proven potential mainly for touching the working stiffs, radio would transcend *all* classes.[45]

And finally, the press. Assuming a minimal degree of literacy within its audience, it could be variegated and more finely tuned to social classes even than radio, ultimately reaching almost every target group. Varieties would be in a range, from newspapers that included deft Nazi slogans in the Party press for the converted, to those containing delicately phrased pro-Nazi arguments, the logic of which could not escape even the highly educated. It would carry images borrowed from the medium of art, could reproduce parts of grand literature or serialize trivia with a hidden Nazi meaning. Moreover, the Nuremberg Gauleiter Julius Streicher's vulgarian weekly broadsheet *Der Stürmer* showed early that it could incite hatred by printing vile caricatures of German Jews.[46]

LITERATURE

In 2009 the American cultural and literary historian Sander L. Gilman expressed an opinion about Nazi literature. He declared that "writing about the mass of literature of the Nazi period today is simply uninteresting."[47] He went on to say that writers like Josef Magnus Wehner, Hans Zöberlein or Kurt Eggers "arguably do not represent 'real' literature in Germany from 1933 to 1945." Gilman did not give his reasons, but presumably he thought of shallow content and imperfect form – literature that was not in the main German tradition of the twentieth or nineteenth century. But even if these were his reasons, whatever German writers produced by way of prose or poetry truly was literature; whether it was good or bad today is another issue. Prose and poetry written by Nazi authors in the years of the Nazi regime, or by writers living in the Third Reich during all or part of that era, was genuine German literature, whether it was derivative, original, or a combination of both, and regardless of its quality.

Admittedly, there was virtually no literature with contemporary, Nazi, settings, at least not until 1940.[48] Writers of novels, for instance, felt too close to circumstances constantly in flux to afford themselves a measured, objective perspective; if they reported on precarious or negative phenomena in their stories to remain in a contemporary groove, such as the Röhm Purge or concentration camps, they knew they would be censored. References to Nazi symbols, personages, or events therefore occurred in writings set before 1933, the year of the political watershed, about which writers could safely report at a distance and with a sense of perspective. In novels of the Party's Kampfzeit, the Nazi Time of Struggle from 1919 to 1933, which obviously had the Weimar Republic as their historical frame, Hitler appeared frequently, followed by Joseph Goebbels and Horst Wessel – they were the most immediately recognizable Nazi leaders of the 1920s and early 1930s, and the most charismatic.[49]

Novels with historic fixed points and post-industrial scenarios typically began during World War I, moved into Freikorps situations (1919–25), and dealt with specific problem areas of the Weimar Republic. Zöberlein, Edwin Erich Dwinger, and Werner Beumelburg specialized in this kind of fare. They suggested, or drew outright, the connection between imperial warrior and para-military Freikorps and SA or SS man; some of their novels were already published in the 1920s but reprinted, to great success, after 1933. All this qualified them as Nazi literature. The fact that those three authors, like others of their ilk, were former soldiers lent a high degree of authenticity to their work.[50]

Two features of this work, which characterized the authors as fascistic, were the glorification of war in the interest of a patriotic (read: chauvinistic) German cause, and the construction of chain-of-command situations in which an authoritarian leadership personality was at the top. A third was the depiction of a single individual, say a soldier in that chain of command, as insignificant, save as part of a larger community, as in a platoon, foreshadowing the Nazi Volksgemeinschaft. For Ernst Jünger the world war had had a lofty, moralizing, effect: "German Man faced a stronger power: he faced himself. Thus this war was, above all, a means to realize himself."[51] Edith Gräfin Salburg glorified the soldier who died "a hero's death in the highest sense"; it was important for a soldier "to grow, above and beyond his own personality, to forget his self in the service of the whole."[52] Dwinger recalled a sense of community with the doomed student volunteers of the famous battle of Langemarck (November 1914) and he, Beumelburg, Heinrich Zerkaulen, and Heinz Steguweit sketched scenes of abject obedience between soldiers and their superiors.[53] As corollaries to the events of World War I, the shameful Treaty of Versailles and the alleged stab in the back by the home front were equally dramatized.[54]

From the disbanded imperial army early in 1919 so-called Freikorps were formed, small groups of paramilitaries led by storied and battle-seasoned commanders, usually of middle rank. They were initially authorized by the incipient Weimar Republic as auxiliary homeland police but after 1920 fought on independently and illegally, mostly in the East, against Bolsheviks, Balts, and Poles who were seen as occupying German soil in cahoots with the Western Allies. Hyper-nationalist Freikorps espoused Hitler and his early movement and sometimes wore painted swastikas on their steel helmets. In his pathography of the Freikorps, Klaus Theweleit has cast them in sharp relief, especially their obsession with cruelties, the significance for them of "blood" as a collateral of wounds and death as well as a life tonic and racial glue, and their view of women, the white-uniformed ones of whom (nurses) were mothers and sisters to be defended, and the red-flag-carrying ones (Communist Red Front fighters) were whores to be killed, all with phallic rifles.[55]

The essence of the hyper-nationalist Freikorps was caught by Zöberlein in his novel *Der Befehl des Gewissens* (*The Command of Conscience*) in 1937, as the troops express their frustration over having been betrayed by the republican government after the November 1918 armistice, which declared them illegal, and in waiting for a Führer to end their demise. Dwinger in his novel *Die letzten Reiter* (*The Last Riders*, 1935) portrayed Sergeant Wollmeier as he took great care to explain to his comrades why he was a early follower of the Nazi movement. And Herbert Volck in his novel *Rebellen um Ehre* (*Rebels for Honor*) in 1939 explicated the Freikorps ethos as the troops were standing up, in Latvia, to "Asian Bolshevism": "Any good officer can command soldiers, but to lead hearts – not everyone. He who only gives orders without letting on his own readiness for death, for him the volunteers will soon be saboteurs."[56]

Some Freikorps, such as Albert Leo Schlageter, were known to have committed sabotage against the French, during their occupation of the left bank of the Rhine.[57] Accordingly, these men and their actions were idolized in the neo-nationalist literature flooding the Third Reich.[58] Anti-French resentment was further glorified in novels highlighting alleged rapes of German women by French colonial troops as part of the occupation army, cases in which the suspects were denigrated as "Negroes," whereas in reality those troops were partly light-skinned Indochinese and Maghreb Arabs.[59]

World War I losers and Freikorps concentrated their anger on the Weimar Republic, which had allowed a Versailles peace and French occupation troops to come to pass. Their fury and contempt became the subject of much popular Third Reich fiction. Conditions in the republic were caricatured in a variety of ways, in ever more lurid detail. Topping all were the descriptions of "asphalt culture," an alleged negative hallmark of the Weimar era. Herbert Volck earmarked "coffee houses, bars, bodegas, dance clubs for the evening, luxury cabarets" for criticism, next to "the new Negro dances, the blaring jazz music, the new fashions."[60] Zöberlein indicted "waiters in black tuxedos," the "wicked eyes of painted demi-monde women," the proliferation of "French champagne" for those with money.[61] As part of this subculture degenerate books (and films) created by benighted liberals stood out, led by Erich Maria Remarque's *All Quiet on the Western Front*, with its openly pacifist theme.[62] Ernst Wiechert deplored the "blurred humanity" of the Weimar era, which Ernst Jünger characterized as responsible for an "optical delusion" of the masses through its elective franchise.[63] Economic dislocations because of the enemy blockade, inflation, the mischief wrought by November traitors, had caused the deracination of formerly well-adjusted strata of society, so that as a result of those foul processes an army of war cripples was now in the streets while academics, war heroes, shopkeepers, and unskilled laborers went jobless.[64] Besides the Jews, the chief culprits for those maladjustments were said to be the Communists and their paramilitaries, the hated Red Front, many of whose members, nonetheless, were described as potential or real Nazi converts.[65]

Anti-Weimar sentiment expressed in these novels precipitated anti-democratic feeling and culminated in authoritarianism, ultimately personi-fied by Adolf Hitler. In Wiechert's novel *Das einfache Leben* (*The Simple Life*, 1939) the former imperial navy captain Thomas von Orla secludes himself in the forlorn East Prussian countryside, far away from the big cities, recog-nizing as his authority in the world a retired general who affects the clipped parlance of Frederick the Great. Von Orla himself represents authority for Bildermann, a former sailor, who has followed him unquestioningly into the hermit's world, as if the Great War were still ongoing.[66] For Ernst Jünger in his essay *Die totale Mobilmachung* (1934), a "merciless discipline" imposed on individuals would lead to a total mobilization of the masses determined not by democracy, but the demands of authoritarianism.[67] Werner Bergengruen, in his novel *Der Grosstyrann und das Gericht* (*The Great Tyrant and the Court of Law*, 1935), drew the outlines of an omnipotent ruler – albeit set back in time – who kills a monk in his domain, then orders a search for the murderer. He psycho-terrorizes his subjects, who begin seeing the killer in almost every neighbor. Slowly Bergengruen transfigured the Great Tyrant, one who rules by fiat, as something naturally befitting him, who creates laws without justifying them, changing territorial infrastructure at will. He loves mega-building construction like the Führer. In the end the tyrant declares in his self-convened court of law ("das Gericht") that "the killing of Fra Agostino lies beyond everyday jurisdiction" – a timely defense of the Röhm "purge" that had just occurred. Bergengruen's concluding interpretation of the ruler might have explained historic tyrants, but it also, not coincidentally, read like a justification of the Führer: "He has to act according to the principles of his essentiality, not to rules that have originated outside his being."[68] Significantly, Rosenberg's *Völkischer Beobachter* celebrated Bergengruen's book as a "Führer novel of the Renaissance period."[69]

Those were the post-industrialist writings. Pre-industrialist prose and poetry concerned themselves with the racial origin of the Germans, by way of Ahnenpflege, or ancestor worship. This meant examining the roots of the German people as far back as possible, as far as could credibly be maintained that there was an unbroken line between early Germanic ethnicity and its culture, on the one side, and the contemporary Volk, on the other. Since such a connection was precarious at best not only because of the racial intermingling by the Germans with other ethnicities over the centuries, but also because the earliest tribal qualities could be ascertained only with difficulty, "historic" novels (rather than poetry) usually contained more fiction than was scientifically defensible. Ancestor respect really was uncritical ancestor idolization, imputing to the old Germanic tribes properties that in all probability they never possessed but which suited the Nazi weltanschauung. Here, clearly, fiction supplanted fact.[70]

One popular genre in this field was Viking iconography as practiced by Werner Jansen, Will Vesper, and Hans Friedrich Blunck. The physician and SS colonel Jansen was a rabid anti-Semite; his novel *Die Insel Heldentum* (*Island Heroism*, 1938), full of kin and tribal feuds and of extreme brutality, recorded the downfall of the Vikings in Iceland. Much as they may have been fatuous and foolhardy, they obeyed the laws of their blood, knowing that "the individual was nothing, the clan everything."[71] The novel reflected laws of thought and feeling, judged the Nazi literary critic Norbert Langer.[72] Walter Best of *Das Schwarze Korps* declared it mandatory reading for every SS man, because Jansen was able to show that "the historic course of our past makes sense, with its death and downfall, only once the heirs of this history can learn their lessons from it."[73] The novelist Vesper's heroes were Icelanders, individuals who traveled to Iceland or figuratively rubbed shoulders with Germanic gods.[74] Blunck, a successor to Heinrich Mann as president of the poets' section at the Prussian Academy of Arts in 1933, portrayed in his novel *König Geiserich* (1936) the ideal qualities of early Germanic leaders. The historic King Geiserich (AD 389–477) was endowed with selfless love of his people, statesmanlike wisdom, moral and physical fortitude. On his march through Spain, the transfer of his Vandal people to north Africa and his reign near Carthage, including fateful exploits such as the Sack of Rome (410), Geiserich stayed unmarried, the better to serve his Volk – an unmistakable compliment to Hitler.[75]

Imaginings about Vikings could easily be pulled forward in time to reflect inherited Germanic customs in the Early or High Middle Ages. Opaquely set in the dark agrarian German West around 1350 is Josefa Berens-Totenohl's novel *Der Femhof* (*The Law Estate*, 1934), in which Magdlene, the daughter of Wulf, a well-established peasant and antecedent of Nazi hereditary farmers (Erbhofbauern), preserves the blood and traditions of her ancestors as an only child. Magdlene falls in love with a hired hand who once killed a man in an attempt to salvage his rightful property. The girl's father, opposed to the union, stabs the suitor after a Feme court has condemned him to die.[76] Allegedly Feme law constituted the juridical system of Germanic tribes; it was, significantly, resurrected by illegal Freikorps fighters in the 1920s who would pronounce sentence and then kill traitors in their midst. (Both Martin Bormann and Rudolf Höss, the first commandant of Auschwitz, spent years for Feme murder in republican jails.) Berens-Totenohl made certain that the Wulf family had progeny after the young man's death, by having had him mate with the daughter against her father's will, so she will become pregnant with the dead man's son. The author thus demonstrated the usefulness of Feme and the priority of an unbroken bloodline from times of yore to, putatively, Wulf's forward-moving genealogy – consequently, she produced a follow-up novel. Her overall message was that one can formally transgress the community's customs and must be punished accordingly, but more importantly, beyond one's individual happiness, one has to ensure the kin's longevity.[77] This book was extremely popular in the Third Reich, selling more than 250,000 copies.[78]

The illicit copulation and out-of-wedlock birth of Wulf's grandson introduce thematic elements underlying most of the literature by völkisch authors before and during the Third Reich, whether in more archaic or contemporary settings. References to Vikings, Old Germans, and ancestor bloodlines typify Nazi-era writings.[79] They were complemented by literary stratagems involving images of women, eugenics, race-consciousness to the point of xenophobia, love of the countryside, (East European) settlement, handcrafts, and a concomitant hatred of the city and its attributes. Aesthetic considerations aside (Saul Friedländer has, correctly, characterized the essence of this melange as kitsch), all add up to a pattern of male-dominated archaic structures and anti-intellectual impulses, a seemingly anti-modern world ruled by blurry emotions.[80]

Much of Nazi literature was marked by biopolitical, organological obsessions. In the Germanocentric orbit of these authors the mother, as in Magdlene Wulf's image, was the fount of all life worthy of living. For women, in Nazi ideology and as mirrored in the literature, this was their main function. Another, secondary one, was serving as the male's helpmate, a partner, just as eugenic as erotic. Pictures of mothers, to be revered, are in many Nazi novels, nowhere more so than in Walter Bauer's *Das Herz der Erde* (*The Heart of the Earth*, 1933), where this picture was reduced to the level of cliché.[81] Bauer extolled the mother beyond the allowable limits of sentimentality: in a quasi-masturbatory action the pregnant Alma "undresses and feels the night breeze around her, senses the power of her body." A few pages later comes the rhetoric: "I have recognized you, Mother. Should her breasts quench his thirst no longer? She was his mother." Later Alma, viewing herself in the shop window, sees herself as "strong, brown, motherly, healthy."[82] The cult of the mother, fertility itself, was serviced excessively in other novels, by Jansen among the Icelanders, Steguweit during the world war where Germany incarnate was equated with Mother, by Otto Paust among the Freikorps, and Karl Benno von Mechow, Hans Carossa, and Wiechert in the flat republican countryside.[83] The SA bard Heinrich Anacker summed it up for the nationalists in a poem where a mother had given birth to three sons to die for Germany, and Hans-Jürgen Nierentz in another poem, as he commended demure women patiently waiting for their babies to be born.[84]

In plot scenarios where the girl, the mother, a vessel for procreation favored by völkisch eugenicists, could have been treated purely in erotic terms, as an object of lust, the writers often bowed out, lest they be accused of pornography in the manner of the Naturalists or Expressionists: Hauptmann and Halbe, Schnitzler and Wedekind.[85] As the solely erotic potential was played down, girlfriends and even wives were emphasized as "comrades," pragmatic helpmates to the man.[86] Other than that, they were infantilized and thereby marginalized, lest they threaten the organic hierarchy with males on top.[87]

The ramifications of eugenic laws disobeyed were described as a natural consequence of this stress on corporeality. Ideally, in these genderized scenarios, both men and women were held up as models of eugenic health for the Volksgemeinschaft, who must forgo sexual congress both in and out of marriage if found hereditarily diseased. In Betina Ewerbeck's novel *Angela*

Koldewey (1939) this is the fate of the painter Martin whom the medical student Angela cannot wed on account of hereditary illness in his family.[88] (Ewerbeck was the wife of leading SS physician Kurt Blome, later a defendant at the Nuremberg Doctors' Trials.) Edwin Erich Dwinger had one of his Freikorps leaders preach: "The unhealthy begins with the cosseting of the poor; the preference of sick people leads to suicide!"[89] Friedrich Griese assumed an air of gravity in his novel *Die Weissköpfe* (1939) when he wrote about the birth of freaks of nature in the olden days: "The child was carried outside and deposited at a hidden spot in the woods; at times it was drowned or buried alive, in order to induce a quicker death."[90] Ewerbeck's and Griese's books were published in 1939, just as the Nazis were embarking on their euthanasia of disabled children, condemned as "lives not worthy of living."[91]

Racial purity was another requirement of eugenic zealots. In the heavy air of xenophobia, the Jews were targeted first, as potential race defilers, chief among them those from eastern Europe who had entered Germany increasingly after World War I, although assimilated German Jews were by far in the majority. Then came black people and, at some distance, Gypsies.[92] Hitler's early Munich mentor Dietrich Eckart was feted because he was believed to have moved the "Jewish Question" into the center of national attention. Jews often became the subject of novels in which the alleged betrayal of the German people in general and the imperial army in particular after November 1918 was lamented. A seeming consequence was the Jews' ongoing involvement in corruption schemes of all manner and, coupled with that, their sexual improprieties toward "Aryan" women.[93] The proverbial jazz age of the 1920s, argued völkisch authors, was a result of Jewish manipulation of jazz music, which had been invented by the Negroes.[94]

The nationalists' fear of black people was less intense because only a negligible number of them, stemming from Germany's colonial past, were living in the country before and after 1933. However, they were a legitimate eugenic concern in the catalogue of völkisch phobias. It was above all the one-time South African resident Hans Grimm who fanned the flames of Negro hatred as he warned about the dangers of racial miscegenation in his books, starting with *Volk ohne Raum* (*People without Space*), first published in 1926 and going on to sell 330,000 copies during the Third Reich. What followed were stories such as *Lüderitzland*, in 1936, in which the Germans of South West Africa (today's Namibia) were glorified, as the native Hereros, victims of the first

German genocide in 1903–4, were reviled. "Caffers" smelled, judged Grimm, and colored girls, sexually uncontrolled, constantly schemed to seduce white men. Hanns Johst cautioned against "black-white mésalliances" as in Marseilles in 1936: "eighteen thousand half-breeds were registered for school in this city this year."[95]

Reading about allegedly hostile foreign neighbors became a popular pastime among Germans after 1933. Looming mysterious, the Soviet Union was at the top of many readers' lists, not least because Jews were said to be lurking there and pulling all the strings. They were notoriously said to be conspiring with the ruling Communists in oppressing German minorities, decent peasant folk who had been settled in the Crimea and Caucasus under Catherine the Great or later. Germans, not Russians or Ukrainian Kulaks, were described as victims of Kremlin-engineered famines killing millions; moreover, Germans were the victims of feral mountain tribes hunting them down. If they were not identified as Jews, native Russians were linked to Tartars, devoid of agreeable physical features and acceptable manners, and always addicted to vodka.[96] With the Sudeten crisis nearing in 1938, novels were also published on behalf of the German minorities in Czechoslovakia, with the Czechs, in particular, portrayed as cunning rogues.[97] Thus a psychological platform was built for Hitler to justify his yearning for eastern conquest to his Volksgemeinschaft the more easily.

In his various books Grimm polemicized against the British and the French, whom he characterized mainly as unscrupulous in trade and ruthless in staking out territorial claims. A similar case, but depending less on colonies, was argued by Karl Aloys Schenzinger in his novel *Anilin* (1937), in which he cast German scientists as inventors fighting against unfair English competition.[98] In novels about the British and French, arguments against the former remained mostly mercantilist, while in opposition to the latter they were predominantly intellectual and moral: the French had introduced the Enlightenment, a so-called Age of Reason that could be said to be corrupted if measured against practices of debauchery and perversion as seen in Paris.[99]

There is a fine anti-intellectual thread that runs through all of this literature, corresponding with the anti-rationality, the irrationality found in Nazi ideology itself. "Thinking leads to quagmire," the count says to Captain von Orla in Wiechert's *Das einfache Leben*, while Orla has been trying to find "the miracles of the universe."[100] Von Mechow cast doubt on "a learned philosophy from the writing desk," and in Tüdel Weller's novel *Rabauken* (*Ruffians*, 1938) any talk about Freud and psychoanalysis can only come from Jews.[101] In Will Vesper's *Geschichten von Liebe, Traum und Tod* (*Stories of Love, Dreams, and Death*, 1937), finally, an academic career was contrasted negatively with a course of "common sense."[102]

The natural home of the intellectual was an urban environment, and so it follows that particular scorn was reserved by writers in the Third Reich for the city, as opposed to the countryside. To these neo-Romantics, the city served like a prism showing, in concentration, all the wicked things they so objected to. Wiechert once likened a city's houses to "graves in a dead land."[103] For him, summarized one of his peers astutely, everything that was not nature met only with refusal. Conversely, "everything that comes from there is absolutely perfect."[104] The city was anonymous and soulless, for authors such as Will Vesper, Fritz Stelzner, and Kuni Tremel-Eggert.[105] A seat of brothels and illicit sex, it was not conducive to childbirth and child-rearing; it was full of Jews and the idle pleasures proffered by corruption and despoliation. Only Communists could find their homes there.[106]

What flourished in the country as opposed to the industrialized, anonymous city? Apart from farming, it was the old trades and crafts, anything men and women did with their hands. Significantly, the virtues of artisanship were exalted in many novels of the time, as well as in several poems. At the base was Hitler's maxim of the equality of workers of brain *and* of fist ("Arbeiter der Stirn und der Faust"). In Wiechert's East Prussian solitude, Captain von Orla resorts to a life of fishing, woodland-clearing, and carpentry.[107] Woodwork, saddle-making, masonry, and tin-smithing were favorite handicrafts mentioned by these writers.[108] As Heinz Steguweit wrote jubilantly: "Proudly spoke the carpenter to the poet/We are of one stock/As I work away with saw, plane, and wood/With hammer, nail, or bolt/You woodwork well with words."[109]

The glorification of manual work corresponded with how Nazi poets and novelists rhapsodized about country, village, and soil. The Nazi rural ideal was initially not Hitler's own brainchild but derived from tortuous thinking by one of his early lieutenants, the agronomist Richard Walther Darré; still, the Führer (and Goebbels) used it to appeal to large masses in agricultural areas.[110] On the other hand, idolizing the countryside was

hardly an invention of the Nazis. It was part of the German literary tradition going back to pre-industrial times and was solidly in denial of any
changes wrought by the Industrial Revolution. Already in the late nineteenth century, writers such as the Bavarian Ludwig Thoma and the Styrian
Peter Rosegger had been the redoubtable champions of the countryside.
Goebbels is known to have favored reading Thoma.[111]

Motifs of the country in books by German writers between 1933 and
1939 appear as carved into a primitive woodcut: they revolved around what
the farmer daily lives on and lives with, his soil and its fruit, his work animals
(nothing motor-driven), cattle to feed off or to sell. The (extended) family
who support him, and whom he bears the responsibility to support, consists
of his spouse, his children (preferably sons, as heirs), sometimes in-laws and
grandchildren and, in an age of absent machinery, the live-in hired help. The
language these archaicized people speak is heavy with local dialect, they
hardly read, their food is simple fare. They go to church in their Sunday best,
they meet communally for beer or wine, or important family festivities. Wives
are mostly subdued, daughters often more so, frequently to be married off
against their will; acquaintances are few but ties between them strong. As in
the High Middle Ages, ancient curses linger, there are premonitions of doom,
especially if evil has been committed. Providence looms – a force Hitler
always loved to invoke. Natural catastrophes are braved, with survival not
always certain. But the farmer and his kin persist on the soil they revere, as the
patriarchal structure is threatened most severely, sometimes irrevocably, by
influences from a nearby town. In all, rural scenarios are static, frozen in time
and space; they lack dynamics, the pulse of the city, the pulse of modernity.[112]

In his poem "Flieg, deutsche Fahne, flieg!" ("Fly, German Banner, Fly!"),
Hans-Jürgen Nierentz encapsulated the fetishization of the "Blood and
Soil" concept as it became literary stock-in-trade during the Nazi period.
The poem drew the line between a German peasant's love of soil and the
blood he might have to shed on his march to gain more Lebensraum in the
European East. It spoke of the Führer on the verge of leading farmers with
their pickaxes and spades, through a German land already packed with
soldiers, from one border to the next.[113] The poem was unabashedly militant, warning already in 1936 of aggression that was to take place in an
easterly direction three years later. Then, in 1938, Hans Friedrich Blunck
published his novel about the sixteenth-century Teutonic Knight Wolter

von Plettenberg and his barely victorious battles against Tsar Ivan the Terrible.[114] This was just a year before Hitler invaded Poland, and three years before he marched into the Soviet Union.

THE PRESS AND RADIO

Virtually no newspaper or journal was allowed to publish anything it wanted in Germany after 1933, no matter how trivial the contents. Several of the Third Reich's authors held jobs with the German press, some earning their chief livelihood there. One of the latter was Friedrich Sieburg, who after 1916, as a twenty-three-year-old, had piloted a plane in World War I and then become a writer in Berlin. In the mid-1920s he had joined the right-liberal *Frankfurter Zeitung* and at the beginning of the Nazi regime was its correspondent in Paris. Himself tending to the political right, Sieburg defended the National Socialists to foreign critics and did this with such conviction that in 1939 Berlin appointed him to the Foreign Service.[115] Sieburg had proved his conservative faith not just with the articles he sent to his Frankfurt paper, but also with a few books. In one, he lambasted humanism and liberalism as being associated with the French Enlightenment, not suited to "the new Germany."[116] In another, he praised the qualities of Portugal's dictator António de Oliveira Salazar, who appeared to him as a führer personality of the highest order.

Sieburg likened Salazar to Hitler when he wrote that the former economics professor was an unassuming man without pomp and circumstance who had been forced by necessity to become the autocratic ruler of his country, not by personal ambition. His fight against Communism was much to his credit, and while he was leading his nation on a promising path, one of the tasks ahead of him was finding a solution to the race question. For one grave mistake the Portuguese conqueror Alfonso de Albuquerque had made in the early sixteenth century was to have encouraged the intermarriage of Portuguese sailors and settlers with colored natives in the newly won overseas colonies, the result of which could still be seen in the streets of Portugal today.[117]

Sieburg and his colleagues everywhere in the editorial rooms of German newspapers after 1933 took their cues from the Schriftleitergesetz of October 1933 as well as from the directives being regularly passed down from the

Propaganda Ministry. A new Nazi news bureau, Deutsches Nachrichtenbüro (DNB), aided in the pre-screening and streamlining of information to be supplied to the reading public, via a totally coordinated German press.[118] News was often twisted or totally falsified, and official copy was dictated to the editorial offices by Berlin. An example of the latter is a directive of December 1935 that ordered editorials in favor of a Goebbels publication, a collection of his speeches, because so far in a free market the book had found only a faint resonance.[119] In 1937, during the civil war in Spain after Guernica had been destroyed by the German Condor Legion, the public was to be told that Spanish planes had bombed the Basque town.[120] During the growing German offensive against the Czechs over the Sudetenland in the fall of 1938, when the Sudeten-German politician Wilhelm Baierle had been assassinated, German papers were enjoined to print that news prominently on their front pages and hint at the likely complicity of German emigrants (who would never miss a chance to vilify Nazi politicians).[121] How well these instructions worked in everyday journalistic practice is shown by a remark Goebbels confided to his diary. On November 10, 1938, after the anti-Semitic pogrom initiated by the Promi, the newspapers had been charged with downplaying the event. Instead, thought Goebbels, one might write that here and there windows had been smashed, and "synagogues incinerated themselves or had somehow burst into flames." There should be no full-page spreads and no pictures reproduced, with nothing on the front page. Individual commentaries were to be allowed but should center on the "understandable anger of the population" and the fact that "a spontaneous answer had been given after the murder of the legation counselor," Ernst vom Rath, in Paris. After his orders had been heeded, Goebbels noted, delighted: "The German press is magnificently helpful. It knows what is at stake."[122]

Did all newspapers in the Third Reich conform to such rulings to the same extent? There is evidence to suggest that among them the *Frankfurter Zeitung* (FZ) was the one most unyielding to Goebbels's demands, because of its long bourgeois-liberal tradition, the staying power of some writers and editors resisting censorship several years into the regime, and the minister's own calculation that the Nazis needed a more traditional-looking organ as window-dressing for the world.[123] Indeed, Sieburg himself never joined the Party, and two other important editors had reason to distrust the Nazis: Benno Reifenberg who was half-Jewish, and Dolf Sternberger who had a

Jewish wife.[124] The paper had once belonged to German Jews and possessed a powerful legacy of Jewish contributors. It was only when the prominent Jewish writers Walter Benjamin and Siegfried Kracauer had stopped working for the firm that Goebbels allowed it to stay open, but even he could not save it entirely; for Hitler himself, who always detested it, finally had it closed down in 1943.[125]

There were several bourgeois newspapers, less resilient, that were allowed to stay on in cities like Cologne, Hamburg, and Berlin, such as the *Deutsche Allgemeine Zeitung* (DAZ), *Berliner Zeitung* (BZ), and *Neue Rundschau* (NR).[126] It is a measure of the level of immersion in National Socialist ideology, forced or voluntary, affecting the entire German press that organs such as the DAZ published favorable reviews of the "Degenerate Art" exhibition in July 1937 or the FZ celebrated Hitler's march into Austria in the spring of 1938.[127] The FZ first printed Hitler's bombastic proclamation on the occasion of the Anschluss and then gave its approval in a long article culminating in these sentences: "Without much ado, as frank as it was decisive, the proclamation of the Führer and Reich Chancellor demonstrates what occurred last night in Austria. The resolutions that have been made have taken place within the security of action that never left the path of a quiet and orderly solution."[128] On Hitler's fiftieth birthday, April 20, 1939, Sternberger compared the Führer's historical greatness as a statesman to that of Caesar, Barbarossa, and Napoleon.[129] Thenceforth, follow-up articles backing Hitler poured oil onto the fires of aggression against Poland.[130]

Placing, as they did, a great deal of emphasis on being rooted in the soil, especially in the countryside, the Nazis made sure to coordinate newspapers in smaller, provincial towns and in agrarian regions, to the extent that they had not already been eliminated.[131] In order to keep them weak and under control, their official status as bearers of government communications was taken away from them; those functions were now delegated to the Party press. Furthermore, the regime had to come to terms with small to medium-size Catholic newspapers, which remained a touchy problem despite Hitler's concordat with the Pope in September 1933.[132]

It is clear then that for Goebbels, the press was ideal for his chief propaganda uses, first to communicate to the people administrative rulings or specially tailored news as a measure of control, second to entertain them, thus keeping them mollified and at peace with the regime. Hence even trade, family, and hobby journals were put to the service of the state. To stay with the example of the Austrian Anschluss: In March 1938 this event was memorialized by an engineering journal, the illustrated family magazine *Der Rundblick*, and the *Silesian Monthly*. A beekeepers' journal printed "Ein Volk! Ein Reich! Ein Führer!" on its first page and then declared the Anschluss "a watershed event also in the history of German beekeeping."[133]

Although the Nazi Party acquired many newspapers after shutting others down, it maintained its own broadsheets in a favored position. The three most important ones were *Völkischer Beobachter* (VB), *Der Angriff*, and *Das Schwarze Korps*. Regionally, there were papers modeled on the VB and adapted to local circumstances and events, such as the *Westdeutscher Beobachter*, located in Cologne. The *Völkischer Beobachter* had been started during Dietrich Eckart's and Alfred Rosenberg's early days in Munich, with them as editors and later Hitler as publisher, and it was the official organ of the Nazi Party.[134] It appeared daily, eventually in two chief editions from Munich and Berlin, printing Party communiqués and dealing with life's occurrences from a strictly Nazi point of view: a totalitarian tool interpreting the world order according to totalitarian criteria and shaped to totalitarian rule. Every Party member was expected to subscribe to it; nonmembers did well to do so, in order not to raise suspicion. Its contents were simple and attuned to the masses, its vernacular unrefined. In matters cultural (feuilleton), discussions were unsophisticated; it catered to all the Nazi stereotypes: that the Enlightenment as a contrivance of the French was abhorrent, that the jewel of music was Romantic music and Germany excelled in this, that Expressionism was degenerate. In all, the VB reflected the unimaginative train of thought of its molder Rosenberg, who remained chief editor until the end.[135] It had sold more than 41,000 copies daily by February 1932, and thereafter its numbers rose rapidly.[136]

Der Angriff (*The Attack*) was a weekly paper Goebbels had founded in his capacity as Gauleiter of Berlin in 1927; it appeared as a twice-weekly from 1929 and a weekly from 1930. Often prohibited in the republican period, it was rather in the SA style, heavy with local news. "Tight, clear, sharp, and radically edited, thus suiting the Berlin mentality," said Joseph Goebbels, it was directed at the working man. With sales of 30,000 copies weekly in 1928 and over 60,000 in 1934, its tone was much ruder than the VB's, and it concentrated even more heavily on the alleged evil of the Jews.[137]

Of more consequence for the spreading of Nazi propaganda, because it was molded by journalists more sophisticated than those working for *Der Angriff*, was the SS's *Das Schwarze Korps*, which was under the curatorship not of Goebbels but of Himmler. Outside the SS, it had a more limited readership than *Der Angriff*, but it could easily be subscribed to and was available at news stands. In style it was often witty, and it printed captivating photographs. It was a tabloid directing itself to the converted, but rather more on the educated side. Whatever went on in Himmler's empire it usually left alone, because anything on his watch was top secret. Only rarely did it let on what the Third Reich was really all about, in terms of its totalitarian constraints and imperialist ambitions, yet in doing so the tabloid remained cagey.[138] A good example of this is its reportage about concentration camps in the Reich. Obviously bothered by what Jewish émigrés were saying about the camps abroad, *Das Schwarze Korps* attempted to keep the record straight. In its edition number 7 of 1936 it clarified, about the camp inmates: "Here we have a collection of race defilers, rapists, sexual deviants, habitual criminals who have spent the largest part of their lives behind penitentiary walls, as well as other individuals who have placed themselves outside the Volksgemeinschaft." The paper offered to make a gift of these people to any country interested in welcoming in its midst "a rich collection of notorious criminals and declared enemies of every order."[139] The latter category would include political prisoners that the paper did not choose to specify.

Even though the press acted as a uniform platform for the political purposes of the Reich, structurally it remained decentralized. By contrast, radio appeared centralized as early as 1933 and was effectively more so as the regime progressed. This was because radio was even more useful for propaganda than newspapers, as even illiterates could be swayed. Realizing that, Reich Chancellor Franz von Papen's authoritarian regime had nationalized radio as early as 1932. As soon as leading Nazis recognized radio's potential as "the cultural SS of the Third Reich," the nation's broadcast stations were acquired by the RRG, as that organ itself became an integral part of the Promi early in 1933. Broadcast workers were incorporated into the Radio Chamber of the RKK that fall.[140] Radio passed its baptism of fire in Nazi political control early in February 1933 when Hitler and Goebbels spoke at the Berlin Sportpalast to woo voters for the March 5 election that would clear the path for the Enabling Law of March 23. To address "twenty or thirty million Germans listening to their radios," gushed the playwright Erich Ebermayer, "without a doubt constitutes a great success for Hitler. What an instrument of mass propaganda radio is today!"[141]

In order to expand broadcasting efficiently, Goebbels had to weigh up a set of balances. In a totalitarian tyranny, a good balance would be achieved by gauging how many listeners might want to afford themselves an outside window by listening to foreign stations, against those without such interests. Allowing an outside window would pose no risk for Goebbels as long as it did not upset the internal peace, given that, as the leaders were well aware, emigrant Jews and visiting journalists were spreading negative news about Germany abroad. Just to be certain, already in the first few months of 1933 the Nazi regime developed a Volksempfänger (VE, a people's receiver as in Volkswagen, the people's car of 1938), which was powerful enough to handle centrally sourced German broadcasts, including of course political messages, but too weak to accommodate foreign stations. The VE 301, as it was soon called, reminding listeners of January 30 (Hitler's rise to power), was to be marketed for a relatively modest 76 Reichsmark, so that as many German citizens as possible would buy it. Not least because of this financial break for economically challenged strata of society, the number of listeners in Germany increased from just over four million in early 1933 to close to fourteen million in late 1939. This meant that by early World War II, 70 percent of German households possessed a radio receiver – among the highest rates in the world.[142]

However, because there were always sufficiently affluent Germans around to purchase stronger sets, the opportunities for foreign-radio reception never ceased. Already in 1937 one-third of all the radios were multi-circuit superhets.[143] Those were capable not just of pulling in the various medium-wave German regional stations along with the national long-wave Deutschlandsender, but also the BBC with its superb news service, Beromünster from Zurich with its neutral matter-of-fact broadcasts, and Radio Luxemburg with its fashionable jazz programs – on all the wave bands. Goebbels, who complained in April 1937 that German radio offerings had deteriorated, knew that his carefully calibrated balance was in danger, for "the listeners are hearing foreign stations."[144]

Goebbels's system of balances was complicated, and hardly ever was he able to achieve an optimal situation: keeping his German clientele willing to embrace the most hard-hitting political propaganda while rendering it sufficiently docile with the right doses of palliative entertainment. Such an aim was overarching; beneath were more modest and more realistic goals of equilibrium between words and music and, broken down, serious versus light music as well as, in broadcasts featuring the spoken word, current-affairs spots as opposed to radio plays, children's hours, and quiz shows.

Goebbels's skill at weighting these factors developed only after time, with a trial-and-error method he began after 1934, to questionable overall effect. During all of 1933, radio was enthusiastically if crudely employed to broadcast political news, the public speeches of regime leaders, especially those of Hitler and Goebbels, and airings of public events. To hear those, and more, in areas with relatively few private sets such as in the provinces, many Germans had to congregate in public places like town halls or proprietary Party pubs and listen communally without a stir. The day of the Nazi rise to power (January 30), the Führer's birthday (April 20), May Day (May 1), Reich Party rallies (every September), and the 1923 Hitler Putsch remembrance day (November 9) were highlights of the official calendar, with large forced public turnouts. Throughout all of 1933, military marches of all types were everywhere on the air, led by Hitler's favorite *Badenweiler*. And the marching sound of SA boots was reproduced, as a unique tribute to Hitler's paramilitary troops, who in those early days were helping the regular police in the roundup of public enemies.[145]

By the end of the first year in power the regime leaders realized that too much emphasis on politics in a public medium such as broadcasting could dismay the upper-class Besitz- und Bildungsbürgertum, on whose skill in administration and the higher professions they relied and many of whose members still had to be fully won over. Moreover, less than refined programming did not leave too good an impression on potentially friendly neighbors such as France and Britain whom Hitler, at first, had no reason to offend. Hence, in order to improve the overall quality of radio, Goebbels by early 1934 cut down on the political crudities and embarked on a campaign of promoting serious music, beginning with a Beethoven cycle in February, followed by rich programs of music by Bach, Handel, Mozart, and Bruckner. That summer featured a special Wagner cycle, his music interwoven with prose by Wagner's acolyte and son-in-law Houston Stewart Chamberlain.[146] It helped that at this particular juncture the mature Richard Strauss was president of the Reich Music Chamber. His music too was generously featured, along with that of the next two most eminent contemporary composers, Hans Pfitzner and, at quite a distance, Paul Graener.[147]

However, from 1934 onward Goebbels's programming policy proved erratic; he found it difficult to find his ideal balance, especially against the backdrop of changing politics and not always entirely sure what the people would put up with. Hence his directives moved from here to there. For example, his objective to loosen up the program during 1934 while at the same time improving its quality led to those classical-music cycles as well as the establishment of a sophisticated studio jazz band, the Golden Seven, in Berlin by December 1934. Whereas this must have impressed London and Paris, protests from among more ordinary folk in Germany as well as from Nazi leadership hardliners caused the abolition of jazz on the radio by the fall of 1935; the Golden Seven were dismissed.[148] Convinced as ever that music had as political a function as any other medium, Goebbels then broadly ordered more light-music content at the expense of serious fare, at the same time reducing the proportion of word content in broadcasting.[149] Then, in mid-1938, after Radio Munich had been airing several hours of light music along with only forty minutes of chamber music daily, Goebbels suddenly changed his mind again, calling for "more serious, less entertainment music. Transmissions of operas and symphonies. A serious program."[150] Clearly, the Anschluss of Austria and palpable tension ahead of the Sudetenland showdown provided his rationale. Later that year radio content consisted of more than 68 percent music and 16 percent current affairs.[151] But once more Goebbels changed his mind, finding this not suitable enough and asking for the lighter programming to be increased.[152] This was in July 1939 when the Nazis were in full rearmament. Sensing that a new global war was not popular, the Nazis, so one may assume, pre-emptively wanted to assuage the population.

FILM AND STAGE

The cinema addressed its audience with moving images *and* sound. What were the essential differences between it and radio? Its marketed product was fixed on celluloid in space and time and could be used repeatedly. Because of a story line, film seemingly had a higher pure-entertainment value with propaganda taking second place. However, propaganda was just as effective in film when dedicated, ideologically aligned, pictures were issued and when, more insidiously, hidden political or social-behavior messages could be conveyed, as a by-product of the lead narrative. Hence Kracauer was right to claim in 1947 that "all Nazi films were more or less propaganda films – even the mere entertainment pictures which seem to be remote from politics."[153]

German film was in a crisis when during the first half of 1933 Goebbels attempted to come to grips with its organizational and financial problems, let alone aesthetic or ideological deficiencies, as he saw them. Economically, the film industry was virtually bankrupt in January, as a result of the ongoing Depression and, from the end of the republic, its deteriorating quality. Several changes were implemented to fix it institutionally, culminating in the creation of a proper Reich Film Chamber within the RKK in the fall. Centralization was accompanied by fiscal stabilization, for instance by increasing ticket prices from an all-time low of 10 pfennigs to 60 pfennigs and then 1 mark, thus removing unprofitability for individual theater owners. Already from 1932 to 1936, films grossed 90 million marks in earnings, of which the distributors received close to 28 million.[154] Withal, from 1933 to 1939, the number of film viewers rose from 245 million to 624 million and, to accommodate them, the number of cinemas increased from roughly 5,000 to 7,000.[155]

In content and format, films in the ascendant Nazi dictatorship inevitably continued the patterns of the republic for lack of something revolutionary at hand; innocuous films from the Weimar era that had been completed after January 1933 were allowed to be shown (in contrast to the problematic ones that had to be banned). Hence the tried and proven genres of large costume films, historical period pieces, operettas, melodramas, or comedies continued to be made, with the traditional Ufa company, formerly of Alfred Hugenberg's holding concern, occupying a quasi-monopoly until newer or smaller firms under the aegis of Goebbels had reaffirmed themselves: Tobis, Berlin-Film, Wien-Film, Bavaria, and Terra. One of these pictures was *Viktor und Viktoria* (1933), a musical comedy featuring Renate Müller, who became a favorite actress of Hitler's until her alleged suicide, reportedly because the Gestapo was after her and her Jewish lover. Another was *Ein Lied für Dich* (*A Song for You*, 1933), an operetta film starring the half-Jewish tenor Jan Kiepura, directed by the Jew Joe May, before he left

Europe for Hollywood, where he failed miserably. Yet a third movie was *Maskerade* (1934), a lavish Austrian costume feature directed by Willy Forst and starring Olga Tschechowa, with sets by the Jew Oskar Strnad.[156] Most of the actors performing in German films from 1933 to 1939 were holdovers from the Weimar period, with only very few of them professing Nazis.[157] One of these was Jenny Jugo of *Ein Lied für Dich*; she was a frequent guest of the Goebbels family and also of Hitler, as was Madame Tschechowa, a niece of Anton Chekhov. Those who had been National Socialists before the Nazi takeover included the young actor Veit Harlan, and most likely Luise Ullrich, Mathias Wieman, and Paul Hartmann. After January 1933, many became close acquaintances of Goebbels and Hitler, such as Anny Ondra, the wife of boxer Max Schmeling; the couple were ensconced as Goebbels's neighbors on the Schwanenwerder peninsula in Berlin-Wannsee. Today their true beliefs are revealed beyond doubt by entries in Goebbels's detailed diaries, less so in the apologetic if not outright specious memoirs of the stars themselves. After World War II they would maintain that as artists they possessed the privilege of being apolitical, more importantly that as *actors* they had to remain neutral, in order to better assume the identity of a saint or a villain, a Communist or Nazi.[158]

That this was a lame excuse when in fact many actors had exposed themselves politically in the Weimar Republic, and would again in the Third Reich one way or another, is shown by the prominent Heinrich George, who played a Communist father in the first true Nazi film of note, *Hitlerjunge Quex*, in 1933. In fact he played a Communist who slowly comes to see the light of National Socialism that has already guided his boy Rudi for a while. George had been a dedicated Marxist in the Weimar years and on the blacklist of the Nazis; under Hitler he turned quickly to promote his celebrated career as a dyed-in-the-wool National Socialist, for all to see.[159]

Analogous to the ritualistic Party droning heard on the air waves throughout 1933, the German movie industry hastened to manufacture the equivalent in Nazi films. For the industry, to be seen as loyal was the most convincing stance. After at least one forgettable attempt, the first significant example in a series of Party films was *SA-Mann Brand*, premiered on June 14 at Berlin's Ufa-Palast, with Hitler present at the second showing. The film followed a thematic pattern already observable in the plots of Kampfzeit-commemorative novels: Nazi fighters before January 1933, usually SA, were celebrated in their big-city brawls against the Red Front, with Jews as wire-pulling villains behind the scenes, often in the garb of Soviet commissars sent abroad by Moscow. There was a conversion theme in that individual Marxists could be saved; intrinsically valuable and having merely been seduced, they are brought over to the other, Hitler's side, frequently within the framework of a love relationship or by way of resolving generational conflict, a motivational dynamic signally involving the Hitler Youth. For the *Brand* picture, reliance on republican resources was clear in the choice of actors Heinz Klingenberg, once a collaborator of left-wing Hertha Thiele, and Otto Wernicke and Wera Liessem – both participants in Fritz Lang's *Testament des Dr. Mabuse*, now banned. Wernicke played the SPD father of Brand who is won over, as is Liessem's character as Brand's future paramour. As in all of those Party films, a Hitler Youth type played a major role; it is either he or the SA man who will fall in a sacrificial death for the cause.[160]

Hitlerjunge Quex was based on a successful novel by Schenzinger completed just in time in 1932.[161] It had a very similar theme, celebrating the martyr death of Herbert Norkus, who had been killed by the Red Front in Berlin in January 1932, and was premiered in Munich in September 1933, again with the Führer attending.[162] Here, along with the generational conflict, the Communist conversion motif was repeated, given not only that former Communists in the Reich, lest they end up in a concentration camp, still had the choice of moving over to the Nazi fold, but also that formerly Communist adolescents were welcome in Baldur von Schirach's Hitler Youth.[163] The country-versus-city trope was, if anything, re-emphasized in the narrative and, as in *SA-Mann Brand*, the political-education theme was paramount. The effect of both films was tested on a random group of German youths by 1934. Not surprisingly, Brand and Heini Völker, the *Quex* lead character, revealed themselves as exemplars both for boys and girls, in the first group to reinforce the will to martial prowess, and in the second to educate young women to serve as assistants to the males – this theme also a subject of many Nazi novels. Hence the reaction of a sixteen-year-old sales girl, who said it would be difficult to forget either film, "because we are striving to act the same as the German men."[164] On a certain Sunday morning in Berlin, 70,000 Hitler Youth, boys and girls, saw the movie.[165]

The film *Hans Westmar*, released in December 1933, had been a total embarrassment; in all, Goebbels's reaction to the SA films as templates for further Nazi pictures was negative and in keeping with his feelings about early radio programming. Even though Rosenberg's *Völkischer Beobachter* praised *SA-Mann Brand* as a "successful attempt" to capture the people's sympathy for the SA, Goebbels was concerned that other Nazi institutions viewed such naïve historicization of the movement's "Time of Struggle" as crudely done, without paying due attention to reality.[166] Moreover, he agreed with criticism labeling this emerging genre of political film "kitsch dictated by opportunism" and, while continuing to insist that political messages be projected, wished to elevate cinema's aesthetic standards altogether.[167] He disapproved of SA men stomping through motion pictures or across theater stages, the minister said in 1933, instead wanting them to march in the streets.[168] A few months later Goebbels spoke out against "kitsch" in the film industry, demanding that "more art" be aimed for.[169]

By the end of 1934 a film had been made, to be released in 1935, which combined high aesthetic quality with top propaganda for the regime, but it was not Goebbels's movie. It was *Triumph of the Will*, not a feature film but a documentary, working solely through its pictorial images and a background score, directed by the thirty-two-year-old former dancer and actress Leni Riefenstahl, on Hitler's personal commission. After fulsome praise in the Nazi press, Goebbels had to concede that it was a masterpiece in every respect and, as his diaries amply show, he regretted not having Riefenstahl in his jurisdiction.[170] The film was a celebration of Hitler's coming to power and, between the lines, his successful suppression of an alleged putsch by his long-time lieutenant Ernst Röhm, the leader of the SA.[171] The film bore several hallmarks that have made it into a classic to this day, not the least of which was the ingenious way in which themes of Wagner's music were woven into background sounds composed by the gifted Herbert Windt.[172] About the brilliant photography the American media critic Susan Sontag, who remained reluctant in her overall praise for Riefenstahl, famously judged in 1975 that "in *Triumph of the Will*, the document (the image) is no longer simply the record of reality; 'reality' has been constructed to serve the image."[173] Riefenstahl's subsequent picture about the Olympic Games in 1936 continued this innovative streak, supplying more clues about "art" to Goebbels, but it never achieved the acclaim of *Triumph of the Will*.[174]

The Röhm Purge that destroyed the potential for any SA legend in film helped Goebbels in turning away from mere Party material and finding other movie subjects which, though not as documentaries like in Riefenstahl's œuvre, combined popular appeal with both political propaganda and superior aesthetics, to varying degrees. Arguably the most successful in all three areas was *Der Herrscher* (*The Ruler*, 1937), directed by Veit Harlan and starring Emil Jannings. His presence in it alone guaranteed success; during a Hollywood interlude, he had been the first recipient of an Oscar (Academy Award) in 1928 and, because of his German accent in a new era of sound films had returned to the Reich, subsequently to become the brightest star in the German movie firmament. *Der Herrscher*, based loosely on a play by Hauptmann, was a paean to a tycoon who, as a widower, tyrannizes his family who expect to inherit a fortune after his death, especially if he can be consigned to an asylum beforehand. The ruler, however, takes his secretary as his mistress and then decides to will his business empire to the state.[175] The parallels between the ruler and Hitler here were striking, with both of them, allegedly, having only the well-being of the commonweal in mind.[176] Had the filmmakers been "working towards the Führer"? Upon its completion, Goebbels professed great admiration for the film, and it was hardly surprising he was flattered that Hitler liked it too.[177]

There were several more full-length feature films with a heavy-hitting propaganda line. If *Der Herrscher* dealt with internal German conditions, fixations of the external enemy were equally important. Already in 1933 the movie *Flüchtlinge* (*Fugitives*) was issued, demonstrating the plight of Volga Germans in the Soviet Union after the Bolshevik revolution. This film provided the Nazis with an opportunity to prove, as they thought, the oppressiveness of Soviet rulers in the Kremlin vis-à-vis a pure ethnic German minority; moreover, the magnificently "Aryan" Hans Albers could portray, as Jannings would in *Der Herrscher*, a charismatic leader.[178] Just to drive the message home, *Friesennot* (*The Plight of the Frisians*), a similar film again characterizing Volga Germans as victims, was shown beginning in 1935; during World War II, when Volga Germans were scheduled to be joined by new German settlers in the Crimea, it was credited with having had "a thorough political and educational effect."[179] By 1935, Hitler had announced rearmament, and in 1938 *Pour le Mérite* was completed, a movie involving disillusioned World War I pilots, as they are eagerly awaiting the renaissance of a Luftwaffe after Hitler's assumption of power, with which to defend, supposedly, the German borders.[180]

Especially toward the end of the peaceful period in the Third Reich and approaching the armed conflict, several films appeared that showed the art of underhand propaganda crafted into a seemingly harmless plot, which German filmmakers appeared to have mastered by that time. This trend coincided with the emergence of the Swedish actress Zarah Leander in German movies as the new superstar of the screen, a replacement for Marlene Dietrich who refused to return from America. In a time of increasing international tension the entertainment industry was to show even attractive and privileged women a responsible place in the Volksgemeinschaft, signaling that emancipation or indulging in private pleasures à la Weimar was a thing of the past. Physically, the brunette Leander bore a certain resemblance to Riefenstahl, who had earlier been successful as an entrepreneurial female making movies, yet remained unspectacular after 1936.[181] In the new moving pictures women were seen increasingly as helpmates for their men, sexual partners only with the goal of progeny, and housewives in the kitchen – not as economically resourceful individuals or as playthings. *La Habanera* was one of three pictures Leander filmed in Berlin-Babelsberg in 1937, the first year of her work in the Reich. It introduced a Swedish girl who marries the governor of Puerto Rico, only to escape the island with a Swedish lover and a small son, after the strongman's death. Her new mate, an accomplished physician, reminds her of their home in the European North, where it snowed and where she belongs with her son, rather than the decadent settings of the sweltering Caribbean.[182] *Heimat* (*Home*) of 1938 struck a similar note as Leander's character, a famous singer, returns from the United States to the German provinces, where she performs in Bach's *St. Matthew Passion* in a church and is, thereafter, reconciled with her retired-colonel father. She too has a child, an illegitimate daughter sired by a local German from some time ago, who, like her mother Magda, is now being returned to the fatherland. Leander's tribute here is both to the call of the blood, as the Nazis would have it, and to the superiority of German music, for Bach is not worthy of performance in America, a land devoid of culture.[183] The year 1938 witnessed two other films where women were relegated to inferior positions: In *Die vier Gesellen* (*The Four Companions*), Ingrid Bergman – her one and only role in German film – portrayed a would-be businesswoman realizing, not too late, her true place as being not in an office but at the side of the resolute man she loves.

Compromises are belittled.[184] In *Die Frau am Scheidewege* (*The Woman at the Crossroads*) a female physician must surrender in all respects to a male professorial colleague, who will keep her at heel as assistant and as wife.[185] And in *Frau am Steuer* (*Woman at the Wheel*) of 1939 once again a marriage relationship is sharply genderized when it turns out that husband and wife cannot work in an office side by side and that the woman belongs in a household.[186] During the war to come Hitler kept women in the home even when Albert Speer and Goebbels thought they should help manufacturing ordnance.

The louche Propaganda Minister was the autocratic ruler of the film world, where he used casting-couch techniques to gain the favor of actresses eager for parts. In December 1938, when his affair with the Czech movie star Lída Baarová had just been terminated on Hitler's orders, the eternally envious Rosenberg likened Goebbels to Jewish magnates of years past, "who forced their employees sexually."[187] It was small comfort for the prudish Party ideologue to know that Goebbels was less successful as a sexual predator when controlling the German stage. Here some of the less corruptible, long-established, and older thespians, including some film actors, worked in more conventional play-sets than movies would provide. Goebbels's reign in this sector was more bounded; for example, he could not exert his influence on theaters operating under the aegis of the Prussian Minister President Göring – chief among them the Staatstheater in Berlin – and a few lesser ones under Rosenberg's influence.

Altogether, then, the wooden stages held less interest for Goebbels; even so, they too had to conform to new Nazi norms. Like the film industry and especially the cinemas, they were in bad financial shape in 1933. The cabinet of Heinrich Brüning in the last years of the republic had reduced funds to the state theaters, so they and municipal as well as private stages could not afford to pay their staff any more because of the Depression. Royalties from publishing houses had decreased. Actors, Intendanten, and stagehands all suffered under depleted earnings or were dismissed outright because of low revenue or none at all. Misery at the German theaters, just as unemployment everywhere, lasted well beyond 1933.[188]

After January 1933 a number of changes led to improvements. In keeping with its general promises about the value of German culture and Goebbels's own predefined propaganda uses, state authorities allotted more money to existing theaters, constructed new ones, and commenced "Reich theater weeks" to stir up more interest among the public, for instance by the Hitler Youth.[189] They consolidated insolvent private theaters and refinanced them with state funds, some after former Jewish owners had been driven out as had Max Reinhardt, cowed into abandoning his five private Berlin theaters to new Nazi owners.[190] In the capital, four prominent theaters were singled out as officially pace-setting, to be headed by famous artistes – one being Göring's Preussisches Staatstheater.[191] Moreover, Party leaders used their own organizations to channel new streams of visitors into theaters: Rosenberg his KfdK and follow-up NS-Kulturgemeinde (NSKG), and Robert Ley his "Strength-through-Joy" (KdF) corporation that was subsidized by the state. If in 1934, Ley had been able to commit 1,500,000 visitors, voluntary or not, that figure increased to 7,500,000 by 1938.[192]

As in the case of literature, many plays of the kind the Nazis regarded as in accordance with the new era had been authored in the Time of Struggle, with virtually no chances of being performed. As they now became available, proffered by writers short of ability but rich in Nazi faith, stage directors and drama critics right up to Goebbels found them wanting and ignored them.[193] A goodly number did get performed, however, often by newly hired Party faithfuls, because of the authors' regime connections, a useful political message or, in the Promi's censorial judgment, for the sake of basic popular entertainment to keep the man or woman in the street satisfied.[194] Hitherto unknown actors now also wanted roles, corruption was rife: no sooner had the third-rate actor Otto Laubinger become president of the new Reich Theater Chamber in the RKK in the fall of 1933 than he insisted a young girlfriend of his be given a role.[195]

The new Nazi plays, some of them written before 1933 but rarely or never performed, were all mediocre, yet, in several ways, insidious. In these plays, be they tragedies or comedies, all National Socialist clichés were burnished, as they were in literature and most of the films. Thus in several plays, and usually in primitive plots, the peasant-soil myth was brought forward, with farmers defending their crops to the death against marauding soldiers (as in the Thirty Years War), heroically sacrificing themselves to a flood in a North German dyke community, or resisting a count's exploitation in pre-industrial times. The appearance of a strong leader in those micro-communities was *de rigueur* in these plays.[196] World War I valor was celebrated by profiling the deaths of student volunteers as at Langemarck in 1914, and early Soviet revolutionaries as well as black colonial soldiers were demonized. So were war profiteers, the November 1918 armistice, and the Treaty of Versailles of summer 1919.[197] Ethnic Germans in eastern Prussian territories coveted by Poles after 1918 were applauded, while the Poles were insulted. The same happened for Czechoslovakia.[198] The city was denigrated vis-à-vis the country, and ancestor worship was held in high esteem.[199] Pointing to more modern days, women's rights were ridiculed and the racially and socially homogeneous Volksgemeinschaft was acclaimed.[200] Anti-Semitic slanders abounded throughout those pieces, as did slurs against Sinti and Roma.[201] The monotony of pedestrian titles publishing companies were advertising at the time cannot deceive today's observer into believing that those plays were innocent.[202]

Some plays in the Third Reich were not necessarily Nazi in content but authored by National Socialists and therefore easily performable. Chief among them was Goebbels's own drama *Der Wanderer*, of 1927, which was presented in Leipzig as early as May 1933. It dealt with the exploits of the Wanderer, "a premonitory interpreter of all events," a doppelgänger of Hitler therefore, who is accompanied by "the poet." Unabashedly, the coordinated *Leipziger Neueste Nachrichten* advertised it as a work with a "political and propaganda purpose"; whether it was successful is not known.[203] An early Party man of Hitler's, as it were, was his fatherly friend Dietrich Eckart, who died of alcoholism shortly after the Beer Hall Putsch in 1923. Posthumously, dramas by Eckart were performed promptly after January 1933, a few for the first time. His best-known and originally successful piece, *Peer Gynt* (1912) after Henrik Ibsen, bore the stamp of Expressionism and became a staple of regime stages. Its inherent anti-Semitism alone recommended it now.[204] A lesser Party troll was Rosenberg's adjutant Thilo von Trotha, one of the movement's hopefuls, who used his position of power to have his plays performed: *Engelbrecht*, *Gudrun*, and *Princess Plumpudding*. Von Trotha, from a Baltic baronial family, was enamored of Nordic themes; before he died in a car accident at thirty-four in early 1938, he had formulated guidelines for the New German stage: "The selection of actors will follow racial criteria and accord with ideological principles." Actors had to have a eugenically informed attitude toward their roles, had to be agreeable in looks and young and healthy, not worn out.[205]

A few, genuinely Nazi dramatists showed some promise and might have been successful even in a non-Nazi world. Leading this group was Hanns

Johst, who had made his name as an Expressionist in the republic and whose 1933 play *Schlageter* still betrayed that early influence: "When I hear the word culture, I cock my Browning" – this phrase, famously misattributed to Göring but uttered onstage by Schlageter's Freikorps friend Friedrich Thiemann, could not have been more Expressionist![206] The trouble with Johst, who had dedicated his play to Hitler, was that only one other of his dramas was staged in the Third Reich: *Thomas Paine*, like *Schlageter* repeatedly and to good effect, was performed by first-rate artists such as Gründgens, Minetti, and Fehling, and it enhanced Johst's reputation with the regime.[207] It was a non-issue that the original of this, again rather Expressionist piece glorifying a Führer, had been published in 1927 and Johst had merely adapted it to suit the times. Indeed, the dramatist became complacent as a friend of Goebbels, Himmler, and Hitler, if not of Göring, and neglected serious writing for the remainder of his career under the regime, publishing a few poems and tracts that flattered his ego and his benefactors. Soon to become an SS general, Johst turned from dramatist to pamphleteer.[208]

One of Johst's admirers was Josef Magnus Wehner, who gave rise to much hope as a future Nazi poet of note. Two more were Gerhard Schumann and Eberhard Wolfgang Möller; all three were members of the Nazi Party, the latter two having joined the SS as well. Wehner, born in 1891 and a World War I veteran, had reaped fame with his anti-pacifist novel *Sieben vor Verdun* (*Seven at Verdun*) of 1930, a book in the vein of Heinrich Zerkaulen's war-glorifying work and republished repeatedly in the Third Reich. Wehner was nothing less than influential in Munich, mostly as a theater critic and theoretician.[209] Gerhard Schumann, born in 1911, as a young talent had already received a state prize in 1936. Two years later, in his play *Die Entscheidung* (*The Decision*), he depicted Freikorps morals as opposed to republican intrigues, with the hero, a former imperial captain, falling at the hands of Communist insurgents, during big-city upheavals in 1920.[210] Schumann joined Eberhard Wolfgang Möller, his senior by five years, as a prominent administrator in the Promi. Among other plays, the national book-prize winner Möller authored *Der Untergang Karthagos* (*The Downfall of Carthage*), with its unmistakable Expressionist accents, in 1938; the Phoenicians, about to surrender to Roman invaders, were likened to Jews, and their body politic to nests of corruption in the Weimar Republic.[211]

Möller garnered special Nazi accolades as the author of *Das Frankenburger Würfelspiel* (*The Frankenburg Dice Game*) premiered at the Berlin open-air stage "Dietrich-Eckart-Bühne" in 1936. That stage was the last outlier of the Thingspiele (Thing plays) movement, which originated in 1934, as a way of integrating the audience, as a Volksgemeinschaft writ small, with actors and action. Apart from elements of the German youth movement and Greek open-air theater, the Thingspiel movement had its roots in an older nation-alist theater reform: experimental stage settings by völkisch dramatists Adolf Bartels, Ernst Wachler, and Friedrich Lienhard, who had tried to innovate, beginning with classical plays, under the open skies from the Wilhelmine period onward, with no lasting success.[212] *Thinge* were old Germanic law courts where, so the Nazis fancied, community plays had also taken place.[213]

The Thingspiel was proposed nationwide for summer 1934 by champions of National Socialism, an imagined proxy to the early movement, advocating the involvement of the audience with the stage, in abundant natural settings, on the margins or outside of cities, such as Heidelberg's "Holy Mountain." Thingspiele were to be Nordic choric theater, hymnic, mythic, and cultic, with large groups of actors on the stage chanting in unison and led by choric foremen. With SA or Hitler Youths participating in large numbers and accompanied by fanfaric music, they were to resemble official Party events like the annual September rallies (hence they could be considered, on a smaller scale, a parallel to the Party and Olympic films of Leni Riefenstahl, albeit inferior in their choreographic architecture).[214] Not the least aim of those large-formation plays was to add to the employment chances of out-of-work professional actors, who could address tens of thousands of onlookers at a time.[215]

Das Frankenburger Würfelspiel took place during the summer of 1936 on the Eckart stage in Berlin, as the last of the officially arranged Thingspiele, and as the one thought to have succeeded most.[216] Möller's subject was a medieval trial of traitorous peasants in southern Germany, who are eventually allowed to gamble for their lives by tossing dice. At the end a black knight appears who declares not the peasants but their feudal lords to be guilty – with all the Volksgenossen in the audience reading Hitler into that figure.[217]

By summer 1936, when a foreign audience visiting the Olympic Games could hardly make sense of such a play, Goebbels had already pronounced the Thingspiel movement redundant and called it off. He did this in

September 1935, after the Röhm Purge of summer 1934, which Hitler had used to declare any further revolution from below terminated. Insofar as Thingspiel had stood for revolution, its champions had seen its days. In fact, Thingspiele usually criticized Weimar republican disorders, and that republic and any reason to complain about it were history.[218] But there had been other, incidental, criticisms, all from within the Party. One had been a form-and-content issue, in that the plots themselves had not been originally conceived but adapted from pre-existing radio plays. Nobody seemed to know how to write the right kind of drama for this new, ideological, genre. For the few that were chosen, either the background music blared too loudly, drowning out the choric verses, or the giant loudspeakers were otherwise ill adjusted.[219] Under the open skies, the weather gods had not always smiled, and as a result Germans had been losing interest in the "static and declamatory" plots, unless they had been forced in mass formations to appear. Also, the Thingspiel sites were tardily constructed. If by early 1934 400 sites had been on the planning boards, two years later there were merely 14 extant.[220] In all, the Thingspiel phenomenon had to be considered a failure, and nothing was ever said about it after its demise.

In competition with Nazi-specific plays, how did traditional theater fare? In June 1935, Goebbels stated publicly that it would sometimes be better "to dedicate oneself to the tried and true rather than the new things that are bad, just because something new is new."[221] In theater, Goebbels still needed the classics in order to catch permanently the imagination of an important segment of the population, the educated Bildungsbürgertum. Through the classics he could do best what the star actor Bernhard Minetti later denied had happened, "to legitimize and transfigure the dictatorship using art, in lending a cultural face to the political anti-culture."[222] Goebbels may have enjoyed more popular playwrights like Ludwig Thoma, whose comedy *Moral* he took in at the Berlin Volksbühne late in 1936, but he certainly knew of the necessity to retain the German classic playwrights, chief among them Schiller and Goethe and occasionally even the Naturalists Hauptmann and Max Halbe and certainly, always, William Shakespeare, who was so uncannily convincing in his overall work that even in the nineteenth century the German elite had claimed him as "Germanic."[223] Not least it was necessary, especially at the beginning of the Nazi tyranny, to keep important foreign governments impressed, particularly London and Paris.

To be sure, the Promi wanted classical pieces to be performed, but infused with a new spirit and in a novel style. However this was to be accomplished was not exactly clear, but Naturalist or Expressionist forms à la Weimar were to be avoided and on the stage the leadership principle of the regime had to be manifest. That could be done, by dramaturgs and directors, through a convincing emulation of the Führer (hence "working towards the Führer" was a motto they would follow). In addition, a revamping of the star system would emphasize the actors' corps as a smaller edition of the Volksgemeinschaft.[224]

The works of classical authors, therefore, continued to be performed, at a rate only slightly below that of the republic – twenty out of every hundred plays in the Reich. Schiller remained at the top of the playlists, followed by Shakespeare and then Goethe, whose cosmopolitanism tended to clash with the chauvinism of leading Nazis.[225] Theaters in Berlin, Dresden, Weimar, and Koblenz demonstrated the lasting significance of pre-Nazi playwrights by honoring the classics.[226] If the works of New German Nazi writers were few and far between here, it was a testimony to the proven qualities of the old school, no less than the deficiencies of the ideology-saturated zealots.

MUSIC

The Nazis hated jazz. Rosenberg called it "Nigger step" and Goebbels kept insisting on "melody as the wellspring of all music."[227] In order to remove jazz from the German cultural establishment, they decided to make it obsolete. This was even though they were aware that as an elitist form of music, jazz appealed to a small, upwardly mobile set as well as some upper-class segments of the population in their teens and twenties (from whom, as they knew, future leaders could be recruited). Often embedded in ordinary dance music, jazz was prohibited on the air waves in October 1935, but banning jazz in the public sphere outright was a more difficult proposition, although jazz musicians were already being harassed in the rarefied club atmosphere of *haut* Berlin. Hence, after the demise of the Golden Seven studio combo, the Nazis attempted to enjoin German big bands, society orchestras really, led by the likes of Barnabas von Géczy and Oskar Joost, to liberate their music from jazz-specific traits such as bent blue notes and strongly syncopated rhythms and goad them back to simpler, old-fashioned melodic, harmonic, and rhythmic structures. Beyond that, a nationwide radio-station contest was organized to find the ideal German-jazz band for the Reich by March 1936. At that time, Radio Hamburg's choice and putative winner, the seasoned orchestra led by Fritz Weber, was still regarded as too hot by the Promi administrators. Therefore Radio Frankfurt's candidate was declared the winner, musicians led by the obscure bandleader Willi Burkart. While the well-known Weber kept playing to full houses throughout Germany, no jazz aficionado listened to Burkart and his dowdy men, and the Promi had to admit defeat.[228] A second attempt well into 1937, to have Joost's tone-downed orchestra appointed as the official role model, failed because of the Nazi-obedient bandleader's complacency and administrative bungling in Goebbels's ministry.[229]

Finally, Wilhelm Hartseil, an SA fanatic and functionary of the Leipzig station came up with a scheme to obliterate jazz through social dancing, by publicly performing various newly composed German dance pieces with suitable orchestras and the aid of professional dance instructors. At the same time, the American-imported Lindy Hop or swing dance was to be replaced by New Germanic creations. This series ran from January 1938 to the fall of that year, but it transpired mostly in Saxony. As various groups were invited to play at Radio Leipzig, listeners were encouraged to weigh in with their opinions, commenting on what was, even by the modest standards of the day, excessively banal music. For Hartseil, affirmative letters were those which substantiated that Jewish and "Nigger" jazz was awful and that instead, one now had recourse to true German alternatives, newly created songs and dance patterns such as the "Railway Dance." Hartseil presented the responses, as they suited his purpose, to the authorities and immediately found himself rebuffed.[230] Thereafter, storm trooper and Hitler Youth musicians tried, in the last months before the war, to revive the entire effort, but with no results.[231] To all intents and purposes, the Nazis had failed to find a German substitute for jazz, which henceforth went underground and, by hook or by crook, survived the national defeat of 1945.

Of the Golden Seven combo, Willi Stech, its first pianist, had been the one recognizable National Socialist. Did his regime affiliation change the nature of the jazz he played? By all accounts, he swung like the rest of the studio musicians. This observation offers itself as a corollary to earlier findings that in the Third Reich the relationship between the political conviction of a creator and his creation was neutral: Nazis did not of necessity perform Nazi music. In fact, so far, as was seen earlier, "Nazi music" has been next to impossible to define. Nonetheless, what other influences could a Nazi performer have had on the art he produced? Is it conceivable that, because he was a Nazi, he was preferred as a musician over others who were not Nazis but would have performed much better? Then again, were there Nazis in the musical-performance world who were optimally qualified and would have functioned at the peak of their resources, whatever the political system?

There is evidence for more than one scenario in the Third Reich; in dealing with musician biographies, sharp profiles are difficult to delineate. Our random group of musicians who would have been successful professionally under any regime includes Günther Ramin, Li Stadelmann, Tiana Lemnitz, Maria Ivogün, Michael Raucheisen, and Elisabeth Schwarzkopf. Insofar as they had already made a career for themselves in the republic, they did not need National Socialism to advance themselves after 1933. This holds true for the church organist Günther Ramin, born in 1898, who was established at the famous Leipzig Thomaskirche already at twenty, and a professor at twenty-three. Perhaps because he thought he needed to ingratiate himself with Hitler's politicians in the Third Reich, less out of conviction as a member of the Confessing Church than crass ambition, Ramin collaborated early with Rosenberg's NSKG and performed at Göring's wedding to actress Emmy Sonnemann in April 1935 as well as at the 1936 Reich Party rally. On a tour of the United States in 1933, he made light of Jewish émigrés' laments.[232]

The harpsichordist Li Stadelmann, two years younger, was an accomplished chamber musician already in the late republic whose one obsession was rivalry by gifted Jews; however, she was confident that "our German masters will find German interpreters." In her case, genuine Nazi beliefs may be taken for granted, as she moved in the vanguard of a Bach revival cult, one of the characteristics of the Nazi music scene.[233] She mirrored the career of soprano Tiana Lemnitz, born in 1897, who after stints in Aachen, Hanover, and Dresden joined the Berlin Staatsoper in 1934, and was renowned for her brilliant signature role as Eva in Wagner's *Die Meistersinger*. Hitler heard her many times and was enthused, appointing her, the Party comrade, Kammersängerin in 1937.[234] Her colleague Maria Ivogün, discovered by Bruno Walter in her early twenties just before World War I, was a favorite of Richard Strauss's and a sensation as Zerbinetta in his opera *Ariadne auf Naxos* at Covent Garden in 1924. Hitler too had praised her highly already before the turn of the republic, when she had just changed from opera to lieder singing, accompanied by her husband Michael Raucheisen, an inveterate Nazi. The multi-talented Raucheisen (piano, flute, and violin) had toured internationally with the half-Jewish violinist Fritz Kreisler in the 1920s – in 1945, only the English piano accompanist Gerald Moore would equal him. After 1933, the couple were choice party guests of Hitler and especially Goebbels.[235] Ivogün's star pupil was Elisabeth Schwarzkopf, Dame of the British Empire at her death in Austria in 2006. Born in 1915, she was instantly meteoric. At age twenty, already at the Berlin Opernhaus, she became a Nazi student leader, beginning a steep operatic career that eventually would take her to a lead position in Dresden under Karl Böhm and provide her entry to the highest Nazi ranks. She became the mistress of SS general Dr. Hugo Jury, the culture-loving Gauleiter of Lower Danube toward the end of the war, having reached the threshold of an even greater career of international stardom.[236] Today, everyone would concede that Schwarzkopf would have achieved that pinnacle of success even if the Nazis had not been in power. Nazis or not: The music of any one of those artists would have contained true substance.

By contrast, there were musicians whose art suffered because of some preoccupation with Nazi ideology or politics. Violinist Gustav Havemann, for one, would have done better had he concentrated entirely on his musical career, as he had done as a professor and principal of a renowned string quartet in the Weimar Republic. But in 1932 he bet on the Nazi horse and then became a functionary of the KfdK, leading its symphony orchestra of unemployed musicians. Having entered Goebbels's RMK in important positions, he habitually neglected his violin-playing, opting instead for mediocre if lucrative conducting. An inveterate womanizer, friend of the bottle, and caught up in the Hindemith affair of 1935, on the side of the composer – in itself a token of integrity – the fifty-three-year-old musician lost his official functions and then resumed his career as a violinist, a shadow of his former self.[237] Robert Heger, too, four years younger, betrayed his musicianship, not as a conductor, his main métier, where he was passable, but as the composer he strived to be (five operas), with his work *Der Verlorene Sohn* (*The Lost Son*), premiered in Dresden in 1936. All of his operas, writes Erik Levi, followed the late-Romantic tradition, "without achieving any distinctive originality." What compromised him as a musician, however, after Kapellmeister experience in Vienna and Berlin, was that with *Der Verlorene Sohn* he wanted to establish an edifice to refugees from formerly German territories – in his own time Strasbourg, from which his family was displaced by the French, and for many contemporary Nazis West Prussia, now in Poland.[238]

Rosalind von Schirach was touted as the "ideal image of a Nordic-Aryan singer" early in the Third Reich. The thirty-seven-year-old may be forgiven for having changed from the Berlin Opernhaus to the more demanding Staatsoper in Berlin in 1935, because she was the daughter of a theater Intendant and sister of Reich Youth Leader Baldur von Schirach. However, among musicians she was better known as a Nazi activist than a singer, having spent much of her time organizing a powerful Nazi employees' cell at the Opernhaus since her debut there in 1930. She was assisted in this by her lover Gerhard Hüsch, who as an excellent baritone preceded her from the Opernhaus to the Staatsoper in 1934 and thereafter was much in evidence as an interpreter of Nazi songs, such as "The Swastika" and "Germany Awake!"[239]

An artist who was the epitome of compromised musicianship in the Third Reich was the pianist Elly Ney. A child prodigy born in 1882, she had won the Mendelssohn prize in 1901 and had a full career until 1930, being featured on many concert tours in the United States. Like Stadelmann, she developed a phobia against Jewish colleagues, stemming from early experiences with her teacher, Isidor Seiss, whom, by his smell, she called "racially alien." When in early 1933 she was asked to concertize in Hamburg in place of the young pianist Rudolf Serkin, who as a Jew had already been banned, she regarded this as an insult. A member of several Nazi organizations, her specialty was performing for the Hitler Youth, not without long-winded ideological introductions, and then playing chiefly Beethoven. With her typically "massive display of temperament," her mop of Beethoven-like hair, she was already past her prime and supported to the high extent that she was primarily because of Nazi loyalties.[240]

Whether Nazi-beholden or not, musicians in the Third Reich re-created only the music written for them to play, and it had no political color. When one turns to composers, one finds that among the younger ones, say those born around the turn of the twentieth century, those with any degree of prominence after 1933 tended to be both adventurous in their music-writing beyond the limits of the tried and true, *and* personally eager to adjust themselves to the new regime. A first group comprised composers whose music was, if innovative, not significant enough to be lastingly remembered after 1945. A second group was more successful in that respect, yet only three names are worth mentioning in these pages, as they are also almost forgotten, with one important exception, Carl Orff who, by virtue of a single composition, lives on in the world of opera and concert halls today.

To the first group belonged Hugo Distler, who joined the NSDAP in May 1933 as a twenty-five-year-old and became a lecturer at the Musikhochschule Stuttgart in 1937. Like Hindemith in the late 1920s, he was fascinated by neo-Baroque approaches to composition; he experimented with pentatonic and whole-tone scales. This pushed him to some limits of conventional harmony, although he condemned the atonality of the Second Viennese School (led by Schoenberg) as "going against nature." Distler was hoping for a renewal of Protestant church music and, ironically, like other composers in this group, allied himself with National Socialism to achieve this. He spoke of "the greatness of the political events after 1933," enthusiastically instructed scores of malleable Hitler Youths and guest-conducted for Robert Ley's Nazi Shop Organization (NSBO) in the German Labor Front – the very same outfit von Schirach and her lover Hüsch had been hustling for. Distler composed celebratory cantatas in memory of Hitler's assumption of power and contributed to many Hitler Youth songbooks.[241]

Distler's older colleague Johann Nepomuk David openly acknowledged the influence of the Second Viennese School, as well as Ravel and Stravinsky. Also a teacher of the Hitler Youth, he wrote a piece based on an aphorism of Hitler's meant to evoke "fealty" to the Volk, which he himself premiered on the campus of his conservatory.[242] Ernst Pepping was born in 1901. Impressed, like others, by the austere structure of an older music genre, he too sought new musical forms somewhere between post-Romantic tonality and Modernism. "Art as much as the new politics of the day is inspired by the same will," proclaimed Pepping, "with the purpose of forming a new community."[243]

In this cohort, Wolfgang Fortner is probably best remembered, if only as the teacher of the illustrious avant-garde composer Hans Werner Henze. Born in 1907, Fortner was a wunderkind and early on impressed by Bach, yet his musical curiosity eventually led him to the study of Stravinsky and the dodecaphonist Anton Webern. Teaching youths in Heidelberg, he came to direct the Hitler Youth orchestra there on a regular basis, while getting involved with Schoenberg's twelve-tone row, the pursuit of which he undertook more seriously only after the national catastrophe in 1945.[244]

Worthy of mention in the better-remembered second group are Rudolf Wagner-Régeny, Werner Egk, and Carl Orff. Rather more traditional in his music-writing, the thirty-three-year-old Wagner-Régeny had his first opera *Der Günstling* (*The Favorite*) performed in 1935 after strong patronage from Rosenberg's NSKG. Wagner-Régeny accepted a subsequent Nazi offer to write a replacement score for Mendelssohn's "Jewish" incidental music to *A Midsummer Night's Dream* by Shakespeare. In 1941 the composer would move from Berlin to Vienna and there become a protégé of (by then) Gauleiter von Schirach. Wagner-Régeny made his mark as a Modernist of sorts – less with his own music than the adoption of librettos and scenic stage works from Caspar Neher's (that friend of Brecht and Weill). His attempts to curry favor with the Nazis culminated in his opera *Das Opfer* (*The Sacrifice*) in 1941, after a text by Eberhard Wolfgang Möller, in which an "Aryan" woman, Agnetha, chooses death over "race defilement," hence avoiding her fate as the mother of a racially impure "bastard."[245]

Much better known than Wagner-Régeny in his own time was Werner Egk, who could not deny pre-1933 influences by Schoenberg, the avantgarde conductor Hermann Scherchen and, especially, Stravinsky. For that reason, he had a tenuous relationship with Nazi culture wardens during the first years of the Reich while in Munich. In 1935 he premiered his opera *Die Zaubergeige* (*The Magic Violin*), which was pointedly anti-intellectual, favoring the country over the city; his character Guldensack could easily be recognized as a repulsive Jew. Egk handily won plaudits and a dubious cash prize for an orchestral ballet performed at the 1936 Olympics, and at the 1939 Reich Music Festival in Düsseldorf he collected another major prize for his new opera *Peer Gynt*, which ultimately pleased Hitler. Egk's greatest concession to the regime, whether he was ever a believing Nazi or not, was his tenure as section leader for composers at the RMK, after July 1941. It was then that he officially denounced "the time of atonality," although he himself, while never in the dodecaphonic groove, had always honed an angular musical style, which fellow composers sometimes ridiculed as labored, stretching traditional diatonic limits.[246]

Carl Orff, like Hindemith born in 1895, was Egk's teacher for a while; he too had been impressed with Scherchen and Stravinsky and had briefly communed with Brecht. Stravinsky committed to Orff his pronounced sense of rhythm, which then characterized Orff's first substantial composition, *Carmina Burana* of 1937. This would remain Orff's masterpiece and, perhaps not coincidentally, put him on track as the only Third Reich composer "whose music has survived in the international repertory," in the judgment of Berkeley musicologist Richard Taruskin. In 1997, at an international panel at the Guggenheim Museum, in which I participated, Taruskin declared that he had "no problem with calling *Carmina Burana* Nazi music."[247] This statement alluded once more to the complexity of the essence of Nazism in music, broached earlier in these pages. Strictly speaking, Orff's "Modernism," in his signature work as well as some others to follow, was not comprised of elements the Nazis clearly abhorred, such as dodecaphony and jazz (bent notes), but of features that resonated with their mode of indulging sights and sounds, as well as manufacturing and conveying propaganda: a sensuality, in-your-face physicality, ostinato rhythms, melodic economy, rudimentary diatonicism, repetition, and monophony, scored to serve as a fount of new folk music (Volksmusik) and simplistic music in the home (Hausmusik) – all generically akin to a peculiarly Nazi aesthetic found, in whole or in parts, elsewhere in Nazi music from 1933 to 1945, and even in the other arts such as literature and painting. Consequently, Orff, if somewhat late in coming, enjoyed enthusiastic Nazi acclamation for his work, reaping substantial benefits such as a cash prize for his own substitution of *A Midsummer Night's Dream* music (1939), as well as a posh sinecure from Viennese Gauleiter Schirach from 1942 to the end of the regime.[248]

Virtually all the composers mentioned so far, and assuredly all musicians, at one time or another acted in official Nazi functions, wrote or played pieces for Nazi formations and celebratory occasions. Would this have rendered them Nazis and their music colored by Nazism? The former, as in the case of Egk, is sometimes in doubt but cannot be excluded: still, there is a fine line between political opportunism and faith. The latter possibility is more certain, particularly in cases where pieces were crafted for specific Nazi purposes. Unambiguous exemplars would be Wagner-Régeny and Orff's Mendelssohn substitutions.

Many times after 1933 respected musicians were placing their art in the service of the rulers. Infamously, for instance, the Berlin Philharmonic

Orchestra was on call for the annual Reich Party rallies as well as for Hitler's birthday celebrations (after 1936), under star conductors ranging from Karl Böhm to Hans Knappertsbusch and Wilhelm Furtwängler.[249] At the inauguration of the Reichskulturkammer in November 1933, Furtwängler officiated along with the baritone Heinrich Schlusnus.[250] Even on lesser occasions, such as when the "Strength-through-Joy" leader Robert Ley was scheduled to speak, as he did in November 1936, a philharmonic orchestra along with Wagnerian baritone Rudolf Bockelmann was on hand to musically enhance the event, in this case with a rendition of Hugo Wolf's song "Beherzigung," after lyrics by Goethe.[251]

There were of course musical devices that served the Nazi state exclusively. The most prominent was the Nazi Symphony Orchestra, founded in 1932, whose members performed in SA mustard-colored tuxedos. It was exceptionally busy, not only, as originally chartered, in the provinces; from 1933 to 1939 it gave a performance virtually every other day. It played for Reich Party rallies and, routinely, many other National Socialist festivities.[252] Composers such as Cesar Bresgen, at a Hitler Youth conservatory in Salzburg, and Bruno Stürmer, in an equivalent function in Kassel, almost exclusively wrote and performed music for Nazi events, while Georg Blumensaat's specialty was composing for Thingspiel stagings, such as they were.[253]

With the aim of creating new Nazi-specific music, competitions were encouraged for ambitious young talents. Part of this effort was to force the transmutation of heavily political songs into folk culture, making them common knowledge so that Volksgenossen would whistle them in the streets. The "Horst Wessel Song," best known by its opening words "Die Fahne hoch" ("The Flag on High"), which had actually been created by Wessel before his death, was to be treated in this way (through forced renditions and never-ending repetition), as was the ditty "A Hitler Man is a-Marching."[254] Evidently, the creation of new, naturally to be intoned, Nazi folk songs for the Volksgemeinschaft was so important that Hitler himself, in rare instances of personal micro-management, decided to define the tempo at which a "Horst Wessel Song" was to be sung, as well as to attract new composers by offering a prize.[255] There were indeed new folk songs issued; one was "High Night of Clear Stars Above" (1936), produced by the Hitler Youth bard Hans Baumann and designed to supplant the Christian evergreen "Stille Nacht" ("Silent Night").[256] With some success, so it seems: the hymn was popular in many German circles long after World War II.[257]

Older, more traditionalist composers also put their skill to regime use, particularly if after the political watershed of 1933 they thought their time had come. Such happened with the neo-Romantic Paul Graener, born in 1872, who functioned at the first 1938 Düsseldorf Reich Music Festival, both as composer and keynote speaker.[258] After years of what he thought had been neglect, his work was praised as "being nurtured by the purest forces of Germandom" in the Third Reich. Earlier, however, this self-taught musician had had to follow a stony path in Germany and also in England as conductor in a London Haymarket varieté.[259] Back in the fatherland, his two major operas, *Don Juans letztes Abenteuer* (1914) and *Hanneles Himmelfahrt* (1927), received only scant attention during the Weimar Republic, Graener having failed to create for himself, by the standards of Erik Levi, "an individual identity" in the manner of his contemporaries Strauss, Pfitzner, or Max Reger. After having helped establish the KfdK in Berlin during 1932, Graener became Egk's predecessor as composers' section leader in the RMK and a vice-president of that body. With the office came the perks: this staunch enemy of any kind of Modernism had his works performed much more frequently in the Third Reich, now right after Strauss and Pfitzner, at least on radio.[260]

Rather more a composer of orchestral works and chamber music was Max Trapp, who was in his late thirties when by the middle of the 1920s he had completed seven symphonies and a violin concerto. These were influenced by Brahms and early Strauss, hence squarely in the late-Romantic tradition. In 1922, at a time when Schoenberg was announcing a revolution in music by introducing the twelve-tone system, Trapp insisted that for his part he strove for melody – hosanna in the ears of Goebbels, who later proclaimed that melody was the essence of all music.[261] To gain more recognition for his work Trapp too joined the Berlin KfdK in 1932 and in 1934 became a member of the reconstituted Prussian Academy of Arts. Wilhelm Furtwängler, an opportunistic servant of all regimes, for the sake of money and seducible women, premiered Trapp's concerto for orchestra (opus 32) in 1935, and three years later Trapp contributed a cello concerto to the Düsseldorf music festival. By the end of the Third Reich he had reaped many Nazi honors and his works were more frequently performed than one might have expected, in a free society, from a composer of mediocre rank.[262]

The two most firmly established composers in the Third Reich were Richard Strauss and Hans Pfitzner. Yet they too served the regime, albeit Strauss much more than Pfitzner. Strauss, "the Reich's highest-ranking musician" even after his fall from official grace in 1935, as the Berlin musicologist Albrecht Riethmüller reminds us, played an individually designed "Olympic Hymn" to Hitler privately before its premiere at the 1936 Olympic Games. He conducted his very own *Festliches Präludium* (*Festive Prelude*) at the Düsseldorf music festival in 1938, as he had done during the November 1933 opening of the Reich Music Chamber.[263] He was needed for Nazi cultural representation, such as when his opera *Elektra* was conducted alongside the overture to *Le furie d'Arlecchino* by the Italian Fascist Adriano Lualdi at a festival in Dresden in May 1937.[264] (Arguably, Lualdi was the most orthodox, unforgiving, Fascist of all Italian musicians.)[265] Pfitzner's most egregious gift to the Third Reich was during the war, when he composed and performed a tailor-made homily for Hans Frank, the ruthlessly anti-Semitic governor-general of Occupied Poland.[266] Both Strauss and Pfitzner had their reasons. Strauss needed to cozy up to the regime because his daughter-in-law was Jewish and he wanted to continue his accustomed commercial success. The maladroit Pfitzner, in Jens Malte Fischer's opinion "a born anti-Semite," believed the Nazis owed him something and, vainglorious as he was, singled out for special attention only those leaders who had expressed their love of him.[267]

On opera and concert stages, Strauss and Pfitzner continued to dominate the music scene in the Third Reich. Astonishingly creative, Strauss wrote five operas during this period, in addition to orchestral works and conducting, but in certain respects he was already past his prime. Pfitzner, always less prolific, composed some instrumental pieces but no operas, and stuck mainly to guest-conducting.[268] Apart from the contemporary activities of these iconic figures, the ubiquity of their earlier compositions for the concert platform and opera stage underlined the importance of works in Germany written in a traditionalist style before 1933, and often before 1900. It meant that anything new or "National Socialist" that other composers were trying to write after the Hitler-engineered regime change, composers who were younger than Strauss and Pfitzner, on balance did not catch on.

Beyond the aesthetics, the continued and even increased flow of conventional musical works signaled improved employment opportunities for artistic and administrative staff at German performance venues in the cities as much as the provinces – just as drama had done for the theater.[269] By virtue of performances arranged by Robert Ley's "Strength-through-Joy" program (in the DAF) alone, the number of concerts increased more than fivefold in the Reich from 1934 to 1938, and the number of staged operas almost thirteenfold. Thousands of unemployed workers in the music industry were now off the dole.[270]

The overall offerings of Berlin's Philharmonic Orchestra and all three opera houses did not deviate significantly from the Weimar republican repertoire, "especially in their adherence to a core of standard favorites dominated by nineteenth-century German symphonies and Italian operas," observes musicologist Pamela Potter.[271] Notable in this context is the music of Bach, Beethoven, and Bruckner. It was their work that had the best potential for guaranteeing that German music "is so very different from all music in the world." This claim by pro-Nazi poet Rudolf Binding early in the Third Reich could best be honored by Bach because as the most supreme composer the world had ever witnessed he, as a German, implicitly had to be identified with the Führer. Bach stood in the line of ancestor worship as it was then being institutionalized by the regime. His main instrument had been the organ, which was being hailed as the king of instruments by National Socialists (and played royally well by Ramin for the Führer and for Göring, who himself acquired a house organ). Moreover, Bach's compositions in melodic linearity and counterpoint were transparent as no other, perceived as the very opposite of "atonality." Beethoven ranked second in this canon of officially sanctioned classics, mostly for the heroic element. To the exclusion of the special-status Wagner, Bruckner came third in the regime leaders' collective taste, even though other traditional composers were performed more often, not for any musical reasons but, again, by the logic of ancestor worship, because Hitler adored the work of an ancestor from Linz. Even though such reverence was rooted in territorial kinsmanship rather than musical comprehension, Hitler mouthed that Bruckner was the greatest organist of all time.[272]

In opera, the Nazis' preference was for Wagner, Verdi, Puccini, Mozart, Albert Lortzing, and Strauss, but not necessarily in that order, and not necessarily everywhere.[273] As with theater and orchestral music, during the entire Third Reich there was hardly a change in the operatic repertoire from the entire Weimar period. A top-notch stage, serving the elevated classes, would play more genuine opera, while the provinces succumbed to operetta-like dross. To illustrate – not a hard statistic – Göring's Berlin Staatstheater in the week of March 12 to 19, 1939, offered works by Strauss on three occasions, Wagner twice, and Lortzing and Puccini once. In the nether region of Koblenz, on the other hand, the total of annual repertory for 1937–8 consisted of Mozart, Gluck, Puccini, Tchaikovsky, Donizetti, and Pergolesi/Stravinsky, along with an equal number of rather more lightly weighing tunesmiths.[274] Every so often, Lehár's *Merry Widow*, Hitler's personal favorite, would perforate the programs. Again one could argue that this was but another case of "working towards the Führer" in cultural society; as such, the mandate was transmitted by osmosis.

Wagner was played during the Third Reich, but not, of course, because his music was *ipso facto* "fascist," as Theodor W. Adorno maintained in 1945. In truth, it was not fascist, and, as Alex Ross has warned, it cannot be assigned the role of a "Muzak of genocide."[275] Rather, Hitler's idiosyncratic taste in Wagner was responsible for the continued presence of a solid Wagnerian repertoire and secure existence of the Bayreuth Festival in uncertain times; that taste had developed before fascism. At the top of the operatic programs, Wagner was actually surpassed by Verdi until 1939, and Bayreuth almost went under in the face of financial troubles but for Hitler's extreme generosity. Although performances of Wagner operas were perfunctory at Party and State events, in the Nazi hierarchy leaders like Rosenberg intensely disliked them, Goebbels barely tolerated them (despite the blushing praise in his diaries), Göring was indifferent, and stooges of all ranks often snored through them, to Hitler's abject embarrassment.[276]

The Bayreuth Festival of 1933 occurred in July after trepidation by the managers working for Winifred Wagner that it might not be held for a lack of financing; the deflation years of the Brüning administration had virtually bankrupted the venture. After Hitler and other Party and State organizations finally granted large subsidies, the festival attracted fewer people because the usual patrons, now enemies of the state, had stayed away: Jews, homosexuals, liberals, and left-wingers, as well as throngs of Austrians (because of a border embargo dispute). The event finished with a loss, Hitler

– a "moderate innovator," in Hans R. Vaget's phrase – having lent his support to the progressive circle around Wagner, Intendant Heinz Tietjen and stage designer Emil Preetorius, who were trying new ideas. Like Riefenstahl, rather than entering Goebbels's RKK jurisdiction, Bayreuth would remain directly under Hitler's control; Party formations bought most of the tickets. Hitler therefore saw good reason to continue utilizing the festivities (and the Wagner family) for his own political purposes, such as impressing high-level visitors from England, Japan, and Italy. In July 1937 special trains carried 2,600 Sudeten Germans from the Czechoslovak Republic to Bayreuth. Propaganda and military uses of the festival's "Green Hill" were to be accentuated after September 1939.[277]

THE VISUAL ARTS AND ARCHITECTURE

Portraits of kings, queens, and presidents hang on the walls of public halls in democracies, including those by name only, to solidify loyalties by the public to the state. In a true dictatorship, there is no governing without a leadership cult, enhancing the status of the solitary ruler. In Nazi Germany, productions by visual artists – among all other cultural contrivances – appear to have served totalitarian governance best. This conclusion follows an examination of other independently employed agents of culture in the Nazi era. Writers, for instance, could glorify the Führer in Time-of-Struggle plots, but it was uncertain how many Germans then would read those books. In music, some 20,000 compositions with political applications were generated, most of them written by crass dilettantes and never recognized. In 1935 Hitler, always on the verge of some withdrawal for charismatic effect, forbade personal dedications to the Führer. There is no known Führer Cantata that became a standard work.[278] In art, however, the best portraits of politicians, chiefly Hitler's own, could be officially displayed or reproduced in print, and one could escape being impressed by those as little as raising one's right arm for the fascist salute, in the public sphere.

There are painted portraits of Göring, Goebbels, Rosenberg, and Hess, among the many of Hitler himself. Two most imposing pictures of him are by Fritz Erler and Heinrich Knirr; they show the Führer in Party uniform, standing upright, with imperious gaze and resolute mien. Erler painted him in the classic SA uniform with cap in hand, before the mighty monument of a naked sword-bearer with a falcon in his open palm. Knirr's Hitler wears a topcoat against the background of a verdant forest the current neo-Romanticists were wont to invoke; Hitler is adorned by a swastika armband and his World War I Iron Cross, and he looks more statesmanlike and less threatening. This portrait was mounted at the "Great German Art" exhibition of July 1937, one of twelve there of the Führer.[279] Another picture at that venue which Hitler had insisted be shown became a veritable cornerstone of Hitler iconography, a painting entitled *In the Beginning was the Word* by Hermann Otto Hoyer. Here Hitler can be seen haranguing a small crowd seated in a dank room in Oberstdorf, Upper Bavaria, where the rookie politician, historically correct, proselytizes for the nascent NSDAP in the very early 1920s. In front of a swastika flag and flanked by an archetypal storm trooper, Hitler, dressed in a simple suit and tie, gesticulates effectively, with onlookers captive – among them, the closest, a woman. Hoyer, whose likeness of himself Hitler later purchased, was barely trained at the Dresden Academy of Arts, wounded in World War I, and an early Old Fighter. He eventually had himself appointed professor by the Führer, dutifully joining the Waffen-SS during the war.[280]

Other pictures of Hitler featured only his head or bust, as did, of course, sculptures.[281] One charcoal drawing of Hitler's head effectively illustrated a Nazi tome full of twisted German history: the great Hohenzollerns, Scharnhorst, Bismarck, Alfred Krupp, Count Zeppelin, and the aviator Baron von Richthofen (the "Red Baron"), with the last section reserved for "The Men of the Third Reich."[282] In yet another full-scale portrait entitled *The Flag Bearer*, also on display in Munich 1937, Hubert Lanzinger placed the Führer on a horse, clad in chain mail and holding a huge swastika flag. The portrait demonstrates to this day, at one and the same time, the ludicrous nature of original Nazi German art beyond common definitions of kitsch, and the depth of evil that lurked behind it.[283] Perhaps the most interesting images from a social-historical vantage point are those depicting Hitler in an interaction with the German people (as did Hoyer's): Hitler among soldiers; Hitler in mustard-brown Party uniform, framed on the wall while Germans are listening to his speech on the people's receiver; Hitler opposite President Paul von Hindenburg on the Day of Potsdam in March 1933.[284]

It may be doubted whether Hitler ever sat for any of these likenesses, as he would have been much too busy. The works were mostly done from photographs or the artist's imagination, and this lack of artistic finesse was often reflected in their overall quality. Such cannot be said of Arno Breker's bust of Hitler's favorite architect Albert Speer, Breker's personal friend; Speer actually sat for the sculptor. Speer was notorious for radiating less charisma than the Führer, and the bronzen head painstakingly reflects this.[285] Portraits of Göring show the man in his full ridiculousness as Reich Hunt Master and "Generalfeldmarschall" (both by Conrad Hommel), done up theatrically in self-designed fantasy attire and hardly to be taken seriously. By contrast, the official Göring biographer Erich Gritzbach produced photographs of the man as an early storm trooper and even a white-coated field marshal, which are quite credible.[286] Unremarkable portraits were also done of Goebbels, Hess, Rosenberg, and Ley. In Goebbels's case, the demon of his essence was difficult to capture on canvas, in marble or in bronze, although Leo von König's Modernist-influenced portrait of 1935 came close.[287]

Altogether, as in the case of pictures showing Hitler with his people, those displaying National Socialist dynamics in action, if comparatively rare, are more interesting than mere personal portrayals. As a creator of portraitures of small Nazi scenarios Elk Eber stood out. This World War I veteran and participant in the 1923 Hitler Putsch began his Nazi artistic career in the early 1920s as a draftsman for the *Völkischer Beobachter* and creator of political posters in the Time of Struggle until 1933. Until the July 1937 Munich signature exhibition, where his famous painting *The Last Hand Grenade* was on display, he had established himself as a pictorial chronicler of exceptionally committed Nazis and their activities within the broader Volksgemeinschaft. In 1938, Eber's composition *Thus Was the SA* was exhibited in Munich (Hitler then bought it), showing a march of an SA troop under a swastika banner, a man in the foreground with his head bandaged, and curious onlookers on the side, among them an admiring young boy – in what was most certainly to be a Berlin Communist stronghold in the late republic.[288] Whereas Eber was fond of illustrating conflict and Nazi martyrdom – he died in 1941 aged forty-nine, after having sketched soldiers and Jews at forced labor during the Polish campaign – these artists dedicated themselves to more prosaic Nazi social topics. In 1938, Franz Eichhorst painted a large mural, covering four walls in a hall of a communal building in Berlin-Schöneberg, *The Face of a Young German*. This was of a young boy beating a drum, in the middle of a group of Hitler Youths, SA and SS men, underneath two huge swastika flags – on the left a member of the upper classes (in a suit and hat in hand) is shaking hands with a manual laborer.[289] Similarly, in a toned-down variation of Eber's genre Georg Sluyterman von Langeweyde, whose preference was for woodcuts, created images of Hitler Youths beating drums and SA men at roll call, as well as a soldier with a hand grenade.[290] Demonstrating national unity as allegedly forced by Nazi leaders and increasing military prowess was a favorite task those painters set themselves. On the part of the artists these works were supposed to demonstrate "a high-minded spirit and a close sense of participation in the fights, goals, and fruits of the German rebirth," wrote the critic Hans Wühr in 1938.[291]

Hitler's Eber acquisition reflected the Führer's taste in German contemporary artists. He also obtained, either for his private or official residences, or for his soon-to-be-constructed, gargantuan Linz Museum, other works by Eber and his compatriots. The last-mentioned artists were less fixated on current events, extolling instead the neo-Romantic ideal that was in vogue in Germany as part of the restorative tendencies after World War I. To them belonged Adolf Wissel, with his agrarian genre pieces such as a peasant family of grandmother, parents, and three children huddled together in a modest living room.[292] Or Hermann Gradl's *High Mountains* for the dining room of the new Reich chancellery: a brook gushing forth in an Alpine setting under foreboding skies.[293] Both paintings could have been done by the nineteenth-century artists Hans Thoma and Ludwig Richter, respectively. In Hitler's Führer building in Munich there hung Adolf Ziegler's triptych *The Four Elements* (1937), which the French ambassador François-Poncet found totally lacking in taste. In allusion to antiquity, Ziegler had painted four nudes in suggestive poses; it was not for nothing that this president of Goebbels's Reich Art Chamber was popularly called "Reich Master of the German Pubic Hair."[294]

Hitler's personal taste in art was undoubtedly influenced by pre-*fin de siècle* currents in Vienna, figures like the academy painter Hans Makart, as his own modest attempts at sketching and painting indicate at the turn of the century, attempts that passed by new Modernist signposts in works through the 1930s. Hitler's watercolor of an old Vienna courtyard of 1911–12, or, on the war path, the French Haubourdin seminar church four years later, is devoid of Impressionist traces, to say nothing of Expressionism – it had just begun. His sketchbook and postcard œuvre shows rudimentary choices in color and a less than perfect sense of perspective. A later drawing of an early storm trooper with Nazi flag is irregular, with the man's chin undeveloped, and his pre-1938 draft of a Volkswagen prototype resembles a mangled toy.[295] As a rule, he did not paint people – as if they had to remain anonymous for him, as the great unwashed; he exhibited "a telling want of feeling for human figures."[296] Altogether, Hitler's output early on comes across like a caricature of the nineteenth-century German masters he admired, albeit less so of Dürer and his Northern Renaissance counterparts – pioneers for other, more educated Nazi greats such as Göring and Hans Frank. And time and again, he alluded to the ancient Greeks and Romans. Hitler implemented such taste on occasions when he opened national art exhibitions, such as the one in Munich in 1937 (when he had allowed his photographer Heinrich Hoffmann to hand-pick the selections according to his own, prejudiced, criteria), and in bombastic annual speeches.[297]

For an overall aesthetic assessment of the New German art one need not look much further than Hitler's collections. The contemporary painting style favored in the Third Reich has variously been described as neo-Romanticism or pseudo-Naturalism, sometimes as neo-Biedermeier. There was an outlier from the mainstream, not unbeloved of Hitler, which could have been called Nazi Realism (in analogy to Socialist Realism), although the National Socialists never used that term. This was a form of obsessive punctiliousness in extension of the New Objectivity à la Dix and Beckmann in the late 1920s; the herald of this in the 1930s was Werner Peiner, who had been an Expressionist and for whom Göring set up a special painters' academy in the Rhenish village of Kronenburg in 1936 with himself as patron, to rear "officers of art." Peiner's likeness of a medieval hunt graced the air marshal's ministry.[298]

Excelling as he did in photographic exactness, Peiner had no peers; most artists in the Third Reich painted – as they had before 1933 – in the neo-Romantic style of Franz Defregger or Hans Thoma, and a few, such as Wolfgang Willrich, in a neo-Gothic manner imitating Dürer, Hans Baldung, or Hans Holbein.[299] After 1933 the main requirement of painting was again being fulfilled, wrote the *Frankfurter Zeitung*'s Carl Linfert, "namely to form what is visibly before our eyes."[300] This meant that what-ever the technique, pictures under the Nazis became representational and literalistic, in their derivative quality devoid of dynamics and seemingly one-dimensional. In such a mode, painting mirrored Nazi literature, just as that literature often echoed Nazi painting.

This intercourse also held true for content. Programmatic themes in the paintings were to reach the viewer like one-way traffic; there was to be no engagement, no discursive experience. "Any kind of problematic is to be opposed," wrote Bruno E. Werner, "there is no place for experiments."[301] And so the motifs of archetypal Nazi painting, reminiscent of Nazi literature, were landscapes, peasant life, women, and animals – all pre-industrial, of course. An additional category, seldom addressed in literature, was heavy-industrial dynamics symbolizing the state, to the exclusion of human individuals.

Wilhelm Leibl and Franz Defregger in particular, wrote the critic Edgar Schindler in 1935, had pioneered the theme of "Blood and Soil" in the previous century and paid special attention to the peasants and their environs.[302] Peasants working the soil appear on canvas, as in the literature or stage plays, in corporeal simplicity exuding eugenic health (blood), devoid of any industrial instruments for tilling and harvesting, such as farm machinery. Their clothing is archaic and the furniture surrounding them hand-crafted. Frequently wearing traditional costumes such as broad-rimmed hats or dirndls, they toil with their oxen (rarely horses, often goats) under heavy skies. Their meals, taken on communally important occasions and as a racially and socially homogeneous unit, are frugal, as *Peasants' Lunch* by Thomas Baumgartner (1892–1962) demonstrates. They possess huge physical prowess, with which to drive their cattle and clear the woodland, they wield pickaxes and lift the weightiest of boulders.[303] By contrast, in the few Nazi pictures of heavy industry (denoting a post-Industrial Revolution phenomenon), humans are either absent or appear virtually consumed by colossal machines and monumental structures like an autobahn bridge in the making. The inanimate monstrosity signified the Nazi state.[304]

Habitually, peasants live and work in surroundings where industrial city-scapes are far away, hence in the Third Reich (as in the nineteenth century) the genre of landscape painting thrived, romantically in the open air.[305] A related genre, animal portraiture, merged with landscape painting, but was given a new twist by the attention now paid to the eagle as a national emblem, and animals fighting for supremacy, for this symbolized struggle as a prerequisite of survival – one of the planks of Nazi ideology. Excelling in this art was Franz Xaver Stahl (1901–77), who had learned the trade of interior decorator, and whose pictures of cows and other animals Hitler was so fond of that he purchased them.[306]

The Social Darwinian leitmotif was continued in the many depictions of women as bearers of fertility and guarantors of future "Aryan" life. National Socialists habitually showed women as mothers, as female companions to the male and sexually inviting courtesans. Mothers could be older women in the vaunted style of Thoma or Leibl or even Dürer, or young wives breast-feeding babies.[307] Those wives were the subject of the painters Johann Vincenz Cissarz (1893–1942), Wolfgang Willrich (1897–1948), and Karl Diebitsch (1899–1985). They each present a young beatific woman holding a new-born to their right breast; the viewer looks on from the left. The background is neutral except for Diebitsch's, who paints a cultivated field and grass, perhaps grain – redolent of fecundity. What is striking about these images is not that they obviously celebrated fertility for the sake of "Aryan" eugenics, but that two of them appear to be copies, with the original patterning itself on a well-used Madonna motif of the Renaissance. Which of the three was an original is difficult to tell, because during the Third Reich all three painters were contemporaries. If Hitler or Goebbels complained, as they did, about a lack of originality in the new art after 1933, these could have served as prime examples.[308]

Even young mothers, young girls, or maidservants in a rural setting were frequently portrayed next to an open clay vessel, to signify fertility – a well-known metaphor from the past but stretched by painters under Hitler. In Leopold Schmutzler's *Farm Girls Returning from the Fields* even a basket worn on the back of one of the three pretty maidens, who in their brown-yellowish country dresses resemble Hitler Youths, serves such a purpose.[309] The sexual allure was made more obvious through an intensification of nine-teenth-century salon painting – nudes that were stylistically eroticized as in Ziegler's *The Four Elements*. Behind a prurient screen, lasciviousness is exuded by the naked young women in Ernst Liebermann's *By the Water*, and those in Ivo Saliger's *Diana's Rest*.[310] Paul Matthias Padua (1903–81) drove these sexual themes to new pornographic heights in his infamous *Leda und der Schwan* (*Leda and the Swan*). This motif too had been known since antiquity, but Padua's explicit depiction of copulation between a naked woman, her face half covered but in ecstasy, and a large white bird conjured up wanton promiscuity; for the sake of future progeny it appeared as if calculated as an aphrodisiac, to incite the sexual lust of German men.[311] In advertising promiscuous sexuality, Nazi literature did not go that far, although the sexual subordination of the woman, to emphasize a male's right to satisfy his lust, was stressed by a few writers (and would be more so in the war to come).[312]

Moreover, sexual attractiveness issued from female nudes sculptured by Nazi artists, although generally speaking sculpture in the Third Reich was reserved for demonstrating the dynamism and heroics of males, which could, of course, exude homoerotic sexuality.[313] Nevertheless, beautiful nude women beckoned suggestively to the viewers, as shaped in sculptures by Georg Kolbe, Richard Scheibe, and Fritz Klimsch. Josef Thorak molded a well-built unclothed female kissing a naked youth.[314] Altogether, however, the German tradition of sculpture had not been broken as much at the beginning of the twentieth century as had painting. Impressionism, Expressionism, or other currents of Modernism had not touched sculpture as much, with the exception of some artists, the most significant of whom arguably were Wilhelm Lehmbruck and Käthe Kollwitz, Barlach, Schmidt-Rottluff and Kirchner, all of whose works were shown at the 1937 "Degenerate Art" exhibition.[315] A representational rather than abstract bust by Scheibe or Kolbe, on the other hand, in the mid-1930s would have looked much like one done in Germany prior to World War I. Thorak and Breker, the Third Reich's greatest sculptors, counted the French artists Auguste Rodin and Aristide Maillol among their masters, as did Scheibe and Klimsch.[316]

Sculpture was a perfect medium for the Nazis, because it could monumentalize in three dimensions what was thought to be ideologically important. Its first interpreter of note after 1933 was Thorak. He was born in Hitler's birth year, 1889, in Salzburg, the son of a master potter. But unlike the later Führer, he found easy entrance to Vienna's Academy of Arts. Having moved to Berlin and striving early on for monumentality, he received his first significant prize from the Prussian Academy of Arts in 1928. Through Hitler's personal architect Albert Speer, Thorak was awarded state commissions, and soon he was sculpting everybody from Paracelsus to Nietzsche, Mussolini to Hitler. The film star Anny Ondra was his model for *The Beauty after a Bath* in 1935. Eventually, Thorak chiseled to perfection giant replicas, often of horses, in a huge studio built for him outside Munich.

His monumental *objets d'art* were to be a proverbial testimony to the greatness of the Third Reich.[317]

It has been written that while Thorak was Hitler's first sculptor of choice, he was later replaced in the Führer's grace by Arno Breker, who became equally fond of monumentalizing to excess. Breker was yet another sculptor, observes Hellmut Lehmann-Haupt, "who confounded bigness with greatness."[318] Born in 1900, Breker received his decisive training at the art academy of Düsseldorf. From 1927 to 1933 he lived in Paris, where he communed with artists such as Robert Delaunay, Jean Cocteau, and Man Ray. After moving to Berlin, he won a silver medal at the 1936 Olympics for statues of athletes and in 1937 became a professor at the Academy of Fine Arts in Berlin. By then a close friend of Speer, he sculpted more and more for the Reich. In an oversized atelier of his own, he made sculptures and reliefs for the new Reich chancellery and other public buildings, such as his male-ego-serving piece *Comradeship*, commissioned by Speer in 1940: "The dramatic sculpture depicts a standing caped man, defiant in his expression, supporting his clearly grievously wounded comrade-in-arms who is unconscious and rests in his friend's arms."[319] It was obvious what especially Thorak and Breker wanted to convey: that German men had to become yet more muscular to fight for Hitler's Reich, and women even more ready to give birth to guarantee the Volk's longevity.[320]

The monumental and heroic qualities of National Socialism and of the Third Reich in gestation, said Hitler, were best expressed in art through architecture.[321] Along with the visual arts this was his favorite kind of cultural expression, before music, film, and everything else. Regarded by many not as an art form but a craft, architecture, like painting and sculpture, was organized within Goebbels's Reich Culture Chamber. Hitler thought that the architecture of the future had to be shaped along heroic and grandiose lines. For this he needed an expert, and that future was more or less guaranteed for him in 1934 as soon as the young architect Albert Speer became his person of reference. With a background in Modernist building, he shared Hitler's overall view of grandeur and of style.

In early 1934, after Hitler's first architect Paul Ludwig Troost had died, the twenty-nine-year-old Speer was placed in charge of one of the few very large architectural schemes that actually came to fruition, at least in part: the Nuremberg Party rally assemblies. Based on earlier plans by Hitler himself and Troost, a huge field with built-up structures was supposed to serve as the Third Reich's venue for annual Party gatherings, also to be integrated with the remodeled city, still reminiscent of medieval times. Everything was designed on a gigantic scale, as monumentalism was the hallmark of Hitler's personal architecture. Final plans for the entire project were outlined as far ahead as 1942. The Colosseum in Rome was the model for a meeting hall, but it was to be much longer and wider. The stadium, planned for about half a million onlookers, was to supersede even the pyramids. As it turned out, Speer merely managed to complete the Zeppelinfeld, for Party, Wehrmacht, and paramilitary parades; it would be host to more than 100,000 Volksgenossen. Other structures for mass accommodation were never quite finished. In keeping with Hitler's own taste, Speer's style was neoclassical, but "deeply influenced by the abstract formal compositions of the twenties." Hitler did not mind, as long as his own greatness and that of the movement he had created was duly emphasized. Never too shy to praise himself, Speer later called his work "a new ordering of genius."[322]

The second architectural milestone of the Nazi era was the House of German Art in Munich, which would be host to the first of a series of "Great German Art" exhibitions, beginning with the one in July 1937. By and large, it constituted an admixture of monumentalism and, with its Doric columns, neoclassical style tempered by touches of 1920s Modernism – Hitler's obsession with ancient Roman and particularly Greek architecture here was especially evident. The building bore Hitler's motto: "Art is a mission requiring fanaticism." Accordingly, it was meant to be the pre-eminent representational token of art in the Third Reich, supposed to raise to a peak the communal spirit within the people, thus tying them closely to the ideals of National Socialism as embodied by the Führer. Objectively speaking, however, as Martin Kitchen has qualified, the House of German Art was styled very much in the manner of international buildings of the era: Paul Philippe Cret's Eccles Building for the Federal Reserve in Washington (1935–7), or Henri Paul Nénot's League of Nations Palace in Geneva (1929–36).[323]

Hitler's third lasting monument of note for the new era turned out to be the new Reich chancellery in Berlin, after he had declared the old one fit only for a manufacturer of cigarettes, with its exterior resembling a fire station.[324] However, this new building was to be the last colossal artifice of any permanence, because it, much like the Nuremberg site, could not be completed as the Third Reich entered the war phase. Hitler's dream of German monumentalism "for eternity" therefore remained a chimera.[325]

The new Reichskanzlei was again a work of Speer. He was commissioned in 1938 and, after nine months, the old building between Wilhelmplatz and Hermann-Göring-Strasse had been enlarged, with a completely new interior. To Hitler's great satisfaction, Speer used all the accouterments of National Socialist grandeur for a structure that would, in the Führer's words, "outlast the centuries": a clear but monumental axis, uniformly gray and heavy-looking stone, two large artworks by Breker greeting the visitor, a marble vestibule, mosaics by Speer's friend Hermann Kaspar in a hall with bright-red floors and walls, and under a glass dome. More halls dominated by marble in red and green and gray and bounded by sky-high, recessed, windows led to heavy mahogany doors opening to the study of the Führer.[326]

The new Reich chancellery project was planned as part of a larger action for the beautification of the capital. Hitler and Speer pored over many blueprints and models, some of them Hitler's own handiwork, to achieve this in the time ahead, with scales that were gigantic by any ordinary human standard. Similar renovations were planned for cities later to be known as Führerstädte: Hamburg, Nuremberg, Munich, and Linz. Hitler and Speer, in collaboration with the Führer's other favorite architect, Munich's Hermann Giesler, planned a so-called Gauforum, a giant stadium for Party activities and adjacent structures, for the capital of all the Party Gaue, the Nazi administrative units of the Reich. Work in Weimar as the Gau capital of Thuringia began in 1936 as a pilot project, with the razing of entire sections of the old town. But nothing was ever finished, either in Weimar or in any other Gau town, or in Linz or Berlin, as World War II began to interfere.[327]

Hitler's personal plans notwithstanding, other great Nazi builders had their own plans for architectural enhancements. Significantly, and contradicting any monolithic theory about architectural style in the Third Reich, the curious combination of monumentalism and neoclassicism with touches of Bauhaus and New Objectivity which had so captivated Hitler and Speer mattered little to builders who felt attracted to the neo-Biedermeier style of Party stalwart Schultze-Naumburg, which Rosenberg's Kampfbund had officially championed in the early regime years. With its characteristic gabled and frequently thatched roofs, this style was now employed increasingly, both for private and official buildings, such as Hitler Youth hostels or rustic governmental housing, or the construction of private villas. Göring's edifice for his first wife Karin, the hunting lodge Karinhall in the northern Brandenburg forest, was built in that woodsy, cozy style (to say nothing of Hitler's own Berchtesgaden Berghof). Yet beyond that traditionalist path Göring, who of course had a more cosmopolitan background, preferred rather modern-looking designs, cool, clean, and sometimes with flat roofs, for his Air Ministry assemblies.[328] The multiplicity of approaches meant that in 1939, before war broke out, when it came to architecture it was truly impossible to point to a singular style and declare it symptomatic of Nazi art.

AN INTERIM ACCOUNTING

When the National Socialists took power in Germany in January 1933 Hitler assured them that they would have a thousand years within which to purge the old culture and create something new. As it turned out, they were given only five and a half years to accomplish this, because after September 1939 the war largely put an end to those efforts. It even took them not one but four years to clean out the old cultural establishment, and even thereafter, traces of it would linger well into the war period. There were the beginnings of an indigenous Nazi culture, but these were marked by trial and error, the lack of original notions, the disappearance of artistic freedom, confused direction by an ineffectual bureaucracy, the dearth of new young talent, and the persistence of old art patterns that had seemingly been written in stone.

After January 1933, a few years into the dictatorship, there were Nazis who readily conceded that the required "National Socialist style" would take longer to evolve than the political sea change. It would be wrong to expect, wrote the novelist Heinz Steguweit, that cultural values of the movement would be ready for application right after the assumption of power, as he cautioned: "First the marriage, then the child!"[329] Several years later Theodor W. Adorno agreed in hindsight, as it were, when he wrote that it would be "erroneous" to assume that there ever sprang to life a specific Nazi culture.[330]

Adorno was referring to music and poetry, but those were not the only arts Steguweit's contemporaries found lacking in Nazi form and substance. By and large, Nazi culture wardens thought all the arts were wanting, even if they conceded early in the regime, as Hitler did for the visual arts, that a grace period was in order for incipient projects to come to fruition.[331] But when this did not happen, as in July 1937, when at preliminary screenings Hitler did not see enough paintings of quality to be included in the first Grosse Deutsche Kunstausstellung, he was furious.[332] And in architecture, regular members of the Volksgemeinschaft found models of Speer's and Hitler's monumental buildings aesthetically awkward and difficult to comprehend.[333]

On behalf of the film industry Goebbels vacillated constantly between full satisfaction and utter despair over the quality of movies that were being produced. In particular, he complained that the new National Socialist spirit had not yet been captured in its work: "the people, the experts, and the N.S. artists are missing," he lamented late in 1936.[334] A specific Nazi essence of life had not yet been reflected in film, echoed the reports of Himmler's Sicherheitsdienst, or SD, the security service of the SS, two years later, and it was admitted that the absence of appropriate film scripts was a function of inadequate personnel recruitment.[335]

For radio, Goebbels's inability to hold a balance between entertainment and propaganda and, within entertainment, between light and high-brow Nazi-conformist content, was a symptom of failure in the gestation of a novel mass-communication medium, judged ideally suited for totalitarian dictatorship. Nor were the supervisors of the new Nazi press satisfied when they stated that the newspaper tree had not yet grown, "which spreads its branches, full of life, over the entire Reich."[336]

With respect to the spoken and the written word things looked hardly better. As a replacement for traditional drama, the Thingspiele failed miserably.[337] In theater, aside from the forced dramatizations of the recent Kampfzeit past, there were no new poets who could write convincing Nazi drama, be it comedy or tragedy, on a permanent basis. "Really good pieces for the stage are sadly lacking," complained Käthe Dorsch, a respected actress and former intimate of Hermann Göring, to Erich Ebermayer, himself a mediocre playwright, in March of 1938.[338] It was necessary for a new generation of German artists to mature, "who would relate naturally to the attitude towards life dictated by National Socialism," read a verdict early in the regime.[339] As for literature, in 1935 the critic Hellmuth Langenbucher spoke despairingly of "that Poet of the Third Reich, still unknown."[340]

As for the pet subject of Alban Berg's former composition student Adorno, no sooner had Goebbels appointed Richard Strauss president of

the new Reich Music Chamber in the fall of 1933, with an extra department for composers, than complaints were pouring in from Party circles
that original music breathing Nazi life was wanting. The music of the
"modern composers" à la Fortner and Pepping did not transport him, grum-
bled Minister Goebbels; newly written pieces for Reich Party rallies did not
measure up.[341] One particular grievance of his concerned opera, the one
medium that would have lent itself elegantly to imparting Nazi lore.[342]

Altogether, then, the lack of substance in artistic output after January
1933 was grounded in two specific circumstances, one in which the most
recent political models that could have served for ideological inspiration
were shop-worn, and the other in which derivative re-creations struck
purveyors of culture as irrelevant. In the first instance, early Nazi iconography became stale. Party archetypes from the Time of Struggle lacked
conviction beyond summer 1934, when Hitler declared closure for the revolutionary movement. And even until the Röhm Putsch, there could be only
so much embellishing of Horst Wessel, whose seedy character – as a failed
university student and sometime pimp – was known to many insiders.
Schlageter, moreover, that earlier Nazi hero, had been thoroughly exhausted
by Hanns Johst, as had the Freikorps and the fatuous SA.[343] As for the
derivative, culture cognoscenti like Goebbels, Hans Severus Ziegler, and
Göring could attach little value to the dramatic theater of Hermann Burte
or the operas of Max von Schillings and Georg Vollerthun; Ludwig Thoma
and Peter Rosegger had written much better novels about peasant life, and
Leibl, Friedrich, and Dürer, after all, had been the better painters.[344]

The regime attempted early on to stem the tide of mediocrity by introducing competitions to ambitious candidates. Hence the coordinated press
was admonished to discover "the best German novel by an unknown
German author," by inviting contributions for serialization. At first less than
encouraging, the exercise was to be repeated every year.[345] In conjunction
with the Promi, the Leipzig publisher Philipp Reclam Junior began the
Dietrich Eckart prize for dramatists; after 800 writers had contributed, only
three received an honorable mention. No one would claim the prestigious
Nazi prize in years thereafter.[346] Rosenberg's NS-Kulturgemeinde, meanwhile, was commissioning new music compositions for interested contest-
ants, whose works, once selected, would be guaranteed a premiere. Here the
results were somewhat better, Rudolf Wagner-Régeny being the most

recognizable of several winners.[347] Robert Ley's "Strength-through-Joy" organization then invited authors to write Thingspiele, but the flood of submitted manuscripts merely highlighted a widespread dilettantism.[348] After another contest, this time for paintings featuring the German Mother, the results were so disappointing that a scheduled exhibition had to be canceled. This event and its demise occurred in 1937, under the sponsorship of Nazi women's leader Gertrud Scholtz-Klink. By 1938, Party and State initiatives were fading, as preparations for war took precedence in the social life of the nation.[349] Two late contests appear to have been one for students of architecture, in honor of Hitler's fiftieth birthday in April 1939, and yet another one for painters, this time on themes from German sagas and fairy tales. Both contests were publicized on September 1, the day of the invasion of Poland.[350]

With more or less established artists failing spectacularly from 1933 through 1939, the regime leaders realized that their safest bets were on recruitment and education of the young.[351] But however much cultural institutions of the Hitler Youth could help in this, time was of the essence in a period when preparations for war began visibly in early 1935 with the introduction of military conscription, and one year later, with Göring's mandate of the Four-Year Plan. What disciplines could one train students in during an incrementally compressed stretch of time? Universities, writers' and music academies, under the immobile and alcohol-besotted Education Minister Bernhard Rust, did not lend themselves to dynamic enrolment and curriculum changes in a hurry. In such a climate, Goebbels reminded himself of his monopoly on theater and film.[352] But a planned Reich high school for dramaturgy remained stuck in inertia.[353] Then, for the cinema, where the cultural overseer Goebbels was most creative, he succeeded in founding an academy, under the direction of the highly motivated actor Wolfgang Liebeneiner, whom Goebbels considered "young, modern, determined, and fanatical."[354] The film academy, under the auspices of the Reich Film Chamber, began operations in March 1938. It taught the arts of drama, specifically acting, using as its base literature by empathetic authors such as Hans Zöberlein, Josefa Berens-Totenohl, Ernst Jünger, and Hans Grimm, interpreted by Nazi conformists like Frankfurt's Intendant Friedrich Bethge. Beyond that, it mandated ideological courses teaching "Our Germanic Heritage," "The Struggle of the National Socialist Movement for Power,"

and "The Shadow of the Jews Over the World."Those courses eerily anticipated the training program some twenty months later for conditioning
police battalions, before they were sent to eastern Poland to kill Jewish civilians.[355] Apart from such thorough ideological indoctrination, not much was
expected from the film academy, neither by film artists nor outside circles,
notably the SS.[356] After its initial trial run, Goebbels had it shut down in the
spring of 1940.[357]

To what extent – to resume an earlier question – were these broken structures, broken processes, and unfinished art projects a consequence of the
inner workings of National Socialist rule? That depended on the degree of
Hitler's interest in a given artistic medium, which was determined less by
what "the masses" thought about it than what the Führer thought himself, as
he was habitually guided by personal tastes.[358] According to our evidence so
far, a correlation existed between Hitler's decision-making in cultural affairs
and his personal identification with the subject: the more he was concerned
about it, the more he became involved in its administration, positively or
negatively, no matter what policy his underlings were favoring. In the case of
the visual arts, for instance, Hitler allowed his closest associates, Goebbels
and Rosenberg (and to a lesser degree Rust and Göring), to extend their
squabbles over Modernism, each of them thinking that he was working
towards the Führer; this situation continued unresolved until he himself, the
would-be painter, made the final call against the movement in July 1937,
thereby sealing the fate of many artists. Hitler made similar, smaller, dictatorial decisions in the visual arts, such as when he forbade Goebbels to display
a Nolde or Barlach in his quarters, or when he acted as the ultimate arbiter
in the choice of paintings for the Grosse Deutsche Kunstausstellung in the
Munich Haus der Kunst. In new architectural construction, characteristically, he reserved final judgment as he saw fit, authorizing and then backing
Troost's work on the new Haus der Kunst building and, later, Speer on the
new Reich chancellery, thereby leaving architectural rivals like Schultze-
Naumburg in the dust. In 1936, Hitler chose Hermann Giesler to commence
the building of a Gauforum in Weimar, as a model for other such projects to
follow, in similar German cities.

Hitler's personal interest in music, more specifically opera, was second
only to that in art and architecture, and, having no formal training in that
discipline either, he made similarly private and not necessarily informed

decisions here. Because he hated the opera-conducting style of the popular Hans Knappertsbusch, a personal whim, he had him barred from achieving ultimate musical success in the Reich.[359] Since he had preconceived notions of what the staging of a Wagner opera should look like, Modernist or not, Hitler backed the progressive ideas of Heinz Tietjen and Emil Preetorius in Bayreuth in 1933, and not on a musical basis but more on visual impulse. Similarly, he endorsed Egk's *Peer Gynt* opera in 1939, overruling Göring's personal objections, to discipline his field marshal and, possibly, because something in Egk's composition (or, more likely, the scenarios) struck a chord. And he ruled on the tempo of the Horst Wessel song out of his own personal sense of rhythm, hearing not harmonies but visualizing columns of marchers.

Arguably the next important art form for Hitler was film. Hitler was active, next to Goebbels, as a censor, determining what movies were suitable for the public, dismissing some, such as *Das Leben kann so schön sein*, according to criteria based on aesthetics as much as on social-political intent; these were never fully explained but were unquestioningly accepted by Goebbels. Those criteria also guided Hitler's decision regarding Riefenstahl: the images she produced were exceptional, pioneering in the art world of filmography as much as propagandistically valuable. Hence, as much as Goebbels would have wanted to rule over Riefenstahl's creative domain, Hitler reserved her talents for himself.

The strong interaction between personal aesthetic preference and policy in Hitler's case furthermore explains why the Führer by and large ignored an art form such as literature. Notwithstanding his interest in history, geography, and military lore, and although he may have passed as an author of non-fiction himself, he possessed no flair for *belles lettres*. The Führer had no use for certain recurring motifs characteristic of some new Nazi literature, such as stories about Germanic ancestors or quaint tales within rural settings. In the first instance, Hitler was well aware that Himmler and Rosenberg, who both thought they were aiding the Führer's cause in their own way and therein rivaled each other, held a certain passion for Germanic prehistory. They even ordered the excavation of wooden structures allegedly built by Germans many centuries ago, in their attempts to prove a time-honored past for the German Volk; Hitler ridiculed them but let them be. He himself held, as he attempted to explain during a January 1942 monologue, that Indo-Germans were ancestors of Greeks from classical times, whose stone architecture he so loved.[360] In the case of peasant themes for books, Hitler had no original understanding of the farmers' world, and hence was not interested in literature featuring "Blut und Boden" motifs. As much as Goebbels sometimes tried to change Hitler's mind about the arts, Reich Peasant Leader Richard Walther Darré could have done so in this area (he had presided over propaganda efforts toward farmers in the Time of Struggle), but Hitler disliked and never received him. Nazi literature therefore developed under Goebbels, the former journalist, Argus-eyed, whom Hitler trusted, because in all the cases concerning culture that mattered he concurred with Hitler – and when he did not, as regarding Modernism in the visual arts, Hitler could overrule him, whether this meant an affirmative nod to Goebbels's rival Rosenberg or not.

The gubernatorial "working towards the Führer" machinery, with Hitler weighing in when he thought it necessary, was well oiled by the time World War II began and was running, quasi on auto-pilot, until the spring of 1945, radicalized and creating self-destructive havoc in its path. This certainly applied to politics and military leadership,[361] but was less visible in the cultural arena. This was because Hitler's role here receded under stress, and his helpers by now had learned how to administer things by rote, to compromise, and either to allow or ignore gross irregularities. For example, almost a whole army was used in the filming of *Kolberg* in 1944 as a last propaganda effort to motivate the nation, at a time when all troops were needed at the fronts. Of course there were times when Hitler still interceded, as he did routinely with newsreels. He had always taken a personal interest in the final selection of paintings in the annual Munich art shows since July 1937. He decided on the shut-down of the *Frankfurter Zeitung* in 1943. And on one particular occasion he ordered a monthly pension to be paid to his favorite actress Henny Porten, whom Goebbels had long removed from Berlin-Babelsberg because of her non-"Aryan" husband.[362] A very few Jews were fortunate if Hitler closed his eyes, for example whenever the actress Käthe Dorsch or Göring's second wife Emmy Sonnemann-Göring approached the field marshal with a request for special protection. But in the main, Hitler went ahead with his resolve to eliminate the Jews, knowing he could enlist his bureaucrats. Long before, he had singled out Jews to be blamed for what he regarded as irregularities in the German world of culture.

CHAPTER THREE

◆ ◆ ◆

Jews in the Nazi Cultural Establishment

ERMAN ANTI-SEMITISM AFTER World War I and well into the 1920s resulted from a wide belief among non-Jewish citizens that through progressive emancipation since the nineteenth century, the Jews had acquired too many liberties, privileges that made them stand out in German society, usurp certain fields of activity, and exploit the Gentiles. A core conviction among a new breed of German anti-Semites in the 1920s was that their objection to Jews, apart from economics, ought to be based on race, not religion. After the dual revolutions, the great French uprising and the Industrial Revolution, of the past century and a half, "race rather than religion now provided the rationale for anti-Semitism," writes Christopher R. Browning.[1] This brand of Jew hatred was "unusually violent in its imagery, and it tended towards violence." Its protagonists claimed that Jews were over-represented in professions such as finance, law, and medicine, but also in culture and the arts.[2]

For transparent reasons, extreme right-wing citizens such as followers of the empire-beholden Deutschnationale Volkspartei (German National People's Party – DNVP), with the incipient Nazi Party eventually over-taking it, after 1918 published evidence attempting to prove the Jews' predominance particularly in the cultural arena. The Nazis continued to do this well beyond January 1933, as they wanted to generate an anti-Jewish legacy, supported by documentation. In pursuing this goal, they not only exaggerated but falsified facts.

128

Nazi agitators held that the over-representation of Jews in the Weimar Republic had occurred in all branches of cultural activity, even radio, for which field the electrical engineer and functionary Hans Bredow and his associate Hans Flesch were singled out as influential string-pullers. However, Bredow was not at all Jewish, and Flesch, the brother-in-law of Paul Hindemith, only had one Jewish parent. In modern music, to mention a more significant example, the composer Franz Schreker was suspected of being Jewish (even though this was, again, only half true), a man who had dared to take the place of Wagner as the creator of "pompous and musically wholly impotent stage pieces." The visual arts, too, were said to have produced a new generation of Jewish painters, "in the shadow of the senior Max Liebermann," pushing genuine German brushwork into the back-ground. The fact was that next to Liebermann there existed only two Jewish painters of note, Jankel Adler and Ludwig Meidner, who could not come close to that master's reputation. In film, the Nazis claimed, Jews had directed every other German movie by 1932 and 70 percent of all film scripts were authored by Jews. And in theater, they charged, Jewish directors had been so ubiquitous that non-Jewish actors auditioning for roles had been rejected on account of "looking too German." German newspapers, too, had been totally "Jewified." In Prussia, which comprised two-thirds of all German territory, affairs of music, theater, and the press were seen as being regulated from above, in government, by Jews.[3]

According to scholarly consensus today, and as could have been ascertained at the end of the republic, Jews were strongly represented in the creative arts. But it is equally true that, quantitatively, their alleged over-representation cannot be and could not then be computed. Undeniably, Jewish artists and writers put a stamp on the nation's culture in terms of quality and originality, because of their extraordinary energy and inventiveness. This was all the more true in cases where Modernist art was involved, because as outsiders from conventional society, many Jews simply took more chances, were open to experimentation, abstract thought and structures, and new impulses. Because the results of their creative labor were often many times more visible than the productions of non-Jews, the public found it easy to smear them with undue charges of monopoly and exclusionary malpractice. Moreover, Jews in Germany tended to live in the large cities, where most of the new culture of the republic originated. Two American historians have recently described these circumstances succinctly, carefully avoiding any hyperbole. In Alan Steinweis's judgment, Jews in Germany numbered "among the most prominent exponents of artistic modernism in the early twentieth century." And, as Saul Friedländer has put it, "modernism as such flourished in a culture in which the Jews played a central role."[4]

The names of Jewish artists who helped determine the Modernist culture of the republic today are legion. Alfred Döblin, Jakob Wassermann, and Franz Werfel dominated in literature, Arnold Schoenberg and Kurt Weill in music composition, and Erich Mendelsohn, who collaborated with Walter Gropius of the Bauhaus, in architecture. One giant among musicians was Otto Klemperer, who conducted "an unusually wide range of contemporary music," especially during his tenure at the Berlin Kroll Opera (1927–31). Another eminent conductor was Bruno Walter, who rejected serialism in favor of more traditional fare, but was also among the first champions of Gustav Mahler and "actively sought new music."

In the visual arts, the Jews stood out not so much as creators, like Liebermann, but as patrons and agents, such as Paul Cassirer and Alfred Flechtheim. In film, Erich Pommer was an influential producer, and Peter Lorre a pioneering actor. Pommer was responsible for *The Cabinet of Dr. Caligari* (1920) and *Metropolis* (1927), and Lorre starred in *M* (1931), a movie critical of current society that also featured the non-Jew Gustaf Gründgens; like *Metropolis* it was directed by Fritz Lang, whose father was Jewish. Other illustrious figures with a Jewish background from film and stage were Alexander Granach, Elisabeth Bergner, Lucie Mannheim, and Fritz Kortner (actually Kohn). A most acerbic and socially critical film analyst at the *Frankfurter Zeitung* was Siegfried Kracauer, who headed the paper's feuilleton department and frequently invited the essayist Walter Benjamin to contribute his insights on modern culture and politics. Other perceptive Jewish writers such as Kurt Tucholsky worked for *Die Weltbühne*, which supplied brilliant commentary on the state of the arts, society, and politics from a left-wing perspective.[5]

On the stage, Leopold Jessner, born in Königsberg in 1878, was a very instrumental Jewish director and producer who influenced both Expressionist theater and cinema. His first film was *Hintertreppe* (*Backstairs*) of 1921, inspired by *Dr. Caligari*, in which a crippled postman (Fritz Kortner) murders the lover of the maid he adores; the lover was played by Wilhelm

Dieterle, later of Hollywood fame, and the maid by Henny Porten, whom Hitler came to admire and favor despite her half-Jewish husband. The movie, like its 1920 predecessor, was a showpiece of Expressionism at that time, featuring its typical props, sounds, and scenes: a ringing alarm clock, a wielded axe, a deformed murderer played frighteningly by Kortner, and a spectacular suicidal jump from the roof of a building. With it, Jessner influenced the typically Expressionist style of chamber stage play also used in movie-making. Next to Jessner and Kortner, other non-"Aryans" had large parts in the making of this film: Carl Mayer as scriptwriter, Hanns Lippmann as co-producer (along with Porten), Hans Landsberger as composer of the score, Paul Leni (actually Levi) as art director, and, not least, Wilhelm von Kaufmann – Porten's husband – as head of production.[6]

Later, as director of the Prussian State Theater in Berlin, Jessner would produce a set of stairs that made him famous, the "Jessnertreppe," from which an actor playing Caesar would spectacularly fall to his death.[7] These stairs served once more as proof of the ingenuity of Weimar artists of Jewish descent, as they worked with Expressionist shapes and content even when that art form was already on the wane. Jessner's beliefs being staunchly socialist, he was in league with Brecht and Erwin Piscator that theater should instil its audiences with the desire for progressive social change, if not actually revolution. As such, he was a firm believer in the Weimar Republic whose official protection he received, and he performed its favored dramatists: Ibsen, Gorky, and Wedekind. But the combination of socialism and Jewishness that Jessner embodied made him more enemies the longer that republic lasted. Being hounded in speeches and print by conservative and, increasingly, National Socialist enemies, in 1930 he felt pressured to resign from his tenure at the theater that had hired him in 1919, continuing only with difficulty as a freelance director until his untimely emigration, via England and Palestine, to the United States, where he worked in films under assumed names until his death in December 1945.[8]

Extreme right-wing action against German Jews in the culture of the Weimar Republic occurred within the ideological framework that had been set up by the DNVP after 1918, abetted, since 1919, by Adolf Hitler's Nazis. It was in September of that year that Hitler documented his personal anti-Semitism in a letter, while he was still working for an anti-Semitic military; there are no signs that, previous to the Great War, Hitler had been an enemy of the Jews. What made him change his views is not known, but it is certain that in the fall of 1919 he had already called for nothing less than "the removal of the Jews."[9] In April 1920, Hitler met up with the Munich voice teacher Adolf Vogl and his wife Else, who excoriated "the cultural Bolshevism" of the republic, in particular the music of the Jewish Schoenberg, and hence welcomed the anti-Semitic stance of the ascendant Nazi Party directed against "Hebrew Munich." (Vogl was later chosen as the vocal coach for Hitler's half-niece Geli Raubal.)[10] As Hitler developed his own brand of vituperative anti-Semitism, he stated in the pages of *Mein Kampf* during the mid-1920s that the world war would have taken a different course had "twelve or fifteen thousand of these Hebrew people-destroyers" been subjected to "poison gas."[11] Concomitantly, he named specifically the theater and the press as cultural arenas in which Jews were allegedly dominant, where they lacked "culture-generating power."[12] Campaigning, as he did in late summer 1930 for the upcoming Reichstag elections, he identified finance and again the press as areas of undue Jewish representation, undoubtedly with the influential Jewish Mosse and Ullstein dailies in mind.[13]

As if on cue, actual attacks from the extreme right against Jewish personalities and cultural institutions – frequently by a combination of DNVP nationalists and Hitler Nazis – increased after Hitler's release from Landsberg jail, during 1925. In spring of that year a pamphlet appeared in Hamburg, calling for the liberation of the German stage from "the odor of pestilence," by boycotting theaters as long as Jews were active there.[14] A year later the Munich publisher Hugo Bruckmann planned to issue a calendar, contrasting Jews with Germans, "the size of the Jews according to their number, their property, their influence on the stock market, the press and theater."[15] Bruckmann and his wife Elsa were directly inspired by Hitler. By that time Jews were craftily clichéd in völkisch writings, for instance in Will Vesper's play *Wer? Wen?* (*Who? Whom?*) of 1927, which depicted them as dishonest pawnbrokers and usurers.[16] At the Nuremberg Party rally between August 19 and 21, 1927, among speeches rich in invective against Jews, Gregor Strasser's stood out, as he railed against "Jews and Jew-servants" contaminating the ultimate will to resistance in "the press, literature and art."[17] The fiercely anti-Semitic Julius Streicher, Hitler's Gauleiter in Nuremberg, also attacked the Jews in his standard virulent fashion. He had begun to make lists of Jews in Germany, for instance all of those in

Prussia, as well as their institutions, including cultural ones, for further targeting.[18]

The discrimination against Jews in cultural activities was amplified further after Alfred Rosenberg had activated his Kampfbund für deutsche Kultur nationwide in 1928. At the end of that year, DNVP deputies in the Prussian Landtag in Berlin, allied with militant Nazis, applied pressure to effect the final dismissal from his Berlin theater of the director Jessner, because, so their reasoning went, "in most other German stages the German spirit has been supplanted by the Jewish spirit."[19] Under Nazi regional governments of Thuringia, as of 1930, Weimar's new theater director Hans Severus Ziegler censored all Jewish content.[20] Also in 1930, the Nazi sympathizer Paul Fechter, a prominent literary critic, repeated the earlier canard of Jews having displaced German content in art, literature, and theater, and warned of certain reprisals. Similar notes were struck in the last two years of the republic.[21] During this time, Hellmuth Langenbucher, who would become a literary censor in Rosenberg's Party offices later, ominously told the grand old conservative man of letters Paul Ernst about his "fight against Jewry and Jewish influence in our intellectual life," adding that the Jews had not ceased to be "a great danger for our race." One significant symptom of this was alleged to be that "a Jew could not create German poetry, he could merely write poetry in the German language." Clearly, the "Jewish Question" had to be solved. But how to get this done? "Neither killing the Jews nor throwing them out of the country is realistically feasible," mused Langenbucher, "apart from the fact that the first-mentioned action can, naturally, not be on the wish list of any decent person."[22]

ANTI-JEWISH MEASURES

After the Holocaust, the West German actor Axel von Ambesser remarked with apparent compassion that when he had been at the town stage of Augsburg in 1933, five or six of his colleagues were swept out of the theater "by the first wave of anti-Semitism." One Jewish singer had started wearing a necklace with a small cross to document her loyalty to Gentiles, to the amusement of all her colleagues.[23] His friend, the actress Lil Dagover, sounded more hypocritical when she said that it had been understandable when Jewish colleagues were leaving behind their jobs at German stages, for how could one expect them to continue performing in plays or films in Germany![24] Back in 1936, on a visit to Switzerland, the writer Hanns Johst had sounded more cynical and closer to the heart of the matter when he suggested that German Gentile actors should have rejoiced after the removal of heavy Jewish competition. He had been visiting a cabaret in Zurich and those Jews had played wonderfully. Many of them had been chased out of Germany by the new "Aryan" requirements.[25]

Saul Friedländer has called to attention that "the cultural domain was the first from which Jews were massively expelled."[26] This confirms our previously expressed contention that the Nazi leaders thought culture was vital in molding their nation, as content for propaganda. At the beginning, the mechanisms by which German Jews from the world of culture were harassed and ultimately dismissed from their positions, were much the same as those used against Jews in other livelihoods, indeed the same as used against left-wingers, liberals, and Modernists. Apart from spontaneous actions usually by the SA, which came under some control only after the Röhm Putsch in summer 1934, new legislation was put in place, to be expanded into a stretch of time, say after 1935, when non-Jews had already been effectively purged. As in the case of left-minded Gentiles, action against the Jews to all intents and purposes began with the Law for the Reconstitution of the Civil Service of April 7, 1933, even though it was foreshadowed by sudden hostile activities, locally or regionally, as early as February and March.

Paragraph 3 of the law called for the dismissal of civil servants of Jewish descent, with one Jewish grandparent enough to give cause. One month's notice was deemed sufficient, with virtually no financial compensation. Although in 1933 it was stated that exemptions were to be made for World War I veterans, that provision was capriciously handled and soon fell by the wayside. Paragraph 3 was immediately applied to servants of the state, but it was not long after that private contracts were also canceled.[27] Even in 1933 the law was complemented by decrees specifically tailored to the cultural domain, such as that for the creation of the Reich Culture Chamber in September 1933, and the Schriftleitergesetz for journalists in October.[28] Under such combined pressures and other means of persecution, 37,000 of the altogether 525,000 Jews in Germany had left the country by the end of 1933, more than in any of the following years.[29] How many worked in the cultural sectors can only be surmised.

A cultural enterprise that was affected early was the film industry. By July 1933, it had gotten rid of its Jewish employees, Ufa being concerned as the largest company.[30] In Bayreuth, too, Winifred Wagner had to let Jewish artists go, with the exception of just a few, who could not be replaced immediately; they left in 1934.[31] Wilhelm Furtwängler tried to save Jewish members of the Berlin Philharmonic Orchestra, chiefly the famous violin concertmaster Szymon Goldberg, but by 1935 that body of musicians was totally "Aryanized."[32] Eminent members of the Prussian Academy of Arts, such as the (half-Jewish) composer Franz Schreker and the architect Erich Mendelsohn, in so far as they had not yet resigned voluntarily, were kicked out starting in the spring of 1933.[33] A similar fate befell Jewish staff members of museums and their patronage societies, galleries, and professional organizations, such as that for German architects.[34] Often, considerable amounts of money were in play, as in the case of Berlin's Ullstein publishing house. The assets of the owners, the Ullstein family, were expropriated, with nominal amounts being paid to them; hundreds of Jewish workers were let go.[35]

The Nuremberg Race Laws of September 15, 1935, exacerbated the foregoing pseudo-legislation and its consequences for Germans with Jewish roots. They enlarged on the definition of who was to be counted as Jewish by re-specifying who was a full, half, or quarter Jew and laying the foundations for further treatment of those people in a civic context. For the time being, Jews with at least three grandparents, counted as full Jews, were to be most disadvantaged in German society, with the half Jews less so and quarter Jews near a fine dividing line. For example, it would now be impossible for a full or half Jew (the latter a Mischling ersten Grades) to hold any kind of employment by "Aryans" in the Reich, whereas quarter Jews usually lost employment in the state or municipal bureaucracy, but often could carry on in privately owned businesses. Sometimes the upper echelons decided who could stay.[36] This is why, in the cultural area, the professor of German literature Richard Alewyn, with one Jewish grandparent, was dismissed from Heidelberg University in August 1933, and why the composer Carl Orff, with the same status, hid details of his ancestry.[37] While Orff was self-employed, he was always on the lookout for a possible position with a conservatory or theater.[38] Stage director Jürgen Fehling, however, also a quarter Jew, was kept on at the Prussian State Theater because it came under the auspices of Göring, who next to Hitler wrote the race rules.

The Nuremberg decrees also added a sexual dimension by prohibiting marriage and intimate relations between Jews and "Aryans."[39] This would make it easy for National Socialists to put pressure on artists to divorce their Jewish wives, as did actors Gustav Fröhlich and Heinz Rühmann, notwithstanding the quality of their marriages before the separation.[40] It also enabled National Socialists to go after Jewish artists who were living in common law with Jews of the other sex, an additional piece of chicanery imposed on the already careworn non-"Aryan" community. For this reason Germany's most popular actor Hans Albers saw his fiancée, the actress Hansi Burg, move to Britain, and the pre-eminent soprano Frida Leider saw her violinist husband Rudolf Deman move to Switzerland. Both united with their partners only after 1945.[41] Jewish "race defilers" (Rassenschänder) who had slept with Gentile partners could easily be sentenced in a court of law and sent to a concentration camp, men more so than women.[42]

Hence by the fall of 1935, about 200,000 Germans with mixed parentage were still living in the Reich, as opposed to some 450,000 full Jews, with three or four Jewish grandparents and confessing the Mosaic faith.[43] The race laws were received by non-Jewish Germans with equanimity because they seemed to put a definitive end to the impulsive storm-trooper injustices of the SA that had characterized the early phase of the Nazi regime. Even some Jews tended to take that line, although they could hardly be comfortable with how things were in German society, including the creative sector. However, it is interesting to note that only 21,000 Jews left Germany in 1935, 25,000 in 1936, and 23,000 in 1937; the end of 1935 and beginning of 1936 marked the months in which Jews were actually returning from abroad to Germany.[44]

In the wake of the Nuremberg laws, German Jews who adjusted themselves and perhaps were now enjoying the institutionalized cultural offerings of the specially formed Jewish Culture League, took many of the following anti-Semitic measures in their stride. Some went so far as to avail themselves of the services of plastic surgeons, such as those offered by the Jewish firm of Adelheim in Berlin-Charlottenburg (where many assimilated, affluent, Jews lived); it claimed to fix noses, ears, face, and breast irregularities. "Sagging lower eyelids will be removed, without a trace, in 4 days," ran the advertisement.[45] But in the cultural sphere, the pace of active discrimination against Jews accelerated. By 1937, Goebbels was intent on cleansing cultural establishments of all full Jews, if any were left, as well as half Jews and quarter

Jews, the latter of whom were termed "mixlings of the second degree" (Mischlinge zweiten Grades). He was also keen to put pressure on Jews who were married to "Aryans," who hitherto had still been privileged.[46]

By the spring of 1938 things were stirred up again, because after the Anschluss of Austria an additional 190,000 Jews had come under Nazi rule.[47] These included many Eastern Jews, all of the Orthodox faith and many with the attending visible accouterments such as caftans, long beards, forelocks, and side-locks. Instantly, Austrian Jews were treated much more harshly as they came into contact with the new rulers (as the 2015 film *Woman in Gold* has shown explicitly), with some having to clean the sidewalks of Vienna with toothbrushes or their bare hands, supervised by SA or callous Hitler Youths, and others being carted off to German concentration camps without due cause.[48] At the end of June, Goebbels showed himself determined to continue the legalistic path of accretive measures against the Jews, while he was aware that, for instance in Berlin, storm-trooper-like excesses had again been triggered by Party agencies, against governmental guidelines.[49]

By November 1938, Goebbels had conspired with Hitler to stage a coup against the German Jews that was to look like a spontaneous, popular event. It was around the time when Leni Riefenstahl was in Hollywood to make good weather for herself and the Nazis – and was snubbed, marking the beginning of her decline.[50] What happened on November 9 and 10 decreased Germany's standing abroad yet further, and became known as Kristallnacht. The SA was ordered to stage scenes of destruction involving the smashing of Jewish shops and burning of synagogues all over the country, but chiefly in Berlin and other large cities. Otto Jung, heir to a vineyard in Rüdesheim and multitalented on the piano as a connoisseur of both classical music and jazz, was passing through Cologne by train when he viewed much of the damage in the morning of November 10. "What brutality," he thought, what sort of people would do this, was anything like that within the law? After the pogrom, tens of thousands of male Jews were taken, if only for a few weeks or months, to concentration camps. These activities were fully supported in the coordinated German press, including the one-time internationally respected, bourgeois papers, such as the *Frankfurter Zeitung* and *Deutsche Allgemeine Zeitung*, and falsely represented as a consequence of outrage by the Volksgemeinschaft against the Jews.[51]

Apart from the economic and psychological deprivation suffered by Jews during this terrifying protracted, multiple pogrom, the most momentous change in their lives was in the cultural arena, because from that time on they were prohibited from visiting cultural venues or places of entertainment that could have provided solace. Included in these were theaters, cinemas, concert and ballet performances, public lectures, cabarets, museums, fairs, conference halls, sports and bathing facilities. Also, Jewish children were now excluded from attendance in German classrooms, while drivers' licenses were confiscated from Jews on December 3, and their automobiles seized without compensation – just to make certain they remained immobile.[52]

Kristallnacht marked a watershed in the lives of German Jews because by now they had to realize that the Nazi regime was following systematic steps to have them marginalized and perhaps eliminated, the latter in the context of a war that few, "Aryans" or Jews, could visualize concretely at that time. Hence many Jews now sought to emigrate. In an ongoing process of oppression until October 23, 1941, when Himmler officially forbade emigration,[53] ranging from the prohibition of pets to the banning from public transportation, the decimation of Jewish cultural life exacerbated the pain resulting from economic and social opprobrium. By November 19, 1941, Jews had been excluded from the general welfare system. On December 8, Jewish scholars who had attained special authorization to use university libraries had this privilege canceled. Classes at university for Jews were curtailed, and in the following months all radio receivers had to be surrendered; they would go to the Wehrmacht at the front.[54] In January 1939, Hitler allowed his intention to destroy the Jews to show more clearly than ever before when he stated publicly: "Today I want to be a prophet again: If international finance Jewry inside and outside Europe again succeeds in precipitating the nations into a world war, the result will not be the Bolshevization of the earth and with it the victory of Jewry, but the annihilation of the Jewish race in Europe."[55]

THE JEWISH CULTURE LEAGUE

In May 1933, Axel Freiherr von Freytag-Loringhoven, who sat in the Reichstag for the Deutschnationale Volkspartei, which had formed an alliance with the Nazis for government under President Hindenburg in January, said in an interview with a Vienna newspaper that it might be possible to solve the "German Jewish Question." Without wanting to judge the overall quality of the Jews as a "foreign tribe," said the baron, he would have to insist that they henceforth be barred from meddling in matters of "our state and our culture." But as proper compensation, the Jews should be allowed a measure of "cultural autonomy." Officially designated as an "alien people," Jews should administer their own cultural affairs, albeit under German government supervision, yet funded by state subsidies. In proportion to their numbers, German Jews might even be allowed to hold public office. Such a situation would protect them before the law (and, as the baron hinted, avoid spontaneous anti-Semitic outbursts such as recent SA actions), and their secured status would guarantee for them, and for Germany, the respect of the entire world. However, there could be no doubt whatsoever that they would permanently have to "distance themselves from German life."[56]

Apart from serving as fulsome testimony to the anti-Semitism of the German nationalists short of being Nazis, the scheme of Freytag-Loringhoven, who was a well-known Jew hater, demonstrates the extent to which the new rulers, as a government, were willing to go early in the regime in order to marginalize the Jews. Already in June, Hans Hinkel, a former *Angriff* manager who had been charged by Göring and Goebbels with the "de-Jewification" of German culture, after talks with representatives of the Jewish community in Berlin, the Reich's largest, was about to set up a Jüdischer Kulturbund, a Jewish Culture League. It would be staffed by Jewish artists and financed by the Jews themselves – beyond the more generous recommendation by Freytag-Loringhoven of state assistance – and, by producing works of cultural significance, was to benefit Jewish audiences exclusively. Hinkel served in the League's administration as the representative of Göring and Goebbels, while on the Jewish side Dr. Kurt Singer took charge. He was nothing less than a Renaissance man, a neurologist with expert knowledge in music and an accomplished conductor in his own right: in the final days of the Hohenzollern empire he had founded the well-regarded Berlin Physicians' Choir, and until recently he had been an Intendant at the Städtische Oper of Berlin, which Goebbels then had usurped for his own purposes under the label of Deutsches Opernhaus. Jewish notables such as Leo Baeck and Martin Buber were called upon to serve on the honorary presidium of the League. Specially coopted members would pay 2 to 3 marks monthly to help with the financing. Some 2,000 artists and auxiliary personnel, including non-German and baptized Jews, were invited to apply for membership as active performers, but in the end no more than 200 were hired. The season opened with Lessing's 1779 play *Nathan der Weise*, in a dedicated Berlin theater on October 1, and two weeks later the new Jüdischer-Kulturbund-Orchester gave a concert, under the conductor Michael Taube.[57]

In the following months, regional culture leagues were established on the Berlin model in the area of Rhine and Ruhr, with a seat in Cologne, and Rhine-Main with a seat in Frankfurt. Smaller institutions were then founded in Hamburg, Munich, Breslau, Kassel, and other locations, so that by March 1935 Nazi administrators organized altogether forty-six associations under a Berlin-led umbrella union, the so-called Reichsverband der jüdischen Kulturbünde (Reich Association of Jewish Culture Leagues), shortened to Jüdischer Kulturbund. Adherence to this overarching union by all the individual Kulturbünde was to be mandatory, while non-Jews were to be barred. Of those leagues, the Berlin local remained the largest; it had 20,000 active and passive members by early 1934, whereas the one in the small Prussian town of Küstrin had merely twenty-four.[58]

Pronouncements by Jewish functionaries at the time gave rise to the belief that Nazis and Jews were equally responsible for the founding of these organizations. It was held that the Jüdischer Kulturbund would give Jews an opportunity to reflect upon their national and cultural origins, on the question of assimilation with non-Jewish Germans or their difference from, or likeness to, eastern European Jewry. There was talk about a great new beginning, which would require, in Dr. Singer's words, "strength, energy, endurance, and time."[59] But these were glib phrases, designed to please or at least placate the Nazi rulers, for Singer's friends knew very well that the Nazis were the true originators of this scheme, notwithstanding the degree of cooperation by individual Jews, whatever their motivation.

As for the Nazis, the reasons for their actions were transparent. First, potential social unrest among Jews as a result of sudden and severe economic displacement could be contained by providing a new source of income, at least for some of those who were connected to the cultural establishment, and they could then act as models for others. After all, approximately 8,000 Jewish writers, musicians, and artists had been expelled from the German work force already during 1933. This held true even if, ultimately, it was not the "Aryans" but other Jews, passive League members, who were forced to provide for those artists. Significantly, one prerequisite for being hired as a Kulturbund artist in Berlin in 1933 was acute financial need; the honoraria paid to solo artists, though comparatively low, turned out to be barely sufficient for subsistence. At least at first. In Frankfurt, for example, performers received 20 marks per appearance. It was in line with this policy that in April 1938 the Promi decreed that only those Jewish artists could be taken on who were League members and had no other regular income. Even with SS troops standing by, the regime did not wish economic discontent among disadvantaged Jews to erupt into revolt.[60]

Second, from a propaganda perspective outside Germany, the Kulturbund ranked highly. If Jews could be shown to have some sort of cultural autonomy, the Nazis would be able to claim that generosity, not oppression, was the guiding principle of Jewish policy, no matter how severe foreign charges of anti-Semitism were. This was the official tenor of pronouncements by Goebbels, Hinkel, and their minions.[61]

And third, the cultural ghettoization of Jews anticipated their physical ghettoization, and later facilitated tighter policing: creating open, porous ghettoes enabled future transportation to eastern liquidation camps, in this case for Jews from the Bildungsbürgertum.[62] This complemented the incremental eviction of Jews from the individual culture chambers (RKK) spearheaded by Goebbels and Hinkel since their foundation in the fall of 1933, subsequent to the creation of the Jewish cultural organizations. Significantly, as managing director of the RKK, Hinkel played a key role in both ventures. And it was not by accident that many Jewish artists, upon being ejected from or formally withheld entry into the Reich Culture Chamber, were routinely told to seek possible employment by the Jüdischer Kulturbund.[63]

Not to be deceived, the harsh judgment of Herbert F. Peyser, an astute music critic at *The New York Times*, was very much to the point when he wrote about the Kulturbund in December 1933: "Like everything else in the 'new' Germany, it exists by the sovereign permission of the Hitler despotism. Its workings are hedged about by hairbreadth rules and drastic conditions the slightest infraction of which would mean instant dissolution. Reports of its activities are ruthlessly barred from all public prints except a few Jewish journals devoted to the special interests of their coreligionists."[64]

Predictably, as the individual examples of suffering Jews have shown, the authorities meted out capricious and cruel treatment to those German Jews who tried to remain in the mainstream of a national culture they had helped to create and been accustomed to for decades. In an area of cultural endeavor painfully circumscribed by the new rules regarding "Jewish" content, the Jewish Kulturbund planners had to exercise self-censorship to abide by the official guidelines, had to seek Hinkel's or his underlings' approval for any schedules, and always risked SS or Gestapo penalties for infractions.[65] Whenever something went wrong, the regime was wont to punish the Jews. For instance, when in February 1936 Wilhelm Gustloff, the Nazi representative in Switzerland, was murdered in Davos by the Croatian Jew David Frankfurter, the entire Kulturbund was totally immobilized by way of reprisal, on Goebbels's orders, for several weeks. Moreover, in November of that year a revue by the Kulturbund artist Leo Raphaeli planned for Hamburg was abruptly canceled for no apparent reason. After Kristallnacht on November 9–10, 1938, all Kulturbund activities were again suspended until Goebbels saw fit to order the Jews back to work in theaters and concert halls, for fear of inciting an international backlash.[66]

That November, not many Jewish artists were able to comply with that ruling, as a great number had been sent to the camps. Furthermore, their audiences had also dwindled. And Kulturbund events never having been a money-making proposition to begin with, their producers found it increasingly difficult to break even as the passive membership, the audiences, diminished year after year. This was due to emigration, pauperization, incarceration, natural death, and sometimes the murder of Germany's Jews. Periodic reminders, as they went out to musicians, to pay up and stay active as supporting members, had little effect. In any event, the 50,000 Jews organized in culture leagues throughout the Reich by 1936–7 constituted little more than 10 percent of all Jews then still living in the country.[67]

The various pogroms of November 1938 signaled the beginning of the end for the Jüdischer Kulturbund. For Jews to be ordered back to producing drama, films, literature, music, or artworks now was much more difficult than it had been in 1933, even under pressure, but still of their own free will. It taxed the Jews' morale. The Nazis' aim of keeping the Jews locally centralized for purposes of control was still paramount; hence, lacking actors and musicians, the reopened leagues were now reduced to showing films or, in the larger cities, the occasional solo recital, poetry reading, or debut by a string quartet. The Gestapo dissolved the Kulturbund nationally on September 11, 1941. When the deportation of German Jews to the European East began in earnest by October 14 of that year, the idea of a Jewish Culture League had become obsolete.[68]

By the beginning of 1939, when approximately 233,000 Jews were still living in Germany, the Jewish Culture League was active in music, theater, lecturing, film, and publishing.[69] The *Jüdisches Nachrichtenblatt* was being printed, which after Kristallnacht had replaced all other Jewish newspapers and was tightly controlled by Goebbels. But publishing books was more difficult and virtually stalled, because the ever smaller circle of Jews became poverty-stricken and so they had other things on their minds than contemporary literature. In cinema, German and foreign films could be shown, but they too were firmly censored. Already in late December 1938 the American film drama *In Old Chicago* by Henry King (1937) had been offered. In February 1939 in Hamburg, the film musical *Tarantella* (1937) with Jeanette MacDonald was featured, at the cinema in the Jewish community building in the Hartungstrasse. German films were some of those made by the production companies Terra Film, Tobis Film, and Ufa. In Hamburg, from February 28 to June 25, 1939, fourteen films were shown in a total of sixty-nine sittings, for a total of 15,768 patrons. With tickets for sale between 0.60 and 2.00 marks, up to 1,500 marks could be earned per film, which was considered a better than reasonable return. From this point on, to the extent that theater, opera, and even concert music receded in the overall program of the Kulturbund, film and lectures gained in importance.[70]

In the Kulturbund theater of the new Nazi regime, the first play *Nathan der Weise* of October 1, 1933, had set a mood, for while it breathed the spirit of the Enlightenment and counseled tolerance and friendship, indeed "harmonious unity between Christian, Jew, and Muslim," this was exactly the aura the Gestapo wished to dispel. In a self-censorial gesture, therefore, the Kulturbund-generated program guide asked the audience to forgo political discussions in or near the theater, lest the wrath of the authorities descend upon the Jews.[71]

In fact, the Nazis favored Eastern Jewish stage plays (because they were regarded as the essence of Jewishness) or, second-best, those by assimilated German or Austrian Jews such as Arthur Schnitzler and Stefan Zweig.

However, as can also be demonstrated in the case of music, German Jewish audiences were little interested in specifically Jewish authors and their microcosmic Jewish themes, with their pronounced predilection for Eastern Jewish *shtetl* scenarios, notwithstanding a certain revival of specifically Jewish cultural forms in the Weimar Republic.[72] Hence the works of Mendele Mocher Sforim (born in Belarus) or Sholem Aleichem (born in Ukraine) did badly, as the audiences, certainly in Berlin, still preferred visiting German public theaters as long as they were able to. However, Shakespeare could be staged as could Molière, as well as the non-Jewish Modernists Klabund and Kaiser; the Hungarian-Jewish Ferenc Molnár was a great favorite. One after the other, Goethe's plays and works of the Romantic era were forbidden, as Promi and Gestapo intensified their pressure.[73]

From the beginning but against heavy odds, it was music that was paramount in the Kulturbund's overall program; in combination, operetta, opera, and concerts commanded the largest number of performances and, especially in the case of opera, used up the bulk of the budget.[74] Some of the Kulturbund's musicians were outstanding; in Berlin the conductors Joseph Rosenstock and, after his departure – first to Tokyo, then to New York – Hans Wilhelm (later William) Steinberg, excelled, aided by Kurt Singer's own choir, and so did Michael Taube's chamber players. Berlin also had soloists such as the pianist Leonid Kreutzer and the contralto Paula Lindberg, who mostly sang cantatas and oratorios but could also perform in opera.[75] Neither were Hamburg and Frankfurt lacking in fine talent, the former city being the home of contralto Sabine Kalter and the latter that of pianists and composers Rosy Geiger-Kullmann and Professor Bernhard Sekles, Paul Hindemith's teacher.[76] Stuttgart had the eminent pedagogue and choirmaster Karl Adler, and in Mannheim for a few months Sekles's former student, Kapellmeister Max Sinzheimer, coordinated musical activities for the region. "The 'business' here at least keeps me going," Sinzheimer wrote to Carl Orff in early 1934. "I do planning and directing and fancy myself as some sort of Jewish Generalmusikdirektor."[77]

Two interrelated difficulties chronically plagued all musical endeavors. One was that the better the performing artists, the greater the likelihood that they would emigrate, as music is not bound by language. Hence the Kulturbund began to lose ranking musicians as early as 1933; none were ever replaced. From Berlin, Kreutzer went to the United States, and the

Hungarian-born violinist Ödön Partos returned to Hungary; in 1934, Taube left for Palestine. The singer Beatrice Freudenthal emigrated to America from Hamburg in 1936, and a year later Hamburg's music critic and composer Robert Müller-Hartmann sought refuge in Britain. By 1938 few professionals were left, one exception being the bass singer and composer Wilhelm Guttmann, who was to die while performing in Berlin in early 1941. Ludwig Misch, a Berlin critic, conductor, and music teacher, in 1936 considered founding a music school in order to educate recruits, but because of the high rate of emigration by musicians, this venture was doomed from the start. Misch himself instructed groups of pupils in what functioned as ghetto "Jewish schools" in the capital, obviously with some positive results, for the last survivor of one class (all the others had perished) thanked him in 1965, recalling that "during that dark period, when we were excluded from concerts and every enjoyment of art was denied us, you introduced us young people to music and awakened in me personally a great love for music, which did not desert me in the war years to come and ever again thereafter." Misch himself survived during the Third Reich as a forced laborer, because he had an "Aryan" wife.[78]

In order to alleviate the dual problem of attrition and recruitment short-ages, Kulturbund leaders sought to hire Jewish stars from abroad, which would have the added effect of acting as a magnet for some of the more jaded concertgoers. A favorite was the bass Alexander Kipnis of Berlin opera and Bayreuth fame, who had emigrated to the United States in a timely move during 1933 but, cutting short a European tour, was back in the capital in 1934. Thereafter, he appeared annually in various German cities until, three weeks before Kristallnacht, he gave what appears to have been a final recital under the roof of Karl Adler's Stuttgart Kulturbund.[79] Sabine Kalter, now a resident of London, performed in Berlin in the spring of 1937 and then in Hamburg that winter, with songs by Mendelssohn, Mahler, and Dvořák, as well as arias by Handel.[80] The violinist Carl Flesch also traveled from London to his former abode of Berlin, but by the summer of 1936 these journeys had become too difficult. The Gestapo had to authorize each visit, and Flesch's basic honorarium of 1,200 marks could no longer be paid due to an ever-decreasing German-Jewish audience. With the explanation that "time is money," this star performer resolved to decline all further invitations to perform in Germany.[81]

With the possible exception of Berlin during the early years of Nazi rule, Flesch's fee would have been an impossible amount to raise for any of the satellite culture leagues. For apart from having to remunerate their own artists, however modestly, they also attempted to subsidize other causes, such as charity for needy Jews, artists, and even out-of-work physicians. In Berlin a separate orchestra was organized for the newly unemployed (such as businessmen who had once learned to play an instrument as a hobby), and a studio was dedicated to younger composers. Several times the leagues suffered an unexpected loss of money, as when performances were indiscriminately canceled by the Gestapo.[82]

Complicating things further were progressively severe rulings regarding the thematic content of programs the culture leagues sought to adopt. The German censors wanted exclusively Jewish music for exclusively Jewish audiences. But that was difficult to achieve, for, just like the Nazis, the Jews were discovering that "Jewish music" was not an artistic genre in and of itself. Had not Schoenberg himself written to Albert Einstein in 1925 that to his knowledge, at present, "a Jewish music" did not exist? Therefore, derivative definitions were used: libretti written by Jewish authors, a storyline from the Old Testament, or the works of any Jewish composers or those baptized Jewish, among whom Mendelssohn remained dominant. Significantly, the very first concert of the Kulturbund in October 1933 included works by Handel, Mozart, and Tchaikovsky, and from then on combinations of Jewish and non-Jewish content were common. (Some Nazis thought Handel was compromised by his love for England and biblical themes; others, like Alfred Rosenberg, disagreed, claiming that despite his *Messiah*, Handel had been a heathen.) Of the thirty-nine orchestral pieces and oratorios staged by the Berlin league up to February 1938, nineteen were composed by Jews; similar ratios obtained for Frankfurt and Breslau, and probably for other places.[83]

Just like their colleagues from the theater, Jewish musicians practiced self-censorship when they excluded the works of Wagner, Richard Strauss, and Carl Maria von Weber, thought to be proprietarily German. In any event, the Promi had already decreed Wagner and Strauss off limits, along with Hitler's declared favorite Anton Bruckner, from the start. In 1936, after the inception of the Nuremberg Race Laws, the playing of Beethoven by Jews was proscribed. In May 1937, Hinkel berated Jews for performing Beethoven and Mozart, so the latter was ruled unplayable in 1938. Bach and Brahms fell by the wayside during 1937, and Kristallnacht in November 1938 finally spelled doom for Handel and Schumann. Throughout these proscriptions, foreign composers, including Jews, remained on the authorized lists until the end, but in the last few months of the Kulturbund Jews were irrevocably forbidden from performing works by German composers.[84]

Ironically, Arnold Schoenberg, the composer thought by Nazi experts such as Hans Severus Ziegler to epitomize Jewish culture, was just as unpopular among German-Jewish music audiences as among "Aryans." Only rarely were works of that icon of modern music performed anywhere – by Erich Itor Kahn early on in Frankfurt, in Berlin in 1934 to celebrate the composer's sixtieth birthday, in Hamburg in 1935, and again in 1937. These remained isolated events, however, dedicated mostly to Schoenberg's earlier, conventionally harmonic works, especially *Verklärte Nacht* (*Transfigured Night*, 1899). Ludwig Misch, the most influential Berlin diaspora critic, led the way; he disliked Schoenberg, whose music had shown "only slight resilience in our living times." Lesser modern composers of the Mosaic faith, such as Karol Rathaus, fared even worse.[85]

Instead, the works of contemporary but, by international standards, hardly memorable Jewish composers, often local celebrities, were featured, including the likes of Max Kowalski and Ludwig Rottenberg, Hindemith's father-in-law, in Frankfurt, and Jacob Schönberg or Gerhard Goldschlag in Berlin. Apart from the usual Handel with his Old Testament motifs, Yiddish and Hebrew synagogue compositions, some artfully contrived, were presented, to mixed receptions.[86] Mozart's *Le nozze di Figaro*, not a Jewish work by any stretch of the imagination – despite its libretto by Lorenzo da Ponte – was the Kulturbund's first opera production, in late 1933. It was followed, in April 1934, by an opera with a genuinely Jewish plot, Verdi's *Nabucco*, which was succeeded a couple of weeks before the November 1938 pogrom by *Die Pioniere*, hailed as the first truly Jewish opera, a Zionist-inspired Eastern-Jewish-Palestinian stage work by Jakob Weinberg. This pianist and composer, who had been born in Ukraine in 1879, had moved to Palestine in 1922; he was fond of contemporary Jewish themes and attempted to use melody and harmony as found in Jewish religious and folk tunes.[87]

As if things were not already complicated enough, even the Jewish and other non-German productions sometimes did not go smoothly. Once

Mahler's song cycle, *Lieder eines fahrenden Gesellen*, was arbitrarily disallowed for Jewish audiences by a new censor in Hinkel's central office. It turned out that this ill-informed man liked Mahler so much that he thought the composer could not possibly be Jewish, so he put him on the index of forbidden works. No sooner had this mistake been discovered than it was corrected. And there was a particularly sordid incident involving Wilhelm Strecker, the powerful publisher of B. Schott's Musik in Mainz. After the Berlin Kulturbund had requested permission to mount Stravinsky's *Histoire du soldat*, Strecker did not wish to go along with this, lest Stravinsky, whose "Aryan" reputation was shaky in some Third Reich circles, suffer at the hands of fanatical Nazis. Strecker informed Stravinsky: "If you permit the Jewish Kulturbund to perform it, your enemies will gleefully term you, as well as your art, 'Jewish,' spoiling everything we have managed to nurture." To avoid the performance – and to avoid telling why – Strecker planned to charge the Jews a higher fee than they were able to afford for the work. Fortunately for the Kulturbund, the publisher later went back on this. Of many that could be cited, this was a particularly stark example of how Gestapo, Promi, and private "Aryan" interests conspired to make the Jews suffer.[88]

As part of the general downfall of the Jüdischer Kulturbund, the retrenchment of its music divisions was most visible because these had been proportionately the largest and most significant. To be sure, despite the occasional musical highlight, there had always been deficiencies, such as the chronic shortage of wind players and an over-representation of string players.[89] Hence the orchestras of Hamburg and Munich consisted mainly of string sections, a problem Hamburg attempted to solve by joining forces with its Frankfurt counterpart, which regularly took to the road.[90]

The creeping failure of the culture league's musical productions was disheartening to sympathetic observers, but not to the cynical manipulators in Goebbels's and Hinkel's wake. Frankfurt had to give up its accomplished orchestra at the end of the 1935–6 season, mostly for lack of funds. Throughout the Reich music performances decreased by 26 percent, compared to an overall decline in artistic activities of 20 percent in the period from September 1936 to September 1937.[91] By June 1939 the Berlin Jewish opera had been disbanded, even though a scaled-down opera choir, now renamed "chamber choir," continued to present Mendelssohn, Monteverdi, and Eastern Jewish and Hebrew chants and hymns. What was left of the

Berlin orchestras and singers congregated for the last time, for a Verdi cele-bration in July 1941. When the end came, with all other activities already canceled, Nazi functionaries redistributed Kulturbund instruments to SA and SS units; pianos went to Nazi welfare organizations and Wehrmacht sanatoriums. Confiscated phonographs and records were recycled, the latter in the form of bakelite for the German record industry, to service the war effort.[92]

What happened to the Jewish leaders of the Culture League? The first artistic director, Dr. Kurt Singer, eventually left Berlin for Holland where he was caught when the Nazis overran the country. After deportation to Theresienstadt, he died in the camp of an illness. The last important director, Dr. Werner Levie, a Dutch citizen, also went to Holland after the League's demise, but again was caught by the Nazis, so that eventually he died from internment in Bergen-Belsen concentration camp, just after the liberation. At the Kulturbund in Berlin, the main Jewish staffers were arrested and then released, freed to await the fate of other Jews in the capital. Some of the leading artists, so it is reported, who had earned some kind of priority standing with the Nazi authorities, wrote up lists of Jews for the Gestapo, to delay their own deportation.[93] Who these individuals were, whom they spied on, and whether they ultimately saved themselves has not been recorded.

ANTI-SEMITISM IN THE NAZI ARTS

As Jews were living in Germany up to and beyond that point in October 1941 where emigration was closed to them, they were at risk from German citizens who were constantly influenced by anti-Semitic messages in the media. Those media – books, movies, journals, newspapers, or radio – were instruments of entertainment and, simultaneously, vehicles of manipulative propaganda, in keeping with Goebbels's broader objective. Propaganda worked best where it used entertainment, high or low, as a thin disguise.

Music or secondary media with music content could serve such purposes. Platitudes about Jews and music were spread, to be ingested by the general population that did not have the means or desire to check message content for the truth. Hence it was said that German film and operetta had created situations of musical chaos in which "the unchained ghetto collided with Valhalla" and "department store instincts led a general attack against German culture."[94] When this was written, in 1934, the Hitler Youth produced a songbook with anti-Jewish chants, such as: "Germany, awake from your evil dreams/Deny foreign Jews a place in your empire."[95] And there was an SA song originating among Austrian illegal Nazis that told of "Judah's tumbling throne."[96] Certain anti-Semitic clichés had to be upheld, best by repetition; thus it was proclaimed that every Jewish musician in Germany had the right to rent a concert hall privately, in which to produce "atonal music."[97] In the long-established *Zeitschrift für Musik*, Gustav Mahler was maligned as the antithesis of German music, and Bernhard Sekles was disparaged in connection with "Negro blood" – a crude reference to the innovative jazz seminar he had founded at Frankfurt's Hoch'sche Konservatorium in 1928.[98] Another renowned journal, *Die Musik*, concurred, adding that the Germans, the most musical, nay most cultivated people on earth, did not need to be taught in an area that was dominated by "Jews and foreigners," by "Negroes and Orientals."[99] As on other cultural platforms, anti-Jewish polemics reached a zenith in the music world around the time of Kristallnacht in 1938 when Goebbels repeated his invective that Jewry and German music were mutually exclusive opposites and the fight against Jews, which Wagner once evoked, had to be redoubled. Others polemicized anew against Mahler, Schoenberg, and their consorts; and about the Salzburg Festival, which had recently been conquered for the Reich, it was remarked that here a totally Jewish phenomenon had to be "Aryanized" from the ground up.[100]

As far as music was concerned, anti-Semitic venom appears to have been spread equally, regardless of whether it was through low or high culture: the Jews of jazz, a Paul Abraham or Leo Fall of the operetta, and the Nazis' classical-music signature Jews Mahler and Schoenberg were evenly maligned. In the visual arts, as has been noted, an anti-Jewish campaign found it difficult to target the few German Jews who were painters or sculptors. Although an identification of "Expressionism" with "Jews" was attempted during the Expressionism debate up to 1937, it failed to take hold. In literature, there seems to have been a parting of the ways in that sophisticated authors, writing for the educated elite, totally avoided the subject of Jewish issues, whereas mass-market writers such as Hans Zöberlein and Edwin Erich Dwinger aligned themselves with the raucous anti-Semitism (Radau-Antisemitismus) of the early storm troopers and allowed it to linger beyond the SA's demise in 1934, by offering rough-cut negative clichés of Jews.

A number of books for adolescents by Julius Streicher's companion Ernst Hiemer, a former primary-school teacher, was in the same groove, as he urged them, on the verge of adult Party service, to consider Jews like animal pests such as grasshoppers damaging a German farmer's crops. Hiemer's message was unabashedly eliminationist in 1940 when he stated about drones threatening virtuous bees that after the application of pest control "they were vanquished. They were killed or chased off."[101] Because Goebbels disagreed with the crudity if not the spirit of such recommendations, as late as May 1943 he was hoping for "a series of anti-Semitic novels" from reputable authors, even if they were not as obviously National Socialist as run-of-the-mill Party writers.[102]

One might indeed ask why authors such as Ina Seidel, Ernst Wiechert, Hans Carossa, Werner Bergengruen, or Wilhelm Schäfer did not openly engage with the "Jewish Question," which had been on everyone's mind at least since 1918. That they were not anti-Semites is hardly a credible explanation, for if they had not been outright Nazis even before 1933, they had been German-völkisch, deutschnational. Until 1933 and its subsequent dissolution, the DNVP had been known for its strong affinity with anti-Semitism, only in a more armchair fashion, with the racial argument toned down. German-völkisch nationals were without exception anti-democratic; conversely, the Jews were seen as the main force behind democracy.[103] One explanation could be that for those authors, ignoring the "Jewish Problem" entirely was tantamount to a resolution of the issue at a higher, abstract, plane: since Jews, especially assimilated Jews, were not treated positively as being a full and natural part of the German people, their absence in narrative made them stand out, as it were. One might therefore say that Jews were being slowly and elegantly obliterated by a purposeful passing over; those writers did not soil their hands. In this context it is interesting to note that Ernst Wiechert was sent to Buchenwald concentration camp on the order of Goebbels in 1938. In his case it is often believed that this was because he resisted the regime, presumably because of its anti-Semitic policies, among other noble reasons. Yet such was not the case. He was incarcerated for a couple of months as an educational measure, so Goebbels had decided, not because of what he had published, but because he had protested against the captivity in Sachsenhausen of Martin Niemöller. This former U-boat commander and anti-Semitic leader of the Confessing Christians had been an avid Nazi before 1933 and had since come to resent Hitler, not because he was, perhaps, anti-Christian, but because Hitler had threatened the institutional independence of the Confessing Church. The deeply religious Wiechert (most DNVP members had been practicing Protestant Christians) entirely sympathized with Niemöller.[104] Again, there is nothing to be found about Jews in the republican agrarian still-life he painted in his novel *Das einfache Leben*; but a careful reading about the circumstances of Captain von Orla's wife suggests that she, a cocaine addict, had fallen in with the perverted city crowd, the perversion having been accomplished – this was standard fare among conservatives – by the Jews.[105]

In the cruder literature, German Jews were portrayed according to preconceived stereotypes. Prefacing those was the theme of Jews who had benefited from World War I by staying behind the lines and engaging in political and economic corruption: that Jews had shunned combat at the Western and Eastern Fronts was a deep-seated prejudice.[106] In due course, many popular books described the Jews as the furtive rulers of Germany after the war – active in politics of the state, the economy, the banks, the universities, art, and culture. Jews were pictured as continuing to profit illicitly from the trade with left-over army provisions and materiel, by driving up interest rates and causing and benefiting from the huge inflation of 1919–23.[107] Complementarily, the Jews of the First Austrian Republic were also defamed.[108]

Much of this anti-Semitic propaganda of course had the effect of preaching to the converted. Some of the writers here, like Dwinger and Herbert Volck, were veteran Freikorps fighters, and tens of thousands in their target group, notably in the SA, SS, and as inactive former imperial army soldiers, were one-time comrades. As most Freikorps fighters had come into contact with Eastern Jews during combat in Upper Silesia, Poland, or Latvia, describing signifiers such as caftans and side-locks derogatorily in great detail guaranteed a mass of readers on the extreme and mostly under-educated Nazi flank.[109] The next-favorite ploy was to portrait Jews as mountebank brokers of agrarian products and cattle in the countryside – the German expression "Viehjude," cattle Jew, was ingrained – as was the image of the lowly Jew as the door-to-door small-time wheeler-dealer, perhaps peddling used buttons and suspenders.[110] Jews were further pictured as saboteurs of the German civic order on call from Moscow, and every historic clash between the SA and

Communists was characterized as having been instigated by Eastern Jews who were Soviet agents.[111] In line with such interpretations were gory accounts of Russian secret-service Jews, often as oppressors of the Swabian or Mennonite Soviet minorities in the south-central Soviet Union.[112]

Luridly, many authors placed emphasis on physical features customarily ascribed to Jews by hateful bigotry. A half-Jewish aristocrat was depicted by Anne Marie Koeppen in *Michael Gnade* as born with "black, kinky hair"; he had "thick pursed lips" and an "oriental nose." After sexual intercourse with "Aryan" women, his sperm would consequently produce Jews with the very same features, ad infinitum.[113] (Koeppen's book conformed to the lessons of the highly successful post-war novel, *Die Sünde wider das Blut* (*The Sin against the Blood*) by the early Nazi Gauleiter Artur Dinter, which enthused hordes of racists and right-wing eugenicists.)[114] According to Tüdel Weller's *Rabauken*, the Berlin Wannsee beach was populated by creatures with "spongy faces" and "hair like great apes." All Jews had "hooked noses."[115] In Otto Paust's *Nation in Not* (*Nation in Peril*, 1936) the evil Jew was Herr Silberfisch, "a heavy, thick-set man with curly hair," speaking "foreign German" and attempting to impress a Gentile girl.[116] The veteran Freikorps fighter Hans Zöberlein, in his novel *Der Befehl des Gewissens* (*The Command of Conscience*, 1937), had the "Aryan" lovers Hans and Berta shockingly confronted with Eastern Jews: "Across the street, which Hans and Berta are walking along in reflective silence, suddenly tramps a noisy mob of Yiddish-mumbling Eastern Jews, with their suitcases and packets. Obviously, a fresh transport from Galicia has just arrived at the station, disgorging its louse-infested, greasy contents into town. And here comes the riff-raff, with smeary, long caftans and flattened round hats, under which gush out long ringlets, framing the cheeks of smirking faces, with their trash bags over arms or shoulders – they are chipper, as if this had always been their home."[117]

One of the most damaging accusations against Jews has always been the sexual one. However much detractors thought inappropriate Jewish sexual behavior was grounded in the Old Testament (citing especially the sexual exploits of ancient Jewish kings, namely David or Solomon), in the Weimar Republic they locked on to the alleged role Jews played in the flourishing sex business, chiefly brothels and the white-slave trade, in the demi-monde culture of nightclubs, cabaret, and light operetta, and in the perpetration of what they called pornography in literature, citing Schnitzler, Sternheim, or Wedekind.

Hence one of the main fictions presented in Nazi literature after 1933 habitually was the Jews' uncontrolled lust and their concentration on the insemination of young "Aryan" women, by any means of seduction, as a ritualistic goal. This accorded with Dinter's classic pattern in *The Sin against the Blood*. Starting with Jews in the ancient world, Werner Jansen described "Hebrews" gathering at a food emporium in Egypt, "where the dancers come as a bonus."[118] The Jewish real-estate agent Knopfstein, wrote Edith Countess Salburg in her novel *Eine Landflucht* (*Flight from the Land*, 1939), had little else on his mind during the 1920s except seducing small-town German maidens.[119] In Gerhard Lorenz's novel *Unrast* (*Unrest*, 1943), Isaak Veilchenduft's obsession was the republican-era premiere of a revue called "A Thousand Sweet Little Leggies."[120] No Jewish political commissar in the Soviet Union, readers were reminded by novelists Karl Hans Strobl and Horst Slesina, forgot after 1917 to avail himself of the prospects for sex with Volga German farm girls. The officer Brodski even wanted to time-share someone's wife, but for the knockout by an enraged, strong Volga German man.[121] In Otto Paust's *Menschen unterm Hammer* (*People under the Hammer*, 1939) a slutty but attractive German girl in the Third Reich appears who has become the groupie of a Jewish lawyer, hanging around for his public appearances in the law courts and serving as his concubine at whim.[122] Hans and Berta in Zöberlein's *Der Befehl des Gewissens* of 1937, two years after the Nuremberg laws, correctly sized up Berlin's Wannsee swimming scenario according to Nazi criteria: it was a hunting ground used by adolescent male Jews to catch German girls. Berta hit the nail on the head: "These Jew pigs are ruining us, contaminating our blood." And: "It's scary to think that German girls just don't get it."[123] Goebbels closed public bathing facilities for Jews at around this time.

In his novel *Rabauken* (1938), Tüdel Weller used the figure of his Jewish Dr. Singer once again to illustrate the Jew's sexual appetite for beautiful German girls, but also his intellectual ability for arcane abstraction and his capacity for camouflage. It takes the young German hero Peter, a former Freikorps fighter, several encounters to find out Singer's true "race," particularly since Singer appears to reason like an "Aryan."[124] Other völkisch authors used these and other alleged properties of Jews to construct within their plots a "Jewish Question," which was then argued for and against and won, naturally, by the racially conscious Nazi protagonist in the narrative. A "Jewish Question" had to be solved especially among the young, to lead irreversibly to Adolf Hitler, his movement, and the new state. Goebbels's propaganda machine wanted the arts to deal with important Jewish issues in such a creative way.[125]

Almost certainly because for Goebbels literature could not portray the Jews convincingly at more sophisticated educational and social levels, he decided, starting in the immediate pre-war era, to render the "Jewish Question" in film, which would attract a larger audience. There is evidence that Goebbels had come to that conclusion by the time of Kristallnacht in November 1938; the fight against Jews was paramount in his mind, and he ordered German film companies to start conceiving anti-Semitic movies.[126] Hitler's threatening January 1939 speech accelerated this development. The first of three such films of considerable significance was *Die Rothschilds*, based on a plot by the well-positioned writer Mirko Jelusich and directed by Erich Maschneck. Structurally, this also marked a change for the film industry as a whole, for until 1940 films had not yet been very closely tied to current events, but this was now changing markedly with the urgencies posed by war. Jews and war: What greater urgency was there now than the one presented by the problem of Jews in a Europe under arms? This would be the principal theme in future of Goebbels's newly minted weekly, *Das Reich*.

In *The Rothschilds*, the ideological Ufa filmmakers attempted to view the Jewish-race issue through the prism of time, by examining the internationally plutocratic Rothschild family. "The path of the Rothschild bank serves as a proxy for the path of Jewry during the last 150 years," wrote *Das Reich*'s reviewer Jürgen Petersen. The Rothschild name would evoke the specter of international finance-dictatorship, war speculation, and influence-peddling in political decision-making, he maintained. Purportedly, the British banker Nathan Rothschild had made millions by manipulating the London stock exchange with early, unexpected (false) news of Napoleon's victory at Waterloo in 1815. The film paralleled an earlier stage play by the Nazis' favorite Eberhard Wolfgang Möller, which in turn inspired it.[127] Once the protagonist Rothschild had made his fortune at the stock exchange, he had become complicit as a wheeler-dealer in cahoots with shady British politicians and military leaders, for the real victors at Waterloo had been the Prussians under Marshal Blücher, argued the film along with Petersen. All told, this movie, which opened in Berlin during July 1940, persuasively demonstrated for Petersen "the criminal basis of Jewish power." Particular credit was ceded to the impersonators of the Jews – the actors Erich Ponto, Carl Kuhlmann, Albert Lippert – but also to lesser, younger players, such as Bernhard Minetti, as Napoleon's sinister chief of police.[128]

The film turned out not to be popular in Berlin, possibly because the Jew Rothschild was victorious in the end – a finale with which Goebbels certainly could not be happy. Its run was therefore cut short, but also because another film in the making was about to open, one that should not be rivaled by a movie of lesser rank. That film was *Jud Süss*, directed by Veit Harlan and starring any number of excellent German actors.[129] After World War II, because of the explosive nature of its plot, several among those actors insisted they had participated in the film against their will, notably Harlan himself, Ferdinand Marian (who played the Jew Süss), and Werner Krauss (who simultaneously posed as Rabbi Löw and other Jewish characters). But if anyone, it was only Marian who appeared credible in this regard. It is known that he got vehemently drunk after having been pressed into the role by Goebbels, that he demolished furniture in a rage – and that he most probably took his own life after the war, as he drove his car into a tree in October 1946, in what many saw as bitter remorse.[130]

The film was based on several earlier poetic adaptations of the biography of the historic Joseph Süss Oppenheimer, whose tragic fate during the early eighteenth century could easily elicit sympathy. In the film the Jew Süss travels from Frankfurt to Stuttgart to serve as Duke Karl Alexander of Württemberg's finance secretary. Süss collects the taxes of the population and governs them harshly, while catering to every personal whim of the tyrant, including the procurement of mistresses. When Süss himself wishes to marry Dorothea, the daughter of Counsellor Sturm, she refuses him; she is already engaged. The plot thickens when Faber, the fiancé, is tortured, an oppositional burgher hanged, and Süss rapes the blond "Aryan" woman, who thereupon drowns herself. (This was one of several "drowning" roles the Swedish actress Kristina Söderbaum, Harlan's wife, played in Nazi films, wherefore the people baptized her "Reich Water Corpse.") After the duke's sudden death from debauchery, the rebel leaders of the enraged people of Württemberg have the Jew tried, condemned for having had sex with a Christian woman, and strung up in a church steeple.[131]

The *Frankfurter Zeitung*'s Carl Linfert judged that the "moral aim" of this story, as shown by the Nazis on the screen, had been to identify the Jew as the exponent of evil incarnate, in particular to demonstrate the creepy insinuations of assimilated Westernized Jews who at the core had remained Eastern Jews – insinuations into the völkisch fabric of the German people in order to exploit them.[132] Karl Korn of *Das Reich* concurred, in as far as "this great film project" had come to grips with the, often ignored, difference between Western and Eastern Jews and, at the same time, their organic interdependence, the acute dangers of which the German people constantly had to be alerted to.[133]

To the same extent that Goebbels had shown himself delighted with the making of the movie, lauding Harlan throughout the filming accordingly and calling the finished product "a really big hit of genius," it turned out to be a great success with German audiences throughout the Reich, starting in September 1940.[134] Everyone praised the narrative, direction, and technical execution, and the acting. The film was thought to be so horrifyingly realistic that in cities such as Leipzig, Karlsruhe, and Dortmund the question was posed whether youths under legal age should be allowed to see it. In a German population of seventy million, over twenty million did watch the movie from 1940 to 1943.[135]

Jud Süss was fiendishly aligned with way stations on the Nazis' incremental anti-Semitic policy path since 1933. The physical separation of Jews in a historic Stuttgart ghetto reflected the legal split between Jews and "Aryans" by the force of the civil service law of April 1933 that had destroyed the livelihood of potentially employable Jews through the cancellation of their job qualifications. Süss's ravishing of Dorothea Sturm signified what was declared to be a crime after the Nuremberg race legislation of September 1935, namely Jews having sexual relations with "Aryan" Volksgenossen. The upheaval of the Gentile masses against Süss and his compatriots that led to his imprisonment paralleled and in retrospect legitimized the alleged revolt of the German people against synagogues and Jewish stores during November 1938. Süss's terrifying execution, showing a criminal in an act of non-defiance trapped in a cage on a church steeple, rope around his neck, portended death to all Jews, as the extermination of Jews in conquered Poland had already begun and Berlin's Jews were slated for deportation to eastern killing sites one year hence. A sub-theme here was the message provided by Süss himself, as he refused to convert to Christianity, that a Jew would always be a Jew, no matter what religion he adhered to. This was in line with the Nazi zealots' argument that perceived differences between Eastern, assimilated and, indeed, baptized Jews, were in practice meaningless, as a Jew always remained a Jew. Immutability of race was the literal meaning of the Nuremberg laws.[136]

Imparting such striking similes with realistic force, the film constituted ideal propaganda, fit for the schooling of future executioners. Hence it was shown for training purposes to the SS in German concentration camps and after 1942 also in Auschwitz, where, according to SS witnesses later, it inspired a still harsher treatment of inmates. In Berlin, demonstrators chanted after the film was shown: "Chase the Jews from the Kurfürstendamm!" and Hitler Youths in Vienna almost stoned to death an old Jew.[137] "The population," judges Peter Longerich, "by and large was motivated to accept the 'Jewish policy' of the regime, in large pre-conceived campaigns, which followed upon one another in waves." Thus the film *Jud Süss* was a constituent element in the "step-by-step radicalization" of anti-Semitic persecution, which Longerich and other historians have been able to delineate.[138]

And so was a third film, *Der Ewige Jude* (*The Eternal Jud*). It originated more or less concomitantly with *Jud Süss* and *The Rothschilds*, namely after Kristallnacht, and the reason for not one but three anti-Jewish films at that time has often been discussed by film historians. Contrary to some beliefs that there was a functional relationship between them, especially between *Jud Süss* and *The Eternal Jew*, they did not develop in any common technical or organic context, for this is nowhere discussed by the authorities, including Goebbels himself. Rather, they came about as a matter of policy to craft three somewhat different films for, possibly, different audiences, with all of them hewing to the new, sharpened, anti-Semitic policy directives, each appearing for a premiere more or less around the start of the new war. If *The Rothschilds* was the least vituperative of the films, *Jud Süss* made its anti-Jewish arguments blunter, and *The Eternal Jew* aimed to accomplish, in the guise of a documentary, with even more firmness what its two predecessors had already thematized: that the Jews were evil, threatening the Germanic racial community by plots of intrusion, and therefore had to be eliminated.

Hence to a certain degree Bill Niven's judgment that *The Eternal Jew* was "a documentary version of *Jew Süss*" makes sense, although exactly because of its "pseudofactual evidence," which was not to come across as "pseudo" for the spectators at all, it was to be a much harder-hitting picture.[139] Thematically, it was grounded in the "Eternal Jew" exhibition that had been opened in Munich in November 1937, and was the result of a combination of several film types: documentaries from recent newsreels, excerpts from German and American feature films, especially filmed scenes of Polish Jews in certain surroundings and committing certain actions. It also, for contrast, included allusions to German high culture such as examples of "Nordic" art and snippets of music by Johann Sebastian Bach; there was suggestive narration and exhortation; effective use of color by transmuting spurned Expressionist artifacts from the "Degenerate Art" exhibition to merely black and white; and the clever use of the filmic technique of dissolve: Jewish characters melding in and out of one another – hence the metamorphosis of the caftan-clad, side-locked Orthodox Eastern Jew with his yarmulke into the urban Western, assimilated businessman in Berlin, clean-shaven and wearing bespoke suits of the finest cloth. Showing the "metamorphosing" of the Polish ghetto Jew at several stages was of the utmost importance to the Nazis, as this once again drove home their argument that Jews were out to infiltrate the German master race until they looked, talked, acted, and smelled like it. To depict the Jews' original state more convincingly, the filmmakers had brought in direct comparisons with subhuman species, with insects and especially rats; at one point, the movie is crawling with rats. This was over and beyond what the two preceding films had been attempting to do, and the overpowering effect was not lost on Albert Brodbeck, the film critic of the *Deutsche Allgemeine Zeitung*, as he commented that the faces of various Jews, captured on film traversing recently conquered Polish roads, could "not very well be compared with other human faces."[140] The horrible nadir of the film came at the end when *shechita*, the kosher slaughtering of animals, forbidden in the Reich since April 1933, was shown, with a cow as an infinitely suffering creature and streams of blood. The idea here was to demonstrate the habitual, inherited, cruelty of Jews but also, metaphorically, to suggest that their eternal, universal aim was to enslave the whole of mankind.[141] The truth is that *shechita* was invented to spare slaughtered animals pain, as the jugular artery was cut quickly.[142]

Goebbels was entirely pleased with the outcome of the filming, after the movie had opened on November 28, 1940, at Berlin's Ufa-Palast, yet it was not popular with the general public.[143] Lest this be mistaken for a humanitarian streak among the Volksgenossen, it should be emphasized that the viewers' objections were anchored in aesthetics, not morality. They especially thought that the depiction of rats was overkill and felt physically sickened after watching the final scenes with the kosher butchers. Audiences in Munich, Halle, Königsberg, and Berlin appreciated the "factual information" – that Jews were responsible for the highest rates in crime, notably prostitution; that Jews played such a predominant role in the United States; that eastern ghettoes were *this* filthy – but they tired of being overwhelmed by the Jews' acts of cruelty, especially to animals, and by their disgusting appearance. The people's main argument against the film, which even the security service of the SS (SD) appeared to sympathize with, was that *Jud Süss* had already told Germans a lot and that it was redundant to overstate the obvious.[144] If this was indeed the reaction, Goebbels could rest assured that one way or another, using any one of the three films made thus far, the regime leaders had taught their lessons well. The floodgates to the Final Solution could well be opened, with not too many citizens wondering why the Jews were disappearing from the streets. Preferentially, it was in locations of Poland – where Jews were to be annihilated *en masse*, and where Wehrmacht and SS troops were stationed – that this film appeared in public cinemas.[145]

In the old German Reich, rather than films and literature, it was the press and, with it, radio that kept the campaign against the Jews going, a campaign that increasingly targeted Jews living outside of Germany after the war had begun. After all, a campaign against *German* Jews would become increasingly unnecessary after the start of the Polish operation. Before September 1939, the press, in shaping anti-Semitic content, oriented itself loosely around current events involving German Jews, including the staggered proscriptions. The prominent *Kölnische Zeitung* started it off in May 1933 by publishing an open letter by the renowned poet Rudolf Binding (who thought nothing of cohabiting with the Jew Elisabeth Jungmann) to the French Nobel laureate Romain Rolland, in which Binding attempted to accentuate Germany's singularity in its incipient fight against Jews: "Many key positions in science, art, and the economy in Germany were occupied by Jews, and they exploited this in such a way that they supported only their tribal compatriots, disregarding an equality of races themselves." This was after Rolland had lamented the Reich's racism, also in the *Kölnische Zeitung*. According to Binding, those German-Jewish efforts were abetted by "elements from the East," taking advantage of Germany's impotence and poverty, and these developments had not even stopped after Hitler's taking of power because Jewish writers beyond Germany's borders fell in line.[146] By fall, regional broadsheets like the *Augsburger Postzeitung* hailed the advent of the Schriftleitergesetz by pointing to an abuse Jewish journalists had practiced in the past, citing "freedom of the press."[147] Meanwhile, the top radio executive Eugen Hadamovsky reminded his listeners that the broadcasting system was in the process of liberating itself from "the salons of Jewish literati and stock market Jews," amongst whom mass communication on the airwaves had originated.[148]

Proprietary Nazi newspapers had a field day manufacturing stories around new "Aryan" paragraphs, which limited civil freedoms for German Jews. For example, *Das Schwarze Korps* in the spring of 1935 welcomed the closing of the Berlin cabarets Katakombe and Tingel-Tangel as Jewish artists fell victim to the employment bans. After the pronouncement of the Nuremberg laws later that year, which claimed to have created the tools for identifying Jewish sex crimes and their perpetrators, Julius Streicher's obscene tabloid *Der Stürmer* serviced the old cliché of male Jews as predators by reporting about the alleged exploitation of a nineteen-year-old, pregnant, "Aryan" housewife. Its message to non-Jews was that "the Jew" had, once again, revealed himself as the creature he always was: "the devil in a human shape."[149]

Bourgeois newspapers printed copy on cue. The *Deutsche Allgemeine Zeitung* in Berlin hailed the permanent removal from the theater of Max Reinhardt and Leopold Jessner and, around the time of the Munich "Degenerate Art" exhibition in summer 1937, the *Münsterischer Anzeiger* gratefully acknowledged the eradication of "the cliquish Jewish press" and "the shameless art dealers and their protégés."[150] In November of that year the DAZ readily endorsed the recently opened exhibition in Munich, "The Eternal Jew," which, the pronouncedly Nazi newspaper *Westdeutscher Beobachter* rejoiced a few weeks later, had drawn 150,000 visitors.[151] In March 1938 came the Austrian Anschluss. In future, celebrated the formerly professional trade organ *Börsenblatt des Deutschen Buchhandels*, the new territory would benefit from the "blessings of anti-Jewish legislation" and from the cleansing of all regional culture of all Jews.[152] After Kristallnacht toward the end of November in that year, both press and radio intensified their anti-Semitic attacks.[153]

The allegedly international character of Jews in the aggregate "World Jewry," as it had already been dramatized in the films *The Rothschilds* and

The Eternal Jew, would become the main object of a Nazi analysis of the "Jewish Question" in the German press throughout World War II. In the Reich itself, there were only 250,000 Jews left by September 1939, and they would soon be made to disappear. Consequently, both Hitler and Goebbels concluded that "anti-Jewish propaganda aimed toward the outside world ought to be substantially reinforced."[154] Among others, this was one of the reasons why the weekly newspaper *Das Reich* was founded in May 1940, for in his lengthy editorials, usually repeated over the radio, Goebbels could acidly engage with what he visualized as Jewish problems, reaching an educated audience in Germany as well as many interested foreign readers.[155]

Among the first such articles was a very poignant one entitled "Mimicry," which appeared in the July 20, 1941, edition of *Das Reich*, a few weeks after the Wehrmacht's invasion of the Soviet Union. With it Goebbels established the tenor of future anti-Semitic attacks by emphasizing the chameleon character of the Jews, their ability to adjust to every situation. One would have to be very experienced to catch them at their game of camouflage, for they would pose behind many masks. With respect to the current crusade, the world had to be reminded that it had been the Jews who had raised the specter of Bolshevism, and that gratitude was due to the Nazi Reich for combating them. However – this would become a refrain – Goebbels also railed against the plutocratic Jews of London and Washington, said to be allied with the Jewish Bolsheviks. This was the extended family of the Rothschilds, these were the second cousins of those Jews in the Polish ghettoes, shown in *The Eternal Jew*. "They are the same Jews, who, on either side, whether openly or in disguise, set the tone and loudly hold sway ... they practice mimicry."[156]

American, British, and especially Soviet Jews remained the subject of rhetorical abuse in Goebbels's lead pieces during the next few months, while German military fortunes were in the ascendant. True to the rules of effective propaganda, stereotypes were associated with each territory and themes were repeated time and again. In the Soviet Union, Jews were said to be immediately behind Stalin and the rest of the Communist leadership and to be particularly active as controllers of the secret police. In Britain and the United States, some Jews were cabinet members such as Leslie Hore-Belisha in London, others were advisers to Roosevelt and Churchill and invariably, they were said to be following merely their plutocratic instincts.

They were controlling politics for the sake of their own wealth. In the western hemisphere, German-Jewish emigrants were standing behind the enemy governments, in fact they were said to be responsible for fanning the flames of armed conflict in the first place.[157]

These very issues were addressed in the most malicious article Goebbels was ever to publish in *Das Reich*, "Die Juden sind schuld!" ("The Jews are at Fault!"), on November 16, 1941. For the regime, this was the highly important culminating moment of anti-Semitic policy, as the emigration of German Jews had just been proscribed and the yellow Star of David on Jewish clothing introduced. For the Jews, this meant an existential turning point: perdition or survival, since evacuation to the East was a certainty, barring a miracle. There was a hint of physical elimination at the end of the article, where Goebbels mentioned the necessity of "finally having to be done with them," but their eventual murder was not alluded to until May 1942, when Goebbels's *Angriff* announced that the war would end "with the extermination of the Jewish race."[158] Goebbels himself reiterated this when a few weeks later he wrote in *Das Reich* about "the extermination of their race in Europe."[159]

After the German defeat at Stalingrad and in the expectation of invasions by the Western Allies in early February 1943, *Das Reich* in barely hidden desperation continued to harp on the same well-used themes, but in shriller tones. The Jews were natural scapegoats. Three weeks after the epochal disaster Goebbels maintained that the Jews of the western plutocracies had created the conditions which led to the most recent catastrophe with the prospect of further dangers.[160] To provide a picture of Jews in America in sharper relief the newspaper's correspondent in neutral Portugal, Margret Boveri, an admirer of Ernst Jünger, in May 1943 published an article entitled "Landscape with a Double Bottom," dealing with "the influence and deception by American Jewry." (At that very time, American troops were threatening the Vichy Caribbean island of Martinique, and German radio was broadcasting torrents of anti-Jewish diatribes, and the Auschwitz death mills were running at high speed.) In the article, Boveri instructed the Reich's readers about "the core of the Jewish problem in the United States," the "strong positions of power" held by American Jews in every sector, and the resultant "anti-Semitic currents" in the country. She detailed negative qualities of the American Jews to the point where anti-Semites in Nazi

Germany would have to recognize close, unsavory, similarities, and talked about the divisions between assimilated and unassimilated Jews, emphasizing the antagonisms against Eastern Jews in central Europe. Perfidiously mentioning personalities such as Henry Morgenthau, Jr. (treasury secretary), Samuel Rosenman (presidential adviser), and Felix Frankfurter (supreme court justice), she appeared to provide insider details regarding the domination of President Roosevelt by Jewish cliques, just as Minister Goebbels had intimated. Her article ended with a word about the "decaying influence" of Jews throughout American society. For the cognoscenti who would habitually read *Das Reich*, Boveri possessed especial credibility, for her mother, though unloved by her, was a native-born American.[161]

Goebbels emulated Boveri when in November 1943 he printed a polemic against Jews in Britain. He repeated the legend of Jewish war guilt and insisted that among the British people presently, anti-Semitism was unstoppable.[162] But on the whole, *Das Reich* became more defensive in its anti-Jewish stance, probably in the knowledge that it was moot to rant against a people now in the process of total obliteration. Curiously, one last anti-Semitic piece was by Carl Linfert, who had earlier commented on German art and written a positive review of *Jud Süss*. His was a critique of the Jews' alleged role in more recent European history and their unchangeable character as a foreign body. The essence of anti-Semitism anywhere in Europe, Linfert wished to remind his readers, lay in the Jews' cultural incompatibility with whatever was their host country. Jews who themselves were incapable of cultural achievements had been caught in the attempt to insinuate themselves into the culture of others. The outstanding question currently was, wrote Linfert in January 1945, a few months before the Nazi Reich's collapse, whether the foreign body would survive, or the organism this body had infested. That was said to be a struggle not even yet near its climax.[163]

HUMAN TRAGEDIES

The gradual radicalization of anti-Semitic policy, including the use of the Kulturbund as a manipulative instrument, would call for many victims. One of them was the sixty-four-year-old journalist Theodor Wolff, a brilliant stylist and editor-in-chief of the *Berliner Tageblatt* at the Jewish Mosse publishing empire. He was also a co-founder of the liberal post-war German

Democratic Party (DDP); hence Wolff had been on the Nazis' blacklist from the beginning. He traveled to Zurich in March 1933, and, after having been rejected for residency, in December he went from there to Nice. When the town had become Italian after Mussolini's invasion of southern France in 1940, Wolff was arrested by the Fascist administration in May 1943 and handed over to the Gestapo. He spent time in Dachau and Sachsenhausen concentration camps before dying from his injuries in a Jewish hospital in Berlin, supervised by the SS, later that year. Already in May 1933, his writings had fallen prey to the student book burnings.[164]

There were not that many Jewish visual artists still living in Germany in the 1940s; nevertheless, Otto Freundlich was one the Nazis caught up with in 1943, after he had left his homeland. The thirty-year-old had moved to Paris in 1908 and there was drawn to the Cubists – Picasso and Robert Delaunay among them. Freundlich hailed Picasso as "one of the first to liberate painting from the slavery of perspective." He himself became a devotee of the two-dimensionalist canvas. Even so, as of 1910 he also produced sculpture, for example *Man's Head* and *Woman's Head*. By 1914, he had fallen in with left-wing and pacifist groups and after World War I became an admirer of the Soviet Union. Back and forth in France and Germany, he was in France after 1924, as a German but hating his country. The Nazis had seized upon his work by 1937, when they showed one of his watercolors at the "Eternal Jew" exhibition, which they opened in Munich in November and sent around Germany through 1939. In 1937, also, Freundlich's *Head*, another watercolor, was included in the "Degenerate Art" exhibition, and when the exhibition guide was printed, it was his sculpture, *Der Neue Mensch* (*The New Man*), which was used as the cover illustration. After the invasion of France in 1940, Freundlich was interned by the French as an enemy alien but escaped, and with his wife he was able to hide in the eastern Pyrenees. There he continued to draw, to paint, and to write. But in March 1943 he was arrested by the Vichy police and, via the Drancy concentration camp, sent to the Maidanek extermination camp in Poland, where he died at the age of sixty-five.[165]

As much as Jewish painters were under-represented in the German art world, Jewish actors were over-represented in cinema and on the stage. And the older a Jewish actor was, the smaller were his or her chances of escaping the clutches of the Nazis. The biography of Lilli Palmer helps to illustrate this. She was the daughter of a Jewish surgeon in Berlin. Barely nineteen years old, she was supposed to have her debut in a Darmstadt stage play in spring of 1933, directed by Arthur Maria Rabenalt. As Palmer tells it, Rabenalt and the theater director got wind of the fact that the local SA was planning to sabotage the performance during opening night, because a Jew was taking part. Rabenalt frantically tried to inform the SA chief that Palmer was in order because of her father's World War I record (which, by the stipulations of the April civil-service law, did *not* apply to a suspect's children). It was only at the last moment that the SA chief could be reached and a band of storm troopers in the first row during the show was observed to remain quiet. A few days later the aspiring actress took a train to be with her sister in Paris; her international acting career started from there.[166]

Fate was less kind to Walter Weinlaub, but he was already older, born in 1901 in Upper Silesia. Having made it through the Depression at the end of the republican era, he founded a small theater in his home town of Kreuzburg. Already in January 1933, SA troopers were disrupting the performances, until Weinlaub was beaten and almost stabbed to death. He managed to leave town overnight, staying in Amsterdam, Prague, and London, before landing in Hollywood, where, under the name of Wicclair, he struggled to resume his calling against many odds.[167]

The actors Julius Seger from Munich and Eugen Burg from Berlin had neither the youth nor the resources to leave Germany for their own safety. Seger was already in his fifties when he was dismissed from the Munich Kammerspiele in 1933. Here he had been a popular mainstay in minor roles, as on other Munich stages, for a stretch of thirty-odd years, interrupted only by service at the front. By 1941, Seger was assigned to a forced-labor detail in Upper Bavaria by the authorities. In 1942 he was taken to the Theresienstadt camp, until two years later he arrived in Auschwitz where he was killed.[168] Burg was born Eugen Hirschburg in 1871 in Berlin; he converted to Protestantism, calling himself Eugen Burg. He was the father of Hans Albers's girlfriend Hansi Burg. A veteran of many stages, including the Deutsches Theater in New York, Burg had made his first silent movie in 1915, the comedy *Robert und Bertram*, also starring Ernst Lubitsch. Later Burg starred with many famous German actors, such as Otto Gebühr and Olga Tschechowa, and not so famous ones, like a young Marlene Dietrich. He also played Sherlock Holmes, Arthur Conan Doyle's master detective. In the 1920s he had helped to train Hans Albers, with whom he filmed several movies toward the end of the republic. But that happened also to be the end of Burg's own movie career; in 1933 he was suspended from all work. The Nazis caught him as he was attempting to flee the Reich and in January 1943 he was sent to Theresienstadt. Despite Albers's intervention, Burg, already nearly blind, was murdered by camp guards in November 1944.[169]

Jewish writers at first sight seem to have done better than journalists or actors, for many were self-employed. As one looks to well-known figures such as Franz Werfel, Stefan Zweig, and Lion Feuchtwanger, it is clear that they had the means to emigrate. But they did so at great risk and with almost no prospects of thriving abroad, as writing in the German tongue was all they knew. A writer who freelanced but also worked for the stage was Edgar Weil, who was at the Munich Kammerspiele. After the police had detained him, he departed for Amsterdam in 1933, with his author wife Grete following two years later. Still, after their invasion of the Netherlands and after Grete had managed to escape, the Nazis transported Weil to Mauthausen concentration camp, where, like Seger, he was murdered.[170] Rudolf Frank also wrote for the theater, besides being a stage director, critic, and writer of feuilletons. Born in 1886 in Mainz as a descendant both of Jacques Offenbach and Heinrich Heine, he worked in Berlin and there was arrested by the Gestapo in 1933. Because he knew Otto Laubinger of Goebbels's Culture Chamber, he was released, after which he stayed with his family on minimum subsistence until 1936, when he decamped for Vienna. From there he made it to Switzerland in 1938, but until 1945 remained at risk of being deported.[171] While in Berlin's Moabit prison Frank had briefly encountered Erich Mühsam, the satirist and critic, who was a friend of Heinrich Mann, Feuchtwanger, and Wedekind – an anarchist and, for the Nazis, the epitome of Jewish depravity. In 1930, Mühsam had premiered a play in Munich that excoriated a National Socialist assumption of political power. Two years later Goebbels warned that Mühsam was the type of enemy who would immediately be arrested after the Nazis seized power. So it comes as no surprise that the fifty-four-year-old writer was apprehended on the very day of the Reichstag fire, February 27, 1933. The SA and SS kept him in custody, torturing him brutally, before they hanged him in the latrine of Oranienburg concentration camp in July 1934.[172]

One older writer got away, probably because he was very famous. He was Alfred Mombert, a Heidelberg jurist with many creative interests, who had dedicated himself to geography and ethnology, philosophy and religious studies. His volumes of poetry included *Der himmlische Zecher* (*The Heavenly Boozer*, 1909) and *Der Held der Erde* (*The Hero of the Earth*, 1919), which reminded admirers of the work of Rainer Maria Rilke and Stefan George. Mombert had to serve in the war after 1917 and lost much of his fortune during the post-World War I inflation. In 1928 he was elected a member of the Prussian Academy of Arts, but was forced out again in May 1933. By 1934, all his books had been prohibited. Still, not reading the signs on the wall, the nationalist Mombert was one of those Jews who thought that their work was "German" enough to lift them above suspicion; he, like the others, totally misinterpreted the Nazis' true intentions. This hubris caused him to remain in Heidelberg, until on October 22, 1940, along with other Jews from Baden, he was deported to the camp in Gurs, southern France. Influential friends, among them Hans Carossa, intervened with the authorities, and a Swiss acquaintance, Hans Reinhart, finally secured for him a Swiss entry visa, which guaranteed the cancer-ridden poet a safe passage to the Idron-par-Pau sanatorium. Mombert died on April 8, 1942, in Winterthur, at the age of seventy.[173]

Among Jewish musicians in the Third Reich several managed to move beyond the Nazis' reach, because music has a universal audience and so they could be engaged outside Germany. Arnold Schoenberg and Kurt Weill, Bruno Walter and Otto Klemperer certainly were the most famous, and among the first to be able to leave. The Hamburg contralto Sabine Kalter also knew this when she was considering leaving the city opera, because she had been tainted by anti-Semitic cartoons already in 1930. However, instead of letting her go right after the civil-service law of April 1933, the opera intendant Albert Ruck kept her on for a couple more years because of her immense popularity with the music-loving elite, while the authorities just stood by. In January 1935, however, under mounting threats, the forty-five-year-old Polish-born singer seized the occasion for a permanent engagement in London and left the Reich forever.[174]

Stars of higher forms of culture were afforded better opportunities for engagement elsewhere than purveyors of lower entertainment, who often were economically more at risk. Germany had many Jews working in dance-band, cabaret, and varieté ensembles, and some of those also traveled internationally. Among them were the Weintraub Syncopators, originally an amateur schoolboy band of five in 1924, who together mastered a considerable number of musical instruments. They were the true pioneers of jazz in Germany. Its leader Stefan Weintraub himself excelled on piano, drums, guitar, xylophone, vibraphone, celesta, and ukulele. When in 1927, Friedrich Hollaender decided to use the Syncopators in his revues, they were catapulted to fame. While Hollaender played the piano, Weintraub switched to drums. In 1930 they were briefly featured in Josef von Sternberg's film *Der blaue Engel* (*The Blue Angel*), for which Hollaender had written the score. In February 1933 they performed in Berlin's Wintergarten, but began a tour in March first to Prague, then Switzerland and Denmark. When they played in Rotterdam in September, they decided not to return to Germany. They were dispersed internationally, with Weintraub settling in Australia, trumpeter Adi Rosner in the Soviet Union, and composer Franz Wachsmann in Hollywood; there Wachsmann changed his name to Waxman, to become a world-famous movie composer, eventually winning two Academy Awards.[175]

With so many outstanding German-Jewish artists leaving Germany, it is no wonder the Nazi authorities were complaining about a lack of local talent. Another was the trumpet player Sigmund Petruschka, who had performed with his band Sid Kay's Fellows in Berlin's large entertainment complex Haus Vaterland since the late days of the republic. Dismissed there after the law of April 1933, he continued mainly as a composer and arranger, in 1935 shaping Theo Mackeben's tango "Speak Not of Faithfulness," played at the Berlin press ball in the spring, under the auspices of Minister Goebbels. Thereafter, ostracized from the Reich Music Chamber, Petruschka worked for Berlin's Jewish Culture League, even producing an exclusively Jewish record label, Lukraphon, which sold records only to Jews. Illicitly, Petruschka kept on creating arrangements for other "Aryan" clients, until January 1938 when he finally managed to leave for Palestine.[176]

How precarious things could become for artists even with merely a partial Jewish background is shown by Heinz (Coco) Schumann's example. Schumann's father Alfred was an "Aryan," a carpenter with a World War I record who converted to Judaism for the sake of his Jewish wife Hedwig. Her father, Louis Rotholz, was the proprietor of a beauty salon in Berlin's Scheunenviertel (Barnyard Quarter), where the poverty-stricken Jews lived, many Orthodox and originally hailing from the European East. Coco, born in 1924, grew up in the Mosaic faith in the Scheunenviertel. He characterizes it in his memoirs: "The Barnyard Quarter had a prickly atmosphere for roaming around. It was a poor but lively place where everyone had to see how he would get through the day."[177] Immediately after Kristallnacht, Coco tried his skill at his uncle Arthur's drum set, which he had left behind after fleeing from his hair salon on Alte Schönhauser Strasse. Inspired by the legendary Weintraub Syncopators, by 1940 Coco was servicing several of the clubs open for Wehrmacht soldiers around the Kurfürstendamm in various combos, casually switching to guitar. Jazz was neither officially forbidden nor expressly permitted; it was silently tolerated due to popular demand and for the sake of the armed forces' morale. By September 1941, Coco was compelled to wear the yellow Star of David, because he had celebrated bar mitzvah and because both his parents were counted as Jews, but he surreptitiously put it in his pocket. "My blue eyes and Berlin wise-guy talk did not fit the stereotype of the typical Jew," so he reminisces.[178] After Goebbels's proclamation of total war in February 1943 the SS conducted a raid on Rosita Bar, Coco's gig, looking for deserters and minors. An SS man stood at the bandstand, clapping his hands in enthusiasm. This brought out the devil in Coco. "I stood up and said, 'Actually, you have to arrest me!' He looked bewildered. 'Why?' 'Well, I'm a Jew, I play swing and I'm a minor.' He laughed out loud and could not stop laughing at this stupendous joke. The entire bar roared with him."[179] However, in March 1943, Coco Schumann was accused of failing to wear the Star of David, performing forbidden music, and seducing "Aryan" women. He was sent to Theresienstadt and from there to Auschwitz. There he survived because at the selection ramp, the SS camp physician Josef Mengele had chosen him for a work detail as a plumber. Yet he ended up playing a guitar left behind by condemned Gypsies, in one of the bands put together for the pleasure of the SS. On April 30, 1945, the day of Hitler's suicide, Coco Schumann and a few other musicians who had survived, after a harrowing death march found themselves in Bavarian Wolfratshausen, just before their final liberation by the Americans. Music had saved his life.[180]

In the end, the fate of Jews connected with German culture was no different from that of Jews in other walks of life, the same measures of discrimination and death applying to all. But there were differences of nuance. In the Third Reich, there was no Jewish equivalent of the Kulturbund in other human activities, say for those who worked in finance or former government employees. From the Gestapo's point of view, the early corralling of "culture Jews," as the Nazis derogatorily called them, made sense in view of subsequent annihilation logistics, but why they should have been singled out has still not been satisfactorily explained. To be sure, their visibility in a Nazi-controlled organization did grant the Jews opportunies for showcasing their skills, for so many of them were talented musicians, filmmakers, writers, and visual artists. Their talent could be, for certain Jews, a lifeline, insofar as they might be known abroad and therefore given a chance to emigrate. The most accomplished of them, such as Sabine Kalter and Sigmund Petruschka, actually did emigrate. They were the lucky ones. By contrast, Jewish physicians, for instance, did far worse because they were driven out of their profession by their own "Aryan" colleagues *before* the requisite legislation was in place.[181] This treatment was perhaps balanced out several years later, because these doctors had a greater chance of survival in concentration and extermination camps such as Auschwitz, where they were needed for medical duty (for example, to prevent epidemics that would also harm SS personnel).

What is so significant after a review of Kulturbund activities is that, first, apart from the logistical numbers, it was used as an instrument of chicanery by the Nazi administrators, for instance in the wake of Kristallnacht, so that even Jews who were easily placated at first must have become suspicious of Nazi intentions. Second, the sudden end of the Culture League in the fall of 1941 does point to strategic Nazi planning, as it signifies a high degree of synchronization between "Judenpolitik," the running of the war, and the calculated application of cultural activities for Germans in Germany. It was in September of that year that the Wehrmacht had come to the end of a long streak of military good fortune and, with a doomed march on Moscow in progress, to the beginning of its eventual demise. With the Jews finally out of the way, what was believed to be German culture could now be applied even more unabashedly to propaganda – propaganda content that would segue into a flood of lies by the time the Nazi leadership had nothing more to hold on to.

◆ ◆ ◆

CHAPTER FOUR

War and Public Opinion, Propaganda, and Culture

F OR THE NAZI regime the primary purpose of German culture after September 1, 1939, was to serve all branches of the war effort. This was expected to occur against the backdrop of an interaction between war events, the people's collective mood, and Goebbels's need for propaganda. As Richard J. Evans has written, propaganda was "to keep people fighting and make sure they conformed, even if only outwardly, to the demands the regime made on them."[1] Indeed, it became Goebbels's priority to watch the public frame of mind, as it was influenced by war scenarios and changing living conditions at home, and apply, as necessary, carrots and sticks of propaganda, ideally in various forms of cultural activity. These developments took place in three overlapping war phases: first, the time of conquest between the surrender of Poland and Field Marshal Rommel's finite successes in North Africa in summer 1942; second, the events before and after the defeat at Stalingrad (February 2, 1943) to the fall of Mussolini in July 1943; and finally the denouement until the German surrender of May 1945.

The German attack on Poland started on September 1, 1939, without a declaration of war, after an incident at Gleiwitz (Gliwice) radio station early in the morning was used to justify it. It was a caper worthy of the Propaganda Ministry, but it was only involved on the sidelines. Under the supervision of Reinhard Heydrich the SD had dressed Polish-speaking concentration-camp inmates in Polish army uniforms, delivered them to the Gleiwitz radio station in Upper Silesia on the border with Poland, killed them, and laid them out in such a fashion as to make them appear to be Polish attackers. An aggressive announcement in Polish was then spoken into the station's microphone, to be picked up by the German broadcast system and distributed throughout the land. Significantly, the Gleiwitz broadcast itself, as far as broadcasts go, was a cultural activity, delivered by the artistic medium of the airwaves. To all intents and purposes, the public believed "Polish aggression" and overwhelmingly was awed by Hitler's first lightning victories.[2]

Although the outbreak of war as such was not popular with the German people – in no way can it be compared to the beginning of World War I, which had caused such widespread jingoistic feeling to take hold – the people were quickly calmed by a streak of military successes. In April and May of 1940, as Denmark and Norway were overrun by the Wehrmacht and SS and the march on Paris was under way, whatever skepticism there had been turned to joy. Artists in Germany took note: "In 1940 there was a not inconsiderable euphoria," recalled the film actress Hilde Krahl, "for Germany seemed to be winning the war."[3]

Goebbels, who ultimately controlled the Gleiwitz radio station, monitored the general mood carefully from the very beginning, aiming for balance – not outbursts of fanaticism but a measured and disciplined sense of optimism.[4] Realizing that millions of regular Germans, not the social elites, bore the bulk of the burden on the military as well as home fronts, he assigned, as early as September, priority to light-entertainment programs, for instance on the radio – as he had already done in peacetime.[5] In November he defined culture unequivocally as "a sharp spiritual weapon for the war," as well as something that would console the human soul in adversity.[6] To drive his points home, Goebbels convened a group of artists in Berlin in January 1940, reminding them of "the duties of cultural creators in wartime."[7] And in July he demonstrated what this meant in practice: executives of the press, of radio and film were told to be responsible for correct reporting and portrayal, in this case, continuing to foment hatred against France, which had just been conquered.[8]

To be sure, as far as the average German was concerned, not everything was going swimmingly. From the beginning of the war, men and women complained about shortages in raw materials, goods, and food. From

September through November 1939, shoes, coal, and potatoes were in short supply, and by May of the following year the seemingly chronic scarcity of potatoes was compounded by a shortfall of eggs and leather.[9] In August 1940 the surveys of the SD substantiated the public's perception of insufficient bread rations (to be doled out using food stamps).[10] As embarrassed as Goebbels was by these deficits, all he could do was to admonish the citizens to hold back and make do with what they received, as in a sacrifice for a greater good. He usually dispensed this advice in the pages of *Das Reich*, as he did in October 1941, when the protracted deficiency of potatoes, and now also cigarettes, had to be downplayed.[11]

"Look where we are today," Himmler boasted to his wife Marga with a view to Germany's military situation in summer 1941.[12] Yet despite undeniable advances at the fronts, including the surrender of France, Belgium, and Holland, military concerns were creeping into the public mood as well. As the people vainly expected a campaign against Britain to be under way, Goebbels realized that sensationalist coverage in the media would have to give way to more sober reportage.[13] In any event, he thought that the line between public contentment and dismay was a very fine one and could easily be crossed to the downside; hence he redoubled his resolve to raise public morale and keep it high. Media such as film and theater, which were popular as never before, would help in this, and the Führer himself strongly agreed.[14] But Goebbels was becoming less certain about which approach to take in propaganda, especially concerning the changing fortunes of the military. When at the end of December 1941 he decided that the people needed "clarity and openness" in the news (rather than patriotic hyperbole), he may have realized that he had gone too far just a few weeks earlier when he had favored obfuscation in the case of the death of Ernst Udet. The celebrated General Udet, formerly of Göring's Richthofen Squadron, a World War I flying ace, former lover of Leni Riefenstahl, and the people's hero, had committed suicide in November out of frustration over the failure of the Luftwaffe against the British and on the Eastern Front; he was given a state funeral. To assuage the people's suspicion, Goebbels had wanted to camouflage his death as the result of an accident.[15]

British air raids beginning in 1940 turned out to be a major challenge to Goebbels's propaganda machine and his efforts to bolster German culture. In May the people suffered a raid over Aachen which, however modest, met with absolutely no anti-aircraft defense; a previous attack on Düsseldorf had not triggered any alarm.[16] On July 9, Goebbels dictated to his diary that there had been British air raids in western and northern Germany, "this time quite successfully, the people are furious."[17] In any case, he was now well aware that Germans in town and country wanted Britain to be bombed into submission quickly and that they wanted civilians, not military installations, to be hit. In September, for the first time, London was targeted in the "Blitz," which was welcomed as the beginning of Göring's strategic vengeance, long awaited. When in November the Luftwaffe struck Coventry and Birmingham rather effectively, the SD security service recorded even greater satisfaction among the German people, who were buoyed by graphic press and radio accounts. They were now placing bets that the most important British industrial towns would be systematically destroyed.[18]

Until mid-summer of 1942, public alarm over intensifying air raids coupled with dismay over consumer restraints forced by shortages was balanced by further military victories, Goebbels's patronizing admonitions, and soothing offerings specifically in the light-entertainment arts. In the first half of 1942 two cities were particularly hard hit by raids, first Thomas and Heinrich Mann's home town of Lübeck in the north, in March, and then, a few weeks later, Cologne in the Rhineland, close to Goebbels's birthplace of Rheydt. Lübeck suffered the highest air-raid casualties in the war so far, exceeded thereafter by Cologne, which was hit by the first 1,000-bomber raid. With regard to Lübeck, Goebbels, surely not thinking of the Mann brothers but of patrician timber framework architecture, fountains, and museums filled with Nazi art, announced that the British had made a special effort to destroy sites of culture, more precisely German culture.[19] To repeated grumblings during the spring that essential goods were chronically absent from store shelves, Goebbels replied in *Das Reich* that luxury for Germans had become out of bounds and they had better get used to bearing material shortages and deprivations.[20] Indeed, apart from consumer goods, coal for home-heating was also suffering critical bottlenecks, along with the lack of potatoes and produce; in the country, farmers were starting to complain about insufficient seeds. These conditions applied before food rations, especially in the case of potatoes, were officially cut once more. Goebbels acknowledged the hardships, but again counseled endurance, with the help of culture, "our moral and spiritual pillar and strength, during probation and success."[21]

The summer of 1942 represented something like a climax for the Reich's overall military campaign. North-western Europe and parts of the Balkans were occupied by the Axis powers, and advances in the Soviet Union were giving rise to hope. Until this time, a plan had been developed for Japanese and German troops to meet up in south-central Asia in a bold effort to invade British-controlled South Asia. The idea was to push through southern Russia into Afghanistan, to be met by German and Italian troops who would have crossed from Italian-held Libya, over the Suez Canal, into the Middle East and further. But Hitler's dream of world domination ruptured when panzer general Erwin Rommel lost the battle of El Alamein to the British general Bernard Montgomery in early November, thereby ceding territory in Egypt and effectively stalling his advance on Suez. Coterminously, the Wehrmacht's 6th Army under General Friedrich Paulus was on its way to Stalingrad: auspicious developments in the eastern theater of war, but fated to fail because of German hubris, the incompetence of their allies, and Soviet superiority.[22]

Whereas in April 1942, Goebbels, already alarmed by the Wehrmacht's adverse fortunes in the East and in North Africa, publicly gave credit to the home front for "being willing and obediently ready to do what is expected of it," in July he had to admit privately that the people were justified in lamenting the lack of foodstuffs, recognizing, in particular, that older women in Germany were in need of more cigarettes.[23] In July and August hopes were temporarily raised by the successful repulse of the Allied attack on Dieppe and what then looked like a fleet and smooth Wehrmacht movement toward Stalingrad.[24] In fact, by early September the people were counting on a quick victory in that theater, a victory that would mark a turning point in this increasingly burdensome conflict.[25] Such a victory was all the more welcome as a second harsh winter in the inhospitable East was dreaded by Wehrmacht soldiers and their loved ones back in the Reich alike.[26] All the greater was the disappointment, therefore, when further on in the month, in spite of evocative headlines on the radio and in the press, a decisive victory over the Red Army was still not materializing. Goebbels realized, as he communicated to his news staff, that once again too sensationalist a coverage of current events had been allowed to slip through. It would henceforth be mandatory to "emphasize the seriousness and severity rather than, as has been the case, breakthroughs and extensions."[27]

Despite Goebbels's constant search for balance in reporting and somehow keeping the peace on the home front, the Stalingrad campaign, accelerating after September 1942, took place at two levels: a realistic military one that was kept from the public, and a fictitious one projected on a screen of propaganda. As for reality, the Wehrmacht had entered the city on the Volga and were fighting Soviet forces there up until November, yet they were engaged with Red Army units already stationed there and in heavy hand-to-hand combat. "Streams of blood in the streets," noted Thomas Mann in his diary, who from his exile in Los Angeles was keenly following the conflagration, "much of it German."[28] By the time the Germans finally controlled almost all of the nearly destroyed city, their army had suffered huge losses. Outside Stalingrad, after regrouping, the Red Army began a concerted attack on the Wehrmacht caught within the city on November 19, and three days later, after a successful pincer operation by three Soviet army groups, Stalingrad was encircled. By January 1943, Stalin had temporarily relieved Leningrad in the north, which had been besieged by German forces since September 1941. By January 1943, also, after three months of fighting in snow and ice, the Wehrmacht in southern Russia had lost more than half a million men, either killed or wounded. Hitler, who refused General Paulus permission to break out of the city with his 6th Army, was still believing Göring's promise that Stalingrad could be well supplied from the air, with 300 tons of provisions per day, but the enfeebled Luftwaffe managed barely a third of that. And even though the Führer could not make good on his promise to send relief troops under General Erich von Manstein, he forbade Paulus to capitulate. The Soviets began invading the city on January 10, 1943, and the German forces inside were split in two. On February 2, Paulus, three days after having been promoted to field marshal by Hitler to prevent him from surrendering, capitulated on his own authority, handing over 90,000 men to the Soviets, from an army originally almost 250,000 strong. The rest had fallen or died of disease and hunger. Of those taken prisoner, most perished soon after: only 5,000 eventually made it back to Germany.[29] "Anyone who experienced Stalingrad," said Lieutenant Hans-Erdmann Schönbeck later, who had been flown out wounded in January, "was unable to believe in Hitler from there on."[30]

Goebbels knew as early as September 1942 that the people were becoming more worried because of the continuing Allied air raids and the bad turns the eastern campaign was starting to take, for letters from the front, even after being censored, were carefully scrutinized, and furloughed soldiers' stories also spread. "By and large," Goebbels noted, "the German people are aware of the fact that it will be impossible to defeat the Soviet Union militarily this fall and winter. Therefore they are getting used to the idea of a very harsh and serious winter in the East."[31] Attempting dissimulation, the minister instructed his propaganda team not to remind the German people of Stalingrad by mentioning it too often, hoping thereby it would disappear from people's minds. Instead, "new headlines" should be found and dwelled on.[32] In order to further help divert attention from the noxious focus of Stalingrad, Goebbels once again turned to the cultured media. He organized a poets' meeting in storied Weimar where he himself, putting on a positive air, gave one of his morally solidifying pep talks, in this case tailored to encourage intellectuals, which he assumed poets were, but also appealing to broader segments of the population, at least within Weimar.[33] Concurrently in *Das Reich*, he launched a think piece featuring a fictitious soldier from the front on home leave. Disingenuously, Goebbels pictured him as confronted with a reality he can hardly fathom, for civilian life is continuing almost normally. The streets and houses are clean and in good repair, streetcars and trains are running as usual, if with a few restrictions, and "cinemas, theaters, concert halls, and restaurants are open, in fact are overflowing." Seeing this, the soldier cannot acknowledge that anyone has any reason to complain; what may irk the civilian appears as but a trifle to him.[34]

Keeping up the propaganda screen upon which to project something positive, however duplicitous, became more difficult for Goebbels after the demise of the Wehrmacht at Stalingrad in November. Therefore, as Jay Baird has explained, Goebbels, rather than saying anything at all, preferred to make no public mention of that crisis; Nazi propaganda "completely ignored the Soviet encirclement of Stalingrad."[35] Only on January 13, 1943, three days after the Red Army had begun to pour into the city and tension at home had become unbearable, did Goebbels and Hitler agree that the German public had to be told something, that the veil of secrecy surrounding the terrible events so far somehow had to be lifted.[36] For both men were realizing that on the basis of whatever news they had, the German people were beginning to doubt not only the army's fortunes in the East, but decisions taken by the senior leadership as well. Some were asking detailed questions, such as: Why was Stalingrad not evacuated while there was still time? Why was the Red Army's strength so obviously underestimated? Why was its pincer-movement offensive of last November not detected? Would Stalingrad not become "a turning point in the war" and, worse, if Germany lost the war would this not result in the Reich's complete collapse? Not surprisingly, in certain regions of the country the SD recorded evidence of a deep feeling of depression.[37] The "Hitler Myth," so durable during peacetime, was in danger of dissolution.

By the end of January news dispensed cautiously by the official media, regarding the 90,000 men handed over to the Soviets, had already overwhelmed some citizens, although the leadership was withholding the last letters out of Stalingrad for delivery to loved ones' homes, in order to keep the exact circumstances of the defeat hidden and manipulate public opinion further.[38] Goebbels, in close cahoots with Hitler, was considering how to ward off possible emotional and physical reactions by desperate Volksgenossen in urban and agricultural settings, as they gradually realized the enormity of the eastern catastrophe. Thus the minister and his Führer went on the offensive themselves, creating the "Myth of Stalingrad" that ignored certain facts and instead falsified others, ultimately declaring that each soldier in that endeavor had died a hero's death, as a gift to the German people who were invited to emulate their sacrifice. (That Paulus and tens of thousands of his men had walked into Siberian captivity without a fight was scrupulously suppressed.)[39] The whole tragic event was stylized as, technically, a military defeat yet a moral victory for the German people and their political leadership, who had been offered and would accept lessons from Valhalla's gods over the direction of their lives in future. Even on January 31, two days before the official capitulation on February 2, Goebbels published a photograph of five Wehrmacht grenadiers in *Das Reich*, shrouded in white fatigues, as they worked their way through a snow-covered ditch at a location near Stalingrad, giving the impression that, as the newspaper claimed, they were "ready for counter-attack."[40]

Immediately after the surrender Goebbels made certain that no "mourning, sentimentality, or brashness" would set in, for, instead, the heroism of Führer, Wehrmacht, and Volk had to be celebrated. The cultural media were essential for this. For three days, but no longer, a national memorial would be held, with appropriately serious music on the airwaves, while theaters, cinemas,

179

and light-entertainment venues were closed. These measures were carefully designed: "The entire German propaganda will have to generate a myth from the heroism of Stalingrad, which will form a most precious part of future German history."[41] Indeed, as far as the public was concerned, these measures seem to have had their desired effect. In Berlin, the teenager Barbara Felsmann noted in her diary: "This week, there was mourning for our heroes at Stalingrad, from Wednesday to Saturday. There were no movies, no theater, and no entertainment whatsoever." But just a day later: "Today is Sunday and I visited Inge Schulz. We sauntered down Frankfurter Allee and then went to the Ufa movie and saw a very pretty film with Marika Rökk and Viktor Staal; it was *Hab mich lieb*. Back home again at 7:30."[42] The dispassionate matter-of-factness of these sentences was a testimony to Goebbels's propaganda skills. For now, his calculating strategy was working.

In the following days, Goebbels endeavored to build on the newly created Stalingrad myth. He extolled the heroism of the fallen men and declared them the historic European vanguard against the steppe. Their sacrifice was a textbook model, their "deepest tragedy" possessed the power to forge greater reserves for the German future. Stalingrad had the ingredients for a national object lesson of the highest calibre, and cultural activities had to assist in such a transformation.[43] Already a week after Paulus's capitulation Hitler had agreed that musical concerts, film, and theater were more necessary than ever. Because, as he told his minister, "if we now cause our cultural life to fall down, the people will lapse into a state of gray hopelessness."[44]

Goebbels's further guidance of his people was supported by the insinuation that a national heroic sacrifice such as occurred at Stalingrad would create the necessary will for endurance, coupled with a supreme hope in the future potential of Nazi arms and resources, including new offensives. For such an outcome, leading to ultimate victory, the full cooperation of all men and women at the home front was essential. This was the tenor of his famous Sportpalast address, "Do You Want Total War?," which became a major media event, piped into every German household with at least one receiver. Goebbels performed like a 1960s rock star, his voice rising to a crescendo at the climax, as his rhetorical questions and screaming acclamations brought the stadium down at the finale. To be on the safe side, he had ordered claques to mix in additional responses such as claps and shouts of approbation along with the audience's shouts, all through amplifiers and loudspeakers, and extra Promi staff had been ordered to appear. But the fanaticism of his listeners was genuine, "suddenly they all let themselves go, screamed, stamped in approval, flailed their arms. The racket was unbearable," recalled Goebbels's secretary Brunhilde Pomsel.[45]

In the aftermath of the speech, the public mood was positive, and the political as much as the military leadership seemed to have been inspired with a new confidence.[46] Goebbels, fully cognizant of the power of repetition in propaganda, reiterated his main points in *Das Reich* articles and on the radio, in order to keep morale high.[47] This lasted until the defeat of the Axis armies at Tunis and Bizerte early in May 1943, with Goebbels trying to make light of the Wehrmacht's loss of the North African position later in the month, as public expectations were again subsiding.[48] On July 10, American, British, and Canadian forces landed in Sicily.

Then, from Mussolini's fall in July until the formal capitulation on May 8, 1945, the Third Reich experienced an uninterrupted series of disasters that, try as they might, Goebbels's propaganda mavens found impossible to gloss over, let alone explain. In the absence of positive occurrences, it would become increasingly difficult for the minister himself to invent credible subterfuges; his appeal to heroic communal sacrifice after Stalingrad simply was not working. For example, there was no overlooking the shortages of civilian supplies, which had plagued the Reich for years. A new cut in meat rations after the defeat at Tunis, as Goebbels admitted to himself, was as unpopular as it was necessary.[49] This was compounded in June 1943 by renewed deficiencies in fruits and vegetables, resulting in long queues of housewives as ugly reminders to the authorities.[50] Late in July the regime decreed a reduction of tobacco supplies for the Reich population as a whole in favor of consumers in the heavily bombed west of the country, further creating ill will in the rest of Germany.[51] At the same time, British air raids were seen as being responsible for a dearth in textiles, as transport avenues such as railways had been bombed.[52] Although by October Goebbels had announced more generous Christmas rations, a month later the people were smarting under a renewed lack of produce, in particular potatoes again.[53] These difficulties persisted through 1944, when, in April of that year, the journalist Ursula von Kardorff still spotted idle spendthrifts making a show of conspicuous consumption in Berlin – something Goebbels had been harping on about for months. Kardorff, who earlier had supported the Nazis, now found it necessary to criticize the regime, and this would not be the last time.[54]

Incremental air raids and their consequences made the situation for Germans worse, especially in urban areas. In January 1943, as the Stalingrad disaster loomed, Berlin withstood its first truly serious air attack by the Allies, and then again in early March.[55] In June, Krefeld in the Rhineland was hit, Goebbels being aware that people were now seriously questioning the role of Göring in the air war and doubting Hitler's competence even more.[56] In July the Germans, including Goebbels, were horrified by the terrible fire-bombing of Hamburg, with a loss of 40,000 lives.[57] Although German citizens were furious especially with the British (who specialized in bombings at nighttime), and were ready to lynch individual pilots who had parachuted from their stricken planes, their anger also targeted the Nazi leadership, namely Göring, for having reneged on the earlier, oft-repeated, promise of "vengeance."[58] Two additional black days came for Berlin on November 22 and 23, when 776 Royal Air Force bombers attacked, enveloping the entire city in a ball of fire and setting asphalt aflame. Cultural hallmarks were hit, such as the legendary Romanisches Café where formerly artists had met, the giant revue palace Scala and numerous concert venues, to say nothing of cinemas and theaters. Von Kardorff came upon bodies of people trapped in residential cellars, charred beyond recognition.[59] By 1944, moreover, the Allies had found ways to destroy sites further to the east in Germany, using bombers with a greater range; hence Nuremberg of Nazi lore was struck on January 2, 1945, and Dresden on February 13 and 14, when 25,000 people perished in a firestorm. On February 9 the cultural town of Weimar was also bombed. Hundreds of lives were lost, while the Goethe Museum, the Schiller House, and the iconic Herder Church of St. Peter and Paul were all severely damaged.[60]

On the military fronts since summer 1943, there was steady deterioration, which Goebbels largely acknowledged privately, while still attempting to suggest victory to his flock publicly. Hence, while he conceded on July 17 that Germans were justified in deploring the difficulties on the Eastern Front, and two days later even remarked to himself that this was the first time in the war that Wehrmacht summer offensives had not been successful, on July 25, using his favorite broadsheet, he again pointed to Wehrmacht feats in Sicily and Russia.[61] The SD's sobering judgment in November was that contrary to what Goebbels's propaganda units were reporting from the theater of war, the army was constantly retreating from the Eastern Front and U-boats were failing to attack enemy ships.[62]

The Allies' early successes on French soil after D-Day, June 6, 1944, further depressed the German public mood.[63] By this time Goebbels believed he had a new effective propaganda weapon in the shape of the V-1 rocket, which raised hopes among Germans that retribution against Britain was finally at hand.[64] It was seemingly perverse that the assassination attempt on Hitler on July 20 briefly restored some sympathy for the regime; the average German's individual bonds to the Führer were strong, however.[65] This notwithstanding, disappointment set in again after the rockets proved ineffectual, even as improved miracle weapons were being announced.[66] Public opinion regarding a German Final Victory sank to a new low in August, when the Allies invaded the South of France. The fall of Paris later that month further dismayed the German home front, for by now it was clear that the complete occupation of their country by the enemy was only a matter of time.[67] Ursula von Kardorff, still writing for her Nazi-controlled newspaper in Berlin, showed herself doubtful that new V-rockets that had apparently been ordered would be able to make a difference. Few people could have believed Goebbels, when at Christmas 1944 he assured readers of *Das Reich* that in the foreseeable future victory would drop into the lap of the German people "like a ripe fruit."[68]

By late summer 1943, Goebbels was beginning to lose the effectiveness of his cultural-political ploys. Whereas until this time he had thought he had ample reason to gloat over the positive reception his articles in *Das Reich* were receiving from the people – richly documented in venal diary entries – SD analysts of public opinion told him in September to think again.[69] Two lead articles of his in August that had hewed to the old theme of defiance and proclaimed near victory had been found fallacious, an obvious attempt at deception of the home front. According to the SD, which was run by Himmler who disliked Goebbels, the minister's contributions had been publicly discussed "in a spirit of aversion. He has frequently aroused hopes before, hopes that to date remain unfulfilled."[70]

Hitting on *Das Reich* was significant because it was Goebbels's personal mouthpiece, arguably the most important of the minister's media weapons, one which had a history of high credibility within Germany, if not abroad.

As the war progressed, Goebbels found it less feasible to utilize cinemas, theaters, concert halls, opera houses, and light-entertainment venues to the same degree he had been able before, because of constant bombings and the resultant loss of civilian life, logistical complications, and the need for more personnel to serve actively at the fronts. Therefore, after the assassination attempt on the Führer in July 1944, and as Goebbels was now general plenipotentiary for total war, with "the widest powers to move and direct the civilian population," he decreed full closure of public cultural institutions effective September 1 of that year. Excepted were some films, the broadcasting of censored news and carefully tailored music offerings, and selected newspapers, such as *Das Reich*, for the continued dissemination of propaganda. This decision also met with a mixed reception among the people.[71]

Goebbels long ago had become cynical, not least about the artists in the Reich themselves. The man who had loved being lionized in their midst at normal times, dismissed artists outright in one of his last diary entries. "I am very discontented with their political attitude," he wrote on March 30, 1945. "But it would be wrong to expect brave conduct from them. After all, they are artists, meaning totally unaffected by things political, not to say devoid of character."[72] Clearly, Goebbels's insight was tantamount to a confession that propaganda by now had lost its edge as a pliant tool with which to manipulate the German people, and this stood in direct relation to the mounting losses at the fronts on the one hand, and the progressive deterioration of quality of life for civilian Germans on the other.

MOVIES FOR GUIDANCE, INDOCTRINATION, AND DISTRACTION

After September 1939, Goebbels saw himself vindicated in believing that film was "one of the best instruments to lead the people," not to be underestimated as "a means of education," particularly in war.[73] Indeed, it could not have escaped him that more and more, German men, women, and teenagers were filling cinemas in town and country.

The films produced by Goebbels's movie factories during the war thematically lacked the martyrology of the Time-of-Struggle productions at the beginning of the regime. The new purpose now was to condition the people to endure war and war-related experiences, all in a spirit of belief in a greater imperialist idea and self-sacrifice for the leadership's militarist aims. As before 1939, with the movie industry's help, the "Führer Myth" had to be upheld. However, the minister was fooling himself if he thought the people visited the movies to receive political instruction or to be educated; in the first years of the war they went to relax after strenuous work in the consumer or the war economy, and even before Stalingrad they went to escape the ever more dreadful realities of air raids, loss of loved ones at the fronts, and an impending defeat. Yet escapism was exactly what Goebbels did not want the people to engage in; at all times they were to refresh themselves in body and soul, in order to sustain ever greater challenges. Hitler's alleged heroism was to be a model.

In his diaries during the war years Goebbels rejoiced over the fact that movie theaters were increasingly popular, even, astoundingly, after heavy air raids. He himself did everything to help this development along; in devastated areas after 1942 he used mobile film stations, and where it was possible, provisional cinemas were erected over the rubble of bombed-out ones, such as in Berlin. In addition, in large cities film screenings were reduced to one a day, starting in the mornings or at noon, which meant, however, that some working people had to miss out.[74] Still, Goebbels deceived himself as to the real extent of the damage done to the film distribution infrastructure, for even at the end of 1944 he thought that film screenings were still in the ascendance.[75] In reality, they were down. Film attendance had risen from almost 624 million viewers in 1938 to just over 892 million in 1941, then rose to its highest point of 1,116 million in 1943, but from thereon fell off. The number of theaters increased from 5,446 in 1938 to 7,043 in 1941 and stood at 6,561 in 1943, only to decrease palpably one year later.[76]

As for quality, Goebbels, having recognized only a relative degree of progress in filmmaking during the six years after the beginning of Nazi rule, was of the opinion that there had been some improvements made by mid-December 1939. In one of the rarer instances of cultural decision-making in wartime, Hitler now proved him wrong by pointing to severe deficiencies with the film industry in a meeting, which was also attended by Alfred Rosenberg, who was positively brimming with schadenfreude.[77] Gritting his teeth, Goebbels had to resign himself to the possibility that the movie-buff Führer was correct and henceforth he tried to implement even more changes. This was difficult, for after all, the Third Reich had failed in the task of promoting genuine talent, lacking, as Hitler had not failed to notice, young geniuses in the arts, especially National Socialist arts. In the years ahead, Hitler was to be proven right. Witness, for example, the mass of inferior Nazi-inspired film scripts that Goebbels reviewed, and the absence of strikingly talented new film professionals, Nazi or not: all this stood in stark contrast to the Weimar Republic. Although by 1943 Goebbels had reached a certain level of satisfaction with his film professionals in Babelsberg, Vienna, and Munich, he saw himself constantly engaged in "reform."[78] Among directors, he most praised Veit Harlan and Wolfgang Liebeneiner, approving their advancement to professor status, but they had been rising stars already in the republic; and among actors he loved Werner Krauss, Heinrich George, and Emil Jannings, who had been pillars of the Weimar establishment and were opportunistic turncoats as Nazis. There were a few hopefuls among the young males, such as Horst Caspar and Joachim Gottschalk, but they were anything but Nazi-minded. Caspar was one-quarter Jewish, and Gottschalk killed himself in November 1941, along with his Jewish wife and son, who had been scheduled for deportation.[79] Among young women, it was even less certain who would emerge with eternal star power, especially because Goebbels was in the habit of making actresses out of nubile playmates. There were several who were "discovered," not because they had graduated from an acting academy or had prior experience on the stage, but because they were employed in a related branch of the film industry and then got noticed. One was the irresistibly attractive, seventeen-year-old Margot Hielscher, who worked as a costume designer for Terra Film in 1936, before she was chosen for her first small role, alongside Zarah Leander, in the anti-British film *Das Herz der Königin* (*The Heart of a Queen*), in 1940. According to my conversation with Hielscher in the 1980s, in order to seduce her, Goebbels had told her that she reminded him of Vivien Leigh (she rather wanted to be Katharine Hepburn), and then invited her to a secret trysting place; whether he was eventually successful with her was not divulged.[80] Clearly, by prioritizing other qualities over talent, Goebbels and his staff had made a mistake, and their film academy, founded in 1938 under Liebeneiner, went to pot. Whatever factor he himself acknowledged – toward the end of his life Goebbels had to admit defeat in the film business.[81]

Replacing "martyrology," the new guide word for war was now "heroism." One of the first films singling out soldiers as heroes, who would create more Lebensraum, at the same time portrayed Germans behind the front, at home, at what the Nazis always liked to call the "home front," and showed organic ties between civilians and warriors. The film, made in 1940, was entitled *Wunschkonzert* (*Request Concert*), after a famous and long-running radio program initiated in October 1939, on which listeners back home communicated with troops in the field, conveying greetings to and fro and fulfilling musical wish lists. *Wunschkonzert* starred the nineteen-year-old Dutch-German ingénue Ilse Werner, the niece of a senior SS general. She later, typically, maintained that she had been drawn into the "giant, all-encompassing propaganda machinery" willy-nilly, starring in the film as Inge Wagner, the love interest of two Wehrmacht officers; one of them, Herbert Koch (played by Carl Raddatz) – who later gets his girl – she meets at the Berlin Olympics.[82] The movie cleverly showed footage from Riefenstahl's documentary with Hitler at the stadium (his only appearance in a feature film). Rather than being able to marry Inge in 1936, Herbert is sent on a mission with the Condor Legion to Spain, and after September 1939 fights on the German military fronts, always without seeing Inge; she nevertheless, incredulously, remains true to him. Intermittently, Herbert meets a comrade who is a rival for Inge's affections, and there is a young music teacher who, as a soldier in France, plays the church organ, that king of instruments, in a place his lost company is supposed to find. During that performance, the organist is killed by an enemy grenade but saves his comrades. Heroism was shown to triumph. The film, including a corny song by the operatic bass-baritone Wilhelm Strienz, was extremely popular because it highlighted scenes of victory for the German armed forces (including U-boats and aircraft); it succeeded, for the time being, in bonding civilians at the home front to the soldiers, with whose constant victories, exemplified in the film itself as well as during its run at movie theaters, the public could easily identify. The main theme was to be taken seriously: soldiering takes precedence over civilian life, and in war as well as at the home front, the völkisch community subsumes the individual. A special message was issued to women, to be repeated untold times during coming feature films: their individual happiness had to take second place, as their soldier husbands or boyfriends had to leave them behind, in search of Germany's greater military and political goals, but for the future benefit of all.[83]

Pictures were an important vehicle for hammering home to civilians their priorities during wartime: fighting and the art of military combat took precedence over women and love interests. The film *Stukas* (1941), directed by Karl Ritter, like Udet and Göring the veteran of a World War I flying squad, exemplified this function. The movie dealt with the early World War II career of several members of the Luftwaffe corps, one of them a physician. When they are not in the air lustily performing stunts, they are not chasing girls but attending the Bayreuth Festival and, unbelievably, playing passages from Wagner's *Götterdämmerung*, arranged for four hands, on a piano, even in the open air. (The pronouncedly anti-Semitic Ritter was distantly related through his father-in-law to Wagner's brother Albert.) Here, very pointedly, women are pushed into the background; at the end, Nurse Ursula, who accompanies an aviator to a Bayreuth showing, is aghast that her date wants to leave the performance early in order to rejoin his squadron. But since *Wunschkonzert* had already come out half a year earlier and Germany is currently victorious on all fronts, the nurse will surely understand – as will the audience – what the priorities are.[84] Apart from acrobatics in the air, this film distinguished itself by "hand-in-hand synergy of music and warfare," German music serving as the epitome of culture throughout the world.[85]

Other contemporary films endeavored to celebrate male gallantry in combat for what it was, to the exclusion of all females, as well as hinting at plausible enemy targets.[86] As military activity became more extended, however, German propaganda found it increasingly necessary to identify Germany's main enemies more specifically for the public. Hence *Heimkehr* (*Homecoming*) was made, and released by October 1941, a movie starring Carl Raddatz (Ilse Werner's officer heart-throb in *Wunschkonzert* and one of the Wagnerian aviators from *Stukas*) and Paula Wessely. This propaganda film set out to vilify the Poles and, as the occasion presented itself, malign Yiddish-speaking Eastern Jews as well. The thirty-four-year-old Wessely, a Reinhardt seminar graduate and long established on German-speaking stages and in film, played Maria Thomas, who becomes the heroic leader of a troupe of Volksdeutsche after their men are incapacitated, ethnic Germans long settled in Poland and, in this film, victimized by the Polish majority just days before Hitler's invasion of the country. Escaping certain death only by accident in the area of Lemberg (Lwów), Maria is credited with having lifted the Germans' morale to the greatest heights in adversity and for having faced off Poles and Jews. The film not only spelled out for the German viewing public who was, for the time being, external Enemy Number One, but also neatly demonstrated German woman's role as helpmate to her men (in this case, Maria's fiancé is murdered and her father blinded, as she courageously perseveres). Wessely, who devoted extraordinary energy in character-acting for that movie, was never asked about this xenophobic part after the war, as she was set to begin her second stellar career in the German movie world.[87]

Emil Jannings was the star of a film stereotyping Great Britain as the new enemy, for the Germans were having a difficult time bombarding it into submission. Not without imagination, the Promi used Britain's alleged role in the Boer War of 1899–1902 to sully the national character, in this case by accusing Britain of land-grabbing and construing an ethnic and moral affinity between the largely Dutch and German-related Boers and main-stream Germans. The main message the Nazis wanted to convey in the film, *Ohm Krüger* (*Uncle Krüger*, 1941), was that the British had invented the concentration camps, because archetypes of these camps had been used to intern women and children of Boer families, whose men were meeting other, more terrible, fates elsewhere.[88]

To win its arguments, the Promi situated the film within a larger propaganda effort to discredit the British on human-rights grounds. This was done through the use of documentary evidence, difficult to verify, relating to the South African conflict. In 1940 the Promi's official Dr. Wilhelm Ziegler, a specialist on the "Jewish Question," had published a coffee-table-sized collection of documents regarding the Boer War, including the German translation of a report by the early English human-rights advocate Emily Hobhouse, whose original of 1901 she had authored for perusal by the British Parliament. Ziegler reproduced, in a disturbing German facsimile version of that original, what Hobhouse had experienced, in the "concentration camp" of Bloemfontein: "Next, a girl of twenty-one lay dying on a stretcher. The father, a big, gentle Boer, kneeling beside her; while, next tent, his wife was watching a child of six, also dying, and one of about five drooping. Already this couple had lost three children in the hospital, and so would not let these go, though I begged hard to take them out of the hot tent."[89] Germans who read this account and other testimonies of inhumanity in 1940 were well conditioned to accept anything else that the movie starring Jannings was ready to impart to them about British atrocities.

Emil Jannings played Paul Krüger in the film, the retired Boer president awaiting his end in a Swiss sanatorium and, in retrospect, telling his story of events. Jannings protested immediately after World War II to Klaus Mann that he had taken on Krüger's role "against my will, merely under pressure," and only "after a special order" issued by Goebbels.[90] This was yet another attempt at whitewashing, for it had been Jannings himself, an early acolyte of Hitler and Goebbels, who had suggested the making of such a film some-time in the past.[91] Indeed, in 1943 he explained that he had wanted to portray Krüger as a man who had "commenced a struggle that was being completed in our time," and ultimately, in order to expose "the methodology of British territorial aggrandizement."[92] Goebbels had accepted Jannings's proposal with enthusiasm and rewarded the star richly during the making of the film, a production largely controlled by Jannings himself.[93]

This movie, highly profitable, attained its political goal of inveigling the population against the English, giving further rise to hopes for a successful invasion.[94] Apart from anti-British bile, the film advocated the Great-Man theory of history through its biography of the heroic (and German-rooted) Krüger, an approach already attempted in pre-war genres, such as *Der Herrscher*, with obvious allusions to Hitler. There were several more such films during the war, ideally using two historic models: Bismarck and, also well tried before, the Prussian King Frederick II (customarily called the Great).

The film about Bismarck's dismissal as imperial chancellor in 1890 appeared at a time when Germany's military fortunes were at a crisis point, in 1942; Hitler's supreme-command decisions were to be accepted in a way that Bismarck's foreign-policy directives had not been, and, as history's nemesis, Kaiser Wilhelm's subsequent policies had led to the disaster of World War I.[95] So in *Die Entlassung* (*The Dismissal*), with Liebeneiner as director, Jannings again played the main role of Bismarck, whose greatness would be shown as through a prism right at the end of his career. This was an artistic twist on which Goebbels prided himself, as he eschewed showing Bismarck's whole life through a biographical sketch. Reflections during Bismarck's last three days or so as chancellor, until 1890, thought Goebbels, would drive the main points of this great personality home for all.[96] The redoubtable Werner Hinz played Kaiser Wilhelm II, and Werner Krauss was the *éminence grise* in the Foreign Ministry, Secret Councillor Friedrich von Holstein, remembered by historians as a sinister figure. Krauss felt qualified for this part, because, as he said later, he was good at portraying demons, Shakespeare's Shylock, for instance, and, one might add, the various

Jews he impersonated in the film *Jud Süss*. Demon or Jew, said Krauss, after his "Shylock" everyone could picture for himself "what the Jew would look like, should he ever come back."[97] Patting himself on the back, when the film was completed in June 1942, Goebbels thought it was "a work of art of the very first order."[98]

As difficult as it would have been always to coordinate cultural matters with current events, the Nazis did attempt this in order to get full use out of their propaganda potential. Where they succeeded was around early summer of 1942 (just before the time of *Die Entlassung*), when Harlan produced his film about Frederick II's fortunes in battle during the Seven Years War (1756–63), which he had started by attacking Saxony but soon had Maria Theresa of Austria opposing him. For military historians the significance of his campaigns was that against all odds, especially after defeat by the Russians and Austrians at Kunersdorf in early 1759, he had won this war, retaining territory he had acquired earlier. He won it after disagreements with his marshals, especially General Friedrich August von Finck following the defeat at Maxen (1759), when Finck was cashiered and he was replaced as supreme commander by Frederick himself.[99] This served as the blueprint for Goebbels's main themes in *Der grosse König* (*The Great King*) of 1942, in which the highlights and low points of Frederick's seven years of heroic strife were retold. The film was supposed to inspire the German armed forces, and with them, all news-sharing civilians at home, with a redoubled belief in Hitler, after the Wehrmacht had had to concede defeat in its months-long siege of Moscow in the first half of December 1941, and Hitler's supreme position had been somewhat shaken by severe disagreements with his generals. Among those had been aces such as Franz Halder and Heinz Guderian, Fedor von Bock and Erich Hoepner. In fact, Hitler had not only dismissed Hoepner from his tank command post at the Russian front, as he had Guderian, he had even thrown him out of the Wehrmacht. Moreover, he had replaced General Walther von Brauchitsch, as chief of the army (OKH), with himself.[100] The movie, although it pleased Hitler and Goebbels because of the obvious parallels with Frederick's destiny, was not popular with the German officer caste, especially the generals, and it annoyed the Austrians among them, Frederick's historic foes.

This film about Frederick II, starring Otto Gebühr, who had played him in previous filmic homilies about the rapacious Prussian ruler, was to serve as a reminder, especially to the Wehrmacht officer corps, that the Führer knew best as supreme commander, even as he was seemingly held up by adversity. Way and above any other personality, Frederick was the figure in human history with whom Hitler identified the most, as pictures of the Prussian king everywhere in his surroundings demonstrated. Frederick was suited to show – as did Gebühr in the film – not just the leader's uncanny wisdom, his infallibility in the face of the greatest risks, but also the human isolation he had to suffer as the greatest price for his genius. At the same time, Frederick was portrayed as a ruler dearly loving his people, much as Hitler himself claimed to be advancing the destiny of his people.[101]

Around 1941, eugenic issues came to the fore in Germany, demanding propagandistic amplification. Film would serve such purposes well. Hence *Friedemann Bach* of 1941 featured another Great Man in the background, yet it was meant to teach the Nazi ideological lesson that physically degenerate persons were unfit to live. In the movie, Wilhelm Friedemann Bach is the weakling son of his mighty father Johann Sebastian, more than metaphorically hovering over him, a man of great talent who is fated to perish due to bad genes somewhere in his ancestry, abetted by an unfavorable environment (migrant artists; debauched court). That he was portrayed by Gustaf Gründgens, who in spite of his ambiguous sexuality was employed in Göring's Staatstheater at the sufferance of the Prussian Minister President, today strikes one ironically, but on screen Gründgens served well to illustrate the regime's cause.[102]

The necessity of ridding the Volksgemeinschaft of lives unworthy of living was exemplified even more strongly in *Ich klage an* (*I Accuse*) of summer 1941, co-scripted and directed by Liebeneiner, as news of the Nazi euthanasia program had filtered through to the population. Virtually every citizen had a family member in an asylum with an inherited disorder such as manic depression or hereditary deafness who could be slated for "mercy-killing," or knew someone in their circle of acquaintances who was affected. The killing program initiated in 1939 by the Reich chancellery head, Goebbels's friend Philipp Bouhler, had officially been stopped by 1941, but it continued surreptitiously. Hence Goebbels had Liebeneiner make a film in which the wife of a physician falls ill with multiple sclerosis and, after asking for it, is administered a toxin by her husband. He thereupon is taken to court by his best friend, also a doctor. The principles of the case are argued hither and yonder before judges with the ultimate aim of persuading the public of the benefits, albeit harshness, of killing the seriously disabled.[103] Paul Hartmann, Mathias Wieman, and Heidemarie Hatheyer, all future stars of West German film, acted in this movie with great dedication, which Liebeneiner's widow Hilde Krahl in 1998 disarmingly declared to have been a contribution to the question not of forced killing but "assisted suicide."[104] By January 1942, after extensive showing in the entire Reich, the SD reported a consensus among the majority of Germans, who approved in principle "that people severely suffering from non-curable diseases be led to a quicker death, by way of legal directives."[105] As if in a totalitarian dictatorship of Hitler's making, public approval was still necessary, and "legal directives" mandatory!

The place of women in a militarized Reich became another important topic for the German film industry after 1939. There were differing viewpoints to be reconciled. The earlier theme of woman as comrade to the male was continued, but in a modified form. Women also went on to be seen as child-bearing vessels; hence sexuality was stressed within that context. But since soldiers were increasingly viewed as men entitled to sexual diversions apart from procreation, both male and female sexual types seeking affairs were portrayed, usually to the advantage of men. This approach did not necessarily single out the pre-war figure of the vamp in film, such as Zarah Leander might have played it, but concentrated on unmarried and sometimes married young women who were willing to give themselves to soldiers, in happy subordination. The propaganda makers were often on thin ice here, because extramarital relations between soldiers and German women were in danger of destroying marriages and the conventional family, an outcome the Nazi leadership officially frowned upon.[106]

The multitude of films featuring girls and mature women after 1939 reflected those, often conflicting, concerns, ultimately leaving the women to suffer. In *Auf Wiedersehen, Franziska* (*Good Bye, Franziska*, 1941), by Helmut Käutner, later vaunted in West Germany, Marianne Hoppe portrayed a single woman who becomes the mistress to a roving war photographer. Nonetheless, even after he has married her and become a father, he will not permanently settle down. He roams the world, seeking adventures in photography, armed conflict, and sex, until finally he has had enough, consenting to stay at home with his wife in Berlin. However, as soon as

Hitler's war has broken out, he is called to the front, leaving Franziska, once more, alone, yet quite contented with her man's new role. Having accepted the part of the understanding wife, she will wait faithfully for the return of her soldier husband from the front.[107] She is assisting him to serve the war effort in the same way that Hanna Holberg is helping her pilot fiancé serve his squadron in *Die grosse Liebe* (*The Great Love*) of 1942 (or Ilse Werner's character is waiting for her officer in *Wunschkonzert*). The fact that Leander played Holberg, a nightclub singer, hinted at excitement: the demi-monde of light entertainment and casual sex rather than a domestically fortified, conventional relationship, particularly since the pilot first gets to know her via a one-night stand (in *Franziska*, in a similar mode, it is the woman who seduces the man during their first night, another throwback to the titillating vamp motif). Beyond the scenes of risqué sexuality, the women in both films will settle down and wait demurely for their men, for the commencement of a normal, boring civil union (and, consequentially, pure-"Aryan" brood).[108] But women as playmates for the fighting men on furlough, without reference to existing or future marriages, were also shown, for example in *Zwei in einer grossen Stadt* (*Two in a Big City*, 1942), in which two uniformed buddies meet a pair of willing girls randomly in Berlin, to enjoy them in scenes of frolicking and intimacy, with the full consent of the film-going public. Apart from the sexual element, the film constituted a huge entertainment asset, for soldiers and civilians alike, of the kind Goebbels wanted his subjects to benefit from for their future endurance.[109]

Women in Nazi-made films continued to be effective for sheer entertainment, as they had been before the war. After 1939, however, light-entertainment movies were even more important as instruments of diversion, in line with Goebbels's idea of recreational activities in order to brave bombardments and the loss of loved ones at the front. A typical film of this kind, with that underhanded political purpose, was *Kora Terry* starring Marika Rökk, of 1940, which, with its revue-cum-adventure plot, could have been made in the 1920s.[110] *Baron Münchhausen*, released in 1943, was a post-Stalingrad effort lavishly made in color (only the second German color film on the screens), shown when aerial bombing was intensifying dramatically. One could get lost in the dream world of Baron Münchhausen's poetic lies during this over-length film if one allowed escapism to prevail; from today's perspective it is doubtful whether it fortified Germans' nerves to boost their morale, as Goebbels had intended this kind of film to do.[111]

The truth is that any films shown after the middle of that fateful year of 1943 had been designed with certain defeat in mind, as Goebbels himself must have known very well before Stalingrad that the war was lost. A movie such as Harlan's *Kolberg*, patterned on the Napoleonic Wars, during which Prussian armies fought against fierce odds, only to be victorious in the War of Liberation, was conceived by the minister as early as 1942, made at great cost and finally shown in March 1945, when no one in the Reich could still be encouraged to hold fast.[112] Perhaps cynically, Goebbels allowed the film *Die Degenhardts* to be released in 1944, presenting a Berlin family that made do in very dire straits, somehow hoping to survive the chaos everywhere.[113] It is claimed, but not proven, that Goebbels himself had had a hand in scripting the book for the last film ever made in Nazi Germany, *Das Leben geht weiter* (*Life Goes On*), which was never completed for popular consumption. It documented the breakdown, under air raids, of a group of Berlin apartment dwellers, during the last weeks of existence in the capital, possibly intended to spread solace, hinting at survival. By some accounts Liebeneiner continued making the film (starring his wife Hilde Krahl) against all hope, because he knew it could keep him and his colleagues from being deployed much more dangerously in the war effort. He kept "filming" when he knew the cameras were running empty. After May 1945, bits and pieces of celluloid were found, documents of a Nazi film empire broken asunder, but not enough material for this particular work to be pieced together and resurrected in the studios.[114]

Although German film audiences continued to rush to the cinemas until the very end, where they still existed, in order to escape an oppressive world around them, German films became ever more flawed, vessels with flimsy content that failed to convince the public that a heroic Final Victory would be in sight. Women, adolescents, and old men alike were becoming more suspicious of the discrepancy between propaganda and reality, as enemy bombs, especially in built-up areas, continued destroying dwellings and livelihoods, often causing many deaths. Front-line soldiers on furlough, when they attended the films, found a much-needed change of atmosphere but invariably told their civilian neighbors that reality out there, in the war, was horrifyingly different from the dreams Goebbels was continuously delivering to them.

THE COMMUNICATION ARTS: RADIO, PRESS, AND NEWSREELS

At the beginning of the war Goebbels remarked that newsreels were a "propaganda weapon of the first degree," the main area of applied culture, in fact, that Hitler chose to take an active interest in during the course of the conflict.[115] An innovation of World War II in the mass communications field, newsreels were produced by so-called Propaganda-Kompanien or PK (propaganda companies); they were far superior to prototypes in World War I and surpassed, in type and scope, anything the Third Reich's enemies could come up with. The Wehrmacht's propaganda companies secured news footage from the military fronts that radio and press could feed on, but their main task was to supply material for the weekly newsreels preceding every feature film.

The four extant private newsreel companies had been centralized for better content control in the Promi by May 1935; this proved to be a boon some fifteen months later when the Olympic summer games could be the focus of attention and, apart from Leni Riefenstahl's efforts, exploited for Goebbels's own propaganda purposes.[116] When by the summer of 1938 German-Czech tensions rose over the question of the Sudetenland, the regime leaders' interest in newsreels increased, and by the fall the Propaganda-Kompanien were created. This meant sending news experts – journalists, photographers, cameramen – to all three branches of the military and, eventually, the Waffen-SS to be weapon-trained; by the spring of 1939 a newsreel central office had been instituted in the Promi. An agreement regarding the division of labor was reached between Promi and Wehrmacht: in a combat zone, the latter would direct PK personnel for the gathering of newsworthy material, whereas the Promi would then edit and distribute it. PK members, thus schooled in weaponry, would potentially be able to fight at the fronts if necessary, but that was not their primary duty.[117]

The first test for the PK men came during the Polish blitzkrieg in the fall of 1939, when much usable material was gathered, showing the harrowing defeat of the Polish army, many of them on horseback shooting at tanks, and the accompanying triumph enjoyed by German soldiers.[118] But Goebbels, still not experienced in this medium, was criticized by Hitler in December for his handling of the footage, in the course of the Führer's censure of feature films that month, because it did not show enough enemy destruction

at the front.[119] In June 1940 the four newsreel companies were further coordinated uner the new label of "Deutsche Wochenschau," with the firm
Ufa-Tonwoche being put in charge.[120] As exciting film shots, photographs,
and war reports came back from the western campaign, especially France,
Hitler, who evidently wanted to see only scenes of total victory, was mollified,
as it could not have escaped him that the German public had discovered that
watching combat newsreels had become a new diversion, helping to fill the
cinemas.[121] As far as Goebbels was concerned up to and including the summer
months of 1941, it was easy for him to produce superb newsreels at a time
when the German front experienced nothing but victories. Scenes of adversity
for the German soldiers could not be presented; if the truth turned out to be
negative, it could not be shown, instead being replaced by manipulated
reports.[122] Ideally, Goebbels favored emotionally saturated comments based
on real-life footage, such as the following remarks on scenes after the French
campaign in the spring of 1940: "Captured tanks, air planes, heavy and heaviest artillery, masses of ordnance in endless fields are being caught by the
camera," and, with Hitler on his way back to the capital after the signing of the
armistice at Compiègne, "the Führer's train is moving through the rejoicing
countryside: everywhere he is being offered love, faith, and gratitude. Berlin's
avenues have been transformed into a flower carpet: the victorious field
marshal is being received by his people while bells are ringing festively."[123]

The production of suspenseful newsreels flattering the Germans became
more complicated by August 1941, after the Wehrmacht had reached the
western edges of Leningrad; Germans on the home front expected the city
to fall quickly from that point onward, but it was in vain.[124] At this time
Goebbels found it still easier to bend the truth and make up stories in his
weekly lead articles for *Das Reich* rather than to present camera footage of
glorious German troop advances. Ignoring war events, he could always, in
Das Reich, prefer to deal with topics such as foreign policy or what he called
British perfidy. Privately, he arrived at sobering conclusions regarding merely
a qualified deployment of on-site camera work after the advance on Moscow
had slowed down, stalling after mid-December.[125] By early 1942 the newsreels staff, rather than concentrating on front-line action, was beginning to
choose diversions by turning to scenarios on the home front, such as the
campaign to collect woolen clothing for the Eastern Front, or Goebbels's
own business trips within the Reich.[126] In May the minister was praying for

a summer offensive in order to be able to generate attractive footage and copy.[127] Nonetheless, despite all the difficulties the production of newsreels had now been increased, from the original 20,000 meters a week in the beginning to 30,000 meters; the size of the PK now totaled 13,000 men.[128]

By the time the propaganda companies were ordered to follow the Wehrmacht's move on Stalingrad, from late summer to December 1942, the frequency of newsreel offerings in German cinemas, once so popular, was already on the wane. One of the factors increasingly affecting the newsreels was Hitler's absence from them. This was in line with his growing reticence: he was not showing himself much publicly anymore and also gave fewer speeches over the radio, which might have risked the carefully constructed "Hitler Myth."[129] After the defeat at Stalingrad in February 1943, the propaganda companies were hard pressed to film German advances, let alone victories, much as Goebbels might push for them. As in other media, the details of surrender at Stalingrad were not mentioned, but this historic tragedy was to spur further actions in other theaters of war.[130] In a report from the Italian front a gunner in the back of a Stuka dive-bomber had his camera attached to the barrel of a machine gun, ready to shoot or to film. After the plane had dropped its bombs, along with many other Stukas, on the port of Valletta in Malta, his mission report read like a victory fanfare – Goebbels must have been pleased.[131] But such images did not square with other, negative pictures that the newsreels had to offer: on April 28 footage from the Deutsche Wochenschau newsreel showed a crestfallen Hitler who, so Goebbels lamely explained earlier, had overworked himself for his Volk.[132] Indeed, the minister by now had to be extremely careful not to turn this earlier instrument of triumph into a document of defeat. In June 1944, German cameramen were reduced to recording the specifics of the Allied D-Day landings. In the process they transformed shame into glory by capturing images of Allied prisoners on the Normandy beaches: Canadian paratroopers and Scottish airborne troops secure in German hands.[133] Around this time, production facilities for the newsreels' PK teams had been heavily bombed.[134] Subsequent films in German cinemas dealt with heroic German defense actions, the workings of V-1 rockets (V-2s were shown only from an unclear distance because they were not really functional), and, finally, east German civilian refugees attempting to escape from the advancing Russians.[135] On March 27, 1945, the final filmic portrait of the

Führer was shown, as he decorated a battle-worn group of Hitler Youths in the chancellery, just a week before.[136]

At the end of 1943, the SS-PK man Loss posted a photograph of a young ethnic German family with two toddlers, as they were traveling up the Danube from Romanian Dobrogea towards the Reich. Fittingly, the image was printed in *Das Reich*, but similar PK photos were distributed to other branches of the newspaper media, the diehard Party press as well as the formerly bourgeois gazettes.[137] Next to newsreels, newspapers were, of course, conceived by the Nazi leadership as yet another vital propaganda weapon to control and energize civilians in time of war. After September 1, 1939, the already rigid controls over all the newspapers were further tightened, as new wartime requirements touching on content, diction, and secrecy took hold. There were smaller and medium-sized conferences to discuss these issues, all held in Berlin and chaired by Goebbels's state secretaries and press plenipotentiaries or by the minister himself.[138] Directives issued there were supplemented by acts of self-censorship, which some papers were especially encouraged to engage in, such as the *Frankfurter Zeitung* (FZ).[139] Overriding all possible subject matter was the motto of "Kampf" ("Struggle"), while Goebbels insisted on loaded words, such as "horror" for England, which were to guide future stories.[140] Much as in the movies, and not surprisingly, specific leitmotifs were suggested, such as Bismarck the Iron Chancellor or Frederick the Great.[141] The "diabolical system of Bolshevism" became another leading theme after the invasion of the Soviet Union on June 22, 1941.[142] Throughout all this, Goebbels micro-managed, as he was wont to do. He took to task individual journalists like Karl Silex, the chief editor of the *Deutsche Allgemeine Zeitung* (DAZ), Ursula von Kardorff's Nazified daily, for alleged irregularities, and prescribed content, color, and tone for future reportage.[143] He himself launched articles in certain papers when it pleased him, such as the one in the FZ in May of 1942, which had as its object "the economic and operational possibilities of an attack on Moscow," a new offensive, after the Wehrmacht had had to retreat.[144] As early as February 1941, however, Goebbels had realized the limits to such an altogether restrictive approach in journalism, as writers were increasingly lacking in individual initiative and losing enthusiasm for their jobs. One year later he realized that this problem of motivation had become even worse, to the point where no person with a sense of honor left would want to opt for journalism as a profession.[145] Notwithstanding the feelings of Goebbels, the former journalist, Hitler for once was enthusiastic about the way the entire press in the Reich had been shaping up by now, apart from his grudge against the "Jewish" FZ.[146]

As all German newspapers, journals, and magazines, to the extent that they were not actually suspended after September 1939, adjusted themselves to the more stringent Promi guidelines, one of the most remarkable changes was in the balance between political and feuilleton-entertainment content, as the latter was sharply reduced in favor of the former.[147] And when there was a story that should have been left in the realm of, say, poetry, it was dragged into the nether regions of politics and war. For example, at the time the Maginot Line was penetrated by the Wehrmacht in May 1940, Goethe's hero Count Egmont was characterized by one Thuringian newspaper not in romantic terms, but purely as a "political fighter" for the Dutch, his people, who, ironically, were not the attackers, as was the Nazi army, but were themselves oppressed by the occupying Spaniards.[148] There were other articles in the press that extolled eugenics, around the time of Nazi experiments with euthanasia, and others again, such as in the *Deutsche Allgemeine Zeitung*, *Berliner Tageblatt*, and *Frankfurter Zeitung*, which accompanied the establishment in Frankfurt of Rosenberg's Institute for Research into the Jewish Question, in March 1941.[149]

Along with *Das Reich*, the FZ was leading all the other papers in reportage about the progress of the war. Enthusiastically, it wrote about "every assault and every act of violence, justifying each one with long-winded, hairsplitting explanations," as the neutral *Neue Zürcher Zeitung* observed a few months after the Reich's final collapse.[150] The FZ, especially under its influential editor Rudolf Kircher, engaged in "optimistic post-war planning for a victorious, Nazi-conquered Europe."[151] After the armistice with France in 1940, Walter Best went on behalf of the DAZ to Paris and thereafter reported to Goebbels about the French: "a tired, dying people without support, without faith in its own strength and hence without any future."[152] Four years later, when France was invaded by the Allies, the DAZ immediately obliged Goebbels's directive to write about this event positively, as if to signal a unique opportunity for Germany to vanquish the enemy.[153] This was in keeping with the minister's tendency at the time merely to interpret adversity as an opportunity for Final Victory. Other formerly bourgeois papers – to say nothing about the Party press – played their own part in hailing Germany's martial prowess: from the *Berliner Illustrirte Zeitung*, which focused on a Nazi pan-Germanic Europe, to the *Münchner Neueste Nachrichten*, which welcomed successes after battles in the Białystok–Minsk area, they all followed Goebbels's order of positive war-reporting to the letter.[154]

Under the Nazis and during the war, the German press experienced not only a qualitative but also a quantitative disaster. For newspaper suspensions, begun in 1933 and accelerating around the war's outbreak, were continued, one technical reason being the increasing scarcity of newsprint.[155] The rulers used such contingencies to rid themselves of organs that had always been a thorn in their side, no matter how Nazified those newspapers had become. Hence in May 1941, 550 papers were closed, followed by another 950 in the spring of 1943; after August 1944 each paper was merely allowed four pages, and from March 1945 two pages.[156] All, at one time liberal, dailies published in Dresden were reduced to one page by March 15, 1943, and the *Frankfurter Zeitung*, as much as it had tried, was closed that fall, on Hitler's personal orders, as he could never forget its Jewish origins.[157]

Another reason for this particular closure must have been that the FZ, in aesthetic appeal and content, simply had resembled *Das Reich* too much, for Goebbels desired a monopoly on both style and story. To be sure, in some ways *Das Reich* was meant to serve as a role model for that part of the Nazi press catering to educated readers, as the formerly bourgeois papers did. Then again, for Goebbels this weekly had a very special function. "The more radical the views we publicize in *Das Reich*," he noted at the height of the war, "the more upscale and inoffensive must be its layout."[158] What this meant was that a plurality if not a majority of articles in the paper had to be visually appealing to the educated elite as well as foreign readers (say in neutral countries like Switzerland or Sweden), by maintaining a polished style, on the one hand. On the other, its messages had to be factual and reasonable, avoiding Nazi pathos or any kind of nerve-shattering, brutal news. Nonetheless, if one read the paper carefully, the brutality of a totalitarian dictatorship shone through its lines. However, a superficial perusal could convey (as the FZ or DAZ often did) a less threatening and even enlightened impression. How was this uneasy balance obtained in practice? With very few exceptions, Goebbels himself demonstrated it in his lead articles, whether they were about Germany's war combatants, home-front morale, or even the Jews: he used brilliant, well-measured, language and exercised contextual constraint.[159]

Many articles in *Das Reich*, which habitually excelled through its feuilleton, were not immediately offensive, such as the review of cultural events, social situations, or of many books. German lifestyle by region, folklore, and customs was often discussed, film reviews were frequent. One such example was a sympathetic portrait of the contemporary composer Werner Egk.[160] Another was an article on Frederick the Great in the Great Man-theory manner; it was patterned on the film about Frederick the Great, *Der grosse König*, and succeeded as much as the movie did in suggesting flattering parallels between King and Führer.[161] But the articles Goebbels really wanted his readers to comprehend were those with a hard political message, however veiled, and those that stated the stark realities of war and imperialist domination, sometimes even in a ferocious vernacular, to the point where even neutral readers might nod their approval. To this category belonged a piece by *Das Reich*'s Washington correspondent Paul Scheffer a year after the beginning of the war that stated, contrary to the facts, that "opponents of the totalitarian states, in their heart of hearts, have always wished for this war to come about."[162] With its aesthetic cachet *Das Reich* could be used to disseminate, credibly, lessons about some of the more sensitive subjects the regime wanted its readers to learn, for instance in racial terms. Hence in February 1941 the university lecturer Ludwig Ferdinand Clauss defined the Nazi völkisch community and warned against those who placed themselves outside it – by neglecting "racial hygiene" or acting in an "un-Nordic" manner. (Clauss had recently mentored the anthropologist Dr. Bruno Beger, who in 1943, as an SS captain, would travel to Auschwitz to select inmates for a skeleton collection at Strassburg University, which purpose he denied in a conversation I had with him in 1963.)[163] At the beginning of the battle of Stalingrad there was an article by chief editor Eugen Mündler glorifying Hitler and naming the Jewish scourge, in commemoration of the Nazi assumption of power ten years earlier.[164] And after the failed coup of July 20, 1944, SS-Obersturmführer (First Lieutenant) Hans Schwarz van Berk praised the miracle that had saved the Führer from assassination, pointing to the circumstance that Hitler had been rescued by Providence several times before and therefore was untouchable.[165]

Ultimately, conscious of their power of insinuation with a more sophisticated segment of the population, Goebbels and his *Reich* editors sought the occasion to broach subject matter of a less conventional, even more explosive nature, which they wanted to be shared, understood, and agreed upon. Apart from Goebbels's own sinister stories about Jews, as discussed in the preceding chapter, others included news about the SS and its security service, the SD, disseminated in calculated, measured doses. Thus in February 1941, after the rush of invading Denmark and Norway, the establishment of the Waffen-SS company "Nordland," which came to include many Norwegian volunteers, was celebrated, in the spirit of partaking in the joy over a greater Germanic Reich now in the process of gestation.[166] A month later the Jewish ghetto in Warsaw was described as being inhabited by Semitic people possessed of "a lack of discipline, and of dissoluteness – a macabre panorama" – a people, then, who, fortunately, had been sequestered from the rest of the population and who were kept in check by SS soldiers, servants of order, marching down the streets to the cheerful tunes of military bands.[167] At that time also, *Das Reich* applauded the smooth cooperation between the Hitler Youth and SS in setting up agrarian labor units in the East.[168] Describing Russian partisans as "bandits," who, according to Hitler's Barbarossa Decree of May 13, 1941, should be "peremptorily shot," became a bit riskier twelve months later, yet the need for the SD-Einsatzgruppen to completely eradicate these bandits was described convincingly in some detail.[169] The author of the article, SS-Obersturmbannführer (Lieutenant Colonel) Wilhelm Spengler, one of the SS specialists at the newspaper, also wrote about the ongoing resettlement of ethnic Germans west of conquered Russian territory, in an equally persuasive manner.[170]

By virtue of such frank content alone, detailing Nazi violence and violators, *Das Reich* apologists after 1945 cannot be said to have been justified in maintaining that this paper compared positively with the run-of-the-mill Nazi press, mainly – so it was argued – because of its aesthetically more pleasing format, the generally toned-down nature of its contributions vis-à-vis cruder publications like Julius Streicher's *Stürmer*, and the Nazi-neutral articles of some of its contributors. Hence it was often maintained that because writers such as Theodor Heuss, Eduard Spranger, Manfred Hausmann, and Max Planck published essays in *Das Reich*, this organ was a crypto-platform of an alleged circle of "inner emigration," even "inner resistance." Quite the contrary, because the essence of the paper was aggressively National Socialist, judging by articles composed by SS officers such as Spengler and Schwarz van Berk, let alone Goebbels, this reflected, and still reflects, badly on those of its authors who defined themselves as "non-Nazis"; they were essentially fence-sitters, who opportunistically wanted to secure for themselves a position of safety once Hitler turned out to be victorious after all, yet, at the same time, would meet with approval in a newly established democracy.[171]

Goebbels had most of his lead articles from *Das Reich* broadcast over the national network.[172] He had good reason; in December 1939 he declared radio, the "cultural SS" of peacetime, to be the most important cultural-medium weapon of the war, most specifically for "the preservation of our morale."[173] At other times, he might have said the same about film or the newsreels. But radio's superb value in wartime was self-evident. For the sake of the greatest possible efficiency, broadcasting, technically administered by the RRG, was removed from the Reich Culture Chamber and placed under the direct control of the Promi.[174] By June 1940, regional programming was sharply reduced in favor of uniform, centralized, content and, as the German borders were increasingly pushed outward, so did the number of stations increase and the corresponding number of listeners grow.[175]

Goebbels continued to be vexed by the problem of balancing content he had faced before, but in general he managed to change the ratio of music to words in programming in favor of music, a situation in which, furthermore, light-entertainment fare pushed back any highbrow offerings.[176] His rationale for this was plausible: the elites, who had had to be pursued in the 1930s in the interests of administering the state, had been won over or were demure and now dispensable; the state was an unassailable dictatorship. They stood in contrast with huge masses of lower and lower-middle classes, who bore the brunt of the fighting at the military fronts and had to be cosseted. They did not care to hear Beethoven sonatas or poems by Goethe, instead they preferred hit-parade tunes and traditional dance music, as well as the hugely popular Tünnes-and-Schäl jokes of the minister's home turf.

Early on, Goebbels was therefore fortunate with the establishment of "Wunschkonzert," on which the extremely popular, eponymously named, film (1940) would be based, for the enjoyment of soldiers and members of the home front, as a staple of Reich broadcasting. It built on a simpler version of the late 1930s, in which civilians had been able to request, by sending in letters, a certain piece of music to be played on the radio, in return for monetary offerings to Nazi charities. In the new context of the 1940s these donations were continued and equivalent music was requested and played, but now this became a dialogue between the military and home fronts: soldiers could ask about their loved ones in town and country, and their relatives and friends could convey to the soldiers personal greetings by name and the latest family gossip. Somewhat anticipating modern American late-night talk shows, the events were staged within the format of lavish, expensive appearances, with the participation of most of Germany's film stars and other eminences of public culture, high and low, who would present live performances of song or dance or humorous anecdotes and reminiscences, emceed always by the same two show-business figures, who became household names. The entire phenomenon was meant to demonstrate the unity of all Volksgenossen at home and on the front line, hallowed, as it were, by constant victory, and blessed, vicariously and sometimes through popular appearance, by Party leaders of all ranks, if not the Führer himself, who even before this war, unlike Mussolini or Stalin or latter-day potentates, had been maintaining the admiration of the public through his remoteness. "Wunschkonzert" ran from October 1939 to May 1940, was suspended during the summer, and then ran again between October 1940 and May 1941. It was obviously identified with blitzkrieg and blitz victory, the enthusiasm over which inspired it, but then, in the early summer of the third year of the war, when it was painfully clear that the conflict was not yet over and sterner times lay ahead, Goebbels canceled it. Besides, British air raids were now making such broadcasts ever more difficult.[177]

As a wartime news service, German broadcasting underwent a development very much analogous to that of the propaganda companies. That is to say that when military fortunes favored the nation, its operations would thrive, but when the going at the fronts got tough, dissimulations, lies, or silence replaced matter-of-fact coverage of events. Between 1939 and 1941 radio still reveled in victory announcements and featured military marches much like those of the early period of the regime; special broadcasts from the front and addresses by Party leaders, including Hitler (even if they were decreasing), were everyday occurrences. Certainly this early on, the German people were with Hitler and the successes of his Wehrmacht all the way, and in particular they loved to hear reports about conquered foreign territories.[178]

Nevertheless, at the turn of 1941, as England was not invaded but instead launched more air raids over Germany, and as news of Hitler's embarrassment at the gates of Moscow filtered through – not necessarily on the air waves but from soldiers' letters from the front or comments when on leave – German broadcasting experienced its first serious setback. News services became less popular, and the forced cheerfulness of many radio shows was increasingly being resented. When, after a special Goebbels directive to air "optimistic pop tunes," Zarah Leander repeatedly offered her hit from the film *Die grosse Liebe*, "This Cannot Make the World Go Under," people became irritated.[179] Goebbels, constantly at odds with himself for a properly balanced radio program, be it the right mix of words and music or ideal proportions within musical pieces, decided to revamp his programming once again by delegating experts in their respective fields at radio central in Berlin, for instance the Weintraub Syncopators veteran, jazz pianist Georg Haentzschel, for dance/entertainment and Michael Raucheisen for serious music, early in 1942.[180] But as he allowed for an even greater share of light music for the benefit of the troops, Goebbels was forced to buy into a jazzier overall sound, because, as he told me in the 1980s, the experienced Haentzschel knew about the jazz and swing tastes of many soldiers, especially the elite pilots who were trying to bomb Britain into submission. Goebbels too must have become aware of the rumor that in the past, German pilots had listened to jazz on the BBC while flying toward the British Isles for a bombing mission and then carefully tried to avoid hitting radio facilities, to assure themselves of being entertained by Benny Goodman's clarinet on their way home.[181] But allowing Haentzschel, with his newly formed German Dance and Entertainment Orchestra (DTU) comprising the choicest of Germany's dance-band musicians, to hold sway also meant incurring the wrath of parochial German listeners, who were habitually complaining about "Jewish jazz."[182]

The second major crisis that affected radio, which also affected other information media, occurred around Stalingrad in early 1943. Already in doubt as to how far he could go with his strategy of broadcasting mostly entertainment, Goebbels forbade light music to be broadcast for a period of four days, scheduling only the classics.[183] Yet true to his fabrication in *Das*

1. Wassily Kandinsky's oil canvas *On White II* (1923), created while on the Bauhaus faculty in Weimar. Kandinsky was a pioneer of abstractionism in the visual arts and a leader of the German Expressionist school. Vitriol was poured on him by Nazis opposing Weimar Culture even before 1933.

2. An unidentified house, probably in the French Hainaut-Cambrai region, during World War I, a watercolor allegedly by Bavarian regiment soldier Adolf Hitler. The signature is unlike the monogram Hitler later affixed to documents. If this is indeed Hitler's work, it shows his dilettantish craftsmanship, for instance his lack of perspective.

3. Composer Carl Orff in 1920, at the age of twenty-five. It was in Munich in this year that he composed his first song cycle based on lyrics by Franz Werfel and where he was later influenced by Bertolt Brecht and other representatives of Weimar Modernism.

4. The actress Hansi Burg in 1926, long before her flight to England as a Jewish refugee from Nazi persecution. After she returned to a defeated Germany in 1945 in a British army uniform, she reclaimed her lover, famous actor Hans Albers, who had been mentored by her father.

5. Carola Neher, Rudolf Forster, and Valeska Gert on the set of the film *The Threepenny Opera*, directed by W. G. Pabst in 1931. A fugitive from Nazism in 1933, Neher was to die on the way to Stalin's Gulag in 1942. It is said that her former lover, the Communist Bertolt Brecht, had a chance to save her but he refused.

6. At a gymnastic exhibition in Stuttgart, 1933. From the right at the front: Propaganda Minister Joseph Goebbels, Nazi Party Treasurer Franz Xaver Schwarz, Reich Sport Führer Hans von Tschammer und Osten, and, with arm uplifted, Vice-Chancellor Franz von Papen. Physical fitness was writ large in the Nazi Reich.

7. A charcoal drawing of Adolf Hitler by H. Oloffs, based on a photograph by Hitler's personal photographer Heinrich Hoffmann. Hoffmann, in whose Munich studio Hitler first met Eva Braun, a shop assistant, possessed the exclusive right to take pictures of the Führer.

8. Poet and dramatist Bertolt Brecht, most likely in exile during the 1930s, place unknown. The ornery Brecht experienced difficulty adjusting to any of his new refuges – Denmark, Sweden, and the United States – and returned unhappily from New York to Europe in 1947, eventually settling in Communist East Berlin.

9. Hubert Lanzinger's oil portrait of Adolf Hitler, known as *The Standard Bearer* (1934). The painting was included in the first "Great German Art" exhibition in Munich, summer 1937, with Hitler's express approval. The damage done to the picture under Hitler's left eye stems from a bayonet wielded by a U.S. army soldier in 1945.

10. The front page of Nuremberg Gauleiter Julius Streicher's anti-Semitic weekly *Der Stürmer*. Apart from showing ugly caricatures of Jews, this issue from May 1934 typically warns of a Jewish murder plot against the non-Jewish world and parrots the Nazi Party's oft-repeated slogan, "The Jews are our Misfortune!"

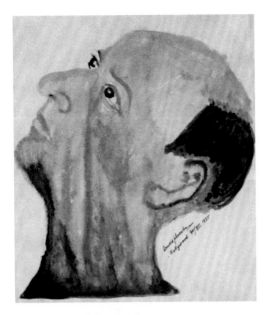

11. The composer Arnold Schoenberg's self-portrait, painted in exile in Hollywood, December 30, 1935. Apart from being the founder of twelve-tone serialism, Schoenberg was an accomplished painter who created many works, mostly in an Expressionist style.

12. Adolf Hitler in Nazi Party uniform, Nuremberg Lord Mayor Willy Liebel, and the Führer's favorite architect, Albert Speer, at the Nuremberg Reich Party rally site, around 1936. This site was one of the few monumentalist projects actually realized by Hitler and Speer.

13. Marlene Dietrich and Erich Maria Remarque in Paris in 1937, where they conducted a stormy love affair. At the time, Dietrich was at the nadir of her Hollywood film career. Still, she refused Goebbels's offer to return to Berlin to become the Reich film diva.

14. The Jewish Otto Freundlich's sculpture *Der neue Mensch* on the cover of the exhibition guide to the Nazi "Degenerate Art" show in Munich, July 1937. The exhibition sealed the death of Modernism in the Third Reich. The guide cost 30 pfennigs, but entrance to the show was free. Freundlich himself was to perish in the Maidanek extermination camp during the war.

15. The cover of the exhibition guide to the Nazis' "Degenerate Music" show staged in Düsseldorf, May 1938. Nazi culture expert Hans Severus Ziegler wrote the text explaining the – mostly defamatory – illustrations, all aimed at Modernist artists.

16. A page from the "Degenerate Music" exhibition guide showing Carl Hofer's allegedly degenerate painting of a jazz band next to Paul Klee's equally despised art work *Musical Comedy*. At the top of the page it says: "'Degenerate Art' and degenerate music hand in hand."

17. Elk Eber's painting *Thus was the SA* (1938) depicts SA storm troopers, most likely in the proletarian Wedding section of Berlin, after a street battle with the Communist Red Front, in the Nazi Time of Struggle before 1933. They are marching through KPD-dominated territory, as the back wall shows. Between it and the marchers are angry workers, one threatening the SA with a clenched fist, but also an approving man with his wife and blond son, who appears to be impressed and pondering joining.

18. Ilse Werner, as a wholesome young woman rooting for the Führer, in the center of a poster for the war propaganda film *Wunschkonzert* (1940). To the left and right is pictured her Wehrmacht officer heart-throb, played by Carl Raddatz, who was to star in many post-1945 West German films; less so Werner, save for some roles in television.

19. Ferdinand Marian as the Jew Süss in the Nazi propaganda film of the same name, 1940. Marian claimed later that he had been forced into this role by Goebbels against his will. As if to lend credence to this, he drove a car into a tree on a West German roadway in 1946, killing himself. Or was it just an accident?

ERNST HIEMER

20. The cover for Ernst Hiemer's book *The Mongrel and Other Thought-Provoking Tales* (1940). Julius Streicher's collaborator, Hiemer claimed that Jews inhabited bastardized dogs and rapacious species such as snakes and grasshoppers, and that they changed their exteriors like chameleons – all pictured around the mongrel on the book cover. For anyone who does not believe the Nazis regarded Jews as subhuman, this is proof from the realm of culture.

21. Wolfgang Willrich's painting of panzer general Erwin Rommel, with tanks in the background, 1940–1. This was a victorious time for Hitler's conquests, and Willrich's painting is a prime example of National Socialist Realism. The convinced Nazi Rommel was forced into suicide after the July 1944 plot on Hitler, although his links with the resistance had been peripheral and primarily because of Hitler's military failures.

22. A Luftwaffe correspondent from a Nazi Propaganda-Kompanie back from a front mission, handing his film reels to a motorcyclist for speedy processing and newsreel film showings in German cinemas, around 1941. The Nazis perfected this particular news network until the news began turning into lies and these efforts backfired.

23. The poet Gerhart Hauptmann being modeled by Arno Breker, Hitler's favorite sculptor, October 26, 1942. Hauptmann's wife Margarete is standing to the right, Breker's Greek wife Demetra is facing her husband. The former social critic Hauptmann enjoyed being celebrated during the Third Reich's military glory days.

24. Franz Eichhorst's painting, *The Memory of Stalingrad* (1943), of which, allegedly, Hitler was very fond. The painting's theme played to the myth of Stalingrad, which held that by sacrificing their lives there, German soldiers were ultimately advancing the fortunes of the Reich.

25. Hans Albers in the lead of the 1943 film *Baron Münchhausen*. The film's purpose was to provide recreation for the German people and ultimately to strengthen their morale in anticipation of the Final Victory. At a time when economic resources were needed in the war and at the home front, this was the most expensive German feature film to date.

26. Nobel laureate Thomas Mann making an anti-Nazi broadcast in Los Angeles, 1943. Mann's recorded speeches were flown to London and broadcast to the German people by the BBC. Mann's committed daughter Erika helped in this venture.

27. Film actress Margot Hielscher as she continued her career in 1950s West Germany. She admitted to a seduction attempt by Joseph Goebbels, which ultimately may or may not have been successful. During the 1950s, as she later confessed, it was Hans Albers who was sexually pursuing her.

28. Actor and theater director Gustaf Gründgens as Mephisto in Goethe's drama *Faust II*, in 1959. Gründgens's early-cemented fame as the most prominent German thespian continued after 1945, despite obviously close ties to the Nazi regime. A crass opportunist if not a true believer in National Socialism, he was never seriously questioned.

29. Composer Werner Egk shortly before his eightieth birthday in May 1981. Egk had been a functionary in Goebbels's Reich Music Chamber and, after a flawed denazification trial, became a well-respected professor in Berlin, while his one-time friend Carl Orff rose to unalloyed world fame on account of his secular oratorio *Carmina Burana*.

30. Author Ernst Jünger at an official celebration after receiving the Bavarian Maximilian Order (in addition to his World War I Blue Max of 1918) in 1986. Contemptuous of democracy and an unqualified admirer of men at war, in the 1920s Jünger had invited Hitler to visit him, but the future Führer never showed up. Jünger died in February 1998, one month shy of his 103rd birthday. He topped Leni Riefenstahl, who expired in 2003, 101 years old.

Reich that Stalingrad was not a pause indicating a turn in Germany's war fortunes, but rather a convenient event upon which to construct a heroic myth, he returned to the agenda of the past of broadcasting lighter music (accompanied by increasingly falsified news broadcasts), suggesting optimism, only to find that civilians at home were turning to radio less for relaxation than to be forewarned about imminent bomb attacks. Soldiers, on the other hand, enjoyed their own well-placed and generously funded "soldier stations," such as Soldatensender Belgrad, which could do as they pleased in an entirely military jurisdiction.[184]

Unlike the movies, radio could not, in the years from 1942 to 1945, supply the German public with a make-believe world it might retreat to, dreaming of better times; its tightly controlled contents could not even faintly approach the evocation of escapist fantasy. In this period, light-entertainment fare became even less popular as it was demonstrably worthless; instead, Germans turned increasingly to enemy broadcasts such as the BBC's to enquire about the real state of the war, even though they knew, if they spread such news, they could be condemned to death.[185] An additional complication turned out to be of a technical and administrative nature. Like cinemas, radio sets were lost in bombing raids and could not easily be replaced; they were surrendered to the troops; radio stations had to be closed because the staff were needed at the fronts; resources such as audiotape were becoming scarcer.[186] In the news department, German civilian trust was disappearing from anything the RRG was broadcasting about the war, which was dominated more and more by themes of Allied invasion, even as Goebbels toned down the lighter side of music somewhat in favor of classical pieces. Altogether, there were too many stories told about heroes having fallen for the fatherland, while the soldiers themselves relied exclusively on their own Soldatensender and what they could pick up, at far less risk, from enemy broadcasts at the fronts. Also, there were stories about gunners who habitually listened to enemy broadcasts using the special receivers inside their tanks.[187] By 1944–5, German radio was almost exclusively broadcasting apocryphal reports.[188]

One of the most important services radio rendered to the Third Reich in those last years was when Goebbels used it on July 20, 1944, to inform the German people that the Führer was alive after an attempt at a military putsch. For a change, this message was true.[189] But Hitler returned to the pattern of faked news again when in a speech before the microphone on January 1, 1945, he asserted that the Germans would have no reason to capitulate, for the hour would arrive, "in which victory will decisively come to the one who has proved most worthy of it: the Great-German Reich."[190] Among the last of these specious news items on Nazi radio was the one from April 30, when a speaker dispassionately reported that the Führer had died a hero's death in the defense of Berlin.[191]

MUSIC AND THEATER IN THE SERVICE OF WAR

During World War II music in Germany was also used heavily for propaganda purposes, as much of it could be directed by the state and musicians, either out of fear or voluntarily, complying with the objectives of the totalitarian regime.[192] One consequence was that the quality of music deteriorated, if it had not done so already before the war. Technical and logistic factors were instrumental in this. For example, many musicians were needed to staff an orchestra, and Germany traditionally had many orchestras at big-city and provincial levels, sometimes even more than two in one place. As male musicians had to be drafted, their units were reduced in size or totally dissolved; amateur musicians, often females, were coopted. Large buildings usually were required to stage concerts, operas, or recitals, and they were of course immobile, unlike a film trolley. For the purposes of propaganda, Goebbels was less enthusiastic about live music events, which were becoming scarcer and of diminished quality; recorded music could be transmitted over radio more easily, cheaply, and safely, especially after the RRG had begun using AEG's earlier invention of Magnetophon tape-recording facilities effectively after 1941. Recorded music was repeatable – an important aspect of propaganda, for instance when broadcast stations broke into Liszt's symphonic poem *Les Préludes* every time there was a victory announcement, even though Liszt was Hungarian.[193]

Moreover, once bombs began falling on German cities, visits by the public to concert venues fell off markedly. In time, many concert halls would be destroyed; those that were left by 1943 increasingly performed to audiences during the day, when fewer people could attend a concert or an opera, with musicians often playing wrapped in coats and hats to facilitate an easy getaway to air-raid shelters. Entire orchestras were shifted geographically, allegedly for safety reasons, as was Duisburg's from the acutely endangered Rhineland to Prague in 1943, depriving the public of musical performances in some cities.[194] In late November 1943, during one of the heaviest air raids on the capital so far, Berlin's cherished Scala, a mainstay of revue and operetta and often hosting jazz acts, was bombed to the ground. On the eleventh anniversary of Hitler's assumption of power, January 30, 1944, Berlin's Philharmonie suffered the same fate. The Staatsoper was destroyed, for the second time, in early February, 1945, and the Dresden opera two weeks later. By that time, Goebbels's cancellation of all public performances was in effect, albeit with exceptions.[195]

Altogether, the performance of serious, classical, music (Ernste Musik) was not as important to the Nazi regime as it had been during peacetime. As in other media such as radio and film, once war started there had to be a shift to performances of music as entertainment, keeping the masses humored through a congeries of lighter fare: operetta, popular tunes, folk and dance music, and even jazz.[196] In February 1942, Richard Strauss, the embodiment of classical music, was taken to task by Goebbels on the Promi premises because he disagreed with the minister's policy favoring music as entertainment. Goebbels rudely told Strauss, "stop babbling about the significance of Ernste Musik! This will not revalue your stock! Tomorrow's culture is different from that of yesterday! You, Mr. Strauss, are of yesterday!"[197] Goebbels's attitude explains why live jazz was never forbidden even during wartime, mainly so that soldiers could be distracted while on furlough by the surviving German jazz bands. They usually performed in specially permitted nightclubs in large cities such as the Berlin Rosita Bar, where Coco Schumann was nearly arrested in February 1943 during a raid by the SS. Besides, the DTU was to become an officially representative orchestra of the state, with its musicians to be remunerated on the scale of the Berlin Philharmonic.[198] Regional prohibitions of jazz music, such as Gauleiter Mutschmann's for Saxony in spring of 1943, were therefore of negligible consequence.[199]

Trouble with Goebbels over the type of music to be served up to German audiences during the war was only one of several vicissitudes besetting Strauss after 1939. He had been replaced as head of the Reich Music Chamber in the RKK by the unexceptional conductor yet solid Nazi Peter Raabe in 1935, after loosely enforcing anti-Jewish membership stipulations and employing the Austrian Jewish writer Stefan Zweig as librettist for his opera *Die Schweigsame Frau*. As anti-Semitic regulations were more harshly enforced by the regime during wartime, Strauss personally came to suffer because of the protection he extended to his Jewish daughter-in-law and his attempts to save her Austrian grandmother from extermination camps (in vain, she died somewhere in the eastern Holocaust). But in order to keep his personal and professional life balanced, Strauss had to continue doing the bidding of the Reich, whose goals were becoming increasingly military. Materially always out for himself, he had to keep himself marketable to the regime. Knowing that the Nazis valued him as an internationally credible representative more than any contemporary artist, Strauss continued to offer his services. He officiated at competitions for young composers, allowed himself to be the subject of an impressive documentary film, and composed a *Festmusik* for the Axis ally, imperial Japan, which itself was waging an aggressive war in the Pacific. Not least to offset the influence of the vacillating Goebbels, Strauss invited the patronage of Vienna Gauleiter Baldur von Schirach and the governor of Occupied Poland, Hans Frank, who would later be hanged for war crimes in Nuremberg.[200] Indeed, Strauss remained on the opera and concert programs, along with Richard Wagner, as one of the most performed composers and was annually featured at the newly reopened Salzburg Festival.[201] On December 5, 1941, Goebbels, rather self-satisfied, confided to his diary that Strauss was toeing the line again. One should retain a good relationship with him, for after all, "he is our greatest and most valuable, most representative musician."[202]

Hence Strauss continued to top the ranking of musicians in the Third Reich. Second, as before 1939, came Hans Pfitzner, Strauss's frustrated nemesis, at least in terms of official prestige, if not actual performances.[203] Pfitzner continued to agonize over a personal dislike by Hitler, which dated from the early 1920s (Hitler had thought he looked like a rabbi); also, his misanthropic personality and gross sense of entitlement grated on most Party greats. However, unlike Strauss, he subscribed to Nazi ideology by and large and understood Germany's quest in wartime. His newly composed *Kleine Symphonie* in G major, opus 44, from November 1939 was thought by the *Völkischer Beobachter* to be a special gift "in a difficult time of war."[204] There were always regional Party chiefs who supported him. One in particular was Gauleiter Arthur Greiser in Posen, or Poznań (publicly hanged by the Poles in 1946), one of the most vicious of Hitler's satraps in the occupied East. His wife Maria was a concert pianist – which led to a Posen Music Week in September 1942, with Pfitzner taking center stage. Eager for an expeditious career, the young soprano Elisabeth Schwarzkopf sang for him there. There were also "Pfitzner Weeks" and "Pfitzner Schumann Festivals." The apex of these politicized music events was a visit by Pfitzner to Hans Frank's government castle in Cracow in November 1942, to which the composer had traveled in the governor's personal railway car and where he performed especially for that music-loving martinet. Pfitzner collected his share of cash prizes and was elevated to culture senator of the Third Reich – an empty title as it turned out, but flattering this composer's stupendous vanity.[205]

Next in line in the unofficial hierarchy of musicians during the war was Carl Orff, who, after his initial success with *Carmina Burana* in 1937, was becoming ever more prominent. In a musical landscape bereft of new compositions, by 1945 this secular oratorio would stand out as the single universally important work produced during the entire span of the Third Reich. Afraid of being found out as a quarter-Jew, Orff was hedging his bets. Like Pfitzner, he collected sizeable cash prizes, including the monthly sinecure from Gauleiter von Schirach, and he was accorded special favors by the regime. In 1941 a Promi directive went out that Orff performances henceforth be especially well reviewed in the German press; he attended discussions in the Propaganda Ministry and RMK President Raabe interceded on his behalf, to preserve a private telephone line, which, during the war, like a car, was usually prohibited. But he also maintained acquaintance with persons who eventually became involved in active resistance against the regime. Fortunately for Orff, his music was played frequently in broadcasts, and in 1944 the Promi offered him a composition contract for what it called "combat music."[206] Thus was music scheduled to serve the war effort directly. Also by 1944, Orff had secured a place on the precious list of exemption from war service, and he had personally come to the attention of Minister Goebbels.[207] Rediscovering, as he did periodically after 1933, his much earlier taste for the moderns, Goebbels, after catching Orff's magnum opus on the radio, dictated a memo in September 1944: "In the case of Carl Orff we are not at all dealing with an atonal talent. On the contrary, his 'Carmina Burana' exhibits exquisite beauty, and if we could get him to do something about his lyrics, his music would certainly be very promising. I shall send for him on the next possible occasion."[208] This was at a time when Goebbels had already shut off most other opportunities for public performances.

Orff's fellow traveler Werner Egk fared similarly well. If, among musical Modernists in the Third Reich, Orff must be ranked at the top, Egk, at some distance, certainly came second. Under the Promi's wartime emphasis on entertainment music, several compositions by Orff and Egk recommended themselves, for example Orff's fairy-tale opera *Der Mond* (1939) and Egk's playful *Die Zaubergeige* (1935). Both men were featured prominently in the composers' list by the prestigious publisher Schott.[209] Assuredly more opportunistically than from Nazi conviction, Egk had been able to act much more aggressively than Orff in assuming the RMK office responsible for composers in June 1941, as his racial pedigree was spotless. In the years following he performed various other services for the regime, particularly the Hitler Youth and SS. Conducting his own works abroad in the interest of war propaganda became his specialty. Hence in June 1941 he presented his opera *Peer Gynt* in Prague, and *Joan von Zarissa* was offered under his direction at the Paris Opéra at least thirty times.[210] These tours were officially sponsored by the Promi as part of the war effort, because "for the French," said Goebbels in early 1942, "cultural propaganda is still the best kind of propaganda. I shall therefore strengthen it even more than before."[211] As a result, not only did the calculating Egk make inordinately large amounts of money, but he was also exempted from war service and earned the Military Order of Merit in 1943, a distinction he was able to share with dyed-in-the-wool Nazi musicians Michael Raucheisen and Elly Ney.[212]

In the classical sector, apart from the newer composers who had established themselves earlier in the Third Reich, the field remained fallow. As in so many other areas of creativity after 1933, no new talent was on the horizon, and certainly no Nazi-specific talent. This is why Strauss and Pfitzner still towered over everyone while Orff and Egk, sometimes composers of undeniable originality, were able to fortify their already well-established positions. Goebbels himself attempted to encourage younger composers such as Gottfried Müller. Born in 1914 and originally a Protestant church musician like Hugo Distler and Wolfgang Fortner, Müller early on had written cantatas based on words by the Führer, and was doing so again, for choir and orchestra, during the war. A winner of state prizes and touted by insiders as the new hopeful of Nazi music, Müller's work was finally, in 1944, regarded as "too polyphonic" by the minister. "Our modern musicians overuse their resources and thereby lose track of the melodic line," he criticized.[213] There were attempts to support new genius through a program called "Composers in Uniform," featuring on radio any and all composers who had served at the fronts, on the chance that a few might be outstanding, but this strategy yielded no results.[214] Goebbels suggested competitions, offered prizes, granted auditions and new commissions, all to no avail.[215] Ultimately, he was more successful with the genre so dear to his heart in those days, hit tunes, film and operetta melodies – anything one could hum easily. He, who was an expert in the seduction of women to the accompaniment of recorded, schmaltzy, music (and himself played some piano to that effect as well), guided the hand of popular tunesmith Norbert Schultze in the creation of ditties against the Soviet Union and also England, and encouraged other efforts toward that end.[216] Schultze's colleague Herms Niel was charged with a similar task targeting France.[217] Realizing that no new usable compositional work could be generated by the talent at hand, fresh recruits or not, Goebbels decided to play it safe by investing some energy in the resurrection and remodeling, where appropriate, of older German music, in order to suit the National Socialist mold.[218]

If composers became more dependent on a Nazi state waging a world war, instrumentalists were even more so. Individual artists became more acutely aware than ever that if they displeased their rulers, they could be dispensed with and sent immediately to the fronts, or, in the case of women, deployed to the war industry. And scores indeed were. Even top musicians had much to fear, such as the conductor Hans Knappertsbusch, whom Hitler always considered more fit to lead a military band and whom, toward the end of the war, Goebbels could barely use to conduct symphonies, and certainly not operas. Goebbels, who soon despaired of searching for new, extraordinarily gifted musical talent as he did in film, kept more established musicians on their toes by periodically reviewing their performances, sometimes in accordance with Hitler. Hence already in 1942, the opera singers Rudolf Bockelmann and Josef von Manowarda were considered to have lost prestige, while the bass Wilhelm Rode at the Berlin Opernhaus was relegated to directing. Luckily for the up-and-coming bass-baritone Hans Hotter, he was deemed very promising and earmarked, by both Hitler and Goebbels, for the Bayreuth Festival.[219] Many orchestra members were fortunate in that radio still needed orchestral music even after Goebbels's shutdown of public performances in September 1944; they could otherwise have long lost their jobs and been employed in the service of a more immediate military victory.[220]

It is therefore understandable that even pre-eminent musicians vied with each other to curry favor with the regime and try to serve its wartime ends, in order to render themselves indispensable. The extreme Nazi fanatic, pianist Elly Ney, took this more seriously than most when she published Open Letters to "my dear soldiers," in which she thanked the Wehrmacht for the individual letters she had received. She conjured up the "combative unity between soldier and artist" and expressed gratitude for being able to serve both "Führer and Volk."[221] Beyond that, she reminded her audience that Hitler had demanded that music be harnessed for the continued development of a national life.[222] While Ney meted out her advice and professional services on whatever occasion she deemed suitable, there were other, fixed, Party dates that had to be musically enhanced. At the top was Hitler's birthday every April 20, when, as before the war, the Berlin Philharmonic, often under Wilhelm Furtwängler, officiated, either live in the Führer's presence or on radio. Other musicians did so as well. On April 20, 1940, for example, Clemens Krauss directed the Bavarian State Orchestra on radio; he was followed by singers Erna Berger and Wilhelm Strienz, and the light-music orchestra of Radio Berlin under conductors Barnabas von Géczy and Hans Rosbaud. The music corps of Hitler's personal bodyguard, the SS-Leibstandarte, also contributed; doubtless they played the *Badenweiler Marsch*.[223] There were other regime events, and even state-sanctioned films, to accompany performances for which, either during filming or at premieres, musicians, instruments in hand, were summoned to appear.[224]

Hans Hotter's possible delegation to Bayreuth was realistic, because singers and conductors could be sent to perform there on Winifred Wagner's or Hitler's own volition. After 1939, the annual Bayreuth Festival was redefined as a sort of cultural war game, as was the music festival in Salzburg after 1940. In 1940 the Salzburg Festival was halted, because in the previous season, after the Anschluss of Austria, the summer event had lost its habitual foreign, especially Jewish, clientele, and had not proved spectacular. For 1941, Hitler and Goebbels decided to reopen the Salzburg Festival merely for soldiers, Nazi nurses, and armaments workers, and perhaps their dependants. The official rationale behind this, as the film *Stukas* tried to insinuate, was that a festival touting the war industry would refresh soldiers with a dose of culture and enable them to fight better at the fronts, while at the same time the very same soldiers were given the opportunity to defend German high culture, as it unfolded on the Salzach River. Under this alliance of "Art and Sword," 20,000 uniformed men and women attended the event from August 2 to 24, 1941, and similar numbers in the two years following, led through a swastika-bedecked town and its historic sites by bands of Hitler Youth. The Salzburg events scheduled for August 1944 were canceled in the aftermath of Claus von Stauffenberg's assassination attempt on Hitler of July 20, and as part of Goebbels's overall prohibition against public performance that fall. From the beginning the festivities served as a showcase for Mozart and, to a lesser extent, Richard Strauss, mostly under the baton of Strauss's craven devotee Clemens Krauss; but the pieces chosen were hardly for the amusement of the Wehrmacht and nurses team of Brown Sisters, as the operas *Der Rosenkavalier* and *Arabella*, and even the more lyrical *Magic Flute*, were hardly to their taste. In all, the Salzburg festivities were a success neither for the war-stressed audience nor for Goebbels, in whose exclusive domain they were staged, because he found the Modernist Krauss personally precocious and musically prone to risky experimentation.[225]

There could have been no question of a competition between Salzburg and Bayreuth because the latter subsisted, in the name of the venerated Richard Wagner, under Hitler's personal suzerainty. Essentially, it served the same purposes as the Salzburg Festival, but Hitler cared for the members of the Wagner family as old friends and did not wish to see them suffer as civilians in a war economy. While Winifred Wagner's younger son Wolfgang briefly served in the Polish campaign and was wounded, the Führer had exempted his protégé Wieland Wagner and given him free rein. Under Winifred's and Heinz Tietjen's artistic direction Wieland, in his twenties, worked in the design department at Bayreuth, the proponent of an old-fashioned style even Hitler had not supported any more, and usually at odds with his more progressive superiors. As in the case of Salzburg, festival tickets were bought by Party and State, to be distributed to soldiers and armaments workers, but the proceeds came to benefit the Wagner family. Eventually, this was resented by the inhabitants of a town who saw their streets filling up with endless queues of uniformed people, guessing, wrongly, that soldiers were having a good time at their expense when in fact they should be serving at the front lines. They need not have worried, for the audience, mostly in field-gray and comprising the lower and middle classes, usually resented being marched from a special train to the Bayreuth Festspielhaus and back, without free time of their own and having to endure hard-to-take Wagnerian droning for hours on end. In addition, they had to sit through academic lectures. They could not have noticed that, in terms of programming, the Wagner canon was skewed: no *Parsifal*, for instance, but repeatedly *Die Meistersinger*, as that was considered more digestible fare. Like Salzburg, the Bayreuth Festival was suffering increasingly from the military conscription of stage personnel; in 1943 the vast chorus was filled with members of the SS Viking Division. July 1944 saw the last festival season during the war. Bayreuth suffered severe bombing in early April 1945, although the Festspielhaus, unlike the town below, was spared. In any case, it was off-season, and there were no performances. The town was entered by U.S. troops on April 14.[226]

Salzburg and Bayreuth were preferred stages for the Nazi leaders to try to impress their soldiers and workers with high culture, but they were not the only ones. The entire infrastructure of live theater was utilized during the war to serve such purposes, increasingly after September 1939, so that by 1941, 23 percent of all performances in the Reich were dedicated to Wehrmacht and Party ancillary organizations, and workers in the armament industries, of both genders.[227]

In general, and not surprisingly, theater was accorded the same war duty as other branches of German culture, be it film or music, namely to provide relaxation, strength, and solace to a war-sustaining population. How well could it do that, compared to those forms of media? Representatives of the Nazi regime expressed no doubts: "When artists work on stage, a people marches," was one slogan, and in the *Völkischer Beobachter* Gustaf Gründgens, the vaunted Intendant of Göring's Prussian State Theater, pronounced the theater arts to be a part of the German defense system.[228] His colleague Heinz Hilpert from Goebbels's Deutsches Theater, down the road from Göring's superior establishment in Berlin, seconded Gründgens by suggesting a more effective führer model for the Reich's stages: an artist would have to integrate himself into the ensemble as would any German into the Volksgemeinschaft, he lectured, and the Intendant of an ensemble was nothing if not its führer.[229] Artists and soldiers were a unit, it was held, and theatrical content should be adapted to the new necessities of the state, gearing itself, for example, to eugenics, as that was a wartime priority starting in 1939.[230] As late as 1943, Hitler himself agreed with his minister of culture to these interpretations of theater, even though it became clearer by the day that the sacrifice of human resources was unavoidable to uphold the fronts.[231]

Although, due to the expansion of the original Reich territories, the number of theaters grew, as did the amount of visitors until 1943, the stages were beset by several difficulties after September 1939.[232] For one, even during expansion conscription always threatened to diminish personnel, a danger greater than for cinemas and even movie-making, because theater productions required more man-hours and on the whole were much more labor-intensive. Second, theater experienced a near existential crisis, because its Promi-ordered drift to light entertainment compromised its traditional pride of place in high culture. This deflated the morale of seasoned theater workers.[233] And third, theater faced recruitment problems both among dramatists and from an actor's perspective – problems inherited from peace-time – as competent plays, and playwrights, especially of the Nazi persua-sion, were few and far between.[234]

Except, possibly, for new war-specific pieces, theater in Germany after the beginning of the conflict by and large was even more mediocre than in peacetime, as random sample pages of the Nazi periodical, *Deutsche Theater-Zeitung*, easily demonstrate. The issue for September 14, 1939, for instance, featured photographs of the Aachen and Frankfurt/Oder theater directors Otto Kirchner and Hermann Grussendorf, no titans in their field, next to advertised plays by convinced Nazis Gustav Frenssen, Walther Gottfried Klucke, Walter Stang, Thilo von Trotha, and Fritz Wolfsdorf, and then highlighted the seasonal programs of provincial backwaters Innsbruck, Coburg, and Regensburg.[235] As for the classics, Goethe, Hebbel, and Kleist fell off against Schiller, until his dramas, redolent of themes of liberty, at Hitler's own instigation were pushed into the background after 1941.[236] Shakespeare and Shaw, as English and Irish playwrights respectively, were quickly banned (although the Nazis had early on claimed Shakespeare as "Nordic"); ignoring French and Russian plays was de rigueur. And as for Fascist Italy, when in May 1940 Mussolini's co-authored play about Count Cavour was presented at the Berlin Staatstheater, with Werner Krauss in the title role, Goebbels drily remarked: "The Duce obviously is better at making history than dramatizing history."[237]

As the political occasion demanded, pro-Nazi bards adapted well to the needs of war, and even directors of previously untarnished reputation hastened to do the regime's bidding. Hence the old Freikorps poet Edwin Erich Dwinger, soon in SS uniform and a PK specialist, authored a drama *Der letzte Traum* (*The Last Dream*) based on his novel *Die letzten Reiter* (*The Last Riders*); the play was as anti-Soviet as the novel and had its timely premiere, at Stettin, in October 1941, just months after Hitler's invasion of Russia.[238] Also in 1941, Gründgens premiered *Alexanderzug* (*Alexander's Train*), by the Hitler Youth poet Hans Baumann, in which Alexander the Great's campaigns were interpreted as a marvellous parallel to Hitler's own; Gründgens, who simultaneously portrayed Secretary of State Joseph Chamberlain in the anti-British film *Ohm Krüger*, himself played Alexander.[239] At that time, Germany was still drunk on victory. A little later, Herbert Reinecker of the SS-PK penned another drama against the Soviet Union, in favor of Russian ethnic Germans – that theme so exalted by Nazis – and had it premiered just before the fall of Stalingrad, an unfortunate turn of events the author had not foreseen.[240] Only two weeks after that disaster the Nazi author Gerhard Schumann presented his new play *Gudruns Tod* (*Gudrun's Death*), a Viking epic from the High Middle Ages. In it a fictitious queen called Gudrun stabs herself to death, in a play as full of kitsch as it was ill crafted, a denouement of drama starkly symbolic of the precarious state in which the Reich with its uncertain military exploits now found itself.[241]

BOOK AND SWORD

In the spring of 1939 a German girl with the Nordic name of Irmingard, straight out of Wagnerian mythology, was given a birthday present by her mother. It was Erich Gritzbach's biography of Göring, which the mother commended "to dear Irmingard in great times." The mother had chosen a very popular book, detailing Göring's life and career thus far, and with interesting photographs. The volume Irmingard received, published the year before and in my possession, was already in its nineteenth edition; at least 340,000 copies had been printed to date.[242] It was this kind of litera-ture that became extremely popular in the months before and after the beginning of World War II, because the German politicians behind it, espe-cially Hitler and Göring, were being idolized, with the "Hitler Myth" at its pinnacle. As the months went by, more and more books were in demand, publishers expanding and booksellers becoming wealthy.

Not to be overlooked, one reason for this was economic. Books were purchased by the civilian population and members of the armed forces to a large extent because there was too much money in circulation. People did not know what to do with it, because fewer and fewer consumer goods were being produced over time or they were becoming so scarce as to be had only with restrictive coupons. Books, on the other hand, required no coupons.[243] As for civilians, ever more women on the home front were buying books, as they had more time on their hands. One of them explained as early as September 1940 that she needed an engaging novel, "in order not to have to stay up at night waiting for enemy planes and then sit around idly later in a cellar."[244] Hence, as Goebbels had divined, it was light, entertaining fare that was most sought after, rather than heavy reads such as Party manuals, and the German book industry was under great pressure to publish it, even if paper stock was becoming ever scarcer. Around the turn of 1941 publishing was entering a crisis, as demand for popular novels at home and from the front could hardly be filled anymore, with the soldiers always receiving priority in aggregate shipments – and wanting more. By early 1943, Goebbels, who oversaw most of book publishing, was forced to close down publishers; the demands of "total war" that he proclaimed on February 18 called for stepped-up inductions into the forces and armament factories, leaving the ranks of paper manufacturers and book publishers thinned out, not to mention writers. In January 1944 the new-book depositories in Leipzig, a major publishing center, were bombed, marking the beginning of the end for new German literature. From September 1, the beginning of Goebbels's ban of cultural activities, no more new editions were permitted.[245]

Five years previously, in September 1939, a writer by the name of Martin Raschke was well on his way to becoming a major star in the Nazi literary firmament. He was twenty-five when in 1930 he decided to freelance as an author, after having tried university studies in vain for two years. Raschke moved back to his home town of Dresden and wrote for several journals and the radio, but his first book of any significance appeared only in 1935. In this novel Raschke, by this time a committed National Socialist, portrayed Reinhold Berger, a young man on an Upper Lusatian farmstead close to the Czech border, who is haunted by the Bohemian mountains that are not yet part of the German landscape. His interest is bolstered by the knowledge that Klara, the daughter of Sudeten German peasants and his sweetheart, lives beyond those mountains. When Reinhold and Klara get together, either on the German or the Czech side, they agree on their path for the future: they will marry and have "many kids." Reinhold dislikes girls whom he cannot visualize as mothers. Raschke's book was an unabashed plea for a union of the Sudetenland with the German Reich, four years before this actually happened. For him, it was rationalized by "Germans living on either side of the border and tilling the earth in the same way." He grieved over a Sudeten German family who had lost young women through marriage to Czech men and whose children "could hardly understand their mother tongue."[246]

In his book Raschke serviced the racialist clichés of fellow Nazi writers, with some of whom he corresponded: Hanns Johst, Will Vesper, Wolf Braumüller. Besides the agenda of Czech annexation and fecundity for the Volk he idolized agricultural skills, the strength of fertile German soil as opposed to barren cities, and argued for German ancestor worship. Raschke, who impressed his many friends as exuding intelligence and charm, greeted the coming of war enthusiastically.[247] He became a disciple of Hitler's idea of a German-led Europe, a Greater Europe, a Grossgermanisches Reich under Nazi suzerainty.

In his second significant work, the novella *Der Pomeranzenzweig* of 1940, Raschke described in somewhat garbled prose how Hubert, a wounded aviator returning from the Polish campaign, visits the home of his brother and sister-in-law, Gertrud. They are the proprietors of a large garden center in Dresden. As Hubert and Gertrud fall in love, the gardener, instead of defending his marriage, resigns himself to failure and resolves to train for the front. Thereafter, Hubert cannot bring himself to consummate his love with Gertrud, who then decides to poison herself. Yet Hubert pre-empts that by shooting first her and then himself. The lurid, convoluted, ending is pure kitsch by any standards, but apart from aesthetics, Raschke has caused Hubert, ever so firmly, to make a case for comradeship: Hubert cannot deceive his brother while both of them are soldiers in the Wehrmacht, sexual passion be damned.[248] After the novella's publication, Raschke was hailed by Nazi critics as "a foremost epic poet in our writers' ranks."[249]

Raschke himself was conscripted into one of the army's propaganda companies. By all accounts, he cherished having been drafted; along with his wife, a Mary Wigman School dance instructor, he agreed that the eastern campaign was necessary and had to be won for Germany. Thus he made himself available for a special mission planned by Goebbels's Party office in Berlin.[250] Then, in November of 1943, he was shot in the abdomen near Nevel, on the Russian front. He was rushed to a combat support ambulance, but it took too long to get him there. His official death notice dates from November 24, 1943.[251]

Raschke's work epitomizes what was significant in German contemporary literature just before and during the years following the Third Reich's invasion of Poland. In his Sudeten-themed novel the subtext was about völkisch values subsumed under the fetish of "Blood and Soil," gaining renewed strength, the respect one owed to one's tribal ancestors, fertility, and the love of children for a continuation of the racial stock, as well as and not least, dedication to rural-based artisanship. Martial struggle, to assert the right of the strong, was already foreshadowed on the eve of the German-Czech crisis. In his subsequent early-war novel, Raschke stressed the priority of active combat for the sake of the fatherland, camaraderie among soldiers, self-sacrifice, and the subservience but also camaraderie of women in a male-oriented, leader-dependent, community.

Had he lived and not died serving in the armed forces, Raschke might well have turned out to be the golden boy of National Socialist literature, the search for whom – in analogy to other arts – regime leaders had commenced in the mid-1930s, a search that was still ongoing at the height of the war. It was symptomatic of deficiencies in Nazi contemporary literature and music that contests were held and meetings scheduled to distill candidates for that golden-boy status. The themes that leaders of the regime wanted brilliant writers to deal with continued to be those sustained in the 1933–9 period, such as history with relevance to Nazi weltanschauung, depredations by the enemy, criticisms involving the urban environment, and race issues. But beyond those, ideas concerning Greater Germany should now be written about, as the warriors of the Reich had made some conquests with prospects of eastern settlement, while the lives of pre-eminent Party comrades who had served as Nazi pioneers for decades should become the subject of regime-sanctioned hagiographies – all with the aim of creating an official, enduring legacy.[252]

Even though, paradoxically, recruitable literary prodigies were dying, like Raschke, in ever greater numbers at the fronts, the leaders decided to source them.[253] In 1941, Alfred Rosenberg participated in a competition organized by his newspaper, the *Völkischer Beobachter*, to find an exceptional new novel; he read four of the best entries but was disappointed to find them all wanting.[254] Goebbels tried one better by transforming the Weimar-based poets' convention held in 1938 into a combination of martial rally and writing workshop, to be staged every fall. As the poet Manfred Hausmann recalled for the readers of *Das Reich* in November 1940, all participants of that first congress were exhorted, by Goebbels and his associates, to heed that they were facing a total war, for the duration of which "the book belongs to the sword, the sword to the book, the poet to the soldier and the soldier to the poet."[255] Although such a banal mantra did anything but imply the highest standards for would-be champions of the pen, two more such congresses were organized, for the fall of 1941 and 1942 respectively, playing host even to foreign authors who were sympathetic to the regime and mastering the German language, during which Führer, Volk, and Fatherland were conjured up and the war was glorified. Still, no genius materialized.[256]

Two men even more prolific than Raschke who might have qualified as *poeta laureatus* during the war were Hanns Johst and Ernst Jünger, but whereas the one became lazy resting on his laurels in a Lake Starnberg villa, the other largely withheld himself, even as a soldier. Both wore Nazi uniforms. At war's beginning Johst was the president of the Reich writers' union in Goebbels's RKK, a post that gave him little to do, as the RKK manager Hans Hinkel and even Goebbels ran day-to-day affairs. Johst himself became the subject of his few reports. An SS general even then, he reveled in his personal friendship with Hitler, armaments chief Fritz Todt, and his soulmate Heinrich Himmler.[257] In 1940, Johst accompanied Himmler on inspection trips to Occupied Poland and reported about them in the most casual of styles, which was to document how he hobnobbed with Nazi grandees as a matter of course. "I was sitting next to the Reichsführer for eighteen hours, as he was steering his small BMW." Having arrived in Poland, Johst listened to one of Himmler's pep talks to his troops, who were already engaged in murdering Polish and Jewish civilians on a day-to-day basis: "The Reichsführer-SS is speaking. Every word of his is marked by brilliance, which is more than all the munitions factories in the world are able to produce. He commands: 'Never be soft . . . never be cruel!'"[258] Despite such testimony, Goebbels later dismissed what Johst told him he had experienced in the occupied territories as naïve, thinking his RKK section chief a lightweight unfit for political office or poetic laurels.[259] Although he considered himself a bard, indeed a historian of the SS, who counted himself as one of Himmler's closest friends until the end of the Reich, in future Johst won no further traction within the regime at large, let alone the reading public, as he had virtually ceased getting anything published.[260]

Johst's one-time Expressionist colleague Ernst Jünger was infinitely more complicated and sentient. As the German writer W. G. Sebald reminded his readers in 1999, Jünger had helped intellectually to usher in the Nazi era through his writings in the 1920s, which concerned themselves with the glories of warfare and the construction of a political totality – anti-democratic and fascistic.[261] He had been in touch with Goebbels then, and sent one of his books to Hitler with the inscription, "To the national Führer Adolf Hitler." At Jünger's invitation, Hitler almost met with him, but at the last minute the Führer did not show up.[262] Although not particularly against Jews, Jünger was an abject racist. He ultimately decided that Nazis were below his standard socially and aesthetically, and formally eschewed them. Nonetheless, even when keeping more to himself than did Johst, Jünger continued, after 1933, to be fascinated by fascist phenomena and war, and on the whole almost every utterance of his applauded Hitler's doing away with democracy in Germany.[263] The literature he wrote identified him, then as now, as a sadistic voyeur of inequities and irregularities in nature, including not just his pet species, insects, but also, in some queer analogy, the life of human beings, as a fastidious observer of the details of the Darwinian struggle for survival, where victims, their convulsions, sores, bloodletting, and death struggles, elicited for him more interest than the healthy normality of victors. In war scenes, he was fond of describing in detail the dead and the dying, with their tortured twists and turns, the corpses, as they succumbed to putrefaction, with flies and maggots eliminating human flesh. He hardly gave any thought to wounded soldiers who had been healed through medical attention. Acts of human kindness did not register with him.[264]

Jünger had been, like the "Red Baron" Manfred von Richthofen and Göring, a recipient of the Pour le Mérite, the First World War's rarest, highest medal. His elitist writer's attitude demonstrated, morally, contempt for humanity at large, from individuals to communities, and aesthetically, a perverse fascination with the morose and decaying, not just in war, aspects of which he was wont to examine and record down to the last detail. He was happiest when he could set himself apart and place himself somewhat exceptionally within a male-dominated band, such as that of warriors, where condescension towards if not disdain of women was commonplace, down to their sexual exploitation. When war broke out in September 1939, Jünger, in the words of Saul Friedländer "a connoisseur in matters of violence," volunteered to be reintegrated into the German army as a captain, eventually seeking a comfortable place for himself in occupied Paris, where he lived like a prince in luxury hotels and gourmet restaurants, savoring his favorite wine, Châteauneuf-du-Pape.[265] He acquired a Jewish mistress, Camilla, whom his knowing wife, Perpetua, back near Hanover had to suffer, and fantasized about all manner of sex with underage girls, whom he considered ideal "bed-warmers," and whom he found worthy of autopsic attention even as partisans, killed on the Russian front.[266] Sexual gratification combined with blood lust may have been the motivation for seeking out the execution of at least one German deserter, the minutiae of whose death Jünger recorded painstakingly, not least in order to sell it as literature later.[267] In keeping with his pre-war character, he again lived the life of a spiritual sadist whose finely calibrated instrument of comprehension was a limitless imagination beyond standards commonly accepted by humankind. The literary critic Peter de Mendelssohn persuasively suggested in 1949 that Jünger wanted to precipitate evil, in order to contemplate, analyze, and describe it.[268] He certainly wished to market it commercially as well. What a contrast Jünger's Paris occupation diary, a sybaritic testament, was to Heinrich Böll's modest, private notes, contemporaneous from the Eastern Front in 1943, a silent monument to his adored young wife Anne-Marie, in which he recounted one manifestation of war horror after another.[269]

Like Johst's, Jünger's literary output during the war was negligible. He composed that war diary, early parts of which he published first in *Das Reich*, thereafter in book form in 1942, with the rest, which revealed his opportunistic relationship both with the French collaborators and fringe members of the German military resistance group around Stauffenberg, in 1949.[270] Those latter contacts, as tenuous as they may have been, as well as an account of Jünger's meeting with Picasso in 1942, helped a great deal in his elevation to the official status of near-resistance fighter in the early Federal Republic.[271] In reality, like several of his colleagues, he had been an opportunistic fence-sitter who cunningly managed to draw capital from his genuine dislike of Hitler, notwithstanding the fact that he would have done so even more famously had the Führer won the war. This dislike is palpable in his novella *On the Marble Cliffs*, where the Head Forester, really a cruel headhunter, still elicits obvious fascination for him.[272] But after the war, it was Böll, not Jünger, who received the Nobel Prize in Literature, in 1972.

The narcissistic Jünger was a household name in the literary circles of Nazi Germany, and although he did not attend the Weimar writers' conferences himself, his work there was quoted with authority.[273] But because of his idiosyncratic, aloof personality, even Goebbels, who had greatly admired him in the Time of Struggle, found him difficult to utilize. Even though he fully valued Jünger's renewed voluntary war service, such as it was, the minister, having just appraised the writer's recent war diaries, thought that he had indulged in "fruitless hogwash." This about a man who, as far as Goebbels was concerned, once had published "good and effective volumes." It would be necessary again to get a hold of him, "to let him know where things are at."[274]

The war became a principal focus for German authors, who, like Johst and Jünger, often wrote about their own experiences. In 1939 the Freikorps-seasoned Werner Beumelburg published a report about German involvement in the Spanish Civil War; the Condor Legion's destruction of the republican-held village of Brunete in July 1937 was described in vivid language resonant with brutality.[275] This language presaged what was to come in the literature. In the treatment of the Western and Eastern Fronts, and of conquered territories, certain common themes predominated: a glorification of battle per se, the soldiers' love for their commanders, the putative chivalry of German soldiers facing their opponents and civilian populations, and a cavalier attitude toward the weaker sex. With respect to the first, the poet Manfred Hausmann, only briefly at the front, glorified "Kampf" as an idea and likened it to a gentlemen's sport.[276] Soldiers in the west expressed their admiration for one young general, who was from the "Ostmark" (Austria) and a glowing devotee of Hitler. In the east, an SS motorized battalion was able to survive a massive attack by Soviet tanks only after the most intrepid leadership by their commander.[277] Having captured some English troops, wrote one German soldier, the Germans had treated them infinitely more courteously than victorious Frenchmen were treating the Germans now; and in the Ukraine, wrote H. G. Rexroth, the Wehrmacht always treated civilians with great kindness.[278] Young women, especially in conquered western territories, were described as deserving of a soldier's protection, whereby the possibilities for sexual adventures were left open, but such adventures had to be conceded, as one published letter to a cheated wife made clear. This situation was in keeping with what in other media had been asserted as the prerogative of the Nazi male warrior: his right to polygamy once he realized it. This was something that adventure-seeking German "Blitzmädel" speculated on, once they were sent to the fronts to help the armies, as telephone operators or secretaries in uniform; but in France, at least, they had to take second place to ever willing collaborationist young women, who would bed down, perhaps for chocolates or cheap perfume, with Wehrmacht soldiers at the blink of an eye.[279]

Writers were guided by the specifics of each location. Whereas a race-conscious German author would stress the dangers in the west emanating from French colonial black soldiers, who were said to resemble animals more than humans, in the east such dangers originated with "Tartar" Red Army fighters, whose slit eyes and pronounced cheekbones were seen as proof of their subhumanity. (Any Kirghiz, Turkman, or Mongol – Inner Asian, but also ethnic Russian – could be called a Tartar.)[280] Derogatory characterizations were published especially after observing Soviet prisoners of war, with disastrous consequences for their fate in German POW camps.[281] Whereas Jews in the west were not mentioned, presumably because they were considered a liability of the Vichy government set up after the Compiègne armistice of June 1940, and because they were hardly distinguishable from the French in Paris, this was different in the east. Here Jews were an integral part of the opposing armed forces because of their assumed role as political commissars in the Red Army and their predominance in partisan ("bandit") units. Besides, civilian Jews were highly visible, beyond large urban centers, as inhabitants of *shtetl*, with their caftans, side-locks, and beards. Those observations called for rich, even exaggerated, depictions. In such situations, there were several conscious efforts by German soldier-writers to identify Jews, especially at a time when they were falling prey to SS-Einsatzgruppen actions, most of them in affinity with the Wehrmacht. Perceived as such, fraudulent Jewish egg wholesalers and winemakers in eastern Poland irked Josef Martin Bauer, for example, as he was pushing southeast with his platoon; later he encountered Jews, clearly as part of the Soviet bureaucracy, lording it over ethnic Germans and pressing non-Jewish women into sex. Published in 1942 and distributed *en masse* to the German forces, Bauer's book *Die Kraniche der Nogaia* (*The Cranes of Nogaia*) may have inspired many a German soldier in the live torching with flamethrowers of Jewish partisans, and the shooting of women, children, and old people into ditches they had had to dig themselves.[282] These impressions were written down, as were others, with obvious eliminationist intent.

Other, serious, non-fiction literature that both soldiers and civilians might be interested to read was usually freighted with heavy ideology. Under the weight of an armed Nazi weltanschauung no free spirits could write, and craven writers' pieces adhered to fixed, pre-set patterns and were not discursive. Most of these books, while not unambitious, were, potentially, tailor-made for serialization in *Das Reich*. However, with the hope of any luck on their side under RSK censorship controls and due to limitations of paper stock, their authors had to have connections higher up to be able to get published at all.

One favorite topic discussed under these conditions was the idea of the Great-Germanic Reich, meaning a new Europe ruled by National Socialist Germany. For this Reich racial uniformity was stressed, hence the books were permeated with diatribes against Jews and (French) Negroes. Hitler's supposed genius as a generator of culture *and* as a politician was often the main theme, pandering to the established "Hitler Myth." Germany's present foes were also downgraded, starting with the Bolshevik-ruled Soviet Union, which was always equated with Asiatic hordes, followed by money-bags England, degenerate France, and a happy-go-lucky (meaning infantile) United States. Against the latter, precise arguments on a cultural level, apart from basic politics and race analysis, were thought to be most effective. A specialist in this field was the SS member Giselher Wirsing, an ultra-conservative author with the closest connections to think tanks in the SD, who worked first as an editor for the *Münchner Neueste Nachrichten* and then for the Wehrmacht (Occupied Territories) propaganda sheet *Signal* – and who subsequently became co-founder and chief editor of the official Protestant weekly *Christ und Welt* after the war. Imperiously, he claimed that all of American culture could be reduced to films and radio and five books, among them the Bible and self-help volumes. For this reason alone, wrote Wirsing, Japan was correct in seeking a reconfiguration of the Asia-Pacific state order.[283]

Finally, in the realm of fiction lesser authors predominated after September 1939, writing lightweight literature, which was in keeping with the overall market for books during the war. Older, more established writers held back, being more interested in outwardly adjusting individual belief systems, either out of conviction or opportunism. Hans Carossa, for example, in 1941 agreed to chair the Nazis' newly established international writers' union, an intended rival to the international PEN club and protected by Goebbels, but to make doubly sure, he also published a paean to "the courageous fighter and Führer who currently is bearing everybody's fate."[284] Like others, he too would claim an "inner-emigration" status after the war. The well-respected authors Agnes Miegel, Wilhelm von Scholz, and Ina Seidel all offered poems specifically glorifying Hitler.[285]

For lighter fiction, three authors approached the acceptable aesthetic and ideological norms in those years but were unexceptional. Yet they provided a compass of Nazi comportment of the kind Goebbels's censors would recommend. They served up all the clichés and stereotypes already known from Nazi writers in peacetime. Emil Strauss's *Lebenstanz* (*Life's Dance*) of 1940 harked back to the 1920s when social and political unrest had ravaged Germany. Durban, a former Freikorps fighter, longs to settle down with the right woman and raise children in the countryside, as he has come to hate the city. He only suspects shady dealings generated by Jews there, whereas he is interested in Nordic sagas.[286] In 1943, Gerhard Lorenz portrayed a character he called Jansen in *Unrast*, a weak north German with potentially good genes (*Erbgut*), who, again in the 1920s, is uprooted, unable to find a steady job as a painter of representational art. He meets various women, among whom a city girl who smokes and is sexually provocative fascinates him most, but he ponders marriage carefully. Another of his female acquaintances is the tubercular wife of a physician who, because of her condition, has managed to settle down away from the city in the countryside, although this will probably not save her life. Jansen eventually marries a sturdy blonde, "a buxom, heavy-boned creature" who works in arts and crafts, a down-to-earth occupation therefore wrought by hand not brain, who can provide comradeship to Jansen and bear him many children.[287] And in Frank E. Christoph's *Sehnsucht nach der Heimat* (*Longing for Home*), also of 1943, the Austrian smith Bruckner emigrates with Fränzi, his blue-eyed and blond young wife, to Venezuela, where he observes the sloth of Negroes and the deceitfulness of Creoles. After considerable struggle, much of it conditioned by race, both decide to return to Germany at a time just after the Anschluss, when they are able to live in the "Ostmark" as Greater German Reich citizens and Bruckner's previous Austrian jail record has been erased.[288]

ART AND ARCHITECTURE

Judging by Speer's and Hitler's 1930s blueprints, architecture could have become the great showcase of culture for the National Socialists, had they not waged war, or had they waged a war that would have been completed after the first lightning victories in the east, and then the west, by 1940. In that case, Speer could have continued his ruminations on architecture in the Third Reich, which he had started so confidently in 1940, but which were to become the testament of unfulfilled longing in the very same year, as Britain began bombing Germany and raw materials had to be committed not to buildings but to an extended war effort.[289] There were other planning exercises, which all remained idle, for example regarding fortresses to be manned by newly settled German peasants in a conquered east.[290] It took the Nazi leaders about three years until they realized they had to win a world war quickly in order to act as great master builders once again. Resigned to inertia, Goebbels wrote in May of 1942: "With a heavy heart, the Führer has said goodbye to any kind of building activity. He is not having any fun any more, because nowadays we have to come to grips with other great difficulties and architecture can be resumed, on a large scale, after the war in any case. Currently, it has been stopped on all fronts; all we can do now is work for victory. Once we have victory, we may resume that task in the shortest of time."[291]

Operating in different physical conditions, the visual arts did not face such constraints. Officially, German art during the war period continued to orient itself according to the standards established by the "Great German Art" exhibition series founded in July 1937. These shows provided for the German public similar diversions as movies, theater, and concerts, and were intended by Goebbels and Hitler as such. At the same time, they gave mediocre yet Nazi-approved painters an opportunity to advertise their products and even to sell them – realistic propositions because, as in the case of the book market, Germans were eager to spend their money on something tangible that might perhaps grow in value, to be acquired without ration stamps and, especially during the height of wartime, as a feasible alternative to other forms of recreation that were now shut off. After September 1939, there had not been much recreation left; private automobiles had had to be surrendered to the war effort, and travel outside Germany, even to neutral states like Switzerland or Portugal, was not permitted, and even if it had been, could not be financed with foreign currency that banks were ordered to withhold.

During this period, a show was held in Munich between July 16, 1939, and February 18, 1940, which drew in 422,234 visitors – some 30,000 fewer than a year before. But this figure rose to 603,975 for another show in 1940–1, and to 705,228 for another a year after that. In 1942–3 there were 846,673 visitors to a show, and it was only then that the trend began to reverse itself, ostensibly because of the increasing air raids and a change in fortune on the battlefields, but for other reasons as well. For a 1943–4 show 700,000 visitors still showed up. As for an exhibition that started in July 1944 and, despite Goebbels's culture boycott for September, continued into spring of 1945, the ticket count is not known. The number of exhibited works also increased in the same period, from around 1,500 in 1939 to 1,900 in 1941, only to fall off to under 1,800 in 1943.

Part of an explanation for these astonishingly high numbers would be, as in the case of the Salzburg and Bayreuth festivals, that entire blocs were led through the exhibition halls, in this case school classes and Party formations such as Hitler Youths and Nazi-organized groups of women. Nothing, however, is known specifically about soldiers' attendance numbers. Most of them would have shared Hitler's taste. From July 1940 to March 1941, when, in absolute numbers, the biggest jump in visitor numbers to an exhibition occurred, many Germans went on their own accord; they interpreted the fact that Hitler had not canceled the exhibition as a sign that after the defeat of France the war was coming to an end, hence the exhibition served as a token celebration. This turned out to be one of the Third Reich's many delusions.[292]

As in the case of other entertainment media permitted by the Nazi state, the public-participation peak for art exhibitions was reached sometime in 1943 after the defeat at Stalingrad. Apart from the obvious dangers that enemy air raids posed, artists were finding it increasingly difficult to secure materials for their work, not just canvas and paints and brushes but also metals and stone for sculptures. Transporting works of art to and from

shows was the responsibility of the artists, and this proved a burden especially when, as happened most of the time, those works were rejected as
unsuitable. Over the years, artists' studios were bombed and works destroyed,
even though the Munich Haus der Deutschen Kunst miraculously never
sustained a hit. The regime found itself in a quandary on the issue of reim-
bursement, and for how much, when designated exhibition items were lost
to artists because of the vagaries of war.[293]

This was a question not only for the Haus der Deutschen Kunst but also
smaller shows organized on behalf of the regime by municipalities or state
and Party ancillaries. There were regional and city-based exhibitions of more
modest scope, for instance one in Görlitz about "Man and Landscape,"
another in Thuringia featuring Bavarian artists, both in 1940. In 1941,
Darmstadt organized an exhibition of paintings, "Artists in Field-Gray"; this
and other shows exhibited animal retrospectives and numerous landscapes,
some also portraits and nudes, but nothing out of the ordinary.[294] Artworks
were painstakingly geared to the standards set by Hitler in 1937 through his
artistic advisor, the photographer Heinrich Hoffmann. It had been Hoffmann
who had selected most of the artifacts for that year's archetypal Munich
exhibition, as he uncannily hit upon Hitler's own taste in art, that of the
nineteenth-century academic painters. In the judgment of historian Jonathan
Petropoulos, Hoffmann was an "artistic dilettante" often duped by forgeries.[295]
But Hitler elevated him to the status of professor in 1938, and during the war
he was assisted, for the Deutsche Kunst shows, by Gerdy Troost, a former
arts-and-crafts student only in her thirties, now also promoted to professor,
whose much older, deceased, husband had designed the building. Yet often
Hitler himself interfered, making the very final selection.[296]

Many German artists could easily adapt to the stipulated historicist
themes and styles, and many turned out paintings by rote to suit such
requirements, hoping to be successful in exhibitions, especially the most
important annual one in Munich. That one, however, was more miss than
hit: among the 7,000 artists who competed for a Munich spot between
1938 and 1944, only one-third eventually succeeded.[297] This, and the ever
growing vicissitudes caused by war and strained logistics created discontent
among certain artists, who were either hoping for state contracts with
money attached in order to make a decent living or, if they could afford it
financially, attempted to smuggle into their artwork certain elements of

what was long called "degenerate art." However, those latter efforts were quickly detected not only by Goebbels and Hitler himself, but also by enforcers of the Reich Art Chamber and spies among the SD. It is ironic that Hoffmann's own son-in-law, the Gauleiter of Vienna Baldur von Schirach, tried in 1940–3 to steer a different course from Munich and Berlin by occasionally patronizing what was suspected to be modern art, yet ultimately he had to toe the line. In Berlin, too, certain artists tried to defy the official line of what was regarded as the Bavarian diktat, but in the end Goebbels and his art police proved much too powerful.[298]

One criticism by painters was that not enough contemporary motifs could be detected in officially sanctioned works of art, in particular scenes of war.[299] These comments were obviously connected to a sense of frustration over state contracts that did not materialize, but were in reality quite unfounded, because every show in the Haus der Kunst from 1939 onward was well represented by paintings about war.[300] In fact, next to nineteenth-century landscape painters, portrait and genre painters, and those who unsuccessfully tried for an Expressionist comeback, the group of war painters was the most original, because its members continued a new trend that in Germany had been creatively nurtured, by the likes of Elk Eber, in an atmosphere of imminent war even before the fall of 1939.

Who, then, were the artists whose works were exhibited during the war and often purchased by Party and private clients, and what did they create? Of particular interest today are those who depicted scenes of warfare or worked on themes featuring soldiers, in order to inspire both the front-line combat troops and civilians at home. This is how Goebbels wanted it: to convey "the great community experience of war."[301] As a consequence, already by 1940, the number of artworks with military and martial motifs at the Munich art show was almost six times higher than it had been in 1937.[302] Their creators were, exclusively, male, and all were already well known; their style was what we may call National Socialist Realism. About the five men and their work discussed here, *Oxford Art Online* characteristically has scarcely a comment, which is one measure of its objective standards. Current extreme right-wing or militaria websites, on the other hand, have various commentaries, and this proves helpful, especially alongside a reproduction of the paintings; yet with such sources, even the biographical details have to be approached with caution.

Elk Eber, who had painted SA men on marches and the like before 1939, produced images of the German advance against Poland and in 1940 was featured in a Berlin exhibition entitled "The Polish Campaign in Pictures and Portraits." Among the twenty works he offered, one entitled *They Are Coming* was probably reproduced in a 1944 art compilation. This picture was of a group of four Wehrmacht soldiers awaiting the onslaught of the enemy, with one comrade lying hunched under a greatcoat, obviously dead. The work, possibly a charcoal sketch, shows the frontman ready to throw a hand grenade; the soldiers behind him, one without a helmet, bear expressions of tension, but also of fear. Their hard-edged faces have been drawn in a Realist style with brutalist inflection, stereotypically Nazi – with prominent noses and square jaws. For his efforts Eber received an art prize from the SA in February 1940.[303]

Eber's colleague Wolfgang Willrich submitted the portrait of a living legend, Colonel Werner Mölders, the first pilot in aviation history with a hundred enemy air hits, who crashed in November 1941 at the age of twenty-eight. Just before Mölders's death, Willrich created a realistic likeness of him, as he looked out of his cockpit window onto the airfield, clad in leather cap and that typical white scarf the elitist Luftwaffe pilots fancied, ready to take off. (It was Mölders who had persuaded Goebbels to allow more jazz to be played for the soldiers.) Later, while a regular soldier in the army, Willrich portrayed navy personnel – Admiral Karl Dönitz and U-boat commander Günther Prien, another legend – and later generals Erwin Rommel and Heinz Guderian. In 1944, after Willrich had starred in several exhibitions, the Army High Command (OKH) assigned to him the theme of "That's Why the German Soldier Fought," which, after his capture by the Americans in 1945, was published under the Perón dictatorship in Argentina between book covers four years later.[304]

Beyond mere human portraiture, the pictures evoked the barbarism of war as something tough but embraceable, to paraphrase Ernst Jünger. There were often artworks in which the individual human figure receded, behind masses of soldiers and piles of machinery. Ferdinand Spiegel created a fresco entitled *Tank*, in which four panzers are moving forward threateningly, blasting into the sky, under which is shown a mound of horses and men, reminiscent of Frederician battles, all entangled and intertwined, all shooting and killing each other. Spiegel, born in 1879, had begun with peasant scenes and he also painted soldiers' portraits, some of which Hitler bought, for approximately 4,000 marks each.[305] A gruesome portrait was painted by Franz Eichhorst, *Artillery Firing on Warsaw*, in which two mobile units manned by scores of Wehrmacht soldiers shoot into a black background. Albeit gruesome, it was still to be welcomed, for the Germans won that battle. (Eichhorst later painted an equally chilling *Memory of Stalingrad* in 1943, which, curiously, Hitler also purchased – a faceless row of emasculated soldiers in a ditch towered over by the half-naked figure of a young recruit, his eyes almost covered by a bandage, topped by a soldier with a rifle, next to an approaching tank: ostentatious martyrs for a patriotic cause.)[306] Yet another such painter was Wilhelm Petersen of the SS-PK, who drew a blurry charcoal rendition of hand-to-hand combat, eerie and breathing terror, where humans were not recognizable as humans. Petersen also created shadowy charcoals of Waffen-SS soldiers engaged in battle, ready to tell of the thrills of war if ever they survived.[307]

Apart from many of the war painters, Hitler personally preferred, as he had before, traditional artists who were repeatedly invited to exhibit in the annual Munich show of the Haus der Deutschen Kunst and whose paintings he was likely to purchase, with many in his entourage following suit. All he had to do was tell his personal photographer, "Professor" Hoffmann, who did the Führer's bidding. One such painter was the Bavarian Sepp Hilz, who achieved official fame with a *Peasant Venus* he exhibited in 1939; Goebbels bought it at the height of the war, for 15,000 marks, and it was made into a commercial postcard.[308] Hilz was born in northern Bavaria in 1906, the son of a painter and church restorer. As an apprentice to a locally well-known painter-craftsman in Rosenheim he was taught to copy images by Albrecht Dürer, Lucas Cranach the Elder, and Albrecht Altdorfer. Eventually, after three semesters at a Munich arts-and-crafts school, Hilz became active as an independent artist all over Upper Bavaria, painting, after 1930, in the style of one of Hitler's favorites, Wilhelm Leibl. Hilz acquired fame as the "peasant painter."[309] Nationally prominent, he was represented twenty-two times in the Munich art exhibitions, from 1938 to 1944. In 1942 he showed his *Weather Witch*, a mischievously smiling, naked, young woman curled up in the darkish heavens, holding a lighted candle behind her and flying over frightened peasant folk. Pure kitsch from a Modernist or any-school point of view, it enthused Hitler so much that he bought it for 35,000 marks.

Other works of Hilz's were purchased by Bavarian Gauleiter Adolf Wagner, Foreign Minister Joachim von Ribbentrop, and Reich Marshal Göring, who all had virtually limitless government expense accounts. (This type of state-treasury robbery was the typical form of Nazi upper-echelon corruption.) In 1943, Goebbels committed to paper: "Once again the Führer is full of praise for the pictures of Sepp Hilz."[310]

Today one wonders what Goebbels and Hitler were so excited about. When the dice are cast, both *Peasant Venus* and *Weather Witch* resemble other paintings of the contemporary genre. Although the *Venus* is pruriently nude without causing pornographic offence, certainly not by the standards of 1930s Germany, her image is similar in style to a work by the Viennese artist Erwin Puchinger, *Fountain in the Mountain*, in which a young girl – it could have been the *Venus* dressed up in a dirndl – glances coyly down to a Tyrol-style fountain scene. The *Weather Witch* painting, moreover, looks like one done by the contemporary Innsbruck master of the brush Heinrich Berann, entitled *Mountain Monster*, in which a man in black trousers and boots is visible, climbing skittishly over rocks under the weight of huge dark bags, set off threateningly against a moody sky. Granted, he does not have a terrified audience underneath, as does Hilz's witch picture, but his presence is terrifying enough.[311]

Another painter popular with the regime in those years was Willy Kriegel; in March 1941, Goebbels acclaimed him as "the Dürer of our time."[312] Kriegel, born in 1901, came from Dresden, where he had attended a masterclass with Oskar Kokoschka. Possibly because he had been influenced by Otto Dix, Kriegel was one of the early victims of the Nazi artist Wolfgang Willrich, but he redeemed himself by the beginning of the war, as Magda Goebbels discovered him, recommending him to her husband. Kriegel is a telling example of what happens once the private tastes and whims of politicians take over in an authoritarian state, dictating styles and artists to consumers. Although Kriegel's specialties were pictures of animals and flowers, Goebbels appreciated his landscapes most. Soon, Hitler too was convinced: Kriegel, a Nazi Party member since 1933, was awarded the title of professor by the Führer in 1943. Twenty-one of his works were exhibited in Munich over the years, of which Hitler himself purchased twelve, for prices of up to 25,000 marks each. Ribbentrop acquired others, and so did Goebbels. For their purchases, these politicians had to account to no one, while the favored artists became very rich. During the final phase of World War II, Hitler himself placed Kriegel on a special list of elite artists exempt from conscription; only twelve men were on it, and Kriegel was one of four painters.[313]

This type of capricious state patronage by a seasoned kleptocratic regime did not extend to all Nazi-conforming artists, as the leaders of the regime kept on deciding what would politically serve them or not. Again, this was in keeping with the nature of an authoritarian, if not to say totalitarian, state system. Even someone who had once been singled out for favors could quickly fall from grace. During World War II, this would become the fate of four painters: Paul Matthias Padua, Hans Schmitz-Wiedenbrück, Constantin Gerhardinger, and Adolf Ziegler.

Padua's daring picture *Leda and the Swan* had been selected by Hitler personally for the Haus der Deutschen Kunst exhibition of 1939; eventually it was bought by the vulgar bigamist Martin Bormann, chief of the Führer chancellery.[314] In 1940, Padua painted a rousing battle scene, commemorating the invasion of Belgium starting on May 10 of that year. The picture showed the commander of a Wehrmacht platoon, standing over his men ready to charge ahead, as he is beckoning them, with an outstretched arm, to meet the challenge. Padua later painted a likeness of a naked Diana, sleeping, as she is guarded by two nude young women, one of whom, with full breasts, is facing the onlooker in a sexually inviting pose. Although Hoffmann would mention him again briefly in his 1943 retrospective of recent Munich shows, Padua had incurred the criticism of Goebbels in December 1940, who thought that his painting *Mars und Venus* had been too daring and executed sloppily. Indeed, as one examines that work today, it was obviously not one of Padua's outstanding efforts, as the outlines of the figures are blurred, with the colors carelessly applied.[315]

Two years later, in 1943, artists as well as political leaders were becoming more nervous, as the defeat at Stalingrad had stung and living and working conditions were more trying under air raids. What with possible stays in shelters, painters were painting less steadily and cutting corners, as had Padua with his *Mars*, and the regime leaders, moody because of war's bad fortunes, reacted ever more critically. This would be the experience of Hans Schmitz-Wiedenbrück, born in 1907, who in 1941 exhibited an ambitious triptych with manual laborers holding pick-axe and spade, next to navy, artillery, and air men and, on the right, a farmer steering oxen.[316] It was to symbolize, as did so many artworks of the Third Reich, the unity between all social classes along with, in this particular case, the priority soldiers had to assume in a time of armed conflict.[317] But in 1943, Hitler himself once again decided what was art and what was not, what was well done and what fell short of what he defined as craftsmanship. For the Munich show starting that summer he denounced several artists Hoffmann had already preselected, on account of their slipshod work, and had them removed from the rosters. Among them was Schmitz-Wiedenbrück, whom Goebbels, who liked him regardless, had nominated at the Führer chancellery for a professorship. While Hitler turned down the candidacy, he at least allowed the artist to exhibit in Munich once again, for all it was worth, in summer 1944.[318]

Things took a sharper turn with Schmitz-Wiedenbrück's colleagues Gerhardinger and Ziegler. Early in 1943, Professor Gerhardinger, who had exhibited regularly from 1938 on, had refused to submit samples of his work for the Munich exhibition because he was afraid they would suffer in one of the bombing raids on the Bavarian capital. The case paralleled the plight of another artist, the jazz and studio pianist Peter Kreuder, who refused to perform concerts in the Rhineland after the fall of 1943 because of the bombs falling there.[319] In Gerhardinger's case, as Goebbels remarked to himself, Hitler was incensed because, "for all its generosity, the National Socialist leadership sees a limit where national interests are at stake." As a consequence, Gerhardinger lost his professorship, whatever that had been worth. When Ziegler, who thought he had some status because of his founding role with earlier Nazi art exhibitions and works the Führer liked, complained on behalf of Gerhardinger in a letter to Goebbels, his *Four Elements* that had so amused François-Poncet were removed from Munich's Führer building and Ziegler was sent to Dachau concentration camp for some weeks, until Hitler himself had him released.[320]

Throughout the 1940s, the Propaganda Minister was of the opinion that in the visual arts, contemporary sculpture took precedence over painting, as far as quality was concerned.[321] The truth is that in many ways sculpture, even before September 1939, had shown itself capable of demonstrating, over and above the most ornate of paintings, power, authority, and manliness. Two sculptors in particular, Josef Thorak and Arno Breker, cast in stark relief those properties during wartime and skillfully added martial accents.

The Austrian Thorak continued his monumental sculptures, many of which were of horses and female nudes, during the war in his giant studios and was represented at every Munich exhibition until 1943. At that point he appeared to have passed a critical remark about the regime, from the repercussions of which Albert Speer had to rescue him. Nonetheless, he became wealthy from all the state commissions, private sales, and other favors. Hitler bought a bust of Nietzsche from him for 50,000 marks. Thorak, who reported an income of 343,000 marks in 1943, acquired Schloss Prielau near Salzburg, paying only 60,000 marks for it, after it had been wrested from its Jewish owner, Hugo von Hofmannsthal's widow Gerty, née Schlesinger. Like Breker, Thorak's name was placed, near the end of the war, on the list of indispensable persons, shielding him from conscription.[322]

Already in February 1940, Goebbels had noted that Thorak paled in comparison with Breker and that the latter was thought by Hitler to be "the greatest sculptor of our time," after the minister himself had introduced him to the Führer.[323] Be that as it may, from everything we know today it can be maintained that Breker was the most successful of all the visual artists during the war and, probably, the most important creator of any objects of culture for the entire Reich, all disciplines considered. His significance for Nazi weltanschauung *and* totalitarian rule cannot be overestimated, since he consistently chose for his themes heroic ones, of men and sometimes of women.[324] Hagiographically, one contemporary biographer credited Breker in 1943 with always capturing "the essential" in his work, which he likened to a Michelangelesque mold, thus having expressed most realistically the "new lifestyle of the German people." More prosaically but succinctly, Jonathan Petropoulos has recently characterized Breker's œuvre as driven by "a heightened sense of anger," and as a manifestation of "glorified aggressive warfare."[325] Showing approximately the same number of works at the Munich art exhibition over the years as Thorak, anywhere from forty to fifty all told, in which busts of Hitler and other Nazi greats were prominent, Breker certainly was the richer of the two and probably the richest of all Nazi artists.[326] Breker enjoyed special favors that later turned into gold, such as being selected to accompany the Führer on his tour to conquered Paris, along with architects Hermann Giesler and Speer, on June 23, 1940. Here Breker was on hand in the Führer's Mercedes, to explain to Hitler architecture and artwork, which, as an old denizen of pre-war Paris bohemia, he knew intimately.[327] Later, in addition to the estates he owned in Germany, Breker was given a town house in Paris that had previously belonged to the perfume doyenne Helena Rubinstein, an American Jew, but was now expropriated by the Third Reich without compensation.[328]

CULTURE TO THE FRONTS

Goebbels's utilitarian view of culture in German society and politics was nowhere more evident than at the military fronts, where there was a decline in the quality of art, music, and drama due to the wartime conditions. Irrespective of their quality, however, cultural diversions were needed as a palliative for soldiers in war.

The organizational framework for Truppenbetreuung ("Caring for the Troops") was created in the late 1930s in a cooperation between the Wehrmacht and KdF, the "Strength-through-Joy" division of the German Labor Front (DAF) under its leader Robert Ley. It had offered up the Volksempfänger (VE; radio receiver), held out promises of a Volkswagen (KdF-Wagen), and offered workers mass entertainment and holiday cruises. At the beginning of the war the Promi joined forces with officers under Goebbels, who instructed Hans Hinkel to recruit artists and oversee a broad program of cultural recreation for military personnel and, secondarily, (German) armaments workers. On Ley's side Bodo Lafferentz eventually officiated, an SS lieutenant colonel with a PhD in economics and later the husband of Richard Wagner's attractive granddaughter Verena, whom Hitler, "Uncle Wolf," always fondly called "Nickel." The cooperation between those three administrations until 1944 was relatively smooth, except for routine differences; such as between the Promi and KdF over emoluments for the artists, with the former wanting to pay out less than the latter thought they were worth, or between the Promi and Wehrmacht, over specially established soldiers' radio stations, whose programming Goebbels tried in vain to oversee. Ultimately, the Reich treasury, becoming rich from all kinds of robbery, including plundering artworks from occupied territories, was responsible for the overall financing.[329]

The raw statistics concerning these events are impressive, even if one considers that many of those who performed hardly deserved the name of artist and many performances, whatever their quality, became routine as they were repeated over and over again. From September to December 1939 alone 12,400 events were staged; throughout 1940, 137,802 performances were recorded. Until July 20, 1944, the day of the assassination attempt on Hitler, Lafferentz published in *Der Angriff* that 836,000 shows had been performed.[330] In no other instance could Goebbels claim with greater authority not only that German culture mattered to bolster morale, but that it would be essential for a Great-German reordering after the war's conclusion.

After registering a dearth of artist volunteers for cultural diversions at the fronts, Goebbels announced in early August 1940 that he expected all artists "to put themselves at the disposal of the great work of Truppenbetreuung, with all their hearts."[331] Indeed, artists had already been working for the program in the rearguard of troop advances both on the Eastern and Western Fronts, and then in the occupied territories such as Norway. Cologne had sent the popular Millowitsch stage ensemble to the west; the Reich Symphony Orchestra with its musicians in mustard-brown Party tuxedos had been playing Wagner, Bruckner, and Beethoven. Very well-known artists had gone on tour, among them the actors Lil Dagover and Rudolf Platte, and the musicians Hans Knappertsbusch, Rudolf Heger, Elly Ney, and Wilhelm Kempff. Other units had included the Berlin and Dresden Philharmonics, the Leipzig Gewandhaus, as well as the opera troupes of Weimar, Hamburg, and Stuttgart, and the Frankfurt theater. And the Salzburg and Bayreuth festivals were clearly an inland extension of Truppenbetreuung, even if they were financed separately.[332]

As was noted before, much of the troop entertainment revolved around books. Goebbels was right when he observed in February 1942 that "the U-boat mate, when he rises from the machine room, dirty and smeared with grease as he is, will not reach for *The Myth of the 20th Century*."[333] Along with Hitler's *Mein Kampf*, couples would be handed this opaque volume by Alfred Rosenberg at their wedding and at baptisms (financed by municipalities and making both authors indecently rich), but soldiers wanted something much lighter.[334] The same applied to brochures about "colonial policy, geopolitics, race science and Fascism."[335] Soldiers preferred to be handed cheap romances of the doctor-and-nurse or secretary-and-boss variety, on thin paper and costing up to 50 pfennigs, next to humorous works authored by the likes of Heinrich Spoerl and the ancient Wilhelm Busch. "Us soldiers, we want kitsch," wrote one trooper from the front, reminding the authorities at home that print had to be large enough to be deciphered on a rattling train. Many of the books designated on the home front for the soldiers were then made available to the troops in special "front bookstores," some of them mobile; one of those was able to transport over 3,000 volumes, with about half of them in a trailer. In France, sixty stationary bookstores at the beginning of 1942 grew to ninety-eight by the end of 1943, complemented by any number of literature buses. In Norway book barges lumbered across the fjords. In 1943 altogether, there were 300 stationary stores, apart from the books-on-wheels. These outlets also carried musical records, pens, and paper, but the number of books never seemed to be enough, so that only 20 percent of total troop demand could be satisfied. Already by January 1940, 8.5 million books were reported to have been specially collected for the front, and after Rosenberg had been appointed Minister for the Occupied Territories in 1941, he weighed in with book donations of his own, chosen by his censorial Party offices and said to have been in the millions.[336]

Next to books, radio, recorded music, and film were important. As for broadcasting, the Wehrmacht established its own stations, manning them with radio personalities and staff of its own choosing; among those stations Soldier Radio Belgrad, where eventually the song "Lili Marleen" was born, was the most discriminating and the most popular, attaining even legendary status.[337] But other broadcasts for the front came from Goebbels's radio stations, and he himself made sure that thousands of extra receivers were collected, many confiscated from German Jews, to be distributed at the front lines. The same applied to shellac records and gramophones: in Berlin alone, in December 1941, 350,000 records and 2,000 record players were centrally assembled under the auspices of the Promi, to be transported to the front. "As one can see," noted Goebbels smugly, "the German people are prepared for any kind of sacrifice, as long as one addresses them properly." By way of films, which were shown both in stationary and mobile theaters, movies with ideological content such as *Jud Süss* and *Heimkehr* were preferred, putting into practice Goebbels's dictum of culture for a people's education, but equally and understandably, the soldiers enjoyed light-entertainment fare such as comedy.[338]

As relaxing as the military found films and recordings, it was live entertainment that interested them most. Not least because of Goebbels's

August 1940 appeal to German artists, approximately 14,000 of them were observed to be occupying themselves with Truppenbetreuung tasks in any given month by the middle of 1942.[339] While established theaters such as the Landestheater Saarpfalz in Kaiserslautern dedicated themselves completely to the servicing of troops, in this case those stationed in the west as early as September 1939, the KdF created itinerant stages moving in behind the advancing troops. The municipal theater in Minsk was cleared of native artists by the new Nazi governor Wilhelm Kube and occupied, successively, by the corps of German local theaters, such as that of Landsberg/Warthe. One of the first plays performed in Minsk was Kube's own *Totila*, hitherto unknown. Before long, artists' hostels ("Künstlerheime") existed in important centers of occupied countries, such as Bordeaux, Athens, Oslo, and Riga. In the fall of 1941, Hinkel launched Künstlerfahrt, a Berlin-based program for the benefit of the wounded, and from the fall of 1942 until May 1944 an artists' barge cruised along the north-western coast of Norway, defying British air raids, mines, and U-boat attacks. The offerings of that show-business industry came to include mostly light entertainment, such as revues and operetta, peasant plays, and unsophisticated comedies of the kind the previously cited unknown soldier had demanded, but also, in much lower numbers, symphonic concerts, solo recitals, and chamber-music evenings. (In this category, many reputable actors such as Olga Tschechowa, Mathias Wieman, and Paul Hörbiger made a specialty of prose recitations and poetry readings.) Throughout, so-called Bunte Abende (variety shows) predominated, mixed-show stagings with Wunschkonzert content, where quizzes followed dance numbers, funny stories, and pop-tune renditions, and the military audience, including of course the Amazon corps of uniformed Blitzmädel, was encouraged to participate.[340]

There were several problems with Truppenbetreuung, however, which damned the entire venture to perdition from the beginning – conceptual and structural ones independent of war events, and others more directly related to military strategy and execution. One endemic difficulty prevailing until the end of the Third Reich was the loose and non-committal nature of the contracts between the Wehrmacht, KdF, and Promi, which affected staff hirings, financial compensation, and coordination in the field. All three agencies differed, for instance, on the degree of quality inherent in culture fit for troop entertainment, with the Wehrmacht expecting a substantial level of high culture, perhaps supplied by pianists Elly Ney and Wilhelm Kempff for classics-loving officers. The Promi, on the other hand, as in civilian life, wished for a predominance of light entertainment, while the KdF, used to serving the working and lower-middle classes from peacetime, eschewed learned culture on principle. Another example of skewed logistics arose from a discordancy plaguing various planning boards: whereas Goebbels decided, in the wake of the July 1944 coup attempt, to close Truppenbetreuung in early September of that year, along with other cultural activities, several units continued on their own, probably supported by KdF and, locally, certainly the Wehrmacht, so that cultural diversions to boost troop morale were going on even in the spring of 1945.

To add to these troubles, there were no obvious chains of command and obligatory allocations of duties in the personnel sector; at the beginning of the Truppenbetreuung scheme visual artists, musicians, and actors could rely on whatever prestige they had, to participate or withhold themselves at will. This was demonstrated in January 1941 when Goebbels, during a visit to the time-honored Josefstadt theater in Vienna, decided on a whim to engage the entire ensemble for a tour in France. Fearing that their set schedules would be interrupted, the directors of the theater argued that currently their performances were fixed and that the actress Paula Wessely, whom Goebbels wanted in particular, was busy filming *Heimkehr* in conquered Poland. Eventually the minister had to relent, especially since the main director then was the prominent Heinz Hilpert, usually in Berlin, and Goebbels had to take solace in the theater's promise to communicate the names of actors and directors who were presently not working. Hence a comprehensive Josefstadt theater tour never materialized.[341]

Earmarking Paula Wessely for performances at the front was symptomatic of the personnel politics that went awry under Ley's and Goebbels's leadership. Because at first an artist could not be conscripted for service, the laws of a free-market economy came into play: as the demand was great, virtually every ballet dancer, pianist, or actor could charge the fee that he or she desired. Commensurate with such a practice was a gradual dilution in the quality of performances, as artists cut down on their presentations and relaxed controls. Fees for unknown singers or two-bit actors were reaching stratospheric proportions, so that Goebbels, at the beginning of 1942, complained that artists had the nerve of demanding anywhere from 300 to

500 marks for merely declaiming a poem. During that year, therefore, he decided that no one be paid more than 75 marks per day, and later still he decreed that 800 marks per month was an acceptable wage. But as a result of this policy many artists decided not to come forward any more, because, as one twenty-year-old rookie actress cockily remarked, with the 1,600 marks she was earning monthly at her home theater there was no need for her to risk performing at the front.

After 1942, therefore, it benefited artists more to be in fixed employment, for instance as performers onstage or filming at Babelsberg, Vienna, or Prague; in that case they could only be conscripted for troop service for a maximum of six weeks, either at the modest rates Goebbels had prescribed or pro bono. This favored established veterans of the stage such as the actress Olga Tschechowa or the pianist Wilhelm Kempff, who were regularly engaged within the Reich; but it was unfair to lesser-known artists, who likely had shorter contracts or were unemployed, and thus were coerced to join Truppenbetreuung. Fixed employment also favored artists such as most painters, sculptors, and authors, who had little to offer soldiers by way of entertainment and were left alone, although such individuals were always prone to be drafted into the armed forces directly or forced to serve in the armaments industry. In all, Truppenbetreuung offered a drab picture in 1943 when many members of the creative class who should have been there had managed not to be sent directly to the fronts with all their inherent danger, and where they were liable to witness unsettling scenes, such as the horribly wounded, the treatment of Soviet prisoners of war, or the liquidation of partisans and even Jews. At that time, the quality of cultural performances at the front had sunk to such low levels that actors and musicians were sometimes laughed out of the officers' messes and makeshift auditoriums by the troops. More and more, soldiers tended to prefer entertainment by indigenous artists, such as Dutch ones in occupied Holland and Ukrainians in south-east Russia. So much for the superiority of German culture in wartime![342]

How did individual artists fare under these circumstances? Paula Wessely's brother-in-law, the film heart-throb Paul Hörbiger, who had celebrated the birthday of Goebbels's wife Magda in 1935 in the presence of Hitler by singing to the accompaniment of Luise Ullrich's accordion, fully welcomed the Anschluss of his native Austria in 1938; he was to make a total of seventy-three films during the Third Reich. He is not known to have put himself at the disposal of Goebbels to serve at the front for the less than generous conditions set in 1942, but the SD kept a file on him, noting, by July 1943, that while he was a candidate for Truppenbetreuung, he should be watched closely for his "known alcoholic excesses." Regardless of whether he had ever made money at the fronts before 1942, Hörbiger was being kept in check by Himmler's controllers.[343] His colleague Tschechowa – arguably an even closer intimate of Goebbels and Hitler – all of whose films, according to Speer, the Führer watched, undoubtedly took advantage of earlier lucrative junkets behind the front lines, as she intimated in a retrospective of 1943. Tschechowa styled it heroically: She had been "honored" to be allowed to play "for our soldiers," she said, as they were so "receptive" to anything artistic. After all, they were in a struggle, "with the whole of man being challenged." After the war she admitted that she had performed in Paris, Lyons, Lille, and Brussels – all of these being relatively peaceful sites after Belgium's and France's capitulation to the Nazis.[344]

The film-script author and dramaturg at Göring's Staatstheater, Eckart von Naso, was twice in Russia, once in Norway, and then in Paris, offering readings from classics of German literature. He used the plenitude of German marks with nothing to buy in the Old Reich to acquire cognac and cigarettes on the black market beyond its borders, butter, real coffee, and tea. To be sure, opportunities for morally questionable enrichment were ample in those conquered territories, then plundered by the Nazis in other obnoxious ways. Gertie Schönfelder, a little-known singer from the Berlin Scala with no lasting prospects of work, was sent in a band to entertain the Wehrmacht and Waffen-SS in the eastern Jewish enforced ghettoes. Led through those venues, she took advantage of the Jews' plight by having them work for her for free; on one occasion, a Jewish master shoemaker custom-made a pair of boots for her, of the finest, softest leather, as she rhapsodized to me many years later.[345]

Thus many artists attempted to appease the regime leaders and derive substantial material benefit for themselves at the same time. A few then used these experiences after the war, as did von Naso, to portray themselves as resistance fighters of a kind when they reminisced. Perhaps the most blatant example of this was furnished by Göring's token genius director at the Staatsoper, Gustaf Gründgens, already described earlier as a left-leaning spirit in his younger days. With his sexual exploits monitored by the regime (the way it kept an eye on Hörbiger's alcohol consumption), Gründgens fabricated brilliant theater under the Prussian Minister President's patronage, while taking advantage of an "Aryanized" estate near Berlin, which became his (and his wife Marianne Hoppe's) residence. In 1941 and 1942, Gründgens went on the Truppenbetreuung circuits with the ideologically neutral play *Das Konzert* by the Austrian Hermann Bahr – in the relative safety of occupied Holland and Norway. Doubtless, this star of all stars was well remunerated. But even in 1941 he bragged about this as an act of personal exertion and sacrifice. Publicly, he said that he had become active in a war, "to be or not be," that he had measured his histrionic talents against "the reality of wartime experience." He had looked into the eyes of men that had "seen death and perceived things sharply." He was a hero to have withstood and mastered such situations, suggested Gründgens, who wanted to go public with Bahr's play – and his own memoirs – after the end of the regime.[346]

Gründgens, who in 1936 had already been caricatured in the novel *Mephisto* by Klaus Mann, his former lover, was a sophisticated manipulator, and he was already in his forties when he said this. Two ingénues of the film world were Ilse Werner and Margot Hielscher, one born in 1921, the other in 1919. As noted earlier, Werner had starred in the film *Wunschkonzert*, thematically if not logistically a feature of the entire troop entertainment program. Werner writes that she was inducted into Truppenbetreuung at a time when there were already scores of wounded soldiers. After 1942, singing and reciting in military hospitals was an ever more frequent aspect of caring for the troops, who were irremediably in retreat. Werner remembers the shock she experienced when in 1943 she started singing, "Why does every man look at me so lovingly," only to realize that her audience consisted of blind men in uniform. According to her testimony, this twenty-two-year-old could hardly hold back her tears.[347] Hielscher, too, had to croon, so she revealed, about a year later as she was filming in Prague, where the Babelsberg crews had moved for safety. There was an infirmary in nearby Pilsen. A young wounded soldier, on his deathbed, wanted to hear her film song "Women are no Angels." She recalls: "I did this, really tried hard hoping my voice would not break. But he died before my eyes. Ever since then this song, my signature melody, is tied to the image of this dying boy, and it took years for me to be able to sing it freely again."[348]

Today we cannot be sure whether Ilse Werner and Margot Hielscher really experienced the pain they so graphically described after the war, not least for commercial gain and fame and to gather sympathy for themselves. Barely beyond their teenage years, they had certainly been abused as young sex symbols by unscrupulous political leaders in ventures that now were woefully falling apart, and had been left with the unenviable role of picking up some of the pieces. In an interview in June 1988 with a successful and affluent Margot Hielscher at her bungalow, in the tony Munich district of Bogenhausen, a stone's throw from Thomas Mann's former villa, the now famous West German film diva was not aware of the devious purposes to which Goebbels had put the entertainment industry, nor was she cognizant of its demise.[349] During the conversation I had with her then, she did not understand that, in wartime, films had deceitfully hidden roles to play. Such as her *Das Herz der Königin* (*The Heart of a Queen*) in 1940, with Germany about to invade Britain – essentially a propaganda film against the island kingdom, meant at the time to convey the false truth to Germans that it was corrupt and ruled by rapacious imperialists. But neither was Hielscher aware of the failure of such efforts, in this case by a film that even then was attacked by critics on its aesthetic grounds alone.[350] Hence she could not see that even the best cultural content up to 1945 had not worked as propaganda to bolster German public morale, in fact that the more the Reich's internal and external fortunes had deteriorated, the more such cultural diversions had been exposed as deceptive and mendacious. Instead, when asked about those final months of working in film for the Reich, long after she had established her credentials as a pliant actress with her predatory boss, Hielscher rejoiced in hindsight about the safe conditions of filming in Prague (after she had spent an equally safe time filming in Vienna); she gloated over the wonderful food she and her film crew had enjoyed, and the limitless amounts of alcohol, and the dance-on-the-volcano revelries. She said that she had been very aware of being well protected in Prague, as no enemy bombing raids could threaten anyone's lives, everyone was well paid and able to buy consumer goods long gone in Berlin. What a privileged situation Hielscher was enjoying in those final months of the war, indeed. But when asked if her good fortune as a film actress from 1940 onward was possibly due to the lack of competition formerly posed by young Jewish actresses like Lilli Palmer, who now had to suffer the travails of emigration, quite apart from those who had actually been killed, the actress fell silent. It was a thought that during her entire Nazi career may never have crossed her mind.

CHAPTER FIVE

◆ ◆ ◆

Artist Émigrés

A S HAS BECOME evident from preceding chapters, emigration from Germany was a fixed component of the Third Reich narrative. In that context, "emigration" may be a euphemism, because it usually denotes an orderly process of leave-taking from the home country and the approved and regulated arrival in a new host country, even if it causes economic and psychological hardship for the émigré. But the exodus from Germany between 1933 and 1941 was not orderly and occurred almost always under political rather than economic pressure, even though there could not have been a single emigrant whose forced withdrawal was not, at the same time, accompanied by financial sacrifice. There were two other demographic characteristics of this modern human flood. It constituted the largest departure of Germans from their home country since the abortive revolutions of 1848–9. Moreover, the emigrants, who because of the pressures applied to them should more properly be called refugees, belonged for the greater part to a single ethnic grouping, the Jews, whether they were assimilated into German mainstream society and sometimes baptized Christians or had been born in Austria or the European East and originally were Orthodox Mosaic. If outside pressure may be easily understood as a catalyst for emigration, the question arises how many Germans, Jewish or not, left the Third Reich motivated by individual conscience. Since Jews must be immediately classified as a victim cohort, this question would concern the so-called Aryans, some of whom might not have been bothered by the Nazi regime had they stayed in Germany after January 1933, although nothing was a certainty. One such person who could have belonged in this category was Harry Graf Kessler; independently wealthy and a reclusive homosexual, he might have been left alone, even in homophobic Nazi Germany. As it turned out, Kessler, via Mallorca, moved to France.[1] Another was the writer Thomas Mann, but he was married to a Jew who would have come under scrutiny. A third was Bertolt Brecht (also with a Jewish wife whom he constantly betrayed), who professed Communism, which, had he continued to uphold it in Germany, would have landed him in a concentration camp.[2] Besides, Communism advocated its own brand of totalitarianism, hence Communists who left for the Soviet Union were exchanging one inhuman political system for another. Such a people transfer would not have occurred under circumstances upholding human rights and freedoms.

Mann and Brecht were two exceptional writers who had been setting the pace, already famous in Germany and the world long before 1933, who found getting out of Hitler's Reich and continuing to make a reasonable living abroad not beyond their capabilities. In that sense both – Brecht less so than Mann – were atypical of the vast majority of musicians, painters, writers, and personalities from film and stage who, mostly Jewish, had to leave, having to overcome severe obstacles, usually of two kinds. One was to manage and survive the process of departure, with all that this entailed on German soil, where, for example, entry visas for a foreign country had to be obtained and, eventually, over 90 percent of an emigrant's financial assets had to be surrendered to Nazi authorities, including the payment of a "Reich flight tax." The other was to secure a suitable welcome in the host country, with the aim of becoming naturally integrated in a new, and strange, society, even if one planned to return. Ideally, this process would ultimately result in commensurate employment in some form of cultural activity, humane acceptance by new neighbors and employers and, not least, potential social mobility for one's offspring (such as the child Peter Gay, the future historian) through tolerance and the requisite formal education.[3] In all these matters, those countries reacted in a variety of ways, with none that could be said to have been ideal from a humanitarian perspective. Not least, how a cultural immigrant was treated depended, to a large degree, on their disposition, skills, prior levels of training, linguistic ability, and willingness to adjust. Altogether, the story that follows is not a happy one, even for those artists and intellectuals whom fortune had smiled upon.

All told, the emigration from Europe of German-speaking men and women due to the Nazi regime affected approximately half a million individuals, including academics, artists, and intellectuals. After having sustained many encumbrances due to National Socialist harassment before they could cross the borders, in addition to difficulties imposed by putative host countries such as visa delays, scores of new problems had to be overcome by immigrants upon arrival in their land of exile. Here economic difficulties easily ranked first, because the entrenched Depression from the late 1920s had led to widespread unemployment and nationalist politicians were reacting by invoking restrictive immigration laws.[4] Among those emigrants Jews overwhelmingly were in the majority. Until the annexation of Austria in March 1938, 129,000 Jews left the German Reich, followed by 118,000 from both countries in 1938–9; and after the outbreak of war until 1945, when this had become all but impossible, just over 31,000 fled. According to Werner Röder and Herbert Strauss, altogether 278,000 German-speaking Jews left the Reich during Hitler's dictatorship.[5]

Which were the main host countries of this involuntary exile, and what were the complications specific to them? In the East there was the Soviet Union, which drew mostly Communist emigrants, and not too many of them. One of the few was Friedrich Wolf, a multitalented physician and author of poetry, stage plays, and novellas who had helped put down the Kapp Putsch in Berlin during March 1920 and later joined the German Communist Party (KPD).[6] Another was Carola Neher, a beautiful German actress who emigrated to the Soviet Union at the age of thirty-two shortly after Hitler's rise to power; she had once collaborated with Brecht, a lover, and Kurt Weill. Denounced as a Trotskyite by fellow German expatriate Gustav Baron von Wangenheim during Stalin's purges, she died of typhus in June 1942 on the way to the Gulag, after years in prison.[7]

The Czechoslovak Republic (CSR), once part of the Habsburg Empire, appealed to many German emigrants because of its Western values and pro-Western leanings, guaranteeing a lifestyle congenial to Berliners and Viennese; it had been the seedbed of much of German culture. Although it required no entry visa, residency, until Hitler's invasion of the region by early 1939, was granted only to refugees traveling directly from Germany.

Unemployment was rampant in the CSR, and work permits or financial support were very hard to obtain.[8]

Sweden was open to political refugees for asylum, but here there was no special consideration of Jews; even so, once there, Jewish exiles suffered from indigenous anti-Semitism and the hostility of Swedish Jews. Here, too, the authorities cited unemployment as a reason for non-admission. Still, in November 1938, at the time of Kristallnacht in the German Reich, 1,200 German and Austrian emigrants were living in Sweden, of whom about 800 were allowed to work. However, the Swedes tightened their entry conditions by the time the war broke out, so altogether there were only 4,600 refugees in the country by May 1945.[9]

If Switzerland was seen as anti-Jewish, this too may have reflected a more general xenophobic stance. For an outsider, except perhaps someone world-famous, it was clear that possibilities for gainful employment did not exist here; the notorious Alien Police (Fremdenpolizei) made certain that permanent residence was granted only to those, like Thomas Mann or Erich Maria Remarque, who could prove financial independence. But even then new competition was feared, as Gottfried Bermann Fischer found out when he wanted to move his father-in-law's Fischer publishing company to Zurich. Nonetheless, there were approximately 10,000 German-speaking refugees in Switzerland during the war, some of whom even enjoyed a transitory right of asylum.[10]

In France, native anti-Semitism was enhanced by the xenophobia of French Jews (about half of the total Jewish population), who hated immigrant Jews from eastern Europe and resented more coming in from Austria and Germany, right into the Vichy era. Restrictions took hold under all cabinets, with the exception of the short-lived administrations of the Jewish Prime Minister Léon Blum, between 1936 and 1938.[11]

As for the United Kingdom, even though, as a parliamentary democracy, one might have expected it to be a most welcoming sanctuary, it accepted only a modicum of refugees until the November 1938 pogrom. The reason was, once again, xenophobia, in particular anti-Semitism, combined with unemployment fears, for many Britons were then on the dole. Overall, there were at least 55,000 German-speaking people in the country by the war's beginning, until, during the Wehrmacht's invasion of France, Belgium, and the Netherlands, widespread anti-German public opinion took hold.

Paradoxically, the Jews, formerly of Germany and Austria and shunned by their home countries, now found themselves victimized in Britain as "enemy aliens." After the new Prime Minister Winston Churchill had issued the order "collar the lot," newcomers from these two countries (and from Fascist Italy separately) were interned, and many were forced to undertake dangerous voyages, for what was meant to be temporary internment, to Australia and Canada. In the end, Great Britain was host to 78,000 immigrants, with virtually all of the detained free by May 1945.[12]

Because Britain had been handed the territory of Palestine as a mandate by the League of Nations after World War I, it was able to curtail German-Jewish immigration to that traditional Zionist haven as well; but despite all the odds, between 1933 and 1941 approximately 55,000 refugees arrived at those Middle Eastern shores. Whatever could have been done to facilitate work for those newcomers the British were observed to prevent; those immigrants had the best chances of employment who chose to toil with their hands – not exactly something artists and intellectuals were used to doing.[13]

In North and South America conditions varied. In the North, Canada proved uncompromisingly resistant to any kind of immigration from central Europe, especially where Jews were involved. The reasons were traditional Jew hatred in the ultramontane province of Quebec, alongside an anti-Semitic bureaucracy under the cabinet of Prime Minister Mackenzie King, who himself was obsessed with an idiosyncratic idolization of Adolf Hitler. When in May 1943, *The New York Times* passed the judgment that Canada, along with the United Kingdom, could do a whole lot more for the Jews of Europe, one senior official in Ottawa was heard to remark that the newspaper was not to be taken seriously, since everyone knew it belonged to Jews and was controlled by Jews.[14] Particularly grim conditions prevailed in Central and South America: bureaucratic red tape, corruption, xenophobia, and lack of work commensurate with talent.[15] As for the Caribbean – it was difficult to be granted residency there, because of prejudices, bureaucratic barriers, and widespread corruption on the part of island governments. Peter Gay remembers that only fate prevented him from boarding the refugee ship *St. Louis* in the spring of 1939. He had arrived with his family in Havana, Cuba, on a different ship a few weeks earlier (and later migrated to the United States). The *St. Louis* became sadly famous, as it docked in Havana without permission to discharge its émigré passengers, who subsequently were also refused by immigrant authorities in Miami (and later in Canada). The steamer had to return to Europe and landed with its human cargo of 936 in Belgium. About a third of those who were not fortunate enough to settle in the United Kingdom were thereafter caught in occupied western Europe by the Nazis, interned, and murdered.[16]

If between 1933 and 1945 only a few hundred refugees managed to make it into Canada, the United States accepted approximately 132,000 German-speaking immigrants – the highest absolute number of any country in the world.[17] This occurred against a background of tight restrictions leveled at immigrants in the historic past, when quotas had been working against Jews and southern Europeans. That trend had begun, for the twentieth century, with specific pieces of legislation in 1921 and 1924 and was resumed between 1929 and 1937, in cumulative steps, in the wake of the Great Depression, although emigrants from Austria and Germany, including Jews, were now less affected, because they did not exceed any nationality quotas. This changed after the November 1938 pogrom; in 1939–40 the Austrian and German quotas were fully met. After Himmler had prohibited the exodus of Jews from the Reich in October 1941, and again after America's entry into the war that December following the attack on Pearl Harbor, refugee immigration was reduced to a trickle. In any event, at all times there were specific difficulties for Jews trying to reach the United States; obtaining American sponsorship as a precondition for a visa was only one of several; another was the forewarning that any would-be newcomers would be met by rampant anti-Semitism.[18]

Altogether, so it has been ascertained, the United States took in nearly 48 percent of all exiles from German-speaking areas, Great Britain took 10 percent, Palestine 8 percent, and Switzerland 4 percent. Somewhat over 7 percent of all the immigrants to the United States were academics, intellectuals, or artists in one form or another. Among the last-mentioned, some 682 were journalists and writers, 465 were musicians, and 296 visual artists.[19]

POLITICAL, ECONOMIC, AND PSYCHOLOGICAL BARRIERS

In the mid-1930s, Klaus Mann, Thomas Mann's oldest son and himself a refugee, asked a serious question: "What would a neurologist from Berlin do in Australia, what a lawyer from Frankfurt in Guatemala?"[20] Mann's query addressed the frequent incompatibility of German or Austrian training with professional job certifications specific to refugee countries. This applied the higher and more specialized one's formal education was. For example jurists, who had been trained in Roman law and often had assumed positions in government and administration, in the United Kingdom had to master the Anglo-Saxon law code, which necessitated re-education, leaving many as lower-level law clerks. Similar stipulations were in force in the United States and Sweden.[21] Physicians fared somewhat better, because the medical arts are more universal than the juridical ones and, in this case, professional codes did not deviate so significantly from country to country. Putting it more succinctly: there was only one way to remove an inflamed appendix. A professional adjustment being a relatively minor matter, England had admitted over 100 refugees to a medical retraining course of studies already in 1933, although the competition was fierce.[22] Something similar was happening in the United States, where physicians constituted the largest proportion of all exiles, individual cases of hardship notwithstanding.[23] Wilhelm Reich, for instance, a one-time pupil of Sigmund Freud, after arriving in New York from European exile in Oslo, received a position as associate professor of medical psychology at the New School of Social Research in the spring of 1940. But no sooner had he started there than he occupied himself with what he abstrusely called "orgon energy," allegedly a power deriving from sexual orgasm and empirically quantifiable. Over this he had a row with Albert Einstein, who was based at the newly founded Institute for Advanced Studies in nearby Princeton, and it was not long before Reich was dismissed from the New School, on the way to losing his mind and being institutionalized.[24] Dr. Käte Frankenthal, who was thrice condemned by the Nazis as a Jew, a lesbian, and a Freudian psychiatrist, arrived in New York in 1936, after frustrating sojourns in France and Switzerland. Nowhere in Europe had she been allowed to practice medicine, and her stay in New York did not spare her the experience of first selling ice cream on the streets and then going from door to door peddling stockings, before an established colleague took her in as an assistant.[25] Heinrich Simon, the elderly proprietor of the *Frankfurter Zeitung*, emigrated via Switzerland and Palestine to New York in 1934, and there found nothing more than a job as a music teacher. One day in May of 1941, as he was walking home, he was accosted by thugs and barely made it to his apartment. Having sustained mortal wounds to his head, he died that same night; his killers were never found.[26]

In that respect the physician and writer Dr. Martin Gumpert proved more successful, as he had possessed a practice in Berlin and, once in New York, underwent an English-language examination, after which he was allowed to practice medicine again. What helped him was that New York State, of all states in the American union, for a while had the most tolerant admissions policy for medical doctors.[27] An author of several books, Gumpert was periodically a romantic partner of Erika Mann and a friend of Klaus Mann, and hence attuned to the artistic interests and activities emanating from the circle surrounding Thomas Mann, spanning not just New York but southern California as well.[28]

Mentioning Gumpert, Klaus and Erika Mann in one breath calls for some caution. Any references to the unusually creative members of Thomas Mann's extended family could suggest a generalization, namely that any biography of exiled German and Austrian artists, intellectuals or academics in opposition to Hitler would have to be characterized by success. This all the more so, since in hitherto existing literature many such individuals have been associated with "paradise," usually denoting California.[29] But for every Thomas Mann there existed scores of writers of both genders who were far removed from the triumphs of that prince of letters, and for every Bruno Walter there was a multitude of unknown conductors jobbing away in some orchestra or dance band.[30] The author Franz Werfel, another famous writer, had such ordinary, even deplorable circumstances in mind when he remarked that he viewed his own success as an undeserved piece of luck, after his bestselling novel *The Song of Bernadette* had come out in print in 1941. "Most others are faring badly," he warned, "they have to defeat many obstacles, with hardly any hopes of victory."[31] Hence it seems advisable to deal, from the point of view of a social history of culture, not just with the vagaries confronting well-known writers such as Thomas Mann and Franz Werfel, but also to look at lesser-known artistic émigrés who were denied good fortune.[32] One question that will have to remain open, however, is whether all the difficulties refugees encountered after their exodus were due to exile rather than tied to their personalities, no matter what the social and political environment they found themselves in.

Distress caused by immigration and employment regulations, but also the rigors of travel, befell almost everyone, even, to some extent, the very famous.

Artists in particular – and here they differed from some professions such as physicians – were not really essential to society in their countries of exile, as the native artists knew all too well; their potential for rivalrous jealousy was always a threat. Hence the new arrivals suffered more from regulations. In the United States, artists fell into the general category of immigrants issued merely temporary visas, which could be exchanged for permanent ones only after crossing the border for a second time, from Mexico or Canada.[33]

Various other difficulties plagued would-be residents of the United Kingdom. It was rare for someone like Sigmund Freud – an international celebrity – to be allowed to add his signature to those of other prominent signatories of the Charter Book of the Royal Society, which was brought to him after his arrival on British soil in 1938.[34] By contrast, when another former national of Austria, the journalist and author Arthur Koestler, finally managed to reach England's shores after frustrating attempts to enter legally from Portugal, he knew that as a former Communist and current Enemy Alien he would immediately be arrested, which is exactly what happened. And this after Koestler, who had already worked as a correspondent for an English newspaper, had been held in French detainment camps during 1940.[35] Moreover, following the disaster of her acting debut in Darmstadt in 1933, the young Berlin actress Lilli Palmer, after several stressful months in Paris, was allowed into England only after hesitation on the part of suspicious border officials, even though she could produce a valid employment contract. When finally she started working for a London film company, that contract made the renewal of a residence permit obligatory every three months.[36] After the beginning of the London Blitz, such oppression became even worse. Palmer's much better-known colleague Elisabeth Bergner, formerly of Vienna, Munich, and Berlin, by 1941 even had to check in weekly with the police, notwithstanding her newly acquired British citizenship.[37] In Palestine, residency conditions for immigrants applied that were similar to those in England, as well as in Sweden, where musicians were singled out for obstruction by the red tape of bureaucracy.[38]

As far as musicians who arrived in Britain are concerned, some music historians have made a special study of Jewish composers such as Berthold Goldschmidt, Mátyás Seiber, Hans Gál, and Franz Reizenstein, who for long periods faced particular misery there, for reasons still unexplained. The Berlin composer Goldschmidt, who had had such a prodigious start in

Germany, was virtually stalled in London (much like the Frankfurt composer Erich Itor Kahn in New York, who slogged away as a lieder accompanist). The BBC contributed substantially to these difficulties. Thus in 1940 some native composers, led by John Ireland and Ralph Vaughan Williams, pressured the broadcasting monopoly to confidentially blacklist 73 Austrian and 239 German-born colleagues, figures soon updated to 117 and 248 respectively. Between 1933 and the end of 1945 only six orchestral pieces by refugee composers were accepted for broadcasting on the radio.[39]

Once in a new country, the refugees usually had to get to grips with a new language. Musicians and visual artists sometimes had an easier time with that, like the composer Ernst Krenek and painter George Grosz once in the United States, who thought that expressing themselves through their art was paramount – yet even they conceded difficulties in daily social intercourse.[40] The violinist Rudolf Kolisch was condescendingly invited by the music critic Olin Downes to play chamber music with him in New York, with Downes himself at the piano. But Kolisch saw the career of his Kolisch Quartet, specializing in works by Schoenberg, destroyed by Downes's reviews once he had declined the invitation, early in the 1940s.[41]

Actors were more seriously challenged by the barriers of language, because that was their principal vehicle of communication. Even very prominent actors such as Bergner and Fritz Kortner, who began their exiles in England, could never rid themselves of their German accents, despite elocution lessons. They got by on their past reputations, due to their personal charm (granting Bergner a significant edge over the often grumpy Kortner), and because they still managed somehow to impress theater audiences.[42] Their German compatriots Albert Bassermann and Curt Goetz, however, who lost their allure because of their strong accents, simply could not compensate for linguistic deficiencies and got irreversibly stuck professionally.[43] Some actresses like Marlene Dietrich, Lotte Lenya, and Bergner, to the extent that they portrayed femmes fatales and the like, could sport an accent, but theater pieces or movies with German female spies in them, for example, were rare (an already much older Lenya later famously starred as Colonel Rosa Klebb in the James Bond movie *From Russia with Love*).[44] About his wife Lenya's attempt to emulate American parlance, Kurt Weill quipped as late as 1949, "it is too difficult for actors with her originality."[45] Great actors were fully demoralized once they had to play minor roles because of their chronically faulty pronunciation, never having learned a foreign tongue properly and thus being excluded from major roles thereafter.[46]

There were peculiar properties of language that German and Austrian writers, dramatists, and actors were conscious of, and which eluded them in different ways. German possessed certain inflections they had been used to but which now, in an English- or Swedish-speaking world, they were deprived of, as those were untranslatable. Refined or even colloquial English, on the other hand, was characterized by qualities, such as a certain idiomatic brevity, which these immigrants could never master.[47] Hence Max Reinhardt's wife, the actress Helene Thiemig, complained in Los Angeles that one had been "alienated from one's own language," and Lion Feuchtwanger concurred by saying that certain turns of phrase in German were simply not translatable.[48] Notwithstanding Feuchtwanger's further observation that once removed from the German mainstream, a writer would be bypassed by the changes in the German language over time, Thomas Mann continued to write in German, even though he took a great interest in Americanisms. Brecht did likewise, for what he had to say, often didactically, had to be formulated in his native idiom.[49] Stefan Zweig, who also wanted to continue writing in his native tongue, worked himself into a conflict after realizing, in England, that German had become the vernacular of oppressing barbarians. "We writers of the German language," he lamented, "feel a secret and tormenting shame because these decrees of oppression are conceived and drafted in the German language, the same language in which we write and think."[50]

This had something to do with age: the younger a person was, the more easily he or she could adjust to their adopted language. This was demonstrated by both Arthur Koestler, born in Budapest in 1905, and Klaus Mann, born in Munich one year later. Koestler published his first novel in English, *Scum of the Earth*, successfully in 1941, and Mann, who right after the war would send reports to the U.S. Armed Forces paper *Stars and Stripes*, asked why he should be writing in German in America, if the Germans themselves wanted to tear his tongue out.[51] He wished to write in American English, said the younger Mann, in order to adequately express the changed situation of the emigrants – his father Thomas praised him for that, as he also applauded his first-born Erika who, the Nobel laureate thought, was so admirably fluent in English.[52]

So it comes as no surprise that difficulties with a new language contributed substantially to professional failure in countries of exile, and this in every artistic medium. Technical language complexities and thorny matters of translation were compounded, moreover, by genre-specific issues, as Carl Zuckmayer found out. This successful author of stage and film dramas fared poorly as a lecturer in stage drama at the New School in New York, because he could not answer questions relating to American dramaturgic practices. For instance, how many minutes would have to pass before the love or sex subject (his wrong translation of the love or sex *interest*) was introduced. Before he lectured in New York, Zuckmayer had worked in Hollywood as a scriptwriter – as did many of his compatriots – but he had found this like working on an assembly line and had given up. Eventually this German writer, who had one Jewish parent, retreated to a farm in Vermont.[53] In Britain, the Berlin playwright Julius Berstl found the format of English "salon plays" difficult to get used to: tea was served in act one, cocktails were served in act two, and whiskey in act three.[54]

Artists who, like Zuckmayer, fell short at academic institutions because they lacked the requisite pedagogical experience or could not fit in as teachers, were common among the highly cultured émigrés. Stefan Wolpe was a left-leaning composer who deplored the ignorance of his colleagues at the Jerusalem Conservatory, when he wrote in 1938: "The fakers of a new Jewish culture show contempt for the powerful, rich music-cultural heritage of Europe," and he called them illiterates squatting on the ill-gotten fruits of their ignorance.[55] His colleague Krenek, equally interested in dodecaphony as Wolpe, said he had discovered "the stuff of dilettantes" when he came upon a young American composer who, he thought, had been seduced by ignoramuses. Krenek found himself in a deplorable situation at Vassar College in Poughkeepsie in New York State, where he was being spied upon; not surprisingly, his contract was allowed to lapse in 1942.[56] And the painter and photographer László Moholy-Nagy, once a renowned teacher with the German Bauhaus faculty, was out of a job as founding director of the New Bauhaus – the American School of Design, in Chicago – after it had to close its doors for lack of money in 1938.[57]

Artists such as Moholy-Nagy needed a certain, culturally predetermined, sounding board that could simply not be transferred from central Europe to foreign countries. Because he thought no one in London cared about good art, Kurt Schwitters, a pioneer of the Dada movement, became a depressive in England: "Only a few friends know what good art is." Similarly, economically deprived German refugee artists made no impression with their art in provincial Sweden. Of course none of them were known in that new country, including Peter Weiss, who at that time tried his hand at oil painting, before he became an internationally famous dramatist much later. As unknown artists these émigrés felt useless, just like those German musicians in England who simply could not secure employment for themselves, try as they might.[58]

Despite all the odds, one-time greats continued in their quest for recognition, money, and fame. Elisabeth Bergner was successful on London stages until in 1940 she played "Boy David" in an eponymous play written for her by the creator of *Peter Pan*, J. M. Barrie – which the critics savaged. Thereupon she left London for Hollywood with her husband, the director Paul Czinner, but Hollywood's aura sickened her. When she was summoned by the mogul Louis B. Mayer in anticipation of a prospective film part and asked to turn around slowly and lasciviously, she stormed out of the room and moved with Czinner to New York. By the time she returned to Britain after the war, she had lost her former appeal.[59]

The famous if ever controversial Brecht fought his own demons. During a first visit to the United States in the fall of 1935 his musical *Die Mutter*, with a score by Hanns Eisler, was rehearsed by New York's Theater Union on Broadway. But its members violently disagreed with him, so that Brecht returned to Europe in a huff. He was back in America at the start of 1942, this time in southern California. At first he tried his luck as a film scriptwriter, but none of his drafts were accepted. His subsequent attempt to stage, together with his former collaborator Kurt Weill, *The Threepenny Opera*, as an Afro-American street ballad starring Paul Robeson, went awry. And when a Hollywood film about Reinhard Heydrich's assassination in June 1942 in Prague, *Hangmen Also Die*, was released to the public, Brecht's credits as co-author were missing, much to his dismay.[60]

Brecht's relationship with Fritz Lang, who had directed the film, was, at best, a terse one. Lang's own productivity suffered and his artistic profile in Hollywood was on the wane because he never appeared without his signature monocle, which lent him the air of an authoritarian Teuton. He certainly behaved like one, for instance when his American film crew wanted a break for lunch and he adamantly refused. The first of his film scripts, dating back to 1934, was turned down by his superiors at MGM, so that he resorted to B-movies. No one bothered to remember the former Fritz Lang who had made *Metropolis* and *Dr. Mabuse*, film classics of the Weimar era. Lang typically could not comprehend that in Hollywood, unlike formerly in Babelsberg, the directors did not make the big decisions, but producers and the mighty men like Mayer who owned the film companies did. Instead, Lang found that he was being dictated to and that he had to work within a certain time limit – not at all Lang's style, when he was used to being his own boss.[61]

Despite the problems experienced in Hollywood by artists like Bergner, Tinseltown naturally attracted immigrant actors who, even if eventually successful, went through very hard times. Walter Weinlaub, who had been chased out of German theaters by the SA, arrived in Hollywood to take a job as a dishwasher, potato peeler, toilet cleaner, and postman's helper.[62] Even after they had landed a part on a movie set, these actors continued laboring in after-hours jobs as taxi drivers or barkeepers. As Hitler showed himself to be more belligerent, Austrian or German Jewish actors with thick German accents eventually became successful portraying Nazis in anti-Nazis movies, the most prominent of which would turn out to be *Confessions of a Nazi Spy*, starring the Hollywood-entrenched (Jewish) American Edward G. Robinson, in 1939. The director was Anatole Litvak, originally Russian-born but recently from Berlin, who had already made his name in the Old Country. The plot consisted of the smashing of a Nazi fifth column in America, with the crime-buster played by Robinson, joined by the likes of Francis Lederer (the Nazi villain), Hans von Twardowski, and Lotte Palfi. During the planning of the film, 150 German émigré actors had thrown their hats into the ring, hoping to be hired by the Warner Brothers studio. Some who were hired changed their names for fear of Nazi reprisals against relatives left behind in Germany. This turned out to be one of altogether 180 anti-Nazi films produced in Hollywood until 1945, ironically providing more work for persecuted Jews in Nazi roles, something they knew how to value economically but fretted over emotionally, the experience proving too close to home.[63]

One formerly great central European show-business entrepreneur, Max Reinhardt, tragically foundered, after being confronted by huge obstacles. A resident of the United State since 1934, and having done some work for the

Hollywood Bowl, he created the first of four movies, *A Midsummer Night's Dream*, which was financially risky even though artistically sound. In 1937, Reinhardt produced, together with Werfel and Weill, the Broadway musical *The Eternal Road*, which, also of high quality if much too long, flopped again at the box office. Next, Reinhardt opened an actors' academy on Sunset Boulevard in Los Angeles, for which he contracted the film directors William Dieterle and John Huston, as well as the formerly Viennese composer Erich Wolfgang Korngold as instructors. Greta Garbo too was to make an appearance, certainly to take in what was going on and perhaps to learn something. Alas, nobody showed up. After the academy had declared bankruptcy, Reinhardt once again turned to Broadway, where he produced the musical *Rosalinda*, an adaptation of Johann Strauss's *Die Fledermaus*, which actually was well reviewed. The premiere of this production by the New Opera Company occurred in October 1942, and a month later Reinhardt was busy with a Jacques Offenbach adaptation, *Helen Goes to Troy*. But then, a year later, he died, having been bitten by a dog with rabies, and having been laid up in a New York hotel room with few visitors. He was seventy years old, ostracized by former pupils and colleagues who, long residents of America, were now thriving in Hollywood as film personalities, movers and shakers.[64] "In reality, he died twenty years ago," remarked Alma Mahler-Werfel, not without bitterness, as she herself had to make ends meet in exile.[65]

There was a strong negative correlation between professional precariousness and economic well-being. To say that not everyone did as well in both regards as Thomas Mann is a truism, as he drew on his private fortune back in Switzerland and since 1938 received consulting and lecturing fees in the United States until, after 1944, royalties from his tetralogy *Joseph and His Brothers* boosted his earnings yet further. His friend Feuchtwanger also was an exception, since he was able to resort to non-German royalties, so that, when it became necessary, he could easily exchange a villa on the Côte d'Azur for an impressive residence in Los Angeles.[66] Kurt Weill hit it rich in 1943, after the triumph of his musical *One Touch of Venus* on Broadway, and so did Franz Werfel with his bestsellers *Embezzled Heaven* and *The Song of Bernadette*.[67]

All four of those knew, however, that they were the chosen few. Most of the artist refugees were indigent; virtually all of them were living on the edge, beyond even the impecuniousness customarily expected of disciples of the muses.[68] Even formerly famous artists fell into this category, among them Brecht, Alfred Döblin, and Heinrich Mann. The unsteady Brecht had to support a family of four, to say nothing of female companions, and with earnings of 125 dollars a month in those years this was hardly possible.[69] Like Brecht, Döblin and Heinrich Mann were chronically underpaid as scriptwriters in Hollywood, with Mann having to bear the additional cost of dealing with the alcoholism of his wife, Nelly Kröger. In 1943 in New York, George Grosz was financially as badly off as Max Reinhardt, who took pains to explain to his son Gottfried how it felt to be unable to pay telephone bills or to drive with threadbare car tires.[70] Both Krenek and Zuckmayer for years did not know how to get by, Zuckmayer having received a $1,000 advance from the Viking publishing company, for a book that was never to be written. "We were just one step above pauperization," wrote the bestselling author years later.[71]

Hence a brutal retooling frequently was the order of the day. In the mid-1930s, Koestler worked as a handyman in Paris, musicians in Tel Aviv would sell hotdogs or open a hat store. Julius Berstl, after considerable experience in Berlin theater, managed to stage his play *Der lasterhafte Herr Tschu* (*The Licentious Mr. Chu*, 1922) in London, but when he could not live on the proceeds even for one month, he began weaving scarves for the black market.[72]

Consequently, these artists' moods became even more unstable and they took to criticizing, often unreasonably, what was new to them and they thought they could not stand. One object of disdain, in America, was the stodgy white bread, which they held to be inedible. For many refugees this became a symbol of decline from European civilization, enough to cause depression. For Brecht as late as 1944, this was significant enough that he planned a film, together with Charles Laughton, which he wished to call "The King's Bread."[73] Everything was better at home, was the émigrés' constant complaint, if natives asked them how they were doing, and Bergner wrote to her fatherly friend George Bernard Shaw that she felt "hopelessly European." "Pride will have a fall, Liesl," he replied.[74]

In countries such as England, the United States, and Sweden these central European artists and intellectuals had to abide what they saw as manifestations of provincialism, certainly in low culture but also in what passed as high culture.[75] In the United States, to escape from an environment suffused with "The American Way of Life," and failing to integrate easily, some tried to isolate themselves in colony-like settlements and met in

European-style salons. Alma Mahler-Werfel held a salon (in Los Angeles and later in New York), and so did Salka Viertel (in Los Angeles) – diasporas within diasporas – that were conceived on the elite principle and barred lesser, unknown, compatriots.[76] Yet even these salons did not serve their purpose of social support and spiritual sustenance for fellow travelers if other, vaunted, émigrés made a point of staying away from them – as did the overly critical Marlene Dietrich from Viertel's salon in Hollywood.[77] The soprano Lotte Lehmann from nearby Santa Barbara also never showed up there, although she was, individually, friends with Bruno Walter and members of the Mann family – sometime guests at Viertel's. Salka Viertel, once an acting student at the Reinhardt seminar in Berlin, had separated from her husband Berthold Viertel, a poet, screenwriter, and director, eventually living with Reinhardt's son Gottfried. Berthold Viertel, originally from Galicia like his wife and la Bergner, was yet another artist who had found the United States unbearable, preferring to make his way in England where, as he said later, he found himself unable to create anything of real significance.[78]

In England other trivialities plagued the newcomers. Artists and literati from Vienna, for instance – notably Stefan Zweig – missed their coffee houses, and for many the English went to bed too early and nobody cared to drop by and say hello.[79] In the United Kingdom one had to accept that the human boundaries between immigrants and native-born subjects of the Crown were higher than in America, because the British paid heed to formality, as Oskar Kokoschka found out. In order to infiltrate the British art world, he had managed to be invited for tea by the director of the Tate Gallery and was then asked to donate a painting. Kokoschka had, instead, expected to be asked to sell one. Later the artist received the CBE (Commander of the Order of the British Empire), which, jested the British cultural historian John Willett, was usually awarded to second- and third-ranking figures of the art world, as well as obscure major-generals.[80]

One who particularly suffered in Britain was Stefan Zweig. Because he was of the opinion that its citizens, in spite of their good will, could not understand the changed central European geopolitical situation, he retreated into self-isolation. Somehow he found it impossible to get close to H. G. Wells and that devotee of German culture, Shaw, both of whom he admired. When the war broke out, he was just sitting there, "immobile, staring into empty space like a condemned man in his cell, walled in, chained to sense-less, impotent, waiting and waiting." Later he moved to the attractive little city of Bath, but did not stay there long. In 1940 he traveled with his new wife, Lotte, to far-away Brazil, and from there, already resigned to isolation, he kept up sporadic contact with émigrés in the United States.[81] His name-sake Arnold Zweig felt equally isolated in Palestine, but now he despised the Hebrew language and, unlike before, hated Zionism.[82]

Depression and frustration suffered by the exiles were exacerbated by tensions dividing larger and smaller groups. Edward W. Said, himself a refugee from Palestine, has in more recent times called this a situation in which exiles were exiled again by other exiles.[83] Such exile within exile, whether real or perceived, may have been short-lived, nonetheless for those affected it meant their world was falling apart. Both Feuchtwanger in *Exil* and Klaus Mann in *Der Vulkan* have tried to describe such feelings in their literature about exile.[84]

These tensions were often caused by personality clashes, of a kind that would have occurred in the home country, but other tensions seem to have been specific to exile. Arnold Schoenberg, for example, could not forgive Bruno Walter for neglecting his compositions in concerts he conducted in exile, and in a circular to friends of 1934 the composer called Walter "a repugnant pig," adding, "whenever I think of him, I get sick."[85] Nine years later Weill called Marlene Dietrich a "stupid cow," after she had turned down the main role in his musical *One Touch of Venus*.[86] Weill also disdained Otto Klemperer, as did Paul Hindemith when he was traveling from his Swiss exile to the United States. "The Klemperer couple could be observed fighting with one another openly and clandestinely," Hindemith carped, "in which Johanna almost always had to capitulate, in her frequent and unsatis-fied thirst for something alcoholic."[87]

Alma Mahler-Werfel was Gustav Mahler's widow, Walter Gropius's ex-wife, Oskar Kokoschka's former mistress, and now married to Franz Werfel. Not Jewish herself, but having had to flee her native Vienna in the company of her persecuted Jewish husband, she took on the whole world every day in a mood of abject resentment. Seemingly paradoxically, she was a former confidante of the authoritarian Austrian ex-chancellor Kurt Schuschnigg and, still, a great admirer of Mussolini. She paid tribute to the early, successful, Nazi campaigns in the war and would annoy Werfel, whom she sometimes whistled for when she wanted to see him, and acquaintances with her praise for Europe's fascists. In Chicago, Moholy-Nagy, who was Jewish, had disagreements with his former Bauhaus boss Ludwig Mies van der Rohe, who was not, after Mies had left the German Reich and joined him. And although Fritz Lang thought he could rule over the denizens of the movie world, he felt inferior to the émigré intellectuals, in particular those who frequented the get-togethers at the houses of Thomas Mann, Salka Viertel, and Alma Mahler-Werfel. So he usually retreated into a corner with a martini in hand.[88] Stefan Zweig was shocked once when Hanns Eisler and Brecht appeared in his London apartment, acting like rowdy hoodlums. But apart from his contempt for these two idiosyncratic artists, Zweig disliked the entire group of emigrants, whom he called the last wave and the most terrible, "all these writers who never really were writers."[89]

A particular problem of interpersonal relations in America affected the Jews in their dealings with each other. Here anti-Semitism increased considerably between 1938 and 1946, for which Hollywood served as a prism. The Jews from eastern Europe had built up the film industry, which did not prevent influential moguls such as Samuel Goldwyn from inviting German-Jewish film practitioners to Hollywood, at the beginning of Nazi rule.[90] But then the already established eastern Jews pronounced their devout Americanism, in order to be seen as good patriots and thus to pre-empt anti-Semitism; this again did not go down well with the newly arrived Jews. To avoid tensions between established eastern Jews and the new arrivals from central Europe, Fritz Lang emphasized the non-Jewishness on his mother's side and played on their Catholicism, whereas Fritz Kortner, who had been born in Vienna as Nathan Kohn, sometimes thought he was patronized by eastern Jews and, at other times, ignored.[91]

Given Thomas Mann's Olympian status, relationships between individuals with him at their center were most sensitive and could be prone to all manner of misunderstandings, jealousy, and ill will. He himself had to contend with those who always begrudged him his place in the sun, but he also had ideological foes such as Brecht and the psychologist Erik Erikson, who believed he had betrayed Germany. At the end of the 1940s, Alma Mahler-Werfel, who was a dreadful schemer and whom Mann's wife Katia described as "by nature fairly evil," provoked an alienation between the novelist and Schoenberg. The composer justly accused Mann of having passed him over in his new novel *Doktor Faustus*, as the historic founder of the twelve-tone serial technique. This, after Mann had sought out Schoenberg's advice about music theory, including the inner workings of dodecaphony.[92]

Thomas Mann had demonstrated earlier how his haughtiness could potentially damage relationships, in his dealings with the satirical draftsman and painter George Grosz and the budding author Arthur Koestler. Grosz happened upon the Manns during their visit to New York in 1934. He had made the mistake of appearing late for lunch at a restaurant with Thomas and Katia Mann and then behaved quite out of order. During their conversation Mann, as was his wont at that time, insisted the Hitler regime would not last long, whereas Grosz, much more realistically, disagreed. As one reviews details of this meeting today, it is clear that the senior, mature novelist could have resorted to a more forgiving attitude and have ended the encounter in a conciliatory mood.[93] Koestler visited Mann a few years later in Switzerland, to interview him as the journalist he then was. But the novelist was unapproachable, behind a "wall of protection – courtesy and coldness," with which he intimidated the younger writer, adding insult to injury when he compared himself to Goethe. Koestler judged later that, unlike Dostoyevsky, Mann had shown no sympathies for the lowly and the downtrodden of this world.[94]

Thomas Mann's personal coldness, combined with egocentricity, often came through in his private dealings with his family, in his villa in Pacific Palisades, California. He cherished moderate drinking on a daily basis, but he could not stand his sister-in-law Nelly, who came from a demi-monde background, especially after excessive consumption of alcohol. He called her vulgar. Thus he attended her funeral, after her suicide in December 1944, only out of respect for his older brother.[95] As far as his relationship with Heinrich was concerned, it was always a tense one, apart from the problems with Nelly. His son Klaus, too, was a problem for Thomas Mann, as he was an unstable, homosexually often promiscuous young man with a high degree of sensitivity, who wanted so much to be like his father and who agonized over so many of the ills of exile, including the knowledge that he was half-Jewish.[96]

The degree of marginalization suffered by the exiles, when they were forced by economic necessity to work in menial occupations instead of their artistic vocation, frequently depended on how they compared the new cultural landscape to the central European one, and what consequences arose from this. One measure on which these could be based was the dichotomy between higher and lower culture, to which they were exposed – as in classical versus light music, or serious stage play versus comedic film. These consequences could also be based on a quality evaluation within a certain genre, perhaps by negatively comparing the conservatory training of American musicians with that of German ones. Often such individual judgments were interdependent, with the end effect of reinforcing the overall culture shock.

This culture shock turned out to be not just subjectively painful, but also detrimental in the marketplace, especially when artists had been forced to doubt their own professional integrity. Such doubts did not befall everyone, certainly not Hindemith, who established his own yardstick; he downgraded American popular culture as a matter of course and even as an emigrant argued for the natural superiority of German Music.[97] As the American music critic Joseph Horowitz has convincingly demonstrated, Hindemith's judgments were reinforced, at another level, by Theodor Adorno's definition of popular culture (Gebrauchskultur), in the course of which America's indigenous art form, jazz, presented itself to him as a cultural disgrace. Here he was seconded by other central European geniuses like Walter, who admired few American composers, and the pianist Rudolf Serkin.[98] By Adorno's benchmark, whoever, as a former European artist, was subjecting himself to these questionable artistic currents, as did the new Broadway composer Weill, was compromising his art. Indeed, buttonholing Weill as an "Americanized" composer who sold his European tradition for commercial gain has been an exercise western musicologists have been engaging in even during more recent times, notwithstanding that the co-creator of *The Threepenny Opera*, who began his career as a composer of serious music, never saw himself that way.[99] And neither did Korngold, who wrote racy scores for Hollywood films and tried to return to classical composing in his late work, desperately hoping for new recognition.[100] George Grosz too has been accused of having watered down his art and hence damaging his artistic persona, by painting more contemplatively in America and forsaking the brilliant acerbity of his Weimar satirical work.[101] Analogous to these cases one could ask, as critics have done of Stefan Zweig and Lion Feuchtwanger, whether the "literature of exile," which called for a certain adaptation to a lower standard predominating in the new country, not least because of hoped-for financial success, had perforce to be at a lower aesthetic level.[102]

Quality differentiation was something Schoenberg had to concern himself with, as he realized that his newly conceived construct, dodecaphony, was a European phenomenon not in tune with the current musical experience common in America. Not least, in California this experience was determined by patterns set by local women's clubs, whose members resisted being exposed to new music. Yet this was necessary, for these conservative women could dispense foundation funds with which traditional concerts were financed.[103] As those committees could not be persuaded in favor of Modernism, Schoenberg had had to resign himself to his twelve-tone compositions being overlooked in America and be content, instead, with performances of his tonally oriented works like *Verklärte Nacht* (1899/1917). So he was learning to get by. Although he kept complaining that even his German colleagues such as Klemperer and Walter would not perform his twelve-tone works in the United States, he wisely denied instruction in the new skill to his students at the University of Southern California and UCLA.[104]

As already indicated, for many refugees their exile turned out to be a tragic journey heading towards depression and alcoholism, illness and death. "Emigration is a serious disease on its own," noted Alma Mahler-Werfel in November 1943, "and that our friends have departed from us prematurely is not surprising."[105] As early as April 1933 the art impresario and critic Harry Graf Kessler had spoken, while in Paris, of a "numbing pain" that would resound like an unstoppable bass instrument.[106] On the fingers of his hand Arnold Zweig counted the number of his friends who were now deceased: Erich Mühsam, Samuel Fischer, Kurt Tucholsky. "Our numbers are diminished. We are getting poorer."[107]

The physical and psychological privations of exile took their toll on the health of the refugees, to the extent that one can reasonably say that many died before their time. Among them was Kessler, for example, who succumbed to a heart and lung disorder in 1937 in the south of France, aged sixty-nine.[108] Werfel, a notorious smoker and drinker, suffered a severe heart attack in September 1943 and, after several more attacks, died in August 1945 at just fifty-six. His widow Alma did not attend the funeral, as she was heavily depressed. Not least because this formerly famous beauty was drinking a bottle of Bénédictine liqueur every day, she put on considerable weight and developed diabetes, which she cynically declared a "Jewish affliction" that should not have affected her.[109]

Alcoholism, accompanied by all manner of psychic depression, became the emigrant's disease *par excellence*. Already in Paris in May 1939 the Austrian poet Joseph Roth had become its victim; he had been addicted since 1933, and most friends agreed that he had systematically killed himself with alcohol.[110] Grosz, who while in exile preferred a nefarious cocktail of absinthe and bourbon, did not die in America, but death caught up with him in Berlin in July 1959.[111] Throughout his life Koestler was a heavy consumer of alcohol, which did not help his depression. He tried several times to take his own life, once, in the spring of 1940, in France, with morphine tablets he had been given by Walter Benjamin. Benjamin poisoned himself a few months later; his suicide came as a result of his failure to escape from France into Spain. Exile Hannah Arendt has judged that he simply did not want to live any more, and above all, he hated America, where he would have been made a public spectacle of everywhere, as the "last European."[112] Koestler's suicide was belated, but it came nonetheless: he and his wife killed themselves with barbiturates in London, in 1983.[113]

Loneliness and nervous breakdowns also caused the suicide of Stefan Zweig and his wife, in Brazil in February 1942. This time Thomas Mann, who was not exactly a fan of Zweig's, was moved, even if he gratuitously made the point that the life of a public person was not merely a private affair.[114] Mann knew what he was talking about because his son Klaus was always risking his health, chain-smoking and ingesting alcohol and drugs. What a tragic contrast between father and son, one a giant in his field, the other constantly in his shadow striving for world fame, achieving little in comparison but enough even for his contemporaries to be educated and entertained! At the beginning of 1949, Klaus Mann was working on his autobiography *The Turning Point*, which would be published posthumously. He remembered his last meeting with Ernst Toller, the dramatist and one-time revolutionary of the Bavarian Soviet Republic (1919), a German Jew who had hanged himself in a New York hotel room in 1939. At the time, wrote Klaus Mann, he was asked to speak standing next to Toller's coffin. "I did not dare to look him in the face. I was afraid. I was ashamed of my tears. For whom were they? Were they for him, who finally was allowed to sleep?"[115] It was not much later after he had composed these lines that Klaus Mann took his own life, in Cannes. "I still don't know how I shall continue with life," wrote Erika Mann to her friend Lotte Lehmann, because at times she had been inseparable from her brother. "But I know I have to, even though no one can actually think about me without him. We were parts of one piece, as only siblings who are very close can be."[116]

FALSE REFUGEES?

The question poses itself: Who exactly was an artist refugee from Nazi Germany? As has been shown, a narrow interpretation of the term would identify artists and certain intellectuals such as theater critics who were forced out of the Third Reich on or after Hitler's assumption of power on January 30, 1933, on ideological-political, sexual-preference or racist grounds, sometimes all three. A somewhat broader definition might include children of other refugees who became artists in the new host country, or children of refugee artists who did not. While it is moot trying to arrive at a binding definition, it might be illuminating to deal with characters on the fringes who, for one reason or another, are habitually counted in the group of artist émigrés. Four cultural icons offer themselves for closer examination; they had different backgrounds and, after their exile, different roles to play; by previously accepted criteria none of them fit the picture of the main groups of refugee artists above. They were Marlene Dietrich, Erich Maria Remarque, Fritz Busch, and Lotte Lehmann.

Marlene Dietrich, born in Berlin in 1901, one year before Leni Riefenstahl, whom she knew and avoided early in her career as did Riefenstahl in reverse, had played roles in several silent films in Babelsberg until she was discovered by Josef von Sternberg during 1929 for his main role of Lola Lola in *Der blaue Engel* (*The Blue Angel*). Sternberg originally was a Viennese Jew who, after much hardship, had made his way to the top as a director of films in Hollywood. As he was only 5 feet 4 inches tall, he had added the "von" to his name to give him some air of distinction. It was Sternberg who had directed Emil Jannings in *The Last Command* of 1928 in the role of Rasputin, which won the German actor the first Academy Award earlier in 1929.[117] With *The Blue Angel*, filmed as the first German sound movie in both English and German, Sternberg wanted to put Heinrich Mann's novel *Professor Unrat* (1905), a work critical of bigotry in Wilhelmine society, on film. Jannings himself played Professor Rath, a high-school teacher who falls for the vixen Lola Lola, totally succumbs to her sexually, and, having quit his profession, is exploited until he dies a shameful, if ludicrous, death. Dietrich, in an understated role as a coolly seductive cabaret singer, became a big name after the film was premiered at the Gloria-Palast in Berlin, on April 1, 1930. Immediately after that premiere, the new-born star boarded ship to sail for the United States, where she rejoined director von Sternberg for further filming in Hollywood.[118]

Legend has it that Dietrich traveled to the United States because of the National Socialists, that she was an opponent of the Nazis and the Third Reich from the beginning, and was fiercely against returning to Germany to live and work there. Some of this, mostly the events after 1939, is true; the Dietrich who promoted American War Bonds and joined the American GIs toward the end of the war to keep their spirits up in the final battles against Hitler's tyranny is a proven figure of history.[119] But the main question here is about her motive for leaving Germany for Hollywood in the spring of 1930. That move had nothing to do with the Nazis. At that time, they were still only a small party, its success blocked by a relatively healthy economy until the Depression in the fall of 1929, and representing 2.6 percent of the German population in the Berlin Reichstag. Granted, this would grow to 18.3 percent after the elections of September 14, 1930, but that was still a few months away.[120] After *The Blue Angel* had been shown to huge popular acclaim, the Nazis' first significant reaction to it was only in July 1930, through an article in the *Völkischer Beobachter*, culminating in an attack on the Jews. That was directed against Sternberg, as the Jewish producer of smutty films – a genre the Weimar film industry was accused of specializing in generally. The twin reasons why Dietrich left for Hollywood were that she thought she was stuck professionally with Ufa Film in Berlin, having developed a feeling of resentment even before November 1929, when the film was beginning to be made. Moreover, after von Sternberg had entered her professional life, she fell for him personally as well; both being married (she to Rudolf Sieber, an assistant film director in Berlin), they had an affair mostly consummated at his Berlin hotel, which Dietrich was in no hurry to deny, and since she believed he was nothing short of a genius and a wonderful influence on her, future episodes with him in Hollywood would be both romantically rewarding and professionally fruitful. (Dietrich's idea then was to establish a new life in Hollywood for herself and have her husband and their child Maria Elisabeth join her.)[121]

Even before her departure from Germany, Dietrich must have realized, of course, that what she stood for in the German film world was anathema to Nazi weltanschauung. Even then she was openly bisexual, having had an affair with the popular Berlin comedienne and cabaret personality Claire Waldoff, and had Jewish friends.[122] If she had stayed in Germany after 1930 and up to 1933, it is possible that she would have adjusted to Nazi rule and, in particular, to Goebbels's ways in Babelsberg – like many others, including (reluctantly) Hans Albers, the supporting male character in *The Blue Angel*, and (enthusiastically) Emil Jannings. She might even have eclipsed Riefenstahl, who had been hoping for the Lola Lola role in the film, but then went on to star in her own self-directed movie, *Das blaue Licht* (*The Blue Light*). That impressive work of 1932 notwithstanding, Goebbels could see that Riefenstahl was attracted to Hitler himself and hence he attempted repeatedly to recall Dietrich from Hollywood and make her the number one star actress in his Babelsberg empire. Dietrich certainly had the potential for this; this role was later filled by Zarah Leander. Dietrich is known to have joked several times in Hollywood that if she wanted, she could return to Germany at once, and her true feelings in Hollywood are not known, because there she suffered both romantic disappointments and professional crises. However, she did apply to become an American citizen in 1937, causing a vicious polemic in Julius Streicher's smutty tabloid *Der Stürmer*, and thereafter, from what one could observe, she identified with solid American values, the most important of which was democracy. Anyone who wished to see her as a refugee from Nazism after that could have been justified.[123]

In contrast to Marlene Dietrich, Erich Maria Remarque had an anti-fascist pedigree when he left Germany, settling in a house in Porto Ronco, near Ascona on the Swiss side of Lago Maggiore, in 1931. He had been born in 1898 and lived through World War I as a soldier, though less at the front lines than he later suggested. But he lost close friends at the front, which imprinted many a horror on his mind. Unlike Ernst Jünger, he saw the soldiers not as heroes who championed war for war's sake, but as victims in conflagrations that ought to be avoided. Thus he came to write his third and most famous novel, *Im Westen nichts Neues* (*All Quiet on the Western Front*), as a convinced pacifist, but not someone overtly interested in politics. After serialization in 1928, he published it as a book the next year. "It was a confession of personal despair," observes Modris Eksteins, "but it was also an indignant denunciation of an insensate social and political order, inevitably of that order which had produced the horror and destruction of the war but particularly of the one that could not settle the war and deal with the aspirations of veterans." After its appearance, the instant success of the book enabled Remarque to leave behind him a shifty ten years in odd jobs and indifferent public-school teaching, and a flaky first novel he later disowned. Multitalented, he could also write poetry, paint, and play the piano and organ – all his life he loved music. At the same time, this middle-class youth from provincial Osnabrück was socially insecure if eagerly upwardly mobile, aspiring to social prominence and sometimes wearing an officer's uniform and fancying a baron's title he had no right to. Handsome and always fastidious with clothes, in 1925 he married the beautiful dancer and actress Ilse Jutta Zambona, of Italian-Danish descent.[124]

When his pacifist novel appeared, it sold 640,000 copies in the first three months and within one year had been translated into some twenty languages. Immediately, Remarque was controversial in Germany, with most on the political right accusing him of insulting the German army, and some on the left of enriching himself by glamorizing the Kaiser's battlefield. The Nazis, even before the auspicious national vote in September 1930 that made them the second-largest party in the Reichstag, were already vocal enough to put up fierce opposition. Their anger increased when Universal Studios in Hollywood made a movie of the novel that year. Maxwell Anderson, Kurt Weill's friend, wrote the screenplay, and the film won two Academy Awards. During its world premiere in Berlin, Nazi storm troopers at the behest of Goebbels disrupted its German version, releasing white mice and tossing beer bottles and stink bombs into the Mozartsaal cinema. After further turbulence organized by the Nazis, republican authorities banned the film in December 1930, as dangerous to the public peace. Goebbels renewed this ban early in the Third Reich, while copies of Remarque's famous novel went up in flames during the May 1933 book burnings.[125]

Granted, Remarque had become instantly rich and famous at the age of thirty, and he began a lifestyle as an internationally feted show-business star. He acquired all the accouterments of luxury such as exotic cars, sojourning in France and, eventually, the United States, while holding on to his house in Switzerland. In both Europe and America, he was to carry on a serious affair with Marlene Dietrich, mostly between 1937 and 1940. One might wish to think that Dietrich, during the late 1930s, was politically sensitized by Remarque, conditioned into accepting an anti-fascist value system on behalf of universal humanity, as the author had developed it for himself years before, even though he remained, outwardly, apolitical. For there is no question that Remarque's chief motive for securing permanent residence in Switzerland between 1931 and January 29, 1933, the day of his final departure from Germany, unlike Dietrich, had not been professional frustration and romantic longing, but the realization that in a Germany drifting irremediably to the extreme right, there was no future for a confirmed democratic pacifist. Hence classifying him as an artist refugee would be more justified in Remarque's case than in the case of Dietrich.[126]

The cases of conductor Fritz Busch and soprano Lotte Lehmann are different to those of both Dietrich and Remarque because, before they left for foreign shores, they attempted to negotiate a deal with the Nazi regime. To conceal this later, they concocted dissembling narratives. Whereas Busch tried to remain in Nazi Germany on his terms, the Austrian and American resident Lehmann attempted to accommodate herself from the outside. Their faked legacies today cast their claims as refugees in serious doubt.

On March 7, 1933, Busch, a World War I veteran with no regrets and politically on the right, was conductor of the Saxon State Opera in Dresden. According to memoirs both he and his wife Grete had carefully composed, he was dismissed that day, after combined machinations by both the SA and the Saxon regional government, on account of his alleged opposition to the Nazi Party early in the Weimar Republic. Following these events, Busch went into self-imposed exile and continued working in Buenos Aires, Copenhagen, and Glyndebourne in England.[127]

What is true is that the Nazis objected to Busch for a number of reasons, even before January 1933. His younger brother was Adolf Busch, a concert violinist, who had married a Jew and taken up residence in Basel in 1926. Adolf Busch was a declared enemy of the Nazis, befriending the brilliant young Jewish pianist Rudolf Serkin (the object of contempt for Elly Ney), who later married the couple's daughter.[128] As for Fritz Busch, a sizeable faction of Nazi deputies in the Saxon Landtag since the end of the republic had clamored for cutting the culture budget, affecting the state opera much more heavily than he himself considered necessary. Moreover, the conductor was accused of patronizing Jewish friends and artists, of spending excessive time on leave as a guest conductor, mainly in Berlin, and of claiming an exceptionally generous salary as well as considerable vacation time. The latter charges could be documented, but Busch was entitled to these privileges contractually since before 1933. There were several personal intrigues against the Busch family in Dresden, preceding his dismissal in March.[129]

Although members of the Dresden opera orchestra had been pressured by the local government to take a stand against Busch, one musician wrote to Richard Strauss that Busch had always been "very popular with the orchestra."[130] Minor irregularities were conceded in the letter, however, of the kind that could easily have been settled by either side.[131] The pro-Nazi music publisher Gustav Bosse admitted that Busch may have stepped out of line, because, as alleged, he was constantly striving to move away from opera in favor of concert performances, especially in Berlin. Still, Bosse deplored that a conductor of Busch's caliber had been "tarnished in this manner."[132]

Bosse, who resided in Regensburg in southern Germany, was not able to see through the cabal that was at the bottom of this affair, and the point about "opera" was really moot. The facts were that behind the scenes a link was being constructed between the conductor and Göring, who, under the influence of his fiancée the actress Emmy Sonnemann and his major-domo in cultural affairs, Heinz Tietjen, wished to attract Busch to Berlin. Sonnemann had been friends with the Busch couple during their earlier years at the Stuttgart Opera, and when Busch had moved to Dresden in 1922 and the actress to nearby Weimar, the three of them continued their friendship. By 1932, Sonnemann had been bringing along her "chap," the stunt flier and businessman Hermann Göring, who was already high up in the Nazi Party hierarchy. Before the clash of March 7, 1933, she had telephoned Busch from Berlin, to tell him of Göring's interest in hiring him. As acting Interior Minister of Prussia and Minister President-designate, Göring was able to employ more than one music director in the capital. Hitler was not expected to interfere, as long as his favorites, the conductors Krauss and Furtwängler, were not affected.[133]

After the Dresden debacle Busch visited Göring a few times, as the latter seemed to hold out hope for a new job as opera director in Berlin. A close reading of archival sources suggests that Busch would have accepted any such position and not have left Germany at all. But Furtwängler, after all, stood in the way in Berlin, and another, potential, role for Busch in

Bayreuth as festival director did not suit his plans. Besides, he had already been approached by the Nazis to do some publicity work for them in South America.[134]

In each of their books, the Busch couple maintain that the telegram inviting the conductor to stage a German opera season at the Teatro Colón in Buenos Aires came as a godsend just as he was being forced to give up his Dresden position.[135] Yet archival documents show this to be an outright fabrication. For although Busch had been invited to Argentina in the 1920s, this latest invitation had been rigged with the assistance of Reich authorities, after Busch had repeatedly consulted with Hans Hinkel. At that time Hinkel, who later worked exclusively for Goebbels, was also in Göring's employ as commissar in the Prussian Ministry of Education (responsible for "de-Jewifying" German culture). Since Göring could not find a space for Busch in Berlin, the plan was for him to give several performances in Buenos Aires. He was to be placed in the company of German artists objectionable to the Nazis, including Jews, to give the impression to the South Americans of a much larger tolerance in the regime for unwanted persons than actually existed. Whether Busch knew it or not, on his tour to South America, which lasted until late 1933, he was constantly observed by a specially appointed Nazi mole.[136]

After the return from Argentina, Busch hoped to be rewarded with an appropriate post in Berlin.[137] This, however, did not happen, so Busch now had to content himself with whatever European offers came his way, as well as repeated tours of South America. By 1934 he was able to assume the musical directorship of the Glyndebourne Opera in Britain – a prestigious if not a lucrative venture. Busch was soon earning his principal income in New York at the Metropolitan Opera, in Buenos Aires, and at the Royal Opera in Copenhagen. Having failed to obtain Swiss citizenship, even with the help of Thomas Mann, who was a close friend of his violinist brother Adolf, he took out Argentinian papers in 1936. Until the outbreak of the war Busch received several offers from the Germans to conduct in the Reich, but now he turned them down. Prevented from international travel by hostilities, he settled permanently in Argentina in 1941, with, as he thought, a spotless anti-Nazi record.[138]

The lyric soprano Lotte Lehmann, born in 1888 near Berlin, after several seasons in Hamburg had become the star of the Vienna Opera by the early

1920s and was the reigning diva in Europe by the beginning of the 1930s. Highlights of her midlife career included singing the lead role in Richard Strauss's new opera *Die Frau ohne Schatten* and performing in some of his other works. All the same, around this time she was becoming restless, casting about for new, exciting, opportunities beyond Austria, whose citizenship she had attained. Always impressed by wealth, titles, and fame, she was open to influence by other, perhaps even more prominent, personalities. After her first engagement in the United States, when she was sailing back to Germany on the ocean liner *Bremen* in December 1930, she chanced upon Marlene Dietrich who was returning to Europe for the first time since the premiere of *The Blue Angel*. At that moment, the stately Lehmann desperately wanted to be like her, and wanted her attention. On the promenade deck of first class, whenever the new Hollywood star sauntered by, Lehmann would intone, softly, but with what she thought was a raunchy voice, Lola Lola's song: "From head to toe, I'm made for love ..." Alas, the glittering Marlene, once demurely trained in the classics on the violin, pretended not to see the older woman and paid no attention to this novel rendition of her famous movie song.[139]

Nonetheless, a couple of years later the opera singer thought she could change her fortunes for the better. For an explanation, our narrative must move forward to 1966. In that year, Lehmann published an article in which she told her many followers that at the start of the Nazi regime she had received a call from Göring, summoning her from Vienna to Berlin for a few guest appearances; money was no object. After an interview with Göring himself, for what appeared to be a permanent changeover at his Berlin State Opera, Lehmann was eventually promised "a fantastic amount," plus a villa, a generous life pension, a castle on the Rhine, and a riding horse. Lehmann wrote that she half agreed to a contract, taking Göring's provision – that she never sing outside Germany again – not very seriously. She said she laughed at his last remark that no critic would be allowed to write bad reviews about her, otherwise he would be "liquidated."

When the final version of the contract arrived, so the article continued, "it contained no word about all that Göring had promised," causing Lehmann to complain to Berlin and reserving, among other things, her right to perform outside Nazi Germany. According to the article, Göring dictated a reply, "a terrible letter, full of insults and low abuse. A real volcano of hate and revenge."

Lehmann concluded her story with the remarks: "This was the end of Germany for me, Hitler's Germany!" Despite attempts to get her back, the singer never returned to the Third Reich.[140]

Lehmann's 1966 article, which made her look like a victim of the Nazis, was based on real events, but they had taken a totally different course. As documentary evidence discovered in an obscure Viennese archive reveals, the meeting took place on April 20, 1934, with Göring, in his capacity as head of the Prussian State Opera, and Generalintendant Heinz Tietjen, Göring's major-domo in cultural affairs. It was the result of efforts by Göring, Tietjen, and Strauss to effect some reforms in the state opera system that could have included the hiring of new stars. Berlin conductors Furtwängler and Robert Heger heard about this and Heger, a personal friend of Lehmann's from his Vienna days, encouraged Lehmann to put out feelers, since she was known to be interested in new opportunities. As in the 1920s, the singer was concertizing frequently in Germany, and the regime change in January 1933 did not affect her in the least. In so doing, she chose a different course from her friend Arturo Toscanini, who had an early falling-out with the Nazi regime, and from her old mentor, Berlin-born Bruno Walter, who had been physically forced out of Germany. One of Lehmann's highlights in the Third Reich was singing, on November 13, 1933, under Furtwängler's direction, as Strauss initiated the Reich Music Chamber in Berlin. Strauss's friend, the storm trooper and music critic Hugo Rasch, enthused in the *Völkischer Beobachter* that the singer's art was opening a new era of Nazi-organized music in the Third Reich, as he was especially impressed with her "unblemished way with song."[141] And on November 9 of that year, a Nazi holiday, Lehmann had performed at the Leipzig Gewandhaus from which Walter had been expelled not so long before.[142] Unsurprisingly, at the end of the first year of Nazi rule Lehmann received a letter from Walter's wife Else, in which she chided the singer for her insensitivity, merely for the sake of money, while artists with a conscience such as Toscanini were attempting to impose sanctions on the Hitler regime. "How I deplore the fact that you sing so much in Germany," she wrote. "You know very well that all artists who have been excluded from Germany, Aryan and non-Aryan, German and foreign, heart-warmingly declared their mutual solidarity and stayed away. It would have pleased me if you, too, had joined that protest and intermittently had turned your back on Germany."[143]

After Lehmann had discussed with Heger how to initiate for her a change from Vienna to Berlin without making it look obvious that it was she who was behind such an action, Heger contacted Furtwängler who then approached Göring. There was a further to and fro via letter, cable, and telephone, as a result of which Göring had the singer flown to Berlin on his private airplane on April 20, 1934. After the meeting with Göring, Lehmann showed herself very satisfied and talked to her German agent Erich Simon about a new deal, as good as sealed. The poor Jew, himself already on the run, had no choice but to congratulate her. Then on tour, she waited in London for the first draft of the contract from Berlin which, when it arrived, sorely disappointed her. The suggested conditions were not attractive to her, and her emoluments were far below the level of generosity touched on by Göring in Berlin and mentioned earlier to her. She conveyed her disillusionment to Tietjen, who on May 16 sent her a devastating reply, implying nothing less than greed and pomposity on her part. Disappointment on the Berlin side was encapsulated in Göring's condemnation that Lehmann as a quasi-Berliner and "a racially arch-German artist" had not felt German enough to consider serving the German people as a point of honor. After several more counter-arguments, some of them touching on money, the initial offer to Lehmann was withdrawn.[144] Subsequently, she was declared *persona non grata* by the government of the Third Reich, never allowed to return, which made it possible for her later to declare that she was a victim who had been persecuted personally by the most senior leaders of the Nazi regime. Without knowledge of the true circumstances, all her followers later pandered to that myth.[145]

How did all this have a bearing on her emigration and status as an exile? As further events unfolded, it became clear that to the extent the Nazi authorities came to resent Lehmann, she herself wanted to be regarded by the world as an enemy of the Third Reich, in order to further her chances of finding a safe haven, assuming that a career in Europe was becoming increasingly fraught with danger. Having lived in New York as a freelancing guest artist off and on since the fall of 1930, and having established valuable ties there with Jewish agents and accompanists, she was lucky enough to be in America when Austria was annexed to the Reich in March 1938. By then her carefully constructed legend could be instantly put to use to assuage suspicious Americans and deceive fellow emigrants, current or potential, especially the Jews among them. After the death of her husband Otto Krause in 1939, she moved permanently to the luxuriant coastal town of Santa Barbara in 1940 with her woman companion, a member of New York's high society. Lotte Lehmann became an American citizen in 1945. While, throughout the duration of the Third Reich, she acquired, technically, the status of an exile in America, she was hardly in the same category as genuine fugitives from fascism.

THE CASE OF THOMAS MANN

Thomas Mann condescendingly approved of the matronly Lotte Lehmann, whom he met occasionally either in Santa Barbara or Los Angeles, in the company of his daughter Erika or their mutual friend Bruno Walter, and whom, in a typically ironic overstatement, he once labeled a "splendid person." Whereas Mann truly admired the singer's art, he found her personally shrill and cloying, while she, not well read, was intimidated by his erudition and deterred by his cold formality.[146]

On the other hand, Mann disliked Marlene Dietrich and Erich Maria Remarque, whom he came across as a couple in the Warner Brothers film studio in Hollywood in April 1939. Remarque, who thought Mann had a "miserly face," probably resented the older novelist's arrogance, chafing at Mann's position as the most celebrated German émigré writer. Mann had noticed Remarque's indifferent behavior, anything but deferential, and was annoyed. About Dietrich he said almost nothing – with his homoerotic inclination, he was not given to commenting about strikingly attractive women. And yet, perhaps he resented her because when Dietrich had been cast as Lola Lola, Trude Hesterberg, his brother Heinrich's mistress at the time, had been overlooked.[147]

Thomas Mann's exile from Nazi Germany had begun in earnest in 1938, after the annexation of Austria in March, when he and his wife Katia were on their fourth sojourn in the United States and he decided not just to sever himself from the Third Reich but to devote his international prestige to acting against it. Arriving at this conviction had not been easy for him. He had halted a European lecture tour at the beginning of 1933 in Switzerland, as a group of influential and nationalist-minded artists and literati, mostly from Munich, had issued a letter citing objections to his mildly critical views of Richard Wagner – the subject of his talk.[148] The Manns remained in Küsnacht near Zurich, hesitating, until 1936, because a complete break with Hitler's Germany would mean a loss of book sales in the Reich, which were considerable.[149] Already during these early years of the regime, a younger generation of Germans, conditioned by Nazi education, did not know anymore who Thomas Mann was.[150] In 1933 the faction under Goebbels had wished him to collaborate in the manner of Richard Strauss. Therefore, his books were not consigned to the flames in May 1933, in contrast to the works of his older brother Heinrich, a known Marxist. There is also some truth to the Manns' argument that after a quiet return to Germany he might have exerted some mitigating influence there. That this was an illusion, however, was brought home to him in a series of letters from Erika, culminating in one dated January 26, 1936, in which she urged her father to terminate his status as "a non-genuine, half" emigrant, to finally declare himself and take an unambiguous stand against the Nazis. Mann thereafter became more vocal against the regime and promptly lost his German citizenship, accompanied by the loss of his honorary doctorate from Bonn. But in the same year he also acquired Czech citizenship for himself and Katia, which would enable them to travel further, in the south of France and northern Europe, for instance, and then North America.[151]

Among refugees from the Third Reich, Mann consistently exemplified a best-case scenario from many vantage points. Not the least of these was professional success. To achieve it, he was allowed – a solitary privilege granted only to him – to commence teaching courses at Princeton University, as "Lecturer in the Humanities," and to go on lecture tours throughout the United States, beginning in the spring of 1938 and continuing until he felt he could make enough money just through sales of his books. Whereas the teaching commitments at Princeton had petered out by 1941, he was appointed to a prestigious consulting position at the Library of Congress in 1942, which was merely nominal but paid him an excellent salary.

On his university lecture tours from 1938 to 1943 he was consistently paid $1,000 per lecture, sometimes more, and he would be feted as the guest of institutes of higher learning from coast to coast, with highlights always in New York, Chicago, and Los Angeles. His usual topics were political; early on he had a lecture prepared, "The Coming Victory of Democracy," which hinted at the downfall of Hitler's dictatorship as being close at hand, and, later on, so-called freedom lectures entitled "War and Democracy" and "How to Win the Peace." Apart from universities, there were speaking engagements at other prestigious venues, such as Carnegie Hall in New York, where the "Victory" speech was announced for Friday, May 6, 1938, at 8:45 p.m. Mann read the prepared lectures in comprehensible but strongly accented English, which improved over the months; although he hated questions, they were usually permitted and answered with the help of interlocutors, only Erika at first and later also hosts on the road. Occasionally, Mann was asked to speak about his own novels, such as the very popular *Der Zauberberg* (*The Magic Mountain*), sometimes at German departments in American universities, and it must have come as a nasty surprise to him that many of those had a German nationalist bent, some to the point of being pro-Nazi.[152]

Moreover, Mann was forever fortunate to be able to continue his career as a novelist almost as if nothing had happened, because he had the support of his old German publisher Samuel Fischer until his death in October 1934 in Berlin; the firm was duly expatriated to Austria, Switzerland, and then Sweden by his son-in-law Gottfried Bermann Fischer. In America, Mann's publisher was Alfred A. Knopf in New York, who had exclusive rights to all English translations of his books. Hence, even though Mann was interrupted by his extensive lecture tours and the vagaries of moving from Switzerland to Princeton and then to Los Angeles, he was still able, during his American exile, to begin and complete five novels, the two most important of which were the fourth part of his *Joseph* tetralogy and *Doktor Faustus*. Many devotees of the novelist – who had received the Nobel Prize in 1929, from Henrik Gustaf Söderbaum, secretary of the Royal Swedish Academy and father of Kristina Söderbaum, who, as an irony of history, would later aid her husband Veit Harlan in the making of pro-Nazi films – eventually would consider *Doktor Faustus* to be Thomas Mann's most important work. He first conceived this as a novella in February 1941 and finally began writing it two years later, in May. There were few émigré writers who came close to Mann's high level of production in fiction, both in terms of quality and material rewards, the next two outstanding ones being Werfel and Remarque.[153] In fact, many exiled writers continued their craft by writing novels about exile, as did Feuchtwanger and Klaus Mann, thereby signifying that the break in their professional past was considerable. Some of those novels were decidedly inferior in quality, like Feuchtwanger's *Exil* or, in English, Salamon Dembitzer's *Visas for America*, excepting, perhaps, Klaus Mann's *Vulkan* and Anna Seghers's *Transit*.

Thomas Mann's uniqueness in a potentially hostile world of exile was also determined by the protection he enjoyed through Agnes Meyer, the wealthy and influential wife of the *Washington Post* publisher Eugene Meyer. This much younger woman with German roots from New York had been impressed by Mann during a previous visit to the United States, and from 1938 onward looked after his well-being in an extraordinary fashion, arranging the Princeton and Library of Congress appointments and other contacts. Eventually, she served as a financial guarantor, providing peace of mind for Thomas Mann as he built his own house in the Pacific Palisades suburb of Los Angeles, at 1550 San Remo Drive, in 1941. Nevertheless, Mann had good reason to feel annoyed by her stream of letters and, at one time, a daring show of physical intimacy, but he kept his faith with her, answering almost every letter. It is fair to say that he sold his soul to Agnes Meyer, even allowing her to inspire the last part of his *Joseph* tetralogy. But then again, what was he to do if he wanted to remain vocal against Nazi Germany in the public manner to which he was now accustomed? He needed her money to help out others who asked for his aid, and to help mankind to survive the fascist onslaught against the free world, which he sometimes believed would collapse in ruins. Surely, a Faustian quandary! It is, however, a fact that when Mann finally left the United States to return to Europe permanently in 1952, Agnes Meyer was one of several important reasons.[154]

Writing, publishing, and lecturing throughout all of North America, Thomas Mann loved traveling in the huge, comfortable trains, like the Sky Chief, that took him, always first class, from one city to another. They appeared to him as some kind of symbol of the goodness of a working democracy in the country that had now taken him and his family in. Among all the artist refugees in the United States, he may have been the only one to feel this way, not just because the others could hardly afford to travel first class and therefore did not have the leisure to contemplate the benefits of this democracy. The fact that there is hardly a complaint in Mann's diaries about those arduous trips and there is, instead, such praise for the luxury Pullman cars conveys how genuinely this author endeavored to understand the new foreign country and how he tried to fit in. Seemingly little things, which threw many of his fellow refugees off, delighted or at least interested him, such as the typically American breakfasts (ham 'n' eggs), often in a drugstore on the road. Here the novelist, notwithstanding his inbred aristocratic bearing, rubbed shoulders with ordinary people in a demonstration of democracy in action. This was notwithstanding that in his Los Angeles home he could employ a Viennese refugee cook, that he always availed himself of a black servant couple from the South, and that he could afford to be chauffeured anywhere in his own Buick.[155]

Thomas Mann cherished democracy, which he himself had only begun to understand and even champion as recently as 1922, and he saw it ideally embodied in President Franklin D. Roosevelt, who became possibly the only living person, after 1933, whom he chose to look up to. He was invited to see and speak with him three times, as early as 1935, but whenever they met he failed to understand why Roosevelt had not read his works nor why he, the master politician, would not be interested in Mann's views on history and politics.[156] This may have poured cold water on the flames of his American love, and during his entire period there, he suffered other inconveniences, misunderstandings, and bouts of doubt. Some of these, as for the other refugees, had to do with the peculiarities of East and West Coast climates. Whereas he felt Princeton, like New York City, to be often muggy, the Californian sameness and predictably sunny weather tired him out easily and he tended to find the consistently gorgeous landscape boring.[157] On the whole, he thought the United States an incoherent ethnic compound, artificially stitched together, as a "colonial land, with the accomplishments of technical know-how."[158] As he wrote to Bermann Fischer, he considered its people naïve in their never-ending optimism, both materially and for a better, feel-good future.[159] Over the years, he was disturbed by this (America lacked the qualities of European tragedy and decay that he himself was expert at conveying in his novels), and already in the early 1940s he wagered more comparisons with Europe. He decided in the end that Switzerland would be the most congenial country for his temperament and lifestyle, and he condemned Munich, most certainly because of the 1933 open letter contrived by his resentful nationalist-minded peers attacking him for his criticism of Richard Wagner.[160]

From his pristine Olympian peak the high-strung Mann found it difficult to abide fellow refugee artists in day-to-day encounters, let alone regard them benevolently, because he found them wanting, each and every one. Since he applied a stringent set of standards to his own behavior in society (always in suit and tie, even at the writing desk) and, what was more, to his creative work ethic, he constantly found fault with members of his cohort, as he had already before 1938 in the case of Grosz and Koestler. He enjoyed social gatherings at the houses of friends and colleagues, where food and drinks were served and everybody, inevitably, spoke German – not least because he could fancy himself as the center of attention. Typically, he noted, after a party at the house of the novelist Vicki Baum in Hollywood in April 1938: "Almost exclusively German-speaking guests. Architect Neutra. The comedian, musician and actor Dr. Klemperer, Schönberg etc. Long conversation before dinner. Buffet dinner. At the end Bali film with youths in ritual trance. Convulsions. – The beautiful young male Indian dancer. – At home with Colin. Late."[161] As frequently throughout his diary entries, Mann found it impossible to repress cynical observations about others: the conductor Klemperer, a manic-depressive and mostly unhappy in America, was often observed to act and talk strangely in the company of others, in order to provoke.

When Thomas Mann, mostly on the U.S. East and West Coasts, engaged with people in conversation and debate on the subject of exile, he expressed strong opinions, sometimes also about persons not in his immediate vicinity. In the case of the poet Joseph Roth, for example, Mann denigrated his lonely death in Paris in May 1939 as that of a "drunkard," without showing any trace of empathy.[162] Mann's relationship with Brecht was consistently acrimonious, even before their controversy in May 1943 about who in Germany should be blamed for the rise of National Socialism.[163] He judged Zuckmayer's writing skills as "mediocre," and even found fault with his friend Albert Einstein's lecture at Princeton University, which he characterized as "very incomprehensible."[164]

And as much as Thomas Mann liked Werfel as a friend – probably the closest friend he had after the writer Bruno Frank and Bruno Walter – Werfel got on his nerves more than once and he disdained his literary output. When in December 1942, Werfel, in the middle of a group of guests, loudly decreed that a peace was in sight after the imminent debacle of National Socialism, Mann was exasperated, blaming an obviously lesser man who had dared to make political predictions in his presence.[165] Hence it comes as no surprise that Mann declined to back a possible candidacy of Werfel for the Nobel literature prize, and he usually cringed when the powerful Alma accompanied her husband. It was clear that Mann, as in the case of Remarque, found it difficult to abide Werfel's American financial success.[166]

Mann sustained a special relationship with Theodor Adorno and Arnold Schoenberg, toward the middle of the 1940s, while in the process of writing *Doktor Faustus*, a novel inspired by a modern musical theme. Although he had always been interested in classical music, especially Wagner, he possessed only scant knowledge of the violin and little of the piano, on which, nonetheless, from early on he was fond of noodling themes from *Tristan und Isolde*. As already noted, next to conversations with the twelve-tone innovator Schoenberg, and apart from musicological information he received, he also gained considerable insight into harmony and music theory through talks with Adorno. As a musician and music critic in his former life, Adorno had been a pupil of Schoenberg's student Alban Berg, and now, although he was engaged with Max Horkheimer, on the East Coast, in the formulation of a new social philosophy, he liked to help Mann out. Yet a third musician useful to Mann was the composer Hanns Eisler, who had also studied under Schoenberg.[167]

Schoenberg, Eisler, and Adorno had Jewish roots, and what appears to have been their smooth relationship with Mann highlights his fundamental sense of tolerance of different ethnicities, cultures, and apposite ideologies (as he had demonstrated in his evaluation of American society in general); this was so important in the diaspora of fugitives from European fascism. Eugene Meyer, who looked upon the charitable actions of his wife Agnes towards Mann with benevolent bemusement, was also Jewish. This is not to say that Mann was entirely free of conventional anti-Semitism, of the kind that Germany's educated classes easily harbored against Jews from the last thirty years of the Wilhelmine Empire. Mann had been much more strongly anti-Semitic in his youth, but he had married a Jewish girl from a closely acculturated, even privileged, family, and in his private circle of relationships an anti-Jewish stance was not discernible, at least not at that time. It was only on certain occasions in America that Jews he did not know well but found easy to stereotype got under his skin, of a type he had known in Europe and obviously disliked.[168] His was a selective caution against Jews.

He was genuinely shaken when his in-laws, Alfred and Hedwig Pringsheim, were driven by the Nazis from their Munich mansion on Arcisstrasse, forced to stay in close quarters near Lake Constance, until in October 1939 they were allowed to seek refuge in Switzerland, all of their fortune having meanwhile been confiscated.[169]

Several American Jewish organizations assisted Mann in the planning of his speaking tours, such as the Wise Temple in Cincinnati, the Shalom Temple in Chicago, and the Young Men's and Young Women's Hebrew Association in St. Louis – where up to 3,000 people came to hear him.[170] Jews were also instrumental in Mann's work with refugee organizations and the monthly political broadcasts he did for German listeners via the BBC from October 1940 on. In these he made certain to address the terrible fate of European Jews as it was unfolding before him, such as when he deplored the transport of French Jews from Vichy France to the death camps of the European East in September 1942. At a time when most people outside Germany claimed ignorance, Mann, significantly, was conversant with these crimes. These broadcasts were also listened to by exiles, particularly in Britain.[171]

Mann showed solidarity with other refugees when German immigrants without American citizenship were required to have themselves registered as "Enemy Aliens" under the existing Alien Enemy Act, recodified after World War I. After the German declaration of war on the United States in December 1941 presidential proclamations 2526 and 2527 under this act provided for Italians and Germans in America to be apprehended, restrained, and secured. Hence in February 1942 he joined other prominent exiles such as Walter, Toscanini, and Einstein in sending a telegram to Roosevelt to draw attention "to a large group of natives of Germany and Italy who by present regulations are, erroneously, characterized and treated as 'Enemy Aliens'." These people had fled to the United States because of "totalitarian persecution" and therefore had lost their citizenship. "Many of these people, politicians, scientists, artists, writers, have been among the earliest and most farsighted adversaries of the governments against whom the United States are now at war." The signatories wanted the president to draw a line "between the potential enemies of American democracy on the one hand, and the victims and sworn foes of totalitarian evil on the other."[172] Roosevelt, however, left the restrictions in place, having wisecracked that "as a lot of opera singers," Italians were not to be feared, whereas Germans were different – "they may be dangerous."[173] Restrictions meant, for instance, that for an affected person there was a local curfew of 8:00 p.m. and that he or she was not allowed to travel more than five miles from their private residence without official permission.[174] Despite such entreaties as Mann's and Einstein's, however, the strictures remained in place until the refugees had acquired American citizenship or until the end of the war, whichever came first.

Despite his personal hauteur, Mann remained generous in listening to cries of help and extending empathy and tangible assistance to many refugees where he could. In 1940 already he was receiving "mountains of mail, mostly distress signals."[175] He wrote a letter to a close acquaintance, the prominent New York journalist Dorothy Thompson, to ask for assistance to be extended to Annette Kolb, a writer and Munich friend of Katia Mann's; Kolb had left Germany already in 1933 and her works were on the Nazi blacklist.[176] In April 1941, Mann considered a request from Fritz Stiedry, a Jewish conductor who had arrived in the United States via the Soviet Union and in New York kept up the New Friends of Music Orchestra, for which he needed funds.[177] He wanted $20,000, which Mann thought he might get from Agnes Meyer. It is doubtful that she gave such a large amount. But Mann asked for just $1,000 a couple of months later, for "emigrant aid," which she promptly paid.[178] And in 1943 he conceived the plan for a "New School" on the West Coast, to assist "the impecunious writers."[179]

Mann's capacity for personal empathy was large in principle because he himself was highly sensitive and used to suffering. Apart from the psychological difficulties due to the fundamental change in moving from Europe to North America and then constant moves on the North American mainland, his physical constitution deteriorated over time. Sixty-three years old when he arrived in the United States to stay, he had to fight all manner of health irregularities and a few serious ailments, aggravated by uncertainty regarding his future. Although in this respect he resembled fellow refugee artists, there were two distinct differences from many of them. First, he never succumbed to alcoholism, even though he was consuming hard liquor and beer on a daily basis and during Prohibition took leather cases with spirits along on the trains.[180] Second, thanks to sufficient personal wealth and excellent connections, he could avail himself of first-class medical help speedily and at all times. Mann was also unique in that he had been interested in the etiology of human disorders for a very long time and thought he could interpret many of their symptoms, as he had showed in his novels *Buddenbrooks* and *The Magic Mountain*, and was to show again in his last great work, dealing with the demise of the syphilitic Adrian Leverkühn in *Doktor Faustus*. But only in some respects was the composer Leverkühn an image of himself.

Mann confessed to suffering from depression (as did, for instance, Stefan Zweig), although it is uncertain whether he had clinically defined manic depression, with its high peaks and deep lows, like Otto Klemperer. If so, Mann would have been especially creative during psychic highs, and his inspiration must have lain fallow during lows. There are indications in his diaries from his American period that such a correlation did exist. For example, he felt "unwell" when he was struggling with his *Joseph* manuscript in the morning of September 23, 1940, while in Brentwood, in the Greater Los Angeles area; in the afternoon, he dictated letters to Katia, without changes to his darkish mood.[181] Less than six months later, back in Princeton, he found himself "bored, lacking concentration, and tired"; the *Joseph* chapter he was laboring on, in the morning and the afternoon, just did not want to take shape.[182] At that particular time, this condition seems to have affected his work for at least a week.[183] In June 1942, the assassination of Heydrich (who had once wanted to put him into Dachau) and the subsequent murder of hundreds of Czech hostages affected him so severely that he decided to stop working in the afternoons, something that Mann, being the creative thinker that he was, would not endure in years to come.[184] In November of 1944 he again suffered from inertia, the inability to think constructively about his new *Doktor Faustus* novel, as he was complaining about a lack of energy on eventless days.[185]

Depression was most obviously linked to consciousness, knowledge, and memory that directly affected a writer's thoughts. Moreover, Mann periodically felt pain from digestive disorders that he tried to relieve with milk of magnesia, chicken broth, tea, or a brandy.[186] There were other ailments, such as bronchial catarrh, compounded by heavy smoking – Mann was habitually fond of expensive cigarettes and a good cigar.[187] One of his worst problems, albeit not life-threatening, was a tooth-decay condition requiring oral root surgery, which dragged on, from April 1941, for months and years and required complicated and expensive treatments.[188]

If his own creative work as a novelist was affected by these maladies, it is not clear how they influenced Mann's views on everyday politics, including the ongoing war. Did stomach pain invoke pessimism regarding the future of the free world when Hitler suddenly attacked Poland, and did relief from toothache inspire hopes of Allied victory upon Rommel's withdrawal from North Africa? Mann himself provided at least one example pointing in the direction of such correlation. On August 3, 1941 he wrote to Bermann Fischer that he had suffered from too slow a pulse, low blood pressure, and malfunction of his thyroid glands. For the remedy, he had taken medications and now felt much better. This against a world-war backdrop that bode ill for Hitler's Reich, after the Nazi invasion of the Soviet Union which, Mann rightly pointed out, had unsettled the German people and even made Wehrmacht generals uncomfortable.[189]

At that juncture, Mann had established himself irrevocably in European, particularly German, affairs, as a man of vision, aesthetically and ethically, who in North America had no equal. This was due to the writer's appearances in the United States previous to the decisive spring 1938 visit, as he was already known then, alongside the long-since emigrated Einstein, as the most prominent German thinker who had removed himself from the Reich. American journalists who approached Mann accepted as a matter of course that he could enlighten them, and through them the American public, on the phenomenon of European fascism, the more so since they themselves, as Erika Mann remarked on later, had few clues and were aware that no matter how many Americans there may already have been against it, there were others, especially Americans of German descent, who were for it.[190] Mann therefore was forced into the role of a political interpreter, even a clairvoyant, that he at first did not really know how to fill. He granted a significant series of interviews in April 1937, at the end of his third American visit, including one to Agnes Meyer, who was working as a correspondent for her husband's daily, *The Washington Post*. When in the summer Mann published an article in a Zurich journal, an English translation, facilitated by Meyer, was printed simultaneously in *The New York Times*. That paper purported to present Mann, as he opened a "war on Nazi concepts," as a Third Reich opponent *par excellence* and declared in a brief preface that he had found the Nazi dictatorship "already confounded." In that very long piece of penmanship, in which Hitler was not mentioned once, Mann posed mainly as a champion of culture who declared, valiantly, that "we want to be artists and anti-barbarians," intent on defending values of a free and open world, one that his idol Goethe could identify with. Upon close analysis, his was less a political than an aesthetic declaration, by which National Socialism appeared to have been generated as an accident of history rather than the consequence of decades of Germanocentric malfeasance, abetted by the machinations of an ascendant demagogue. Hesitating to accept fascisms such as Nazi creed and rule as something permanent, Mann declared that "the hypnotic spell which for a time emanated from these uniformly depressing ideas which are called 'fascistic' is on the wane. As an intellectual fashion, fascism can already be considered antiquated." All the same, as if this were easily done and could be wrought beyond the realm of politics, Mann promised that "we shall help to prepare for a German power and a German State in which the German intellect can cheerfully participate, thereby realizing a genuine totality."[191]

But as he had done before, Mann was to undergo a political education. After World War I, he had renounced a chauvinistic, ultra-conservative position to throw in his lot with the democracy of the Weimar Republic.[192] And during his erstwhile stay in Switzerland he opted late, but he did opt publicly against Hitler, whom, in a public address after the electoral success of the National Socialists in the September 1930 elections, he had not even mentioned.[193] The relative political naïveté characterizing the *New York Times* exposition which, in the final analysis, minimized the fascist danger rather than accentuating it, was already less apparent in an interview he gave to that paper on his fourth arrival in the United States in February 1938. Now he was honest enough to admit that he did not "work politically" and would rather "prefer to talk about literature." As far as the politics went, he was sufficiently prescient to realize that Hitler's current exploits in Austria (the Anschluss was three weeks away) would not satisfy the dictator's imperialist appetite and that Czechoslovakia "will come next." He also, correctly, identified America as a "lone bulwark against the destruction of liberty and freedom," but again committed the mistake of seeing in Nazism merely a singular "error of history." Yet at least he had, this time, mentioned Hitler by name.[194]

From March 1938 to the fall of 1940, Mann's political opinion vacillated between precarious conjecture and well-educated guesswork, a fragile position for a man considered a sort of pundit by the American public, a role he may have doubted for himself. As he prepared for his pro-democracy and anti-Nazi speeches at American institutions in late March 1938, he deplored Hitler's annexation of Austria, again assuring himself that this was only the beginning of Nazi imperialism, while insisting publicly that a war in Europe was rather improbable. "No one wants it," he maintained from the end of May, claiming that Hitler was incapable of war and France too torn to wage it.[195] This was irrespective of Hitler's view, expressed already in *Mein Kampf* (which Mann had obviously never read), that "struggle" was a fundamental plank of Nazi ideology – "the essence of the Nazi system," as Ian Kershaw later defined it – and oblivious to circumstances in which France had signed military mutual assistance pacts with eastern European nations since the early 1920s, should contingencies arise.[196]

During the Sudeten crisis in the fall of 1938 and into the spring of 1939, Mann was adamant that in a pinch the Czechs would fight for the status quo, claiming at the same time that France and Britain would withdraw from conflict, despite prior alliances with the CSR. As for the latter point, he may have been aware that France's intention of honoring the agreement with the Czechs was weak and British politicians were well aware of this. After Hitler had duped Prime Ministers Édouard Daladier and Neville Chamberlain in Munich, Mann thought wrongly (contrary to what previously he had said after the Anschluss) that Hitler was now satiated and a war out of sight. However – and this again was prescient – he allowed that within a year of March 1939 a European war was possible.[197]

That March, Mann published an essay about Hitler in the men's magazine *Esquire*, which brought into focus, on the one hand, gaps in the author's historical knowledge, combined with an uncertain political instinct at that time, culminating in an underestimation of the Führer, yet also, on the other hand, the beginnings of some fundamental comprehension. In stilted (translated) English he claimed that Hitler was "a catastrophe" and "a man ten times a failure, extremely lazy, incapable of steady work; a man who has spent long periods in institutions; a disappointed bohemian artist; a total good-for-nothing," and someone who had "neither technical nor physical discipline." But he conceded Hitler "a gift of oratory. It is oratory unspeakably inferior in kind, but magnetic in its effect on the masses: a weapon of definitely histrionic, even hysterical power, which he thrusts into the nation's wound and turns round: He rouses the populace with images of his own

insulted grandeur, deafens it with promises, makes out of the people's suffer-
ings a vehicle for his own greatness, his ascent to fantastic heights, to unlim-
ited power, to incredible compensations and over-compensations." Hitler,
said Mann, had annexed Austria only as a move against "the venerable
Freud, the real and actual enemy," and through all of his political misdeeds
he had brought the German people up against him.[198]

That Hitler was a "catastrophe" was now the free world's general
consensus, but even his worst enemies at the time would not have called the
Nazi Führer lazy or incapable of steady work, certainly not after World War
I. Moreover, unless Mann meant prison, it was historically verifiable that
Hitler had never been institutionalized. Mann could have read up on this
not only in *Mein Kampf*, which would have had to be used with caution, but
also in two recent biographies of Hitler, by Konrad Heiden and the less
credible Rudolf Olden. The first (one of eventually two volumes) had been
published in German earlier in 1936 in Zurich, Mann's European abode,
and the second, also in German, in Amsterdam in 1935. Both were reviewed,
as translated narratives, in *The New York Times* on May 24, 1936.[199] From
these titles alone Mann could have gleaned that Hitler, though of "bizarre
appearance and eccentric behaviour" (Volker Ullrich) and keeping irregular
hours in bohemian circles, especially early on in Munich where Mann
himself resided, had worked extremely hard at becoming a politician, in
order to snake-charm the masses.[200] Heiden, for instance, gives this, correct,
impression as he writes about Hitler's early career in Munich, from the time
he left the army in 1919 to the putsch of November 1923.[201] Ultimately,
having succeeded at politics by having applied immense self-discipline
proved to be his genius. Mann implicitly acknowledged this when he
referred to Hitler's awesome speech-making, but he belittled it to make him
laughable, when in fact, as the sociologist Max Weber had shown much
earlier, a successful speaker for the masses frequently was a man, more like
a shaman who did not fit a gentrified, conventional mold. In truth, Hitler's
"hysterical power" was the secret to his charisma, which had made him into
the leader of half the European continent.[202] As for Sigmund Freud, Mann
had no evidence that Hitler had ever seriously concerned himself with that
pioneer in psychiatry, nor could Hitler have known, quite apart from
Freud's Jewishness, the difference between analytical (Freudian) and organic
psychiatry.[203] And Mann's contention of a split between the German people

and the Führer denied the very popularity Hitler had been enjoying among his subjects, at least from 1933 to early 1939 – the consequence of those political skills Mann seemed to want to question. On the other hand, Mann had put his finger firmly on the leader's charismatic qualities as those that worked effectively on his people, without actually saying so.

Mann continued his mixed political analyses and prophesies, as during the summer of 1939 when Hitler was obviously preparing himself for war, by playing down this possibility, arguing either that European nations did not want to fight or were militarily helpless. When the Nazi-Soviet Pact was signed on August 23, he interpreted this to mean that Hitler wished to avert war and the Soviet Union was uninterested in a partition of Poland.[204] The opposite was actually true: Hitler was burning to attack Poland and, something contained in a secret protocol but already thought likely by other observers, attempted to assuage Moscow by offering Stalin the eastern half of that state, both sides proceeding with partition in late September.[205]

As the war commenced after September 1, Mann again underestimated Hitler by thinking that it would not last very long, as the Germans could not even endure one winter.[206] But further into the conflict, Mann's confidence in Hitler's ineffectualness diminished, as he took the dictator's pact with Moscow seriously, beginning to think that eventually Nazi Germany and the Soviet Union would combine to fight the United States. Around this time Mann started to think more clearly about a possible intervention in the war by Roosevelt, in fact he became somewhat obsessed with that until Hitler actually declared war on America on December 11, 1941. The first such notion is expressed in his diary in the middle of April 1940, and a month later he reasoned, quite realistically, that America's entry into the war was the more probable the more reckless Hitler, with millions under arms, showed himself. But would America not come to the rescue too late? During the fall of France in summer 1940, Mann realized that war would continue regardless of a large-scale Hitler victory, and by September he wanted the United States in the conflict more strongly than ever, even crediting Roosevelt with the power of ultimately toppling the dictator.[207]

In October 1940, Mann began his regular broadcast recordings for the BBC, in which he came out squarely contra Hitler, in the combined role of conveyer of objective news and spiritual guide to what, in the majority, he still viewed as a controlled and victimized people. This entailed more sober reportage, more thoughtful judgments, and fewer emotional asides, even though his texts, as a moral compass, were much marked by compassion. Hence he spoke for the record, in July 1942, of Hitler's inability to achieve victory, as he himself would "always prevent it," as indeed Hitler had done before the gates of Moscow in December 1941 and would again at Stalingrad, the demise of which Mann now saw approaching as early as the fall of 1942.[208] It is possible that two years earlier, in the fall of 1940, Mann's news sources had improved, from radio commentator Raymond Gram Swing, whom he apparently listened to on CBS, from *The New York Times*, *The Washington Post*, and the journal *The Nation*. It is likely also that he now relied more on informed new sources from neutral Sweden and Switzerland – mostly newspaper clippings and letters that were sent to him.[209]

By early summer of 1943, because the United States was in the war and no more armistices or peace arrangements were looming, Mann was of the opinion – sooner than other pundits – that Nazi Germany was militarily finished. In August he distanced himself from the declaration of certain émigrés, supported by Brecht, which differentiated between the Hitler regime and its "allied classes" on the one side, and "the German people" on the other.[210] Several months later, as he now believed the German people were not merely victims but collectively complicit in the war, his sense of propriety allowed him to approve of the plan of Roosevelt's Secretary of the Treasury, Henry Morgenthau, for a division and reduction of Germany, turning it into a vast sheep pasture, to forestall renewed aggression. He continued to hold this view into early 1945, when some Allied representatives were actually devising alternative plans, providing for a gradual reintegration of the once fascist state into a civilized member of the family of nations.[211]

In a final evaluation of Thomas Mann's role as an artist refugee from Nazism it is incumbent to balance the extremes of his self-perception with reality and then, perhaps, compare that with the average artist refugee. Mann was, by all accounts, an aloof and distant man who gave himself an air of untouchability and grandness. To those who did not know him better, he expressed this unmistakably during his interview for *New York Times* readers when in February 1938 he stated that "where I am, there is Germany."[212] In constant self-reflection he accepted his persona as unique, insisting that in company he be treated preferentially and with the greatest respect. He cherished being compared to Goethe and he himself made frequent references to him, especially as he was completing his Goethe novel, *Lotte in Weimar*, following his arrival in America in 1938.[213] After receiving enthusiastic letters about this book from colleagues he typically was beside himself with joy, and in October 1940, as he was about to begin his anti-Hitler broadcasts, he treasured the remark by an unknown American soldier that he was "not only the greatest living writer, but the greatest living man in our history."[214] At the height of the summer in 1943 he relished the notion of fellow emigrants that after a final victory over Hitler he be appointed to lead Germany, presumably as president of a new, democratic, commonweal, cognizant of past cultural achievements. He himself was suitably ironic when during a visit from Martin Gumpert they talked "much about my Führer future in Germany, from which God may save me."[215]

Suitably ironic! In fact, Mann must have been much relieved when a few months later not himself but a certain Carl von Habsburg was said to be in the running to be Germany's new head of state.[216] This circumstance must have reminded him once more that at the core he was a poet, not a politician, and that it was as a poet that he had been endowed with extraordinary gifts some called genius. Knowing this, yet also knowing about his private insecurities, he had said as early as December 1929, during the Nobel Prize ceremonies in Stockholm, that it was not he himself who was being honored, but "the German spirit, German prose."[217] Mann had put the accent on "German" because he knew, as did all the literati, that those individuals he had portrayed in *Buddenbrooks* and *The Magic Mountain* were particularly German characters in very German relationships, and that he had written about those unambiguously as a German author who knew German mores and traditions well. In that sense, he was placing himself as the heir to Goethe, not only by virtue of the Nobel Prize, but also because Mann embodied the same blend of innovation, as shown in boldness of style and content, and conservatism. Goethe had been an enlightened chancellor of the duchy of Weimar, but he had also harbored conservative inclinations, as in the death sentence he upheld for an unwed mother who had killed her child; Mann, who during his American exile even sympathized with socialism and after 1949 recognized the Communist German Democratic Republic, never ceased to be the son of a patrician Lübeck senator, a conservative at heart. Hence Mann found it natural to identify with Goethe, as he did already during that interview with *The New York Times* in August

1937, when he said: "We want to be artists and anti-barbarians," and, further, "the artist," said Goethe, "must have an origin, must know from what he stems." In the same interview Mann mentioned Richard Wagner, a fellow artist, as an inspiration, so that it was clear how he saw himself as a successor to both Goethe *and* Wagner, notwithstanding the criticism he was known to have leveled against the composer earlier on.[218]

It is against this background that one has to understand Mann's statement that Germany was wherever he was, which at first sight is so redolent of hubris. For he added immediately that he carried his German culture in him. Since these sentences were meant to challenge Hitler, they implied that Mann, exemplifying a true German cultural tradition following Goethe, saw himself in the United States, away from fascism, as warranting a Germany without Hitler. Figuratively speaking, being on this moral high ground, he was saving both culture and Germany.[219] Mann's New York publisher Knopf recognized this when he maintained that nowadays the writer was "Hitler's most dangerous foe."[220] This was a few months before Mann wrote in *Esquire* that as uncomfortable as it felt, there existed a symbiotic relationship between himself and Hitler, whom he, again ironically, called "my brother," not only because, however justified, both saw themselves as artists and accomplices in their undying love of Wagner, but also, even more so, because they represented opposite poles aesthetically, and certainly ethically.[221] They were Cain and Abel, except that in this case, Abel would survive. Justly so, because Adolf Hitler stood for intolerance and the domination of humankind, whereas Mann represented democracy and freedom. To have expressed this often privately and publicly from 1933 to 1945 and beyond, and having said it with emphasis and logic, made the Nobel laureate stand out from among all the other refugees from tyranny.

◆ ◆ ◆

CHAPTER SIX

Transfer Beyond Zero Hour, May 1945

Uring the early years of the Third Reich, Joseph Goebbels would have wanted Thomas Mann to return to Germany in order to help uphold the country's reputation around the world in the arts. Having received his doctorate in German literature in 1922, Goebbels knew about Mann's cultural significance early on, in fact he enjoyed reading him, especially his *Buddenbrooks*, at the very time he was moving close to the new Nazi Party in the mid-1920s. This was notwithstanding the fact that he considered Mann prone to favoring themes of decadence and decay, and that the loss of such a great literary talent to the cause of the Weimar Republic with its parliamentary democracy was deplorable.[1] That Mann was not a Modernist in the manner of other writers who were commanding much attention at that time, and some of whom he liked, was not an issue for Goebbels, as he appreciated Mann's more traditionalist literary approach. Hence Goebbels should have been happy had Mann decided not to leave Germany at all or to return to it later, as he then could have supported Mann's personal motto that wherever he was, there was Germany, or its axiom, there was German culture. It is very likely that had Mann accommodated himself to the dictatorship from 1933 like Richard Strauss, who did not contemplate emigration, German cultural matters during the regime would have taken a different course – more favorable to Goebbels than what he actually got. This is provided Mann would have written the same high-quality novels as he produced in exile, without interference by the regime leaders. The prestige of the arts under the Third Reich could have been considerable.

Obviously, Mann did not want to be the representative of what he regarded as a traditional, time-honored culture in a Germany ruled by Nazis. It is therefore not without irony that after they were defeated, he still refused to return to the land of his birth, assuming there a position of cultural authority. There is no question that certain factions wanted him back in Germany, to help with the rebuilding of the country and to be an example to new, budding writers. This was, especially, the view of those officers of the U.S. occupying forces in the American zone (Office of Military Government, United States, or OMGUS) concerned with cultural affairs, although they feared that Mann might be repelled by unacceptable living conditions.[2] Knowing the superior lifestyle to which he was accustomed in the United States, this could have been a reason for him to hold back, but what was decisive for him was that influential Germans rejected his putative position of authority. In the bigger picture, his situation was tied into the whole thorny question of emigrating versus sticking it out in Germany; the latter was now being advocated by writers Walter von Molo, Frank Thiess, and even the sometime Nazi Manfred Hausmann, as the best way to have withstood the Nazis. It was Thiess who in August 1945 popularized the neologism "inner emigration" when he wrote in a Munich newspaper that even as an opponent of the regime, having stayed in Germany had enriched his character and was preferable to having watched "German tragedy" unfold from the "theater boxes of abroad."[3] However, Mann may not have known that von Molo and Thiess, like Hausmann, had made well-calculated concessions to Goebbels and other Nazi administrators. During the final phase of the war Mann had claimed that the German people should bear some measure of guilt after all for having supported the Nazis, and he reacted with uncommon acrimony in October by saying he was in fear of a country that had become foreign to him. He would find it difficult to engage with those who had compromised their beliefs and besides, "books that had any chance of being published between 1933 and 1945 now are less than valuable and not worthy of being opened. Blood and ignominy stick to them. They should all be pulped."[4]

Thomas Mann returned to Germany from Los Angeles for the Goethe festivities in Frankfurt and Weimar in the late summer of 1949, not least with a view to resettlement. But his visits there, marked by his customary hauteur, did not go over well with his hosts in either West or East Germany.[5] His labored justification for emigration and his pro-democracy preaching could not convince critics such as Erich Kästner (another "inner emigrant" who had been well paid for his script for the lavish 1943 *Baron Münchhausen* film, under the pseudonym of Berthold Bürger), who had earlier published his view that Mann was known mostly for his characterizations of sickly, decadent creatures and had better remain in America.[6] Mann, who had always been grateful for the asylum Switzerland had granted him early on, had mentioned a return to Zurich several times in his diaries from late in the war. So it came as no surprise that he decided to move back there in 1952, when conditions in the United States, especially the political witch-hunt for Communists, became unbearable for him.[7]

Once again, Thomas Mann's situation was exceptional, as he was in the fortunate position of being able to either accept or reject an offer of residence in Germany. The vast majority of writers who might have wanted to return did not have this choice. They were unwelcome in a society that allowed entrenched Nazis to carry on and merely accorded the benefit of the doubt to pre-1933 established bourgeois authors such as Hans Carossa. On the other hand, this being a new democracy, it did not encourage but neither did it hinder the formation of some younger writers into what they themselves called Gruppe 47 ("Group of 1947"). Those were mavericks who decided to wage a new beginning, predicated on rejecting anything that smacked of the Third Reich. But even these innovative writers, who were semi-officially led by the unexceptional novelist Hans Werner Richter and included Günther Grass, Ingeborg Bachmann, and Walter Jens, and who were of a generation that could still have been conscripted into the Wehrmacht, wished to have nothing to do with older compatriots outside their circle. They possessed a "youthful coolness," explains a former member of this coterie, the Munich cultural-affairs critic Joachim Kaiser; they wanted to revive, on their own, "language and literature" that the Nazis were said to have destroyed. And anyone with a literary past from the Weimar Republic, they decided, was not for them either.[8]

Nor were other exiled writers invited back, including Mann's children, Lion Feuchtwanger, and Bertolt Brecht, not least because there remained a latent strain of anti-Semitism in West Germany, and there existed the

301

beginnings of a new xenophobia. While (the non-Jewish) Brecht eventually found a new home in East Germany, which developed different standards for reintegrating former exiles into a new, Communist-led, society (and which would accommodate other artists as well, on dubious and Soviet-determined conditions),[9] the western trizonal part of Germany, and later the Federal Republic, did not want many of these exiled writers. Klaus Mann, in jurisdictions such as West Germany's where homosexuality was punishable by law, was rejected as a contributor for new newspapers like Munich's *Süddeutsche Zeitung*. Also, his novel *Mephisto* was banned from publication in West Germany, a judgment vigorously supported by Peter Gorski, the former lover and adopted son of Gustaf Gründgens (Mann's erstwhile lover), after the celebrated actor's death in 1963, on whom Mann had based his novel. The ban was in force until 1981, during which time one could read the novel only in earlier editions published in Holland and East Germany.[10] Although the formal basis for the West German judgment was character defamation rather than an anti-homosexual motive, homophobia was rife in the new German cultural establishment and played a role in Klaus Mann's rejection as an author.

Beyond that sentiment, there existed an almost demonic energy with which others went after prominent émigrés. Erich Maria Remarque was picked over critically by *Der Spiegel* and *Die Zeit*, supposedly liberal journals, and condemned, even in his home town of Osnabrück, for his latest novel, *Der Funke Leben* (*The Spark of Life*), which excoriated concentration camps.[11] A would-be returnee from exile like Alfred Döblin was marginalized to the point of having his work excluded not only from bookstores but also anthologies, for example school textbooks that habitually still featured Nazi-prone writers like Friedrich Griese and Josefa Berens-Totenohl. No newly formed German publisher wished to publish, or reprint, those questionable émigrés.[12]

Such mistrust regarding would-be returning refugees extended to all the other arts as well, even if the Soviets, in their zone of occupation, initially made self-serving exceptions. In the Trizone (the American, British, and French areas of German occupation following the end of World War II), led by OMGUS, it had been deemed necessary to resurrect a corrupted film industry by inviting back former exiles from Hollywood to come and help out. However, it proved difficult to appoint a U.S.-authorized commissioner who would then persuade fellow exiles to return. Detlev Sierck, who had made *La Habanera* with Zarah Leander in 1937 before leaving for Hollywood and taking the name of Douglas Sirk, traveled to Germany but was not tempted to stay, since there he discovered "no profound break" with the past, merely a failure to confront recent history.[13] The Americans then prevailed on Erich Pommer, who had produced *The Cabinet of Dr. Caligari* in 1920 and permanently settled in Hollywood after leaving Germany for France in 1933. Pommer supervised the resumption of the film industry in the American zone, but failed to permanently attract important expatriates such as Peter Lorre or Lilli Palmer, much less Marlene Dietrich.[14] Lorre, whose Hollywood career was going downhill after the war, actually made one film in Germany in 1951, *Der Verlorene* (*The Lost One*), which analyzed the Nazi phenomenon "in a series of rather perfunctory clichés," according to *The New York Times*; it did badly at the box office and that sealed Lorre's fate in the Old Country.[15] Those actors who insisted on returning to Germany, such as Walter Weinlaub, who now called himself Walter Wicclair, had become unknowns, and upon introducing themselves to German actor associations that could advance their cause were rebuffed.[16] Even Curt Bois, a one-time student of Max Reinhardt who had played a pickpocket in *Casablanca* alongside Ingrid Bergman in 1942, was snubbed.[17]

Moreover, the celebrated architect Walter Gropius was looked upon with suspicion when in August 1947 he gave a lecture in Berlin's Titania-Palast. Gropius had recommended his friend Hans Scharoun, who had lain low in the Nazi period, as a mentor to younger colleagues undertaking new architectural projects, but was told that those colleagues needed "no suggestions."[18] Interest or compassion was also lacking in the music industry, especially where Modernist dodecaphony was involved. Jews like Erich Wolfgang Korngold, Ernst Toch, or Hans Gál were not approached, and even the non-Jewish Ernst Krenek had his *Zwölftonkontrapunktstudien* (1940) published by Schott only belatedly, in 1952.[19] Whereas the master Schoenberg did not even bother to attempt a return to Berlin or Vienna, Egon Wellesz, also a noted champion of dodecaphony and now ensconced in Oxford, obliged his bona-fide anti-Nazi colleague Karl Amadeus Hartmann in Munich (who was now campaigning against the conventional, primal music of Carl Orff), by sending him his twelve-tone *In Memoriam* string quartet for performance. Wellesz must have registered with bitter-sweet feeling that the Berlin Philharmonic premiered his First Symphony, a diatonic work, under the politically unobjectionable Romanian Sergiu Celibidache in March 1948, but it was not exactly a homecoming.[20]

THE DEMISE OF CULTURE

All of Wellesz's string quartets could have been considered part of the canon of German modern music until 1945, had the composer been allowed to remain in the country. Obviously Hartmann thought so, or he would not have wanted them to replace Orff's music, of which only *Carmina Burana* would later be regarded as an outstanding work produced in the Third Reich, in fact as the only outstanding work of music, even surpassing Strauss's – and as such it was a composition that for discerning critics reflected fascism per se. Joachim Kaiser's sarcastic verdict of 2008 that Furtwängler conducted music better than ever from 1941 to 1945 because musicians played and people listened as if there was no tomorrow, if vaguely credible, would serve as a shameful measure of human motivation.[21] After the German capitulation in May 1945, the pickings in other areas of creativity were correspondingly slim.

None of the films made between 1933 and 1945, even the overtly non-political ones, could today be considered classics, except for one or two by Leni Riefenstahl, which are immediately recognizable as ideologically compromised. The same is true for theater productions, even if a very few stage directors, Heinz Hilpert and Jürgen Fehling and also Gründgens, occasionally produced near-masterpieces. In the visual arts, Modernism was to all intents and purposes stifled in this period, and even politically neutral paintings, from an aesthetic vantage point, only reflected mediocrity. In literature, some books such as Werner Bergengruen's *Der Grosstyrann und das Gericht* (*The Great Tyrant and the Court of Law*, 1935), made for stimulating reading, but it had a political subtext potentially friendly to fascism; after 1933, there were no equivalents of Ernest Hemingway, James Joyce, or Selma Lagerlöf in Germany. In architecture, the really great innovations had occurred in Germany before 1933, through the Bauhaus and from other architects, while the monumental style identified with the Third Reich, inasfar as it could be realized before the outbreak of war, constituted infantilist regression. Radio made some headway technically because of the introduction of tape-recording devices (and even television, invented in this period), but as far as content was concerned, it deteriorated especially after 1939, as increasingly ineffectual propaganda and outright lies overshadowed all other broadcasts. The same can be said about the press, whose journalists, even the formerly bourgeois ones, wrote in order to please Goebbels and avoid being sent to concentration camps. Those claiming after 1945 to have written for readers hostile to the Nazi regime, who knew how to read criticism "between the lines," thereby concocted one of the more bizarre figments of fantasy by capitulating fence-sitters after the national catastrophe. Articles in *Das Reich* or any other Nazi newspaper, or, for that matter, Bergengruen's *Grosstyrann*, fail to reveal "between-the-lines" content pointing to the inalienable rights of humankind or the need for anything remotely democratic. If there had been any such suggestions in the press before May 1945, the former journalist Goebbels, not stupid, would have uncovered them and arrested those responsible.[22] Few journalists in fact suffered significantly at his hands for providing copy that fell short of Nazi standards, or crossed the line. In the few cases where they incensed the regime, they were demoted or transferred to another journalistic post.[23] Any journalist who had to endure a long jail term, or worse, would have had to be regarded as a true resister, not someone who was attempting alleged opposition from within. Few journalist resisters are known.

Cultural matters in Nazi Germany worked first in helping to prop up the popularity of the regime during its early victories in the war, but then failed to support the war effort with the ultimate aim of making victors out of soldiers. They also failed to support German occupation structures in conquered territories, whether under Himmler, Rosenberg, or the military governments; the anticipated European "New Order" never came into being.[24] At the height of the war poor quality in all areas of culture in Germany was discernible to the extent that sophisticated outsiders, like the Italian Fascist philosopher Ernesto Grassi, exclaimed that the Nazis' ideal of "a Nordic culture" did not exist.[25]

To a large extent this decrease in quality, of course, was the result of missing talent as a consequence of having driven out the old masters and having failed to put new and younger ones in their place – because none could be raised. But beyond forced emigration, through which such great artists as Thomas Mann and his family were lost, the demise of culture in the Third Reich was also caused by an absence of leadership in all artistic endeavors, a condition observed by a Berlin scriptwriter as early as October 1933 – and ironic for a country that prided itself on being a "Führerstaat."[26] For the Reich as a whole, unified, central leadership was absent from an administrative foundation that was prone to fissures from the beginning and only fractured further as the regime developed, revealing ever more crippling operational deficiencies under Gestapo terror and a war that went off the rails. Historians of institutions during the Third Reich have noted the divisions and subdivisions that characterized the governance of many affairs of politics and society from 1933 to 1945, including culture, whose fragmenting pattern was, in one sense, a reflection of overall conditions. Apart from Goebbels's well-documented quarrels with Rosenberg over competency in cultural matters beginning in 1933, the Propaganda Minister's rivalry with Göring regarding their respective Berlin stages, and Robert Ley's encroachments on popular culture through the DAF programs, were other examples of structural tension. Additionally, because Bernhard Rust's ministerial portfolio included not only formal education, which Goebbels had little interest in, but museums and public libraries, which he was keen on, there was friction between the two men in those areas. Furthermore, Max Amann, as head of the Party-owned Eher-Verlag, nominally controlled nearly 80 percent of the German press, and Otto Dietrich, though a titular section head in the Promi, was press chief of the NSDAP and therefore craved institutional independence. And as soon as Martin Bormann was appointed head of the Führer chancellery after Rudolf Hess's flight to Britain in spring 1941, he began to meddle in cultural affairs. This list of individuals who wielded power in cultural affairs does not even include squabbles over the direction of artistic matters by agencies beyond Goebbels's purview, such as Himmler's fight with Rosenberg over prehistorical artifacts (they also disagreed over the mythic Atlantis as a source of Germandom), or the stand taken by Poland's Governor General Hans Frank against the SS in cultural matters, especially music performance (he was a connoisseur of the classics).[27] But even within individual cultural disciplines, there was no organizational uniformity. To take music as an example, apart from Rust, who was in charge of the conservatories, and Hitler's idiosyncratic interest in Bayreuth, Himmler's SS research center "Ahnenerbe" had a music department as did Rosenberg, who (like Ley) also sponsored performances; while Goebbels oversaw two offices often in rivalry with one another, the Reich Music Chamber in the RKK and

Heinz Drewes's censorial apparatus planted directly in the Promi. Meanwhile, Goebbels (along with Rust) envied the Hitler Youth its autonomy in music education and vied with its leaders for control over public concerts.[28] All these ministers and Gauleiter, even if they thought they were "working towards the Führer," were contributing to chaos at the end.

To the extent that Goebbels had made propaganda qua culture responsible for the flourishing of the Third Reich both before and during the war, culture's failure could be said to have been not just a reflection of the regime's disintegration, but an essential cause as well. Within this context, after identifying a clique of accountable politicians such as Goebbels and Göring, the question of Hitler's own agency once again arises. Given his already moderate role in cultural decision-making before 1939, which was possible because of so many satraps working (seemingly congenially) towards him, and a less complicated government machinery at that time, he showed even less interest in cultural affairs once the war was under way. Overall, this was wholly in keeping with his incrementally inadequate governance of home affairs. The exceptions were isolated sectors of the visual arts, some architectural daydreaming, and the Bayreuth Festival. "For five years now I have been disconnected from the other world," he crowed in August 1944, "I did not visit a theater, listened to no concert, and did not watch a film. I live for the sole task of waging this war, because I know: If no man with an iron will gets behind it, this struggle cannot be won."[29] Because of the pronounced paucity of Hitler's final judgments in the area of cultural bureaucracy after September 1939, his underlings felt they had an even freer hand and, consequently, through contradictory resolutions, duplications, and negligence, worsened the already heavily corroded infrastructure of culture management.

BEYOND ZERO HOUR

Such culture management, because of the pervasive chaos, ended months before the German capitulation of May 1945. Many Germans attempting a new beginning thereafter assumed a Zero Hour that separated those efforts from the vanquished Reich, with no aspects of which they wished to be associated. They may have been inspired by the doyen of German historians, Friedrich Meinecke, who claimed as early as 1946 that the extinction of Nazi "anus culture" would prepare the path for change.[30] Ignoring such a bad example of culture through political and cultural amnesia was thought helpful to many who wanted to safeguard a better future for themselves. Those included the cultish Gruppe 47 members, whose memory lapses even attached to the 1920s; they could make no mental connections, for example, to Jewish intellectuals of the Weimar era who might have inspired them, because throughout the Nazi regime they had been prevented from knowing any Jews.[31]

Whether on purpose or involuntarily, these Germans wanted to wipe the past "from memory," in Adorno's phrase.[32] They were oblivious to streams of continuity, especially in cultural matters, from the Weimar Republic to the Third Reich, from there to the new democratic West Germany, and from the Weimar Republic, leaping over the Nazi regime, again to post-1945 Germany. That various iterations of pre-existing mainstream culture, in all the arts, had been transferred into Nazi Germany, many of them stifled by the time of World War II, is undeniable. At the extreme Modernist flank of that culture, the Nazis had called a halt with their "Degenerate Art" exhibition of July 1937 – at least in the visual arts. At the extreme reactionary flank, the literature of Freikorps fighters, begun after 1918, established the pace well into the 1940s. Somewhere in between, genuine Nazi arts flourished that had been initiated by German fascists in the 1920s. Beyond that, Nazis after 1933 related to the nineteenth-century Romantics, for instance Schiller and Hölderlin.[33] Other, if not identical, lines of continuity can be detected in music, film, architecture, and theater.

As for a transition from 1932 to the late 1940s, passing over the Third Reich, at least in the Western zones of the occupying powers there was no Zero Hour. In architecture, for instance, the homey, comfy villa style of Paul Schultze-Naumburg, which had been established in pre-republican times and flourished in the 1920s, was transposed unadulterated after the war and became very popular, as new houses were rebuilt on the ruins.[34] In music, a development similar to that in the Weimar Republic was observable. Diatonic compositions were resumed (they had continued under the Nazis), as were experiments in dodecaphony (which had largely been discontinued), but those experimenters were few and only reluctantly allowed into the mainstream.[35] It is ironic that Hans Werner Henze, that giant of modern music, was a student of the erstwhile Nazi Wolfgang Fortner, who experimented with Schoenbergian twelve-tone composition even before 1945, but made his Third Reich mark as a Church and Hitler Youth musician.[36] In the visual arts, the Modernism of the 1920s inspired Modernism in the early Federal Republic, with abstraction becoming a hallmark of new paintings.[37] Many new films of the incipient democracy, long after licenses had been granted by the occupying powers, quoted not masterpieces of Expressionism such as *The Cabinet of Dr. Caligari*, but classics of the, later, Ufa-Film era. Actors such as the celebrated Hans Albers, whose attempt to avoid kowtowing to the Nazis was much less successful than he later liked to insist, even though the regime had separated him from his Jewish girlfriend, claimed that in terms of style and spirit, he was continuing after the war from where he had left off in 1932. (Even the girlfriend, Hansi Burg, returned to him from London in a British uniform after the war, to chase Albers's current inamorata from his table and his bed.)[38]

Of great significance would have been a transfer of Nazi culture, or artists working under Hitler, into post-war Germany, certainly the western part. This transfer actually did occur, in two ways. First, ideologically Nazi artists and their art segued into post-war society under cover and continued championing fascism, with a view to undermining the new democracy; their numbers were relatively few, however. Second, and in greater numbers, some artists who had been Nazi sympathizers adapted to the new political regime and made a point of changing their ideology, whether this was genuine or faked.

With respect to the first transfer: Much has been written about the political success of West Germany's democracy after 1960, which grew in tandem with an enlightened politics and culture critical of the Nazis; in particular an outspoken form of literature evolved, in which members of Gruppe 47 like Heinrich Böll participated and which championed individual human rights and freedoms. But concentrating on that angle of history alone can make one forget that the path leading towards 1960, almost a return to the parliamentary democracy of the best years of the Weimar Republic, was less than smooth. One difficulty true democrats have had to overcome was the fact that certain facets of culture under the Nazis persisted, sometimes in conjunction with a reactionary politics that attempted to exploit gaps in the constitutional and social fabric, as it was overseen by the first post-war chancellor, Konrad Adenauer.[39]

Adenauer, having suffered in the Third Reich as a retired mayor of Cologne, was known to give quarter to former Nazis in government and appeared to tolerate them at other levels of society, as long as he was in need of expertise in the rebuilding of the country. Full-time Nazi functionaries such as Hans Globke and Theodor Oberländer were in his party, the Christian Democratic Union (CDU), as well as his cabinets. Globke had helped author official Nazi documents to cement the race legislation of 1935, while Oberländer had advocated the cleansing of the European East of Poles and Jews.[40] Moreover, the Free Democratic Party (FDP), alongside outright Nazi holdovers such as the Socialist Reich Party (SRP), became a place of refuge for former National Socialists.[41] Erich Mende, one of the FDP leaders who had served as an officer in World War II, in 1951 called for the end of a preoccupation in the public mind with the bogeymen of an allegedly evil Nazi past.[42] This at a time when a serious examination of the past was more than a decade away.

In 1946, 40 percent of Germans said that Nazism had been a good idea, just not well executed, and in 1952 one-third of West Germany's citizens still acknowledged some admiration for the Führer.[43] In such an atmosphere, National Socialism for many was not yet a phantom of the past but a recent, albeit dormant, reality that had to be re-animated, and the "Hitler Myth" still had currency. A structured, critical, retrospective of Jews as victims of genocide was far off.[44] Especially former Nazi literati who now were free-lancing exploited this atmosphere, as they had recourse to neo-Nazi publishers and once more found an audience among right-wing Germans. Often they themselves were the publishers, as was Herbert Böhme, a former highly placed SA leader and poet who now co-founded a new journal, *Nation Europa*, and started the radical-rightist publishing firm Der Türmer.[45] His published books, often reprints of older tomes, were authored by the likes of Hans Grimm, Friedrich Griese, Edwin Erich Dwinger, and Hans Friedrich Blunck. As not all copyrights had been dissolved by the occupying Western powers, publishers formerly beholden to the Nazis such as the Deutsche Verlags-Anstalt in Stuttgart, Piper in Munich, and Bertelsmann in Gütersloh continued operating, often steered by their old authors. Grimm himself, a convener for the SRP, organized a congress of former Nazi writers, the "Lippoldsberger Dichtertage," on the Weser river, in 1949. There he towered over them as an intellectual *éminence grise*; his most prominent guest arguably was Erwin Guido Kolbenheyer, who had won twelve Nazi literary prizes, more than any other writer. Yet another Nazi poet, Gerhard

Schumann, proprietor of the neo-Nazi Hohenstaufen Verlag, founded an Europäischer Buchklub that managed to attract 200,000 subscribers. These writers were implicitly supported by old Nazi literary scholars such as Hermann Pongs, Benno von Wiese, Paul Fechter, and Heinz Kindermann, who also guided much of the course of literary studies at the universities, until a fundamental discussion led by younger scholars, foremost among them Karl Otto Conrady, began reforming the field at the Germanists' annual convention in Munich, as late as 1966.[46]

There were Nazis in other fields who resorted to the mentality of trench warfare. In the visual arts, for example, the scabrous cartoonist and poster designer Hans Schweitzer, under the Nordic, freaky, name "Mjölnir" had worked for *Der Angriff* and the *Völkischer Beobachter*, creating "the hard-faced, heroic storm trooper, known as the 'Mjölnir type,' whose opposite image, the bloated, leering Jew, he adapted from nineteenth-century models and invested with a new viciousness." During his denazification tribunal Schweitzer praised the Nazi regime for having opposed modern art that had departed "from nature," defended the reduction of "excessive Jewish influence" in German art and society, and praised concentration camps as "necessary emergency measures against spies and other internal enemies."[47] Once appointed a professor by Hitler, he now served as an illustrator for extreme right-wing newspapers in West Germany, while insinuating himself into the federal press bureau in Bonn as a poster draftsman.[48] And the former SS officer Count Klaus Baudissin, who had been the nemesis of the artist Oskar Schlemmer and other Modernists, lived as a retired municipal government worker on a pension in northern Germany – a pension he had finagled for himself after suing the city of Essen in a year-long trial.[49]

Shapers of culture who had served the Nazis and now wanted to quietly integrate into West German society found various ways to do so, depending on their expertise, whom they knew and, ultimately, their chosen path toward earning a living. No one had stood as high under Hitler as Albert Speer, and, ironically, no one succeeded more spectacularly in attaining fame and fortune even after twenty years in prison. Speer did not re-enter the civilian world as the architect he had once been, but as an author of titillating memoirs and a media star who lied about important functions of the Nazi regime. The most grievous falsehoods were that he had not known about Auschwitz and, similarly, that he had not been present at Himmler's infamous speech of October 1943 to the Gauleiter at Posen, during which the annihilation of the Jews was made crystal-clear.[50]

Another impressive ascent was managed by Elisabeth Noelle, who, intimate with Adenauer's CDU and a sycophant of Ernst Jünger, attained a chair in political science at the new university of Mainz, a French creation of 1946, along with the founding directorship the following year of the, eventually famous, Allensbacher Institut für Demoskopie on Lake Constance. That she also worked as a visiting professor at the University of Chicago between 1978 and 1991 is not without irony. Born in 1916, Noelle had attended the University of Missouri on a Promi scholarship in 1937–8, where she had studied journalism and the emerging American techniques for monitoring and shaping public opinion. While there, she wrote for a local student newspaper that "National Socialism is opposed to the mixing of races because it sees herein a danger to the maintenance of national character."[51] From 1940 to 1941 she was a staff writer for *Das Reich* and, among others, wrote an article about American society. Here she engaged in exile-baiting and railed against Eleanor Roosevelt, who allegedly was forcing the American public to adopt a "Jewish standpoint." About the prominent columnist Walter Lippmann she remarked that as "a Jew of German origin" he was "most clever in factual deception," and she accused the broadcaster Dorothy Thompson of "fake logic" and "furious rhetoric." Hewing to a popular National Socialist cliché that was also adopted by her colleague Margret Boveri two years later, she described Jews as being behind the American press, such as the *Chicago Daily News*, as well as controlling the film industry, radio, and all the theaters. How exactly she was able to found her institute in 1947 and gain access to the faculty in Mainz awaits discovery, but what is already certain is that she was always heavily supported by the CDU, with Adenauer's government and subsequent cabinets routinely contracting her for her demoscopic research (which, some scholars have contended, resembled Himmler's SD reports on the public mood in Nazi Germany, suggesting a direct influence).[52]

In West Germany, journalists like Noelle found it relatively easy to slip into positions with a newspaper newly licensed by the occupation authorities, because they were all looking for staff with writing experience. With her past plausible closeness to the SD, Noelle was not far removed from Giselher Wirsing, the SS officer who had worked for the *Münchner Neueste Nachrichten* and was especially mandated by Himmler to analyze the situation of Jews and Palestine for the SD.[53] In 1938 he had followed in the footsteps of Adolf Eichmann's exploratory visit of 1937 to Palestine. But come 1945, Wirsing had effectively changed his spots, becoming chief editor for the conservative Lutheran weekly *Christ und Welt*. Still, his past would overtake him. In 1959 his continuing connections to SS veterans led him to one Dr. Horst Schumann, who was practicing medicine in Ghana, "the loneliest person I have ever met." In April that year Wirsing published an article about Schumann, extolling the selfless acts of this Samaritan and calling him "a second Dr. Schweitzer." But instead of having done Schumann a favor, he had involuntarily exposed him as SS-Sturmbannführer Schumann, the notorious Auschwitz physician who had forced "euthanasia" procedures and sterilization on male inmates. It took the Federal Republic until 1966 to have Schumann extradited to Germany, where he was put on trial in 1970. Wirsing stood by dumbfounded; he died in 1975.[54] For his part, Schumann was released from prison in 1972 due to his deteriorating health and died in 1983.

Many Nazis from areas of cultural endeavor managed to secure for themselves a safe spot for a fresh beginning. Alfred Baum, for instance, who had been a deputy director during the filming of *Jud Süss*, advanced to become chief of the new democratic radio station Sender Freies Berlin, while music critic Walter Abendroth, a dyed-in-the-wool anti-Semite who, among other feats, had hailed the 1938 Düsseldorf Reich Music Festival with tributes to Goebbels and Hitler, in 1948 took over the features section of the newly founded weekly *Die Zeit*.[55] Hans Egon Holthusen, an SS and Party member and aspiring writer, succeeded in an even more illustrious career when in 1961 he became director of the New York Goethe House, which was sponsored by the German government, and, later still, a professor of German at Northwestern University in Illinois.[56] Holthusen had prepared for such steps in 1949 by castigating, in a book about Thomas Mann, the "stupid devilries" of National Socialism.[57] Mere opportunistic word play! For as a soldier in the Wehrmacht, while vanquishing Poland, Holthusen had written: "Gradually the conquered country was revealing its nature. The further we moved from the German border, the deeper sank the population into a kind of pre-civilized condition."[58] This had been his personal justification for the Nazis' push into Eastern Europe.

Moving into a university seems to have been a comparatively easy strategy for a number of cultured Nazis. Some of them actually originated from there, such as the journalism teacher Emil Dovifat, who had hailed the limitations on freedom of the press introduced by Goebbels starting in the fall of 1933.[59] After 1945, the professor helped Adenauer found the CDU in Berlin and took over a chair in journalism at the Free University, which he had also helped to found (along with Meinecke). In order to avoid embarrassing questions, Dovifat had redacted his own textbooks, written during the Nazi period, eliding anything that could compromise him.[60] The music writer Joseph Müller-Blattau, however, who had collaborated heavily with the SS "Ahnenerbe" and had held a chair in the core Nazi university of Strassburg, resorted to a different tactic, as he had lines and passages blacked out in his *History of German Music*, now freshly used in the seminars, as he changed to a professorship in Saarbrücken in 1952. As a leading German musicologist has noted, that *History* was remarkable not so much for the text that had been rendered illegible as for the passages still left intact.[61]

In music itself, as is widely known, all the great composers, conductors, singers, and instrumental musicians with the conspicuous exception of Elly Ney overcame their problematic Nazi ties, to be allowed to perform in public again without major interruptions: Furtwängler, Strauss, von Karajan, Knappertsbusch, Gieseking, and Schwarzkopf. In the opinion of denazifying bureaucrats working in the summer of 1945 for the Americans, it was "silly to dismiss a flutist of the Philharmonic orchestra only because he nominally belonged to the Nazi Party, one important reason being the scarcity of musicians overall."[62] What held true in this case for Berlin was a credo all over Germany's occupied zones: the traditional belief that music as such was more or less apoliticial meshed with the sentiment that this art was paramount in calming and re-educating a misled populace. This fitted well with Meinecke's 1946 dictum that *German* music was, after all, a most superior art and ought to be nurtured, rather than penalized. Yes, "great German music" was able to help denazify, claimed Meinecke, not realizing the hubris inherent in that statement.[63] Hence even musicians who had deliberately worked for the regime, such as the Hitler Youth composer and prize-winner Bruno Stürmer, soon were in employment again, ironically at the Darmstadt modern-music festival, having most likely lied, as the need arose, to the authorities about prior political affiliations.[64]

In film, too, as with the press, radio, the universities, and the music scene, the new authorities needed the old experts. After 1945 German film was not seriously invested with a propaganda mandate as it had been under Goebbels, but apart from its time-honored duty to entertain, as in the Third Reich, it was needed for education. This explains why many formerly dedicated Nazi actors, after a relatively brief hiatus dictated by the victors (least urgently in the Soviet zone), were able to resume their career. Even though the *Jud Süss* film director Veit Harlan, as the most exposed Nazi in the movie industry, had to undergo two trials because of Nazi collaboration, he was ultimately acquitted in both and resumed making pictures. The acquittal proceedings in his case remained the most controversial ones for entertainers caught up in the justice system, and were deemed by critics as nothing less than scandalous.[65] Leni Riefenstahl was ruled as merely a Nazi sympathizer after four denazification procedures. In 2002 she was tried in, but then released from, a civil suit because of the Auschwitz fate of Roma Gypsies she had employed in the Nazi portion of her extended feature *Tiefland*, released only in 1954 and to moderate acclaim.[66]

As the occupation authorities attempted to size up the National Socialist proclivities of actors and directors, as well as the Nazi qualities of the films themselves, they made many omissions and errors of judgment, because of their inability to read the subtle propaganda subtexts Goebbels and his film advisors had embedded in seemingly innocuous narratives. Formerly Nazi-committed actors and directors intentionally encouraged overall obfuscation or engaged in self-invention: the actress Lil Dagover grandly declared she had never voted for Hitler; Wolfgang Liebeneiner quickly offered to direct the filming of the vacuous Trapp family saga that included their escape from the Nazis; Heinz Rühmann and Gustav Fröhlich had divorced their Jewish wives for their own advancement and their current opportunist drive toward a stage comeback was abetted shortly after the war by new film directors.[67] Hence, although several films were banned, such as *Der Herrscher*, *Die grosse Liebe*, and of course Party movies like *SA-Mann Brand*, those starring Rühmann were still shown, including *Die Feuerzangenbowle* (*The Punch Bowl*), a 1944 masterpiece of the escapism-to-steel-yourself genre in the manner of *Baron Münchhausen*. Like *Münchhausen*, the film was widely shown again starting in the late 1940s.[68] Whereas this was suitable light entertainment, the promised educational value was wanting.

Many early decisions to spurn or not to spurn film actors, actresses, and other personnel after the war were also based on happenstance or lack of judgment, and those decisions often favored the guilty at the expense of the less politically committed. Jenny Jugo, for instance, formerly a close friend of Hitler and Goebbels, was thought too popular by the American authorities to be removed from the silver screen, whereas the relatively innocent Ilse Werner, who had starred in the, now banned, *Wunschkonzert* movie, was immediately ostracized by the film industry.[69] Later, when her ban was lifted, her attractiveness as a young actress had been superseded by the public's fascination with newer faces – Sonja Ziemann, Hildegard Knef (teenage mistress of the last Nazi film-imperium director and SS officer Ewald von Demandowsky), or Swiss actress Liselotte Pulver with her tomboy innocence.[70] Somehow Margot Hielscher pulled through, but right after her Zero Hour she had cleverly allied herself with Gene Hammer, a big-band leader from Texas who played for the American troops; she became his girl-friend and lead singer. Part of a larger re-education effort through culture, Hammer and Hielscher were helping OMGUS to re-animate American jazz in Germany by performing in concerts and nightclub acts, to which young Germans were invited.[71] Other known Nazis, such as the enigmatic Sybille Schmitz, first were banned and then had trouble being offered roles; in her case, in 1955 an alcohol problem and dependence on heavy drugs led to Schmitz's suicide, at the age of forty-five.[72]

Seldom, therefore, were members of the film industry prosecuted for Nazi transgressions and punished accordingly. One was Marianne Simson, the Moon Woman in the *Münchhausen* film, a ranking Hitler Youth leader and reputedly one of Goebbels's favorite concubines. In 1944 she had tried to seduce a Wehrmacht officer who had confided to her his closeness to the circle of Count von Stauffenberg, Hitler's would-be assassin. Upon being rejected, she denounced him to the Gestapo, and he almost paid with his life. In 1945, aged twenty-four, she was arrested by the Soviet authorities and imprisoned. After her release in 1952, Simson was offered smaller roles in theaters in the southwest of Germany, keeping a low profile until she died, unremembered, in 1992.[73]

CONJURED VICTIMHOOD

During his trials and in his autobiography, Veit Harlan insisted that Goebbels had forced him to make the *Jud Süss* film and that he had finally consented under pressure, in order to forestall the worst that might happen. In fact, he claimed to have changed many of the film's scenes from being highly injurious to Jews to less offensive footage. This, Harlan implied, had ultimately made him into a sort of resister from within, certainly someone who had wrought more good than had he succeeded in avoiding Goebbels's mandate (in other words, had the film been made by a less sympathetic director). The opposite was true: Harlan was lying on all counts, twisting the facts, for rather than mitigating them, he had wilfully accentuated the anti-Jewish themes.[74]

To have remained in the system in order to prevent the worst was the first line of defense for many former Nazis, also in the cultural arena. To have stayed on as an inwardly detached person, as an "inner emigrant" awaiting calmer times, was the second best excuse, but still a favorite tool of self-exculpation. As already mentioned, both arguments were used against Thomas Mann and many of his lesser refugee peers, by German cultural players who, while not murderers in the SS mold, after 1945 had a lot of explaining to do. An extreme variant of the hold-out position would have been to style oneself as a *victim* of the Nazi regime, when in fact indifference, complicity, or co-conspiracy had been in play.

Let us consider that particular argument in some detail: The victim defense reflected an attitude held by Germans who felt they were wronged during Nazi rule, particularly the war period when, so they said, they had suffered primarily at the hands of Allied bombing raids. Indeed, "terror fliers" during the last months of the war, meaning those Allied pilots who had escaped from their stricken bombers by parachuting onto German soil, had been at the mercy of Volksgenossen ready to lynch them instantly on the ground. As Theodor Adorno remarked early on, the bombardment of Dresden or Hamburg was a useful alibi for German apologists to discount the crimes of Auschwitz in an overall reckoning.[75] Next as culprits came the Red Army, whose members had driven Germans from the eastern parts of the Reich, raped up to two million women and girls, and killed thousands of civilians. Third only came the Nazis themselves, whose propaganda had not succeeded in calming the population, which had suffered from the loss of relatives, shortages of consumer goods, cramped quarters, and an overall disturbance of peace and quiet. After 1945 Germans not only found themselves bombed out, but facing the shame of unconditional surrender, dissolution of their armed forces, and embarrassing "denazification."[76] Those who suffered allegedly also included Germans who had come to realize the evil nature of the regime and now blamed its leaders as the true culprits and saw themselves as victims of a grand betrayal.[77] This was the tenor of the treatise by Meinecke (an anti-Semite early in his career), as he set a strong Zero Hour and viewed "the German catastrophe" as the deplorable result of a perverted governance that was an accident, having had nothing to do with the continuity of, otherwise wholesome, German history.[78] With his apologist's stance, in substance much like Thomas Mann's beliefs before 1943, Meinecke signaled a demonizing approach to the most recent past, defining the present as morally unsullied, if forcibly skewed and subdued. This attitude was to merge later with a larger German self-consciousness as a people who had extinguished their collective memory of what really happened, which resulted in an eventual "inability to mourn," mourn their participation in recent history that is, as Alexander and Margarete Mitscherlich described it in some detail in 1967.[79]

Not least because of such intellectual backing as Meinecke's, a new martyrological subculture had developed already in the late 1940s, pervading society well into the 1960s, with the writing of books and newspaper articles and the making of films, some of the visual arts and certain contributions to broadcasting, for example in radio plays. Film was an early medium to succumb to this wave. The new genre of "rubble film" strove to show Germans in their involvement with – or, more often, detachment from – the Nazi phenomenon as seen from a contemporaneous perspective, one in which the geographic depictions were fields and streets buried under ruins, amid which surviving Germans attempted new beginnings. Those images were accompanied by self-pitying reflections on the recent past – who had done what, and perhaps why. But if someone responsible was found it was either a dead Nazi like Hitler or a person outside one's private circle who had yet to be called to account. Moreover, in a phase when Nazi leaders were being put on trial in Nuremberg and one could point to them as guilty, such films did not identify their creators as those responsible, nor the Germans as a whole as viewers; rather, these films exculpated them. This, for instance, was the tone of the first movie of this kind (and the first German movie after capitulation in May 1945), written and directed by Wolfgang Staudte, *Die Mörder sind unter uns* (*The Murderers are Among Us*). Staudte, born in 1906, had participated in the making of *Jud Süss*, *Pour le Mérite*, and the Hitler

Youth film *Jungens*, and obviously used this new approach self-servingly, to legitimize himself in the eyes of the Allied victors.[80] His film was made during 1946 in Babelsberg by the newly Soviet-licensed DEFA company, in which a Wehrmacht returnee (Ernst Wilhelm Borchert, born 1907, and a former SA trooper) observes his one-time commanding officer, whom he had witnessed ordering civilians to be shot, from his own moral high ground. In rare scenes reminiscent of the Expressionism in *The Cabinet of Dr. Caligari* this former surgeon restarts life in the ruins with a returned concentration-camp inmate (an unbelievably well-preserved twenty-one-year-old Hildegard Knef as obviously not a *political* ex-prisoner, judging by her utterings). He is trying to come to grips with his former life and the putative guilt of his superior, who is made to look exactly like Himmler, now a struggling small businessman converting old steel helmets into cooking pots. The doctor accuses this man of war crimes he had obviously committed but neglects to search for fault in himself as a compliant member of the very Wehrmacht execution squad in question, nor does he scrutinize Nazi society or politics in general. The ending projects private bliss for the new-found lovers as the businessman keeps screaming "I am innocent!"[81] Subsequent rubble films, in which the inhabitants especially of the three Western occupation zones recognized themselves as victims, helped reinforce Meinecke's interpretation of the Third Reich as a diabolic concert of criminals one could easily distance oneself from, in order to continue with an agenda of healthy harmony. In time, however, viewing people who persevered among the rubble against all odds constituted so dire a scenario that the German public, aspiring pioneers of an economic miracle, tired of these films around 1950. Thereafter they favored, instead, along with a rerun of Ufa period movies such as *Der Kongress tanzt* (*The Congress Dances*, 1931), another novel genre, the "Heimat" (homeland) films. Those concentrated on harmony and bliss: the German heath, forests, and mountain pastures, savvy fox hunters or veterinarians in lederhosen, Tyrolean jackets, and fedoras, who sing Volkslieder accompanied by accordions, with innocently pretty girls in braids and dirndls deserving to be chastely wooed and married. Both genres represented escapism of the highest order tailored for their times. The "Heimat" films were thematically related to the Nazi "Blut und Boden" rural-happiness movies of a mere decade earlier; they were even further removed from a genuine moral stock-taking than the rubble films had been, but they guaranteed meat-and-potatoes comfort and a quiet conscience in which to enjoy Hitler's Volkswagens, which were finally for sale.[82]

A collective sense of responsibility, let alone guilt, about what had been conjured by Germans between 1933 and 1945 was missing in other sectors of the arts as well. Starting with the preservation of cultural artifacts in the universities, many art and music professors complained after the end of the war: the prehistorian Herbert Jankuhn, already in a new professorship at Göttingen University as of 1956, styled himself as a sacrificial servant of Himmler's pro-Germanic science and complained about the Americans, who had beaten him close to deafness in the Langwasser internment camp.[83] Mistreatment in Allied internment camps was also a grievance of the former Thingspiel author Richard Euringer, who had to endure a writing ban until 1946 but then dedicated himself to the reworking of his older prose.[84] The sculptor Arno Breker, who continued to earn big money after 1945, claimed that he had lived in a ghetto during the Nazi period and that he had helped the persecuted, but he also thought he was wrongly ostracized from West German society because of his active engagement with the new radical right.[85]

In painting, an exorbitant scam was perpetrated around Emil Nolde. Because of the supervision he had had to endure during the last years of Nazi rule, he was able, with the help of several prominent assistants, to reinvent himself as the Nazi victim extraordinaire. He was allowed dedicated exhibitions that emphasized his role as a victim, one in 1950 having been urged by Theodor Heuss of the FDP, the former contributor to *Das Reich*, who as a member of the Deutsche Staatspartei had voted for Hitler's Enabling Law in the March 23, 1933, Reichstag, and now was the President of the Federal Republic. It was Heuss, too, who upon reintroducing the Pour le Mérite as the new republic's highest honor, made sure that Nolde was among its first recipients. Before his death in 1956 the painter re-edited his 1934 memoirs, cleansing them of all xenophobic, in particular anti-Semitic, content.[86] Publications by sympathizers featured Nolde's, admittedly striking, paintings (including some he had done in his hermit phase); they were meant to document his fundamentally anti-fascist character. That he had been too close to the National Socialists was explained in one book as the "political misunderstanding" of a "totally inexperienced and wholly naïve person," while his anti-French sentiments were denied and charges of anti-Semitism repudiated. In 1968, Siegfried Lenz's spurious portrait of Nolde, exonerating him completely, was published and turned into a two-part costume drama by ARD television channel 1 in 1971. On the occasion of the book launch Lenz's friend, the (quarter-Jewish) SPD leader Helmut Schmidt, sent a letter, congratulating him and stating that Nolde's inclusion in the "Degenerate Art" exhibition in July 1937 had caused his own break with National Socialism at the age of seventeen.[87] As late as February 1982, Schmidt's chancellery office in Bonn organized a Nolde exhibition, at whose opening he cemented the legend of the painter as persecuted by the Nazis.[88] Even posthumously, Nolde's stature as a martyr was complete.

THE "INNER EMIGRANTS"

As for the "inner emigrants" who waited out the regime while being critical of it, not proving opportunistic and later possessing the modesty to claim no spoils for victim status – among artists they were rare indeed. Scholars have counted among them Ricarda Huch, who lived mostly in Jena with her husband after her resignation from the Prussian Academy of Arts in early 1933. She continued to publish on historical subjects, making a point of mentioning the persecution of Jews in the Middle Ages, which incurred the wrath of the irascible but power-starved Rosenberg, so nothing happened to her.[89] The quarter-Jewish theater director Jürgen Fehling, working under Gustaf Gründgens in Berlin, was possibly another "inner emigrant"; signs of non-compliance with the Nazis were there on the one hand, yet also thematic concessions, on the other. He was immediately allowed to direct Goethe's *Urfaust* in a small theater in Berlin, in October 1945.[90] One poet who kept himself out of sight in the Third Reich was Rudolf Alexander Schröder, potentially a real enemy of the homophobic Nazis because he was homosexual. The composer Karl Amadeus Hartmann did not perform his works in public; he lived secluded with his small family in Munich and Kempfenhausen on Lake Starnberg, supported by wealthy parents-in-law.[91]

Those artists who claimed "inner emigration" status insisted on never having been associated with National Socialism. "No one had ever been a Nazi," observed Peter Viertel, Salka's son, caustically, while monitoring public opinion in the American zone of occupation for the Office of Strategic Services (OSS) in 1945.[92] This group would include the East

Prussian poet Agnes Miegel, who said she had been "apolitical," after having joined the Party in 1940 and having published poetry ardently in favor of the Führer.[93] It also included Sepp Hilz, that most beloved of Hitler's painters who had created *Weather Witch* and *Peasant Venus*, had enchanted the highest Party cadres with his work and became very rich doing it. Hilz passed the denazification process easily after having declared he never made "political paintings" (which was, technically, correct) and having stressed his work for the Catholic Church, which he did, unbeknownst to anyone, down south in rural Bavaria.[94]

Today Gerhart Hauptmann may be said to have been the prototype of the "unpolitical" German claiming to have endured dictatorship in spiritual isolation, and trying to profit from it. Hauptmann had come to fame as one of the pioneers of Naturalism who late in the Wilhelmine Empire spoke up for the dispossessed, especially with his play *Die Weber* (1892).[95] Having received the Nobel Prize for literature in 1912, Hauptmann fitted well into the democracy of the Weimar Republic. Come 1933, however, he fully supported the new regime, most certainly driven by fear, like Thomas Mann, of losing his immense income from books sold in Germany. Declaring himself for Hitler early on, Hauptmann hailed the Reich's exit from the League of Nations in October. Days later he participated in the opening ceremonies of Goebbels's Reich Culture Chamber along with Furtwängler and other artists, and he publicly backed the Anschluss in 1938. Hitler's victory over France in 1940 found him ecstatic. When Hitler invaded the Soviet Union a year later, Hauptmann sent a "Greeting to the Front," broadcast by Radio Breslau. Officially the playwright, who, like Strauss, had a Jewish daughter-in-law, was silent on the persecution of the Jews, but in private he ranted against them, especially his one-time friend, the critic Alfred Kerr (who had fled to London). Once confronted with the German Jews' suffering, Hauptmann was contemptuous of "a few Eastern Jews," labeling them "not so important," and he denounced Jewish emigrants to the United States who would pretend to represent German culture.[96]

The Nazis themselves were divided over Hauptmann's significance for the New Order. Not surprisingly, Rosenberg hated this former pacifist and champion of the Naturalist school, a forerunner of Modernism in Germany, as alien to what was to become a new culture and discouraged the staging of his plays. But Rosenberg's powers being confined, Hitler had himself encouraged the premiere of a new Hauptmann play, *Die goldene Harfe* (*The Golden Harp*), in Munich, in the fall of 1933.[97] Besides, Intendanten such as Friedrich Bethge in Frankfurt believed that Hauptmann had already changed his style, adapting it to the new requirements of drama.[98] As far as Goebbels was concerned, he agreed with Rosenberg that Hauptmann's official profile would have to remain low, respecting the writer's own reservations. Of course he was conscious of Hauptmann's international market value, just as he was of Strauss's and would have been of Thomas Mann's. Goebbels therefore had made no moves to prevent the performance of some of Hauptmann's dramas particularly after 1939, when it had become obvious that the Nazis' own young dramatists were not delivering. In June 1942, after a private dinner at the minister's home, Goebbels voiced his appreciation of Hauptmann's ongoing enthusiasm over the progress of the war and expressed confidence in his own ability "to win him fully over to the National Socialist regime."[99] Like Strauss and Pfitzner, Hauptmann hobnobbed with Governor General Hans Frank, the slaughterer of Poland, a person "with deep human dispositions," whom he thought to be "an educated man, anxious to improve his extensive knowledge." He also liked Baldur von Schirach, who invited him to Vienna for festivities on the occasion of Hauptmann's eightieth birthday in November 1942, after he had collaborated with Goebbels in putting on more official festivities in Breslau. On that occasion, Hitler had sent a vase, with Hauptmann reciprocating by calling the Führer "the one sent by the stars to realize the destiny of Germany."[100] This was less than three months before the Wehrmacht surrendered at Stalingrad.

After the Soviets had overrun Hauptmann's village of Agnetendorf in Silesia, they embraced the Nobel laureate who had suddenly found his way back to his socialist-liberal roots, sufficiently so for the Communists to claim him as one of their own. Hauptmann emphasized his apolitical and former pacifist nature to the new masters, as he had already done in the presence of the writer Erich Ebermayer in February 1934, when he had said, after being questioned: "I am no politician. Neither am I a political poet," and had continued, "I am a poet. Just a poet. And beyond that I am a German."[101] When, in 1967, East German literary critics found themselves in a bind, trying to explain why their culture maven Johannes R. Becher had wooed Hauptmann right after the war, they echoed the playwright's own refrain of "inner emigration," namely that he had lived "withdrawn during the Nazi era."[102]

MAKE-BELIEVE RESISTERS

Finally, there were those artists who had maintained a comfortable lifestyle within the Third Reich and now, after May 1945, claimed to have resisted it all along. One leading artist was the composer Werner Egk, the functionary from the RMK who now contended that his position had enabled him to protect his (supposedly anti-Nazi) colleagues by preventing adverse legislation and thus doing good instead. During his denazification tribunal in 1946–7 he fabricated a story of having tried to sabotage the Nazis toward the end of the regime. He made much noise about having opposed them as part of a clandestine cell at the Berlin Staatsoper and running courier services to a group in Paris, transmitting details about concentration camps and "crimes against humanity."[103] There was in fact no such cell at the opera nor did that group exist. Nor, as claimed before the tribunal, had there been an attempt by Egk in the spring of 1945 to notify the advancing American troops of local Nazis in the Munich suburb where he was then living.[104] On the contrary, once, at a crucial time, Hartmann had asked Egk to take some mail to his brother in Switzerland, a former card-carrying Communist, but Egk had refused. Egk wanted Hartmann to appear as a material witness at his tribunal, but Hartmann in good conscience could not help him, merely consenting to act as a character witness in writing, but never appearing in court in person.[105]

Although Egk's one-time teacher Carl Orff had no official appointment under the Third Reich, after the war he also alleged his opposition to the Nazi regime by having, along with the Munich psychology professor Kurt Huber, "founded some kind of a youth group." The group Orff was referring to in an interview with the OMGUS interrogation officer Newell Jenkins in early 1946 was the White Rose of 1942–3, an anti-Nazi resistance group that Huber had established together with Hans and Sophie Scholl and other students from Munich University. (Huber and the Scholls, along with their co-conspirators, were murdered by the Nazis.) Orff had told Jenkins that story because he wanted the chance to enter public service in the budding democracy of the American zone; for that to happen he had to be removed from a blacklist. As it turned out, Orff then decided against serving in public office (as Württemberg theater intendant in Stuttgart). Having been cleared politically, his new opera, *Die Bernauerin*, was allowed to be premiered in Stuttgart on June 15, 1947.[106]

Both Egk and Orff integrated themselves well into the West German cultural establishment. Orff enjoyed his customary position as a pre-eminent composer and Egk filled an important professorial post at the Berlin Hochschule für Musik, after the denazification tribunal had accepted his stories of alleged resistance.[107] The unbelievable naïveté of the Americans evident in so many of these rehabilitation cases was matched by British and French ignorance or nonchalance and complemented, in the Soviet sector, by shrewd calculation regarding the immediate value of potential Nazi turn-coats. In the American zone, the victors' attitude, combined with German tolerance, also led to leniency for Hans Knappertsbusch, who overcame the initial charges that he had been a Nazi collaborator. There is evidence that he had had a hand in the dismissal of Jewish conductor Bruno Walter as Munich Generaldirektor in 1922; the fiercely anti-Semitic maverick conductor then occupied that position himself. Throughout the 1920s in Munich his rabid hatred of Jews revealed itself further, as the music director, a brilliant Wagner interpreter, aligned himself more closely with the rising National Socialists, although he never joined the Party. In early 1933 it was Knappertsbusch who was instrumental behind the conspiracy to oust Thomas Mann from the Bavarian capital. Then, to the extent that Hitler came to favor Clemens Krauss as chief conductor of the Munich Opera, Knappertsbusch's position was endangered, and, Hitler never having liked him for musical reasons, had his contract terminated in 1936. But the maestro was allowed to relocate to Vienna and continued to guest-conduct all over the Reich thereafter, including, after the outbreak of World War II, in occupied territories and for Hitler's birthday.[108]

Although there remained doubts around Knappertsbusch, in the summer of 1945 OMGUS appointed him once again to the position of Munich Generaldirektor, in the belief that he was currently the cleanest of all the high-ranking German conductors. Using his 1936 dismissal from Munich and counting on his former vast popularity with the Munich audience, Knappertsbusch had portrayed himself as ideally suitable. But realizing their embarrassing mistakes later in 1945, the Americans dismissed him again. In 1947, Knappertsbusch aired his opinion that he had been unjustly treated, adding "we were, everyone in his own fashion, resistance fighters, who through some miracle never got caught." And so in 1948 a German court reversed the OMGUS ruling and reinstated Knappertsbusch in

Munich. While there, he eventually received the enhanced Order of Merit with a star from the Federal Republic, after having served as the first post-war conductor at the Bayreuth Festival, in 1951.[109]

There are egregious examples of artists, writers, and intellectuals who played a dual role, attempting to navigate the Third Reich in the safest and most comfortable way, all clamoring for resistance status after the war and claiming to have salvaged a part of the common good. In reality, they were cynically trying to ensure the best of two opposing worlds for themselves: one, in which Hitler would be victorious and they could profit from what they would procure for the Nazis; the other, in which the Allies would triumph, where they would have something to show proving they had been opposed to the Nazis.

One of those who burned their candles at both ends was the film script-writer Erich Ebermayer, who found himself threatened at the start of the regime because, like Gründgens whom he knew well, he was homosexual. But from the outset of the new Reich, Ebermayer was aware that he held two trump cards, and the fact that he played them seriously exposed him as a man prone to graft and corruption: both Philipp Bouhler, the Nazi functionary, who organized the "euthanasia" program, and Fritz Todt, the engineer who built the autobahns, were his cousins, the last-mentioned by marriage. Throughout his (allegedly secret) diaries, written between 1933 and the beginning of the war, Ebermayer made no apologies for the way in which he attempted to square the circle by falling in with stalwarts of the Nazi system while honing pre-regime contacts with Jews or democrats, such as Klaus and Thomas Mann, and preserving his homosexual lifestyle.[110] The upshot of this was that he was allowed, increasingly, to enter the lucrative world of film scripting at Berlin-Babelsberg, carefully avoiding the most overtly political assignments. In an extraordinary show of advertising his formula to Thomas Mann, he traveled to Küsnacht in late February 1936 for a meeting with the novelist, over lunch and coffee. Mann judged that his guest was "an insignificant drip, who is just bedazzled over the success of his *Traumulus* film with Goebbels and Hitler."[111] That movie, just released in Germany and creating a major trajectory for Ebermayer's future success, was one of the reasons why the scriptwriter continued in the good offices of the Nazis, because, as he said cynically, if he had not been able to write the script, some Party hack would have done it. To calm his conscience after having been admonished by Mann, Ebermayer chronicled: "The problem of inner emigration!...What would I have subsisted on after having emigrated? Is there not already enough emigrants' misery in the world? But above all, do not Germans like us, whom Thomas Mann recognizes as 'decent,' those of us who have remained, do they not face an important task: to help the true, the real Germany through the filth of these times, into a new future? Is it nothing to stay in Fortress Germany, in order to undermine it from within, to weaken the power of evil wherever we can and throughout this to remain true to ourselves, in spite of daily danger to body and soul?"[112] This was, of course, the classic argument Mann would have to face some ten years later, from writers like Frank Thiess and Walter von Molo, who as opponents of the regime were just as dubious as Ebermayer. Taking this position always allowed them, as it allowed him, to partake of the sweet fruits of accommodation to a fascist Germany, fruits like, as in Ebermayer's case, enjoying the sight of, and intimately befriending, attractive Hitler Youths, and benefiting from Goebbels's 1936 edict prohibiting cultural (film) criticism.[113] Ebermayer, having preserved what was most dear to him, wrote many a film script after 1945. A lawyer by training, he also defended Emmy Göring and Winifred Wagner in denazification tribunals.[114]

This excuse of claiming to do good from within the system was used many times over by artists after 1945 to retroactively justify their immoral existence, whatever the degree. Like Orff, Werner Bergengruen claimed to have assisted the White Rose resistance group in Munich by helping to distribute their illicit flyers, though there is not a shred of evidence he did so.[115] The journalist Karl Korn guaranteed a soft landing for himself by participating in the founding of the *Frankfurter Allgemeine Zeitung* in 1949 and becoming its features editor well into the 1970s. Back in 1940 he had written against Jews obsessed with "Talmudic nihilism" and had enthused over the film *Jud Süss* because it had shown that now "the Jewish problem in Germany has been mentally solved."[116] Then, in *Der Spiegel* in 1960, Korn reinterpreted the term "Talmudic nihilism" as an act of resistance, because it had connoted "covert" language warning fellow Germans how Jews were being ill-treated. He was referring to the literary style of inferring between the lines deployed in the novella *Auf den Marmorklippen* by his paragon, the "anti-nihilist" Ernst Jünger, as Korn later explained in an encomium.[117]

"Slave language" (a phrase originally attributed to Jünger) was also supposed to have been employed by the journalist Hubert Neun when reporting on Jews in the Warsaw Ghetto in 1941. Only such language would reveal, in hidden form, the exceedingly deplorable aspects of their living conditions there, he betrayed to *Der Spiegel* twenty-three years later. There was no other means of alerting the public, and his method had been an act of opposition.[118] But what exactly did Neun write in *Das Reich* in March 1941? He justified the removal of the Jews from "other city dwellers" of the Polish capital, and their subsequent isolation. This had calmed civilian life in Warsaw, as the "enormously repulsive multitude of every Jewish type of the East" had now been seen through.[119] After 1945, Neun assisted Elisabeth Noelle at the Allensbach Institute and in 1961 became a Bundestag deputy for the CDU.[120]

The list goes on. The Nazi poet Gerhard Schumann, Nazi theater director Gustaf Gründgens, and, of course, Nazi Wehrmacht captain Ernst Jünger, employing various subterfuges, asserted after the war that they had resisted the regime.[121] Like Meinecke and Bergengruen, who transfigured the Third Reich into a "Satanocracy," thereby abstracting it from the regular stream of German history and absolving its subjects of guilt, the author Hans Carossa demonized the regime as something atypically German and explained his role in it as that of an intrepid regulator, which was why he had assumed the leadership of Goebbels's international writers' union.[122] Besides, some things about Hitler had been salutary, Carossa argued, for example the execution of the Holocaust. "He had millions of Jews, adults and children killed, and thus effected that all good people on this earth turned to Jewry with boundless compassion. Without his rampage there would, perhaps, not be a state of Israel today." After all, Hitler had been unjustly treated by the Jews, because of insults hurled by Jews abroad – no wonder German Jews had to suffer the consequences.[123] Here not the murderer but the victim was to blame.

Today, given the complex wartime circumstances, it is difficult to sketch the outlines of the ideal, the artists who would have maintained their artistic integrity in the Third Reich, refused to collaborate with the regime, engaged in acts of resistance, and not have felt like a casualty after World War II.[124] Perhaps, cynically, one can say that this role could have potentially been filled by Käthe Dorsch. Born in 1890, a one-time fiancée of Göring in 1917, she remained a well-liked actress in Germany even after 1945. It is documented that after 1933 she helped many artists who became targets of one

regime leader or another. This was made possible due to her enduring prox-
imity to the Reichsmarschall, who found it difficult to deny her interven-
tions. She acted in several films under Goebbels, none of which were outright
propaganda films, with perhaps the exception of one costume drama, *Trenck,
der Pandur* (1940), in which she portrayed the Austrian empress Maria
Theresa and soldiering and war were glorified. (It was banned in West
Germany until 1953.) But because almost all the films made in this period
helped oil the Nazi machinery of governance, one cannot dismiss Dorsch's
film cameos as harmless. Well in tune with the times' right-wing trends, she
remained close to Göring after her love affair of 1917, a man known as an
authoritarian and anti-Semite. She remained on social terms with both
Goebbels and Hitler, was appointed an actress extraordinaire in 1939 and
given an honorific place on the list of exemptions from military and home-
front service in 1944, as she continued looking up to these men and their
politics.[125] Still, the aid she rendered has to be acknowledged.

Perhaps the conundrum may be solved by contemplating two opposing
statements on the matter, by persons who considered themselves artists,
intellectuals, persecuted by the Nazi tyrants. The first is by the poet and
essayist Gottfried Benn, who after 1935 had thought he could find succor
by joining the Wehrmacht. In 1950, attempting to justify his earlier position, he wrote disingenuously: "I maintain that many of those who stayed
on and continued in their posts did so because they were hoping to preserve
their spots for those who had left, in order to pass them on once they had
returned."[126] Five years earlier, the Austrian-born physicist Lise Meitner,
who had had to emigrate to Holland, then to Sweden from Berlin in 1938
because she was Jewish, wrote to her long-time associate Otto Hahn, who
had remained in the Reich to keep working on the atomic bomb and ended
up with his colleagues in the British Farm Hall detention center in
Godmanchester, near Cambridge, in the spring of 1945: "All of you have
worked for Nazi Germany and never even tried some passive resistance.
Certainly, to assuage your conscience, here and there you helped some
person in need of assistance but you allowed the murder of millions of innocent people, and no protest was ever heard." This, a more valid and honest
judgment than Benn's, could have applied equally to every writer and musician, every painter and actor, every journalist and filmmaker, who, after
January 1933, opted to stay in Nazi Germany.[127]

◆ ◆ ◆

Culture in Three Tyrannies

T HE OPENING OF this book maintained that the relationship between
culture and tyranny is a complex one, and indeed questioned whether
culture was even possible in a dictatorship. Examining the place of
culture in other despotisms against the background of the Third Reich
might offer some enlightening perspectives. In Fascist Italy, unlike in Nazi
Germany, culture had been a constituent element in the formation of the
new authoritarian state since before 1922, the year of Benito Mussolini's
infamous but theatrical March on Rome. The flag-waving poet Filippo
Tommaso Marinetti combined political and cultural aspirations on the platform of the Futurist movement, which became part of Mussolini's evolving
ideology. A formative element of this movement was a vision of modernity,
symbolized by the interaction of machine-age inventions such as the airplane
with day-to-day politics, which together signified youth, dynamics, violence,
and a crass rejection of the Liberal age prior to World War I. Hence
technology and modernity (in contrast to the aesthetically intellectualized
movement of "modernism" in the parallel Weimar period, much of it associated with democracy) became catchwords of the new-born, defiantly anti-
democratic, Fascist era. As a precursor of dictatorial Nazi practices, Mussolini,
in developing a police state that had established its main contours by 1924,
set up corporatist structures to administer the arts and letters ("Syndicalism").
Re-created in the RKK of Goebbels, this emphasized national cultural

events such as patriotic exhibitions, and forced an artist-state consensus that the Nazis later claimed was reconfigured in a racial, culturally determined Volksgemeinschaft. Under the Duce until the early 1930s cultural exhibitions focused on Italian artists, and unlike in the Third Reich, foreign influences such as American films (and jazz) were tolerated, avant-garde music like Schoenberg's was performed, and non-Italian authors were read. An aesthetic pluralism characterized Fascist Italy into the 1930s, but such pluralism was stamped out under Hitler's tyranny beginning early in 1933.[1]

The fact that culture, despite the appearances of autonomy, was marshaled in the service of the state had become obvious at least by 1932, when in Italy the Fascist dictatorship of Mussolini had been fully launched, paralleled in Germany by Hitler's rise to power the following year and the first of Stalin's purges in the Soviet Union in 1936. In 1932 in Italy a Futurist-inspired painting of machinery, airplanes, and ocean liners symbolized ten years of Fascist rule, and an official "Exhibition of the Fascist Revolution" allowed avant-garde art to illuminate the political landscape. By this time Fascist iconography featuring images of the Duce was deeply entrenched, in various melodramatic, imperious poses, in films, and in popular culture, perhaps on beer steins; this was very unlike the austere Hitler, who generally disliked overly dramatized reproductions of his image. The populist Duce was the recipient of praise in works of music dedicated to him, for instance the Ninth Psalm for chorus and orchestra by Goffredo Petrassi, in 1934. Mussolini himself had now assumed a more strident role at the heart of cultural censorship, especially in literature and theater, similar to but not as dogmatic as the role Hitler was then playing in the visual arts. Earlier than the Nazis, however, the Fascists had come to the realization that their form of art had so far been disappointing, and in 1936 they also rued the failure of their literature, despite such pretentious novels as Giulietto Calabrese's *Nozze fasciste: Il romanzo fascista* (1934), which depicted the life of an exemplary young Italian family, characterized by black shirts, shotguns, and wide-hipped maternal fecundity.[2]

A new dimension, politically as well as culturally, was added to Italian authoritarianism, driving it more in the direction of totalitarianism by the specter of war in 1934, even earlier than in the case of Germany. During that year it became clear that Mussolini coveted territory in North Africa. As part of the Fascist ideological canon colonial imperialism had a history going back to the pre-1922 Futurists, who patterned much of their imagery on Italy's conquest of Libya in 1911, and an appetite for more North African land throughout the 1920s.[3] It gave rise to Fascist imaginings of African natives as biologically inferior, sexually subversive, and fit to be exploited, dreamt up out of a self-arrogated right to safeguard (a fictitious) humanity. This had manifested itself culturally in 1932, for example, when the Afro-American cabaret dancer and singer Josephine Baker was banned from performing in Italy. The German parallel was in the racist condemnation of Jews, Gypsies, and black people by the Nazis, which had gradually developed since the humiliation through the Treaty of Versailles and led to ramifications in the treatment of "Jewish" culture by the late 1920s. The Duce's 1935 invasion of Ethiopia was predictably marked by unspeakable atrocities; cultural symbolism, as in Giannino Antona-Traversi's play *L'offerta* (*The Offering*, 1935), which celebrated a missing soldier's body, condoned aggression aesthetically and morally, as would German art for the Führer's eastern campaign from 1941.[4]

Because of its Ethiopian adventure Fascist Italy was drawn into the pro-Axis orbit, whereupon its cultural pluralism, already attenuated, was further shattered. Once the Fascists started supporting General Franco's Nationalist forces in the Spanish Civil War, depictions of animal-like black people and Spanish republican fighters multiplied in their art; in 1937 the reverberations from Hitler's "Great German Art" exhibition in Munich encouraged Fascist hardliners in the arts to allow more cultural currents to flow from their northern neighbor. In 1936 the anti-Semitic Fascist functionary Roberto Farinacci was instrumental in a meeting of the Fascist Grand Council on November 19, during which Mussolini announced "that the time had come to introduce racial policies in Fascist literature and doctrine." Under pressure from the Führer, Fascist politics aligned itself with Nazi legislation by way of discrimination against Jews; the Roman race laws of November 1938 coincided with the monstrosity of Kristallnacht. For Italy, the cultural ramifications amounted to a removal of Jews from the professions, including journalism; from education, including art academies; and from the artists' syndicate.

The Pact of Steel forged early in 1939 between Germany and Italy ushered in a climate congenial to more Fascist-beholden artworks. Inevitably, the venal, publicity-crazed Mussolini would feature in the foreground: in a painting *People Listening to a Speech by Il Duce on the Radio* (1939), or in a film (1941) showing sailors in a sinking submarine, celebrating their leader before drowning, in heightened verisimilitude – what one may call examples of Fascist Realism. These images were imbued with anti-Semitic implications, and the self-proclaimed avant-garde Futurists, maintaining their former claim to modernity, now emphasized their own anti-Semitic feelings. Emblematic of these developments was a competition in 1940 for "best racial monograph," about which one of the runners-up later reminisced that he had "dedicated many hours of study to racism." Jews were not allowed to participate in the Florentine Maggio Musicale festival in 1939, and in 1941, like *Jud Süss* in Nazi Germany, a momentous anti-Semitic film was on the Fascist drawing boards.[5]

But that filming never took place; Fascist Italy lay broken in 1943. With all the censorship and restrictions on culture forced upon its creators, the arts and letters in that country never came under the same degree of pressure as they did in the Third Reich, although, as there, they also never attained sovereign originality either. One reason surely was that – similar to Germany with its porous gubernatorial structures and unlike the centralized Soviet Union – Italy had a multitude of cross-defeating agencies and culture bosses who varied in their conceptions of art (and in their belief in pro-Fascist political symbols); for example, a Fascist intellectual such as the Hegelian philosopher Giovanni Gentile would differ significantly in his views from a Party hack like Farinacci.[6] Yet in the final analysis these agencies were embedded in a political system that was, in comparison with Hitler's and Stalin's, considerably less brutal and more forgiving.[7]

As far as culture was concerned, the Soviet Union constituted yet another proposition. German cultural influences there were less pervasive than in Italy and, for reasons of war, virtually absent after 1940. If anything, it was the other way around: Wassily Kandinsky, who started with the Weimar Bauhaus in the very early 1920s, had first worked with the Russian revolutionary artists under culture commissar Anatoly Lunacharsky; and Moholy-Nagy's Constructivist background, possibly through the short-lived Hungarian Soviet Republic of 1919, was also indebted to revolutionary art under the Bolsheviks.[8]

There were also progressive, modern artists before the Bolshevik Revolution and under the tsars, and they continued their work in the optimistic belief that their art would help to shape a new, Communist society, with the new government backing them. Kazimir Malevich painted bold geometric shapes with strong colors, inventing a school of painting he called Suprematism around 1915. Vladimir Tatlin, inspired by Picasso's Cubist collages in Paris during 1913, helped found Constructivism that year, where pieces of material – glass, wood, or metal – were made into *objets d'art*. Vladimir Mayakovsky thought his new poetry could establish a discourse with the great unwashed, while Vsevolod Meyerhold and Sergei Eisenstein thrived in experimental theater and film. It was a time of youthful merriment as well, reminiscent of Dadaism in the Weimar Republic. Eisenstein later remembered how "greased pigs were let loose among the members of the audience, who leapt on their seats and screamed. It was terrific. Goodness, how we enjoyed ourselves!"

Another movement in popular culture close to the bottom of the social scale originated during the revolutionary years – the Proletkult. It utilized circus acts, folk songs, and primitive movies with proletarian content to further the new egalitarian political goals. Many of these efforts fused with those of the modern bourgeois artists, but, as it turned out, Lenin and his clique, especially the watchful Lunacharsky, with functions like Goebbels's or Rosenberg's, suspected there was too much independence in these artistic currents that they might not ultimately be able to harness. Hence both movements, to all intents and purposes, were snuffed out by orders from on high as early as 1920, causing the exodus abroad of many members of the creative class, such as Marc Chagall and Kandinsky, whereas others, like Malevich and the painter and poet Pavel Filonov, stayed on in the Soviet Union and just barely survived.[9]

The pattern in the Soviet Union thus far resembled that of culture early on during the Third Reich when Modernist experiments were officially canceled, even after a certain lapse of time. In Italy, of course, things were different because vengeful rogue elements embraced the avant-gardists, bending them to their purpose, with their art adapted to the brutalisms of an emerging Fascist ideology, aiming for totalitarianism. The situation changed in the Soviet Union, however, when Lenin, through the spirit of his New Economic Policy (NEP), allowed for a type of cultural pluralism the Italians also tolerated for a while, one that was typically absent from Nazi Germany. After 1920, therefore, under the Communist regime more traditional forms of culture flourished again, such as classical music, theater, and opera; and the vaunted jazz made its appearance in Soviet cities in 1922, although these were imperfect performances. But Lenin's political doctrine underlay much of this culture – high and low. Yakov Protazanov's 1927 film *The Forty-First*, for example, was adapted from a civil-war story about a female Bolshevik sniper who, having killed forty White soldiers, adds another notch on her rifle after she has shot her lover, a young aristocrat whom she had initially sheltered because of his good looks. Nevertheless, during this period of apparent relative freedom between 1921 and 1928, censorship in the Soviet Union was firmly in place, especially regarding new literature, which was always suspect, and particularly books by foreign authors.[10]

Joseph Stalin's rise to power after Lenin's death in 1924 meant the elimination of his fiercest rival Leon Trotsky and the beginning of what has been called the Cultural Revolution in 1928. What this amounted to was a complete denial of the frail freedoms that had been granted in the NEP era, so that novel experiments like jazz were trampled underfoot, private sheet-music publication was stopped in 1929, libraries were purged, and Gypsy music was prohibited in broadcasting.[11] Stalin started establishing dictatorial rule through the initiation, economically, of the first Four Year Plan and, culturally, a broad program of Socialist Realism that aimed for a true representation, in the arts and letters, of Soviet personages and material achievements. Chief among the former was of course Stalin himself, who wished to establish a Stalin Cult as an instrument of power, something vaguely akin to the "Hitler Myth."[12] But whereas, in the cultural arena, Stalin always tended to force a strong representation of his self, Hitler increasingly enhanced his aura by his physical absence.

The most significant artistic discipline for Stalin, as certain visual arts were for Hitler, came to be literature, in which he always took an enduring personal interest, to the point of reading plays and novels in manuscript carefully before allowing publication. One reason for this (apart from being a promising poet when young) was Stalin's upbringing in the traditional Russian canon, Pushkin, Chekhov, and Tolstoy, even if his passion had mostly been for revolutionary pamphleteering; in this he resembled Mussolini, whose true trade was journalism. More importantly, however, as the Soviet Union, after the years of cultural turbulence until about 1932, was poised under Stalin to gradually advance along a steadier, totalitarian path, he capitalized on the power of the written word as a constituent element of national law and order. Paintings of Stalin with pen in hand near a green-shaded lamp, signifying intelligence and erudition, are among the most compelling portraits of the tyrant posing as benevolent ruler. They rival photographs of the Führer gazing at exhibits in the "Degenerate Art" exhibition in Munich, in July 1937. The novelist Maxim Gorky, finally returned from self-exile in Italy in 1932, until his death in 1936 became Stalin's most trusted companion in cultural affairs, similar to Hitler's Albert Speer, who helped to assure for the Third Reich the supremacy of the visual arts, especially sculpture and architecture. But architecture also became more important under Stalin. As high towers were built in Moscow and other cities, for instance, the Supreme Leader assumed the stature of a vigilant watchtower over the nation's fortunes.[13]

Stalin embarked in 1932 on a series of steps that put in place organizational critiques of writers that culminated in the Committee on Arts Affairs, directly controlled by the Supreme Council of Soviets, in 1935. In good time, similar controls were patterned on these steps for all the other Soviet arts. In their totality, they greatly resembled the institutional controls that Hitler imposed, through Goebbels, on German culture creators with the foundation of the RKK in this period (with Fascist Italy clamping down harshly on the eve of its racial war campaigns in North Africa as well).[14]

The political purges that Stalin initiated in 1932, and which grew to cataclysmic proportions between 1936 and 1938, found their cultural equivalent in the fight by the Supreme Council's department of cultural affairs against what was called Formalism, anything deviating from Soviet-prescribed literalist representation. Its henchmen terrorized authors as much as filmmakers and musicians, already famous artists and mostly good Communists, such as the poets Anna Akhmatova, Ossip Mandelstam, and Boris Pasternak. The reign of terror entrapped those and many other artists. Some like Mandelstam died in camps, others like Mayakovsky committed suicide, while the great theater actor, director, and producer Meyerhold was tortured and shot.[15] It has been claimed that these early Russian purges encouraged Hitler toward his own Röhm Purge in the summer of 1934 and that this action again in turn motivated Stalin to reinforce his terror between 1936 and 1938 (when German actress Carola Neher's tragic fate in captivity had already been sealed); what is certain is that Hitler did not single out creative individuals for special punishment, as Stalin seems to have wanted to do. This suggests that the Russian tyrant accorded even more significance to the potentially undermining influence of great writers and artists, as being a threat to his power, than did the Führer.

The Great Purges came to an end as war was dawning, without heavy censorship and yokes of repression having been lifted. But after 1941 the Soviet Union's cultural elites were solidly behind Stalin's effort to win the war against Nazi Germany, with Soviet Jewish culture connoisseurs aware of the Nazis' attempts to eliminate Jews. Hence filmmakers and journalists such as Eisenstein and Ilya Ehrenburg – many of them Jewish – willingly served the patriotic cause. Artists were enlisted.[16] That situation was no different from the one in Germany where painters like Ferdinand Spiegel were working for the Nazis and, to a lesser extent, Fascist Italy. After the war, Stalin's glum grip on culture did not lessen (there was another anti-Formalist wave in the late 1940s), and it was even strengthened by anti-Semitic outbursts from the despot himself. It eased up only in March 1953, following Stalin's death, after he had been accusing a clique of Jewish doctors of wanting to assassinate him.

From the point of view of culture alone, the Communist regime in the Soviet Union represented the worst of three tyrannical situations. A number of factors point to that conclusion. First, no one other than Stalin ever gave the appearance of being so totally conversant with and personally interested in controlling arts and letters in the quest for a spiritual elixir to nurture the nation's life, even if deficiencies of a new, regime-specific, culture were lamented here as in Germany and Italy.[17] Second, even before judging hunger-induced mass murder on the one side against Jewish genocide on the other, no dictator was as cruel as Stalin equally in his civic as in his cultural policymaking, utilizing terror as an instrument of ultimate control. His governing secret, as demonstrated hundreds of times through his show trials, which were supported by elaborate indictments, judgments, and signed confessions (for the attainment of which any torture was justified),[18] lay in the unpredictability of the purgative mechanisms and, to heighten the terror, Stalin's willingness to sacrifice even his most devoted henchmen, without apparent rhyme or reason, from one day to the next. Hitler refrained from this; his personal relationships were more transparent. Altogether, he was known to be too lenient to old Party cronies from the Time of Struggle, for example, no matter what their possible transgressions; hence the Nazi poet Hanns Johst, dependably loyal, never had to fear.

Neither had other literati or musicians in the Third Reich who consistently toed the line. On the other hand Stalin, after criticizing the manner in which his idol, Tsar Ivan the Terrible, had been portrayed in a devotional film, once said that it was good for Ivan to have been "very cruel," and that it would be well to show that cruelty as long as it could be justified.[19] The greatest cruelty of all, of course, was Stalin's determination never to justify his own. Thus he perfected terror.

Such circumstances led, thirdly, to a degree neither seen in Fascist Italy nor in Nazi Germany, to personality twists in the men and women whom Stalin had vowed unto himself to rule over and to use. The most publicized of these cases are those of the police chiefs Genrikh Yagoda and Nikolai Yezhov, and after Stalin's death, Lavrentiy Beria, all of whom had been prosecutors and ended up being tried for treason and executed. In the realm of culture, the tragic figure of Dmitry Shostakovich stands out. The Soviet Union's great hope in contemporary music (along with Sergei Prokofiev), and initially much lauded for his idiosyncratic avant-garde style, Shostakovich was attacked by the anti-Formalists in 1936 over his new opera *Lady Macbeth of the Mtsensk District*. This made him a victim of Soviet cultural policy, but due to his outstanding qualities as a composer and his international acclaim he overcame opprobrium sufficiently to be ensconced as a member of the prestigious Stalin Music Prize committee, whose favor as a beneficiary he himself enjoyed. Scarcely had he been thus established than Shostakovich bowed to anti-Formalist guidelines in his own evaluation of prize candidates. He once more became a defendant during the final onslaught of the anti-Formalists in the late 1940s and then lived out his life as a respected Communist with many official titles. However, although he knew better, he again moved against the avant-garde in 1961.[20] In the annals of culture under Hitler, there were no such complex turncoats.

This was not the only difference in the cultural arena between the Soviet Union under Stalin and the Third Reich. If in a pluralistic, democratic society culture at the extremes is often the most powerful expression of its time, either as assent to existing circumstances or as protest, all three tyrannies were united in a negation of those variable functions. Instead, culture had to be an instrument of autocratic rule, manipulated by political revolutionaries from the top, on the path to or in perfection of totalitarianism. However, whatever regulation against or encouragement of certain cultural trends Nazi Germany may have shared with Fascist Italy and Soviet Russia, the uniqueness of the cultural situation under Hitler consisted logically of sequential steps almost to the end, which contrasted with an arbitrariness of decision-making in cultural affairs under both Mussolini and Stalin.

Thus when Hitler and Goebbels had decided they needed culture as an instrument of power over the population, the destruction of what was termed Weimar culture, embodying the freedoms of modern democracies, to them was a cogent prerequisite, especially because the Jews could be simultaneously eliminated. Against the resistance of many artists and intellectuals opposed to political controls, the leading Nazis, even in the face of dissension within their own ranks, prevailed. Flagrantly conspicuous bookburnings, and by 1938 two signally censorious exhibitions castigating what was called degenerate art and music, were meant to establish new official taboos. These were aligned with novel police and administrative controls, such as the restrictive Reich Culture Chamber.

That chamber was also used to help establish new norms of creativity in a National Socialist spirit. So-called revolutionary standards for specifically Nazi arts were put forward but failed to take hold for lack of original content and human craft, so that recourse had to be had to older movements and patterns, traditionalist and neo-Romantic, mostly reaching back to the nineteenth century. Hitler also condoned such works of art, many of them derivative, although he himself for political reasons only singled out art forms in which he took a private interest: some visual art and architecture, some films such as Riefenstahl's, and Wagner's music, in particular his operas.

Foreseeably from these formative settings, defeat for culture in Nazi Germany – ultimately expressed through the failed grafting of a Nazi-specific ersatz culture – was further accelerated by the exodus or elimination of the uncommonly creative Jews and the course of World War II. Establishing a ghetto culture league for Germany's remaining Jews was a well-calculated slap in the face intended to demean and control those formerly integrated citizens, now seen as racial *and* cultural aliens who had to be entirely removed. In the fall of 1941, when the Jewish Kulturbund was officially dissolved, culture in Germany had been made fully subservient to the requirements of warfare, which now compounded Goebbels's already existing difficulty of superintending culture for political ends. This resulted in a first disruption to the Nazi logic: Most Germans increasingly expressed mistrust in Goebbels's stratagems of conjuring a Final Victory based on "Blood and Soil" culture. Subsequent Nazi planning was irreparably upset when after the defeat at Stalingrad in February 1943, Goebbels, and seemingly an ever-absent Hitler, kept insisting that culture-based propaganda would guide the people.

As early as 1933 a counter-culture to Nazi culture had taken hold, however timidly, in countries where forced emigrants from the Third Reich, mostly Jewish, had sought refuge. But due to the trauma suffered by those German-speaking creative artists, who were often unfamiliar with the new language and culture, and could be the object of disdain and professional rejection, a German culture abroad found little space in which to develop. A notable exception, as mentioned, was the work of the internationally famous novelist Thomas Mann, who became a spokesman for German culture beyond Germany, even a political prognosticator, a moral challenger to Hitler. The fact that he, not to mention a multitude of lesser colleagues, was not welcome in a post-war Germany attempting to emancipate itself from Nazism, was indicative of the intellectual and psychic paralysis that had overtaken many inhabitants of the new western democracy. It would take decades of cleansing and reconstruction to prepare the ground for a complete cultural rebirth.

Notes

PREFACE

1. Keynote speech by Joseph Goebbels at the inauguration of the Reich Culture Chamber (RKK) in Berlin, November 15, 1933, cited in Goebbels, *Signale*, 325.
2. Other active participants were David Scrase, Alan E. Steinweis, Eric Rentschler, Pamela M. Potter, Frank Trommler, and Jonathan Petropoulos. See the articles in Huener and Nicosia, *The Arts in Nazi Germany*.
3. Jost Hermand's *Culture* is a useful introduction but lacks treatment of victims of Nazi cultural policy, as well as documentation, supplying only a "selected bibliography." See the review by Anselm Heinrich in *Bulletin of the German Historical Institute London* 36, no. 1 (2014): 105–9. Lisa Pine's final section on culture in her very readable *Hitler's "National Community,"* 215–78, also serves introductory purposes, but is shorter and lacking analysis. See the review by Joseph W. Bendersky in *American Historical Review* 114 (2009): 228–9.
4. See, for example, Rentschler, *Ministry* and *Use and Abuse*; Hull, *Film*; Welch, *Propaganda*; Niven, *Hitler*; Sösemann, "Journalismus" and "Voraussetzungen"; Schnell, *Dichtung* and *Geschichte*; Prieberg, *Musik im NS-Staat* and *Musik und Macht*; Levi, *Mozart* and *Music*; Potter, *Most German*.
5. Petropoulos, *Art, Faustian Bargain*, and *Artists under Hitler*; Potter, *Art of Suppression*.

ONE – DECONSTRUCTING MODERNISM

1. The latter point has been justly emphasized by Pamela Potter, see further in this chapter at note 136. See also Eksteins, *Rites of Spring*; Herf, *Reactionary Modernism*.
2. Gay, *Weimar Culture*, 105.
3. Ibid.
4. See the photograph in Bergdoll and Dickerman, *Bauhaus*, 52.
5. Kater, *Weimar*, 144–5; Honegger and Massenkeil, *Lexikon*, vol. 4, 95.
6. Kater, *Different Drummers*, 3–28. For the Berlin cabaret scene, see Jelavich, *Berlin Cabaret*, 118–227; on Hesterberg specifically PEM, *Heimweh*, 37–8, 131, 170, 175.
7. Kracauer, *Caligari*, 61–76, 149–50, 162–3, 226–9.

8. Plates in Bergdoll and Dickerman, *Bauhaus*, 115, 191.
9. Hoeres, *Kultur*, 143–5; Hermand and Trommler, *Kultur*, 193–211.
10. Michalzik, *Gründgens*, 48–9; Rischbieter, *Theater*, 228; Spotts, *Legacy*, 34; Petropoulos, *Artists under Hitler*, 216–19. On Weimar-era theater, see also Laqueur, *Weimar*, 174–97.
11. Jelavich, *Berlin Alexanderplatz*, 1–35; Evans, *The Coming*, 411.
12. Volz, *Daten*, 24, mentions this but is silent on the content.
13. Without documentation by Martynkewicz, *Salon Deutschland*, 11. In his 1927 speech at Nuremberg, printed in Rosenberg and Weiss, *Reichsparteitag*, 38–46, Hitler did not mention culture.
14. Bollmus, *Amt Rosenberg*, 27–8.
15. Kater, *Weimar*, 205.
16. Steinweis, "Weimar Culture," 409.
17. See Schultze-Naumburg, *Kampf*, e.g. 10, 12; Meckel, *Animation*, 20.
18. Blunck, "Volkstum," 190.
19. Stern, *Wassern*, 74.
20. Hussong, "*Kurfürstendamm*," 7 (1st quote); Stang, *Grundlagen*, 12 (last two quotes).
21. *Mitteilungen des Kampfbundes für deutsche Kultur* 2 (1930): 36; Klee, *Kulturlexikon*, 616–17; Hille, "Beispiel," 207–11; Dümling, "Hexensabbat," 190–4.
22. On the other hand, Hans Zöberlein wrote novels of that ilk. See his *Der Glaube* (first publ. 1931), and Ketelsen, *Literatur*, 222.
23. Steinweis, "Conservatism," 340.
24. Petsch, "Malerei," 248.
25. *Deutsche Kultur-Wacht*, no. 2 (1932): 13; ibid., no. 4 (1932): 12; ibid., no. 1 (1933): 13; ibid., no. 3 (1933): 14–15; RKK Gustav Havemann (BAB, former BDC); Steinweis, "Culture," 416; Führer, "Cultural Life," 475.
26. Steinweis, "Culture," 417.
27. Moeller, "Filmstars," 155. Trenker and Riefenstahl had been co-stars in *The Holy Mountain* (1926) and *The Great Leap* (1927).
28. Ketelsen, *Literatur*, 219.
29. Schultze-Naumburg, *Kampf*, 13; Blunck, "Volkstum," 200.
30. Wardetzky, *Otto*, 69–75; Klee, *Kulturlexikon*, 402.
31. Petersen, *Strasse*, 8–11.
32. Langhoff, *Moorsoldaten*, 5–6, 82–3; Klee, *Kulturlexikon*, 320 (Mann quote); Föllmer, *Kultur*, 100; song text freiklick.at/index.php?option=com_content&task=view&id=1123.
33. Kater, *Muse*, 278; Bermann Fischer, *Bedroht*, 106 (quote); Hull, *Film*, 30. Kleiber was not Jewish, as is sometimes claimed (e.g. in the otherwise very readable *Third Reich* volume by Thomas Childers, 293).
34. Kirchner, in *LEMO: Lebendiges Museum Online*; Kirchner cited in William Cook, "The Best Thing to Come Out of Davos," *The Spectator Online*, January 18, 2014.
35. Goebbels on May 31, 1934, in *Theater von A–Z, XXII g 6* (1st quote); Bühner in Dreyer and Jenssen, *Demut*, 87 (2nd quote); Engelbrecht, *Kunst*, 64; Schlegel, *Dichter*, 31, 33; Eberlein, *Was*, 33–4; Högg, "Baukunst," 63; Schindler, "Gedanken," 318; Feulner, *Kunst*, 7–8; Lorenz, *Unrast*, 19, 127. A thorough treatment of "asphalt culture" from a Nazi perspective is in Hussong, "*Kurfürstendamm*."
36. Bracher, *Dictatorship*, 193–7.
37. Text in *Reichsgesetzblatt Teil I* (October 7, 1933): 713–17.
38. "Gesetz zur Wiederherstellung des Berufsbeamtentums vom 7. April 1933," *Reichsgesetzblatt Teil I* (April 7, 1933): 175.
39. Klee, *Kulturlexikon*, 351.
40. Stein, *Schoenberg Letters*, 116 (quote); Reich, *Schoenberg*, 187–8.
41. *Tägliche Rundschau*, May 11, 1933.
42. Sarkowicz, "Schriftsteller," 176–8; Brenner, *Ende*, 27–161.

43. Brenner, *Ende*, 63–6 (quote 64: Huch to Schillings, March 24, 1933); Albrecht et al., *Lexikon*, vol. 1, 402–3.
44. Rischbieter, "Schlageter," 213–15; Petzet, *Theater*, 253–4.
45. Rischbieter, *Theater*, 478; Rischbieter, "Schlageter," 216–17; Ketelsen, *Theater*, 75–6. From a critical Nazi point of view see Ziegler, *Wende*, esp. 77–8.
46. Rischbieter, "Schlageter," 215.
47. Thiele interviewed in Gramann et al., *Thiele*, 14–19; "Nachzensur aller Filme, die vor 1933 zugelassen wurden," *Frankfurter Zeitung*, July 8, 1935; Hull, *Film*, 44; Wetzel and Hagemann, *Zensur*, 15–19; Kreimeier, *Ufa-Story*, 302.
48. On jazz, see Nazi choir director Fritz Stein's remarks in *Deutsches Podium* (July 31, 1936): 4, and Stein, "Chorwesen," 285–6. On atonality see Goebbels, *Tagebücher Fragmente*, vol. 2, 534, and vol. 3, 398–9 (quote); Siegfried Kallenberg, "Wiedergeburt der Musik," *Münchner Neueste Nachrichten*, August 18, 1933; Jena speech by Hans Severus Ziegler, May 13, 1936, in Ziegler, *Wende*, esp. 8.
49. Drewniak, *Theater*, 282; Levi, "Opera," 139; Du Closel, *Stimmen*, 409–10.
50. Steinbeck, "Tannhäuser," 134–7.
51. Eckert, *Rundfunk*, 228, 246; Kater, "Controls," 60–1.
52. Speech in Goebbels, *Signale*, 203–4. See also Dressler-Andress, *Reichsrundfunkkammer*, 32.
53. "Die Urteilsbegründung im Rundfunkprozess," *Frankfurter Zeitung*, June 15, 1935; Diller, *Rundfunkpolitik*, 72–5, 96, 108–11, 129–33, 146; Evans, *The Coming*, 402; Grüttner, *Brandstifter*, 316–18.
54. Schäferdieck, *Lebens-Echo*, 88–9.
55. Hadamovsky, *Propaganda*, 58 (1st quote); Drechsler, *Funktion*, 40 (2nd quote), 64 (last quote). For the political uses of Beethoven's œuvre in the Third Reich, see Dennis, *Beethoven*, 142–74.
56. Goebbels, *Tagebücher Fragmente*, vol. 2, 376; Martens, *Reich*, 19; Frei and Schmitz, *Journalismus*, 14; Grüttner, *Brandstifter*, 310.
57. "Schriftleitergesetz. Vom 4. Oktober 1933," *Reichsgesetzblatt Teil I* (October 7, 1933): 713–17 (quote 713); Amann, "Volkspresse," XII–XIII; Hagemann, *Publizistik*, 35–42; Grüttner, *Brandstifter*, 311; Frei and Schmitz, *Journalismus*, 15–23; Sösemann, "Voraussetzungen," 201–8.
58. Frei and Schmitz, *Journalismus*, 17; Sösemann, "Voraussetzungen," 203; Laux, *Nachklang*, 228–9.
59. Kursell, "Kunstpolitik," 4.
60. Högg, "Baukunst," 64 (1st quote); Schindler, "Gedanken," 356 (2nd quote); Schultze-Naumburg, *Kunst*, 43; Hager, "Bauwerke," 19.
61. Miller Lane, *Architecture*, 169.
62. Teut, *Architektur*, 67–70.
63. Miller Lane, *Architecture*, 170–3 (1st quote 172), 181–4; Weissler, "Bauhaus-Gestaltung," 58–62; Nerdinger, "Modernisierung," 19–20; Petropoulos, *Artists under Hitler*, 68–72, 75–87 (2nd quote 80); Nerdinger, "Bauhaus-Architekten," 153–63 (last quote 158). Gropius's attitude is far from that of a political fugitive, as Florian Siebeck suggests: "Wettschulden sind Ehrenschulden," *faz.net*, February 24, 2016.
64. Hitler, *Mein Kampf*, 283; Hitler's 1933 Party rally speech in Dreyer, *Kultur*, 16; 1934 Party rally speech in *Der Kongress*, 102–3; 1935 Party rally speech in Hinz, *Malerei*, 143, 146–7; Hitler in "Die Ansprache des Führers zur Eröffnung des Hauses der Deutschen Kunst," *Mitteilungsblatt der Reichskammer der bildenden Künste* (August 1, 1937): 2–3, 6.
65. Scholz, "Kunstgötzen," 5; Willrich, "Aufgabe," 276–7, 278 (quote), 279, 285.
66. Klaus Graf von Baudissin, "Das Essener Folkwangmuseum stösst einen Fremdkörper ab," *National-Zeitung*, Essen, August 18, 1936; Hermann Dames, "Es wird aufgeräumt!," *Nationalsozialistische Erziehung* (1935): 83; Rave, *Kunstdiktatur*, 53; Brenner, *Kunstpolitik*, 37–8; Lehmann-Haupt, *Art*, 74; Merker, *Künste*, 124; Spotts, *Hitler*, 156–62; Clinefelter, *Artists*, 69; Steinkamp, "Schöpfung," 295–6.

67. Rave, *Kunstdiktatur*, 47–8; Lehmann-Haupt, *Art*, 74–87; Bushard, "Bildhauer," 105.
68. For a definition see Willett, *New Sobriety*, 111–17.
69. Scholz, *Lebensfragen*, 31 (quote); Schubert, *Dix*, 110; Peters, *Neue Sachlichkeit*, 84, 133; Beck, *Dix*, 143; Klee, *Kulturlexikon*, 103.
70. Linfert, "Beckmann," esp. 66–9; Karin Janker, "Wie Hitler Kitsch verherrlichte," *sueddeutsche.de*, June 4, 2015; Klee, *Kulturlexikon*, 36.
71. Karin Janker, "Wie Hitler Kitsch verherrlichte," *sueddeutsche.de*, June 4, 2015 (1st quote); Droste, "Bauhaus-Maler," 131–2; Schlemmer in Lauzemis, "Ideologie," 46 (2nd quote).
72. Hübinger, *Mann*, 123, 138–9, 180, 182; Klee, *Kulturlexikon*, 351–3; Heinrich Mann, in *LEMO: Lebendiges Museum Online*.
73. Ziegler, *Wende*, 76; Brenner, *Kunstpolitik*, 44–5; Strothmann, *Literaturpolitik*, 176; Schnell, *Emigration*, 25; Barbian, *Literaturpolitik*, 47, 250, 254–5.
74. Naumann and Lüthgen, *Kampf*, 3–4; Brenner, *Kunstpolitik*, 48; Strothmann, *Literaturpolitik*, 74; Strätz, "Aktion," 348–53, 363; Sauder, *Bücherverbrennung*, 169–71; Ketelsen, *Kulturpolitik*, 238; Boese, *Bibliothekswesen*, 226–7; Barbian, *Literaturpolitik*, 40.
75. Goebbels's speech in *Deutsche Allgemeine Zeitung*, May 12, 1933; Sauder, *Bücherverbrennung*, 179–80; Evans, *The Coming*, 427–9.
76. "Verordnung über die Errichtung einer vorläufigen Filmkammer. Vom 22. Juli 1933," *Reichsgesetzblatt Teil I* (July 25, 1933): 531–2.
77. Hagemann, *Publizistik*, 62; Hull, *Film*, 30–1 (quote); Baird, *To Die*, 73–107.
78. Kalbus, *Werden*, 102; Heyde, *Presse*, 29; Hull, *Film*, 43–4; Lowry, *Pathos*, 10; Kreimeier, *Ufa-Story*, 268–9; Moeller, *Filmminister*, 107–8; Grüttner, *Brandstifter*, 351–3.
79. Albrecht, *Filmpolitik*, 330–56.
80. Paragraph 13, "Schriftleitergesetz. Vom 4. Oktober 1933," *Reichsgesetzblatt Teil I* (October 7, 1933): 714.
81. Hagemann, *Publizistik*, 37; Abel, *Presselenkung*, 30–1; Grüttner, *Brandstifter*, 309–10.
82. Dovifat quoted in Wilkens, "Urteil," 371; Guido Enderis, "Reich Press Loses Last of its Rights; Must Serve State," *The New York Times*, October 6, 1933.
83. Original text in *Der deutsche Schriftsteller* 1, no. 12 (December 1936): 280–1.
84. Approvingly: Dovifat, *Zeitungslehre Zweiter Band*, 35–36. Critically: Hagemann, *Publizistik*, 60; Strothmann, *Literaturpolitik*, 270–1, 276–7.
85. "Kultur und kein Bildungsphilister!" *Das Schwarze Korps*, February 25, 1937.
86. Rudolf Kircher, "Der Kunstschriftleiter," *Frankfurter Zeitung*, November 29, 1936.
87. Aigner, "Indizierung," 983–1,004; Dahm, *Buch*, 169–71; Barbian, *Literaturpolitik*, 251–7.
88. Payr, *Schrifttumspflege*, 14, 18, 26; Hagemann, *Publizistik*, 42; Brenner, *Kunstpolitik*, 52–3; Strothmann, *Literaturpolitik*, 39.
89. "Theatergesetz. Vom 5. Mai 1934," *Reichsgesetzblatt Teil I* (May 19, 1934): 411–12.
90. Von Schramm, *Neubau*, 22–3; Drewniak, *Theater*, 34; Dussel, *Theater*, 89–95; Levi, "Opera," 139–40; Rischbieter, *Theater*, 218; Grüttner, *Brandstifter*, 347.
91. "Reichskulturkammergesetz. Vom 22. September 1933," *Reichsgesetzblatt Teil I* (September 26, 1933): 661–2.
92. Steinweis, *Art*, 174.
93. Schnell, *Emigration*, 26–8; Dahm, *Buch*, 167–8; Strothmann, *Literaturpolitik*, 179–80; editor in Klepper, *Schatten*, 1; Friedländer, *Years*, 426. In 1937, Klepper had published a two-volume biography of King Friedrich Wilhelm I of Prussia (the "soldier king"), which evinced right-wing, patriarchal, views. See his *Der Vater*; Zimmermann, "Literatur," 400.
94. Kater, *Muse*, 293–4.
95. Abel, *Presselenkung*, 30; case of Dr. Kaspar Rathgeb in Frei, "Berufsgerichte," esp. 122–3, 150.
96. Minutes of broadcast planning committees are in BAK, e.g. R55/696.
97. Fröhlich, "Pressekonferenz," 347–81; Gillessen, *Posten*, 153–5; Sänger, *Politik*, 66–7, 91, 94–5, 149, 154; Frei and Schmitz, *Journalismus*, 30–1. Vollerthun's case is treated in corr. (1936), BAK, R55/223.

98. Härtwig, *Wagner-Régeny*, 43; Levi, "Opera," 156 (quote).
99. Petzet, *Theater*, 262 (Wagner quoted ibid.).
100. Mühr, *Mephisto*, 144–5.
101. Walter, *Hitler*, 175–212.
102. Paragraphs 1 and 2, "Verordnung über die Aufgaben des Reichsministeriums für Volksaufklärung und Propaganda. Vom 30. Juni 1933," *Reichsgesetzblatt Teil I* (July 5, 1933): 449.
103. Goebbels, *Tagebücher Fragmente*, vol. 2, 483; Kreimeier, *Ufa-Story*, 333; Moeller, *Filmminister*, 317–18.
104. Wetzel and Hagemann, *Zensur*, 11; Moeller, *Filmminister*, 332.
105. Goebbels, *Tagebücher Fragmente*, vol. 2, 697.
106. Wetzel and Hagemann, *Zensur*, 24; Drewniak, *Film*, 244. The wife was played by a very young Ilse Werner. Her recollection of Hitler's censorship is in *So*, 86.
107. Goebbels, *Tagebücher Fragmente*, vol. 3, 229, 499; Bucher, "Filmpropaganda," 59.
108. Benn, *Morgue*, 6.
109. Benn, in *LEMO: Lebendiges Museum Online* (quote); Hindemith, in *Oxford Music Online*; Klee, *Kulturlexikon*, 39–40.
110. Benn, *Staat*, esp. 19–20, 23, 26–9, 31–2, 34 (quote).
111. Benn, "Bekenntnis," esp. 15–16.
112. Benn, "Lebensweg," 10; Sarkowicz, "Schriftsteller," 179–81 (quote 181); Ketelsen, *Literatur*, 335–7; Schnell, *Zeiten*, 93–7; Barbian, *Literaturpolitik*, 265–6.
113. Benn's post-1935 life is described well in Petropoulos, *Artists under Hitler*, 128–36.
114. Barlach, in *LEMO: Lebendiges Museum Online*; Barlach, in *ernst-barlach-haus.de*.
115. Paret, *Artist*, 94.
116. Barlach, *Briefe*, 377, 388–9, 396–7, 433; Piper, *Barlach*, 81; Nina Burleigh, "Haunting MoMA: The Forgotten Story of 'Degenerate' Dealer Alfred Flechtheim," *The Observer Online*, February 14, 2012; *alfredflechtheim.com*; Petropoulos, *Faustian Bargain*, 221.
117. Speech of February 16, 1934, printed in Barlach, *Briefe*, 847 (n. 2); Paret, *Artist*, 80–1.
118. Barlach, *Briefe*, 454; Wilhelm Westacker in *Berliner Börsenzeitung*, February 20, 1934, cited in Piper, *Barlach*, 105–6; Blunck, *Kulturpolitik*, 27; Rosenberg, *Revolution*, 8.
119. Barlach to Willy Katz, [September 15, 1934], in Barlach, *Briefe*, 493–4; ibid., 490; Paret, *Artist*, 88–9.
120. Jan, "Barlach," 68–9, 74–5.
121. Barlach to Goebbels, May 25, 1936, in *Briefe*, 636–8; Goebbels's entry for April 4, 1936, in Goebbels, *Tagebücher Fragmente*, vol. 2, 596; Paret, *Artist*, 96–7. See also Petropoulos, *Artists under Hitler*, 6, 48.
122. Barlach, *Briefe*, 663, 713, 721–2, 783; Paret, *Artist*, 95; Barlach, in *LEMO: Lebendiges Museum Online*.
123. Lenz, *Deutschstunde*, see esp. 146–8, 280–2. See, e.g., Nolde, *Mein Leben*, esp. 393–4. Emphasizing the victim theme is Steinkamp, "Schöpfung," 297–300.
124. Nolde, in *LEMO: Lebendiges Museum Online*; Fulda and Soika, "Nolde," 191. Nolde evinced dislike of and ambivalence toward Jews in his memoirs, *Jahre* (1934), 78–79, 101–2, 119–24, 170. On the Secession, see 134, 139–50, on the French, 193–6, 210, 233.
125. Fulda and Soika, "Nolde," 187–8; Paret, *Artist*, 69 (quote); Evans, *The Coming*, 414.
126. Fulda and Soika, "Nolde," 188.
127. Fulda and Soika, "Nolde," 190, Hanfstaengl quote ibid. Ernst Hanfstaengl alleges to have been critical of Hitler's old-fashioned (and ill-informed) taste in art (Hanfstaengl, *Haus*, 70–4).
128. Fulda and Soika, "Nolde," 190, Nolde quote ibid.
129. Admiring: Weigert, *Kunst*, 100. See also Fulda and Soika, "Nolde," 190–1.
130. Hennig, "Judentum," 355.
131. Willrich, *Säuberung*, 135.
132. Steinkamp, "Schöpfung," 298; Fulda and Soika, "Nolde," 191–2.

133. Nolde, *Mein Leben*, 393–4; Nolde, in *LEMO: Lebendiges Museum Online*.
134. Fulda and Soika, "Nolde," 193–4, Ada Nolde quoted ibid.; Fulda, "Transfiguration," 179.
135. Heiber, *Goebbels*, 33–9 (quote 35); Longerich, *Goebbels*, 50, 106–7; Speer, *Erinnerungen*, 40–1; Piper, *Barlach*, 24. See Goebbels, *Michael*.
136. See the well-made argument in Potter, *Art*, 209.
137. Bruno E. Werner, "Der Aufstieg der Kunst," *Deutsche Allgemeine Zeitung*, March 3, 1933. See under Werner, in *Munzinger Archiv*, www.munzinger.de/search/portraits.
138. Alfred Rosenberg, "Revolution in der bildenden Kunst," *Völkischer Beobachter*, July 6, 1933.
139. Hippler, *Verstrickung*, 128; Merker, *Künste*, 131–3; Meckel, *Animation*, 21; Brenner, *Kunstpolitik*, 66–8.
140. Paret, *Artist*, 65.
141. Merker, *Künste*, 134; Hitler's speech in Dreyer, *Kultur*, 16.
142. Eberlein, *Was*, 37; Pinder, "Was" (2nd quote 406). On Pinder, see Klee, *Kulturlexikon*, 414–15.
143. Wendland, *Kunst*, 9; Weigert, *Kunst*, 25–6, 29, 32, 115, 119, 124, 138 (quote).
144. Bollmus, *Amt Rosenberg*, 54–60.
145. Rosenberg, *Revolution*, 13.
146. Hitler's speech at 1934 Nuremberg Party rally in *Der Kongress*, 103; Merker, *Künste*, 136.
147. On the NSKG (Nationalsozialistische Kulturgemeinde, or Nazi cultural community, which changed the KfdK into a Rosenberg-sponsored theater patronage organization, June 1934), and its move toward Ley, see Bollmus, *Amt Rosenberg*, 66–103.
148. Speech "Kunst und Kultur im Dritten Reich," printed in *Der Autor* 10, nos 5 and 6 (May and June, 1935): 11–12.
149. Scholz, "Kunstpflege," 149; Willrich, *Kunst*, 7; Gerlach, "Maler," 8–9; Rosenberg, *Gestaltung*, 333–4; Scholz, *Lebensfragen*, 53–5; Willrich, *Säuberung*, 25.
150. "Ansprache des Führers zur Eröffnung des Hauses der Deutschen Kunst," *Mitteilungsblatt der Reichskammer der bildenden Künste* (August 1, 1937): 2–7 (quote 4).
151. Brenner, *Kunstpolitik*, 73; Merker, *Künste*, 136.
152. Klee, *Kulturlexikon*, 258; Baird, *To Die*, 13–40; Evans, *The Coming*, 417–18; Johst, *Schlageter*; quote in Schoeps, *Literatur*, 126.
153. Baird, *To Die*, 108–29; Hull, *Film*, 34; Kreimeier, *Ufa-Story*, 329; Rentschler, *Ministry*, 60–2.
154. Niven, "Thing," 54; Ketelsen, *Literatur*, 65.
155. Miller Lane, *Architecture*, 191; Schlenker, "Art," 99.
156. Lehmann, "Richard der Dritte," 173–4, 176, 182. The mother of Fehling's father was Anna Emilie Oppenheimer, a daughter of Hamburg Jews (RKK Jürgen Fehling, BAB [former BDC]). Actor Bernhard Minetti, who played Buckingham, falsely maintains in his memoirs that it was Gloster, played by Gustaf Gründgens, who simulated the limp (Minetti, *Erinnerungen*, 113).
157. Steinkamp, "Schöpfung," 298; Fulda and Soika, "Nolde," 191–2; William Cook, "The Best Thing to Come Out of Davos," *The Spectator Online*, January 18, 2014; Barlach, *Briefe*, 718; Piper, *Barlach*, 153; Paret, *Artist*, 131.
158. Goebbels, *Tagebücher Fragmente*, vol. 3, 215; Peters, "Genesis," 113–14.
159. "Ansprache von Präsident Prof. Ziegler zur Eröffnung der Ausstellung 'Entartete Kunst' am 19. Juli 1937 in München," *Mitteilungsblatt der Reichskammer der bildenden Künste* (August 1, 1937): 11.
160. See Willrich, *Säuberung*. Also: Rave, *Kunstdiktatur*, 96, 98; Brenner, *Kunstpolitik*, 108; Merker, *Künste*, 143; Backes, *Hitler*, 67, 73; Peters, "Genesis," 111–12.
161. Rave, *Kunstdiktatur*, 97; Brenner, *Kunstpolitik*, 109; Merker, *Künste*, 145; Backes, *Hitler*, 74; Spotts, *Hitler*, 163.

162. *Deutsche Allgemeine Zeitung*, July 20, 1937; *Münsterischer Anzeiger*, July 22, 1937.

163. *National-Zeitung* (Gross-Essen), July 20, 1937.

164. Lüttichau, "Rekonstruktion," 120–81; Rave, *Kunstdiktatur*, 103.

165. Nolde, *Leben*, 391.

166. *Münchner Neueste Nachrichten*, August 20, 1937; Nolde, *Leben*, 391. On July 23, 1923, a 1,000-gram rye bread cost 16,000 marks in Munich; after the return to normality with the introduction of the rentenmark on October 22, 1924, it cost 0.44 marks (*Statistisches Jahrbuch*, 1924/25, 262).

167. Evans, *Third Reich in Power*, 174.

168. Backes, *Hitler*, 75; Rave, *Kunstdiktatur*, 105; Lehmann-Haupt, *Art*, 80; Merker, *Künste*, 145; Paret, *Artist*, 132; Spotts, *Hitler*, 165.

169. Werwigk, "Gemälde," 121.

170. Lott, "Staatsgalerie," 294.

171. Kardorff, *Aufzeichnungen*, 84.

172. Kaiser, *Entartete Kunst*, 1.

173. Kaiser, *Entartete Kunst*, 6, 8.

174. Kaiser, *Entartete Kunst*, 8–10.

175. Kaiser, *Entartete Kunst*, 10–12.

176. Kaiser, *Entartete Kunst*, 12–14.

177. Kaiser, *Entartete Kunst*, 14–16.

178. Kaiser, *Entartete Kunst*, 16–20.

179. Kaiser, *Entartete Kunst*, 20–2.

180. Kaiser, *Entartete Kunst*, 22–3.

181. Kaiser, *Entartete Kunst*, 24–30.

182. Kaiser, *Entartete Kunst*, 31.

183. "Ansprache von Präsident Prof. Ziegler zur Eröffnung der Ausstellung 'Entartete Kunst' am 19. Juli 1937 in München," *Mitteilungsblatt der Reichskammer der bildenden Künste* (August 1, 1937): 11; *Hamburger Tageblatt*, July 20, 1937 (quote); *Kieler Neueste Nachrichten*, July 20, 1937; *Hamburger Nachrichten*, July 20, 1937; *Münchner Neueste Nachrichten*, August 20, 1937.

184. Marks, "Black Watch," 297–334.

185. Lüttichau, "Crazy," 46 (quote); Shorter, *Dictionary*, 280.

186. *Frankfurter Zeitung*, February 27, 1938; *Der Mittag* (Düsseldorf), July 19, 1938; *Meldungen aus dem Reich*, vol. 2, 275.

187. Werwigk, "Gemälde," 122; Peters, "Genesis," 119; Boelcke, *Kriegspropaganda*, 329.

188. "Erlass des Preussischen Ministerpräsidenten Hermann Göring," *Hakenkreuzbanner*, August 4, 1937, reprinted in Piper, *Barlach*, 204. The quoted phrase in German is "ausgemerzten Gegenstände."

189. "Gesetz über Einziehung von Erzeugnissen entarteter Kunst," May 31, 1938, reprinted in Piper, *Barlach*, 209; Goebbels, *Tagebücher Fragmente*, vol. 3, 401; Lehmann-Haupt, *Art*, 81; Peters, "Genesis," 118–19.

190. Adolf Ziegler, "Entartete Kunst," April 23, 1941, *Mitteilungsblatt der Reichskammer der bildenden Künste* (May 1, 1941): 6.

191. Goebbels, *Tagebücher Fragmente*, vol. 3, 494, 547; Lehmann-Haupt, *Art*, 82–3; Schubert, *Dix*, 120–1; Backes, *Hitler*, 76–7; Spotts, *Hitler*, 167–8; Peters, "Genesis," 119; Petropoulos, *Art*, 76–83.

192. On Schumann: Daverio, *Schumann*, 197; Botstein, "Jewish Question," 445.

193. Klee, *Kulturlexikon*, 617; Dümling, "Hexensabbat," 194–8; Levi, *Music*, 95.

194. Levi, *Music*, 94 (quote); Klee, *Kulturlexikon*, 108.

195. Dümling, "Hexensabbat," 198–200.

196. Speech of February 27, 1937, in Ziegler, *Wende*, 46–7.

197. Dümling and Girth, *Entartete Musik*, 105–10; Prieberg, *Musik im NS-Staat*, 275; Schwerter, "Heerschau," 112–13; Blacher, in *Oxford Music Online*.

198. Goebbels's speech published in *Völkischer Beobachter*, May 29, 1938.
199. Frotscher, "Problem," 426.
200. Heinz Fuhrmann, "Abrechnung mit der entarteten Kunst," *Hamburger Nachrichten*, May 25, 1938; Laux, *Nachklang*, 271.
201. Laux, *Nachklang*, 271.
202. Wolfgang Steinecke, "Entartete Musik – Eröffnung der Düsseldorfer Ausstellung," *Deutsche Allgemeine Zeitung*, May 25, 1938.
203. Levi, *Music*, 95; Ziegler, *Musik*, 21.
204. Ziegler, *Musik*, 17 (quote); Moldenhauer and Moldenhauer, *Webern*, 491, 497–8, 503, 516–17, 531.
205. Schönberg, "Vorwort," in *Harmonielehre*, n.p.
206. Hindemith opposed Schoenberg's atonal conceptions, offering instead innovations within the conventional tonal system. See his *Unterweisung*, published in 1937, esp. 9–27.
207. Ziegler, *Musik*, 11, 17, 25, 31; Levi, *Music*, 95.
208. Dümling, "Target," 60; Prieberg, *Musik im NS-Staat*, 279.
209. Ziegler, *Musik*, esp. 13–16, 22, 24, 26, 29.
210. Dümling, "Hexensabbat," 204–5.
211. Prieberg, *Musik im NS-Staat*, 281.
212. As Jonathan Petropoulos has ably shown in his book *Artists under Hitler*.
213. Kater, *Weimar*, 253–4.
214. The group organizing the auto-da-fé was Deutsche Studentenschaft (DSt), the core organization of all university students in the Third Reich, to which every student belonged automatically. The group backing Expressionism and Barlach was the Nazi Student League (NSDStB), run by the Nazi Party and to be joined voluntarily.

TWO – PRE-WAR NAZI CULTURE

1. Bracher, *Dictatorship*, quotes 235–6.
2. Jäckel, *Hitlers Weltanschauung*, 60–8; idem, *Hitlers Herrschaft*, 63–5. "Volksgenosse" is generally translated as "racial comrade"; it meant all the members of the biologically defined Nazi community ("Volksgemeinschaft").
3. Mommsen, *Beamtentum*, 98, n. 26.
4. Mommsen, "Hitlers Stellung," esp. 51–4, 57, 59–60 (quote). Variants of this, describing the Rosenberg office and the SS, were presented already in 1970 and 1974, respectively, by Reinhard Bollmus (*Amt Rosenberg*, 236–50) and the present author (*Ahnenerbe*, 338–52).
5. Manfred Funke, "Ämterchaos und Weltmachtstreben: Die Debatte über Struktur und Politik des Hitler-Reiches," *Frankfurter Allgemeine Zeitung* (March 20, 1984): 25.
6. Kershaw, *Hitler Myth*, 253–64, last two quotes 253 and 257–8.
7. Kershaw, *Hubris*, 529–31 (quotes 530), 534; Kershaw, *Nemesis*, 27, 311.
8. On Gestapo denouncements, often for personal reasons, see Gellately, *Gestapo*.
9. Kershaw, *Hubris*, 530.
10. Ullrich, *Hitler*, 579.
11. This conversation took place in Munich-Schwabing, a short distance from where the Nazi Party had its institutional origins.
12. Ullrich, *Hitler*, 7. See also Pyta, *Hitler*, 235.
13. Hotter in a telephone conversation with the author, Munich, December 12, 1994; Hotter, *Mai*, 128–9. For more on the post-1919 Hitler and Richard Wagner see Alex Ross's chapter "Siegfried's Death," in his forthcoming book *Wagnerism: Art in the Shadow of Music*, to be published by Farrar, Straus and Giroux. I am indebted to the author for allowing me a preview.
14. Ullrich, *Hitler*, 388–9.
15. Hanfstaengl, *Haus*, 45.

16. Kershaw, *Hubris*, 449.
17. Hanfstaengl, *Haus*, 52–3; Ullrich, *Hitler*, 32, 176, 389–90, 395; Chapoutot, *Greeks*, 262–9; Ross, "Hitler Vortex," 66.
18. Niven, *Hitler*, esp. 9–30, 120–40.
19. Ullrich, *Hitler*, 385–6.
20. Kater, *Composers*, 253.
21. Hanfstaengl, *Haus*, 55–6; Heesters, *Sekunde*, 126; Ullrich, *Hitler*, 32, 389–90, 632; Pyta, *Hitler*, 68–9, 92.
22. Evans, *Third Reich in Power*, 209 (quote). For Bruckner as a mainstay of the symphonic canon, see Painter, *Aspirations*, 167–205.
23. See the near-overinterpretation by Werckmeister, "Hitler," 275, 278; Groys, "Kunstwerk Rasse," 36. Also not convincing: the genius cult subtext in Spotts, *Hitler*.
24. For impressions Hitler intended for posterity, see: Mann, *Tagebücher, 1937–1939*, 477; Kershaw, *Nemesis*, 213; Ullrich, *Hitler*, 726.
25. Schwarz, *Geniewahn*, 21–9; Ullrich, *Hitler*, 7, 33, 402–4; Pyta, *Hitler*, 17, 47–61, 84, 88.
26. Weinheber as observed by dramaturg Eckart von Naso, in *Leben*, 695–7; Klee, *Kulturlexikon*, 387, 588; *Weimarer Reden . . . 1938*, 55–69; Berger, *Weinheber*, 260–340.
27. See Trommler, "Command Performance," 125; Zeller, *Klassiker*, vol. 1, 155.
28. Adolf Hitler, "Verordnung über die Aufgaben des Reichsministeriums für Volksaufklärung und Propaganda. Vom 30. Juni 1933," *Reichsgesetzblatt Teil I* (July 5, 1933): 449 (quote); "Erste Verordnung zur Durchführung des Reichskulturkammergesetzes. Vom 1. November 1933," *Reichsgesetzblatt Teil I* (November 3, 1933): 797, par. 3.
29. Goebbels, *Tagebücher Diktate*, vol. 3, 213 (quote); Goebbels's RKK opening speech (November 15, 1933) in Goebbels, *Signale*, 323–36; Goebbels at the Reichs-Theaterfestwoche Hamburg, June 17, 1935, in *Deutsche Theater-Zeitung*, June 13, 1937; Münster, "Wille," 13–14. Objectively, see Koszyk, "Propaganda," 649.
30. See Evans, *Third Reich in Power*, 122–3.
31. Goebbels in an address on the Ufa film grounds in Babelsberg on April 26, 1933 (*Film-Kurier*, April 27, 1933).
32. Mosse, *Nazi Culture*, 133.
33. Goebbels touched on some of these purposes in his July 5, 1937, speech at the Berlin Krolloper, reprinted in Albrecht, *Filmpolitik*, see esp. 456–7. Also: Goebbels, "Richard Wagner und das Kunstempfinden unserer Zeit," speech of August 6, 1933; Goebbels, "Die deutsche Kultur vor neuen Aufgaben," in Goebbels, *Signale*, 191–6, 323–36; Goebbels's speech at the Reichstheaterwoche Dresden, May 27, 1934, in *Theater von A–Z*, XII e 1–XII e 4; Goebbels at Deutsches Opernhaus Berlin, November 26, 1937, in Volz, *Grossmacht*, 416–26.
34. Minetti, *Erinnerungen*, 107.
35. Goebbels (1st quote) in Hagemann, *Publizistik*, 61; Kolb and Siekmeier, *Rundfunk*, 346 (2nd quote); Traub, *Film*, 6 (3rd quote), 29; Rentschler, *Ministry*, 544–5.
36. Hanns Johst, "Das Theater und die Nation," *Der neue Weg* (April 20, 1933): 128 (1st quote); Karl August Walther, "Das Theater der Zukunft: Erneuerung deutscher Bühnenkunst," *Deutsche Bühne* 1, no. 1 (September 1933): 6 (2nd quote); Liskowsky, "Wiedergeburt," 222 (3rd quote); Nufer, "Erneuerung," 76; Nufer, "Lage," 422; Gerlach-Bernau, *Drama*, 70–2; von Trotha, "Rasse," 2.
37. Schultze-Naumburg, *Kunst*, 24–5 (quote); Engelbrecht, *Kunst*, 156; Willrich, *Säuberung*, 149–51.
38. See Scholz, *Lebensfragen*, 57.
39. Naumann in Naumann and Lüthgen, *Kampf*, 6; Johst, *Standpunkt*, 27; Kindermann, "Geschichtsbild," 556; Langenbucher, *Nationalsozialistische Dichtung*, 22–3; Möller, "Dichtung," 178.
40. As correctly outlined by Strothmann, *Literaturpolitik*, 401.
41. Ross, *Rest*, 307.

42. Herzog, "Musik," 205.
43. Goebbels speaking at the Berlin Krolloper, July 5, 1937, cited in Albrecht, *Filmpolitik*, 461.
44. Musicologist Bryan Gilliam refers to some Nazis' definition of music: "Aryan music was heroic, lofty, organic, uplifting, philosophical, and spiritual" ("Annexation," 590). On this point, see also Riethmüller, "Komposition," 268; Potter, "Music in the Third Reich," 91.
45. Goebbels's opening speech at the first Nazi broadcast exhibition in Berlin, August 18, 1933, "Der Rundfunk als achte Grossmacht," printed in Goebbels, *Signale*, 197–207; Goebbels, "Geleitwort," in Weiss, *Rundfunk*, 9–10; Hadamovsky, *Dein Rundfunk*, 72–3; Hadamovsky, *Der Rundfunk*, 13, 22.
46. Facsimiles in Varga, *Jew-Baiter*, 186–7, 190–5. See Münster, "Wille," 13; Amann, "Volkspresse," XIII, X; Dovifat, *Zeitungslehre Erster Band*, 115.
47. Gilman in *American Historical Review* 114 (2009): 230. Gilman was reviewing the monograph by Jay W. Baird, *Hitler's War Poets*, arguing Baird had missed the point. On the contrary, Baird had dealt with six of the most important writers of the Nazi era: Rudolf G. Binding, Josef Magnus Wehner, Hans Zöberlein, Edwin Erich Dwinger, Eberhard Wolfgang Möller, and Kurt Eggers.
48. Some surfaced after 1939 but was mostly war-related. See Chapter 4.
49. For prose: Volck, *Rebellen*, 263; Goote, *Fahne*, 414; Lohmann, *SA*, 184; Stelzner, *Schicksal SA*, 27; Pantel, *Befehl*, 14–15, 21; Zöberlein, *Befehl*, 448; Dwinger, *Reiter*, 54; Keller, *Nacht*, 47; Steguweit, *Sinnen*, 23; Hagen, *Tonne*, 117. For poetry: Anacker, *Reich*, 45; Burte, *Anker*, 7. Hans Carossa mentions Italian Fascists admiringly in *Geheimnisse*, 176.
50. Gerstner and Schworm, *Dichter*, 59; Pongs, *Krieg*, 8–10. Critically: Baird, *Hitler's War Poets*, 98, 119; Adam, *Lesen*, 140–3. On the genre of World War I Kriegsroman see, critically, Geissler, *Dekadenz*, 17–19; Prümm, "Erbe," 139–41.
51. Jünger, *Mobilmachung*, 34–5 (quote). See Langer, *Dichtung*, 31–2, and, critically, Loewy, *Literatur*, 169–70.
52. Salburg, *Kamerad*, 224.
53. Dwinger, *Reiter*, 118; Beumelburg, *Gruppe Bosemüller*, 71; Zerkaulen, *Hörnerklang*, 187–8; Steguweit in the poem "Soldatenbrief," *Melodie*, 46. Beumelburg's novel is discussed in detail in Busch, *Und*, 105–11.
54. Dwinger, *Reiter*, 49–50; Salburg, *Kamerad*, 194. See Loewy, *Literatur*, 171–2.
55. Theweleit, *Male Fantasies*, vol. 1, 57–8; vol. 2, 185–6.
56. Zöberlein, *Befehl*, 246–7; Dwinger, *Reiter*, 149; Volck, *Rebellen*, 51. From a Nazi-approval point of view, see Trunz, *Dichtung*, 6–7; Langenbucher, *Volkhafte Dichtung*, 533–4. Critically: Schoeps, *Literatur*, 80–3.
57. Schlageter, in *LEMO: Lebendiges Museum Online*.
58. Volck, *Rebellen*, 263; Goote, *Fahne*, 103; Dörfler, *Brücke*, 173–4; Dwinger, *Reiter*, 195–6; Schenzinger, *Anilin*, 349.
59. Stelzner, *Schicksal SA*, 15; Goote, *Fahne*, 99; Schenzinger, *Anilin*, 352. Derogatorily about "Congo Negroes": Jünger, *Mobilmachung*, 29.
60. Volck, *Rebellen*, 105.
61. Zöberlein, *Befehl*, 91. Critically on *Befehl*: Busch, *Deutschland*, 83–7. See also Steguweit, *Unrast*, 220–2, and the allegorical sketchings in Wiechert, *Totenwolf*, 233.
62. Klaehn, *Sturm 138*, 63–5.
63. Wiechert, *Leben*, 314–15; Jünger, *Mobilmachung*, 31. On Wiechert's anti-Weimar republican sentiment see Niven, "Wiechert," 14.
64. According to Zöberlein, *Befehl*, 71, 81; Klaehn, *Sturm 138*, 7–8. The writer Thor Goote's contemporary Kurt Ziesel portrayed Goote as one such victim: *Krieg*, 165–8. Goote, b. 1899, whose real name was Werner von Langsdorff, came from the low nobility. He eventually piloted a Luftwaffe plane and was shot down over the North Sea in July 1940 (Klee, *Kulturlexikon*, 173–4).
65. Hagen, *Tonne*, 82–3; Barthel, *Volk*, 143; Paust, *Menschen*, 240–1; Klaehn, *Sturm 138*, 15; Pantel, *Befehl*, 22. Critically: Stollmann, "Wege," 196, 206–10.

66. Wiechert, *Leben*, 89, 330. Critically: Niven, "Wiechert," 11–13.
67. Jünger, *Mobilmachung*, 13–14.
68. Bergengruen, *Grosstyrann*, 60, 188, 226, 237, 307.
69. According to Zimmermann, "Literatur," 400. See also the positive contemporary critique in Langer, *Dichtung*, 222.
70. For a contemporary justification of this approach, see Blunck, *Kulturpolitik*, 6–9. One current, critical, evaluation of the Nazi manipulation of Germanic myths is Johann Chapoutot's in *Law of Blood*, 32–63.
71. Jansen, *Insel Heldentum*, 187.
72. Langer, *Dichtung*, 179.
73. Best, *Dramaturgie*, 81–6, quote 82.
74. See his *Geschichten*, 18, 103.
75. Blunck, *Geiserich*, esp. 108, 163–5. See Langenbucher, *Volkhafte Dichtung*, 411–12; critically: Werbick, "Roman," 165–7.
76. Berens-Totenohl, *Femhof*, 281.
77. Contemporary interpretation in Langer, *Dichtung*, 203; Langenbucher, *Volkhafte Dichtung*, 143–4.
78. Schonauer, *Literatur*, 88–9; Schoeps, *Literatur*, 101–3; Adam, *Lesen*, 28–89.
79. Salburg, *Landflucht*, 184, 187; Griese, *Weissköpfe*, 247; Weisenborn, *Mädchen*, 22, 62; Wiechert, *Totenwolf*, 17–18; Grimm, *Lüderitzland*, 92; Gmelin, *Konradin*, 18; Carossa, *Geheimnisse*, 11, 21, 30–1. Critical commentary in: Geissler, *Dekadenz*, 17, 39–41; Schwarz, *Aufbruch*, 265; Loewy, *Literatur*, 61–2, 122; Schonauer, *Literatur*, 78–9.
80. In the shifted context of the Holocaust: Friedländer, *Kitsch und Tod*. See also Schonauer, *Literatur*, 90.
81. Curiously enough, Bauer served as professor of German literature at the University of Toronto after World War II. While a student there, I never came into contact with him.
82. Bauer, *Herz*, 98, 124, 172.
83. Jansen, *Insel Heldentum*, 376; Steguweit, *Unrast*, 170; Paust, *Nation*, 98; von Mechow, *Jahr*, 223; Carossa, *Geheimnisse*, 121; Wiechert, *Leben*, 256.
84. "Eine deutsche Mutter spricht," in Anacker, *Reich*, 50; Nierentz partially reprinted in Leuchter, "Nierentz," 196.
85. Typically murky, Nazi-conformist depictions of physical love with the emphasis on procreation are in Carossa, *Geheimnisse*, 120, and Wiechert, *Totenwolf*, 236–9. For the rare exception, love as sexual passion for its own sake, see Weisenborn, *Mädchen*, 52–3; 153–4.
86. Paust, *Nation*, 427 (quote). Also: Klaehn, *Sturm 138*, 24–43, 137–9; Volck, *Rebellen*, 248, 425; Anderlahn, *Gegner*, 60–1; von Mechow, *Jahr*, 219; Zöberlein, *Befehl*, 627; Zerkaulen, *Hörnerklang*, 43, 265, 304.
87. Griese, *Weissköpfe*, 289; Paust, *Nation*, 96; von Mechow, *Jahr*, 28; Lohmann, *SA*, 150–1.
88. Ewerbeck, *Koldewey*, 211–12.
89. Dwinger, *Reiter*, 261.
90. Griese, *Weissköpfe*, 273.
91. As if in anticipation of this: Bauer, *Herz*, 68, 273; Frenssen, *Vorland*, 177–8; Weller, *Rabauken*, 286–7, 321.
92. Gypsies (there was no attempt at distinction between Roma, Sinti, and Lalleri) were treated mostly as thieves and, if female, promiscuous temptresses: Molzahn, *Nymphen*, 23–4, 152; Berens-Totenohl, *Femhof*, 91, 110–11; Tremel-Eggert, *Schmied*, 67, 76. See Schonauer, *Literatur*, 91.
93. Zöberlein, *Befehl*, 333, 338 (quote); Hagen, *Tonne*, 44–5, 165; Salburg, *Kamerad*, 211.
94. Blome, *Arzt*, 23–5; Salomon, *Die Geächteten*, 32; Hutten, *Kulturbolschewismus*, 12–15, 29, 82–91.

95. Grimm, *Volk*; *Lüderitzland*, esp. 101, 152–3; Johst, *Maske*, 196–7. Approvingly and recommending other writings from Grimm's pen: Pongs, *Krieg*, 72; Langenbucher, *Volkhafte Dichtung*, 458–64. A critical view of the German colonial treatment of the Hereros and Nama as the first genocide of the twentieth century is in Christoph Schult and Christoph Titz, "Herero und Nama verklagen Deutschland," *SpiegelOnline*, January 6, 2017.

96. Dwinger, *Gott*, 13, 23, 45, 89–91, 94–5, 103; Barthel, *Volk*, 11–12, 22, 26.

97. See Rothacker, *Dorf*, 18, 40, 85, 108; Zillich, "Dichtung," 1,192.

98. Schenzinger, *Anilin*, 69, 77, 208, 213, 335. Critically, see Adam, *Lesen*, 87–92.

99. Hohlbaum, *König Volk*; Jansen, *Insel Heldentum*, 208; Johst, *Standpunkt*, 8–9.

100. Wiechert, *Leben*, 259–60.

101. Von Mechow, *Jahr*, 79 (quote); Weller, *Rabauken*, 183.

102. Vesper, *Geschichten*, 102.

103. Wiechert, *Totenwolf*, 119.

104. Peters, "Werk," 5. See, e.g., Wiechert, *Leben*, 53, 137.

105. Vesper, *Geschichten*, 104; Stelzner, *Schicksal SA*, 13; Tremel-Eggert, *Barb*, 274.

106. Bauer, *Herz*, 124, 139 146; von Mechow, *Jahr*, 14, 53; Salburg, *Landflucht*, 78–9; Lange, *Weide*, 211; Tremel-Eggert, *Barb*, 333; Weller, *Rabauken*, 63; Wiechert, "Brief," 176; Hagen, *Tonne*, 91.

107. Wiechert, *Leben*, 239, 319.

108. Dörfler, *Brücke*, 36, 96, 105; Lersch, *Pioniere*, 94; Faust, *Maurer*, 85. See Langenbucher, *Volkhafte Dichtung*, 262–3, 268–9.

109. Steguweit, *Melodie*, 47.

110. Darré, an agronomist with shaky job prospects, met Hitler through his friend Himmler and the Artaman settlers' youth movement, becoming Reich Minister for Food and Agriculture in June 1933 (Wistrich, *Who's Who*, 45–6).

111. Entry for August 26, 1937 in Goebbels, *Tagebücher Fragmente*, vol. 3, 249.

112. Varied sample evidence is in: Wiechert, *Totenwolf*, 10; Keller, *Nacht*, 95; Salburg, *Landflucht*, 12; Lersch, *Pioniere*, 35; Griese, *Gesicht*, 316; Böhme, *Kirchgang*, 18, 22, 50, 71–2; Vesper, *Geschichten*, 103; and the poems by Steguweit, "Deutschland," in Echtermeyer, *Auswahl*, 719–20, and "Bauer," in Steguweit, *Melodie*, 33. Affirmatively then: Pongs, *Krieg*, 68–71. Critically now: Trommler, "Command Performance," 120.

113. Nierentz, "Flieg, deutsche Fahne, flieg!," in Echtermeyer, *Auswahl*, 722–3.

114. Blunck, *Plettenberg*, 40–1, 48–9, 77, 272–3. Affirmatively then: Langer, *Dichtung*, 157; Langenbucher, *Volkhafte Dichtung*, 413. Critically now: Werbick, "Roman," 168–71.

115. Sieburg, in www.deutsche-biographie.de/sfz121633.html#ndbcontent; Klee, *Kultur lexikon*, 511–12.

116. Sieburg, *Deutschland*, 140, 157, 208, 217, 268 (quote).

117. Sieburg, *Portugal*, 24, 111–12, 179–82.

118. Leupold, *Neuordnung*, 11; Abel, *Presselenkung*, 38–40; Grüttner, *Brandstifter*, 315.

119. Sänger, *Politik*, 95.

120. Grüttner, *Brandstifter*, 313; Ullrich, *Hitler*, 685.

121. Sänger, *Politik*, 224–5.

122. Sänger, *Politik*, 254 (first three quotes); entry for November 14, 1938, in Goebbels, *Tagebücher Fragmente*, vol. 3, 534.

123. See the book by Gillessen, *Posten*, which makes that point but on the whole is far too apologetic.

124. Klee, *Kulturlexikon*, 433, 532.

125. See the critical remarks regarding FZ by Bernd Sösemann, "Zwischen Distanz und Anpassung," *Die Zeit*, March 6, 1987. Also Evans, *Third Reich in Power*, 141–3.

126. See, e.g., the Nazi-conformist review by Margret Boveri, "Versailles nach 15 Jahren," *Berliner Tageblatt*, January 6, 1935; Bermann Fischer, *Bedroht*, 116; Haffner, *Defying*, 153–4. Not least for apologist purposes, post-1945 Boveri describes typical Nazi pressure tactics against the *Berliner Tageblatt* in *Wir lügen alle*, 538–71.

127. *Deutsche Allgemeine Zeitung*, July 20, 1937.
128. "Die deutschen Truppen sind in Oesterreich einmarschiert," *Frankfurter Zeitung*, March 13, 1938. Hitler's proclamation is printed ibid.
129. "Die Zeitgenossen," *Frankfurter Zeitung*, April 20, 1939.
130. Reto Caratsch, "Die letzten zehn Jahre der 'Frankfurter Zeitung'," *Neue Zürcher Zeitung*, January 19, 1947.
131. Lindemann, "Heimat," 31, 43–4, 47.
132. Frei, *Eroberung*, 136–313; Hale, *Press*, 102–273.
133. Facsimiles of journals in Lehmann, *Gestaltung*, 203, 213, 223, 225 (quote).
134. Hale, *Press*, 15–38; Mühlberger, introductions and subsequent English-language excerpts from VB in *Hitler's Voice*, vols 1 and 2.
135. Münster, *Zeitung*, 89; Dennis, *Inhumanities*, e.g. 127–285.
136. Eksteins, *Limits*, 85.
137. No post-1933 treatment of the paper could be found. It did not change its character after 1933. For its origins, see Münster, *Zeitung*, 94 (quote); Eksteins, *Limits*, 85; Lemmons, *Goebbels*, 21–42.
138. Heiber and Kotze, *Querschnitt*; Grunberger, *Reich*, 63.
139. "K.Z. und seine Insassen," *Das Schwarze Korps*, February 13, 1936.
140. Kolb and Siekmeier, *Rundfunk*, 76 (quote); Hagemann, *Publizistik*, 47; Frei and Schmitz, *Journalismus*, 83–4. The stations were Deutschlandsender (long-wave), Deutscher Kurzwellensender (short-wave), and nine Reichssender: Berlin, Breslau, Cologne, Frankfurt, Hamburg, Königsberg, Leipzig, Munich, and Stuttgart. Saarbrücken was opened in 1935 (Drechsler, *Funktion*, 37).
141. Diary entry for February 11, 1933, in Ebermayer, *Deutschland*, 21–2.
142. Hadamovsky, *Dein Rundfunk*, 119, 122; Weiss, *Rundfunk*, 147–8; Hagemann, *Publizistik*, 45; Ullrich, *Hitler*, 539. Figures from Eckert, *Rundfunk*, 38. Still, in April 1937 a stonemason from Liegnitz, Silesia, at 76 pfennigs an hour, had to work more than 100 hours before taxes, to afford a VE (*Statistisches Jahrbuch ... 1938*, 341). Around that time, a used small Opel P4 motorcar cost ca. 500 marks (Hagen, *Auftrag*, 143).
143. Kater, *Drummers*, 46–7.
144. Entry for April 23, 1937, in Goebbels, *Tagebücher Fragmente*, vol. 3, 121.
145. Hadamovsky, *Dein Rundfunk*, 76; Eckert, *Rundfunk*, 99, 130–2, 179, 242–5; Kater, *Drummers*, 47; Grüttner, *Brandstifter*, 321.
146. Hadamovsky, *Dein Rundfunk*, 75–7; Drechsler, *Funktion*, 36–8, 58–61, 70–1, 74, 79–80, 86–7; Klingler, "Rundfunkpolitik," 44; Frei and Schmitz, *Journalismus*, 85–6.
147. My previous research shows that the percentage of the educated elite class compared with all the other classes joining the Nazi Party declined gradually, from 1933 until 1938, when it rose again (Figure 2 in Kater, *Nazi Party*, 264).
148. Kater, *Drummers*, 48; Frei and Schmitz, *Journalismus*, 86. For an anti-jazz hardliner see Heinrich Glasmeier cited in "Die Programmgestaltung des Rundfunks: Vorträge von Dr. Glasmeier und Dr. Kriegler," *Frankfurter Zeitung*, August 10, 1938.
149. Goebbels, *Tagebücher Fragmente*, vol. 2, 545; Klingler, "Rundfunkpolitik," 45; Koch, *Wunschkonzert*, 58. Goebbels's conviction is paraphrased in Eckert, *Rundfunk*, 247.
150. Entry for June 25, 1938, in Goebbels, *Tagebücher Fragmente*, vol. 3, 465. Radio Munich's program for January 25, 1938, is in Fischer, *Dramaturgie*, 174–5.
151. Münster, *Publizistik*, 85–6.
152. Klingler, "Rundfunkpolitik," 47; Drechsler, *Funktion*, 42.
153. Kracauer, *Caligari*, 275.
154. Carter, *Ghosts*, 92; Lehnich, *Jahrbuch*, 168–9.
155. Rentschler, *Ministry*, 13.
156. Rentschler, *Ministry*, 216; Moeller, *Filmminister*, 153.
157. Bathrick, "State," 295.

158. See, among many, Ullrich in *Schaukel*, who married a count (Wulf Dietrich zu Castell-Rüdenhausen), whose sister Alexandra Hedwig was married to Friedrich Christian Prinz zu Schaumburg-Lippe, of the Promi and later Ribbentrop's Foreign Ministry (213). See also Niven, *Hitler*, 121–40; Klee, *Kulturlexikon*, 468, 563; Stockhorst, *Köpfe*, 375 and the last chapter of this book.

159. Klee, *Kulturlexikon*, 160–1.

160. "S.A.-Mann Brand," *Völkischer Beobachter*, June 16, 1933; Kalbus, *Werden*, 119–20; Moeller, *Filmminister*, 158–9; Tegel, *Nazis*, 53–6.

161. Schenzinger, *Hitlerjunge Quex*.

162. Baird, *To Die*, 108–29; "Hitlerjunge Quex: Die Welturaufführung in München," *Reichsfilmblatt*, September 16, 1933; Kalbus, *Werden*, 122–3; Rentschler, *Ministry*, 54–9, 67–9; Schulte-Sasse, *Entertaining*, 258–68; Tegel, *Nazis*, 57–62; Hoffmann, *Fahne*, 59–63.

163. With respect to this film see the contemporary remarks in Eckert, "Filmtendenz," 23.

164. Funk, *Film*, 104.

165. Kriegk, *Film*, 243.

166. "S.A.-Mann Brand," *Völkischer Beobachter*, June 16, 1933 (1st quote); Goebbels's mixed feelings in Goebbels, *Tagebücher Fragmente*, vol. 2, 433–4. A Party objection to the showing of *SA-Mann Brand* in Frankfurt is mentioned in Rabenalt, *Goebbels*, 40–1, and Tegel, *Nazis*, 55–6.

167. Kalbus, *Werden*, 119–20 (quote; the original German is "Konjunkturkitsch").

168. Goebbels in a Berlin speech on May 19, 1933, reprinted in Albrecht, *Filmpolitik*, 442.

169. Goebbels, *Tagebücher Fragmente*, vol. 2, 552.

170. For the press, see Ewald von Demandowsky, "Das grösste Filmwerk, das wir je gesehen haben," *Der Filmbeobachter (Beilage zum VB)*, March 30, 1935; Rudolf Kircher, "'Triumph des Willens'," *Frankfurter Zeitung*, March 30, 1935; also Kriegk, *Film*, 216–17.

171. On the purge aspect, see Volker, "*Von oben*," 50–1; Tegel, *Nazis*, 77. An early appreciation of the film as art *and* propaganda is in Welch, *Propaganda*, 147–59. See the more current appraisal in Niven, *Hitler*, 71–84.

172. See Vaget, "Nazi Cinema," 36–43.

173. Susan Sontag, "Fascinating Fascism," *The New York Review of Books*, February 6, 1975, www.nybooks.come.ezproxy.library.

174. See Kriegk, *Film*, 218; Welch, *Propaganda*, 112–18; Tegel, *Nazis*, 97; Niven, *Hitler*, 84–94.

175. Hull, *Film*, 115–17; Welch, *Propaganda*, 159–63; Kreimeier, *Ufa-Story*, 306–7; Moeller, *Filmminister*, 173. The actor Will Quadflieg recounts witnessing the charismatic Jannings smashing glass furniture before the filming of a particularly violent scene, to get into the proper mood (*Spielen*, 224–5).

176. That it was a forced comparison was the immediate impression of the British critics. See *Monthly Film Bulletin* (1937): 151. Similarly on the German side: Jasser, "Film," 232.

177. Goebbels, *Tagebücher Fragmente*, vol. 3, 76, 79.

178. Krützen, *Albers*, 237–8; Rentschler, *Ministry*, 76.

179. Kriegk, *Film*, 212 (quote); Welch, *Propaganda*, 242–6; Rentschler, *Ministry*, 76. Hitler saw his Crimean settlement plans temporarily thwarted after Stalin had deported the Volga Germans to Siberia and Kazakhstan in the fall of 1941 (Kershaw, *Nemesis*, 401–3; Pyta, *Hitler*, 372).

180. Kriegk, *Film*, 242.

181. Riefenstahl attempted to make the film *Tiefland* with herself as lead character, but was bogged down by financial and logistical difficulties beginning in 1938 and through the war, so that the movie was completed only in 1954, to moderate acclaim. See Petropoulos, *Artists under Hitler*, 251–7; Klee, *Kulturlexikon*, 440–1.

182. Rentschler, *Ministry*, 125–6, 131–4, 139–41; Nadar, "Director," 72–5; Lowry, *Pathos*, 212.

183. Ascheid, *Heroines*, 186–94; Drewniak, *Film*, 500–1. On the alleged superiority of Bach and inferiority of the U.S.A. see Riethmüller, "Leander," 163, 174–5.

184. Hake, *Cinema*, 198.

185. Heins, *Melodrama*, 79–80.

186. Ascheid, *Heroines*, 143–52.

187. Rosenberg, *Tagebücher*, 267.

188. Von Schramm, *Neubau*, 96. Unemployment among the gainfully employable was at 19.9 percent for all of 1932. At 16.3 percent artists in "theater, music, etc." were below but close to that level. The highest rate was among domestic servants at 99.2, the lowest among mine workers at 0.3 percent (figures in Horkenbach, *Reich*, 507). By 1937, the Reich unemployment rate had been reduced to 5.87 percent, with "theater, music, etc." at zero (figures in *Statistisches Jahrbuch . . . 1938*, 371, 377).

189. Schoeps, *Literatur*, 123; "Erste Reichstheatertagung der HJ," *Der Autor* (April/May 1937): 15; Zander and Willimczik, *Reichstheatertage*.

190. Rischbieter, *Theater*, 225–6.

191. The Deutsches Theater was led by Heinz Hilpert, the Schiller-Theater by Heinrich George, the Deutsche Volksbühne by Eugen Klöpfer, and the Preussisches Staatstheater by Gustaf Gründgens. The first three came under the Promi, the last under Göring. In Munich, the Prinzregententheater (under Promi) was singled out and after March 1938, in Vienna, the Burgtheater (under Promi). See Rischbieter, *Theater*, 227. On Göring's patronage see "Ministerpräsident Goering [sic]: Die Rede an die Theater-Intendanten," *Film-Kurier*, September 13, 1933.

192. Baranowski, *Strength*, 58. See also Robert Ley's speech of November 27, 1935, in Ley, *Deutschland*, 103–4; Dressler-Andress, *Jahre*, 11 (with, likely, inflated figures); Guthmann, *Kunst*, 30. On Rosenberg, see Brenner, *Kunstpolitik*, 90; Dussel, *Theater*, 102–3. KdF = Kraft durch Freude.

193. Corr. Lampel and Schlösser (May 1934) published in Wardetzky, *Theaterpolitik*, 280–1; Herbert A. Frenzel, "Nationalpolitische Tat auf der Bühne," *Hamburger Tageblatt*, October 22, 1935; Walter Gättke, "Hier irrt Herr Bunje!," *Hamburger Tageblatt*, July 20, 1937; von Naso, *Leben*, 618; Drewniak, *Theater*, 212; Schoeps, *Literatur*, 123.

194. On Party theater personnel: Denk, "Zukunftsschau," 448; Drewniak, *Theater*, 217.

195. Ebermayer, *Deutschland*, 241.

196. Nowak, *Bauer*, 9–10, 26, 39–40; Wischmann, *Vogt*, esp. 52; Ahlers, *Sturm*, 14, 16, 34, 40–1, 51, 54–5, here positively the Nazi critic Wanderscheck, *Dramatik*, 251.

197. Zerkaulen, *Jugend*, 32–3, 36, 42, 70, critically Schoeps, *Literatur*, 129–31; Dwinger, *Namenlosen*, 16–17, 83–6; Steguweit, *Petermann*, 9, 11, 21–2.

198. Blachetta, *Kampf*, 25–7, 38–9, 46–7; Felix Lützkendorf, "Vom 'Opfergang' zum 'Alpenzug,'" *Hamburger Tageblatt*, October 22, 1935; Billinger, *Gigant*, 9, 17, 25, 53.

199. Diebenow, *Nacht*, 20–2, 25; Billinger, *Lob*, 38, 40.

200. Huth, *Gesellen*, esp. 80–1, 10, see Wanderscheck's approving comments: *Dramatik*, 269–70; Steguweit, *Baron*; Hinrichs, *Petermann*, 8, 16, 38, 40, 42, 68, 75, 81.

201. E.g. Billinger, *Lob*, 38, 40.

202. See fourteen insipid-looking titles of the Braunschweiger-Bühnen-Verlag Albert Limbach, Berlin, in *Deutsche Theater-Zeitung*, September 14, 1939.

203. Fitz Mack, "Das Stück des Reichsministers Joseph Goebbels," *Leipziger Neueste Nachrichten*, May 16, 1933.

204. Eckart, in *LMO: Lebendiges Museum Online*; "Aus der Arbeit eines Ortsverbandes," *Deutsche Bühnen-Korrespondenz* 4, no. 5 (January 19, 1935): 4; Dresler, "Eckart," 22; Drewniak, *Theater*, 216.

205. Helmuth Merzdorf, "Dichtung aus nordischem Geist," *Hamburger Tageblatt*, October 22, 1935; "Deutsches Volkstheater . . . Plumpudding," ibid.; Alexander Funkenberg,

"Thilo von Trotha," in Zander and Willimczik, *Reichstheatertage*, n.p. (quote); Klee, *Kulturlexikon*, 558.

206. Johst, *Schlageter*, 26; Pfanner, *Johst*, e.g. 243.

207. Johst, *Paine*; Ketelsen, *Theater*, 69; Michalzik, *Gründgens*, 99–100; *Jürgen Fehling*, 144–5; Goebbels's positive reaction (November 1935) in Goebbels, *Tagebücher Fragmente*, vol. 2, 541.

208. See Johst, *Standpunkt* and *Maske*; Johst's three poems in Böhme, *Rufe*, 101, 304, 348. Positively historicizing Johst: Horn, "Johst," 87, 91–2, 105–8, 112; Wanderscheck, *Dramatik*, 54–5, 93–5, 100; Langenbucher, *Volkhafte Dichtung*, 554–9.

209. Hermann Wanderscheck, "Das Theater als Idee," *Deutsche Theater-Zeitung*, no. 84 (July 25, 1937); Baird, *Hitler's War Poets*, 66–95.

210. Paul Kersten quoted in "Gerhard Schumann als Dramatiker," *Deutsche Theater-Zeitung*, no. 8 (January 18, 1939).

211. Möller, *Untergang*, esp. 15, 17, 32, 37, 49, 65, 71, 105–6, 118–19; Frenzel, "Möller," 141, 157–8, 168; Baird, *Hitler's War Poets*, 165–207; Klee, *Kulturlexikon*, 373, 500–1. On the Nazi characterization of Carthage, during the Punic Wars (264–146 BC), as Jewish see Chapoutot, *Greeks*, 293–8.

212. Menz, "Sprechchor," 332, 338; Kater, *Weimar*, 120–4.

213. Stang, *Grundlagen*, 38; Rischbieter, *Theater*, 219.

214. "'Flamme des Volkes'," *Deutsche Bühnenkorrespondenz* 4, no. 42 (May 29, 1935): 2; Kurt Heynicke, "Erfahrung und Meinung," *Der neue Weg* 12 (August 15, 1935): 350; von Schramm, *Neubau*, 46, 48, 51, 65; Schlösser, *Volk*, 57; *Theater von A–Z*, XI c 5; Braumüller, "Heynicke," 3. See the critical analysis by Niven, "Thing," esp. 56–61, and 67–8 on audience integration.

215. Rischbieter, *Theater*, 219; Brenner, *Kunstpolitik*, 103; Niven, "Thing," 55.

216. Goebbels's praise: *Tagebücher Fragmente*, vol. 2, 600, 654.

217. Wanderscheck, *Dramatik*, 33, 121–2; Petersen, *Geschichtsdrama*, 53–5; Baird, *Hitler's War Poets*, 180–3; Menz, "Sprechchor," 340–1; Rischbieter, *Theater*, 224.

218. Menz, "Sprechchor," 339–40; Rischbieter, *Theater*, 222, 225; Niven, "Thing," 62–7.

219. Goebbels, *Tagebücher Fragmente*, vol. 2, 626; Kühn, "Thingspiel," 459–63; Schlösser, *Volk*, 54–5; Stang, *Grundlagen*, 37–8; Krug, "Erziehung," 456–62; Emmel, *Theater*, 23–4.

220. The quoted phrase is William Niven's: "Thing," 76. See Schlösser, *Volk*, 56; Brenner, *Kunstpolitik*, 106; Rischbieter, *Theater*, 220.

221. "Die Kunst im öffentlichen Leben," *Münchener Zeitung*, June 18, 1935.

222. Minetti, *Erinnerungen*, 107. See also text above at n. 34.

223. Goebbels, *Tagebücher Fragmente*, vol. 2, 748; Ledebur, "Shakespeare," 1–12.

224. Kenter, "Regieführung," 744; Künkler, "Probleme," 199–200; Ketelsen, *Theater*, 129–30.

225. Dussel, *Theater*, 280–5; Gadberry, "Dresden," 129–30. On the significance of Schiller for the Nazis (until 1941) see Zeller, *Klassiker*, vol. 1, esp. 164–227, 403–36; Kater, *Weimar*, 243–5. On Goethe: Kater, *Weimar*, 239–41.

226. Playlists: Willi Glindemann, in Werkhäuser, *150 Jahre*, 91 (Koblenz, performed Hauptmann); *Berliner Zeitung am Mittag*, March 11, 1939 (Berlin); Gadberry, "Dresden," 129 (Dresden Reich Theater Week, 1934); *Deutsche Theater-Zeitung*, January 17, 1937 (Weimar, performed Halbe).

227. Rosenberg, *Tagebücher*, July 1936, 185; Goebbels cited in *Amtliche Mitteilungen der Reichsmusikkammer* 5, no. 11 (June 4, 1938).

228. Pohle, *Rundfunk*, 322–3; Stege, "Jazzkapelle," 251; *Das Deutsche Podium* (November 8, 1935): 3, (November 14, 1935): 1,280, (January 24, 1936): 4, (February 7, 1936): 1–2, (February 14, 1936): 3, (March 20, 1936): 3, (April 3, 1936): 1–2; *Der Artist*, (August 28, 1935): 961, (November 14, 1935): 1,279, (February 6, 1936): 129, (February 13, 1936): 156, (February 20, 1936): 189, (February 26, 1936): 228, (March 5, 1936): 244, (March 19, 1936): 304–5, (June 4, 1936): 651–52.

229. Joost-Hinkel corr. (1936), RKK Oskar Joost, BAB (former BDC); *Das Deutsche Podium* (February 28, 1936): 5, (May 26, 1936): 7; Diller, *Rundfunkpolitik*, 198.

230. Wilhelm Hartseil, "Rassestimmen und Hörerbriefe zur Sendereihe 'Rundfunkball des Reichssenders Leipzig' (Neue Wege zum Deutschen Tanzstil)," ms., BAK, Library, Rundfunk, esp. 1, 3, 5–6, 10–15, 18, 24, 35, 79, 102, 123; *Unterhaltungsmusik* (January 6, 1938): 4.

231. *Unterhaltungsmusik* (April 14, 1938): 451, (August 11, 1938): 1,054–5; *Musik in Jugend und Volk* 2 (1939): 33.

232. Ramin, in *Oxford Music Online*; Kater, *Muse*, 175–6; Klee, *Kulturlexikon*, 428–9.

233. Ehlert to Esser, April 4, 1934, BH, MWi/2817; corr. in RKK Li Stadelmann, BAB (former BDC) (quote Stadelmann to Hinkel, August 3, 1933); SMK, 275 and 97/5; Klee, *Kulturlexikon*, 523.

234. Lemnitz, in *Oxford Music Online*; Klee, *Kulturlexikon*, 327–8 (with different career dates).

235. Ivogün and Raucheisen, in *Oxford Music Online*; Klee, *Kulturlexikon*, 251, 430–1.

236. In 1943–4, Schwarzkopf was treated for TB in a sanatorium in the Tatra Mountains. Physician Jury was a TB specialist. See Kater, *Muse*, 61–3, 260 n. 140; Schwarzkopf, in *Oxford Music Online*; Klee, *Kulturlexikon*, 503.

237. Klee, *Kulturlexikon*, 203; Kater, *Muse*, 15, 17, 23–4.

238. Heger, in *Oxford Music Online* (quote); Heger to Lotte Lehmann, July 9, 1933, ATW/15; Laux, *Nachklang*, 244–5; Klee, *Kulturlexikon*, 206; Niessen, "Schauplatz," 136.

239. Hüsch, in *Oxford Music Online*; Klee, *Kulturlexikon*, 246, 474; Berthold Goldschmidt in Csipak, "Goldschmidt," 61; *Die Musik* 26 (1934): 363 (quote).

240. Ney to Robert Ley, July 15, 1943, EB/26 (1st quote); Ney, in *Oxford Music Online* (2nd quote); Klee, *Kulturlexikon*, 391; Kater, *Muse*, 31–3.

241. Distler, in *Oxford Music Online*; Klee, *Kulturlexikon*, 102; quotes in Fischer, "Kirchenmusik," 204, 231.

242. David, in *Oxford Music Online*; Klee, *Kulturlexikon*, 95; Kater, *Muse*, 166–7.

243. Pepping, *Stilwende*, 79–81 (quote); Pepping, in *Oxford Music Online*; Kater, *Muse*, 165–6.

244. Fortner, in *Oxford Music Online*; Klee, *Kulturlexikon*, 144.

245. The German original of "race defilement" is "Rassenschande." Quotes from the contemporary *Deutsche Theaterzeitung* as cited by Klee, *Kulturlexikon*, 577. See also Wagner-Régeny, in *Oxford Music Online*; Honegger and Massenkeil, *Lexikon*, vol. 8, 325–6.

246. Egk as quoted by Anton Würz in *Zeitschrift für Musik* 108 (1941), 725; *National-Zeitung* (Essen), August 18, 1936; Schmitz, "Oper," 382; Egk, in *Oxford Music Online*; Kater, *Composers*, 3–21. Ridicule of Egk was expressed by Hans Bergese (to Orff, March 16, 1938, CM, Allg. Korr.), and Karl Amadeus Hartmann (Elisabeth Hartmann, recorded interview with author, December 13, 1994, YUA, CA ON00370 F0456).

247. Taruskin's quotes: (1) Taruskin, "Carl Orff" in *Oxford Music Online*; (2) author's minutes of panel discussion at symposium, "The Politics of Music: Orff, Weill and Brecht," co-produced by New York City Opera and Works and Process at the Guggenheim Museum, New York, March 16, 1997 (APA).

248. Schmitz, "Oper," 382; Levi, "Opera," 153; Taruskin, "Carl Orff," in *Oxford Music Online*.

249. Aster, *Orchestra*, 120–1, 154.

250. Steinweis, *Art*, 42–9; Piper, *Barlach*, 92.

251. "Tätigkeitsbericht des Präsidenten der Reichskulturkammer, Dr. Goebbels," *Völkischer Beobachter*, November 28, 1936.

252. "10 Jahre NS.-Sinfonieorchester," *Die Musik* 34, no. 4 (1942): 151.

253. Bresgen, and Stürmer, in *Oxford Music Online*; Klee, *Kulturlexikon*, 55, 71; Kater, *Muse*, 71–2, 143–6; Kurt Heynicke, "Erfahrung und Meinung," *Der neue Weg* (August 15, 1935): 350; Riethmüller, "Komposition," 243.
254. Muschler, "Film," 7; Wähler, "Kampflied," 154–6.
255. *Tägliche Rundschau*, May 11, 1933; *Amtliche Mitteilungen der Reichsmusikkammer* 6, no. 4 (February 15, 1939): 9.
256. "Hohe Nacht der klaren Sterne . . . ," in Baumann, *Kamerad*, 68–9.
257. I have this on the authority of my wife, Barbara Kater, née Streit, who experienced this many times in family circles.
258. See Chapter 1 at n. 197.
259. Killer, "Graener," 150; Schmitz, "Geburtstag," 1–3.
260. Graener, in *Oxford Music Online* (quote); Levi, "Opera," 148; Klee, *Kulturlexikon*, 176. In translation, the operas are *"Don Juan's Last Adventure"* and *"Hannele's Ascension"* (after Hauptmann).
261. Matthes, "Trapp," 1,074–5, 1,078–9; Trapp, in *Oxford Music Online*; Honegger and Massenkeil, *Lexikon*, vol. 8, 161.
262. Matthes, "Trapp," 1,078; Büttner, "Reichsmusiktage," 739–40; Trapp, in *Oxford Music Online*; Klee, *Kulturlexikon*, 556.
263. Büttner, "Reichsmusiktage," 738; Riethmüller, "Stefan Zweig," 269 (quote), 273; Steinweis, *Art*, 42–9; Piper, *Barlach*, 92.
264. Martin, *New Order*, 78.
265. Sachs, *Music*, 21–2.
266. Fischer, "Fate," 80 (quote), 85–6. More on Pfitzner in the war in Chapter 4.
267. Walter, *Strauss*, 355–95; Fischer, "Fate," 82–8.
268. Honegger and Massenkeil, *Lexikon*, vol. 6, 260–1, vol. 8, 23–5.
269. Kater, *Muse*, 7–12. For the crucial case of Berlin see Potter, "Berlin Philharmonic," 39–55; Potter, "Musical Life," 93–8.
270. Figures according to Baranowski, *Strength*, 58. See also Ley, *Deutschland*, 107; Dressler-Andress, *Jahre*, 10.
271. Potter, "Musical Life," 97.
272. Hitler, in Linz, was seven when Bruckner died in 1896. See Binding in *Sechs Bekenntnisse*, 19 (quote); Liskowsky, "Wiedergeburt," 222; Herzog, "Musik," 201–3; "Bachfest des Reiches," *Münchener Zeitung*, June 18, 1935; Laux, *Bruckner*, 90–1; Riethmüller, "Bestimmung," 28–69; Ross, *Rest*, 314–16, 335; Dümling, "Michel," 202–14. On Binding's pro-Nazism see Baird, *Hitler's War Poets*, 32–65.
273. Levi, *Music*, 192–3; Drewniak, *Theater*, 328–30; Aster, *Orchestra*, 155; Reinhold, "Repräsentation," 41–2; Dussel, *Theater*, 215.
274. "Wochenspielplan der Berliner Theater," *Berliner Zeitung am Mittag*, March 11, 1939; Werkhäuser, *150 Jahre*, 90.
275. Adorno in March 1945, in *Schriften*, 416. Quote is from Alex Ross's chapter "Prelude: Death in Venice," in his forthcoming book *Wagnerism* (see n. 13 above).
276. Herzog, "Musik," 201, 204; "Zum Abschluss: Festaufführung im Deutschen Opernhaus," *Völkischer Beobachter*, November 28, 1936; Hamann, *Wagner*, 236; Reinhold, "Repräsentation," 42; Werr, *Weltsicht*, 195–7.
277. Vaget, *Erbe*, 457; Hamann, *Wagner*, 231–399; Spotts, *Bayreuth*, 161–88.
278. Collection in BS, Ana/306; Bormann to Kähler, July 4, 1933, ibid.; Rasch to Promi, April 24, 1935, BAK, R55/1177; Goebbels, *Tagebücher Fragmente*, vol. 3, 491; Prieberg, *Musik und Macht*, 180.
279. Reproductions in Schorer, *Kunstbetrachtung*, 145; Schlenker, "Art," 95 (see also 99); Merker, *Künste*, 261. On Erler (1868–1940) and Knirr (1862–1944), see Klee, *Kulturlexikon*, 126, 287–8.
280. The painting is reproduced in Merker, *Künste*, 262. On Hoyer (1893–1968) see Schlenker, "Art," 99–100; Klee, *Kulturlexikon*, 243.

281. See Merker, *Künste*, 260; Hackel, "Annäherungen," 76–7; *Grosse Deutsche Kunstausstellung*, plate 55. Also Adam, *Art*, 105, 171, 224.

282. Frontispiece "Der Führer," charcoal drawing by H. Oloffs after a photograph by Hitler's personal photographer Heinrich Hoffmann, in Mantau-Sadila, *Deutsche Führer*. See also ibid., 202–407.

283. See painting in Adam, *Art*, 18. A regime-beholden description read: "Führer as knight in silver-white armour on horseback, with a fluttering flag in hand" (Bruno E. Werner, "Erster Gang durch die Kunstausstellung," *Deutsche Allgemeine Zeitung*, July 20, 1937). On Lanzinger (1880–1950) see Klee, *Kulturlexikon*, 320.

284. Reproductions in Adam, *Art*, 73, 173; *Kölnische Volkszeitung*, July 22, 1937.

285. See the photograph of Breker, bust-in-progress, and Speer in Adam, *Art*, 197. Also the finished bust in Hackel, "Annäherungen," 76.

286. Images in *Grosse Deutsche Kunstausstellung*, plate 4; Adam, *Art*, 97; Gritzbach, *Göring*, frontispiece opposite title page and plate opposite 192.

287. Reproduced by Petropoulos in *Artists under Hitler*, 19. See also *Grosse Deutsche Kunstausstellung*, plates 5, 56, 57. Wilhelm Otto Pitthan (1896–1967) painted Goebbels in 1938: www.google.ca/search?q=wilhelm+otto+pitthan. The portrait was reproduced during the war: Hans Hartmann, "Das politische Portrait: Wilhelm Otto Pitthan, ein Maler deutscher Staatsmänner," *Das Reich*, January 30, 1944. Max Brüning (1887–1968) published an original etching of a pensive Goebbels in Kalbus, *Werden*, 102.

288. Werner Rittich, "Maler der Kampfzeit und des Krieges," *Völkischer Beobachter*, August 15, 1941; images in Backes, *Hitler*, 79, and Adam, *Art*, 99. On Eber (1892–1941) see Klee, *Kulturlexikon*, 111–12.

289. www.renegadetribune.com/artwork-german-hardship-soldierly-struggle-franz-eichh orst/#&gid=psgal_48164_1&pid=1.

290. Wühr, "Graphik," 165; Merker, *Künste*, 264; Adam, *Art*, 65. Biography of Sluyterman (1903–78) is in Klee, *Kulturlexikon*, 516.

291. Wühr, "Graphik," 164.

292. *Kalauer Bauernfamilie*, purchased by Hitler 1939 (Backes, *Hitler*, 80). See also Schorer, *Kunstbetrachtung*, 172, 180. For Wissel (1894–1973) and Gradl (1883–1964) see Klee, *Kulturlexikon*, 175–6, 605.

293. *Hochgebirge*, in Backes, *Hitler*, 94.

294. Adam, *Art*, 119, 284.

295. Spotts, *Hitler*, plates near 139, and drawings 52, 394.

296. Ross, "Hitler Vortex," 69.

297. Hitler, "Die Ansprache des Führers zur Eröffnung des Hauses der Deutschen Kunst," *Mitteilungsblatt der Reichskammer der bildenden Künste* (August 1, 1937): 4; Hitler's speech at the Grosse Deutsche Kunstausstellung 1938, in Hinz, *Malerei*, 176; Hitler's speech in "Der Führer," 34–5; Hitler utterings in Jochmann, *Hitler*, 387, 398; Lehmann-Haupt, *Art*, 89–91; Merker, *Künste*, 163; Backes, *Hitler*, 90; Schlenker, "Art," 98–9.

298. "Die Begabung des Einzelnen – Fundament für Alle," *Hakenkreuzbanner*, June 10, 1938; reproduction in Schorer, *Kunstbetrachtung*, 175; Petsch, "Malerei," 268 (quote); Klee, *Kulturlexikon*, 409; Adam, *Art*, 101, 166–7; Spotts, *Hitler*, 176, 178. "Realism" may suggest contemporary motifs only, but Peiner (1897–1984) painted in all genres.

299. See Willrich's *Kind aus Schaumburg-Lippe*, in Hansen, "Willrich," 337. Programmatically, Robert Böttcher reproduced Dürer's *Bildnis meiner Mutter* in *Kunst*, 27. See also Sluyterman von Langeweyde's linoleum cut *In einem kühlen Grunde*, in Lehmann-Haupt, *Art*, 95. See Weise, "Aussprache," 405–7. Willi Münch-Khe's *Der Bodenseefischer Leopold Wenck* is of the Peiner school (reproduction in Merker, *Künste*, 252). On Hans Thoma see Julia Voss, "Der gefallene Meister der deutschen Kunst," July 2, 2013, www. faz.net, and his contemporary portrait by Hans Adolf Bühler reproduced in Clinefelter, *Artists*, 63.

300. Linfert, "Sichtbar vor Augen," *Frankfurter Zeitung*, September 29, 1936.
301. Werner, "Erster Gang durch die Kunstausstellung," *Deutsche Allgemeine Zeitung*, July 20, 1937.
302. Schindler, "Blut und Boden," 370.
303. Reproductions, including Baumgartner's *Bäuerliches Mittagsmahl*, in: Wühr, "Graphik," 168; Willrich, *Säuberung*, 152; Schorer, *Kunstbetrachtung*, 179; Damus, "Gebrauch," 98; Merker, *Künste*, 242–3, 251, 274. See also Hinz, *Malerei*, 76–7, 109; Meckel, *Animation*, 44, 70–2.
304. Hermand, "Tümlichkeiten," 108; Schirmbeck, "NS-Kunst," 72; Merker, *Künste*, 280–83.
305. See *Am Massinger See* (*At the Massing Lake*) by Hermann Mayerhofer of Passau, in Schindler, "Blut und Boden," 372, and the commentary in Petsch, *Malerei*, 253.
306. Veronika Wulf, "Einmal 'Weidende Kühe' für Adolf Hitler," *Sueddeutsche.de*, March 12, 2017; Klee, *Kulturlexikon*, 523; Engelbrecht, *Kunst*, 102; Merker, *Künste*, 250; Petsch, *Malerei*, 261; Adam, *Art*, 132.
307. For the first type see Wissel, *Bäuerin* (*Peasant Woman*), in Schorer, *Kunstbetrachtung*, 180, and Hans A. Bühler's *Heimkehr* (*Homecoming*), in Merker, *Künste*, 243. For reference, Böttcher reproduced Leibl's *Drei Frauen in der Kirche* (*Three Women in Church*), in *Kunst*, 17. The connection between Bühler and Thoma is made in "Hans Adolf Bühler, ein Maler deutscher Weltanschauung," *Deutsche Kultur-Wacht* 3 (1933): 13. Bühler's own portrait of his teacher Thoma is reproduced in Clinefelter, *Artists*, 63. Dürer's *Mother* is shown in Böttcher, *Kunst*, 27.
308. Cissarz, *Mütterlichkeit* (*Motherliness*), in Merker, *Künste*, 273; Willrich, *Meine Frau* (*My Wife*), in Hansen, "Willrich," 335; Diebitsch, *Mutter und Kind* (*Mother and Child*), in Schorer, *Kunstbetrachtung*, 181.
309. In Adam, *Art*, 147. See also Karl Schlageter's *End of the Day*, ibid., and Bühler's *Heimkehr*, as in n. 307.
310. Reproductions in Adam, *Art*, 64, 223. Earlier an Impressionist, Liebermann (1869–1960) was no relative of the Jewish painter Max Liebermann. See Klee, *Kulturlexikon*, 331–2.
311. Reproduction in Adam, *Art*, 154. See also Klee, *Kulturlexikon*, 404. For earlier exemplars, see those by Giambettino Cignaroli (1706–70) and Henri Matisse (1869–1954).
312. Exemplary: Frenssen, *Vorland*, 71–2, 136–7.
313. Willrich, *Säuberung*, 157.
314. Reproductions in Adam, *Art*, 15, 191, 194; Merker, *Künste*, 271–2.
315. Stephanie Barron's introduction in Einzig et al., *Sculpture*, 13–28; Kaiser, *Führer*, 19; Heftrig, "Modernism," 273; www.bpb.de/politik/hintergrund-aktuell/141166/vor-75-jahren-ausstellung-entartete-kunst-18-07-2012.
316. Damus, "Gebrauch," 110; Lehmann-Haupt, *Art*, 103.
317. Thorak, in www.meaus.com/josef-thorakenglish.htm; reproductions in Merker, *Künste*, 248–9, 266; Adam, *Art*, 194–6.
318. Lehmann-Haupt, *Art*, 98.
319. www.germanartgallery.eu/m/Webshop/0/product/info/Arno_Breker,Kameraden&id=31 (quote); Breker in *LEMU: Lebendiges Museum Online*; Lehmann-Haupt, *Art*, 97–100; Petropoulos, "Seduction," 205–29; and the reproductions in Petsch, "Malerei," 266, and Adam, *Art*, 8, 14–15, 198–204.
320. See Merker, *Künste*, 297; Lehmann-Haupt, *Art*, 100; Petsch, "Malerei," 263–74.
321. Miller Lane, *Architecture*, 188.
322. Miller Lane, *Architecture*, 192–3 (1st quote); Speer, "Vorwort," 10–11 (2nd quote); Lotz, "Reichsparteitagsgelände," 264–8; Hager, "Bauwerke," 11–12; Thies, *Plans*, 87–9; Merker, *Künste*, 220–4.
323. Kitchen, *Speer*, 31–3; Hitler's motto in Brenner, *Kunstpolitik*, 124; Dresler, *Braune Haus*, 10; Rasp, *Stadt*, 21, 27–8; Chapoutot, *Greeks*, 88–9. Hitler's Graecomania is

documented in his public speeches: see, for 1933, Hitler in Dreyer, *Kultur*, 13–15, and for 1935 in Hinz, *Malerei*, 142–3. Perforce, Rosenberg, who, like Himmler, was a Germanocentric at heart, paid lip service to this in *Revolution*, 10.

324. Adam, *Art*, 252.

325. Hitler quoted in Miller Lane, *Architecture*, 189.

326. In 1938 Kaspar (1904–86) was appointed professor of monumental painting in Munich. Photographs and text in Adam, *Art*, 252–9 (Hitler quoted 254); Speer, "Vorwort," 12–13; Klee, *Kulturlexikon*, 269.

327. Spotts, *Hitler*, 311–85; Kater, *Weimar*, 221–3.

328. Pfeiffer, "Jagdhaus," 19–24; "Nationalsozialistische Baukunst," *Mitteilungsblatt der Reichskammer der bildenden Künste* 4, no. 9 (September 1, 1939): 1; Miller Lane, *Architecture*, 196–208, 215; Damus, "Gebrauch," 116–20; Schäche, *Architektur*, 67–9; Kitchen, *Speer*, 34. Schultze-Naumburg reiterated his well-known views in *Kunst*, 42–4.

329. Werkhäuser, *150 Jahre*, 71 (1st quote); Steguweit, *Sinnen*, 118 (2nd quote).

330. Adorno, *Schriften*, 424.

331. Rosenberg in July 1933 speech, printed in Rosenberg, *Ein Kampf*, 250.

332. Goebbels, *Tagebücher Fragmente*, vol. 3, 167; Backes, *Hitler*, 61, 79–82; Spotts, *Hitler*, 172.

333. *Meldungen aus dem Reich*, vol. 2, 276.

334. Goebbels, *Tagebücher Fragmente*, vol. 2, 722.

335. *Meldungen aus dem Reich*, vol. 2, 116; Lehnich, *Jahrbuch*, 117; Eckert, "Filmtendenz," 25.

336. Lindemann, "Heimat," 35 (quote), 36.

337. Emmel, *Theater*, 23–4.

338. Dorsch to Ebermayer, March 11, 1938, printed in Ebermayer, . . . *und morgen*, 248.

339. Stang, "Nationalsozialismus," 389. See also Billerbeck-Gentz, "Ausschaltung," 10; von Trotha, "Rasse," 2; Schlösser, *Volk*, 54–5.

340. Langenbucher, *Nationalsozialistische Dichtung*, 40. Critically today: Andersch, *Literatur*, 7–8; Geissler, *Dekadenz*, 8–9; Strothmann, *Literaturpolitik*, 10, 391, 394.

341. Goebbels, *Tagebücher Fragmente*, vol. 3, 465–6 (quote).

342. Herzog, "Musik," 203; Ziegler, *Wende*, 13; Schmitz, "Oper," 381–2. Also Vogelsang, *Filmmusik*, 12; Werr, *Weltsicht*, 157.

343. Bade, *Aufgaben*, 16; Haupt, *Dichtung*, 20; Weigert, *Kunst*, 118; Stang, "Weltanschauung," 196; Stang, "Nationalsozialismus," 389; Langenbucher, *Nationalsozialistische Dichtung*, 28; Eckert, *Rundfunk*, 131. Critically: Tegel, *Nazis*, 73.

344. Goebbels, *Tagebücher Fragmente*, vol. 2, 432, 556, 620, 751; vol. 3, 272, 320; Weigert, *Kunst*, 117; Merzdorf, "Romane," 373–4; Ziegler, *Wende*, 13. Critically: Boeschenstein, *Novel*, 3.

345. Bade, *Aufgaben*, 18.

346. Drewniak, *Theater*, 211; Wardetzky, *Theaterpolitik*, 77.

347. Schinköth, "Leistung," 66. Carl Orff had been commissioned after a similar invitation by Frankfurt's lord mayor, the SS officer Fritz Krebs.

348. Brenner, *Kunstpolitik*, 106.

349. Meckel, *Animation*, 86; Fröhlich, "Pressekonferenz," 374–6.

350. *Mitteilungsblatt der Reichskammer der bildenden Künste* 4 (September 1, 1939): 3, 5.

351. Rosenberg in *Völkischer Beobachter*, January 1, 1935; Hans Weigert, "Kunst und Staat," *Deutsche Allgemeine Zeitung*, July 18, 1937.

352. Goebbels, *Tagebücher Fragmente*, vol. 3, 327.

353. *Meldungen aus dem Reich*, vol. 2, 117; Hagemann, *Publizistik*, 65; Wardetzky, *Theaterpolitik*, 77.

354. Goebbels quoted in Klee, *Kulturlexikon*, 331.

355. *Deutsche Filmakademie*, 4, 19–21, 89. The police curriculum is detailed in Browning, *Ordinary Men*, 177.

356. *Meldungen aus dem Reich*, vol. 2, 116.

357. Slansky, *Filmhochschulen*, 162–4.
358. Quote in Petropoulos, *Artists under Hitler*, 42.
359. Kater, *Muse*, 43–6.
360. Hitler in Jochmann, *Hitler*, 214; Bollmus, *Amt Rosenberg*, 153–234; Kater, *Ahnenerbe*, 139–44; Chapoutot, *Greeks*, 7, 30, 69–77.
361. Kershaw supplies examples of this in *Nemesis*, e.g. 462, 469, 514, 576–7, 580–1, 622–3, 688, 838.
362. Katja Iken, "Von Hitler verehrt, von Goebbels kaltgestellt," www.spiegel.de/einestages/henny-porten-erster-deutscher-star-der-ufa-a-1182894.html.

THREE – JEWS IN THE NAZI CULTURAL ESTABLISHMENT

1. Browning, *Origins*, 5.
2. Goldhagen, *Executioners*, 77 (quote); Friedländer, *Nazi Germany*, 107.
3. Menz, *Aufbau*, 2–5 (1st two quotes 4); Stang, "Weltanschauung," 197 (3rd quote); Münster, *Zeitung*, 143–4; Spieker, *Hollywood*, 64; Niewyk, "Cultural Role," 172. Among Jewish painters, one could also mention Otto Freundlich and Felix Nussbaum, both of whom perished in the Holocaust (on Freundlich, see below; for Nussbaum, see Milton, "Culture," 89–95).
4. Steinweis, "Anti-Semitism," 20; Friedländer, *Nazi Germany*, 108. See also Müller-Wesemann, *Theater*, 23–5; Hoeres, *Kultur*, 81; Winkler, "Gesellschaft," 276–7; Niewyk, "Cultural Role," 167–8. Peter Gay pioneered the thesis of the Weimar German Jews as creatively most potent outsiders, in his classic *Weimar Culture*, but later distanced himself from it (see Friedländer, *Nazi Germany*, 107).
5. Peter Heyworth and John Lucas in *Oxford Music Online* (1st quote); Eric Ryding and Rebecca Pechefsky, ibid. (2nd quote). See also Niewyk, "Cultural Role," 169–72; Müller-Wesemann, *Theater*, 22; Du Closel, *Stimmen*, 288; Fox-Gál, *Musik*, XII; Grüttner, *Brandstifter*, 143; Deák, *Weltbühne*, 13–61.
6. Kracauer, *Caligari*, 97, 101–2.
7. Laqueur, *Weimar*, 176.
8. Heilmann, *Jessner*, 402–3, 412; Feinberg, "Leopold Jessner," 114–28; Strobl, *Swastika*, 16–17; Klee, *Kulturlexikon*, 256.
9. Hitler quoted in Jäckel, *Hitlers Herrschaft*, 89; Pyta, *Hitler*, 143–5. In the wake of this pioneering literature, including Thomas Weber's own *Hitler's First War*, portraying a Hitler in World War I without Jew hatred, Weber is correct in referring, in his 2017 Hitler biography, to Hitler's "anti-Semitic conversion" during 1919 (*Becoming Hitler*, 58). See also Longerich, *Hitler*, 68–70.
10. The Vogls' quotes from Pyta, *Hitler*, 160.
11. Hitler, *Mein Kampf*, 772.
12. Hitler, *Mein Kampf*, 332 (quote), 345.
13. Ullrich, *Hitler*, 230–1.
14. Pamphlet cited in Müller-Wesemann, *Theater*, 30.
15. Bruckmann cited in Martynkewicz, *Salon Deutschland*, 426.
16. Vesper, *Wer? Wen?*, 102, 112.
17. Strasser's speech printed in Rosenberg and Weiss, *Reichsparteitag*, 11–13 (quote 11).
18. Streicher's speech printed in Rosenberg and Weiss, *Reichsparteitag*, 9–11; his lists, such as the aggregate one of Jews in Prussia [1930], are at NAW, Captured German Records, T-580/267. I owe my knowledge of these documents to Marc Romanych, of Digital History Archive.
19. Grosse Anfrage, sign. Gieseler et al., December 12, 1928, Sitzungsprotokoll des Preussischen Landtages, quoted in Heilmann, *Jessner*, 395.
20. Müller-Wesemann, *Theater*, 31–2; Kater, *Weimar*, 205–10.
21. Friedländer, *Nazi Germany*, 109; Steinweis, "Conservatism," 343.

22. Langenbucher to Ernst, July 21, 1931, printed in Bähre, "Langenbucher," 254–5.
23. Von Ambesser, *Nimm*, 84.
24. Dagover, *Dame*, 205.
25. Johst, *Maske*, 31.
26. Friedländer, *Nazi Germany*, 12.
27. "Gesetz zur Wiederherstellung des Berufsbeamtentums. Vom 7. April 1933," *Reichsgesetzblatt Teil I* (April 7, 1933): 175–7; "Erste Verordnung zur Durchführung des Gesetzes . . .," *Reichsgesetzblatt Teil I* (April 11, 1933): 195; "Zweite Verordnung zur Durchführung des Gesetzes . . ." *Reichsgesetzblatt Teil I* (May 4, 1933): 233–5; Friedländer, *Nazi Germany*, 27. A German-Jewish reaction playing down the issue is in "Zur Kündigung jüdischer Arbeitnehmer," *C.V.-Zeitung*, May 11, 1933.
28. For their anti-Jewish stipulations, see Hagemann, *Publizistik*, 36; Brechtken, "Experiment," 65; Barbian, *Literaturpolitik*, 193–202; Friedländer, *Nazi Germany*, 328; Steinweis, *Art*, 103–20.
29. Friedländer, *Nazi Germany*, 62.
30. Horak, *Fluchtpunkt*, 7–9; Beyer, *UFA*, 24; Krützen, *Albers*, 149; Tegel, *Nazis*, 73.
31. Hamann, *Wagner*, 273; Werr, *Weltsicht*, 190.
32. Potter, "Berlin Philharmonic," 48; Aster, *Orchestra*, 45–50.
33. See Brenner, *Ende*, esp. 136–7.
34. Teut, *Architektur*, 70; Lauzemis, "Ideologie," 62–3.
35. Erich Kämpfer, "Bei Ullstein nichts verändert," *Deutsche Kultur-Wacht*, no. 12 (1933): 14; de Mendelssohn, *Zeitungsstadt*, 362–3, 380–2; Barbian, *Literaturpolitik*, 53–4.
36. "Reichsbürgergesetz. Vom 15. September 1935," *Reichsgesetzblatt Teil I* (September 15, 1935): 1,146–99.
37. König, *Germanistenlexikon*, vol. 1, 18–21.
38. Kater, *Composers*, 142.
39. Friedländer, *Nazi Germany*, 142.
40. Fröhlich divorced Gitta Alpar in 1935, and Rühmann Maria Bernheim in 1938: Klee, *Kulturlexikon*, 150–1, 456.
41. Klee, *Kulturlexikon*, 16, 326.
42. See "K.Z. und seine Insassen," *Das Schwarze Korps* (February 13, 1936): 10.
43. Friedländer, *Nazi Germany*, 151.
44. Friedländer, *Nazi Germany*, 62; Longerich, *Davon*, 94–5; Grüttner, *Brandstifter*, 148–60.
45. Fascimile of advertisement (1937) in London, "Introduction," 13.
46. See Goebbels, *Tagebücher Fragmente*, vol. 3, 346. The quintessential text on the fate of those Jews throughout the Third Reich is the diary of Victor Klemperer, *Tagebücher, 1933–1945*.
47. Friedländer, *Nazi Germany*, 241.
48. Zweig, *Welt von Gestern*, 367; Berkley, *Vienna*, 259–60; Goldhagen, *Executioners*, 286–7.
49. Goebbels, *Tagebücher Fragmente*, vol. 3, 463.
50. Doherty, *Hollywood*, 302–10.
51. Longerich, *Goebbels*, 393–9; Longerich, *Davon*, 137; Kogon, *SS-Staat*, 209; Kershaw, *Nemesis*, 141; protocol of author's interview with Dr. Otto Jung, Bad Rüdesheim, June 1988, YUA, CA ON00370 F0456.
52. Friedländer, *Nazi Germany*, 285; Sänger, *Politik*, 255; Hamann, *Wagner*, 380; Föllmer, *Leben*, 160; Peter Carstens, "Wo sind die Autos, die Nazis den Juden geraubt haben?" *faz.net*, April 15, 2017.
53. Jürgen Matthäus in Browning, *Origins*, 369.
54. Friedländer, *Nazi Germany*, 285; Koch, *Wunschkonzert*, 146; Grüttner, *Brandstifter*, 160.
55. Reichstag speech of January 30, 1939, as quoted by Friedländer, *Nazi Germany*, 310.
56. Freytag-Loringhoven's interview with *Wiener Neueste Nachrichten* as paraphrased by *Berliner Lokal-Anzeiger* and reprinted in the German-Jewish *Central-Verein-Zeitung*, May 11, 1933.

57. Freeden, *Theater*, 14–16, 19; *Zündende Lieder*, 31–2; Dahm, "Leben," 85–6, 90. Hinkel's vita is in Klee, *Kulturlexikon*, 225–6 (quote).
58. "Aufruf," [1935], LBI, AR-A726/2590; *Jüdische Rundschau*, August 20, 1935; Freeden, *Theater*, 25, 59; Dahm, "Leben," 93, 105, 120; Düwell, "Kulturbund Rhein-Ruhr," 428; Steinweis, *Art*, 121.
59. *Jüdische Rundschau*, July 21, 1936 (quote); *Israelitisches Familienblatt*, Berlin, October 26, 1933; *Schild*, June 12, 1936.
60. Freeden, *Theater*, 22–3, 94; Dahm, "Leben," 87, 89; Walk, *Sonderrecht*, 221; Rosy Geiger-Kullmann, "Lebenserinnerungen," ms., February 1961, LBI, ME/180; Friedländer, *Nazi Germany*, 66.
61. Goebbels paraphrased by Freeden, *Theater*, 61; *Israelitisches Familienblatt*, Berlin, August 1, 1935; *Zündende Lieder*, 36.
62. Gestapo, "Richtlinien für die Tätigkeit des Reichsverbandes der Jüdischen Kulturbünde in Deutschland," August 13, 1934, LBI, AR-A726/2590/63+64; Freeden, *Theater*, 52.
63. Hinkel in *Frankfurter Zeitung*, May 13, 1937; personal files of Wilhelm Guttmann, Erich Rosenow, and Hugo Stern, BAB (former BDC); Dahm, "Leben," 109; Steinweis, *Art*, 122.
64. Herbert F. Peyser, "Germany's Jewish Culture League," *The New York Times*, December 10, 1933.
65. Singer to Berlin Gestapo, September 7, 1934; Gestapo to Kulturbund, September 11, 1934, LBI, AR-C1210/3100; Dahm, "Leben," 114; Steinweis, *Art*, 122.
66. *Hamburger Fremdenblatt*, February 6, 1936; communication by Jüdischer Kulturbund Hamburg, March 10, 1936, LBI, AR-A727/2591; Jüdischer Kulturbund Hamburg, program, November 6, 1939, LBI, AR-A728/2592; Steinweis, *Art*, 123.
67. *Hamburger Israelitisches Familienblatt*, May 21, 1936; Kulturbund Hamburg to "Sehr geehrtes Mitglied," March 1937, LBI, AR-A728/2592; Freeden, *Theater*, 92–3, 104; Dahm, "Leben," 120.
68. Freeden, *Theater*, 160, 163–4; Dahm, "Leben," 245–6, 251, 257; Dahm, *Buch*, 151–3; *Zündende Lieder*, 40.
69. Müller-Wesemann, *Theater*, 179–80.
70. Müller-Wesemann, *Theater*, 181–2, 187–9.
71. Levi, *Mozart*, 91.
72. On the latter, see Brenner, *Renaissance*, 129–211.
73. Molnár, in www.yivoencyclopedia.org/article.aspx; Geisel and Broder, *Premiere*, 16–28, 72, 150–1; Rovit, "Collaboration," 145–6; Rovit, "Jewish Theatre," 198–201; Müller-Wesemann, *Theater*, 190, 213–18.
74. Dahm, "Leben," 121–2.
75. See Rosenstock's obituary by Dena Kleiman in *The New York Times*, October 18, 1985; *Israelitisches Familienblatt*, Berlin, November 2, 1933; *Jüdisches Gemeindeblatt für Berlin*, February 13, 1938; Fischer-Defoy, *Kunst*, 156.
76. "Abend Frankfurter Komponisten," January 27, 1934, LBI, AR-A7049/13; Rosy Geiger-Kullmann, "Lebenserinnerungen," ms., February 1961, LBI, ME/180.
77. Sinzheimer to Orff, January 20, 1934, CM, Allg. Korr.; Dahm, "Leben," 94.
78. Traber and Weingarten, *Musik*, 291, 305, 308, 341, 344; "Jüdischer Kulturbund Hamburg: Abschieds-Abend," November 25, 1936, LBI, AR-A727/2591; *Jüdisches Nachrichtenblatt*, May 2, 1941; *Jüdisches Gemeindeblatt für Berlin*, April 12, 1936; Weiss to Misch, January 3, 1965, LBI, AR-C738/2073. On Misch, see *Oxford Music Online*.
79. *Israelitisches Familienblatt*, Berlin, March 8 and April 19, 1934; *Jüdisches Gemeindeblatt für Berlin*, November 17, 1935, May 3, 1936, May 2, 1937, October 24, 1937, January 16, 1938; "Gastspiel Alexander Kipnis," Düsseldorf, February 9, 1937, LBI, AR-A835/3047; "Alexander Kipnis," Hamburg, February 10, 1937, LBI, AR-A728/2592; "Stuttgarter Jüdische Kunstgemeinschaft," October 15, 1938, LBI, AR-A7276/IV/2/15; Pâris, *Lexikon*, 373–4.

80. *Jüdisches Gemeindeblatt für Berlin*, April 4, 1937; Stefan Wulf in Heister et al., *Musik im Exil*, 154.

81. *Schild*, April 24, 1936; *Jüdisches Gemeindeblatt für Berlin*, May 3, 1936; Flesch to Herr Doktor, July 5, 1936, LBI, AR-7049/2 (quote).

82. *Israelitisches Familienblatt*, Berlin, January 11 and September 13, 1934; *Schild*, October 30, 1936; *Jüdisches Gemeindeblatt für Berlin*, July 12, 1936; Berlin Künstlerhilfe to Kowalski, April 14, 1935, LBI, AR-A7049/4; Jüdischer Kulturbund Hamburg to subscribers, [May 1936], LBI, AR-A727/2591.

83. *Israelitisches Familienblatt*, Berlin, October 26, 1933; "Konzert" at Dr. Meyer's, February 10, 1935, LBI, AR-A7049/13; "Stimmen im Tempel," August 30, 1938, LBI, AR-A7040/13; Freeden, *Theater*, 74, 123, 126. On Schoenberg, see Schoenberg quoted in Tonietti, "Albert Einstein," 1; on Handel see Rosenberg, *Gestaltung*, 281 and Hirsch, "Defining," 35.

84. Hinkel quoted in *Frankfurter Zeitung*, May 13, 1937; Hirsch, "Defining," 29; Freeden, *Theater*, 162; Dahm, "Leben," 115; Müller-Wesemann, *Theater*, 327; Steinweis, *Art*, 122.

85. *Schild*, April 12, 1935; *Jüdisches Gemeindeblatt für Berlin*, September 22, 1934, May 19, 1935, and June 16, 1937; "Konzert," January 31, 1935, LBI, AR-A726/2529; "Klavierabend Bernhard Abramowitsch," November 20, 1935, LBI, AR-A726/2590; Berlin Kulturbund program, March 1934, LBI, AR-A834/3046; Maurer Zenck, "Itor Kahn," 241.

86. *Jüdisches Gemeindeblatt für Berlin*, January 5, 1935, and April 28, 1936; *Schild*, June 28, 1935; "Abend Frankfurter Komponisten," January 27, 1934, LBI, AR-A7049/13; program, "Jüdischer Kulturbund Hamburg," December 1935, LBI, AR-A726/2590; "Konzert Tempelchor," February 1938, LBI, AR-A729/2593; Prieberg, "Davidsstern," 124.

87. *Schild*, November 26, 1933 and April 12, 1935; *Israelitisches Gemeindeblatt*, Berlin, November 23, 1933; Dahm, "Leben," 191.

88. Craft, *Stravinsky*, 243, n. 42 (quote); Dahm, "Leben," 114; Evans, "Rezeption," 91–93, 104, 106–7.

89. *Schild*, October 27, 1933; *Israelitisches Familienblatt*, Berlin, September 13, 1934; *Jüdisches Gemeindeblatt für Berlin*, March 27, 1938; Freeden, *Theater*, 75.

90. "Jüdischer Kulturbund Hamburg," November 12, 1935, LBI, AR-A726/2590; Freeden, *Theater*, 101; *Zündende Lieder*, 33, 37; Dahm, "Leben," 93.

91. Freeden, *Theater*, 102–3 (calculations according to figures, 114).

92. Dahm, "Leben," 242, 247, 255; Prieberg, "Davidsstern," 126.

93. Müller-Wesemann, *Theater*, 192; Rovit, "Collaboration," 15; www.joodsmonument.nl/en/page/546495/0; Klee, *Kulturlexikon*, 514.

94. Herzog, "Musik," 202.

95. Quote from Drüner and Günther, *Musik*, 55.

96. Wähler, "Kampflied," 152.

97. Guthmann, *Kunst*, 44.

98. Muschler, "Vollerthun," 991; Ziegler, *Wende*, 8 (quote).

99. Frickhoeffer, "Musik," 246.

100. Goebbels in *Amtliche Mitteilungen der Reichsmusikkammer* 5, no. 11 (June 4, 1938); Menz, *Aufbau*, 4; Novak, *Salzburg*, 169.

101. Hiemer, *Pudelmopsdackelpinscher*, 11 (quote), 35–42.

102. Goebbels, *Tagebücher Diktate*, vol. 8, 386.

103. Sontheimer, *Denken*, 180–239. For a nuanced discussion of the DNVP's anti-Semitism see Jones, "Antisemitism," esp. 96–7.

104. On Niemöller, the Confessing Church, and Jews, see Conway, *Persecution*, 202–13; Goldhagen, *Executioners*, 108–9, 111–12; Gutteridge, *Mouth*, 91–2, 100–4, 129–30, 287–90.

105. Ernst Jünger emerges as one of the rare high-level (conservative to Nazi) authors who not only was not an anti-Semite, but someone who mostly rejected anti-Semitism. Others would have included, reputedly, Arthur Möller van den Bruck and Oswald Spengler.

106. Goote, *Fahne*, 280; Salburg, *Kamerad*, 74–6.

107. Frenssen, *Recht*, 7–8; Frenssen, *Vorland*, 218; Goote, *Fahne*, 197; Weller, *Rabauken*, 13; Johst, *Schlageter*, 35; Salburg, *Tag*, 41–2; Zöberlein, *Befehl*, 24, 28, 92, 334–5; Steguweit, *Unrast*, 256; Strauss, *Lebenstanz*, 182; Paust, *Menschen*, 170. See also Wanderscheck, *Dramatik*, 111, who comments on Möller's "Karthago" as a Semitized Weimar Republic.

108. Lohmann, *SA*, 136; Keller, *Nacht*, 45; Salburg, *Landflucht*, 211–13.

109. Dwinger, *Reiter*, 76; Volck, *Rebellen*, 95.

110. Goote, *Fahne*, 256, 268; Koeppen, *Erbe*, 138–9; Jansen, *Insel Heldentum*, 216; Anderlahn, *Gegner*, 36–40; von Mechow, *Jahr*, 108–10; Böhme, *Kirchgang*, 93; Lersch, *Pioniere*, 27.

111. Volck, *Rebellen*, 340; Stelzner, *Schicksal SA*, 160; Roth, *Kampf*, 229–31; Pantel, *Befehl*, 32–3, 98–102.

112. Dwinger, *Gott*, 55; Dwinger, *Tod*, 115; Slesina, *Soldaten*, 127–8, 305–6; Brehm, "Kampf," 46; Strobl, *Dorf*, 61, 91.

113. Koeppen, *Gnade*, 41 (quotes), 137.

114. Dinter, *Sünde*. See Kater, *Weimar*, 199.

115. Weller, *Rabauken*, 18, 57, 63.

116. Paust, *Nation*, 294–5.

117. Zöberlein, *Befehl*, 313.

118. Jansen, *Kinder*, 61.

119. Salburg, *Landflucht*, 128–9.

120. Lorenz, *Unrast*, 119.

121. Slesina, *Soldaten*, 128; Strobl, *Dorf*, 295–6.

122. Paust, *Menschen*, 47–8.

123. Zöberlein, *Befehl*, 297–9.

124. Weller, *Rabauken*, esp. 149.

125. Bie and Mühr, *Kulturwaffen*, 35; Stelzner, *Schicksal SA*, 18; Zöberlein, *Befehl*, 512; reflectively Langenbucher, *Nationalsozialistische Dichtung*, 37.

126. Niven, *Hitler*, 165–7.

127. Busch, *Und*, 155.

128. Jürgen Petersen, "Die Rothschilds: Ein Film der neuen deutschen Produktion," *Das Reich*, July 21, 1940. See also the less prolific review by Hans Kraemer, "'Die Rothschilds': Im Ufa-Palast am Zoo," *Berliner Lokal-Anzeiger*, July 18, 1940.

129. Rentschler, *Ministry*, 153; Tegel, *Nazis*, 129; Hollstein, *Jud Süss*, 115; Busch, *Und*, 155; Longerich, *Davon*, 155.

130. Niven, *Hitler*, 167–8; Moeller, *Filmminister*, 243–4; Klee, *Kulturlexikon*, 355–6; Harlan, *Schatten*, 89–95, 100–30; von Cziffra, *Luftballon*, 296–8; Hippler, *Verstrickung*, 199.

131. *Jud Süss*, BAK, FILMSG 1/8336 II. See Niven, *Hitler*, 168–71.

132. Carl Linfert, "'Jud Süss': Der Film von Veit Harlan," *Frankfurter Zeitung*, September 26, 1940.

133. Karl Korn, "Der Hofjude: Veit Harlans-Film 'Jud Süss' im Ufa-Palast am Zoo," *Das Reich*, September 29, 1940.

134. Goebbels, *Tagebücher Fragmente*, vol. 3, 666; vol. 4, 286 (quote), 339.

135. *Meldungen aus dem Reich*, vol. 6, 1,811–12; Culbert, "Impact," 147.

136. *Jud Süss*, BAK, FILMSG 1/8336 II.

137. Courtade and Cadars, *Geschichte*, 187; Rentschler, *Ministry*, 165; Jürgen Matthäus in Browning, *Origins*, 251.

138. Longerich, *Davon*, 52.

139. Niven, *Hitler*, 181. This was also the view of Fritz Hippler (formerly of the NSDStB, see Chapter 1), the film's chief creator, according to Clinefelter, "Construction," 136. Clinefelter convincingly defines the work as a "compilation film" (134).

140. Albert Brodbeck, "'Der Ewige Jude': Uraufführung des grossen Dokumentarfilms," *Deutsche Allgemeine Zeitung*, November 30, 1940.

141. Clinefelter, "Construction," 134–46; Culbert, "Impact," 148–50; Rentschler, *Ministry*, 160; Hollstein, *Jud Süss*, 109–16; Friedländer, *Nazi Germany*, 100. *Shechita* is explained in Bin Gorion et al., *Philo-Lexikon*, 635.

142. Within the context of *Der Ewige Jude*, see the enlightening discussion in Chapoutot, *Law of Blood*, 23–6.

143. Goebbels, *Tagebücher Fragmente*, vol. 3, 619; vol. 4, 306; Culbert, "Impact," 148.

144. *Meldungen aus dem Reich*, vol. 6, 1,917–19. See also Culbert, "Impact," 151–2.

145. See Browning, *Origins*, 510–11 n. 295.

146. Binding's letter to Rolland in *Kölnische Zeitung*, May 20, 1933, reprinted in *Sechs Bekenntnisse*, 11. See Baird, *Hitler's War Poets*, 54–5.

147. *Augsburger Postzeitung*, October 6, 1933, cited in Wilkens, "Schriftleitergesetz," 372.

148. Weiss, *Rundfunk*, 27.

149. *Das Schwarze Korps*, May 15, 1935; *Der Stürmer*, April 1936 (quote).

150. "'Deutsches Theater' – von ehedem: Das Theater der Piscator, Jessner, Reinhardt und Barnay," *Deutsche Allgemeine Zeitung*, August 28, 1936; "Schund am Pranger," *Münsterischer Anzeiger*, July 27, 1937.

151. *Westdeutscher Beobachter*, December 1, 1937; Friedländer, *Nazi Germany*, 253.

152. *Börsenblatt* text reprinted in Bähre, "Langenbucher," 272.

153. "Die Programmgestaltung des Rundfunks: Vorträge von Dr. Glasmeier und Dr. Kriegler," *Frankfurter Zeitung*, August 10, 1938; directives of press conference of November 24, 1938, reprinted in Sänger, *Politik*, 262–3; Longerich, *Davon*, 141.

154. Friedländer, *Years*, 19 (quote), 48.

155. Friedländer, *Years*, 161.

156. See also Friedländer, *Years*, 204–5.

157. Representative samples: Joseph Goebbels, "Um die Entscheidung," *Das Reich*, August 3, 1941; "Die Angeber," ibid., September 14, 1941; "Marathonlauf hinter dem Kriege," ibid., September 21, 1941; "Die sogenannte russische Seele," ibid., July 19, 1942; "Der steile Aufstieg," ibid., September 20, 1942. Echoing these leitmotifs in the public arena were Promi secretary of state Leopold Gutterer in Salzburg ("Unser Kulturschaffen im Kriege," printed in *Deutsche Allgemeine Zeitung*, August 5, 1942) and invited speakers at the Promi-organized poets' meeting in Weimar, summer 1942 (Wilhelm Haegert in Erckmann, *Dichter*, 7–8).

158. Joseph Goebbels, "Die Juden sind schuld!" *Das Reich*, November 16, 1941 (1st quote); Friedländer, *Years*, 337 (2nd and 3rd quotes). See also Goebbels, *Tagebücher Diktate*, vol. 2, 352; *Meldungen aus dem Reich*, vol. 8, 3,007; Steinert, *Krieg*, 245.

159. Joseph Goebbels, "Die motorischen Kräfte," *Das Reich*, June 6, 1943.

160. Joseph Goebbels, "Die Krise Europas," *Das Reich*, February 28, 1943.

161. Margret Boveri, "Landschaft mit doppeltem Boden: Einfluss und Tarnung des amerikanischen Judentums," *Das Reich*, May 28, 1943. Probably misspelling deliberately, Boveri wrote "Samuel Roseman." See, post-1945, and deceptively: Boveri, *Wir lügen alle*. On Martinique and broadcasting, see Klemperer, *Tagebücher 1943*, 74.

162. Joseph Goebbels, "Das innere England," *Das Reich*, November 7, 1943.

163. Carl Linfert, "Fremdkörper: Über einige Ratschläge der Juden an sich selbst," *Das Reich*, January 21, 1945.

164. Silex, *Kommentar*, 122–3; Görtemaker, *Leben*, 63; Klee, *Kulturlexikon*, 608.

165. Edouard Roditi, "The Fate of Otto Freundlich: Painter Maudit," *Commentary*, September 1, 1955 (*commentarymagazine.com*) (quote); Kracht, "Symbol," 9–18, 21–2.

166. Palmer, *Lilli*, 76–85; Klee, *Kulturlexikon*, 404.

167. Helmut G. Asper, "Walter Wicclair (1901–1998)," *Neuer Nachrichtenbrief der Gesellschaft für Exilforschung e.V.*, no. 11 (June 1998): 5–7; Wicclair, *Kreuzburg*, 74–7.

168. Petzet, *Theater*, 252; Klee, *Kulturlexikon*, 507.

169. Krützen, *Albers*, 150–1; "Eugen Burg," www.steffi-line.de.
170. Petzet, *Theater*, 252–3; Kremer, *Holocaust Literature*, 1,290–1.
171. Frank, *Spielzeit*, 331–9; Frank, in tls.theaterwissenschaft.ch.
172. Mühsam, in *LEMO: Lebendiges Museum Online*; *SS im Einsatz*, 66.
173. Elisabeth Höpker-Herberg, "Mombert, Alfred," in *Neue Deutsche Biographie* 18 (1997): 22–3; Carossa, *Welten*, 106–10.
174. *Zündende Lieder*, 136; Lüth, *Hamburger Theater*, 65; Stefan Wulf in Heister et al., *Musik im Exil*, 149–51.
175. Bergmeier, *Weintraub Story*, 5, 7, 9, 13, 23, 31–51; Hollaender, *Von Kopf bis Fuss*, 118; Stauffer, *Forever*, 84–5; Starr, *Red and Hot*, 122, 194–225.
176. Sigmund Petruschka to author, June 28, 1990, YUA, CA ON00370 F0456; sample recording of Sid Kay's Fellows on cassette tape supplied with Christian Kellersmann, "Jazz in Deutschland von 1933–1945," MA thesis, University of Hamburg, 1989; Bergmeier and Susat, "Spitzenband," 34–9.
177. Schumann, *Ghetto Swinger*, 9.
178. Schumann, *Ghetto Swinger*, 30.
179. Schumann, *Ghetto Swinger*, 35.
180. Schumann, *Ghetto Swinger*, 62.
181. Kater, *Doctors under Hitler*, 177–221.

FOUR – WAR AND PUBLIC OPINION, PROPAGANDA, AND CULTURE

1. Evans, *Third Reich at War*, 563.
2. Shirer, *Rise*, 518–20, 595, 599, 601; Weinberg, *World*, 51; Longerich, *Goebbels*, 425–6; Kershaw, *Nemesis*, 221. There were other staged attacks, at two additional border points, but the Gleiwitz incident received the broadest publicity (Gruchmann, *Weltkrieg*, 22).
3. Krahl, *Ich*, 48.
4. Fröhlich, "Pressekonferenz," 377.
5. Fröhlich, "Pressekonferenz," 378.
6. Goebbels quoted in Kallenbach, *Kulturpolitik*, 17.
7. "Autor Ungenannt! Von einem notwendigen Anspruch des geistig Schaffenden," *Der Autor* 15, no. 1 (January 1940): 2.
8. Boelcke, *Kriegspropaganda*, 437–8.
9. *Meldungen aus dem Reich*, vol. 4, 955, 1,070, 1,110; Boelcke, *Kriegspropaganda*, 426; Baird, *World*, 73–4; Steinert, *Krieg*, 119, 121.
10. *Meldungen aus dem Reich*, vol. 5, 1,439.
11. *Meldungen aus dem Reich*, vol. 8, 2,671; Goebbels, "Soldaten im Kampf der Geister," *Das Reich*, October 12, 1941.
12. Heinrich to Marga Himmler, August 31, 1941, in *Himmler privat*, 260.
13. Boelcke, *Kriegspropaganda*, 558.
14. Goebbels's Berlin speech, February 15, 1941, in Albrecht, *Filmpolitik*, 468; Goebbels, *Tagebücher Diktate*, vol. 1, 103, vol. 2, 556; *Meldungen aus dem Reich*, vol. 8, 2,671; Hitler in Jochmann, *Hitler*, 94.
15. Goebbels, *Tagebücher Diktate*, vol. 2, 316, 556 (quote); Wistrich, *Who's Who*, 324.
16. *Meldungen aus dem Reich*, vol. 4, 1,140, 1,164.
17. Goebbels, *Tagebücher Diktate*, vol. 4, 233. See also *Meldungen aus dem Reich*, vol. 5, 1,338–9; Boelcke, *Kriegspropaganda*, 443.
18. *Meldungen aus dem Reich*, vol. 5, 1,563, vol. 6, 1,788.
19. Goebbels's speech, March 28, 1942, in Dresden, printed in Schlösser, *Kunst*, 10; Goebbels, *Tagebücher Diktate*, vol. 3, 583, vol. 4, 422–3; Steinert, *Krieg*, 286; Kershaw, *Nemesis*, 524.
20. *Meldungen aus dem Reich*, vol. 7, 2,301, vol. 9, 3,448–9; Goebbels, *Tagebücher Diktate*, vol. 3, 315; Goebbels, "Das grosse Herz unseres Volkes," *Das Reich*, April 5, 1942.

21. Goebbels, "Rede in München anlässlich der Eröffnung der Grossen Deutschen Kunstausstellung," *Film-Kurier*, July 6, 1942 (quote). See *Meldungen aus dem Reich*, vol. 10, 3,566; Goebbels, *Tagebücher Diktate*, vol. 5, 55; Goebbels, "Ein Wort an alle," *Das Reich*, March 8, 1942; Goebbels, "Offene Ansprache," *Das Reich*, March 29, 1942; Steinert, *Krieg*, 285.
22. Gruchmann, *Weltkrieg*, 176–91; Weinberg, *World*, 348–52; Pyta, *Hitler*, 458–9.
23. Goebbels, "Das grosse Herz unseres Volkes," *Das Reich*, April 5, 1942 (quote); Goebbels, *Tagebücher Diktate*, vol. 5, 73, 138. See also vol. 5, 55; *Meldungen aus dem Reich*, vol. 10, 3,936.
24. *Meldungen aus dem Reich*, vol. 11, 3,985, 4,053, 4,135.
25. *Meldungen aus dem Reich*, vol. 11, 4,188–9.
26. *Meldungen aus dem Reich*, vol. 11, 4,232; Boelcke, *Krieg*, 371.
27. Goebbels according to Boelcke, *Krieg*, 365.
28. Mann, *Tagebücher, 1940–1943*, 475.
29. Langer, *Encyclopedia*, 1,143; *SpiegelOnline*, January 29, 2003; *Der Spiegel* (December 16, 2002): 68; Gruchmann, *Weltkrieg*, 187–94; Weinberg, *World*, 410–17; Pyta, *Hitler*, 429.
30. Schönbeck quoted in Tim Proese, "Schlacht von Stalingrad: 'Menschen fielen vom Himmel'," *SpiegelOnline*, September 23, 2017.
31. Goebbels, *Tagebücher Diktate*, vol. 5, 478.
32. Goebbels quoted in Boelcke, *Krieg*, 371.
33. *Meldungen aus dem Reich*, vol. 11, 4,345–6.
34. Goebbels, "Der Segen der Erde," *Das Reich*, October 18, 1942.
35. Baird, *World*, 179.
36. Baird, *World*, 182.
37. *Meldungen aus dem Reich*, vol. 12, 4,720, 4,750–1 (quote); Baird, *World*, 187–9.
38. Von Kardorff, *Aufzeichnungen*, 24; Rosenberg, *Tagebücher*, 469.
39. Baird, *World*, 184.
40. Caption under photograph, "Härteste Kämpfe an der Ostfront," front page of *Das Reich*, January 31, 1943.
41. Goebbels's directives to the public media of February 3, 1943, as printed in Boelcke, *Krieg*, 435–6. They are reflected in his diary entries of February 4: Goebbels, *Tagebücher Diktate*, vol. 7, 255–6.
42. Felsmann et al., *Backfisch*, 41.
43. Goebbels, "Die harte Lehre," *Das Reich*, February 7, 1943 (quote); "Unser Wille und unser Weg," *Das Reich*, February 14, 1943.
44. Goebbels, *Tagebücher Diktate*, vol. 7, 298, 320 (quote).
45. Goebbels, "Nun, Volk, steh auf, und Sturm brich los!" Sportpalast speech, February 18, 1943, la802607.us.archive.org; Goebbels, *Tagebücher Diktate*, vol. 7, 373–4; Hansen, *Leben*, 83–4 (Pomsel's quote); Boelcke, *Krieg*, 23–5.
46. *Meldungen aus dem Reich*, vol. 12, 4,831.
47. Goebbels, "Die Winterkrise und der totale Krieg," *Das Reich*, March 14, 1943; "Ein offenes Wort zum totalen Krieg," *Das Reich*, April 4, 1943.
48. Steinert, *Krieg*, 383; Goebbels, *Tagebücher Diktate*, vol. 8, 242; Hagemann, *Publizistik*, 263; Goebbels, "Mit souveräner Ruhe," *Das Reich*, May 23, 1943.
49. Goebbels, *Tagebücher Diktate*, vol. 8, 263.
50. *Meldungen aus dem Reich*, vol. 14, 5,406.
51. Goebbels, *Tagebücher Diktate*, vol. 9, 136.
52. Goebbels, *Tagebücher Diktate*, vol. 9, 115, 160.
53. Goebbels, "Der Stichtag," *Das Reich*, October 31, 1943; *Meldungen aus dem Reich*, vol. 15, 6,063–4.
54. Von Kardorff, *Aufzeichnungen*, 120; Goebbels, "Nun, Volk, steh auf, und Sturm brich los!" Sportpalast speech, February 18, 1943, la802607.us.archive.org; Goebbels, "Der totale Krieg," *Das Reich*, January 17, 1943; "Der Blick nach vorne," *Das Reich*, January 31, 1943;

"Die harte Lehre," *Das Reich*, February 7, 1943; "Ein offenes Wort zum totalen Krieg," *Das Reich*, April 4, 1943.

55. Von Kardorff, *Aufzeichnungen*, 78–9.

56. Goebbels, *Tagebücher Diktate*, vol. 8, 511.

57. Goebbels, *Tagebücher Diktate*, vol. 9, 162.

58. *Meldungen aus dem Reich*, vol. 14, 5,575; vol. 15, 5,940, 6,063, 6,093.

59. Von Kardorff, *Aufzeichnungen*, 82; Schäfer, *Berlin*, 36–41; Söderbaum, *Nichts*, 197–8.

60. Kater, *Weimar*, 272–3.

61. Goebbels, *Tagebücher Diktate*, vol. 9, 115, 124–6 (see also for July 26, 162–3); Goebbels, "Die Voraussetzung zum Sieg," *Das Reich*, July 25, 1943. The eastern panzer offensive "Citadel" had started on July 5, but, failing, was called off by Hitler near Orel on July 12, 1943 (Kershaw, *Nemesis*, 591–2; Pyta, *Hitler*, 468–70).

62. *Meldungen aus dem Reich*, vol. 15, 6,063, 6,067.

63. *Meldungen aus dem Reich*, vol. 17, 6,598.

64. Von Kardorff, *Aufzeichnungen*, 138.

65. *Meldungen aus dem Reich*, vol. 17, 6,684.

66. *Meldungen aus dem Reich*, vol. 17, 6,684, 6,687.

67. *Meldungen aus dem Reich*, vol. 17, 6,707; Steinert, *Krieg*, 495.

68. Goebbels, "Die Zeichen der Zeit," *Das Reich*, December 24, 1944.

69. As one of many self-satisfied reactions, see Goebbels, *Tagebücher Diktate*, vol. 2, 440.

70. *Meldungungen aus dem Reich*, vol. 14, 5,699 (quote); Goebbels, "Die Realitäten des Krieges," *Das Reich*, August 22, 1943; "Von der Unersetzlichkeit der Freiheit," *Das Reich*, August 29, 1943.

71. Wistrich, *Who's Who*, 99 (quote); Steinweis, *Art*, 168–71; Diller, *Rundfunkpolitik*, 432; Goebbels, "Der Befehl der Pflicht," *Das Reich*, August 6, 1944; *Meldungen aus dem Reich*, vol. 17, 6,701.

72. Goebbels, *Tagebücher Diktate*, vol. 15, 638.

73. Goebbels, *Tagebücher Diktate*, vol. 3, 187, 525.

74. Goebbels, *Tagebücher Fragmente*, vol. 3, 673; vol. 4, 805; Goebbels, *Tagebücher Diktate*, vol. 9, 62; vol. 10, 338, 370; vol. 12, 147.

75. Goebbels, *Tagebücher Diktate*, vol. 14, 94, 457.

76. Promi State Secretary Leopold Gutterer's remarks in "Unser Kulturschaffen im Kriege," *Deutsche Allgemeine Zeitung*, August 5, 1942; Rentschler, *Ministry*, 13; Moeller, *Filmminister*, 293–4.

77. Goebbels, *Tagebücher Fragmente*, vol. 3, 662–3; Rosenberg, *Tagebücher*, 303.

78. Goebbels, *Tagebücher Fragmente*, vol. 4, 52, 72, 335, 338, 399, 423, 542; Goebbels, *Tagebücher Diktate*, vol. 1, 500; vol. 2, 102, 126, 155, 363; vol. 3, 244; vol. 5, 34–5; Hitler in Jochmann, *Hitler*, 406.

79. Klee, *Kulturlexikon*, 83, 174–5.

80. Kater, *Drummers*, 183–4.

81. Goebbels, *Tagebücher Diktate*, vol. 5, 133; vol. 12, 191, 249.

82. RKK Ilse Werner, BAB (former BDC); Werner, *So*, 22 (quote).

83. *Meldungen aus dem Reich*, vol. 6, 2,007–8; Courtade and Cadars, *Geschichte*, 209–22; Drewniak, *Film*, 396–7; Hoffmann, *Fahne*, 172; Tegel, *Nazis*, 176–7; Koch, *Wunschkonzert*, 162–9.

84. Vaget, "Nazi Cinema," 45–51; Courtade and Cadars, *Geschichte*, 200–1; Drewniak, *Film*, 377–8.

85. Vaget, "Nazi Cinema," 49.

86. Such as *U-Boote westwärts* ("U-Boats Moving West") and *Spähtrupp Hallgarten* ("Reconnaissance Unit Hallgarten"); see Jürgen Schüddekopf, "Neue Filme – vom Publikum her gesehen," *Das Reich*, June 8, 1941.

87. Welch, *Propaganda*, 134–41; Drewniak, *Film*, 320–8; Niven, *Hitler*, 219–20; Steiner, *Wessely*, 111, 121–7. For Goebbels's extremely positive reaction see Goebbels, *Tagebücher Diktate*, vol. 2, 171.

88. See the book by August Schowalter, *Ohm Krüger* (1902), on which the film was based, newly printed and illustrated with screen shots of the film. The plate opposite 237 shows a concentration camp, captioned: "In such concentration camps defenseless Boer women were kept."

89. Facsimile of Hobhouse, "Bericht von Fräulein Emily Hobhouse über die Zustände," [London or Berlin, 1901], in Ziegler, *Humanität*, 85–130, quote 96. The English version cited is the original, by Emily Hobhouse, "Report of a Visit to the Camps of Women and Children in the Cape and Orange River Colonies," n.d., 5, babel.hathitrust.org/cgi/pt?id=uiuc.2776304;view=1up;seq=3. Biographical details on Hobhouse are in www.ofxorddnb.com under Hobhouse, and on Ziegler in Klausch, *Erbe*; and www.munzinger.de/search/portraits under Ziegler.

90. As related by Klaus Mann, who interviewed Jannings in his capacity as a correspondent for *Stars and Stripes: Posten*, 311.

91. Moeller, *Filmminister*, 249–50. See Jannings's opportunistic declaration in Ebermayer, *Deutschland*, 586.

92. Emil Jannings, "Die grosse Aufgabe," in Siska, *Wunderwelt*, 57–8. See also Jannings, "Paul Krüger," in Schowalter, *Ohm Krüger*, 7–12; Hüpgens, "Film," 411.

93. Hull, *Film*, 182–3; Moeller, "Filmstars," 144, 170.

94. Goebbels, *Tagebücher Fragmente*, vol. 4, 540; *Meldungen aus dem Reich*, vol. 7, 2,293–5; Drewniak, *Film*, 337–8.

95. Drewniak, *Film*, 197–9; Tegel, *Nazis*, 198–9.

96. Goebbels, *Tagebücher Diktate*, vol. 2, 176–7, 286, 410.

97. Krauss quoted in Karl Lahm, "Shylok der Ostjude," *Deutsche Allgemeine Zeitung*, May 19, 1943.

98. Goebbels, *Tagebücher Diktate*, vol. 4, 636.

99. Langer, *Encyclopedia*, 503–4.

100. Weinberg, *World*, 270–4, 292–5; Gruchmann, *Weltkrieg*, 128–31.

101. Goebbels, *Tagebücher Diktate*, vol. 3, 187, 207, 340, 400–1, 407, 412–13, 437–8, 499, 577, 589; vol. 4, 135, 407, 579; *Meldungen aus dem Reich*, vol. 10, 3,758–60; Ilse Urbach, "Der grosse Friedrich," *Das Reich*, March 8, 1942; Welch, *Propaganda*, 175–82; Hull, *Film*, 215; Drewniak, *Film*, 191–3. For Hitler's complete identification with Frederick esp. during the war, see Pyta, *Hitler*, 637–43.

102. Hull, *Film*, 185–6; Heldt, "Composers," 124–5.

103. Goebbels, *Tagebücher Fragmente*, vol. 4, 503, 708; Goebbels, *Tagebücher Diktate*, vol. 3, 220; Welch, *Propaganda*, 121–2, 125–30; Moeller, *Filmminister*, 245–9; Niven, *Hitler*, 217–19.

104. Her term is "Sterbehilfe": Krahl, *Ich*, 63. See also the apologist remarks by co-creator Fritz Hippler, *Verstrickung*, 216–17.

105. *Mitteilungen aus dem Reich*, vol. 9, 3,175–6. Gerhard Herzberg had argued similarly already in "Ich klage an/Capitol," *Film-Kurier*, August 30, 1941.

106. See Boelcke, *Kriegspropaganda*, 326; Goebbels, *Tagebücher Diktate*, vol. 2, 114; *Meldungen aus dem Reich*, vol. 16, 6,487; Rabenalt, *Goebbels*, 198.

107. Hull, *Film*, 236–7; Reimer, "Turning," 216–21; Heins, *Melodrama*, 169–73.

108. O'Brien, "Spectacle," 197–208; Moeller, *Filmminister*, 266–7; Nadar, "Director," 76; Heins, *Melodrama*, 177–8, 181–3.

109. Heins, *Melodrama*, 174–5; Goebbels, *Tagebücher Diktate*, vol. 3, 104–5. After having played Sudeten-German Anna in *Die goldene Stadt* (1942), who drowns herself because she has succumbed sexually to a Czech in Prague, Harlan's wife Kristina Söderbaum claimed to have realized how even harmless films helped the regime in goading the people toward support of the war effort (*Nichts*, 197–8). Simplistically and self-exculpatorily: Quadflieg, *Wir spielen*, 113.

110. Quadflieg, *Wir spielen*, 111–12; www.rarefilmsandmore.com/kora-terry-1940#. WULSmsmQyJI.

111. Goebbels, *Tagebücher Diktate*, vol. 7, 308; Krützen, *Albers*, 185–6, 273; Rentschler, *Ministry*, 212.

112. Goebbels, *Tagebücher Diktate*, vol. 8, 365; vol. 14, 386; vol. 15, 542; Liebeneiner and Harlan in "Über die Aktualität des historischen Films," *Film-Kurier*, December 24, 1943; Harlan, *Schatten*, 181–94; Drewniak, *Film*, 194–6.

113. O'Brien, "Celluloid War," 170–4.

114. Christoph Gunkel, "Der letzte Film der Nazis: Lindenstrasse 1943," *SpiegelOnline*, April 16, 2015; Moeller, "Filmstars," 164; Rentschler, *Use*, 140.

115. Goebbels, *Tagebücher Diktate*, vol. 2, 127.

116. Moeller, *Filmminister*, 365; Kriegk, *Film*, 219. The companies were Ufa-Tonwoche (the largest), Deulig-Tonwoche, Tobis-Wochenschau, and Fox Tönende Wochenschau (originally a child of Hollywood's Twentieth Century Fox).

117. Barkhausen, *Filmpropaganda*, 218–19; Bucher, "Filmpropaganda," 53; Moeller, *Filmminister*, 368, 372.

118. Robert Klein in Hippler et al., *Jahre*, 46; *Meldungen aus dem Reich*, vol. 3, 820; Barkhausen, *Filmpropaganda*, 215.

119. Goebbels, *Tagebücher Fragmente*, vol. 3, 663; Rosenberg, *Tagebücher*, 302–3; Moeller, *Filmminister*, 370. Hitler's reason is implied by subsequent Goebbels, *Tagebücher*, remarks.

120. Traub, *UFA*, 110.

121. *Meldungen aus dem Reich*, vol. 5, 1,403, 1,577; vol. 8, 2,673; Bucher, "Filmpropaganda," 54.

122. For Goebbels's official attitude to newsreel work, see his Berlin speech of February 15, 1941, printed in Albrecht, *Filmpolitik*, 472; and his articles "P. K.," *Das Reich*, May 18, 1941; "Nachrichtenpolitik," *Das Reich*, July 6, 1941. Also Bucher, "Filmpropaganda," 55–6.

123. Felix Henseleit, "Die neue Wochenschau: Der Führer wieder in Berlin," *Film-Kurier*, July 11, 1940. See also Goebbels, *Tagebücher Fragmente*, vol. 4, 233.

124. *Mitteilungen aus dem Reich*, vol. 8, 2,873; Goebbels, *Tagebücher Diktate*, vol. 2, 340.

125. Goebbels, *Tagebücher Diktate*, vol. 2, 556. See Bucher, "Filmpropaganda," 57–9.

126. *Mitteilungen aus dem Reich*, vol. 9, 3,167; Goebbels, *Tagebücher Diktate*, vol. 3, 531.

127. Goebbels, *Tagebücher Diktate*, vol. 4, 289.

128. Barkhausen, *Filmpropaganda*, 215, 222; Gutterer in *Deutsche Allgemeine Zeitung*, August 5, 1942.

129. Moeller, *Filmminister*, 394.

130. See Goebbels, *Tagebücher Diktate*, vol. 7, 90, 308; Hoffmann, *Fahne*, 219–20; Bucher, "Filmpropaganda," 60–6; Moeller, *Filmminister*, 395.

131. Siska, *Wunderwelt*, 47–9.

132. Hoffmann, *Fahne*, 221.

133. "Dokument vom Kampf gegen die Invasion: Die Neue Deutsche Wochenschau," *Film-Kurier*, June 20, 1944.

134. Moeller, *Filmminister*, 398–9.

135. Bucher, "Filmpropaganda," 64; Hoffmann, *Fahne*, 223–4.

136. The decoration occurred on March 19, 1945. See Hoffmann, *Fahne*, 228–9.

137. "Die letzten Deutschen aus der Dobrudscha fahren die Donau stromauf zur neuen Heimat im Reich," *Das Reich*, December 8, 1940; Kallenbach, *Kulturpolitik*, 147–53.

138. Heyde, *Presse*, 36; Sänger, *Fäden*, 71; Hagemann, *Presselenkung*, 32–6; Abel, *Presselenkung*, 40, 51–2, 84.

139. Gillessen, *Posten*, 415.

140. Goebbels, *Tagebücher Fragmente*, vol. 4, 250.

141. Boelcke, *Kriegspropaganda*, 280.

142. Boelcke, *Krieg*, 238.

143. Goebbels, *Tagebücher Diktate*, vol. 7, 400; also vol. 3, 240, 387; Hagemann, *Publizistik*, 257.

144. Goebbels, *Tagebücher Diktate*, vol. 4, 291.

145. Goebbels, *Tagebücher Fragmente*, vol. 4, 497; Goebbels, *Tagebücher Diktate*, vol. 8, 101.
146. Hitler on February 22–3, 1942, in Jochmann, *Hitler*, 294.
147. Kallenbach, *Kulturpolitik*, 22–3; Haacke, *Feuilletonkunde*, 149.
148. Kallenbach, *Kulturpolitik*, 54.
149. Kallenbach, *Kulturpolitik*, 165–6; Köhler, *Publizisten*, 305. See Bollmus, *Amt Rosenberg*, 122.
150. Reto Caratsch, "Die letzten zehn Jahre der 'Frankfurter Zeitung': Bemerkungen über die Gefahren des Maskentreibens," *Neue Zürcher Zeitung*, January 19, 1947.
151. Sösemann, "Journalismus," 30.
152. Goebbels, *Tagebücher Fragmente*, vol. 4, 288.
153. Von Kardorff, *Aufzeichnungen*, 137.
154. Goebbels, *Tagebücher Fragmente*, vol. 4, 184; Goebbels, *Tagebücher Diktate*, vol. 2, 199; *Meldungen aus dem Reich*, vol. 7, 2,647; Baird, *World*, 155–6.
155. Goebbels, *Tagebücher Diktate*, vol. 2, 54; Kallenbach, *Kulturpolitik*, 51; Heyde, *Presse*, 31.
156. Brechtken, "Experiment," 68; Frei and Schmitz, *Journalismus*, 38.
157. Laux, *Nachklang*, 297; Goebbels, *Tagebücher Diktate*, vol. 9, 103; Köhler, *Publizisten*, 356.
158. Goebbels, *Tagebücher Diktate*, vol. 2, 209; vol. 7, 381 (quote).
159. The most egregious exception probably was "Die Juden sind schuld!" *Das Reich*, November 16, 1941.
160. Werner Oehlmann in *Das Reich*, June 21, 1942.
161. Ilse Urbach, "Der grosse Friedrich," *Das Reich*, March 8, 1942.
162. Paul Scheffer, "Zwischen Wunsch und Zweifel: Amerikanische Betrachtungen zur Jahreswende," *Das Reich*, December 29, 1940.
163. Ludwig Ferdinand Clauss, "Natürliche Rolle – Gemeinschaftsrolle: Über Anlagen und Erziehungsziel," *Das Reich*, February 9, 1941; Himmler to Bormann, September 8, 1943, BAK, T-175, EAP 161-b-12/94. See Kater, *Ahnenerbe*, 245–54, 425–8.
164. Eugen Mündler, "Der Krieg gibt das Gesetz," *Das Reich*, January 31, 1943.
165. Hans Schwarz van Berk, "Ein Attentat und seine Antwort: Keine Fahne und kein Regiment entehrt," *Das Reich*, July 23, 1944.
166. "Standarte Nordland," *Das Reich*, February 9, 1941.
167. Hubert Neun, "Wiedersehen mit Warschau: Besiegte Stadt zwischen Gestern und Morgen," *Das Reich*, March 9, 1941.
168. "Der Bauer als Lehrherr: SS und Landdienst," *Das Reich*, March 9, 1941.
169. Wilhelm Spengler, "Bandenkrieg im Niemandsland: Vom Einsatz des SD," *Das Reich*, May 3, 1942. The quotation is from Kershaw, *Nemesis*, 357.
170. Wilhelm Spengler, "Volksdeutsche Schicksale," *Das Reich*, August 19, 1942.
171. Pross, "Einleitung," 5; Sarkowicz, "Schriftsteller," 187; Frei and Schmitz, *Journalismus*, 110–13; Abel, *Presselenkung*, 75–82, 85–94. One of Theodor Heuss's (unpolitical) articles was "'Dennoch . . .': Begegnung mit einer Vergangenheit," *Das Reich*, December 1, 1940. See further on this problem in Chapter 6.
172. Goebbels, *Tagebücher Diktate*, vol. 2, 440; vol. 3, 395; *Meldungen aus dem Reich*, vol. 8, 2,774; Klingler, "Rundfunkpolitik," 173.
173. Goebbels, *Tagebücher Diktate*, vol. 3, 670.
174. Par. 1 of "Fünfte Verordnung zur Durchführung des Reichskulturkammergesetzes. Vom 28. Oktober 1939," *Reichsgesetzblatt Teil I* (1939): 2,118; Fischer, *Dramaturgie*, 134.
175. Eckert, *Rundfunk*, 38; Diller, *Rundfunkpolitik*, 375; Klingler, "Rundfunkpolitik," 51–2.
176. Echoing imbalance: Goebbels, *Tagebücher Diktate*, vol. 4, 149, 221; *Meldungen aus dem Reich*, vol. 6, 1,776; Boelcke, *Kriegspropaganda*, 527.
177. The two radio icons were Heinz Goedecke and Wilhelm Krug. They produced their own volume, *Wunschkonzert*, including several (authentic?) fan letters, see 160, 162–4, 167. Also: Goebbels, *Tagebücher Diktate*, vol. 4, 131; *Meldungen aus dem Reich*, vol. 4, 940–1; vol. 5, 1,692, 1,712; vol. 6, 1,889; Koch, *Wunschkonzert*, 100–16, 130–5, 140–5, 157.

178. On content and balance, see Goebbels, *Tagebücher Fragmente*, vol. 4, 118, 683, 685; Goebbels, "Der Rundfunk im Kriege," *Das Reich*, June 15, 1941; *Meldungen aus dem Reich*, vol. 4, 1,118; vol. 5, 1,493–4; vol. 7, 2,533; vol. 8, 2,662; Fischer, *Dramaturgie*, 134, and 178–9 for a sample day's broadcasts (May 27, 1941).

179. Goebbels, *Tagebücher Diktate*, vol. 2, 305, 556; vol. 3, 40 (quote), 92; *Meldungen aus dem Reich*, vol. 9, 3,137, 3,199. The original German is "Davon geht die Welt nicht unter."

180. Goebbels's vacillations toward balance are reflected in Goebbels, *Tagebücher Diktate*, vol. 1, 460, 494; vol. 2, 119–20, 126, 245, 340; vol. 3, 111, 243–4, 249–50. For the revisions, see Drechsler, *Funktion*, 42–3.

181. Das Deutsche Tanz- und Unterhaltungsorchester (DTU) was co-led by Haentzschel and Franz Grothe, both seasoned jazz musicians, with Grothe also receiving a leading post in radio. Haentzschel later composed the film score for *Baron Münchhausen* (1943): Kater, *Drummers*, 126–7; author's recorded interview with Georg Haentzschel, Cologne, October 1, 1988, YUA, CA ON00370 F0456.

182. Goebbels, *Tagebücher Diktate*, vol. 3, 274, 314, 406; vol. 4, 476; Goebbels, "Der treue Helfer," *Das Reich*, March 1, 1942; *Meldungen aus dem Reich*, vol. 8, 3,076; vol. 9, 3,437–9; Kater, *Drummers*, 128–9.

183. "Programmwoche vom 13.–19. Dezember 1942"; minutes of broadcast planning meetings of January 6, February 4 and 11, June 17, 1943, BAK, R55/696; Hinkel to Goebbels, January 25 and February 3, 1943, BAK, R55/1254; Goebbels, *Tagebücher Diktate*, vol. 7, 192, 256; *Meldungen aus dem Reich*, vol. 11, 4,244; Klingler, "Rundfunkpolitik," 152–4.

184. *Meldungen aus dem Reich*, vol. 13, 4,928–9, 4,970; Klingler, "Rundfunkpolitik," 179, 196.

185. Frei and Schmitz, *Journalismus*, 89–90.

186. *Meldungen aus dem Reich*, vol. 16, 6,195; Klingler, "Rundfunkpolitik," 251.

187. Protocol of author's interview with former panzer grenadier Werner Wunderlich, Baden-Baden, September 5, 1986, YUA, CA ON00370 F0456.

188. Klingler, "Rundfunkpolitik," 178, 253.

189. Kershaw, *Nemesis*, 681.

190. Hitler as quoted in Klingler, "Rundfunkpolitik," 248–9.

191. I myself heard this on my grandparents' radio in Wersabe near Bremen, as a seven-year-old boy, ironically while drying wet Hitler stamps on the windowsill.

192. The propaganda value was asserted in Kallenbach, *Kulturpolitik*, 58.

193. Bucher, "Filmpropaganda," 60.

194. *Meldungen aus dem Reich*, vol. 15, 6,174–5; Goebbels, *Tagebücher Diktate*, vol. 9, 56; von Kardorff, *Aufzeichnungen*, 113; Aster, *Orchestra*, 151; Föllmer, *Leben*, 215.

195. *Staatskapelle Berlin, Bach Cantatas Website*; Kater, *Drummers*, 163; Hamann, *Wagner*, 419, 494–6; Aster, *Orchestra*, 149–50. See also Goebbels, *Tagebücher Diktate*, vol. 13, 354.

196. Goebbels, *Tagebücher Diktate*, vol. 4, 409, 419; Leopold Gutterer's remarks in *Deutsche Allgemeine Zeitung*, August 5, 1942.

197. Goebbels quoted in Kater, *Composers*, 252. See also Egk, *Zeit*, 342–3; Julius Kopsch to Franz Strauss, July 21, 1946, RG.

198. Goebbels, *Tagebücher Diktate*, vol. 1, 515.

199. "Verbot des Jazz und ähnlich entarteter Musik in Sachsen. Eine Anordung von Gauleiter Mutschmann," in Lovisa, *Musikkritik*, 220. See also *Chemnitzer Zeitung*, July 5, 1943; *Musik im Kriege* 1 (1943): 75.

200. Walter, *Strauss*, 374–95; Kater, *Composers*, 228–59; Riethmüller, "Stefan Zweig," 267–87.

201. Drewniak, *Theater*, 331–4; Novak, *Salzburg*, 330.

202. Goebbels, *Tagebücher Diktate*, vol. 2, 436.

203. For the latter, see Drewniak, *Theater*, 331–4.

204. *Völkischer Beobachter*, November 22, 1939.

205. Kater, *Composers*, 150–77; Kershaw, *Nemesis*, 250–2, 484–5.

206. Orff to Strecker, May 22, 1941, CM, Schott Korr.; Pietzsch to Orff, May 31, 1941, CM, Allg. Korr.; ["To Whom It May Concern"], sign. Raabe, Berlin, February 20, 1942, CM, Allg. Korr.; Orff to Strecker, May 26, 1943, CM, Schott Korr.; Aulich to Orff, July 23 and October 23, 1943, CM, Allg. Korr.; Scherping to Reichsminister [Goebbels], April 25, 1944, BAK R55/559; Deutsche Wochenschau G.m.b.H. to Orff, June 7, 1944 (quote); Theater am Nollendorfplatz to Orff, July 17, 1944, CM, Allg. Korr.; Ellis, "Music," 133.

207. Goebbels, *Tagebücher Diktate*, vol. 13, 466; entry for August 30, 1944, in "Gertrud Orffs Tagebuch," CM; Rathkolb, *Führertreu*, 176.

208. Goebbels, *Tagebücher Diktate*, vol. 13, 466.

209. "Opern und Ballette für die neue Spielzeit aus dem Verlag B. Schott's Söhne, Mainz," *Deutsche Theater-Zeitung*, September 14, 1939.

210. Entry for March 7–27, June 3–10, June 24, July 2, 5–22, 1943, in Egk's pocket calendar, BS, Ana/410; Drewes to Graener, March 26, 1943, BS, Fasc. germ; Egk, *Zeit*, 349.

211. Goebbels, *Tagebücher Fragmente*, vol. 3, 317.

212. "Military Government of Germany: Fragebogen," sign. Werner Egk, October 16, 1945; Beisler to Kläger, September 23, 1946, AM, Egk; Goebbels, *Tagebücher Diktate*, vol. 13, 333; RKK Elly Ney, BAB (former BDC); RKK Egk, BAB (former BDC); Rathkolb, *Führertreu*, 176. Military Order of Merit = Kriegsverdienstkreuz.

213. RKK Gottfried Müller, BAB (former BDC); Schinköth, "Psalm," 305–9; Goebbels, *Tagebücher Diktate*, vol. 12, 204 (quotes), 234.

214. Goebbels, *Tagebücher Diktate*, vol. 11, 88; Klingler, "Rundfunkpolitik," 185.

215. Goebbels, *Tagebücher Diktate*, vol. 3, 556; vol. 4, 211–12; Leopold Gutterer in *Deutsche Allgemeine Zeitung*, August 5, 1942.

216. Andrew Lamb on Schultze in *Oxford Music Online*; Goebbels, *Tagebücher Fragmente*, vol. 1, 7–8, 23; Goebbels, *Tagebücher Diktate*, vol. 2, 33, 477; Kühn, "Kompass," 366–8.

217. Goebbels, *Tagebücher Diktate*, vol. 4, 172, 175.

218. Goebbels, *Tagebücher Fragmente*, vol. 4, 118; Goebbels, *Tagebücher Diktate*, vol. 1, 386; RKK Georg Schünemann, BAB (former BDC).

219. Hotter in telephone conversation to author, Munich, December 14, 1994; Goebbels, *Tagebücher Diktate*, vol. 4, 408; vol. 12, 204; Picker, *Tischgespräche*, 396. Goebbels's futile search is exemplified in *Tagebücher Diktate*, vol. 11, 77.

220. Diller, *Rundfunkpolitik*, 432.

221. Elly Ney, "Elly Ney schreibt an den deutschen Soldaten," *Zeitschrift für Musik*, 109 (March 1942): 122–3.

222. Ney, "Bekenntnis," 67.

223. Goebbels, *Tagebücher Diktate*, vol. 4, 135; facsimile, "Reichsprogramm des Grossdeutschen Rundfunks zum Geburtstag des Führer 20. April 1940," in Diller, *Rundfunkpolitik*, 347; Aster, *Orchestra*, 120.

224. Drewniak, *Film*, 328, 396, 438; Aster, *Orchestra*, 121.

225. Brown Sisters = Braune Schwestern. See Posch, "Salzburger Festspiele," 451–3; Goebbels, *Tagebücher Diktate*, vol. 2, 265, 519; Hörbiger, *Ich*, 274; Novak, *Salzburg*, 269–77, 328–30, 338–9, 347–8; Levi, *Mozart*, 157–9; Kriechbaumer, *Österreich*, 315–25, 372–3.

226. Spotts, *Bayreuth*, 190–9; *Meldungen aus dem Reich*, vol. 5, 508; vol. 8, 2,675; vol. 15, 5,807–9; Vossler, *Propaganda*, 331–5; Hamann, *Wagner*, 407–49, 460–507; Wagner, *Wagner Theater*, 171, 226, 235–42, 256, 309–13, 320.

227. Drewniak, *Theater*, 86.

228. Werner Kark, "Künstler spielen – ein Volk marschiert: Deutsche Theater in historischer Stunde," *Deutsche Theater-Zeitung*, September 24, 1939 (quote); Gründgens cited in Hans Erman, "Gustaf Gründgens: Krieg und Theaterführung: Der 'VB.' unterhielt sich mit dem Generalintendanten des Staatlichen Schauspielhauses," *Völkischer Beobachter*, October 19, 1939.

229. Hilpert, "Menschenführung," 273, 275–6.

230. Karl Pempelfort, "Theater in ernster Zeit," *Deutsche Theater-Zeitung*, September 24, 1939; Best, *Dramaturgie*, 46–7.

231. Goebbels, *Tagebücher Diktate*, vol. 7, 608; vol. 8, 515.

232. For expansion: Goebbels, *Tagebücher Fragmente*, vol. 4, 509; Goebbels, *Tagebücher Diktate*, vol. 1, 428; vol. 2, 151; vol. 10, 381; *Meldungen aus dem Reich*, vol. 5, 1,680; vol. 9, 3,372; vol. 10, 3,937; vol. 12, 4,766–7; Schlösser, "Lebendiges Theater," 3; Heyde, *Presse*, 31–2; Drewniak, *Theater*, 86.

233. Goebbels, *Tagebücher Diktate*, vol. 4, 300; *Meldungen aus dem Reich*, vol. 5, 1,681; vol. 9, 3,371; Dussel, *Theater*, 245.

234. Goebbels, *Tagebücher Fragmente*, vol. 4, 422; Goebbels, *Tagebücher Diktate*, vol. 1, 124; vol. 4, 579; Künkler, "Probleme," 197, 206. Rosenberg's fiercely anti-Semitic troll Elisabeth Frenzel even expressed fears that German theater, lacking new blood, might still be clandestinely Jewish (*Jude*, 2, 8; on her see Klee, *Kulturlexikon*, 147).

235. Those names were advertised by the Nazis' own publisher Franz Eher Nachfolger. Equally insipid but probably less virulent politically were names publicized by publishers Vertriebsstelle Berlin and Capitol-Verlag Berlin.

236. Wapnewski, *Auge*, 53; Ruppelt, *Schiller*, 41–4, 113–14.

237. Goebbels, *Tagebücher Fragmente*, vol. 4, 152 (quote); Schlösser, "Lebendiges Theater," 3; Dussel, *Theater*, 284.

238. Paul Kersten, "E. E. Dwinger: 'Der letzte Traum': Uraufführung der 'deutschen Tragödie' in Stettin," *Deutsche Theater-Zeitung*, November 2, 1941; Drewniak, *Theater*, 238; Klee, *Kulturlexikon*, 111. On Dwinger in World War II, see Baird, *Hitler's War Poets*, 151–9.

239. Mühr, *Mephisto*, 193–5.

240. In *Das Dorf bei Odessa* ("The Village near Odessa") German-Soviet officials have to choose between service for the Moscow government and loyalty to their village community: See Reinecker, *Dorf*, e.g. 71, 75; *Deutsche Dramaturgie* 2 (1943): 83; Drewniak, *Theater*, 239.

241. Schoeps, *Literatur*, 154–5.

242. Gritzbach, *Göring*.

243. Goebbels, *Tagebücher Diktate*, vol. 3, 376; vol. 4, 507; *Meldungen aus dem Reich*, vol. 3, 582; vol. 4, 949; vol. 5, 1,492; von Schirach, *Kantaterede*, 10; Adam, *Lesen*, 296–7; Friedländer, *Memory*, 258.

244. *Meldungen aus dem Reich*, vol. 5, 1,576.

245. Goebbels, *Tagebücher Diktate*, vol. 5, 94; vol. 7, 542; vol. 11, 47; *Meldungen aus dem Reich*, vol. 10, 3,970; vol. 12, 4,662; Leopold Gutterer in *Deutsche Allgemeine Zeitung*, August 5, 1942; Wezel, "Wunschzettel," 27–30; Strothmann, *Literaturpolitik*, 188; Barbian, *Literaturpolitik*, 247–8, 372; Adam, *Lesen*, 171.

246. Raschke, *Erbe*, esp. 114–15, 120, 144, 215, 242, 246, 249–50, 255. The quotes are 215 and 242.

247. See von Kardorff's sympathetic characterization in *Aufzeichnungen*, 15, 85–6; Fischer-Gravelius, "Erinnerungen," 343. A typical contribution praising people's art is Raschke, "Grenzen der Volkskunst," *Das Reich*, December 6, 1943. See Haefs, "Werkchronik," 239–40.

248. Raschke, *Pomeranzenzweig*, esp. 7, 19, 24, 99, 116–20.

249. Langenbucher, *Volkhafte Dichtung*, 290. See also Steinborn, "Erzähler," 61–4; Langer, *Dichtung*, 139.

250. Raschke, "Europa," 152–3; Raschke, "Briefen," 338, 341; Haefs, "Zeit," 94–6, 100–1; Haefs, "Werkchronik," 259–64.

251. Spezialkatalog Martin Raschke, *Neue Deutsche Biographie Online*.

252. Stöve, "Dichtung," 149; Denecke, "Grenzen," 155; Goebbels 1942 as cited in Strothmann, *Literaturpolitik*, 404; Barbian, *Literaturpolitik*, 366.

253. Deploring the losses: Wilhelm Haegert, "Zum Dichtertreffen 1941," in *Die Dichtung*, 5–6; idem, "Eröffnungsrede zum Dichtertreffen 1942," in Erckmann, *Dichter*, 5.

254. Rosenberg, *Tagebucher*, 383.

255. Manfred Hausmann, "Das Grossdeutsche Dichtertreffen in Weimar: Ein Überschlag und Ausblick," *Das Reich*, November 3, 1940.

256. See Hesse, "Beitrag," 28, 34; Erckmann, "Sinn," 7; Burte, *Reden*, 30.

257. See Johst's published poem "Dem Führer," in Velmede, *Führer*, 56; and his homily to both Hitler and Todt, in *Todt*, 15, 48.

258. Johst, *Ruf*, esp. 8, 19, and 63 (quotes).

259. Goebbels, *Tagebücher Diktate*, vol. 6, 110.

260. Johst aphorisms were published in Casper, *Johst*, see e.g. 7, 35, 68, 92–3. Johst received lame recognition from radio and literary reviews: *Meldungen aus dem Reich*, vol. 10, 3,953; Künkler, "Probleme," 199. On Johst and SS see esp. Düsterberg, *Johst*, 302–5; with Himmler: Himmler's corr. in *Himmler privat*, e.g. 337. See also Steinweis, *Art*, 28; Klee, *Kulturlexikon*, 258.

261. Sebald, *Luftkrieg*, 125. See Jünger's books *In Stahlgewittern* and *Das Wäldchen 125*, as well as *Der Arbeiter*, e.g., on the archetype of the fascist soldier, 107–8.

262. Kiesel, *Jünger*, 280–2; Martynkewicz, *Salon Deutschland*, 426.

263. See the comment on rabble behavior in Jünger, *Strahlungen*, 119.

264. Examples from World War II: Jünger, *Gärten*, 107–8, 129–31, 177 from the Weimar Republic; Jünger, *Kampf*, 14.

265. Friedländer, *Years*, 381.

266. Jünger, *Gärten*, 109, 196 (quote); Jünger, *Strahlungen*, 223.

267. Jünger, *Strahlungen*, 39–41.

268. De Mendelssohn, "Gegenstrahlungen," e.g. 164–6.

269. Böll, *Man*, 28–80.

270. Ernst Jünger, "Aus den Tagebüchern von 1939/40," *Das Reich*, February 9, 1941.

271. Jünger, *Strahlungen*, 138–9. See de Mendelssohn's criticism, "Gegenstrahlungen," 157.

272. Jünger, *Auf den Marmorklippen*.

273. Hesse, "Beitrag," 32.

274. Goebbels, *Tagebücher Diktate*, vol. 2, 315–16.

275. Beumelburg, *Kampf*, 127–30.

276. Manfred Hausmann in Bade and Haacke, *Jahr*, 159–63.

277. Curt Strohmeyer ibid., 374–6; Moser, "Am Rande," 30–2.

278. Horst Merkwitz in Bade and Haacke, *Jahr*, 246–7; Josef Magnus Wehner, ibid., 411–13; Rexroth, *Wehrmutstrauch*, 205; Slesina, *Soldaten*, 84.

279. Friedrich Wilhelm Hymmen in Bade and Haacke, *Jahr*, 178–80; Enno W. Müller-Waldeck, ibid., 263–8; Otto Voigtel, ibid., 393–4.

280. On French colonial troops, see Alfons von Czibulka in Bade and Haacke, *Jahr*, 66–8. On a perceived French racial mix: Fritz Fröhling, ibid., 123.

281. On the physiognomy of Soviet troops, see Rexroth, *Wehrmutstrauch*, 214, 218–19; Dwinger, "Bolschewismus," 13–14; Slesina, *Soldaten*, 23, 76. On Russian POWs, see the authoritative volume by Streit, *Keine Kameraden*, esp. 83–190.

282. Bauer, *Kraniche*, esp. 48, 115–17, 124, 126, 131–2, 189, 197–8; Rexroth, *Wehrmutstrauch*, 146–55; Dwinger, "Bolschewismus," 15; Slesina, *Soldaten*, 26; Brehm, *Geschichten*, 184. On the collusion between the SS and Wehrmacht against Jews on the Eastern Front, see Browning, *Origins*, 215–24, and Jürgen Matthäus in Browning, *Origins*, 247–67.

283. For a paradigmatic sampling of thoughts and concepts, see Brand, *Domen*, 48–50, 74, 124, 142–3, 160, 254–6; Burte, *Reden*, 29; Wirsing, *Zeitalter*, 26, 31–2, 42, 55, 62, 77–9, 120–3, 129–31; Dwinger, "Bolschewismus," 21; Ehmer, "Wirkungen," 26–30, 37–8; Frenssen, *Recht*, 14, 45–6; Nachenius, "Solidarität," 9–10; Schumann, "Krieg," 70–1; von Heiseler, "Oktober 1939," 33–4.

284. See Carossa's contribution to Velmede, *Führer*, 14 (quote), and his post-1945 skin-saving attempt in *Welten*, 117–27. On the ill-fated writers' union and his helmsmanship there, 1941–3, see Martin, *New Order*, 227–62.

285. Agnes Miegel, "An den Führer," in Miegel, *Ostland*, 5–6; Wilhelm von Scholz, "Deutsche Wünsche," in Scholz, *Gedichte*, 316–17; Ina Seidel, "Lichtdom," in Velmede, *Führer*, 16.

286. Strauss, *Lebenstanz*, 37, 109, 154, 177, 185, 232–3, 289–90, 330, 438–9.

287. Lorenz, *Unrast*, 5, 15–16 (quote), 31, 51, 58, 61, 67.

288. Christoph, *Sehnsucht*, 16, 46, 48, 60,162, 166, 284–5, 310–11, 412.

289. Speer, "Vorwort," esp. 9, 13.

290. See Wilhelm Grebe, "Wiedergesundung und Neuausrichtung des ländlichen Bauwesens: Zu dem Bauernhof-Wettbewerb, 1941–42" (September 1942), in Teut, *Architektur*, 277–9.

291. Goebbels, *Tagebücher Diktate*, vol. 4, 418.

292. All figures from Meckel, *Animation*, 39–40.

293. *Meldungen aus dem Reich*, vol. 5, 1,754–6; vol. 12, 4,835.

294. *Meldungen aus dem Reich*, vol. 4, 1,038; Thomae, *Kunst*, 159.

295. Petropoulos, *Faustian Bargain*, 93. See also Schlenker, *Salon*, 130–7.

296. Brantl, *Haus der Kunst*, 100–2, 106–8. On Gerdy Troost see Schlenker, *Salon*, 139–43.

297. Brantl, *Haus der Kunst*, 102.

298. *Meldungen aus dem Reich*, vol. 5, 1,340–1, 1,485, 1,754–6; vol. 7, 2,345–6; Goebbels, *Tagebücher Diktate*, vol. 2, 440; vol. 4, 415; Rathkolb, *Führertreu*, 68–78; Petropoulos, *Artists under Hitler*, 184–9.

299. *Meldungen aus dem Reich*, vol. 12, 4,804–5, 4,836–7.

300. Search www.gdk-research.de.

301. *Meldungen aus dem Reich*, vol. 12, 4,444.

302. Schlenker, "Art," 103.

303. Eber, *Sie kommen*, in Westecker, *Krieg*, 62; artroots.com/art5/elkeberarticle.htm.

304. Willrich, *Oberst Mölders*, in Westecker, *Krieg*, 27; www.cimilitaria.com/Wolfgang Willrich.htm.

305. Spiegel, *Tank*, in Merker, *Künste*, 288; Hoffmann, *Kunstausstellung*, 19; Ferdinand Spiegel in www.germanartgallery.eu.

306. Eichhorst, *Feuernde Geschütze bei der Beschiessung von Warschau*, in Westecker, *Krieg*, 47; galleria.thule-italia.com/franz-eichhorst/?lang=en; www.google.ca/search?q=eichhorst +erinnerung+an+stalingrad; Hoffmann, *Kunstausstellung*, 17.

307. Wilhelm Petersen, *Der Stosstruppführer*, in *SS-Leitheft* 9 (April 1943): 28; *Der Stosstruppkämpfer*, and *Der Nahkampf*, in *SS-Leitheft* 9 (May 1943): near 8; *Posten im Niemandsland*, in Merker, *Künste*, 293. For more on Petersen, see galleria.thule-italia. com/wilhelm-petersen/?lang=en; Christiansen and Petersen, *Petersen*, 5–20.

308. Adam, *Art*, 153.

309. Harm Wulf, *Sepp, der Bauernmaler*, artroots.com/art2/sepphilzarticle3.htm; reproduction of *Bäuerliche Venus*, ibid.

310. Goebbels, *Tagebücher Diktate*, vol. 4, 587; vol. 8, 259, 526 (quote); galleria.thule-italia. com/sepp-hilz/?lang=en; Hoffmann, *Kunstausstellung*, 8.

311. Puchinger, *Brunnenplatz im Berge*, reproduced in Hoffmann, *Kunstausstellung*, 24; Berann, *Bergheuer*, ibid., 31. Interestingly, Adam, *Art*, 153, has reproduced a Hilz picture similar to *Venus*, entitled *Eitelkeit (Vanity)*, and confused it with the original *Peasant Venus*. Although an act of scholarly impropriety, one can hardly blame him for the confusion.

312. Goebbels, *Tagebücher Fragmente*, vol. 4, 558.

313. Goebbels, *Tagebücher Diktate*, vol. 2, 357; vol. 8, 259, 515, 548; Hoffmann, *Kunstausstellung*, 12; Kriegel in hausderdeutschenkunst.de; Merker, *Künste*, 167; www. germanartgallery.eu/m/Webshop/0/product/info/Willy_Kriegel.

314. Petropoulos, *Faustian Bargain*, 261.

315. Padua, *Mars und Venus*, www.artnet.com/artists/paul-matthias-padua/mars-und-venus-kuA1uoL3z7LuwUyDLifUMQ2; Goebbels, *Tagebücher Fragmente*, vol. 4, 445; Klee, *Kulturlexikon*, 404; *Schlafende Diana*, reproduced in Hoffmann, *Kunstausstellung*, 11–12; *Der 10. Mai 1940*, reproduced in Merker, *Kunste*, 256.

316. *Abeiter, Bauern und Soldaten*, reproduced in Adam, *Art*, 162–3.

317. Hinz, *Malerei*, 77, 84; Petsch, "Malerei," 251–2.

318. Goebbels, *Tagebücher Diktate*, vol. 8, 548; www.gdk-research.de/db/apsisa.dll/ete?action=addFilter&filter=filter_kunstler&term=Schmitz-Wiedenbr%FCck.

319. *Amtliche Mitteilungen der Reichskulturkammer*, October 15, 1943, BAK, RD 33/2-2; corr. regarding Kreuder (April–December 1943), BAK, R 55/126; Hinkel to Tiessler, May 4, 1944, RKK Peter Kreuder, BAB (former BDC).

320. www.gdk-research.de/db/apsisa.dll/ete?action=addFilter&filter=filter_kunstler&term=Gerhardinger,Constantin; Goebbels, *Tagebücher Diktate*, vol. 8, 258, 526 (quote); Klee, *Kulturlexikon*, 162, 616; Spotts, *Hitler*, 179; Schlenker, *Salon*, 212–14. Petropoulos, *Faustian Bargain*, 260, writes that a second reason for Ziegler's treatment was that he had been found out as someone who wanted peace feelers with the Western Allies.

321. Goebbels, *Tagebücher Fragmente*, vol. 4, 52; Goebbels, *Tagebücher Diktate*, vol. 4, 417.

322. See the following Thorak reproductions: *Francisca da Rimini* (Hoffmann, *Kunstausstellung*, 33), *Hannele* (Hoffmann, *Kunstausstellung*, 35), [*Man and Horse in Giant Studio*] (Adam, *Art*, 204); also text in Hoffmann, *Kunstausstellung*, 24, 32; Goebbels, *Tagebücher Diktate*, vol. 1, 132; vol. 4, 572; Merker, *Künste*, 167; Petropoulos, *Art*, 169, 242; Petropoulos, *Faustian Bargain*, 266–7. The website for Grosse Deutsche Kunstausstellungen München lists no exhibition for Thorak in 1943 and after: www.gdk-research.de/db/apsisa.dll/ete?action=addFilter&filter=filter_kunstler&term=Thorak.

323. Goebbels, *Tagebücher Fragmente*, vol. 4, 52.

324. As most convincing proof of Breker's war style, see his three bas-reliefs, from the 1940 and 1941 Munich exhibitions, reproduced in Spotts, *Hitler*, 108–9. Also *Schreitende*, in Hoffmann, *Kunstausstellung*, 34; Adam, *Art*, 203.

325. Grothe, *Breker*, 1; Petropoulos, "Seduction," 211.

326. Petropoulos, *Art*, 35; Petropoulos, *Faustian Bargain*, 223–39.

327. Spotts, *Hitler*, 325–7.

328. Petropoulos, *Faustian Bargain*, 233.

329. August, "Stellung," 171–3; Baranowski, *Strength*, 203–4; Drewniak, *Theater*, 87–9; Klee, *Kulturlexikon*, 315.

330. According to Vossler, *Propaganda*, 83–4.

331. Goebbels in *Die Bühne*, no. 15 (August 10, 1940): 1.

332. Vossler, *Propaganda*, 81–2.

333. Goebbels, *Tagebücher Diktate*, vol. 3, 382.

334. Although in the ideological-literature category, Hitler's book topped the charts for the soldiers.

335. Hauptmann Dr. Wernecke's lecture about "Aufgabe und Methodik des Einsatzes der RWU-Filme bei der Truppenbetreuung," published in *Film und Bild* 8, no. 2 (February 15, 1942): 17.

336. Vossler, *Propaganda*, 215 (soldier quoted), 216; Adam, *Lesen*, 297–9; Barbian, *Literaturpolitik*, 364–5; *Meldungen aus dem Reich*, vol. 12, 4,506.

337. Soldatensender Belgrad: Drewniak, *Theater*, 89; Kater, *Drummers*, 126, 176–7.

338. Boelcke, *Kriegspropaganda*, 425; Goebbels, *Tagebücher Diktate*, vol. 2, 340, 523 (quote); Ernst Hellwig in "Soldaten zum Thema Film," *Film-Kurier*, December 24, 1943; Baranowski, *Strength*, 207.

339. Leopold Gutterer's review, "Unser Kulturschaffen im Kriege," in *Deutsche Allgemeine Zeitung*, August 5, 1942.

340. Goebbels, *Tagebücher Diktate*, vol. 2, 114, 525; Vossler, *Propaganda*, 82–3, 297, 317–18, 362; Drewniak, *Theater*, 87–8; August, "Stellung," 188; Baranowski, *Strength*, 205–6.

341. Dillmann, *Hilpert*, 154–5.

342. Goebbels, *Tagebücher Diktate*, vol. 3, 80, 376–7, 395; vol. 5, 161; vol. 10, 106; vol. 11, 582; *Meldungen aus dem Reich*, vol. 9, 3,372–3; Vossler, *Propaganda*, 84, 290–6, 302, 307; Drewniak, *Theater*, 89; Baranowski, *Strength*, 208–9; Goldhagen, *Executioners*, 244.

343. Hörbiger SD entry, July 2, 1943, RKK Paul Hörbiger, BAB (former BDC); Klee, *Kulturlexikon*, 232; Hörbiger, *Ich*.

344. Tschechowa in Siska, *Wunderwelt*, 84 (quotes); Tschechowa, *Uhren*, 179; Klee, *Kulturlexikon*, 559. A similar representation on her own behalf is in the memoirs of grande-dame actress Lil Dagover, *Dame*, 238–9.

345. Von Naso, *Leben*, 718; Klee, *Kulturlexikon*, 387; protocol of author's interview with Gertie Schönfelder, Lindau, June 2, 1988, YUA, CA ON00370 F0456. On Jewish ghetto members' craft productions such as cabinets, gloves, and shoes, before deportations to extermination camps, see Browning, *Origins*, 153–4.

346. Gründgens quoted in Michalzik, *Gründgens*, 104–5; Kitchen, *Third Reich*, 187–9.

347. Werner, *So*, 111–13.

348. Hielscher quoted in Adrian Prechtl, "Deutschlands letzte Diva, Filmstar und Entertainerin: Margot Hielscher," *Abendzeitung*, Munich, August 22, 2017.

349. Protocol of author's interview with Margot Hielscher, Munich, June 4, 1988, YUA, CA ON00370 F0456.

350. "Ballade von Leben, Liebe und Tod: Bericht von der Formung des Ufa-Films 'Das Herz einer Königin'," *Filmwelt* 49 (December 8, 1939): 6–7; Fox, *Film Propaganda*, 167; Tiedt, *Sterne*, 115; Quadflieg, *Wir spielen*, 110–11.

FIVE – ARTIST ÉMIGRÉS

1. Easton, *Count*, 398–406.

2. Brecht's second wife was the actress Helene Weigel, whom he married in 1930.

3. Gay was born Peter Joachim Fröhlich in Berlin, in 1923; he entered the United States with his parents in 1941, eventually becoming a distinguished historian at Yale University.

4. Röder and Strauss, *Handbuch*, XIII, XVII.

5. Röder and Strauss, *Handbuch*, XIX. Against these figures, Anthony Heilbut's compilation appears too high (*Exiled*, 26).

6. Clark, *Moscow*, 156–61; Albrecht et al., *Lexikon*, vol. 2, 480–2.

7. Wegner, *Klabund*, 168–81; Clark, *Moscow*, 151, 211; Lars-Broder Keil, "Deutschlands schönste Frau starb im Gulag," *Die Welt*, February 3, 2017. After 1945, Wangenheim played an important role in the movie industry of the Communist German Democratic Republic.

8. Frankenthal, *Fluch*, 227, 232.

9. Müssener, *Exil*, 61–72, 92, 95; Röder and Strauss, *Handbuch*, XL.

10. Röder and Strauss, *Handbuch*, XLI; Bermann Fischer, *Bedroht*, 120; Frankenthal, *Fluch*, 220; Mann and Mann, *Escape*, 237; Pritzker-Ehrlich, *Emigrantenlos*; Krispyn, *Writers*, 59–62; Mäusli, "Music Scene," 259–70; Palmier, *Weimar*, 154–61.

11. Friedländer, *Nazi Germany*, 220–3; Barron, "Artists," 15–16; Du Closel, *Stimmen*, 268–77; Holz, "Artists," 355–7.

12. Carsten, "Emigranten," 140, 148–50; Wasserstein, *Britain*, 9–10, 81–2, 94, 119–20, 345–9. See also Berghahn, *Refugees*, 121, 129–30, 137; Berstl, *Odyssee*, 182; Fend, "Hans Gál," 174–7; Heilbut, *Exiled*, 26; Hirschfeld, "Great Britain," 4–6, 9–12; Haffner, *Engländer*, 31–2, 102–3.

13. Röder and Strauss, *Handbuch*, XXVIII; Gradenwitz, "Ben-Haim," 120–1.

14. Abella and Troper, *None*, 36, 50–1, 144.

15. Zur Mühlen, *Fluchtziel*, 43–4, 53–9, 75, 86, 96–102.

16. Gay, *Question*, 149–50, 156–9; Friedländer, *Nazi Germany*, 299–300.
17. Röder and Strauss, *Handbuch*, XXIX.
18. Röder and Strauss, *Handbuch*, XXIX; Durzak, "Exilsituation," 147–8; Davie, *Refugees*, 16–17, 21–5, 29, 33–6, 44, 63, 88; Friedrich, *City of Nets*, 47.
19. Möller, *Exodus*, 47.
20. Mann and Mann, *Escape*, 237.
21. Carsten, "Emigranten," 139; Müssener, *Exil*, 96; Davie, *Refugees*, 287–8.
22. Carsten, "Emigranten," 139.
23. Davie, *Refugees*, 257–9.
24. Ollendorf-Reich, *Reich*, esp. 48–64; pre-1933 history in Hoeres, *Kultur*, 64.
25. Frankenthal, *Fluch*, 203–45.
26. Reifenberg, "Jahre," 44; Gillessen, *Posten*, 173.
27. Gumpert, *Hölle*, 276–8; Kater, *Doctors under Hitler*, 211.
28. Der Lühe, *Erika Mann*, 178–80.
29. See Heilbut, *Exiled*; Taylor, *Strangers*; Merrill-Mirsky, *Exiles*; Brinkmann and Wolff, *Driven into Paradise*.
30. For whatever reasons, Walter has overstated the degree of his positive acculturation in America, see *Thema*, 441–3.
31. Werfel quoted in Jungk, *Werfel*, 287.
32. For émigré historians in the United States, this has been done exemplarily by Catherine Epstein, "Schicksalsgeschichte," 116–17.
33. Taylor, *Strangers*, 174.
34. Gay, *Freud*, 631; Tergit, "Exilsituation," 138.
35. Koestler, *Writing*, 513–14; Cesarani, *Koestler*, 145–6, 156–7, 160–2, 170–1.
36. Palmer, *Lilli*, 132–56. See also Berghahn, *Refugees*, 92, 104–5.
37. Bergner, *Bewundert*, 190–1.
38. Milton, "Culture," 87; Gradenwitz, "Ben-Haim," 120–1; Müssener, *Exil*, 293.
39. Raab, "Internierung," 294; Raab Hansen, *Musiker*, 144, 151, 154, 176–8, 218; Du Closel, *Stimmen*, 302, 307, 311–14; Scheding, "Tendencies," 249–50, 255–6; Haas, *Music*, 252–5.
40. Flavell, *Grosz*, 95; Krenek, *Tagebücher*, 105–6.
41. Türcke, "Klänge," 20–1.
42. Bergner, *Bewundert*, 114–15, 147, 180; Kortner, *Tage*, 274–5; Mann and Mann, *Escape*, 60, 352–4.
43. Viertel, *Kindness*, 247; Zuckmayer, *Stück*, 408.
44. Bergner played Catherine the Great once (with a Saxe-Anhalt German accent?); Dietrich and Lenya were more typically femmes fatales. See Bergner, *Bewundert*, 115; Spoto, *Blue Angel*, 130, 172.
45. Weill to Jolles, May 27, 1949, WC, Weill and Jolles correspondence.
46. Davie, *Refugees*, 351.
47. See Willett, "Künste," 186; Karl Stern's observation in Berghahn, *Refugees*, 98; Pross, *Emigration*, 58.
48. Mann and Mann, *Escape*, 303 (quote); Feuchtwanger, "Schriftsteller," 548–50. See also Walter, "Literatur," 84.
49. Vaget, "Wetter," 72; McGilligan, *Fritz Lang*, 293; Kortner, *Tage*, 278; Heilbut, *Exiled*, 34.
50. Zweig, *Welt*, 394; Zweig quoted in Prochnik, *Exile*, 144; Mann, *Tagebücher, 1935–1936*, 218.
51. Cesarani, *Koestler*, 145, 178; Heilbut, *Exiled*, 34.
52. Heilbut, *Exiled*, 206; Vaget, "Wetter," 72–3.
53. Zuckmayer, *Stück*, 409–10, 417, 414–15, 424–5.
54. Berstl, *Odyssee*, 178.
55. Stefan Wolpe in *Stefan Wolpe*, 112 (quote). See also Clarkson, "Stefan Wolpe," 219–44.
56. Entry for March 9, 1939, in Krenek, *Tagebücher*, 105 (quote); Brinkmann, "Letter," 3–20.

57. Wingler, *Bauhaus*, 198–9; Hahn, "Bauhaus," 14–16; Findeli, "Ästhetik," 34–6, 40–1; Engelbrecht, "Moholy-Nagy," 55–7.
58. Schwitters as quoted in Willett, "Künste," 190; Berghahn, *Refugees*, 95–6, 103; Müssener, *Exil*, 296–7.
59. Bergner, *Bewundert*, 193–5; Willett, "Künste," 197.
60. Kater, "Weill und Brecht," 62–7; Heilbut, *Exiled*, 183–5.
61. McGilligan, *Fritz Lang*, 210, 212, 215, 231, 262; Heilbut, *Exiled*, 256–7.
62. Wicclair, *Kreuzburg*, 126.
63. Loewy, *Babelsberg*, 59, 61, 71; Horak, *Fluchtpunkt*, 3–4, 22, 27–8; Doherty, *Hollywood*, 202, 338–45. On refugee composers in Hollywood, see Haas, *Music*, 265–7.
64. Heilbut, *Exiled*, 224; Palmier, *Weimar*, 526–8; Mann and Mann, *Escape*, 300–2; Taylor, *Strangers*, 65–7, 215–18; Kortner, *Tage*, 320; Bergner, *Bewundert*, 230–2; Reinhardt, *Genius*, 304–8.
65. Mahler-Werfel, *Mein Leben*, 367.
66. Taylor, *Strangers*, 148.
67. Friedrich, *City of Nets*, 58; Jungk, *Werfel*, 297; Kater, *Composers*, 65.
68. Jungk, *Werfel*, 297.
69. Heilbut, *Exiled*, 182.
70. Flavell, *Grosz*, 85, 88, 91, 98, 213, 230–1; Reinhardt, *Genius*, 309.
71. Zuckmayer, *Stück*, 400, 418, 419 (quote); Krenek, *Tagebücher*, 105–6; Maurer Zenck, "Challenges," 175.
72. Cesarani, *Koestler*, 100; Der Lühe, *Emigration*, 336; Berstl, *Odyssee*, 177–8, 183.
73. Pfanner, *Exile*, 86–7; Heilbut, *Exiled*, 183–4.
74. Taylor, *Strangers*, 9; Gay, *Question*, 179; Bergner, *Bewundert*, 195 (quotes).
75. Davie, *Refugees*, 58.
76. Symonette and Kowalke, *Speak Low*, 436; McGilligan, *Fritz Lang*, 217; Viertel, *Kindness*.
77. Spoto, *Blue Angel*, 111.
78. Wegner, *Exil*, 102.
79. Willett, "Künste," 186; Berghahn, *Refugees*, 92; Prochnik, *Exile*, 10, 168.
80. Willett, "Künste," 189–90.
81. Zweig, *Welt*, 356–7, 390 (quote), 391; Wegner, *Exil*, 94–5.
82. Zweig, *Insulted*, IX–X; Durzak, "Diaspora," 48; Wolf, "Stationen," 214–15.
83. Said, *Reflections*, 178.
84. See Feuchtwanger, *Exil*; Mann, *Vulkan*; Mann, *Der Wendepunkt*, and Möller, *Exodus*, 14.
85. Schoenberg circular, December 25, 1934, LBI, AR-A7049/10.
86. Weill to Lenya, July 1943, in Symonette and Kowalke, *Speak Low*, 369.
87. Paul to Gertrud Hindemith, March 27, 1939, in Rexroth, *Hindemith*, 224 (quote); Symonette and Kowalke, *Speak Low*, 209.
88. Jungk, *Werfel*, 302–3; Engelbrecht, "Moholy-Nagy," 57; McGilligan, *Fritz Lang*, 216–17. Remarque witnessed the whistling (von Sternburg, *Remarque*, 312).
89. Willett, "Künste," 187–8 (Zweig quoted 187).
90. Carr, *Hollywood*, 238–47.
91. Röder and Strauss, *Handbuch*, XXVI; Heilbut, *Exiled*, 45; Taylor, *Strangers*, 114–15; McGilligan, *Fritz Lang*, 219, 288, 290; Kortner, *Tage*, 304, 347–8; Reinhardt, *Genius*, 304.
92. Heilbut, *Exiled*, 300; Lehnert, "Repräsentation," 398; Mann, *Memoiren*, 132 (quote); Kater, *Composers*, 117–19. Brecht and Mann differed (after summer 1943) over who bore ultimate responsibility for National Socialism in Germany, with Brecht blaming solely the upper, capitalist, classes (Borchmeyer, *Was*, 873–92). See below at n. 210.
93. Grosz, *Little Yes*, 317–21; Flavell, *Grosz*, 117–19.
94. Koestler, *Writing*, 454–6; Cesarani, *Koestler*, 143; Hans R. Vaget in *Thomas Mann, Agnes Meyer*, 30 (quote).
95. Mann, *Tagebücher, 1940–1943*, 445, 546, 775; Viertel, *Kindness*, 279–80.

96. Mann, *Wendepunkt*, 430; Gregor-Dellin, "Exilromane," 460; Lehnert, "Repräsentation," 398; Kurzke, *Thomas Mann*, 474–81. Spotts's most recent *Cursed Legacy* is suffused with striking examples.

97. Rexroth, *Hindemith*, 208–10, 222; Brinkmann, "Letter," 12. On the precariousness of exalting German music see the contributions to Applegate and Potter, *Music*.

98. Horowitz, *Artists*, 77–160. See also Heilbut, *Exiled*, 127–8, 160; Ryding and Pechefsky, *Walter*, 187, 274, 320; Lehmann and Faber, *Serkin*, 77–150; Kater, *Drummers*, 28, 33.

99. Gay, "Jews," 29; Goehr, "Music," 78; Danuser, "Composers," 160; Kater, *Composers*, 83–5.

100. Gilliam, "Opera Composer," 223–5; Korngold, *Korngold*, 92–7.

101. Berstl, *Odyssee*, 164; Mann and Mann, *Escape*, 252–3; Heilbut, *Exiled*, 137–8; Flavell, *Grosz*, 90, 166–7, 214.

102. Wegner, *Exil*, 89, 96; Feuchtwanger, "Nachwort" in *Exil*, 789; Reich-Ranicki, "Feuchtwanger," 443, 446, 450.

103. Viertel, *Kindness*, 210; Crawford, *Evenings*, 4–8, 32; Korngold, *Korngold*, 69.

104. Maurer Zenck, "Challenges," 184–5; Kater, *Composers*, 189–99.

105. Mahler-Werfel, *Mein Leben*, 367.

106. Entry for April 8, 1933, in Pfeiffer-Belli, *Kessler*, 358.

107. Zweig, *Insulted*, X.

108. Easton, *Count*, 406–8; Barzantny, *Kessler*, 275–83.

109. Mahler-Werfel, *Mein Leben*, 350, 361; Giroud, *Mahler*, 151, 154 (Mahler-Werfel's quote); Junck, *Werfel*, 317–18. Apart from her cynicism, Mahler-Werfel had a point: Diabetes is, and was, proportionately higher among Jews. See Efron, *Medicine*, 132–42.

110. Albrecht et al., *Lexikon*, vol. 2, 229–30; Wegner, *Exil*, 100; Bronsen, "Sonderfall," 67–9, 76, 81–2.

111. Zuckmayer, *Stück*, 450; Flavell, *Grosz*, 299–300.

112. Koestler, *Writing*, 512–13; Cesarani, *Koestler*, 161–2; Arendt, *Men*, 170–1 (quote).

113. *The New York Times*, March 4, 1983; Klee, *Kulturlexikon*, 294.

114. "Memorial Gathering Honors Stefan Zweig," *The New York Times*, March 1, 1942; Heilbut, *Exiled*, 44; Junck, *Werfel*, 294–5; Wegner, *Exil*, 98–9; Mann, *Briefwechsel*, 305.

115. Mann, *Wendepunkt*, 450–1.

116. Schaenzler, *Mann*, 520; Erika Mann to Lehmann, Zurich, June 1949, GC.

117. As well as for acting in the 1927 film *The Way of All Flesh* (*Telegraph*, May 16, 2016).

118. Spoto, *Blue Angel*, 53–66; Bach, *Dietrich*, 290–308.

119. Palmier, *Weimar*, 591; Bach, *Dietrich*, 290, 308.

120. Table 2.1 in Falter, *Hitlers Wähler*, 25.

121. Kulturinterview/Archiv, April 1, 2005, deutschlandfunkkultur.de; Spoto, *Blue Angel*, 53–66.

122. Jelavich, *Berlin Cabaret*, 101–4; Bemmann, *Musenkinder-Memorien*, 146; Bach, *Dietrich*, 74.

123. Dietrich's citizenship was granted in 1939. Spoto, *Blue Angel*, 139–40.

124. Von Sternburg, *Remarque*, 61–134; Eksteins, *Rites of Spring*, 283.

125. Von Sternburg, *Remarque*, 147–79; 240; Eksteins, *Rites of Spring*, 276, 287, 298; Longerich, *Goebbels*, 150–1; Ullrich, *Hitler*, 243.

126. Von Sternburg, *Remarque*, 227–8, 241–5; 269–84.

127. Busch memorandum, March 8, 1933, RKK Fritz Busch, BAB (former BDC); Busch, *Pages*, 192–215; Busch, *Busch*, 52–129.

128. German Embassy at The Hague to Auswärtiges Amt, October 18, 1933, incl. memorandum of October 17, 1933, BAK, R55/1181.

129. Lüddecke et al., "Denkschrift," March 18, 1933, RKK Fritz Busch, BAB (former BDC); Busch, *Pages*, 192–208; Busch, *Busch*, 52–62; *Münchner Neueste Nachrichten*, January 19, 1933; *Deutsche Kultur-Wacht*, no. 7 (1933), 13; Stargardt-Wolff, *Wegbereiter*, 283.

130. Posse to Adolph, March 15, 1933, RKK Fritz Busch, BAB (former BDC); Bauer to Strauss, March 20, 1933, RG (quote).

131. Bauer to Strauss, March 20, 1933, RG.
132. Bosse, "Führerverantwortlichkeit," 484–5.
133. Busch, *Pages*, 196–8 (quote 197); Busch, *Busch*, 62–3.
134. Furtwängler to Rust, June 4, 1933, RKK Wilhelm Furtwängler, BAB (former BDC); *Melos* 12 (1933), 257; Busch, *Pages*, 206–15; Rathkolb, *Führertreu*, 101; Prieberg, *Musik im NS-Staat*, 42; Prieberg, *Kraftprobe*, 109–10; Spotts, *Bayreuth*, 170–1.
135. Busch, *Pages*, 211; Busch, *Busch*, 66.
136. Hinkel to Demann [?], October 1933, RKK Fritz Busch, BAB (former BDC); Beussel, "Zeichen," 670; Prieberg, *Kraftprobe*, 110–13; Scanzoni and Kende, *Prinzipal*, 198–9; Shirakawa, *Music Master*, 393.
137. Braun to Hinkel, April 10, 1933; Busch to Hinkel, April 26, 1933; Brandt to Hinkel, September 22, 1933, RKK Fritz Busch, BAB (former BDC).
138. Pâris, *Lexikon*, 104–5; Honegger and Massenkeil, *Lexikon*, vol. 1, 394–5; memorandum about Busch, March 12, 1934, BAK, R55/1181; Mann, *Tagebücher, 1933–1934*, 84, 261, 271, 290, 375; Mann, *Tagebücher, 1940–1943*, 138; Otto Erhardt, "Fritz Busch," in Müller and Mertz, *Diener*, 141; Busch, *Busch*, 77–252; J. Hellmut Freund in Heister et al., *Musik*, 75.
139. Lehmann to Wolfgang zu Putlitz, June 20, 1966, APA; Putlitz, *Laaske*, 231–2.
140. Lehmann, "Göring," 187–99.
141. Fragment, *Völkischer Beobachter*, [November 1933], GC. For the 1933 Bayreuth season Toscanini, already an enemy of Fascist Italy, canceled a planned guest conductorship in protest against Hitler's coming to power (Sachs, *Music*, 227).
142. Gary Hickling, Lotte Lehmann Chronology (Kailua, 2004–6), LLFA.
143. Else Walter to Lehmann, November 29, 1933, ATW/15.
144. See Lehmann-Heger-Furtwängler-Tietjen-Göring-Krause correspondence (1933–4, 1955; Göring's quote according to Tietjen to Lehmann, April 26, 1934, ATW, 17), in ATW/15; ATW/17; ATW/18.
145. Davenport, "Song," 22; "Reich Ban Decreed on Lotte Lehmann," *The New York Times*, November 10, 1935; Lehmann to Hansing, April 10, 1935; September 5, 1936, GC; Lehmann to Lachmann, December 10, 1938, ATW/TNLL; Marboe memo, November 10, 1955, LLFA; Lehmann to Burgau, July 31, 1956, GC; Lehmann to Walter, January 14, 1956, GC; Lehmann to Erika Mann, November 28, 1968, EMA/914/78; Lehmann to Hecht, February 14 and November 23, 1938, GC; Lehmann to Bundestheaterverwaltung, January 18, 1955, LLFA; Lehmann to Klee, February 28, 1955; Lehmann to Shawe-Taylor, November 22, 1974, GC; Lehmann to Marboe, December 29, 1955, CG; Sheean, *Love*, 238; Emmons, *Tristanissimo*, 160; Ewen, *Men*, 148; Geissmar, *Musik*, 244; Erika Mann in Mann, *Briefe*, 622; Varnay, *Years*, 6; Glass, *Lehmann*, xvi; Rasponi, *Prima Donnas*, 484; and, lastly, Kater, *Muse*, 120.
146. Mann to "Frau Sonne" [Lotte Lehmann], August 2, 1941, GC; Mann, *Tagebücher, 1940–1943*, 118 (quote), 281, 303, 447–8.
147. Mann, *Tagebücher, 1937–1939*, 387; Mann, *Tagebücher, 1940–1943*, 121–2; Remarque quoted in von Sternburg, *Remarque*, 312; Vaget, *Amerikaner*, 362. On Hesterberg and Mann: PEM, *Heimweh*, 230; Klee, *Kulturlexikon*, 219–20.
148. This affair, with its background and consequences, has been exhaustively treated in Vaget, *Erbe*, 249–327.
149. This is a point emphasized by Katia Mann after World War II in her *Memoiren*, 107, and Mann himself in interview with *The New York Times*, February 22, 1938.
150. See the telling example for May 1935 in Ebermayer, *Deutschland*, 532–3.
151. The letter is published in Mann, *Vater*, 104–7 (quote 106). See also Mann, *Memoiren*, 100, 105, 107; Ebermayer, *Deutschland*, 101–2; Krüll, *Netz*, 357–9; Vaget, *Amerikaner*, 60–3, 120, 241.
152. *The New Yorker* (May 6, 1938): 5; Mann, *Tagebücher, 1937–1939*, 305, 383; Mann, *Tagebücher, 1940–1943*, 239, 343, 347, 399; Vaget, *Amerikaner*, 221–5, 238–47, 254, 280–1.

153. Mann, *Tagebücher, 1937–1939*, 207, 224, 493; Mann, *Tagebücher, 1940–1943*, 224, 226–7; Vaget, *Amerikaner*, 149; Krüll, *Netz*, 383; von Sternburg, *Remarque*, 322–3.

154. Mann, *Tagebücher, 1940–1943*, 285, 414, 433, 464, 500; Mann, *Tagebücher, 1944–46*, 119; Vaget, *Amerikaner*, 181–7, 207–8, 214–15, 259.

155. Mann, *Tagebücher, 1940–1943*, 63, 332, 399.

156. Mann, *Tagebücher, 1937–1939*, 393; Vaget, *Amerikaner*, 67–156.

157. Mann, *Tagebücher, 1940–1943*, 80, 227, 294; Mann, *Briefwechsel*, 286.

158. Entry for June 30, 1941, in Mann, *Tagebücher, 1940–1943*, 288.

159. Mann, *Briefwechsel*, 212, 219.

160. Mann, *Tagebücher, 1940–1943*, 130, 133, 290.

161. Entry for April 6, 1938, in Mann, *Tagebücher, 1937–1939*, 204. "Colin" was Mann's live-in male secretary at the time.

162. Mann, *Tagebücher, 1937–1939*, 423.

163. Mann, *Tagebücher, 1937–1939*, 242–3; Mann, *Tagebücher, 1940–1943*, 655.

164. Entry for February 26, 1939, in Mann, *Tagebücher, 1937–1939*, 365 (1st quote) and for June 19, 1939, ibid., 409 (2nd quote).

165. Mann, *Tagebücher, 1940–1943*, 506.

166. Mann, *Tagebücher, 1937–1939*, 310; Mann, *Tagebücher, 1940–1943*, 37, 151, 346; Mann, *Briefwechsel*, 307.

167. Mann, *Tagebücher, 1937–1939*, 226, 311; Mann, *Tagebücher, 1940–1943*, 5, 102, 404, 572, 595, 617; Mann, *Tagebücher, 1944–46*, 15; Mann, *Memoiren*, 52, 146–7; Krüll, *Netz*, 201; Vaget, *Amerikaner*, 443–78. On Mann and music, consummately Vaget, *Seelenzauber*, 21–47.

168. Mann, *Tagebücher, 1937–1939*, 221, 270, 436; Mann, *Tagebücher, 1940–1943*, 38, 125, 144, 293, 335–6, 386, 526, 616. See also Kershaw, *Hubris*, 481–2. Adorno used his mother's Corsican maiden name in order to emphasize non-Jewishness.

169. Mann, *Tagebücher, 1937–1939*, 251, 259, 417.

170. Vaget, *Amerikaner*, 250.

171. Vaget, *Amerikaner*, 101–2, 126; Krüll, *Netz*, 375.

172. Printed in Mann, *Briefwechsel*, 301–2.

173. Nagler, "Internment," 75–9 (Roosevelt quoted 75).

174. See the case of Lotte Lehmann: Lehmann to Hope, April 24, June 4 and 10, 1942, CU/2; Rauch to Lehmann, June 4, 1942, GC.

175. Entry for September 27, 1940, in Mann, *Tagebücher, 1940–1943*, 155.

176. Entry for March 7, 1941, in Mann, *Tagebücher, 1940–1943*, 229; Klee, *Kulturlexikon*, 295.

177. Mann, *Tagebücher, 1940–1943*, 257–8.

178. Mann, *Tagebücher, 1940–1943*, 279, 281.

179. Entry for July 14, 1943, in Mann, *Tagebücher, 1940–1943*, 600.

180. See, e.g., Mann, *Tagebücher, 1937–1939*, 193.

181. Mann, *Tagebücher, 1940–1943*, 153.

182. Entry for February 11, 1941, in Mann, *Tagebücher, 1940–1943*, 220.

183. Mann, *Tagebücher, 1940–1943*, 223.

184. Mann, *Tagebücher, 1940–1943*, 437.

185. Mann, *Tagebücher, 1944–46*, 122.

186. Mann, *Tagebücher, 1937–1939*, 427; Mann, *Tagebücher, 1940–1943*, 393, 444–5; Mann, *Tagebücher, 1944–46*, 7, 67.

187. Mann, *Tagebücher, 1940–1943*, 458; Mann, *Tagebücher, 1944–46*, 34.

188. Mann, *Tagebücher, 1940–1943*, 247, 250, 259; Mann, *Tagebücher, 1944–46*, 26, 154.

189. Mann, *Briefwechsel*, 286.

190. Mann, *Vater*, 47.

191. "Mann Opens War on Nazi Concepts; Asks Recruits in Moral Struggle," *The New York Times*, August 15, 1937 (quotes); Vaget, *Amerikaner*, 157–9.

192. "Thomas Mann Speaks in Favour of the Weimar Republik (1922)," alphahistory.com/weimarrepublic/thomas-mann-speaks-in-favour-of-the-weimar-republic-1922; Mann, *Republik.*

193. Mann, *Ansprache,* esp. 11–21, 25–6.

194. "Mann Finds U.S. Sole Peace Hope," *The New York Times,* February 22, 1938.

195. Mann, *Tagebücher, 1937–1939,* 187, 193, 227, 249, 277. Quote is from entry for May 30, 1938, ibid., 230.

196. Langer, *Encyclopedia,* 988, 1,128; Kershaw, *Nemesis,* 229.

197. Mann, *Tagebücher, 1937–1939,* 288, 301, 379; Kershaw, *Nemesis,* 95–6.

198. Mann, "Brother," 31, 133.

199. Anne O'Hare McCormick, "Two Brilliantly Revealing Studies of Hitler's Life," *The New York Times,* May 24, 1936. The books' titles included *Hitler* in both cases, Heiden's having been published in New York by Mann's own publisher, Alfred A. Knopf.

200. Ullrich's quote in *Hitler,* 122.

201. Heiden, *Fuehrer,* 87–182.

202. See, correctly, Jäckel, *Hitlers Herrschaft,* 26, 151. On the charisma of "prophets and heroes, magicians and demagogues, doctors and quacks, leaders of mobs or orchestras or robber bands" in the Weberian sense see Reinhard Bendix's chapter, "Charismatic Leadership and Domination," in his *Max Weber,* 298–328, esp. 299 (quote).

203. Freud is not mentioned in *Mein Kampf,* nor is psychology or psychiatry.

204. Mann, *Tagebücher, 1937–1939,* 390, 452, 456, 461.

205. Langer, *Encyclopedia,* 1,036, 1,135; Kershaw, *Nemesis,* 210–11.

206. Mann, *Briefwechsel,* 240.

207. Mann, *Tagebücher, 1937–1939,* 474, 483; Mann, *Tagebücher, 1940–1943,* 8, 60, 73–5, 103, 142.

208. Mann, *Listen,* 102–6 (quote 103). See also Mann, *Briefwechsel,* 273; Mann, *Tagebücher, 1940–1943,* 254, 261, 266, 275, 293, 475, 484, 487.

209. I am indebted for my knowledge of Mann's sources to Professor Hans R. Vaget of Smith College (written communication of October 30, 2017).

210. Vaget, *Amerikaner,* 427–9. Declaration quoted 428.

211. Mann, *Tagebücher, 1940–1943,* 590; Mann, *Tagebücher, 1944–46,* 6, 74, 145.

212. "Mann Finds U.S. Sole Peace Hope," *The New York Times,* February 22, 1938.

213. Mann, *Tagebücher, 1937–1939,* 291, 327; Mann, *Tagebücher, 1944–46,* 8.

214. Mann, *Tagebücher, 1940–1943,* 4, 25; entry for October 3, 1940, ibid., 159 (quote).

215. Mann, *Tagebücher, 1940–1943,* 597, 600; entry for November 2, 1943, ibid., 645 (quote).

216. Mann, *Tagebücher, 1944–46,* 6.

217. Mann's acceptance speech partially cited in Krüll, *Netz,* 341.

218. "Mann Opens War on Nazi Concepts; Asks Recruits in Moral Struggle," *The New York Times,* August 15, 1937.

219. "Mann Finds U.S. Sole Peace Hope," *The New York Times,* February 22, 1938.

220. Entry for September 26, 1938, in Mann, *Tagebücher, 1937–1939,* 298.

221. Mann, "Brother," 31, 132.

SIX – TRANSFER BEYOND ZERO HOUR, MAY 1945

1. Goebbels, *Tagebücher Fragmente,* vol. 1, 36, 45–6, 145, 483, 489, 492, 504; Longerich, *Goebbels,* 708, n. 99.

2. Chamberlin, *Kultur,* 41. Alfred Andersch was one young writer who welcomed Mann's return for guidance (Vaget, *Amerikaner,* 496).

3. Thiess quoted in Sarkowicz and Mentzer, *Literatur,* 52.

4. Mann quoted in Sarkowicz and Mentzer, *Literatur,* 53.

5. Mann, *Ansprache,* esp. 4, 7, 16; Josef Marein, "Thomas Mann: Goethe-Preisträger östlich und westlich," *Die Zeit,* June 23, 1949; Kater, *Weimar,* 213–15.

6. Sarkowicz and Mentzer, *Literatur*, 54.

7. Vaget, *Amerikaner*, 376–415.

8. Schnell, *Geschichte*, 67–112; Kaiser interviewed by Georg Diez and Dominik Wichmann in *Süddeutsche Zeitung Magazin*: sz-magazin.sueddeutsche.de (quotes).

9. For the music scene, one might mention only Hanns Eisler and Paul Dessau. For the literary scene, Stephan Hermlin (Rudolf Leder) and Stefan Heym.

10. Krüll, *Netz*, 391–2; Spotts, *Legacy*, 256.

11. Von Sternburg, *Remarque*, 354, 365.

12. Sarkowicz and Mentzer, *Literatur*, 54, 61–2.

13. Sirk quoted in Hardt, *Caligari*, 174.

14. Kreimeier, *Ufa-Story*, 440–1.

15. Vincent Canby, "Film: 1951 'Lost One,' Directed by Peter Lorre," *The New York Times*, August 1, 1984 (quote); Hardt, *Caligari*, 174.

16. Wicclair, *Kreuzburg*, 87.

17. Ganz et al., *Bois*, 16.

18. Schäche, *Architektur*, 87–9 (quote).

19. "Studies in Twelve-Tone Counterpoint." See Drüner and Günther, *Musik*, 342–3.

20. Drüner and Günther, *Musik*, 341. On Hartmann's Third Reich struggles, see Kater, *Composers*, 86–110.

21. Kaiser interviewed by Georg Diez and Dominik Wichmann in *Süddeutsche Zeitung Magazin*: sz-magazin.sueddeutsche.de (quotes).

22. Bergengruen himself vitiated his post-war claim of clandestine resistance through anti-Nazi literature by claiming the existence of a "secret language" the "clumsy" (!) SS was unable to read and then by saying that "people in the Propaganda Ministry knew how to read" (*Schreibtischerinnerungen*, 192, 200). See also Lewy, *Harmful*, 192.

23. An example would be Paul Scheffer (1883–1963), who was chief editor of the Nazi-coordinated *Berliner Tageblatt* but in 1936 was fired. He left for the United States, and after 1940, rather than joining the émigré diaspora, served as the freelancing America correspondent for *Das Reich* and other Nazi dailies (Scheffer, in *Deutsche Biographie*: www.deutsche-biographie.de/sfz111236.html#ndbcontent). See Chapter 4 at n. 162.

24. Kater, *Ahnenerbe*, 145–90; Martin, *New Order*, 149–262.

25. Grassi quoted in Martin, *New Order*, 250.

26. Ebermayer's observation on October 15, 1933 (*Deutschland*, 187).

27. This listing owes much to Martin Kitchen's exhaustive register in *Third Reich*, 185. Quarrels between Himmler and Rosenberg are discussed, at length, in Bollmus, *Amt Rosenberg*, and Kater, *Ahnenerbe*. On Atlantis, see Chapoutot, *Greeks*, 35–6.

28. Potter, *Most German*, 225–6, 131–55; Kater, *Ahnenerbe*, 11, 28, 136, 193–4, 401, 409; Bollmus, *Amt Rosenberg*, 77, 88.

29. Hitler at Führer headquarters on August 31, 1944, quoted in Heiber, *Lagebesprechungen*, 277.

30. Meinecke used the term "Afterkultur" (*Katastrophe*, 170–3 [quote]).

31. Joachim Kaiser interviewed by Georg Diez and Dominik Wichmann in *Süddeutsche Zeitung Magazin*: sz-magazin.sueddeutsche.de.

32. Adorno, "Terms," 115.

33. On Hölderlin and Nazis, see Martynkewicz, *Salon Deutschland*, 304–5; Chapoutot, *Greeks*, 138–9.

34. Schäche, *Architektur*, 86–7. An example of this home (from the inside) may be seen in the German heath house shown in the 1954 Deutsche London Film Verleih film *Geständnis unter vier Augen* by André Michel, with Hildegard Knef and Ivan Desny.

35. Drüner and Günther, *Musik*, 341 (esp. Hartmann's quote); Haas, *Music*, 280.

36. Honegger and Massenkeil, *Lexikon*, vol. 3, 137–8; vol. 4, 74–5.

37. Krempel, "Moderne," 332–3; Konstanze Crüwell, "Die Freiheit von Blau, Weiss und Grün," *Frankfurter Allgemeine Zeitung*, March 28, 2017.

38. Kreimeier, *Ufa-Story*, 438–43; Krützen, *Albers*, 285–6.
39. Bark and Gress, *Shadow*, 93–346; Frei, *Adenauer's Germany*.
40. Stockhorst, *Köpfe*, 156, 310–11; Klee, *Personenlexikon*, 186–7, 441.
41. Ulrich Herbert, "Als die Nazis wieder gesellschaftsfähig wurden," *Die Zeit*, January 10, 1997, ZEITONLINE; Ronen Steinke, "Im Bonner Justizministerium arbeiteten besonders viele Nazis," October 9, 2016, Sueddeutsche.de; Sascha Zoske, "Verwaltungswissenschaft: NS-Belastung ist 'immer noch ein heisses Eisen'," September 10, 2017, faz.net; Stockhorst, *Köpfe*, 156, 310–11. The SRP was banned in 1953 as unconstitutional (Wehler, *Gesellschaftsgeschichte: Fünfter Band*, 9, 288, 405).
42. Fröhlich, "Rückkehr," 107.
43. Kater, "Reeducation," 105.
44. Herf, *Divided Memory*, 201–333.
45. Note the alliteration to Streicher's *Der Stürmer*. See Böhme's anthology of Nazi poems, *Rufe*, in which he himself is represented eleven times: 16, 28, 114, 119, 132, 165, 201, 293, 320, 336, 361. See also Klee, *Kulturlexikon*, 58–9.
46. Sarkowicz, "Schriftsteller," 203; Zimmermann, "Literatur," 382; Sarkowicz and Mentzer, *Literatur*, 58–64; Klee, *Kulturlexikon*, 133, 179, 227, 295–6, 500–1; Kater, *Weimar*, 278. Fechter was typical of many German conservative intellectuals: He initially adored National Socialism and esp. *Mein Kampf*, but later became more critical of the regime. Yet his right-wing stance was unbroken beyond 1945 (Zuckmayer, *Geheimreport*, 110–12).
47. Paret, *Barlach*, 99–100 (quotes); Petropoulos, *Artists under Hitler*, 43, 277.
48. Klee, *Kulturlexikon*, 504.
49. Lauzemis, "Ideologie," 67; Klee, *Kulturlexikon*, 31–2.
50. Speer, *Erinnerungen*, 385–6; Brechtken, *Speer*, 366–576 (Posen: 462–3).
51. Simpson, "Historical Context," 151–2, Noelle quoted 152.
52. Elisabeth Noelle, "Wer informiert Amerika? Journalisten, Radiosprecher, Filme," *Das Reich*, June 8, 1941 (quotes); Simpson, "Historical Context," 154–61; Becker, *Noelle-Neumann*, 7–132; Claudia Haas and Henriette Löwitsch, "Neue Vorwürfe gegen Frau Noelle-Naumann," *Die Welt*, September 1, 1997.
53. See text in Chapter 4 at n. 283.
54. Wirsing, in *Christ und Welt*, April 16, 1959. See also Dietrich Strothmann, "Mörder im weissen Kittel," *Die Zeit*, April 1, 1966; Köhler, *Publizisten*, 299–315; Klee, *Kulturlexikon*, 604; *SS im Einsatz*, 369.
55. Berg, *Holocaust*, 203; Abendroth, "Fest der musikalischen Volksgemeinschaft," *Berliner Lokal-Anzeiger*, May 24, 1938; Abendroth, in Munzinger Archiv, www.munzinger.de/search/portraits; Klee, *Kulturlexikon*, 13. Abendroth's Jew hatred shines through his correspondence with his close friend, the grossly anti-Semitic composer Hans Pfitzner, 1933–45, OW, F68 Pfitzner.
56. Holthusen, in Munzinger Archiv, www.munzinger.de/search/portraits; Klee, *Kulturlexikon*, 240.
57. Holthusen, *Welt*, 6. See E. M. Leissner's review in *The Germanic Review* (December 1950): 303–5.
58. Holthusen, "Aufbruch," 106.
59. See Chapter 1 at n. 82.
60. Dovifat in: Konrad Adenauer Stiftung: Geschichte der CDU, www.kas.de/wf/de/37.8079/; Köpf, "Elend," 28–9; Köhler, *Publizisten*, 65–6, 78.
61. Riethmüller, "Stunde Null," 81. See also Potter, *Most German*, 135, 252; Klee, *Kulturlexikon*, 381. See Müller-Blattau's *Geschichte*.
62. Chamberlin, *Kultur*, 51 (quote), 150.
63. Meinecke, *Katastrophe*, 170 (quote), 71. See the contributions in Applegate and Potter, *Music*, and Applegate, *Necessity of Music*.
64. Thacker, *Music*, 52, 79; Haas, *Music*, 282.

65. Harlan, *Schatten*, see e.g. 213–18; Hull, *Film*, 269; Klee, *Kulturlexikon*, 196–7.
66. Riefenstahl, in Klee, *Kulturlexikon*, 440–1; *Holocaust Encyclopedia*, www.ushmm.org/wlc/en/article.php?ModuleId=10007410.
67. Chamberlin, *Kultur*, 46, 67; Dagover, *Dame*, 254; Rühmann, *Das*, 160–3; Moeller, "Filmstars," 165; Klee, *Kulturlexikon*, 92, 150–1, 331, 456–7; Blumenberg, *Leben*, 206–7.
68. Which is when I saw them as a young boy. The films were part of an ambulant film-screening effort in the countryside, organized, in this case, in the British occupation zone. On the banning: Kelson, *Catalogue*, 62, 70, 79.
69. Kelson, *Catalogue*, 88; Werner, *So*, 182; Chamberlin, *Kultur*, 67; Klee, *Kulturlexikon*, 260, 594. Nonetheless, Jugo's film *Königskinder*, 1950, was her last assignment.
70. Söhnker, *Tag*, 271. The married Demandowsky was shot by a Soviet military tribunal in October 1946 (Klee, *Kulturlexikon*, 97, 287).
71. Protocol of author's interview with Hielscher, Munich, June 4, 1988, YUA, CA ON00370 F0456; "Hallo Fräulein," *Der Spiegel* (March 20, 1948): 24; Kater, "New Democracy," 174–8.
72. Hardt, *Caligari*, 190; Schmitz, in www.imdb.com/name/nm0773525/bio; Klee, *Kulturlexikon*, 482–3.
73. "Geschichten zwischen Gestapo-Keller und Buchenwald," *WeltOnline*, January 3, 1998; Klee, *Kulturlexikon*, 514.
74. "Harlan im Zwielicht," *Der Tagesspiegel*, Berlin, April 5, 1949; Rentschler, *Ministry*, 166; Reichel, "Nationalsozialismus," 36; Niven, *Hitler*, 167–71.
75. Adorno, "Terms," 116.
76. Reichel, "Nationalsozialismus," 28. The film writer Ernst von Salomon (a co-conspirator in the murder of Walther Rathenau 1922) expressed his extreme discomfort with "denazification" by OMGUS in his autobiography, *Fragebogen*, e.g. 624–808.
77. The writer Ernst Wiechert vented this sentiment: *Jahre*, 210. More on self-victimization in Jarausch, *Broken Lives*, 188, 191–2, 231–2, 238, 250–1.
78. Meinecke, *Katastrophe*, in particular 170–3. On early anti-Semitism, see Wehler, *Gesellschaftsgeschichte: Vierter Band*, 718.
79. Mitscherlich and Mitscherlich, *Unfähigkeit*, esp. 13–85, 249–62.
80. Klee, *Kulturlexikon*, 527.
81. *Die Mörder sind unter uns*, Sovexport 1946, DVD reissue by Kino-Legenden, vol. 6. Follow-up films were *Irgendwo in Berlin* ("Somewhere in Berlin"), 1946, *In jenen Tagen* ("During those Days"), 1947, or *Liebe 47* ("Love in 1947"), 1949.
82. Helmut Käutner, "Demontage der Traumfabrik," *Film-Echo*, vol. 1 (June 1947): 33; Gustav Zimmermann, "Filmtheater kein Forum Academicum," *Film-Echo*, vol. 1 (July 1947): 49; Kersten et al., *Staudte*, 13; Kreimeier, *Ufa-Story*, 444; Clemens, *Kulturpolitik*, 140–1; Kramer, "Wiederkehr," 286–7; Heins, *Melodrama*, 196–200; Rentschler, *Use*, 6–7, 136–7, 143, 160. Paradigmatic of the Heimatfilm genre is the Berolina production *Grün ist die Heide* (*Green is the Heath*) from 1951 by Hans Deppe, with Nazi-period holdovers Rudolf Prack as forester and Sonja Ziemann as his prospective bride (reissued by filmjuwelen DVD). As a sub-theme, this film bemoaned the recent fate of east German refugees.
83. Author's interview with Professor Jankuhn in Göttingen, May 14, 1963, IfZ, Archiv, ZS/A-25/1-183; Kater, *Ahnenerbe*, 155–58; Klee, *Personenlexikon*, 283.
84. Niven, "Thing," 88.
85. Petropoulos, "Seduction," 212; Petsch, "Malerei," 275.
86. The book appeared in 1957. See Nolde's *Jahre* (1957), where, for example his earlier mention of the Jewish Dr. Schapiere is missing (original 1934 version: "In art this was my first conscious meeting with a person of a different race" [101]), and he omits the favorable mention of an anti-Semitic student club (original version: 160).
87. See Haftmann, *Nolde*, 12–18, quotes 15; Fulda, "Nolde," 183–8.
88. Schmidt's address of February 10, 1982, is printed in *Bulletin: Presse- und Informationsdienst der Bundesregierung*, 19 (March 4, 1982): 150–1.

89. Lewy, *Harmful*, 166–7; Klee, *Kulturlexikon*, 245.
90. Chamberlin, *Kultur*, 126.
91. Author's recorded interview with Elisabeth Hartmann, Munich, December 13, 1994, YUA, CA ON00370 F0456.
92. Viertel, *Kindness*, 282. See the chapter on "Inner Emigration" in Hermand, *Culture*, 143–68.
93. Sarkowicz, "Schriftsteller," 204.
94. "Drei Zentner Wetterhexe," *Der Spiegel* (September 15, 1949): 32.
95. "The Weavers."
96. Lewy, *Harmful*, 180–4 (quotes 182); Ebermayer, *Deutschland*, 262–3.
97. Lewy, *Harmful*, 180–3; Sprengel, *Abschied*, 375.
98. Rathkolb, *Führertreu*, 143.
99. Goebbels, *Tagebücher Diktate*, vol. 4, 500.
100. Petropoulos, *Artists under Hitler*, 121; Rathkolb, *Führertreu*, 74; Lewy, *Harmful*, 181–3 (Hauptmann quoted).
101. Ebermayer quoting Hauptmann in *Deutschland*, 263; Lewy, *Harmful*, 184.
102. Albrecht et al., *Lexikon*, vol. 1, 331.
103. Strobel in minutes of public proceedings, Spruchkammer München-Land, October 17, 1947; Egk to Spruchkammer München-Land, August 5, 1946 (quote); Gsovsky deposition under oath, July 10, 1946; von Borresholm to Kommission für Kulturschaffende, July 12, 1946; Egk in "Anlagen zum Fragebogen," [1947], all in AM, Egk; Egk to Schüler, January 27, 1946, BS, Ana/410.
104. This was a scheme Egk had concocted with Gertrud Orff, Carl's wife at the time. She later denounced it as fictitious in conversation with the author. See Gertrud Orff and Paul Eckstein's depositions under oath, both March 4, 1946, AM, Egk (as samples for several others, all identical); Egk's own description of the scheme in minutes of public proceedings, Spruchkammer München-Land, October 17, 1947, AM, Egk; protocol of author's interview with Gertrud Orff, Munich, August 5, 1992, YUA, CA ON00370 F0456.
105. Author's recorded interview with Elisabeth Hartmann, Munich, December 13, 1994, YUA, CA ON00370 F0456; Hartmann's deposition under oath, March 11, 1946; Hartmann to Spruchkammer München-Land, September 5, 1947, AM, Egk.
106. Author's recorded interview with Newell Jenkins, Hillsdale, NY, March 20, 1993, YUA, CA ON00370 F0456; entry for January 19 and March 5, 1946, in "Gertrud Orffs Tagebuch," CM; Isenstead to Orff, February 28, 1946; Jenkins to Orff, March 26 and November 26, 1946; Preussner to Orff, July 26, 1946; Ley to Orff, May 13, 1947, CM, Allg. Korr.; Evarts to Bauckner, July 16, 1946, BH, Staatstheater/14395; Slonimsky, *Music*, 837; Monod, *Settling Scores*, 54, 65, 67–8, 113.
107. Kater, *Composers*, 29–30, 138–43; Klee, *Personenlexikon*, 126; Klee, *Kulturlexikon*, 115, 400–1.
108. Vaget, *Erbe*, 249–315; Monod, *Settling Scores*, 61–2; Klee, *Kulturlexikon*, 286–7.
109. Knappertsbusch to Leer, December 28, 1947, AM, Pfitzner (quote); Monod, *Settling Scores*, 61–5, 174–5; Vaget, *Erbe*, 315–17; Klee, *Kulturlexikon*, 287.
110. There is much evidence in Ebermayer's diaries, *Deutschland* and . . . *und morgen*, testifying to his closeness to Jews and assumed foes of the regime.
111. Mann, *Tagebücher, 1935–1936*, 259.
112. Ebermayer, . . . *und morgen*, 25–6 (quote), 82.
113. Ebermayer ogled Hitler Youths the way Thomas Mann sized up youthful waiters at table. See Ebermayer, . . . *und morgen*, 127, 136.
114. Klee, *Kulturlexikon*, 112.
115. Bergengruen, *Schreibtischerinnerungen*, 201. The objective White Rose biographer Petry, *Studenten*, 38–9, 57, repeats prepublished memoir fragments by Bergengruen but does not mention the flyer activities. Neither does Bergengruen's, entirely apologist,

post-war so-called documentary, *Schriftstellerexistenz*. The latest objective history of the White Rose mentions Bergengruen's closeness to mentors of the student resisters and Hans Scholl, but no distribution of leaflets: Gebhardt, *Weisse Rose*, 164, 168–9. Jost Hermand, in a chapter ceding credit to a minuscule number of "inner emigrants" such as Ricarda Huch, lauds Bergengruen but does not mention his White Rose involvement (*Culture*, 153–5).

116. Karl Korn, "Der Hofjude: Veit Harlans-Film 'Jud Süss' im Ufa-Palast am Zoo," *Das Reich*, September 29, 1940.

117. Karl Korn, "Der Antinihilist: Durch die Feuerzonen der Technik zum kosmologischen Spiritualismus: Rede zum Schillergedächtnispreis für Ernst Jünger," *Frankfurter Allgemeine Zeitung*, November 16, 1974; "Schillernde Feder," *Der Spiegel* (January 20, 1960): 33. See also Payk, "Amerikakomplex," 193–9; Klee, *Kulturlexikon*, 299–300; text in Chapter 3 at n. 133. The self-serving, self-exculpatory use of "slave language" parallels Bergengruen's employment of "secret language," see n. 22 above.

118. Neun quoted in "Erich Peter Neumann über Hans Dieter Müllers Faksimile-Band 'Das Reich': Der Umstand, Sklave zu sein," *Der Spiegel* (October 1964): 140–1.

119. Hubert Neun, "Wiedersehen mit Warschau: Besiegte Stadt zwischen Gestern und Morgen," *Das Reich*, March 9, 1941.

120. Klee, *Kulturlexikon*, 389. Under the name of Erich Peter Neumann he married Noelle, who henceforth called herself Noelle-Neumann. Allegedly, Neumann was his real name, whereas Neun had been a pseudonym.

121. Jünger qua his, now openly published, alleged Paris contacts with Stauffenberg conspirators such as General Hans Speidel. See his entries throughout *Strahlungen*. See also Sarkowicz, "Apologeten," 438–9; Michalzik, *Gründgens*, 115; Stefan Steinberg, "The Rehabilitation of Gustav [sic] Gründgens," World Socialist Web Site, www.wsws.org/en/articles/1999/12/gust-d29.html.

122. Bergengruen, *Schreibtischerinnerungen*, 131. On Carossa's assumption of office, see text in Chapter 4 at n. 284.

123. Carossa, *Welten*, 31, 159; Schnell, *Dichtung*, 89.

124. See the valid argument in Lewy, *Harmful*, 187.

125. Waibel, *Diener*, 71. There are numerous favorable entries about Dorsch in all the *Goebbels Diaries*.

126. Benn, *Doppelleben*, 103.

127. As Saul Friedländer, *Years*, xxi–xxii, has rightly concluded. He quotes Meitner, xxi.

CONCLUSION – CULTURE IN THREE TYRANNIES

1. For the Italian side, see Stone, *Patron State*, 4–5, 27, 35, 43–54, 65–9, 75; Talbot, *Censorship*, 145–6; Ben-Ghiat, *Modernities*, 7, 70–3; Bonsaver, *Censorship*, 59; Falasca-Zamponi, *Fascist Spectacle*, 31–3, 70, 142–3; Marchicelli, "Futurism," 34–7.

2. The painting was Gerardo Dottori's *Anno X*, reproduced in Stone, *Patron State*, 84. See also ibid., 46, 80–2, 85–8, 108, 133, 156–9; Talbot, *Censorship*, 90, 108, 117, 148–9; Ben-Ghiat, *Modernities*, 47–8; Sachs, *Music*, 146; Bonsaver, *Censorship*, 62, 64, 159, 163; Falasca-Zamponi, *Fascist Spectacle*, 183–4.

3. See the images in Calvesi et al., *Il Futurismo*, e.g. 90–1.

4. Ben-Ghiat, *Modernities*, 120, 125–32; Burdett, *Cardarelli*, 180–2; Bonsaver, *Censorship*, 116–17; Berezin, *Fascist Self*, 207; Falasca-Zamponi, *Fascist Spectacle*, 167–70.

5. The movie was Francesco de Robertis's *Uomini sul fondo* (*Men at the Bottom*). See Bonsaver, *Censorship*, 169 (1st quote), 170–2; Ben-Ghiat, *Modernities*, 9, 26, 121, 148, 156–7, 170 (2nd quote), 173–7, 187, 198; Stone, *Patron State*, 177–83, 191–4, 197–8, 203–5; Sachs, *Music*, 95; Burdett, *Cardarelli*, 8; Falasca-Zamponi, *Fascist Spectacle*, 143.

6. I could make out at least seven agencies which, to varying degrees and at different times, were responsible for the administration of culture: the Ministry of National Education; the Ministry for Press and Propaganda; the Ministry of Popular Culture; police agencies at national and regional levels; regional governors (podestà); PNF offices (Farinacci); Mussolini personally. For personality variances, see Stone, *Patron State*, 66; Bonsaver, *Censorship*, 262–3.

7. Enlightening: Berezin, *Fascist Self*, 14; Sachs, *Music*, 53.

8. Kater, *Weimar*, 140. Alex Ross mentions Richard Wagner's influence on early Bolsheviks such as Lunacharsky in his chapter "Ring of Power," in *Wagnerism* (forthcoming, see n. 13 of Chapter 2).

9. Eisenstein quoted in Berlin, *Soviet Mind*, 51. Also see Clark and Dobrenko, *Soviet Culture*, 4; Vasily Rakitin in Günther, *Culture*, 183–4; Stites, *Popular Culture*, 39–40, 50–1; Starr, *Red and Hot*, 7, 40.

10. Clark and Dobrenko, *Soviet Culture*, 5; John Barber in Günther, *Culture*, 7; Brooks, *Stalin*, 3–5, 23, 30–1; Starr, *Red and Hot*, 45–9, 53; Stites, *Popular Culture*, 47–9, 57, 62.

11. Stites, *Popular Culture*, 72; Clark and Dobrenko, *Soviet Culture*, 50; John Barber in Günther, *Culture*, 7.

12. Examples of strong Stalin-centredness in the arts and letters until 1941 are provided by Boris Groys in Günther, *Culture*, 140–1; Jørn Guldberg, ibid., 152, 168; pictures, ibid., near 138; Clark and Dobrenko, *Soviet Culture*, 117, 141, 291–3, 296–7, 343–4; Frolova-Walker, *Music Prize*, 26–8, 56; Brooks, *Stalin*, 113; Clark, *Moscow*, 304–5, 310.

13. Clark, *Moscow*, 90–93, 114–15; Stites, *Popular Culture*, 71; Clark and Dobrenko, *Soviet Culture*, 5, 108, 120–1, 139–40, 268–9; photographs of Soviet towers in Günther, *Culture*, near 136.

14. Brooks, *Stalin*, 108–9; Clark, *Moscow*, 210; Clark and Dobrenko, *Soviet Culture*, 139–71.

15. Clark and Dobrenko, *Soviet Culture*, 146–8, 209, 243–8, 305–7; Berlin, *Soviet Mind*, 44–45, 72.

16. Clark and Dobrenko, *Soviet Culture*, 348–9, 364–9, 432–6; Stites, *Popular Culture*, 107–12, 119; Frolova-Walker, *Music Prize*, 286; Berlin, *Soviet Mind*, 33, 52; Brooks, *Stalin*, 175, 191.

17. On the last-mentioned problem see Brooks, *Stalin*, 113; Clark and Dobrenko, *Soviet Culture*, 291, 394; Starr, *Red and Hot*, 143; Stites, *Popular Culture*, 73.

18. Enlightening on this aspect: Clark, *Moscow*, 93.

19. Stalin (on February 26, 1947) quoted in Clark and Dobrenko, *Soviet Culture*, 441.

20. Frolova-Walker, *Music Prize*, 40–3, 46, 54, 57, 61, 82, 85, 90–1, 105–6, 113, 122, 231–3, 291–2; Clark and Dobrenko, *Soviet Culture*, 136, 145–6, 318–19; Starr, *Red and Hot*, 59, 126, 149, 162; Berlin, *Soviet Mind*, 7, 22–3; Brooks, *Stalin*, 121–2; www.bbc.co.uk/radio3/shostakovich/timeline.shtml; David Fanning on Shostakovich in *Oxford Music Online*.

Archival Sources

Amtsgericht München (AM)
Egk; Pfitzner

Archiv, Theatermuseum Wien (ATW)
15; 17; 18

Archiv, Theatermuseum Wien, Teilnachlass Lotte Lehmann (ATW/TNLL)
Correspondence

Author's Private Archive (APA)
Miscellanea

Bayerische Staatsbibliothek München, Handschriftenabteilung (BS)
Ana/306; Ana/410

Bayerisches Hauptstaatsarchiv München (BH)
MWi; Staatstheater/14395

Bundesarchiv Berlin (BAB)
RKK (former BDC)

Bundesarchiv Koblenz (BAK)
R55; FILMSG 1; Library, Rundfunk; Microfilm T-175

Carl-Orff-Zentrum München (CM)
Allg. Korr.; Schott Korr.

Columbia University, New York, Rare Books and Manuscripts, Butler Library (CU)
Constance Hope Papers

Elly-Ney-Nachlass, Staatsarchiv Bonn (EB)
26

ARCHIVAL SOURCES

Erika-Mann-Archiv in der Handschriftenabteilung der Stadtbibliothek München (EMA)
914

Institut für Zeitgeschichte München (IfZ)
Archiv, ZS/A-25

Leo Baeck Institute, New York (LBI)
AR; ME

Lotte Lehmann Foundation Archive, Kailua (LLFA)
Miscellanea

National Archives Washington (NAW)
Captured German Records, Streicher Papers, T-580/267

Österreichische National-Bibliothek Wien, Musiksammlung (OW)
F68 Pfitzner

Richard Strauss-Archiv, Garmisch (RG)
Correspondence

Stadtarchiv München, Kulturamt (SMK)
97; 275

University of California at Santa Barbara, Davidson Library, Special Collections, Lotte Lehmann Papers (GC)
General Correspondence

Weill-Lenya Research Center, New York (WC)
Weill and Jolles Correspondence

York University Archives and Special Collections, Toronto (YUA)
CA ON00370 F0456

Bibliography

Abel, Karl-Dietrich, *Presselenkung im NS-Staat: Eine Studie zur Geschichte der Publizistik in der nationalsozialistischen Zeit* (Berlin: Colloquium, 1968)

Abella, Irving and Harold Troper, *None is Too Many: Canada and the Jews of Europe, 1933–1948* (Toronto: Lester and Orpen Dennys, 1982)

Adam, Christian, *Lesen unter Hitler: Autoren, Bestseller, Leser im Dritten Reich* (Berlin: Galiani, 2010)

Adam, Peter, *Art of the Third Reich* (New York: H. N. Abrams, 1992)

Adorno, Theodor W., *Vermischte Schriften II* (Frankfurt am Main: Suhrkamp, 1986)

Adorno, Theodor W., "What Does Coming to Terms with the Past Mean?" (1959), in Geoffrey H. Hartman, ed., *Bitburg in Moral and Political Perspective* (Bloomington: Indiana University Press, 1986), 114–29

Ahlers, Rudolf, *Sturm auf Lehst: Schauspiel in vier Aufzügen* (Leipzig: Der junge Bühnenvertrieb/Ralf Steyer, 1937)

Aigner, Dietrich, "Die Indizierung 'schädlichen und unerwünschten Schrifttums' im Dritten Reich," *Archiv für Geschichte des Buchwesens* 11 (1971): 934–1,034

Albrecht, Gerd, *Nationalsozialistische Filmpolitik: Eine soziologische Untersuchung über die Spielfilme des Dritten Reiches* (Stuttgart: Ferdinand Enke, 1969)

Albrecht, Günter, Kurt Böttcher, Herbert Greiner-Mai, and Paul Günther Krohn, eds, *Lexikon deutschsprachiger Schriftsteller von den Anfängen bis zur Gegenwart*, 2nd edn (Leipzig: VEB Bibliographisches Institut, vol. 1, 1972; vol. 2, 1974)

Amann, Max, "Die nationalsozialistische deutsche Volkspresse," in Carl Schneider, ed., *Handbuch der deutschen Tagespresse*, 6th edn (Leipzig: Armanen-Verlag, 1937), VII–XIII

Ambesser, Axel von, *Nimm einen Namen mit A* (Berlin: Ullstein, 1985)

Anacker, Heinrich, *Wir wachsen in das Reich hinein* (Munich: Eher, 1938)

Anderlahn, Hanns, *Gegner erkannt! Kampferlebnisse der SA. im Jahre 1937* (Munich: Eher, 1937)

Andersch, Alfred, *Deutsche Literatur in der Entscheidung: Ein Beitrag zur Analyse der literarischen Situation* (Karlsruhe: Volk und Zeit, [1948])

Applegate, Celia, *The Necessity of Music: Variations on a German Theme* (Toronto: University of Toronto Press, 2017)

Applegate, Celia, and Pamela Potter, "Cultural History: Where It Has Been and Where It Is Going," *Central European History* 51 (2018): 75–82

Applegate, Celia, and Pamela M. Potter, eds, *Music and German National Identity* (Chicago: University of Chicago Press, 2002)

Arendt, Hannah, *Men in Dark Times* (New York: Harvest/HBJ, 1968)

Ascheid, Antje, *Hitler's Heroines: Stardom and Womanhood in Nazi Cinema* (Philadelphia: Temple University Press, 2003)

Aster, Misha, *The Reich's Orchestra: The Berlin Philharmonic, 1933–1945* (London: Souvenir, 2010)

August, Wolf-Eberhard, "Die Stellung der Schauspieler im Dritten Reich: Versuch einer Darstellung der Kunst- und Gesellschaftspolitik in einem totalitären Staat am Beispiel des 'Berufsschauspielers'," Diss. phil. (Cologne, 1973)

Bach, Steven, *Leni: The Life and Work of Leni Riefenstahl* (New York: Knopf, 2007)

Bach, Steven, *Marlene Dietrich: Life and Legend* (New York: William Morrow, 1992)

Backes, Klaus, *Hitler und die bildenden Künste: Kulturverständnis und Kunstpolitik im Dritten Reich* (Cologne: DuMont Buchverlag, 1988)

Bade, Wilfrid, *Kulturpolitische Aufgaben der deutschen Presse: Eine Rede* (Berlin: Junker und Dünnhaupt, 1933)

Bade, Wilfrid, and Wilmont Haacke, eds, *Das heldische Jahr: Front und Heimat berichten den Krieg* (Berlin: Weltgeschichte-Verlag, 1941)

Bähre, Ralf, "Hellmuth Langenbucher (1905–1980): Beschreibung einer literaturpolitischen Karriere," *Archiv für Geschichte des Buchwesens* 47 (1997): 249–308

Baird, Jay W., *Hitler's War Poets: Literature and Politics in the Third Reich* (New York: Cambridge University Press, 2008)

Baird, Jay W., *The Mythical World of Nazi War Propaganda, 1939–1945* (Minneapolis: University of Minnesota Press, 1974)

Baird, Jay W., *To Die for Germany: Heroes in the Nazi Pantheon* (Bloomington: Indiana University Press, 1990)

Baranowski, Shelley, *Strength Through Joy: Consumerism and Mass Tourism in the Third Reich* (New York: Cambridge University Press, 2004)

Barbian, Jan-Pieter, *Literaturpolitik im NS-Staat: Von der "Gleichschaltung" bis zum Ruin* (Frankfurt am Main: S. Fischer, 2010)

Bark, Dennis L., and David R. Gress, *From Shadow to Substance, 1945–1963* (Oxford: Basil Blackwell, 1989)

Barkhausen, Hans, *Filmpropaganda für Deutschland im Ersten und Zweiten Weltkrieg* (Hildesheim: Olms Presse, 1982)

Barlach, Ernst, *Die Briefe, 1888–1938*, vol. 2, ed. Friedrich Dross (Munich: Piper, 1969)

Barron, Stephanie, "European Artists in Exile: A Reading between the Lines," in Barron, ed., *Exiles and Emigrés: The Flight of European Artists from Hitler* (Los Angeles: Los Angeles County Museum of Art, 1997), 11–29

Barthel, Max, *Das unsterbliche Volk: Roman*, 2nd edn (Berlin: Büchergilde Gutenberg, 1937; 1st edn 1933)

Barzantny, Tamara, *Harry Graf Kessler und das Theater: Autor – Mäzen – Initiator, 1900–1933* (Cologne: Böhlau, 2002)

Bathrick, David, "State of the Art as Art of the Nazi State: The Limits of Cinematic Resistance," in Neil H. Donahue and Doris Kirchner, eds, *Flight of Fantasy: New Perspectives on Inner Emigration in German Literature, 1933–1945* (New York: Berghahn, 2003), 292–304

Bauer, Josef Martin, *Die Kraniche der Nogaia: Tagebuchblätter aus dem Feldzug im Osten* (Munich: R. Piper, 1942)

Bauer, Walter, *Das Herz der Erde: Ein Mutter-Roman* (Berlin: Deutsche Buch-Gemeinschaft, 1933)

Baumann, Hans, *Horch auf Kamerad*, 2nd edn (Potsdam: Ludwig Voggenreiter, 1937)

Beck, Rainer, *Otto Dix: Zeit, Leben, Werk, 1891–1969* (Konstanz: Stadler, 1993)

Becker, Jörg, *Elisabeth Noelle-Neumann: Demoskopin zwischen NS-Ideologie und Konservatismus* (Paderborn: Ferdinand Schöningh, 2013)

Bemmann, Helga, *Berliner Musenkinder-Memorien: Eine heitere Chronik von 1900–1930* (Berlin: Lied der Zeit Musikverlag, 1981)

Ben-Ghiat, Ruth, *Fascist Modernities: Italy, 1922–1945* (Berkeley: University of California Press, 2001)

Bendix, Reinhard, *Max Weber: An Intellectual Portrait* (New York: Anchor, 1962)

Benn, Gottfried, "Bekenntnis zum Expressionismus," *Deutsche Zukunft* 1, no. 4 (November 5, 1933): 15–17

Benn, Gottfried, *Der neue Staat und die Intellektuellen* (Stuttgart: Deutsche Verlags-Anstalt, 1933)

Benn, Gottfried, *Doppelleben: Zwei Selbstdarstellungen* (Wiesbaden: Limes, 1950)

Benn, Gottfried, "Lebensweg eines Intellektualisten (1934)," in Benn, *Doppelleben: Zwei Selbstdarstellungen* (Wiesbaden: Limes, 1950), 9–73

Benn, Gottfried, *Morgue und andere Gedichte* (Munich: Der Bücherwinkel, [1912])

Berens-Totenohl, Josefa, *Der Femhof* (Jena: Eugen Diederichs, 1934)

Berezin, Mabel, *Making the Fascist Self: The Political Culture of Interwar Italy* (Ithaca, NY: Cornell University Press, 1997)

Berg, Nicolas, *Der Holocaust und die westdeutschen Historiker: Erforschung und Erinnerung* (Göttingen: Wallstein, 2003)

Bergdoll, Barry, and Leah Dickerman, eds, *Bauhaus 1919–1933: Workshops for Modernity* (New York: Museum of Modern Art, 2009)

Bergengruen, Werner, *Der Grosstyrann und das Gericht* (Zurich: Verlag der Arche, 1949; 1st pr. 1935)

Bergengruen, Werner, *Schreibtischerinnerungen* (Munich: Nymphenburger Verlagshandlung, [1961])

Bergengruen, Werner, *Schriftstellerexistenz in der Diktatur: Aufzeichnungen und Reflexionen zu Politik, Geschichte und Kultur, 1940–1963*, ed. Frank-Lothar Kroll, N. Luise Hackelsberger, and Sylvia Taschka (Munich: R. Oldenbourg, 2005)

Berger, Albert, *Josef Weinheber (1892–1945): Leben und Werk – Leben im Werk* (Salzburg: O. Müller, 1999)

Berghahn, Marion, *German-Jewish Refugees in England: The Ambiguities of Assimilation* (London: Macmillan, 1984)

Bergmeier, Horst J. P., *The Weintraub Story Incorporated: The Ady Rosner Story* (Menden: Jazzfreund, 1982)

Bergmeier, Horst J. P., and Jürgen W. Susat, "Spitzenband im Hintergrund: Sid Kay Fellows," *Fox auf 78* no. 9 (Winter 1990/91): 34–39

Bergner, Elisabeth, *Bewundert und viel gescholten . . .: Elisabeth Bergners unordentliche Erinnerungen* (Munich: Goldmann, 1978)

Berkley, George E., *Vienna and Its Jews: The Tragedy of Success, 1880s–1980s* (Cambridge, MA: Abt Books, 1988)

Berlin, Isaiah, *The Soviet Mind: Russian Culture under Communism*, ed. Henry Hardy (Washington, DC: Brookings Institution Press, 2016)

Bermann Fischer, Gottfried, *Bedroht – Bewahrt: Weg eines Verlegers* (Frankfurt am Main: S. Fischer, 1967)

Berstl, Julius, *Odyssee eines Theatermenschen: Erinnerungen aus sieben Jahrzehnten* (Berlin-Grunewald: Arani, 1963)

Best, Walter, *Völkische Dramaturgie: Gesammelte Aufsätze* (Würzburg-Aumühle: Konrad Triltsch, 1940)

Beumelburg, Werner, *Die Gruppe Bosemüller: Der grosse Roman des Frontsoldaten* (Oldenburg: Gerhard Stalling, 1930)

Beumelburg, Werner, *Kampf um Spanien: Die Geschichte der Legion Condor* (Oldenburg: Gerhard Stalling, 1939)

Beussel, Ferdinand, "Im Zeichen der Wende," *Die Musik* 25 (1933): 669–75

Beyer, Friedemann, *Gesichter der UFA: Starportraits einer Epoche*, 2nd edn (Munich: Heyne, 1992)

Beyerchen, Alan D., *Scientists under Hitler: Politics and the Physics Community in the Third Reich* (New Haven: Yale University Press, 1977)

Bie, Richard, and Alfred Mühr, *Die Kulturwaffen des neuen Reiches* (Jena: Eugen Diederichs, 1933)

Billerbeck-Gentz, Friedrich, "Die Ausschaltung des Liberalismus am deutschen Theater: Eine Kampfbundrede, gehalten auf der 1. Reichstagung der Deutschen Bühnen in Eisenach, September 1933," *Deutsche Kultur-Wacht* 30 (October 28, 1933): 9–10

Billinger, Richard, *Der Gigant: Schauspiel in fünf Akten* (Berlin: S. Fischer, 1937)

Billinger, Richard, *Lob des Landes: Komödie in fünf Aufzügen* (Munich: Langen Müller, 1933)

Bin Gorion, Emanuel, Alfred Loewenberg, Otto Neuburger, and Hans Oppenheimer, eds, *Philo-Lexikon: Handbuch des jüdischen Wissens* (Berlin: Philo Verlag, 1935)

Blachetta, Walther, *Kampf um eine deutsche Stadt: Ein Spiel aus der Ostmark* (Leipzig: Arwed Strauch, 1933)

Blome, Kurt, *Arzt im Kampf: Erlebnisse und Gedanken* (Leipzig: A. J. Barth, 1942)

Blumenberg, Hans-Christoph, *Das Leben geht weiter: Der letzte Film des Dritten Reiches* (Berlin: Rowohlt, 1993)

Blunck, Hans Friedrich, *Deutsche Kulturpolitik* (Munich: Albert Langen, 1934)

Blunck, Hans Friedrich, *König Geiserich: Eine Erzählung von Geiserich und dem Zug der Wandalen* (Hamburg: Deutsche Hausbücherei, [1936])

Blunck, Hans Friedrich, "Volkstum und Dichtung," in Heinz Kindermann, ed., *Des deutschen Dichters Sendung in der Gegenwart* (Leipzig: Philipp Reclam jun., 1933), 180–205

Blunck, Hans Friedrich, *Wolter von Plettenberg: Deutschordensmeister in Livland* (Hamburg: Hanseatische Verlagsanstalt, 1938)

Boelcke, Willi A., ed., *Kriegspropaganda, 1939–1941: Geheime Ministerkonferenzen im Reichspropagandaministerium* (Stuttgart: Deutsche Verlags-Anstalt, 1966)

Boelcke, Willi A., ed., *Wollt Ihr den Totalen Krieg? Die geheimen Goebbels- Konferenzen, 1939–1943* (Munich: DTV, 1969)

Boeschenstein, Hermann, *The German Novel, 1939–1944* (Toronto: University of Toronto Press, 1949)

Boese, Engelbrecht, *Das Öffentliche Bibliothekswesen im Dritten Reich* (Bad Honnef: Bock + Herchen, 1987)

Böhme, Herbert, *Der Kirchgang des Grosswendbauern: Novellen* (Munich: Franz Eher, 1936)

Böhme, Herbert, ed., *Rufe in das Reich: Die heldische Dichtung von Langemarck bis zur Gegenwart* (Berlin: Junge Generation, 1934)

Böll, Heinrich, *Man möchte manchmal wimmern wie ein Kind: Die Kriegstagebücher, 1943 bis 1945*, ed. René Böll (Cologne: Kiepenheuer und Witsch, 2017)

Bollmus, Reinhard, *Das Amt Rosenberg und seine Gegner: Zum Machtkampf im nationalsozialistischen Herrschaftssystem* (Stuttgart: Deutsche Verlags-Anstalt, 1970)

Bonsaver, Guido, *Censorship and Literature in Fascist Italy* (Toronto: University of Toronto Press, 2007)

Borchmeyer, Dieter, *Was ist Deutsch? Die Suche einer Nation nach Sich Selbst* (Berlin: Rowohlt, 2017)

Bosse, Gustav, "'Führerverantwortlichkeit' oder 'Revolution der Strasse'?," *Zeitschrift für Musik* 100 (1933): 483–86

Botstein, Leon, "The Jewish Question in Music," *Musical Quarterly* 94 (2011): 439–53

Böttcher, Robert, *Kunst und Kunsterziehung im neuen Reich* (Breslau: Ferdinand Hirt, 1933)

Boveri, Margret, *Wir lügen alle: Eine Hauptstadtzeitung unter Hitler* (Olten: Walter, 1965)

Bracher, Karl Dietrich, *The German Dictatorship: The Origins, Structure and Effects of National Socialism* (New York: Praeger, 1972)

Brand, Guido K., *Zwischen Domen und Bunkern: Westeindrücke eines OT-Kriegsberichters* (Amsterdam: Volk und Reich Verlag, 1944)

Brantl, Sabine, *Haus der Kunst, München: Ein Ort und seine Geschichte im Nationalsozialismus* (Munich: Allitera Verlag, 2007)

Braumüller, Wolf, "Kurt Heynicke: 'Der Weg ins Reich': Lothar Müthels politische Spielgestaltung," *Deutsche Bühnenkorrespondenz* 4, no. 48 (July 24, 1935): 1–3

Brechtken, Magnus, *Albert Speer: Eine deutsche Karriere* (Munich: Siedler, 2017)

Brechtken, Magnus, "Ein überflüssiges Experiment? Joseph Goebbels und die Propaganda im Gefüge des Nationalsozialismus," in Christoph Studt, ed., *"Diener des Staates" oder "Widerstand zwischen den Zeilen"? Die Rolle der Presse im "Dritten Reich"* (Berlin: LIT VERLAG, 2007), 49–74

Brehm, Bruno, *Der König von Rücken: Geschichten und Geschautes* (Karlsbad: Adam Kraft, 1942)

Brehm, Bruno, "Unser Kampf im Osten," in *Die Dichtung im kommenden Europa: Weimarer Reden 1941* (Hamburg: Hanseatische Verlagsanstalt, 1942), 35–48

Brenner, Hildegard, *Die Kunstpolitik des Nationalsozialismus* (Reinbek: Rowohlt, 1963)

Brenner, Hildegard, ed., *Ende einer bürgerlichen Kunst-Institution: Die politische Formierung der Preussischen Akademie der Künste ab 1933: Eine Dokumentation* (Stuttgart: Deutsche Verlags-Anstalt, 1972)

Brenner, Michael, *The Renaissance of Jewish Culture in Weimar Germany* (New Haven: Yale University Press, 1996)

Brinkmann, Reinhold, "Reading a Letter," in Brinkmann and Christoph Wolff, eds, *Driven into Paradise: The Musical Migration from Nazi Germany to the United States* (Berkeley: University of California Press, 1999), 3–20

Brinkmann, Reinhold, and Christoph Wolff, eds, *Driven into Paradise: The Musical Migration from Nazi Germany to the United States* (Berkeley: University of California Press, 1999)

Bronsen, David, "Der Sonderfall als exemplarischer Fall – Joseph Roth und die Emigration als Grenzsituation," in Peter Uwe Hohendahl and Egon Schwarz, eds, *Exil und Innere Emigration II: Internationale Tagung in St. Louis* (Frankfurt am Main: Athenäum, 1973), 65–84

Brooks, Jeffrey, *Thank You, Comrade Stalin! Soviet Public Culture from Revolution to Cold War* (Princeton: Princeton University Press, 2000)

Browning, Christopher R., *Ordinary Men: Reserve Battalion 101 and the Final Solution in Poland* (New York: Harper Perennial, 1998, 1st edn 1992)

Browning, Christopher R., *The Origins of the Final Solution: The Evolution of Nazi Jewish Policy, September 1939–March 1942* (Lincoln: University of Nebraska Press, 2004)

Bucher, Peter, "Nationalsozialistische Filmpropaganda im Zweiten Weltkrieg, 1939–1945," *Militärgeschichtliche Mitteilungen* 2 (January 1, 1986): 53–69

Burdett, Charles, *Vincenzo Cardarelli and his Contemporaries: Fascist Politics and Literary Culture* (Oxford: Clarendon Press, 1999)

Burte, Hermann, *Anker am Rhein: Eine Auswahl neuer Gedichte* (Leipzig: Haessel, 1938)

Burte, Hermann, *Sieben Reden* (Strassburg: Hünenburg, 1943)

Busch, Fritz, *Pages from a Musician's Life* (Westport: Greenwood, 1971)

Busch, Grete, *Fritz Busch: Dirigent* (Frankfurt am Main: S. Fischer, 1970)

Busch, Stefan, *"Und gestern, da hörte uns Deutschland": NS-Autoren in der Bundesrepublik: Kontinuität und Diskontinuität bei Friedrich Griese, Werner Beumelburg, Eberhard Wolfgang Möller und Kurt Ziesel* (Würzburg: Königshausen und Neumann, 1998)

Bushard, Magdalena, "Ein Bildhauer zwischen den Stühlen: Gerhard Marcks in den dreisiger Jahren," in Winfried Nerdinger, ed., *Bauhaus-Moderne im Nationalsozialismus: Zwischen Anbiederung und Verfolgung* (Munich: Prestel, 1993), 103–12

Büttner, Horst, "Reichsmusiktage in Düsseldorf: Vom 22. bis 29. Mai 1938," *Zeitschrift für Musik* 105, no. 7 (July 1938): 736–43

Calvesi, Maurizio et al., *Il Futurismo* (Milan: Fratelli Fabbri Editori, 1976)

Carossa, Hans, *Geheimnisse des reifen Lebens: Aus den Aufzeichnungen Angermanns* (Leipzig: Insel, 1936)

Carossa, Hans, *Ungleiche Welten* (Wiesbaden: Insel, 1951)

Carr, Steven Alan, *Hollywood and Anti-Semitism: A Cultural History* (Cambridge: Cambridge University Press, 2001)

Carsten, Francis L., "Deutsche Emigranten in Grossbritannien, 1933–1945," in Gerhard Hirschfeld, ed., *Exil in Grossbritannien: Zur Emigration aus dem nationalsozialistischen Deutschland* (Stuttgart: Klett, 1983), 138–54

Carter, Erica, *Dietrich's Ghosts: The Sublime and the Beautiful in the Third Reich* (London: British Film Institute, 2004)

Casper, Siegfried, ed., *Hanns Johst spricht zu Dir: Eine Lebenslehre aus seinen Werken und Reden* (Berlin: Nordland Verlag, 1942)

Cesarani, David, *Arthur Koestler: The Homeless Mind* (London: Heinemann, 1998)

Chamberlin, Brewster S., ed., *Kultur auf Trümmern: Berliner Berichte der amerikanischen Information Control Section, Juli–Dezember 1945* (Stuttgart: Deutsche Verlags-Anstalt, 1979)

Chapoutot, Johann, *Greeks, Romans, Germans: How the Nazis Usurped Europe's Classical Past* (Oakland: University of California Press, 2016)

Chapoutot, Johann, *The Law of Blood: Thinking and Acting like a Nazi* (Cambridge, MA: The Belknap Press of Harvard University Press, 2018)

Childers, Thomas, *The Third Reich: A History of Nazi Germany* (New York: Simon & Schuster, 2017)

Christiansen, Uwe, and Hans-Christian Petersen, *Wilhelm Petersen: Der Maler des Nordens* (Tübingen: Edition Grabert, 1993)

Christoph, Frank E., *Sehnsucht nach der Heimat: Roman eines deutschen Auslandsschicksals* (Berlin: Hyperion-Verlag, 1943)

Clark, Katerina, *Moscow, the Fourth Rome: Stalinism, Cosmopolitanism, and the Evolution of Soviet Culture, 1931–1941* (Cambridge, MA: Harvard University Press, 2011)

Clark, Katerina, and Evgeny Dobrenko, eds, *Soviet Culture and Power: A History in Documents, 1917–1953* (New Haven: Yale University Press, 2007)

Clarkson, Austin, "Stefan Wolpe: Broken Sequences," in Michael H. Kater and Albrecht Riethmüller, eds, *Music and Nazism: Art under Tyranny, 1933–1945* (Laaber: Laaber, 2003), 219–40

Clemens, Gabriele, *Britische Kulturpolitik in Deutschland, 1945–1949: Literatur, Film, Musik und Theater* (Stuttgart: Franz Steiner, 1997)

Clinefelter, Joan L., "A Cinematic Construction of Nazi Anti-Semitism: The Documentary *Der Ewige Jude*," in Robert C. Reimer, ed., *Cultural History through a National Socialist Lens: Essays on the Cinema of the Third Reich* (Rochester, NY: Camden House, 2000), 133–54

Clinefelter, Joan L., *Artists for the Reich: Culture and Race from Weimar to Nazi Germany* (Oxford: Berg, 2005)

Conway, John S., *The Nazi Persecution of the Churches, 1933–45* (Toronto: Ryerson, 1968)

Courtade, Francis, and Pierre Cadars, *Geschichte des Films im Dritten Reich* (Munich: Wilhelm Heyne, 1975)

Craft, Robert, ed., *Stravinsky: Selected Correspondence*, vol. 3 (London: Faber and Faber, 1982–5)

Crawford, Dorothy Lamb, *Evenings On and Off the Roof: Pioneering Concerts in Los Angeles, 1939–1971* (Berkeley: University of California Press, 1995)

Csipak, Karoly, "Berthold Goldschmidt im Exil: Der Komponist im Gespräch über Musiker-Exil und Musikleben," in Habakuk Traber and Elmar Weingarten, eds, *Verdrängte Musik: Berliner Komponisten im Exil* (Berlin: Aragon, 1987), 43–77

Culbert, David, "The Impact of Anti-Semitic Film Propaganda on German Audiences: Jew Süss and the Wandering Jew (1940)," in Richard A. Etlin, ed., *Art, Culture and Media under the Third Reich* (Chicago: University of Chicago Press, 2002), 139–57

Cziffra, Geza von, *Kauf dir einen bunten Luftballon: Erinnerungen an Götter und Halbgötter* (Munich: Herbig, 1975)

Dagover, Lil, *Ich war die Dame* (Munich: Schneekluth, 1979)

Dahm, Volker, *Das jüdische Buch im Dritten Reich*, 2nd edn (Munich: C. H. Beck, 1993)

Dahm, Volker, "Kulturelles und geistiges Leben," in Wolfgang Benz, ed., *Die Juden in Deutschland, 1933–1945* (Munich: C. H. Beck, 1988), 75–267

Damus, Martin, "Gebrauch und Funktion von bildender Kunst und Architektur im Nationalsozialismus," in Damus et al., *Kunst und Kultur im deutschen Faschismus* (Stuttgart: Metzler, 1978), 87–128

Danuser, Hermann, "Composers in Exile: The Question of Musical Identity," in Reinhold Brinkmann and Christoph Wolff, eds, *Driven into Paradise: The Musical Migration from Nazi Germany to the United States* (Berkeley: University of California Press, 1999), 155–71

Davenport, Marcia, "Song and Sentiment," *The New Yorker* (February 23, 1935): 18–22

Daverio, John, *Robert Schuman: Herald of a "New Poetic Age"* (New York: Oxford University Press, 1997)

Davie, Maurice R., *Refugees in America: Report of the Committee for the Study of Recent Immigration from Europe* (New York: Harper, 1947)

De Mendelssohn, Peter, "Gegenstrahlungen: Ein Tagebuch zu Ernst Jüngers Tagebuch," *Der Monat* 14 (1949): 149–74

De Mendelssohn, Peter, *Zeitungsstadt Berlin: Menschen und Mächte in der Geschichte der deutschen Presse* (Berlin: Ullstein, 1959)

Deák, István, *Weimar Germany's Left-Wing Intellectuals: A Political History of the Weltbühne and Its Circle* (Berkeley: University of California Press, 1968)

Dembitzer, Salamon, *Visas for America: A Story of an Escape*, 2nd edn (Sydney: Villon Press, [1950]; 1st edn [194?])

Denecke, Rolf, "Grenzen und Freiheit der historischen Dichtung," *Bücherkunde* 6 (1940): 154–8

Denk, Ferdinand, "Hans Brandenburgs Zukunftsschau des deutschen Theaters," *Der neue Weg* (1935): 448–50

Dennis, David B., *Beethoven in German Politics, 1870–1989* (New Haven: Yale University Press, 1996)

Dennis, David B., *Inhumanities: Nazi Interpretations of Western Culture* (New York: Cambridge University Press, 2012)

"Der Führer auf der Kulturtagung," in *Reden des Führers am Parteitag Grossdeutschland 1938*, 4th edn (Munich: Franz Eher, 1939), 29–46

Der Kongress zu Nürnberg vom 5. bis 10. September 1934: Offizieller Bericht über den Verlauf des Reichsparteitages mit sämtlichen Reden (Munich: Eher, 1934)

Der Lühe, Barbara von, *Die Emigration deutschsprachiger Musikschaffender in das britische Mandatsgebiet Palästina* (Frankfurt am Main: Peter Lang, 1999)

Der Lühe, Irmela von, *Erika Mann: Eine Biographie* (Frankfurt am Main: Fischer Taschenbuch, 1996)

Deutsche Filmakademie mit dem Arbeitsinstitut für Kulturfilmschaffen (Berlin-Babelsberg: Max Hesses Verlag, [1938])

Die Dichtung im kommenden Europa: Weimarer Reden 1941 (Hamburg: Hanseatische Verlagsanstalt, 1942)

Diebenow, Johannes, *Die Nacht vor der Entscheidung: Ein Spiel aus deutscher Notzeit* (Leipzig: Arwed Strauch, 1933)

Diller, Ansgar, *Rundfunkpolitik im Dritten Reich* (Munich: DTV, 1980)

Dillmann, Michael, *Heinz Hilpert: Leben und Werk* (Berlin: Edition Hentrich, 1990)

Dinter, Artur, *Die Sünde wider das Blut: Ein Zeitroman*, 3rd edn (Leipzig: Im Wolfverlag, Erich Matthes, 1919)

Doherty, Thomas, *Hollywood and Hitler, 1933–1939* (New York: Columbia University Press, 2013)

Dörfler, Anton, *Die ewige Brücke: Roman* (Jena: Eugen Diederichs, 1937)

Dovifat, Emil, *Zeitungslehre I: Erster Band: Theoretische Grundlagen – Nachricht und Meinung – Sprache und Form* (Berlin: Walter de Gruyter & Co., 1937)

Dovifat, Emil, *Zeitungslehre I: Zweiter Band: Schriftleitung – Stoffbeschaffung und Bearbeitung – Technik und Wirtschaft des Betriebes* (Berlin: Walter de Gruyter & Co., 1937)

Drechsler, Nanny, *Die Funktion der Musik im deutschen Rundfunk, 1933–1945* (Pfaffenweiler: Centaurus-Verlagsgesellschaft, 1988)

Dresler, Adolf, *Das Braune Haus und die Verwaltungsgebäude der Reichsleitung der NSDAP. in München*, 2nd edn (Munich: Eher, 1937)

Dresler, Adolf, "Dietrich Eckart," in Paul Gerhardt Dippel, ed., *Künder und Kämpfer: Die Dichter des neuen Deutschland* (Munich: Deutscher Volksverlag, [1937; 2nd edn 1939]), 17–44

Dressler-Andress, Horst, *Die Reichsrundfunkkammer: Ziele, Leistungen und Organisation* (Berlin: Junker und Dünnhaupt, 1935)

Dressler-Andress, Horst, *Drei Jahre Nationalsozialistische Gemeinschaft "Kraft durch Freude": Ziele und Leistungen* (Berlin: Reichsdruckerei, 1936)

Drewniak, Boguslaw, *Das Theater im NS-Staat: Szenarium deutscher Zeitgeschichte, 1933–1945* (Düsseldorf: Droste, 1983)

Drewniak, Boguslaw, *Der deutsche Film, 1938–1945: Ein Gesamtüberblick* (Düsseldorf: Droste, 1987)

Dreyer, Ernst Adolf, ed., *Deutsche Kultur im Neuen Reich: Wesen, Aufgabe und Ziel der Reichskulturkammer* (Berlin: Schlieffen, 1934)

Dreyer, Ernst Adolf, and Christian Jenssen, eds, *Demut vor Gott – Ehre dem Reich – Hochzeit der Künste: Eine Dankesgabe des Europäischen Schrifttums an Hans Friedrich Blunck* (Berlin: Frundsberg-Verlag, [1938])

Droste, Magdalena, "Bauhaus-Maler im Nationalsozialismus: Anpassung, Selbstentfremdung, Verweigerung," in Winfried Nerdinger, ed., *Bauhaus-Moderne im Nationalsozialismus: Zwischen Anbiederung und Verfolgung* (Munich: Prestel, 1993), 113–41

Drüner, Ulrich, and Georg Günther, *Musik und "Drittes Reich": Fallbeispiele 1910 bis 1960 zu Herkunft, Höhepunkt und Nachwirkungen des Nationalsozialismus in der Musik* (Vienna: Böhlau, 2012)

Du Closel, Amaury, *Erstickte Stimmen: "Entartete Musik" im Dritten Reich* (Vienna: Böhlau, 2010)

Dümling, Albrecht, "Der deutsche Michel erwacht: Zur Bruckner-Rezeption im NS-Staat," in Albrecht Riethmüller, ed., *Bruckner-Probleme: Internationales Kolloquium, 7.–9. Oktober 1996 in Berlin* (Stuttgart: Franz Steiner, 1999), 202–14

Dümling, Albrecht, "'Ein wahrer Hexensabbat': Die Ausstellung 'Entartete Musik' im Widerstreit," in Hellmut Th. Seemann and Thorsten Valk, eds, *Übertönte Geschichten: Musikkultur in Weimar: Jahrbuch der Klassik Stiftung Weimar* (Göttingen: Wallstein, 2011), 189–205

Dümling, Albrecht, "The Target of Racial Purity: The 'Degenerate Music' Exhibition in Düsseldorf, 1938," in Richard A. Etlin, ed., *Art, Culture and Media under the Third Reich* (Chicago: University of Chicago Press, 2002), 43–72

Dümling, Albrecht, and Peter Girth, eds, *Entartete Musik: Zur Düsseldorfer Ausstellung von 1938: Eine kommentierte Rekonstruktion*, 3rd edn (Düsseldorf: Der Kleine Verlag, 1993)

Durzak, Manfred, "Die Exilsituation in USA," in Durzak, ed., *Die deutsche Exilliteratur 1933–1945* (Stuttgart: Philipp Reclam jun., 1973), 145–58

Durzak, Manfred, "Literarische Diaspora: Stationen des Exils," in Durzak, ed., *Die deutsche Exilliteratur 1933–1945* (Stuttgart: Philipp Reclam jun., 1973), 40–55

Dussel, Konrad, *Ein neues, heroisches Theater? Nationalsozialistische Theaterpolitik und ihre Auswirkungen in der Provinz* (Bonn: Bouvier, 1988)

Düsterberg, Rolf, *Hanns Johst: "Der Barde der SS"* (Paderborn: Schöningh, 2004)

Düwell, Kurt, "Der Jüdische Kulturbund Rhein-Ruhr, 1933–1938: Selbstbesinnung und Selbstbehauptung einer Geistesgemeinschaft," in Jutta Bohnke-Kollwitz and Willehad

Paul Eckert, eds, *Köln und das rheinische Judentum: Festschrift Germania Judaica, 1959–1984* (Cologne: Bachem, 1984), 427–41

Dwinger, Edwin Erich, "Der Bolschewismus als Bedrohung der Weltkultur," in Rudolf Erckmann, ed., *Dichter und Krieger: Weimarer Reden 1942* (Hamburg: Hanseatische Verlagsanstalt, 1943), 13–22

Dwinger, Edwin Erich, *Der Tod in Polen: Die volksdeutsche Passion* (Jena: Eugen Diederichs, 1940)

Dwinger, Edwin Erich, *Die letzten Reiter* (Jena: Eugen Diederichs, 1935)

Dwinger, Edwin Erich, *Die Namenlosen: Schauspiel* (Jena: Eugen Diederichs, 1934)

Dwinger, Edwin Erich, *Und Gott schweigt . . .? Bericht und Aufruf* (Jena: Eugen Diederichs, 1936)

Easton, Laird M., *The Red Count: The Life and Times of Harry Kessler* (Berkeley: University of California Press, 2002)

Eberlein, Kurt Karl, *Was ist Deutsch in der Deutschen Kunst?* (Leipzig: E. A. Seemann, 1934)

Ebermayer, Erich, *Denn heute gehört uns Deutschland . . .: Persönliches und politisches Tagebuch: Von der Machtergreifung bis zum 31. Dezember 1935* (Hamburg: Paul Zsolnay, 1959)

Ebermayer, Erich, ". . . und morgen die ganze Welt": Erinnerungen an Deutschlands dunkle Zeit* (Bayreuth: Hestia, 1966)

Echtermeyer, Ernst Theodor, *Auswahl deutscher Gedichte von den Anfängen bis zur Gegenwart*, ed. Richard Wittsack, 48th edn (Halle: Buchhandlung des Waisenhauses GmbH, 1936)

Eckert, Gerd, "Filmtendenz und Tendenzfilm," *Wille und Macht* 6, no. 4 (February 15, 1938): 19–25

Eckert, Gerhard, *Der Rundfunk als Führungsmittel* (Heidelberg: Kurt Vowinckel, 1941)

Efron, John M., *Medicine and the German Jews: A History* (New Haven: Yale University Press, 2001)

Egk, Werner, *Die Zeit wartet nicht* (Percha: Schulz, 1973)

Ehmer, Wilhelm, "Schöpferische Wirkungen des Krieges," in Rudolf Erckmann, ed., *Dichter und Krieger: Weimarer Reden 1942* (Hamburg: Hanseatische Verlagsanstalt, 1943), 23–44

Einzig, Barbara, Lynne Dean, and Andrea P. A. Belloli, eds, *German Expressionist Sculpture* (Los Angeles: Los Angeles County Museum of Art, 1984)

Eksteins, Modris, *Rites of Spring: The Great War and the Birth of the Modern Age* (Toronto: Lester and Orpen Dennys, 1989)

Eksteins, Modris, *The Limits of Reason: The German Democratic Press and the Collapse of the Weimar Republic* (London: Oxford University Press, 1975)

Ellis, Donald W., "Music in the Third Reich: National Aesthetic Theory as Governmental Policy," PhD diss. (University of Kansas, 1970)

Emmel, Felix, *Theater aus deutschem Wesen* (Berlin: Georg Stilke, 1937)

Emmons, Shirlee, *Tristanissimo: The Authorized Biography of Heroic Tenor Lauritz Melchior* (New York: Schirmer, 1990)

Engelbrecht, Kurt, *Deutsche Kunst im totalen Staat: Zur Wiedergeburt des Kunsthandwerks* (Lahr: Richard Keutel, 1933)

Engelbrecht, Lloyd C., "Moholy-Nagy und Chermayeff in Chicago," in Peter Hahn and Lloyd Engelbrecht, eds, *50 Jahre Bauhausnachfolge: New Bauhaus in Chicago* (Berlin: Bauhaus-Archiv: Argon, 1987), 51–68

Epstein, Catherine, "Schicksalsgeschichte: Refugee Historians in the United States," in Hartmut Lehmann and James J. Sheehan, eds, *An Interrupted Past: German-Speaking Refugee Historians in the United States after 1933* (Cambridge: Cambridge University Press, 1991), 116–35

Erckmann, Rudolf, ed., *Dichter und Krieger: Weimarer Reden 1942* (Hamburg: Hanseatische Verlagsanstalt, 1943)

Erckmann, Rudolf, "Sinn und Aufgabe des Grossdeutschen Dichtertreffens 1940," in *Die Dichtung im Kampf des Reiches: Weimarer Reden 1940*, 2nd edn (Hamburg: Hanseatische Verlagsanstalt, 1941/43), 5–10

Evans, Joan, "Die Rezeption der Musik Igor Strawinskys in Hitlerdeutschland," *Archiv für Musikwissenschaft* 55 (1998): 91–109

Evans, Richard J., *The Coming of the Third Reich* (New York: Penguin, 2004)

Evans, Richard J., *The Third Reich at War* (New York: Penguin, 2008)

Evans, Richard J., *The Third Reich in Power* (New York: Penguin, 2005)

Ewen, David, *Men and Women Who Make Music* (New York: The Reader's Press, 1946)

Ewerbeck, Betina, *Angela Koldewey: Roman einer jungen Ärztin* (Berlin: Verlag Neues Volk, 1939)

Falasca-Zamponi, Simonetta, *Fascist Spectacle: The Aesthetics of Power in Mussolini's Italy* (Berkeley: University of California Press, 1997)

Falter, Jürgen, *Hitlers Wähler* (Munich: C. H. Beck, 1991)

Faust, Philipp, *Die Maurer: Erzählung* (Berlin-Steglitz: Eckart-Verlag, 1939)

Feinberg, Anat, "Leopold Jessner: German Theatre and Jewish Identity," *The Leo Baeck Institute Yearbook* 48, no. 1 (January 2003): 111–33

Felsmann, Barbara, et al., eds, *Backfisch im Bombenkrieg: Notizen in Steno*, 2nd edn (Berlin: Matthes und Seitz, 2013)

Fend, Michael, "Hans Gál: 'Immer wieder anfangen müssen'," in Hans-Werner Heister, Claudia Maurer Zenck, and Peter Petersen, eds, *Musik im Exil: Folgen des Nazismus für die internationale Musikkultur* (Frankfurt am Main: S. Fischer, 1993), 171–86

Feuchtwanger, Lion, "Der Schriftsteller im Exil" (1943), in Feuchtwanger, *Centum Opuscula: Eine Auswahl*, ed. Wolfgang Berndt (Rudolstadt: Greifenverlag, 1956), 547–52

Feuchtwanger, Lion, *Exil: Roman* (Amsterdam: Querido, 1940)

Feulner, Adolf, *Kunst und Geschichte: Eine Anleitung zum kunstgeschichtlichen Denken* (Leipzig: Karl W. Hiersemann, 1942)

Findeli, Alain, "Die pädagogische Ästhetik von László Moholy-Nagy und seine Rolle bei der Umsiedlung des Bauhauses nach Chicago," in Peter Hahn and Lloyd C. Engelbrecht, eds, *50 Jahre Bauhausnachfolge: New Bauhaus in Chicago* (Berlin: Bauhaus-Archiv: Argon, 1987), 33–50

Fischer, E. Kurt, *Dramaturgie des Rundfunks* (Heidelberg: Kurt Vowinckel, 1942)

Fischer, Jens Malte, "The Very German Fate of a Composer: Hans Pfitzner," in Michael H. Kater and Albrecht Riethmüller, eds, *Music and Nazism: Art under Tyranny, 1933–1945* (Laaber: Laaber, 2003), 75–89

Fischer, Jörg, "Evangelische Kirchenmusik im Dritten Reich: 'Musikalische Erneuerung' und ästhetische Modalität des Faschismus," *Archiv für Musikwissenschaft* 46 (1989): 185–234

Fischer-Defoy, Christine, *Kunst, Macht, Politik: Die Nazifizierung der Kunst- und Musikhochschulen in Berlin* (Berlin: Elefanten-Press, [1988])

Fischer-Gravelius, Gottfried, "Erinnerungen an Martin Raschke," *Das Innere Reich*, no. 4 (1943/44): 343–50

Flavell, M. Kay, *George Grosz: A Biography* (New Haven: Yale University Press, 1988)

Föllmer, Moritz, *"Ein Leben wie im Traum": Kultur im Dritten Reich* (Munich: C. H. Beck, 2016)

Fox, Jo, *Film Propaganda in Britain and Nazi Germany: World War II Cinema* (Oxford: Berg, 2007)

Fox-Gál, Eva, ed., *Musik hinter Stacheldraht: Tagebuchblätter aus dem Sommer 1940 von Hans Gál* (Bern: Peter Lang, 2003)

Frank, Rudolf, *Spielzeit meines Lebens* (Heidelberg: Lambert Schneider, 1960)

Frankenthal, Käte, *Der dreifache Fluch: Jüdin, Intellektuelle, Sozialistin: Lebenserinnerungen einer Ärztin in Deutschland und im Exil*, ed. Kathleen M. Pearle and Stephan Leibfried (Frankfurt am Main: Campus, 1981)

Freeden, Herbert, *Jüdisches Theater in Nazideutschland* (Tübingen: J. C. B. Mohr, 1964)

Frei, Norbert, *Adenauer's Germany and the Nazi Past: The Politics of Amnesty and Integration* (New York: Columbia University Press, 2002)

Frei, Norbert, "Die nationalsozialistischen Berufsgerichte der Presse: Dokumentation," *Vierteljahrshefte für Zeitgeschichte* 32 (1984): 122–62

Frei, Norbert, *Nationalsozialistische Eroberung der Provinzpresse: Gleichschaltung, Selbstanpassung und Resistenz in Bayern* (Stuttgart: Deutsche Verlags-Anstalt, 1980)

Frei, Norbert, and Johannes Schmitz, *Journalismus im Dritten Reich* (Munich: C. H. Beck, 1989)

Frenssen, Gustav, *Recht oder Unrecht – Mein Land* (Berlin: G. Grote'sche Verlagsbuchhandlung, 1940)

Frenssen, Gustav, *Vorland: Der Grübeleien dritter Band* (Berlin: G. Grote'sche Verlagsbuchhandlung, 1937)

Frenzel, Elisabeth, *Der Jude im Theater* (Munich: Zentralverlag der NSDAP, 1943)

Frenzel, Herbert A., "Eberhard Wolfgang Möller," in Paul Gerhardt Dippel, ed., *Künder und Kämpfer: Die Dichter des neuen Deutschland* (Munich: Deutscher Volksverlag, [1937; 2nd edn 1939]), 141–72

Frickhoeffer, Otto, "Die deutsche Musik im deutschen Rundfunk," *Die Musik* 29 (January 1937): 245–49

Friedländer, Saul, *Kitsch und Tod: Der Widerschein des Nazismus* (Munich: Hanser, 1984)

Friedländer, Saul, *Nazi Germany and the Jews: The Years of Persecution, 1933–1939* (New York: HarperPerennial, 1997)

Friedländer, Saul, *The Years of Extermination: Nazi Germany and the Jews, 1939–1945* (New York: HarperCollins, 2007)

Friedländer, Saul, *Where Memory Leads: My Life* (New York: Other Press, 2016)

Friedrich, Otto, *City of Nets: A Portrait of Hollywood in the 1940s* (New York: Harper & Row, 1991)

Fröhlich, Claudia, "Rückkehr zur Demokratie – Wandel der politischen Kultur in der Bundesrepublik," in Peter Reichel, Harald Schmid, and Peter Steinbach, eds, *Der Nationalsozialismus – Die Zweite Geschichte: Überwindung – Deutung – Erinnerung* (Munich: C. H. Beck, 2009), 105–26

Fröhlich, Elke, "Die kulturpolitische Pressekonferenz des Reichspropagandaministeriums," *Vierteljahrshefte für Zeitgeschichte* 22 (1974): 347–81

Frolova-Walker, Marina, *Stalin's Music Prize: Soviet Culture and Politics* (New Haven: Yale University Press, 2016)

Frotscher, Gotthold, "Das Problem Musik und Rasse auf der musikwissenschaftlichen Tagung in Düsseldorf," *Musik in Jugend und Volk* 1, nos 9–10 (July–August 1938): 426–7

Führer, Karl Christian, "German Cultural Life and the Crisis of National Identity during the Depression," *German Studies Review* 24 (2001): 461–86

Fulda, Bernhard, "Myth-making in Hitler's Shadow: The Transfiguration of Emil Nolde after 1945," in Jan Rüger and Nikolaus Wachsmann, eds, *Rewriting German History: New Perspectives on Modern Germany* (Houndmills: Palgrave Macmillan, 2015), 177–94

Fulda, Bernhard, and Aya Soika, "Emil Nolde and the National Socialist Dictatorship," in Olaf Peters, ed., *Degenerate Art: The Attack on Modern Art in Nazi Germany, 1937* (Munich: Prestel, 2014), 186–95

Funk, Alois, *Film und Jugend: Eine Untersuchung über die psychischen Wirkungen des Films im Leben der Jugendlichen* (Munich: Ernst Reinhardt, 1934)

Gadberry, Glen W., "The First National Socialist Theatre Festival – Dresden 1934," in Glen W. Gadberry, ed., *Theatre in the Third Reich, the Prewar Years: Essays on Theatre in Nazi Germany* (Westport: Greenwood, 1995), 121–39

Ganz, Bruno, Helmut Wietz, Gerold Ducke, and Wolfgang Jacobsen, *Curt Bois* (Berlin: Stiftung Deutsche Kinemathek, 1983)

Gay, Peter, *Freud: A Life for Our Time* (New York: Norton, 1988)

Gay, Peter, *My German Question: Growing up in Nazi Berlin* (New Haven: Yale University Press, 1998)

Gay, Peter, "'We Miss Our Jews'," in Reinhold Brinkmann and Christoph Wolff, eds, *Driven into Paradise: The Musical Migration from Nazi Germany to the United States* (Berkeley: University of California Press, 1999), 21–30

Gay, Peter, *Weimar Culture: The Outsider as Insider* (New York: Harper & Row, 1968)

Gebhardt, Miriam, *Die Weisse Rose: Wie aus ganz normalen Deutschen Widerstandskämpfer wurden* (Munich: Deutsche Verlags-Anstalt, 2017)

Geisel, Eike, and Henryk M. Broder, *Premiere und Pogrom: Der Jüdische Kulturbund, 1933–1941: Texte und Bilder* (Berlin: Siedler, 1992)

Geissler, Rolf, *Dekadenz und Heroismus: Zeitroman und völkisch-nationalsozialistische Literaturkritik* (Stuttgart: Deutsche Verlags-Anstalt, 1964)

Geissmar, Berta, *Musik im Schatten der Politik*, 4th edn, ed. Fred K. Prieberg (Zurich: Atlantis, 1985)

Gellately, Robert, *Backing Hitler: Consent and Coercion in Nazi Germany* (Oxford: Oxford University Press, 2001)

Gellately, Robert, *The Gestapo and German Society: Enforcing Racial Policy, 1933–1945* (New York: Oxford University Press, 2008)

Gentile, Emilio, "The Fascist Anthropological Revolution," in Guido Bonsaver and Robert S. C. Gordon, eds, *Culture, Censorship and the State in Twentieth-Century Italy* (London: Legenda, 2005), 22–32

Gerlach, Josef, "Ein Maler im Dritten Reich," *Neues Volk*, no. 9 (1935): 7–9

Gerlach-Bernau, Kurt, *Drama und Nation: Ein Beitrag zur Wegbereitung des nationalsozialistischen Dramas* (Breslau: Ferdinand Hirt, 1934)

Gerstner, Hermann, and Karl Schworm, eds, *Deutsche Dichter unserer Zeit* (Munich: Eher, [1939])

Gillessen, Günther, *Auf verlorenem Posten: Die Frankfurter Zeitung im Dritten Reich* (Berlin: Siedler, 1986)

Gilliam, Bryan, "A Viennese Opera Composer in Hollywood: Korngold's Double Exile in America," in Reinhold Brinkmann and Christoph Wolff, eds, *Driven into Paradise: The Musical Migration from Nazi Germany to the United States* (Berkeley: University of California Press, 1999), 223–42

Gilliam, Bryan, "The Annexation of Anton Bruckner: Nazi Revisionism and the Politics of Appropriation," *Musical Quarterly* 78, no. 3 (1994): 584–604

Giroud, Françoise, *Alma Mahler or the Art of Being Loved* (Oxford: Oxford University Press, 1991)

Glass, Beaumont, *Lotte Lehmann: A Life in Opera and Song* (Santa Barbara: Capra Press, 1988)

Gmelin, Otto, *Konradin reitet: Novelle* (Leipzig: Philipp Reclam jun., 1933)

Goebbels, Joseph, *Die Tagebücher von Joseph Goebbels: Sämtliche Fragmente*, 5 vols, ed. Elke Fröhlich (Munich: K. G. Saur, 1987)

Goebbels, Joseph, *Die Tagebücher von Joseph Goebbels: Teil II, Diktate, 1941–1945*, 15 vols, ed. Elke Fröhlich (Munich: K. G. Saur, 1996)

Goebbels, Joseph, *Michael: Ein deutsches Schicksal in Tagebuchblättern* (Munich: Franz Eher Nachf., 1929)

Goebbels, Joseph, *Signale der neuen Zeit: 25 ausgewählte Reden*, 10th edn (Munich: Eher, 1940)

Goedecke, Heinz, and Wilhelm Krug, *Wir beginnen das Wunschkonzert für die Wehrmacht* (Berlin: Nibelungen-Verlag, 1940)

Goehr, Lydia, "Music and Musicians in Exile: The Romantic Legacy of a Double Life," in Reinhold Brinkmann and Christoph Wolff, eds, *Driven into Paradise: The Musical Migration from Nazi Germany to the United States* (Berkeley: University of California Press, 1999), 66–91

Goldhagen, Daniel Jonah, *Hitler's Willing Executioners: Ordinary Germans and the Holocaust* (New York: Knopf, 1996)

Goote, Thor, *Die Fahne hoch!* (Berlin: Zeitgeschichte-Verlag, 1933)

Görtemaker, Heike B., *Ein deutsches Leben: Die Geschichte der Margret Boveri, 1900–1975* (Munich: C. H. Beck, 2005)

Gradenwitz, Peter, "Paul Ben-Haim: Schöpfer der israelischen Musik," in Hans-Werner Heister, Claudia Maurer Zenck, and Peter Petersen, eds, *Musik im Exil: Folgen des Nazismus für die internationale Musikkultur* (Frankfurt am Main: S. Fischer, 1993), 120–31

Gramann, Karola, Heide Schlüpmann, and Wolfgang Jacobsen, *Hertha Thiele* (Berlin: Stiftung Deutsche Kinemathek, 1983)

Gregor-Dellin, Martin, "Klaus Manns Exilromane," in Manfred Durzak, ed., *Die deutsche Exilliteratur 1933–1945* (Stuttgart: Philipp Reclam jun., 1973), 457–63

Griese, Friedrich, *Das letzte Gesicht: Roman* (Munich: Langen Müller, 1934)

Griese, Friedrich, *Die Weissköpfe: Roman* (Munich: Langen Müller, 1939)

Grimm, Hans, *Lüderitzland: Sieben Begebenheiten* (Munich: Langen Müller, 1936)

Grimm, Hans, *Volk ohne Raum*, 2 vols (Munich: Albert Langen, 1926–7)

Gritzbach, Erich, *Hermann Göring: Werk und Mensch*, 18th–19th edn (Munich: Franz Eher, 1938)

Grosse Deutsche Kunstausstellung 1939 im Haus der Deutschen Kunst zu München, 16. Juli bis 15. Oktober 1939 (Munich: Knorr & Hirth, 1939)

Grosz, George, *A Little Yes and a Big No: The Autobiography of George Grosz* (New York: Dial Press, 1946)

Grothe, Heinz, ed., *Arno Breker: Sechzig Bilder* (Königsberg: Kanter, 1943)

Groys, Boris, "Das Kunstwerk Rasse," in Robert Eikmeyer, ed., *Adolf Hitler: Reden zur Kunst- und Kulturpolitik, 1933–1939* (Frankfurt am Main: revolver, 2004), 25–39

Gruchmann, Lothar, *Der Zweite Weltkrieg: Kriegführung und Politik* (Munich: DTV, 1967)

Grunberger, Richard, *The 12-Year Reich: A Social History of Nazi Germany, 1933–1945* (New York: Ballantine Books, 1972)

Grüttner, Michael, *Brandstifter und Biedermänner: Deutschland, 1933–1939* (Stuttgart: Klett-Cotta, 2015)

Gumpert, Martin, *Hölle im Paradies: Selbstdarstellung eines Arztes* (Stockholm: Bermann Fischer, 1939)

Günther, Hans, ed., *The Culture of the Stalin Period* (Houndmills: Macmillan, 1990)

Guthmann, Heinrich, *Zweierlei Kunst in Deutschland? Der Bund der Verschworenen* (Berlin: Volkschaft-Verlag, 1935)

Gutteridge, Richard, *Open Thy Mouth for the Dumb! The German Evangelical Church and the Jews, 1879–1950* (Oxford: Basil Blackwell, 1976)

Haacke, Wilmont, *Feuilletonkunde: Das Feuilleton als literarische und journalistische Gattung*, vol. 1 (Leipzig: Karl W. Hiersemann, 1943)

Haas, Michael, *Forbidden Music: The Jewish Composers Banned by the Nazis* (New Haven: Yale University Press, 2013)

Hackel, Rainer, "Arno Breker: Annäherungen," in Rainer Hackel, ed., *Im Irrlicht: Arno Breker und seine Skulpturen* (Wetzlar: Büchse der Pandora Verlags-GmbH, 2013), 25–92

Hadamovsky, Eugen, *Dein Rundfunk: Das Rundfunkbuch für alle Volksgenossen* (Munich: Eher, 1934)

Hadamovsky, Eugen, *Der Rundfunk im Dienste der Volksführung* (Leipzig: Robert Noske, [1934])

Hadamovsky, Eugen, *Propaganda und nationale Macht: Die Organisation der öffentlichen Meinung für die nationale Politik* (Oldenburg: Stalling, 1933)

Haefs, Wilhelm, "'Die götterlose Zeit will enden . . .': Martin Raschke als Erzähler im 'Dritten Reich'," in Wilhelm Haefs and Walter Schmitz, eds, *Martin Raschke (1905–1943): Leben und Werk* (Dresden: w.e.b., 2002), 79–106

Haefs, Wilhelm, "Martin Raschke (1905–1943): Eine Lebens- und Werkchronik," in Wilhelm Haefs and Walter Schmitz, eds, *Martin Raschke (1905–1943): Leben und Werk* (Dresden: w.e.b., 2002), 203–81

Haffner, Sebastian, *Als Engländer maskiert: Ein Gespräch mit Jutta Krug über das Exil* (Stuttgart: Deutsche Verlags-Anstalt, 2002)

Haffner, Sebastian, *Defying Hitler: A Memoir* (London: Weidenfeld & Nicolson, 2002)

407

Haftmann, Werner, *Emil Nolde: Ungemalte Bilder* (Cologne: M. DuMont Schauberg, 1963)

Hagemann, Jürgen, *Die Presselenkung im Dritten Reich* (Bonn: H. Bouvier, 1970)

Hagemann, Walter, *Publizistik im Dritten Reich: Ein Beitrag zur Methodik der Massenführung* (Hamburg: Hansischer Gildenverlag, 1948)

Hagen, Peter, *SA-Kamerad Tonne* (Berlin: Nationaler Freiheits-Verlag, 1933)

Hagen, Wilhelm, *Auftrag und Wirklichkeit: Sozialarzt im 20. Jahrhundert* (Munich-Gräfelfing: Werk-Verlag Dr. Edmund Banaschewski, 1978)

Hager, Werner, "Bauwerke im Dritten Reich," *Das Innere Reich* 4, no. 1 (April 1937): 5–21

Hahn, Peter, "Vom Bauhaus zum New Bauhaus," in Peter Hahn and Lloyd C. Engelbrecht, eds, *50 Jahre Bauhausnachfolge: New Bauhaus in Chicago* (Berlin: Bauhaus-Archiv/Argon, 1987), 9–19

Hake, Sabine, *Popular Cinema of the Third Reich* (Austin: University of Texas Press, 2001)

Hale, Oron J., *The Captive Press in the Third Reich* (Princeton: Princeton University Press, 1964)

Hamann, Brigitte, *Winifred Wagner oder Hitlers Bayreuth* (Munich: Piper, 2002)

Hanfstaengl, Ernst, *Zwischen Weissem und Braunem Haus: Memoiren eines politischen Aussenseiters* (Munich: R. Piper, 1970)

Hansen, Thore D., ed., *Ein deutsches Leben: Was uns die Geschichte von Goebbels' Sekretärin für die Gegenwart lehrt* (Berlin: Europa, 2017)

Hansen, Walter, "Wolfgang Willrich," *Das Bild* (1936): 332–7

Hardt, Ursula, *From Caligari to California: Eric Pommer's Life in the International Film Wars* (Providence: Berghahn, 1996)

Harlan, Veit, *Unter dem Schatten meiner Filme: Selbstbiographie*, ed. H. C. Oppermann (Gütersloh: Sigbert Mohn, 1966)

Härtwig, Dieter, *Rudolf Wagner-Régeny: Der Opernkomponist* (Berlin: Henschel, 1965)

Haupt, Gunther, *Was erwarten wir von der kommenden Dichtung?* (Tübingen: Rainer Wunderlich, 1934)

Heesters, Johannes, *Es kommt auf die Sekunde an: Erinnerungen an ein Leben im Frack* (Munich: Blanvalet, 1978)

Heftrig, Ruth, "Narrowed Modernism: On the Rehabilitation of 'Degenerate Art' in Postwar Germany," in Olaf Peters, ed., *Degenerate Art: The Attack on Modern Art in Nazi Germany, 1937* (Munich: Prestel, 2014), 258–81

Heiber, Helmut, *Joseph Goebbels* (Munich: DTV, 1965)

Heiber, Helmut, ed., *Lagebesprechungen im Führerhauptquartier: Protokollfragmente aus Hitlers militärischen Konferenzen, 1942–1945* (Munich: DTV, 1962)

Heiber, Helmut, and Hildegard von Kotze, eds, *Facsimile Querschnitt durch das Schwarze Korps* (Munich: Scherz, 1968)

Heiden, Konrad, *Der Fuehrer: Hitler's Rise to Power* (Boston: Houghton Mifflin, 1944, 1st pr. 1936)

Heilbut, Anthony, *Exiled in Paradise: German Refugee Artists and Intellectuals in America, from the 1930s to the Present* (Boston: Beacon, 1983)

Heilmann, Matthias, *Leopold Jessner – Intendant der Republik: Der Weg eines deutsch-jüdischen Regisseurs aus Ostpreussen* (Tübingen: Max Niemeyer, 2005)

Heins, Laura, *Nazi Film Melodrama* (Urbana: University of Illinois Press, 2013)

Heiseler, Bernt von, "Oktober 1939," *Der Bücherwurm* 25, no. 2/3 (October 1939): 33–4

Heister, Hans-Werner, Claudia Maurer Zenck, and Peter Petersen, eds, *Musik im Exil: Folgen des Nazismus für die internationale Musikkultur* (Frankfurt am Main: S. Fischer, 1993)

Heldt, Guido, "Hardly Heroes: Composers as a Subject in National Socialist Cinema," in Michael H. Kater and Albrecht Riethmüller, eds, *Music and Nazism: Art under Tyranny, 1933–1945* (Laaber: Laaber, 2003), 114–35

Hennig, Albert, "Das Judentum in der Malerei," in Theodor Fritsch, ed., *Handbuch der Judenfrage: Die wichtigsten Tatsachen zur Beurteilung des jüdischen Volkes*, 38th edn (Leipzig: Hammer-Verlag, 1935), 352–5

Herf, Jeffrey, *Divided Memory: The Nazi Past in the Two Germanys* (Cambridge, MA: Harvard University Press, 1997)

Herf, Jeffrey, *Reactionary Modernism: Technology, Culture, and Politics in Weimar and the Third Reich* (Cambridge: Cambridge University Press, 1984)

Herf, Jeffrey, *The Jewish Enemy: Nazi Propaganda during World War II and the Holocaust* (Cambridge, MA: Harvard Univeristy Press, 2006)

Hermand, Jost, "Bewährte Tümlichkeiten: Der völkisch-nazistische Traum einer ewig-deutschen Kunst," in Horst Denkler and Karl Prümm, eds, *Die deutsche Literatur im Dritten Reich: Themen – Traditionen – Wirkungen* (Stuttgart: Philipp Reclam jun., 1976), 102–17

Hermand, Jost, *Culture in Dark Times: Nazi Fascism, Inner Emigration, and Exile* (New York: Berghahn, 2013)

Hermand, Jost, and Frank Trommler, *Die Kultur der Weimarer Republik* (Frankfurt am Main: Fischer Taschenbuch, 1988)

Herzog, Friedrich W., "Was ist deutsche Musik? Erkentnisse und Folgerungen," *Bausteine zum deutschen Nationaltheater* 2, no 7 (July/August 1934): 200–5

Hesse, Kurt, "Der Beitrag des deutschen Schrifttums zur soldatisch-kämpferischen Leistung unserer Zeit," in *Die Dichtung im Kampf des Reiches: Weimarer Reden 1940*, 2nd edn (Hamburg: Hanseatische Verlagsanstalt, 1941/43), 15–34

Heyde, Ludwig, *Presse, Rundfunk und Film im Dienste der Volksführung* (Dresden: M. Dittert & Co., 1943)

Hiemer, Ernst, *Der Pudelmopsdackelpinscher und andere besinnliche Erzählungen* (Nuremberg: Der Stürmer-Buchverlag, 1940)

Hille, Karoline, "Beispiel Thüringen: Die 'Machtergreifung' auf der Probebühne 1930," in Dieter Ruckhaberle, ed., *1933 – Wege zur Diktatur: Staatliche Kunsthalle Berlin und Neue Gesellschaft für Bildende Kunst: Ausstellung im Rahmen der Projekte des Berliner Kulturrats vom 9.1. bis 10.2.1983* (Berlin, 1983), 187–217

Hilpert, Heinz, "Menschenführung im Theater: Rede, gehalten am 14. Februar 1940 vor den Berliner Kunstbetrachtern," *Die Literatur* 42 (1939/1940): 273–7

Himmler privat: Briefe eines Massenmörders, ed. Katrin Himmler and Michael Wildt, 2nd edn (Munich: Piper, 2014)

Hindemith, Paul, *Unterweisung im Tonsatz I: Theoretischer Teil* (Mainz: Schott's Söhne, 1940, 1st edn 1937)

Hinrichs, August, *Petermann fährt nach Madeira: Ein Volksstück in 4 Bildern* (Berlin: Drei Masken Verlag, 1936)

Hinz, Berthold, *Die Malerei im deutschen Faschismus: Kunst und Konterrevolution* (Munich: Hanser, 1974)

Hippler, Fritz, *Die Verstrickung: Einstellungen und Rückblenden*, 2nd edn (Düsseldorf: MEHR WISSEN, 1982 [?]; 1st edn 1981 [?])

Hippler, Fritz, et al., *25 Jahre Wochenschau der Ufa: Geschichte der Ufa-Wochenschauen und Geschichten aus der Wochenschau-Arbeit* (Berlin: Illustr. Filmwoche G.m.b.H., 1939)

Hirsch, Lily E., "Defining 'Jewish Music' in Nazi Germany," in Erik Levi, ed., *The Impact of Nazism on Twentieth-Century Music* (Vienna: Böhlau, 2014), 27–43

Hirschfeld, Gerhard, "Great Britain and the Emigration from Nazi Germany: An Historical Overview," in Günter Berghaus, ed., *Theatre and Film in Exile* (Oxford: Berg, 1989), 1–14

Hitler, Adolf, *Mein Kampf*, 26th edn (Munich: Franz Eher Nachfolger, 1933)

Hitler, Adolf, *Reden des Führers am Parteitag der Ehre 1936*, 6th edn (Munich: Eher, 1936)

Hoeres, Peter, *Die Kultur von Weimar: Durchbruch der Moderne* (Berlin-Brandenburg: be.bra, 2008)

Hoffmann, Heinrich, ed., *"Grosse Deutsche Kunstausstellung": München 1943* (Vienna: Verlag Heinrich Hoffmann, [1943])

Hoffmann, Hilmar, *"Und die Fahne führt uns in die Ewigkeit": Propaganda im NS-Film* (Frankfurt am Main: Fischer Taschenbuch, 1988)

Högg, Emil, "Deutsche Baukunst – gestern – heute – morgen," *Das Bild* (1934): 61–4

Hohlbaum, Robert, *König Volk: Roman der Masse* (Munich: Langen Müller, 1943; 1st edn 1931)

Hollaender, Friedrich, *Von Kopf bis Fuss: Mein Leben mit Text und Musik* (Munich: Kindler, 1965)

Hollstein, Dorothea, *"Jud Süss" und die Deutschen: Antisemitische Vorurteile im nationalsozialistischen Spielfilm* (Frankfurt am Main: Ullstein, 1983)

Holthusen, Hans Egon, "Der Aufbruch: Aufzeichnungen aus dem polnischen Kriege," *Eckart* 16 (April 1940): 104–7

Holthusen, Hans Egon, *Die Welt ohne Transferenz: Eine Studie zu Thomas Manns "Dr. Faustus" und seinen Nebenschriften* (Hamburg: Heinrich Ellermann, 1949)

Holz, Keith, "The Exiled Artists from Nazi Germany and their Art," in Richard A. Etlin, ed., *Art, Culture and Media under the Third Reich* (Chicago: University of Chicago Press, 2002), 343–67

Honegger, Marc, and Günther Massenkeil, eds, *Das Grosse Lexikon der Musik: In acht Bänden*, 8 vols (Freiburg i. Br.: Herder, 1978–82)

Horak, Jan-Christopher, *Fluchtpunkt Hollywood: Eine Dokumentation zur Filmemigration nach 1933*, 2nd edn (Münster: MAkS Publikationen, 1986)

Hörbiger, Paul, *Ich hab für euch gespielt: Erinnerungen* (Frankfurt am Main: Ullstein, 1989)

Horkenbach, Cuno, ed., *Das Deutsche Reich von 1918 bis Heute* (Berlin: Verlag für Presse, Wirtschaft und Politik, 1933)

Horn, Walter, "Hanns Johst," in Paul Gerhardt Dippel, ed., *Künder und Kämpfer: Die Dichter des neuen Deutschland* (Munich: Deutscher Volksverlag, [1937; 2nd edn 1939]), 77–113

Horowitz, Joseph, *Artists in Exile: How Refugees from Twentieth-Century War and Revolution Transformed the American Performing Arts* (New York: HarperCollins, 2008)

Hotter, Hans, *"Der Mai war mir gewogen . . .": Erinnerungen* (Munich: Kindler, 1996)

Hübinger, Paul Egon, *Thomas Mann, die Universität Bonn und die Zeitgeschichte: Drei Kapitel deutscher Vergangenheit aus dem Leben des Dichters, 1905–1955* (Munich: Oldenbourg, 1974)

Huener, Jonathan, and Francis R. Nicosia, eds, *The Arts in Nazi Germany: Continuity, Conformity, Change* (New York: Berghahn, 2007)

Hull, David Stewart, *Film in the Third Reich: A Study of the German Cinema, 1933–1945* (Berkeley: University of California Press, 1969)

Hüpgens, Theodor, "Film der Nation," *Die Literatur* 43 (1940/41): 410–11

Hussong, Friedrich, *"Kurfürstendamm": Zur Kulturgeschichte des Zwischenreichs* (Berlin: Scherl, [1933])

Huth, Jochen, *Die vier Gesellen: Ein Lustspiel in drei Akten* (Berlin: Felix Bloch Erben, 1936)

Hutten, Kurt, *Kulturbolschewismus: Eine deutsche Schicksalsfrage* (Stuttgart: W. Kohlhammer, 1932)

Jäckel, Eberhard, *Hitlers Herrschaft: Vollzug einer Weltanschauung* (Stuttgart: Deutsche Verlags-Anstalt, 1986)

Jäckel, Eberhard, *Hitlers Weltanschauung: Entwurf einer Herrschaft* (Tübingen: Rainer Wunderlich/Hermann Leins, 1969)

Jan, Reinhold von, "Ernst Barlach und die Zeit," *Bausteine zum deutschen Nationaltheater* 3, no. 3 (March 1935): 65–76

Jansen, Werner, *Die Insel Heldentum: Roman* (Brunswick: Georg Westermann, 1938)

Jansen, Werner, *Die Kinder Israel: Roman* (Berlin: Herbert Stubenrauch, 1941; 1st edn 1927)

Jarausch, Konrad H., *Broken Lives: How Ordinary Germans Experienced the Twentieth Century* (Princeton: Princeton University Press, 2018)

Jasser, Manfred, "Film und Schrifttum," *Die Neue Literatur*, no. 5 (May 1938): 230–6

Jelavich, Peter, *Berlin Alexanderplatz: Radio, Film, and the Death of Weimar Culture* (Berkeley: University of California Press, 2009)

Jelavich, Peter, *Berlin Cabaret* (Cambridge, MA: Harvard University Press, 1993)

Jochmann, Werner, ed., *Adolf Hitler: Monologe im Führer-Hauptquartier, 1941–1944: Die Aufzeichnungen Heinrich Heims* (Hamburg: Albrecht Knaus, 1980)

Johst, Hanns, *Fritz Todt: Requiem* (Munich: Eher, 1943)

Johst, Hanns, *Maske und Gesicht: Reise eines Nationalsozialisten von Deutschland nach Deutschland* (Munich: Langen Müller, 1936)

Johst, Hanns, *Ruf des Reiches – Echo des Volkes: Eine Ostfahrt*, 7th edn (Munich: Eher, 1944; 1st edn 1940)

Johst, Hanns, *Schlageter: Schauspiel* (Munich: Langen Müller, 1933)

Johst, Hanns, *Standpunkt und Fortschritt* (Oldenburg: Gerhard Stalling, 1933)

Johst, Hanns, *Thomas Paine: Schauspiel* (Munich: Langen, 1927)

Jones, Larry Eugene, "Conservative Antisemitism in the Weimar Republic: A Case Study of the German National People's Party," in Larry Eugene Jones, ed., *The German Right in the Weimar Republic: Studies in the History of German Conservatism, Nationalism, and Antisemitism* (New York: Berghahn, 2014), 79–107.

Jünger, Ernst, *Auf den Marmorklippen* (Hamburg: Hanseatische Verlagsanstalt, 1939)

Jünger, Ernst, *Das Wäldchen 125: Eine Chronik aus den Grabenkämpfen 1918*, 6th edn (Berlin: E. S. Mittler, 1935; 1st edn 1926)

Jünger, Ernst, *Der Arbeiter: Herrschaft und Gestalt*, 2nd edn (Hamburg: Hanseatische Verlagsanstalt, 1941; 1st edn 1932)

Jünger, Ernst, *Der Kampf als inneres Erlebnis*, 2nd edn (Berlin: E. S. Mittler & Sohn, 1926; 1st edn 1922)

Jünger, Ernst, *Die totale Mobilmachung*, 2nd edn (Berlin: Junker und Dünnhaupt, 1934; 1st edn 1930)

Jünger, Ernst, *Gärten und Strassen: Aus den Tagebüchern von 1939 und 1940*, 2nd edn (Berlin: E. S. Mittler & Sohn, 1942)

Jünger, Ernst, *In Stahlgewittern: Ein Kriegstagebuch*, 16th edn (Berlin: E. S. Mittler & Sohn, n.d.; 1st edn 1926)

Jünger, Ernst, *Strahlungen*, 3rd edn (Tübingen: Heliopolis, 1949)

Jungk, Peter Stephan, *Franz Werfel: Eine Lebensgeschichte*, 2nd edn (Frankfurt am Main: S. Fischer, 1987)

Jürgen Fehling der Regisseur (1885–1968): Ausstellung in der Akademie der Künste vom 28. Oktober bis 26. November 1978, 2nd edn (Berlin: Akademie der Künste, 1985)

Kaiser, [Fritz], *Führer durch die Ausstellung Entartete Kunst* (Berlin, [1937])

Kaiser, Henriette, and Joachim Kaiser, *"Ich bin der letzte Mohikaner"* (Berlin: Ullstein, 2008)

Kalbus, Oskar, *Vom Werden deutscher Filmkunst. 2. Teil: Der Tonfilm* (Altona-Bahrenfeld: Cigaretten-Bilderdienst, 1935)

Kallenbach, Helmut, *Die Kulturpolitik der deutschen Tageszeitung im Krieg: Eine Untersuchung über den politischen Einsatz und die publizistische Einsatzmöglichkeit der Kulturpolitik in der deutschen Tageszeitung, aufgezeigt am Beispiel des Krieges 1939–1940* (Dresden: M. Dittert, 1941)

Kardorff, Ursula von, *Berliner Aufzeichnungen: Aus den Jahren 1942–1945* (Munich: DTV, 1964)

Kater, Michael H., *Composers of the Nazi Era: Eight Portraits* (New York: Oxford University Press, 2000)

Kater, Michael H., *Das "Ahnenerbe" der SS, 1935–1945: Ein Beitrag zur Kulturpolitik des Dritten Reiches*, 4th edn (Munich: Oldenbourg, 2006; 1st edn 1974)

Kater, Michael H., *Different Drummers: Jazz in the Culture of Nazi Germany* (New York: Oxford University Press, 1992)

Kater, Michael H., *Doctors under Hitler* (Chapel Hill: University of North Carolina Press, 1989)

Kater, Michael H., "New Democracy and Alternative Culture: Jazz in West Germany after the Second World War," *Australian Journal of Politics and History* 52 (2006): 173–87

Kater, Michael H., "Problems of Reeducation in West Germany, 1945–1960," *Simon Wiesenthal Center Annual* 4 (1987): 99–123

Kater, Michael H., "Social, Cultural and Political Controls: Radio in the Third Reich," in Theo Mäusli, ed., *Talk About Radio: Towards a Social History of Radio (Colloqui del Monte Verità)* (Zurich: Chronos, 1999), 59–71

411

Kater, Michael H., *The Nazi Party: A Social Profile of Members and Leaders, 1919–1945* (Cambridge, MA: Harvard University Press, 1983)

Kater, Michael H., *The Twisted Muse: Musicians and their Music in the Third Reich* (New York: Oxford University Press, 1997)

Kater, Michael H., "Weill und Brecht: Kontroversen einer Künstlerfreundschaft auf zwei Kontinenten," in Albrecht Riethmüller, ed., *Brecht und seine Komponisten* (Laaber: Laaber, 2000), 51–73

Kater, Michael H., *Weimar: From Enlightenment to the Present* (New Haven: Yale University Press, 2014)

Keller, Sepp, *Zwischen Nacht und Tag* (Jena: Diederichs, 1938)

Kelson, John F., *Catalogue of Forbidden German Feature and Short Film Productions held in Zonal Film Archives of Film Section, Information Services Division, Control Commission for Germany, (BE)*, ed. K. R. M. Short (Westport: Greenwood, 1996)

Kempter, Klaus, "'Objective, not neutral': Joseph Wulf, a documentary historian," *Holocaust Studies* 21, nos 1–2 (2015): 38–53

Kenter, Heinz Dietrich, "Über Regieführung aus nationalsozialistischem Geist," *Die Bühne*, no. 2 (December [1936]): 744–5

Kershaw, Ian, *Hitler, 1889–1936: Hubris* (New York: Norton, 1999)

Kershaw, Ian, *Hitler, 1936–45: Nemesis* (New York: Norton, 2000)

Kershaw, Ian, *The "Hitler Myth": Image and Reality in the Third Reich* (Oxford: Clarendon Press, 1987)

Kersten, Heinz, Katrin Seybold, and Egon Netenjacob, *Wolfgang Staudte* (Berlin: Verlag Volker Spiess, 1977)

Ketelsen, Uwe-Karsten, *Heroisches Theater: Untersuchungen zur Dramentheorie des Dritten Reichs* (Bonn: H. Bouvier, 1968)

Ketelsen, Uwe-Karsten, "Kulturpolitik im III. Reich und Ansätze zu ihrer Interpretation," *Text und Kontext* 8 (1980): 217–42

Ketelsen, Uwe-Karsten, *Literatur und Drittes Reich* (Schernfeld: SH-Verlag, 1992)

Kiesel, Helmuth, *Ernst Jünger: Die Biographie* (Munich: Siedler, 2007)

Killer, Hermann, "Paul Graener 70 Jahre alt," *Die Musik* 34, no. 4 (January 1942): 150–1

Kindermann, Heinz, "Vom Geschichtsbild der Gegenwartsdichtung: Ein Bericht," *Völkische Kultur* 2 (1934): 556–8

Kitchen, Martin, *Speer: Hitler's Architect* (New Haven: Yale University Press, 2015)

Kitchen, Martin, *The Third Reich: Charisma and Community* (Harlow: Pearson Longman, 2008)

Klaehn, Friedrich Joachim, *Sturm 138: Ernstes und viel Heiteres aus dem SA-Leben* (Leipzig: H. Schaufuss, 1934)

Klausch, Hans-Peter, *Braunes Erbe – NS-Vergangenheit hessischer Landtagsabgeordneter der 1. Wahlperiode (1946–1987)* (Odenburg/Wiesbaden: DIE LINKE Fraktion im Hessischen Landtag, 2011)

Klee, Ernst, *Kulturlexikon zum Dritten Reich: Wer war was vor und nach 1945* (Frankfurt am Main: Fischer Taschenbuch Verlag, 2009)

Klee, Ernst, *Personenlexikon zum Dritten Reich: Wer war was vor und nach 1945*, 2nd edn (Hamburg: Nikol, 2016)

Klemperer, Victor, *Tagebücher 1933–1945*, 7 vols, ed. Walter Nowojski (Berlin: Aufbau-Taschenbuch, 1999)

Klepper, Jochen, *Der Vater: Der Roman des Soldatenkönigs*, 2 vols (Stuttgart: Deutsche Verlags-Anstalt, 1937)

Klepper, Jochen, *Unter dem Schatten deiner Flügel: Aus den Tagebüchern, 1932–1942*, ed. Hildegard Klepper (Munich: DTV, 1976)

Klingler, Walter, "Nationalsozialistische Rundfunkpolitik, 1942–1945: Organisation, Programm und die Hörer," Diss. phil. (Mannheim, 1983)

Koch, Hans-Jörg, *Wunschkonzert: Unterhaltungsmusik und Propaganda im Rundfunk des Dritten Reiches* (Graz: Ares, 2006)

Koeppen, Anne Marie, *Das Erbe der Wallmodens: Roman* (Leipzig: Hesse & Becker, [1936])

Koeppen, Anne Marie, *Michael Gnade: Die Geschichte eines deutschen Hauses* (Berlin: Blut und Boden, 1934)

Koestler, Arthur, *Scum of the Earth* (New York: Macmillan, 1941)

Koestler, Arthur, *The Invisible Writing: The Second Volume of an Autobiography, 1932–40* (London: Hutchinson, 1979)

Kogon, Eugen, *Der SS-Staat: Das System der deutschen Konzentrationslager* (Munich: Kindler, 1974)

Köhler, Otto, *Unheimliche Publizisten: Die verdrängte Vergangenheit der Medienmacher* (Munich: Knaur, 1995)

Kolb, Richard, and Heinrich Siekmeier, eds, *Rundfunk und Film im Dienste nationaler Kultur* (Düsseldorf: Friedrich Floeder, 1933)

König, Christoph, ed., *Internationales Germanistenlexikon, 1800–1950*, 3 vols (Berlin: Walter de Gruter, 2003)

Köpf, Peter, "Das Elend der deutschen Zeitungswissenschaft," *Publizistik & Kunst* 39, no. 11 (November 1990): 28–9

Korngold, Luzi, *Erich Wolfgang Korngold: Ein Lebensbild* (Vienna: E. Lafite, 1967)

Kortner, Fritz, *Aller Tage Abend*, 5th edn (Munich: DTV, 1976)

Koszyk, Kurt, "Propaganda," in Carola Stern, Thilo Vogelsang, Erhard Klöss, and Albert Graff, eds, *Lexikon zur Geschichte und Politik im 20. Jahrhundert* (Cologne: Kiepenheuer & Witsch, 1971), 649–50

Kracauer, Siegfried: *From Caligari to Hitler: A Psychological History of German Film* (Princeton: Princeton University Press, 1947)

Kracht, Isgar, "Vom Symbol der Freiheit zum Sinnbild 'entarteter' Kunst: Otto Freundlichs Plastik 'Der neue Mensch'," in Uwe Fleckner, ed., *Das verfemte Meisterwerk: Schicksalswege moderner Kunst im "Dritten Reich"* (Berlin: Akademie Verlag, 2009), 3–27

Krahl, Hilde, *Ich bin fast immer angekommen: Erinnerungen, aufgezeichnet von Dieter H. Bratsch* (Munich: Langen Müller, 1998)

Kramer, Sven, "Wiederkehr und Verwandlung der Vergangenheit im deutschen Film," in Peter Reichel, Harald Schmid, and Peter Steinbach, eds, *Der Nationalsozialismus – Die Zweite Geschichte: Überwindung – Deutung – Erinnerung* (Munich: C. H. Beck, 2009), 283–99

Kreimeier, Klaus, *Die Ufa-Story: Geschichte eines Filmkonzerns* (Munich: Carl Hanser, 1992)

Kremer, S. Lillian, ed., *Holocaust Literature: An Encyclopedia of Writers and their Work*, vol. 2 (New York: Routledge, 2003)

Krempel, Ulrich, "Moderne und Gegenmoderne: Der Nationalsozialismus und die bildende Kunst," in Peter Reichel, Harald Schmid, and Peter Steinbach, eds, *Der Nationalsozialismus – Die Zweite Geschichte: Überwindung – Deutung – Erinnerung* (Munich: C. H. Beck, 2009), 318–34

Krenek, Ernst, *Die amerikanischen Tagebücher, 1937–1942: Dokumente aus dem Exil*, ed. Claudia Maurer Zenck (Vienna: Böhlau, 1992)

Kriechbaumer, Robert, *Zwischen Österreich und Grossdeutschland: Eine politische Geschichte der Salzburger Festspiele, 1933–1944* (Vienna: Böhlau, 2013)

Kriegk, Otto, *Der deutsche Film im Spiegel der Ufa: 25 Jahre Kampf und Vollendung* (Berlin: Ufa-Buchverlag, 1943)

Krispyn, Egbert, *Anti-Nazi Writers in Exile* (Athens, GA: University of Georgia Press, 1978)

Krug, Konrad, "Erziehung zur Gemeinschaft im deutschen Thingspiel," *Volk im Werden* 3 (1935): 453–64

Krüll, Marianne, *Im Netz der Zauberer: Eine andere Geschichte der Familie Mann* (Frankfurt am Main: Fischer Taschenbuch, 1995)

Krützen, Michaela, *Hans Albers: Eine deutsche Karriere* (Weinheim: Quadriga, 1995)

Kühn, Volker, "Der Kompass pendelt sich ein: Unterhaltung und Kabarett im 'Dritten Reich'," in Hans Sarkowicz, ed., *Hitlers Künstler: Die Kultur im Dienst des Nationalsozialismus* (Frankfurt am Main: Insel, 2004), 346–91

413

Kühn, Walter, "Thingspiel, das Spiel der völkischen Gemeinschaft," *Schlesische Monatshefte* 11 (1934): 456–63

Künkler, Karl, "Probleme des Dramas und Theaters," *Nationalsozialistische Monatshefte* 14, no. 157 (1943): 197–207

Kursell, Otto von, "Nationalsozalistische Kunstpolitik," *Deutsche Kultur-Wacht* 33, no. 20 (August 19, 1933): 3–5

Kurzke, Hermann, *Thomas Mann: Das Leben als Kunstwerk* (Munich: C. H. Beck, 1999)

Lange, Horst, *Schwarze Weide: Roman* (Hamburg: H. Goverts, 1937)

Langenbucher, Hellmuth, *Nationalsozialistische Dichtung: Einführung und Übersicht* (Berlin: Junker & Dünnhaupt, 1935)

Langenbucher, Hellmuth, *Volkhafte Dichtung der Zeit*, 5th edn (Berlin: Junker & Dünnhaupt, 1940)

Langer, Norbert, *Die deutsche Dichtung seit dem Weltkrieg: Von Paul Ernst bis Hans Baumann* (Karlsbad: Adam Kraft, 1941 [?]; 1st edn 1940)

Langer, William L., ed., *An Encyclopedia of World History* (Boston: Houghton Mifflin, 1968)

Langhoff, Wolfgang, *Die Moorsoldaten: 13 Monate Konzentrationslager* (Berlin: Aufbau-Verlag, 1947)

Laqueur, Walter, *Weimar: Die Kultur der Republik* (Frankfurt am Main: Ullstein, 1977)

Laux, Karl, *Anton Bruckner: Leben und Werk* (Leipzig: Breitkopf & Härtel, 1940)

Laux, Karl, *Nachklang: Autobiographie* (Berlin: Verlag der Nation, 1977)

Lauzemis, Laura, "Die nationalsozialistische Ideologie und der 'neue Mensch': Oskar Schlemmers Folkwang-Zyklus und sein Briefwechsel mit Klaus Graf von Baudissin aus dem Jahr 1934," in Uwe Fleckner, ed., *Angriff auf die Avantgarde: Kunst und Kunstpolitik im Nationalsozialismus* (Berlin: Akademie-Verlag, 2007), 5–88

Ledebur, Ruth Freifrau von, "Shakespeare: Der dritte deutsche Klassiker in Weimar," in Jochen Golz and Justus H. Ulbricht, eds, *Goethe in Gesellschaft: Zur Geschichte einer literarischen Vereinigung vom Kaiserreich bis zum geteilten Deutschland* (Cologne: Böhlau, 2005), 1–12

Lehmann, Ernst Herbert, *Gestaltung der Zeitschrift* (Leipzig: Karl W. Hiersemann, 1938)

Lehmann, Hans-Thies, "Richard der Dritte, 1937 – eine Skizze," in Gerhard Ahrens, ed., *Das Theater des deutschen Regisseurs Jürgen Fehling* (Berlin: Quadriga Verlag J. Severin, 1985), 172–83

Lehmann, Lotte, "Göring, the Lioness and I," in Charles Osborne, ed., *Opera 66* (London: Alan Ross, 1966), 187–99

Lehmann, Stephen, and Marion Faber, *Rudolf Serkin: A Life* (New York: Oxford University Press, 2003)

Lehmann-Haupt, Hellmut, *Art under a Dictatorship* (New York: Octagon, 1973; 1st edn 1954)

Lehnert, Herbert, "Repräsentation und Zweifel: Thomas Manns Exilwerke und der deutsche Kulturbürger," in Manfred Durzak, ed., *Die deutsche Exilliteratur 1933–1945* (Stuttgart: Philipp Reclam jun., 1973), 398–417

Lehnich, Oswald, ed., *Jahrbuch der Reichsfilmkammer 1937* (Berlin-Schöneberg: Max Hesses Verlag, 1937)

Lemmons, Russel, *Goebbels and Der Angriff* (Lexington: University Press of Kentucky, 1994)

Lenz, Siegfried, *Deutschstunde: Roman*, 4th edn (Munich: DTV, 1974)

Lersch, Heinrich, *Die Pioniere von Eilenburg: Roman aus der Frühzeit der deutschen Arbeiterbewegung* (Berlin: Büchergilde Gutenberg, 1937)

Leuchter, Heinz M., "Hans-Jürgen Nierentz," in Paul Gerhardt Dippel, ed., *Künder und Kämpfer: Die Dichter des neuen Deutschland* (Munich: Deutscher Volksverlag, [1937; 2nd edn 1939]), 173–205

Leupold, Wilhelm, *Die Neuordnung des deutschen Zeitungsverlagswesens* (Munich: Münchener Zeitungs-Verlag, [1940])

Levi, Erik, *Mozart and the Nazis: How the Third Reich Abused a Cultural Icon* (New Haven: Yale University Press, 2010)

Levi, Erik, *Music in the Third Reich* (New York: St. Martin's Press, 1994)

Levi, Erik, "Opera in the Nazi Period," in John London, ed., *Theatre under the Nazis* (Manchester: Manchester University Press, 2000), 136–86

Lewy, Guenter, *Harmful and Undesirable: Book Censorship in Nazi Germany* (New York: Oxford University Press, 2016)

Ley, Robert, *Deutschland ist schöner geworden*, ed. Hans Dauer and Walter Kiehl (Berlin: Mehden, 1936)

Lindemann, Paul, "Heimat und Volkstum in der deutschen Tagespresse," Diss. phil. (University of Leipzig, 1937)

Linfert, Carl, "Beckmann oder das Schicksal der Malerei [1935]," in Martin Freiherr von Erffa and Erhard Göpel, eds, *Blick auf Beckmann: Dokumente und Vorträge* (Munich: Piper, 1962), 57–82

Liskowsky, Oskar, "Kulturelle Wiedergeburt," *Bausteine zum deutschen Nationaltheater* 2, no. 7 (July/August 1934): 219–24

Loewy, Ernst, *Literatur unterm Hakenkreuz: Das Dritte Reich und seine Dichtung*, 3rd edn (Frankfurt am Main: Europäische Verlagsanstalt, 1977)

Loewy, Ronny, ed., *Von Babelsberg nach Hollywood: Filmemigranten aus Nazideutschland: Exponatenverzeichnis: Ausstellung vom 26.5.–9.8.1987* (Frankfurt am Main: Deutsches Filmmuseum, 1987)

Lohmann, Heinz, *SA räumt auf: Aus der Kampfzeit der Bewegung* (Hamburg: Deutsche Hausbücherei, [1935])

London, John, "Introduction," in London, ed., *Theatre under the Nazis* (Manchester: Manchester University Press, 2000), 1–53

Longerich, Peter, *"Davon haben wir nichts gewusst!": Die Deutschen und die Judenverfolgung, 1933–1945* (Munich: Siedler, 2006)

Longerich, Peter, *Hitler: Biographie* (Munich: Siedler, 2015)

Longerich, Peter, *Joseph Goebbels: Biographie* (Munich: Pantheon, 2012)

Lorenz, Gerhard, *Unrast: Roman des Malers Kai Jansen* (Munich: Deutscher Volksverlag, 1943)

Lott, Dagmar, "Münchens Neue Staatsgalerie im Dritten Reich," in Peter-Klaus Schuster, ed., *Die "Kunststadt" München 1937: Nationalsozialismus und "Entartete Kunst,"* 3rd edn (Munich: Prestel, 1988), 289–300

Lotz, Wilhelm, "Das Reichsparteitagsgelände in Nürnberg," *Die Kunst im Dritten Reich* 2, no. 9 (September 1938): 264–9

Lovisa, Fabian R., *Musikkritik im Nationalsozialismus: Die Rolle deutschsprachiger Musikzeitschriften, 1930–1945* (Laaber: Laaber, 1993)

Lowry, Stephen, *Pathos und Politik: Ideologie in Spielfilmen des Nationalsozialismus* (Tübingen: Max Niemeyer, 1991)

Lüth, Erich, *Hamburger Theater, 1933–1945: Ein theatergeschichtlicher Versuch* (Hamburg: Verlag der Werkberichte Justus Bueckschmitt, 1962)

Lüttichau, Mario-Andreas von, "'Crazy at any Price': The Pathologizing of Modernism in the Run-up to the 'Entartete Kunst' Exhibition in Munich in 1937," in Olaf Peters, ed., *Degenerate Art: The Attack on Modern Art in Nazi Germany, 1937* (Munich: Prestel, 2014), 36–51

Lüttichau, Mario-Andreas von, "Rekonstruktion der Ausstellung 'Entartete Kunst': München, 19. Juli–30. November 1937," in Peter-Klaus Schuster, ed., *Die "Kunststadt" München 1937: Nationalsozialismus und "Entartete Kunst,"* 3rd edn (Munich: Prestel, 1988), 120–81

Mahler-Werfel, Alma, *Mein Leben* (Stuttgart: Deutscher Bücherbund, 1960)

Mann, Erika, *Mein Vater, der Zauberer*, ed. Irmela von der Lühe and Uwe Naumann (Reinbek: Rowohlt, 1996)

Mann, Erika, and Klaus Mann, *Escape to Life: Deutsche Kultur im Exil*, ed. Heribert Hoven (Reinbek: rororo, 1996)

Mann, Katia, *Meine ungeschriebenen Memoiren*, ed. Elisabeth Plessen and Michael Mann (Frankfurt am Main: Fischer Taschenbuch, 1974)

Mann, Klaus, *Auf verlorenem Posten: Aufsätze, Reden, Kritiken, 1942–1949*, ed. Uwe Naumann and Michael Töteberg (Reinbek: Rowohlt, 1994)

Mann, Klaus, *Der Vulkan: Roman unter Emigranten* (Amsterdam: Querido, 1939)

Mann, Klaus, *Der Wendepunkt: Ein Lebensbericht* (Munich: Edition Spangenberg, 1981)

Mann, Klaus, *Mephisto: Roman einer Karriere* (Amsterdam: Querido, 1936)

Mann, Thomas, *Ansprache im Goethejahr 1949* (Weimar: Thüringer Volksverlag, 1949)

Mann, Thomas, *Betrachtungen eines Unpolitischen* (Berlin: S. Fischer, 1918)

Mann, Thomas, *Briefe, 1937–1947*, ed. Erika Mann (Frankfurt am Main: S. Fischer, 1963)

Mann, Thomas, *Briefwechsel mit seinem Verleger Gottfried Bermann Fischer, 1932–1955*, ed. Peter de Mendelssohn (Frankfurt am Main: S. Fischer, 1973)

Mann, Thomas, *Deutsche Ansprache: Rede, gehalten am 17. Oktober 1930 im Beethoven-Saal zu Berlin* (Berlin: S. Fischer, 1930)

Mann, Thomas, *Listen, Germany! Twenty–Five Radio Messages to the German People over BBC* (New York: Knopf, 1943)

Mann, Thomas, *Tagebücher, 1933–1934*, ed. Peter de Mendelssohn (Frankfurt am Main: S. Fischer, 1977)

Mann, Thomas, *Tagebücher, 1935–1936*, ed. Peter de Mendelssohn (Frankfurt am Main: S. Fischer, 1978)

Mann, Thomas, *Tagebücher, 1937–1939*, ed. Peter de Mendelssohn (Frankfurt am Main: S. Fischer, 1980)

Mann, Thomas, *Tagebücher, 1940–1943*, ed. Peter de Mendelssohn (Frankfurt am Main: S. Fischer, 1982)

Mann, Thomas, *Tagebücher, 1944–1.4.1946*, ed. Inge Jens (Frankfurt am Main: S. Fischer, 1986)

Mann, Thomas, "That Man Is My Brother," *Esquire* 11 (March 29, 1939): 31, 132–3

Mann, Thomas, *Von deutscher Republik* (Berlin: S. Fischer, 1923)

Mantau-Sadila, Hans Heinz, *Deutsche Führer, Deutsches Schicksal: Das Buch der Künder und Führer des dritten Reiches* (Berlin: Verlag und Versand für Deutsche Literatur Hans Eugen Hummel, n.d.)

Marchicelli, Graziella, "Futurism and Fascism: The Politicization of Art and the Aestheticization of Politics, 1909–1944," PhD diss. (University of Iowa, 1996)

Marks, Sally, "Black Watch on the Rhine: A Study in Propaganda, Prejudice and Prurience," *European Studies Review* 13 (1983): 297–334

Martens, Erika, *Zum Beispiel Das Reich: Zur Phänomenologie der Presse im totalitären Regime* (Cologne: Verlag Wissenschaft und Politik, 1972)

Martin, Benjamin G., *The Nazi-Fascist New Order for European Culture* (Cambridge, MA: Harvard University Press, 2016)

Martynkewicz, Wolfgang, *Salon Deutschland: Geist und Macht, 1900–1945* (Berlin: Aufbau, 2009)

Matthes, Wilhelm, "Max Trapp," *Zeitschrift für Musik* 104 (October 1937): 1,073–85

Maurer Zenck, Claudia, "Challenges and Opportunities of Acculturation: Schoenberg, Krenek and Stravinsky in Exile," in Reinhold Brinkmann and Christoph Wolff, eds, *Driven into Paradise: The Musical Migration from Nazi Germany to the United States* (Berkeley: University of California Press, 1999), 172–93

Maurer Zenck, Claudia, "Erich Itor Kahn: Ein unbekannter Mittler der Neuen Musik," *Musica* 6 (1986): 525–31

Mäusli, Theo, "The Swiss Music Scene in the 1930s: A Mirror of European Conditions?," in Michael H. Kater and Albrecht Riethmüller, eds, *Music and Nazism: Art under Tyranny, 1933–1945* (Laaber: Laaber, 2003), 259–70

McGilligan, Patrick, *Fritz Lang: The Nature of the Beast* (New York: St. Martin's Press, 1997)

Mechow, Karl Benno von, *Das ländliche Jahr: Roman* (Munich: Langen Müller, 1935)

Meckel, Anne, *Animation – Agitation: Frauendarstellungen auf der "Grossen Deutschen Kunstausstellung" in München, 1937–1944* (Weinheim: Deutscher Studien Verlag, 1993)

Meinecke, Friedrich, *Die deutsche Katastrophe: Betrachtungen und Erinnerungen* (Wiesbaden: Brockhaus, 1946)

Meldungen aus dem Reich: Die geheimen Lageberichte des Sicherheitsdienstes der SS, 1938–1945, 17 vols, ed. Heinz Boberach (Herrsching: Pawlak, 1984)

Menz, Egon, "Sprechchor und Aufmarsch: Zur Entstehung des Thingspiels," in Horst Denkler and Karl Prümm, eds, *Die deutsche Literatur im Dritten Reich: Themen – Traditionen – Wirkungen* (Stuttgart: Philipp Reclam jun., 1976), 330–46

Menz, Gerhard, *Der Aufbau des Kulturstandes: Die Reichskulturkammergesetzgebung, ihre Grundlagen und ihre Erfolge* (Munich: C. H. Beck, 1938)

Merker, Reinhard, *Die bildenden Künste im Nationalsozialismus: Kulturideologie, Kulturpolitik, Kulturproduktion* (Cologne: DuMont Buchverlag, 1983)

Merrill-Mirsky, Carol, ed., *Exiles in Paradise* (Los Angeles: The Museum, 1991)

Merzdorf, Helmut, "Geschichtliche Romane," *Nationalsozialistische Monatshefte* 6, no. 61 (April 1935): 373–4

Michalzik, Peter, *Gustaf Gründgens: Der Schauspieler und die Macht* (Berlin: Quadriga, 1999)

Michaud, Eric, *The Cult of Art in Nazi Germany: Cultural Memory in the Present* (Stanford: Stanford University Press, 2004)

Miegel, Agnes, *Ostland: Gedichte* (Jena: Eugen Diederichs, 1941)

Miller Lane, Barbara, *Architecture and Politics in Germany, 1918–1945* (Cambridge, MA: Harvard University Press, 1968)

Milton, Sybil H., "Culture Under Duress: Art and the Holocaust," in Frederick C. DeCoste and Bernard Schwartz, eds, *The Holocaust's Ghost: Writings on Art, Politics, Law and Education* (Edmonton: University of Alberta Press, 2000), 84–96

Minetti, Bernhard, *Erinnerungen eines Schauspielers*, ed. Günther Rühle (Stuttgart: Deutsche Verlags-Anstalt, 1987)

Mitscherlich, Alexander, and Margarete Mitscherlich, *Die Unfähigkeit zu trauern: Grundlagen kollektiven Verhaltens* (Munich: Piper, 1967)

Moeller, Felix, *Der Filmminister: Goebbels und der Film im Dritten Reich* (Berlin: Henschel, 1998)

Moeller, Felix, "'Ich bin Künstler und sonst nichts': Filmstars im Propagandaeinsatz," in Hans Sarkowicz, ed., *Hitlers Künstler: Die Kultur im Dienst des Nationalsozialismus* (Frankfurt am Main: Insel, 2004), 135–75

Moldenhauer, Hans, and Rosaleen Moldenhauer, *Anton von Webern: A Chronicle of His Life and Work* (New York: Knopf, 1979)

Möller, Eberhard Wolfgang, *Das Frankenburger Würfelspiel* (Berlin: Theaterverlag Langen Müller, 1936)

Möller, Eberhard Wolfgang, *Der Untergang Karthagos: Ein Drama in drei Akten* (Berlin: Theaterverlag Langen Müller, 1938)

Möller, Eberhard Wolfgang, "Dichtung und Dichter im nationalsozialistischen Staat," *Das Programm: Blätter des Bayerischen Staatstheaters in München* 3, no. 12 (1936): 178–85

Möller, Eberhard Wolfgang, *Rothschild siegt bei Waterloo: Ein Schauspiel*, 3rd/4th edn (Berlin: Langen-Müller, 1937)

Möller, Horst, *Exodus der Kultur: Schriftsteller, Wissenschaftler und Künstler in der Emigration nach 1933* (Munich: C. H. Beck, 1984)

Molzahn, Ilse, *Nymphen und Hirten tanzen nicht mehr: Roman* (Berlin: Rowohlt, 1938)

Mommsen, Hans, *Beamtentum im Dritten Reich: Mit ausgewählten Quellen zur national-sozialistischen Beamtenpolitik* (Stuttgart: Deutsche Verlags-Anstalt, 1966)

Mommsen, Hans, "Hitlers Stellung im nationalsozialistischen Herrschaftssystem," in Gerhard Hirschfeld and Lothar Kettenacker, eds, *Der "Führerstaat": Studien zur Struktur und Politik des Dritten Reiches* (Stuttgart: Klett-Cotta, 1981), 43–70

Monod, David, *Settling Scores: German Music, Denazification and the Americans, 1945–1953* (Chapel Hill: University of North Carolina Press, 2005)

Moser, Otto Heinrich, "Am Rande," *SS-Leitheft* 9 (June 1943): 28–32

Mosse, George L., *Nazi Culture: Intellectual, Cultural and Social Life in the Third Reich* (New York: The Universal Library, 1968)

Mühlberger, Detlef, ed., *Hitler's Voice: The Völkischer Beobachter, 1920–1933*, 2 vols (Bern: Peter Lang, 2004)

Mühr, Alfred, *Mephisto ohne Maske: Gustaf Gründgens: Legende und Wahrheit*, 2nd edn (Munich: Langen Müller, 1981)

Müller, Martin, and Wolfgang Mertz, eds, *Diener der Musik: Unvergessene Solisten und Dirigenten unserer Zeit im Spiegel der Freunde* (Tübingen: Wunderlich, 1965)

Müller-Blattau, Joseph, *Geschichte der deutschen Musik*, 5th edn (Berlin: Vieweg, 1944)

Müller-Wesemann, Barbara, *Theater als geistiger Widerstand: Der Jüdische Kulturbund in Hamburg, 1934–1941* (Stuttgart: M&P, 1997)

Münster, Hans A., "Der Wille zu überzeugen – ein germanischer Wesenzug in der Volksführung des neuen Staates," in Hans A. Münster, *Die drei Aufgaben der deutschen Zeitungswissenschaft* (Leipzig: Robert Noske, [1934]), 3–22

Münster, Hans A., *Publizistik: Menschen – Mittel – Methoden* (Leipzig: Bibliographisches Institut, 1939)

Münster, Hans A., *Zeitung und Politik: Eine Einführung in die Zeitungswissenschaft* (Leipzig: Robert Noske, 1935)

Muschler, Reinhold Conrad, "Georg Vollerthun," *Zeitschrift für Musik* 100, no. 10 (October 1933): 989–92

Muschler, Reinhold Conrad, "Nationalsozialistischer Film?" *Deutsche Kultur-Wacht* 2/21 (August 26, 1933): 7–8

Müssener, Helmut, *Exil in Schweden: Politische und kulturelle Emigration nach 1933* (Munich: Carl Hanser, 1974)

Nachenius, J. C., "Die germanische Solidarität Europas: Eine Stimme aus den Niederlanden," *SS-Leitheft* 9 (September–October 1943): 9–10

Nadar, Thomas R., "The Director and the Diva: The Film Musicals of Detlef Sierck and Zarah Leander: *Zu neuen Ufern* and *La Habanera*," in Robert C. Reimer, ed., *Cultural History through a National Socialist Lens: Essays on the Cinema of the Third Reich* (Rochester, NY: Camden House, 2000), 65–83

Nagler, Jörg, "Internment of German Enemy Aliens in the United States during the First and Second World Wars," in Kay Saunders and Roger Daniels, eds, *Alien Justice: Wartime Internment in Australia and North America* (St. Lucia, Queensland: Queensland University Press, 2000), 66–79

Naso, Eckart von, *Ich liebe das Leben: Erinnerungen aus fünf Jahrzehnten* (Hamburg: Wolfgang Krüger Verlag, 1953)

Naumann, Hans, and Eugen Lüthgen, *Kampf wider den undeutschen Geist: Reden, gehalten bei der von der Bonner Studentenschaft veranstalteten Kundgebung wider den undeutschen Geist auf dem Marktplatz zu Bonn am 10. Mai 1933* (Bonn: Gebr. Scheur, 1933)

Nerdinger, Winfried, "Bauhaus-Architekten im 'Dritten Reich'," in Winfried Nerdinger, ed., *Bauhaus-Moderne im Nationalsozialismus: Zwischen Anbiederung und Verfolgung* (Munich: Prestel, 1993), 153–78

Nerdinger, Winfried, "Modernisierung – Bauhaus – Nationalsozialismus," in Winfried Nerdinger, ed., *Bauhaus-Moderne im Nationalsozialismus: Zwischen Anbiederung und Verfolgung* (Munich: Prestel, 1993), 9–23

Ney, Elly, "Bekenntnis zu Ludwig van Beethoven," in Alfred Morgenroth, ed., *Von deutscher Tonkunst: Festschrift zu Peter Raabes 70. Geburtstag* (Leipzig: C. F. Peters, 1942), 59–68

Niessen, Carl, "Der Schauplatz der Oper," in Niessen, ed., *Die deutsche Oper der Gegenwart* (Regensburg: Gustav Bosse, 1944), 24–334

Niewyk, Donald L., "The Economic and Cultural Role of the Jews in the Weimar Republic," *Leo Baeck Institute Yearbook* 16 (1971): 163–73

Niven, Bill, "Ernst Wiechert and his Role between 1933 and 1945," *New German Studies* 16 (1990/91): 1–20

Niven, Bill, *Hitler and Film: The Führer's Hidden Passion* (New Haven: Yale University Press, 2018)

Niven, William, "The Birth of Nazi Drama? *Thing* Plays," in John London, ed., *Theatre under the Nazis* (Manchester: Manchester University Press, 2000), 54–95

Nolde, Emil, *Jahre der Kämpfe* (Berlin: Rembrandt, 1934)

Nolde, Emil, *Jahre der Kämpfe, 1902–1914*, 2nd edn (Flensburg: Christian Wolff, [1957])

Nolde, Emil, *Mein Leben* (Cologne: DuMont, 1976)

Novak, Andreas, *"Salzburg hört Hitler atmen": Die Salzburger Festspiele, 1933–1944* (Munich: Deutsche Verlags-Anstalt, 2005)

Nowak, Bruno, *Der Bauer: Ein Spiel der Mahnung* (Berlin: Theaterverlag Albert Langen/ Georg Müller, 1935)

Nufer, Wolfgang, "Erneuerung des Spielplans," *Deutsche Bühne* 1, no. 3 (October 1933): 75–6

Nufer, Wolfgang, "Zur Lage des deutschen Thaters," *Die Bühne* 2, no. 13/14 (July 1936): 419–22

O'Brien, Mary-Elizabeth, "The Celluloid War: Packaging War for Sale in Nazi Home-Front Films," in Richard A. Etlin, ed., *Art, Culture and Media under the Third Reich* (Chicago: University of Chicago Press, 2002), 158–80

O'Brien, Mary-Elizabeth, "The Spectacle of War in *Die grosse Liebe*," in Robert C. Reimer, ed., *Cultural History through a National Socialist Lens: Essays on the Cinema of the Third Reich* (Rochester, NY: Camden House, 2000), 197–213

Olden, Rudolf, *Hitler* (New York: Friede Covici, 1936)

Ollendorf-Reich, Ilse, *Wilhelm Reich: A Personal Biography* (New York: St. Martin's Press, 1969)

Painter, Karen, *Symphonic Aspirations: German Music and Politics, 1900–1945* (Cambridge, MA: Harvard University Press, 2007)

Palmer, Lilli, *Dicke Lilli – gutes Kind* (Munich: Droemer Knaur, 1974)

Palmier, Jean-Michel, *Weimar in Exile: The Anti-Facist Emigration in Europe and America* (London: Verso, 2006)

Pantel, Gerhard, *Befehl Deutschland: Ein Tagebuch vom Kampf um Berlin* (Munich: Eher, 1936)

Paret, Peter, *An Artist against the Third Reich: Ernst Barlach, 1933–1938* (Cambridge: Cambridge University Press, 2003)

Pargner, Birgit, *Marianne Hoppe: "Erst Schönheit, dann Klugheit und dann das helle saubere Herz"* (Munich: Henschel, 2009)

Pâris, Alain, ed., *Lexikon der Interpreten klassischer Musik im 20. Jahrhundert* (Munich: DTV/ Bärenreiter, 1992)

Paust, Otto, *Menschen unterm Hammer: Roman* (Berlin: Wilhelm Limpert-Verlag, 1939)

Paust, Otto, *Nation in Not: Roman* (Berlin: Wilhelm Limpert-Verlag, 1936)

Payk, Marcus M., "Der 'Amerikakomplex': 'Massendemokratie' und Kulturkritik am Beispiel von Karl Korn und dem Feuilleton der 'Frankfurter Allgemeinen Zeitung' in den fünfziger Jahren," in Arnd Bauernkämpfer, Konrad H. Jarausch, and Marcus Payk, eds, *Demokratiewunder: Transatlantische Mittler und die kulturelle Öffnung Westdeutschlands, 1945–1970* (Göttingen: Vandenhoeck & Ruprecht, 2005), 190–217

Payr, Bernhard, *Das Amt für Schrifttumspflege: Seine Entwicklungsgeschichte und seine Organisation* (Berlin: Junker und Dünnhaupt, 1941)

PEM [Paul Erich Marcus], *Heimweh nach dem Kurfürstendamm: Aus Berlins glanzvollsten Tagen und Nächten* (Berlin: Lothar Blanvalet, 1962)

Pepping, Ernst, *Stilwende der Musik* (Mainz: B. Schott's Söhne, 1934)

Peters, J., "Das Werk Ernst Wiecherts," *Die Bücherei* 7, no. 1/2 (1940): 1–28

Peters, Olaf, "Genesis, Conception, and Consequences: The 'Entartete Kunst' Exhibition in Munich in 1937," in Olaf Peters, ed., *Degenerate Art: The Attack on Modern Art in Nazi Germany, 1937* (Munich: Prestel, 2014), 106–25

Peters, Olaf, *Neue Sachlichkeit und Nationalsozialismus: Affirmation und Kritik, 1931–1947* (Frankfurt am Main: Dietrich Reimer, 1998)

Petersen, Jan, *Unsere Strasse: Eine Chronik: Geschrieben im Herzen des faschistischen Deutschlands, 1933/34* (Berlin: Aufbau, 1967)

Petersen, Julius, *Geschichtsdrama und nationaler Mythos: Grenzfragen zur Gegenwartsform des Dramas* (Stuttgart: J. B. Metzler, 1940)

Petropoulos, Jonathan, *Art as Politics in the Third Reich* (Chapel Hill: University of North Carolina Press, 1996)

Petropoulos, Jonathan, *Artists under Hitler: Collaboration and Survival in Nazi Germany* (New Haven: Yale University Press, 2014)

Petropoulos, Jonathan, "From Seduction to Denial: Arno Breker's Engagement with National Socialism," in Richard A. Etlin, ed., *Art, Culture and Media under the Third Reich* (Chicago: University of Chicago Press, 2002), 205–29

Petropoulos, Jonathan, *The Faustian Bargain: The Art World in Nazi Germany* (New York: Oxford University Press, 2000)

Petry, Christian, *Studenten aufs Schafott: Die Weisse Rose und ihr Scheitern* (Munich: Piper, 1968)

Petsch, Joachim, "'Unersetzliche Künstler': Malerei und Plastik im 'Dritten Reich'," in Hans Sarkowicz, ed., *Hitlers Künstler: Die Kultur im Dienst des Nationalsozialismus* (Frankfurt am Main: Insel, 2004), 245–77

Petzet, Wolfgang, *Theater: Die Münchner Kammerspiele, 1911–1972* (Munich: Kurt Desch, 1973)

Pfanner, Helmut F., *Exile in New York: German and Austrian Writers after 1933* (Detroit: Wayne State University Press, 1983)

Pfanner, Helmut F., *Hanns Johst: Vom Expressionismus zum Nationalsozialismus* (The Hague: Mouton, 1970)

Pfeiffer, Richard, "Jagdhaus 'Karinhall'," *Die Völkische Kunst* 1, no. 1 (January 1935): 19–24

Pfeiffer-Belli, Wolfgang, ed., *Harry Graf Kessler: Aus den Tagebüchern, 1918–1937* (Munich: DTV, 1965)

Phelps, Reginald H., "Die Hitler-Bibliothek," *Deutsche Rundschau* 9 (1954): 923–31

Picker, Henry, *Tischgespräche im Führerhauptquartier, 1941–42*, ed. Gerhard Ritter (Bonn: Athenäum, 1951)

Pinder, Wilhelm, "'Was ist deutsch an der deutschen Kunst?' Zu der Schrift von K. K. Eberlein," *Zeitschrift für Kunstgeschichte* 2, no. 6 (1933): 405–7

Pine, Lisa, *Hitler's "National Community": Society and Culture in Nazi Germany*, 2nd edn (London: Bloomsbury Academic, 2017; 1st edn 2007)

Piper, Ernst, ed., *Ernst Barlach und die nationalsozialistische Kunstpolitik: Eine dokumentarische Darstellung zur "entarteten Kunst"* (Munich: R. Piper, 1983)

Pohle, Heinz, *Der Rundfunk als Instrument der Politik: Zur Geschichte des deutschen Rundfunks von 1923/38* (Hamburg: Verlag Hans Bredow-Institut, 1955)

Pongs, Hermann, *Krieg als Volksschicksal im deutschen Schrifttum: Ein Beitrag zur Literaturgeschichte der Gegenwart* (Stuttgart: J. B. Metzlersche Verlagsbuchhandlung, 1934)

Posch, Franz, "Salzburger Festspiele," *Zeitschrift für Musik* 109, no. 10 (October 1942): 451–3

Potter, Pamela M., *Art of Suppression: Confronting the Nazi Past in Histories of the Visual and Performing Arts* (Oakland: University of California Press, 2016)

Potter, Pamela M., *Most German of the Arts: Musicology and Society from the Weimar Republic to the End of Hitler's Reich* (New Haven: Yale University Press, 1998)

Potter, Pamela M., "Music in the Third Reich: The Complex Task of 'Germanization'," in Jonathan Huener and Francis R. Nicosia, eds, *The Arts in Nazi Germany: Continuity, Conformity, Change* (New York: Berghahn, 2007), 85–110

Potter, Pamela M., "Musical Life in Berlin from Weimar to Hitler," in Michael H. Kater and Albrecht Riethmüller, eds, *Music and Nazism: Art under Tyranny, 1933–1945* (Laaber: Laaber, 2003), 90–101

Potter, Pamela M., "The Nazi 'Seizure' of the Berlin Philharmonic, or the Decline of a Bourgeois Musical Institution," in Glenn R. Cuomo, *National Socialist Cultural Policy* (New York: St. Martin's Press, 1995), 39–65

Prieberg, Fred K., *Kraftprobe: Wilhelm Furtwängler im Dritten Reich* (Wiesbaden: Brockhaus, 1986)

Prieberg, Fred K., *Musik im NS-Staat* (Frankfurt am Main: Fischer Taschenbuch, 1982)

Prieberg, Fred K., *Musik und Macht* (Frankfurt am Main: Fischer Taschenbuch, 1991)

Prieberg, Fred K., "Musik unterm Davidsstern," in *Geschlossene Vorstellung: Der Jüdische Kulturbund in Deutschland, 1933–1941* (Berlin: Hentrich, 1992), 113–26

Pritzker-Ehrlich, Marthi, ed., *Jüdisches Emigrantenlos 1938/39 und die Schweiz: Eine Fallstudie* (Bern: Peter Lang, 1998)

Prochnik, George, *The Impossible Exile: Stefan Zweig at the End of the World* (New York: Other Press, 2014)

Pross, Harry, "Einleitung," in Hans Dieter Müller, ed., *Facsimile Querschnitt durch Das Reich* (Munich: Scherz, 1964), 4–6

Pross, Helge, *Die deutsche akademische Emigration nach den Vereinigten Staaten, 1933–1941* (Berlin: Duncker u. Humblot, 1955)

Prümm, Karl, "Das Erbe der Front: Der antidemokratische Kriegsroman der Weimarer Republik und seine nationalsozialistische Fortsetzung," in Horst Denkler and Karl Prümm, eds, *Die deutsche Literatur im Dritten Reich: Themen – Traditionen – Wirkungen* (Stuttgart: Philipp Reclam jun., 1976), 138–64

Putlitz, Wolfgang zu, *Laaske, London und Haiti: Zeitgeschichtliche Miniaturen* (Berlin: Verlag der Nation, 1966)

Pyta, Wolfram, *Hitler: Der Künstler als Politiker und Feldherr: Eine Herrschaftsanalyse* (Munich: Siedler, 2015)

Quadflieg, Will, *Wir spielen immer: Erinnerungen* (Frankfurt am Main: S. Fischer, 1976)

Raab, Jutta, "Internierung – Bombardierung – Rekrutierung: Musiker-Exil in Grossbritannien," in Hans-Werner Heister, Claudia Maurer Zenck, and Peter Petersen, eds, *Musik im Exil: Folgen des Nazismus für die internationale Musikkultur* (Frankfurt am Main: S. Fischer, 1993), 171–86

Raab Hansen, Jutta, *NS-verfolgte Musiker in England: Spuren deutscher und österreichischer Flüchtlinge in der britischen Musikkultur* (Hamburg: Von Bockel Verlag, 1996)

Rabenalt, Arthur Maria, *Joseph Goebbels und der "Grossdeutsche" Film: Ausgewählt, durch historische Fakten ergänzt*, ed. Herbert Holba (Munich: F. A. Herbig, 1985)

Raschke, Martin, "Aus letzten Briefen," *Das Innere Reich*, no. 4 (1943/4): 337–41

Raschke, Martin, *Das Erbe: Eine Erzählung* (Frankfurt am Main: Rütten & Loening, 1935)

Raschke, Martin, *Der Pomeranzenzweig: Erzählung* (Leipzig: Paul List, 1940)

Raschke, Martin, "Junges Europa," *Das Innere Reich* (April–September 1942): 152–4

Rasp, Hans-Peter, *Eine Stadt für tausend Jahre: München – Bauten und Projekte für die Hauptstadt der Bewegung* (Munich: Süddeutscher Verlag, 1981)

Rasponi, Lanfranco, *The Last Prima Donnas* (New York: Knopf, 1982)

Rathkolb, Oliver, *Führertreu und Gottbegnadet: Künstlereliten im Dritten Reich* (Vienna: Österreichischer Bundesverlag, 1991)

Rave, Paul Ortwin, *Kunstdiktatur im Dritten Reich*, ed. Uwe M. Schneede (Berlin: Argon, [1949])

Reich, Willi, *Schoenberg: A Critical Biography* (London: Longmans, 1971)

Reich-Ranicki, Marcel, "Lion Feuchtwanger oder der Weltruhm des Emigranten," in Manfred Durzak, ed., *Die deutsche Exilliteratur 1933–1945* (Stuttgart: Philipp Reclam jun., 1973), 443–56

Reichel, Peter, "Der Nationalsozialismus vor Gericht und die Rückkehr zum Rechtsstaat," in Peter Reichel, Harald Schmid, and Peter Steinbach, eds, *Der Nationalsozialismus – Die Zweite Geschichte: Überwindung – Deutung – Erinnerung* (Munich: C. H. Beck, 2009), 22–61

Reifenberg, Benno, "Die zehn Jahre/1933–1943," in Max von Brück et al., *Ein Jahrhundert Frankfurter Zeitung, 1856–1956, begründet von Leopold Sonnemann* (Frankfurt am Main: Frankfurter Societäts-Druckerei, [1956]), 40–54

Reimer, Robert C., "Turning Inward: An Analysis of Helmut Käutner's *Auf Wiedersehen, Franziska; Romanze in Moll;* and *Unter den Brücken*," in Reimer, ed., *Cultural History through a National Socialist Lens: Essays on the Cinema of the Third Reich* (Rochester, NY: Camden House, 2000), 214–39

Reinecker, Herbert, *Das Dorf bei Odessa: Schauspiel in einem Aufzug* (Berlin: Deutscher Bühnenvertrieb im Zentralverlag der NSDAP, 1942)

Reinhardt, Gottfried, *The Genius: A Memoir of Max Reinhardt* (New York: Knopf, 1979)

Reinhold, Daniela, "Repräsentation und Zerstreuung: Aspekte faschistischer Spielplanpolitik im Musiktheater am Beispiel der Sächsischen Staatsoper Dresden," *Beiträge zur Musikwissenschaft* 28, no. 1 (1986): 39–52

Remarque, Erich Maria, *Der Funke Leben: Roman* (Cologne: Kiepenheuer & Witsch, 1952)

Remarque, Erich Maria, *Im Westen nichts Neues* (Berlin: Propyläen, 1929)

Rentschler, Eric, *The Ministry of Illusion: Nazi Cinema and its Afterlife* (Cambridge, MA: Harvard University Press, 1996)

Rentschler, Eric, *The Use and Abuse of Cinema: German Legacies from the Weimar Era to the Present* (New York: Columbia University Press, 2015)

Rexroth, Dieter, ed., *Paul Hindemith: Briefe* (Frankfurt am Main: Fischer Taschenbuch, 1982)

Rexroth, H. G., *Der Wehrmutstrauch: Aufzeichnungen aus dem Kriege* (Hamburg: H. Goverts, 1944)

Riethmüller, Albrecht, "Die Bestimmung der Orgel im Dritten Reich," in Hans Heinrich Eggebrecht, ed., *Orgel und Ideologie: Bericht über das fünfte Colloquium der Walcker-Stiftung für orgelwissenschaftliche Forschung, 5.–7. Mai 1983 in Göttweig* (Murrhardt: Musikwissenschaftliche VG, 1984), 28–69

Riethmüller, Albrecht, "Die 'Stunde Null' als musikgeschichtliche Grösse," in Matthias Herrmann and Hanns-Werner Heister, eds, *Dresden und die avancierte Musik im 20. Jahrhundert. Teil II: 1933–1966* (Laaber: Laaber, 2002), 75–86

Riethmüller, Albrecht, "Komposition im Dritten Reich um 1936," *Archiv für Musikwissenschaft* 38 (1981): 241–78

Riethmüller, Albrecht, "Stefan Zweig and the Fall of the Reich Music Chamber President, Richard Strauss," in Michael H. Kater and Albrecht Riethmüller, eds, *Music and Nazism: Art under Tyranny, 1933–1945* (Laaber: Laaber, 2003), 269–91

Riethmüller, Albrecht, "Zarah Leander singt Bach: Antiamerikanisches in Carl Froelichs Film 'Heimat' (1938)," in Angelika Linke and Jakob Tanner, eds, *Attraktion und Abwehr: Die Amerikanisierung der Alltagskultur in Europa* (Cologne: Böhlau, 2006), 161–76

Rischbieter, Henning, "'Schlageter – Der 'Erste Soldat des Dritten Reichs': Theater in der Nazizeit," in Hans Sarkowicz, ed., *Hitlers Künstler: Die Kultur im Dienst des Nationalsozialismus* (Frankfurt am Main: Insel, 2004), 210–44

Rischbieter, Henning, ed., *Theater im "Dritten Reich": Theaterpolitik, Spielplanstruktur, NS-Dramatik* (Seelze-Velber: Kallmeyer, 2000)

Röder, Werner, and Herbert A. Strauss, eds, *Biographisches Handbuch der deutschsprachigen Emigration nach 1933* (Munich: K. G. Saur, 1980)

Rosenberg, Alfred, *Blut und Ehre: Ein Kampf für die deutsche Wiedergeburt: Reden und Aufsätze von 1919–1933*, ed. Thilo von Trotha, 26th edn (Munich: Eher, 1942)

Rosenberg, Alfred, *Die Tagebücher von 1934 bis 1944*, ed. Jürgen Matthäus and Frank Bajohr (Frankfurt am Main: S. Fischer, 2015)

Rosenberg, Alfred, *Gestaltung der Idee: Blut und Ehre II. Band: Reden und Aufsätze von 1933–1935*, ed. Thilo von Trotha, 2nd edn (Munich: Eher, 1936)

Rosenberg, Alfred, *Revolution in der bildenden Kunst?* (Munich: Eher, 1934)

Rosenberg, Alfred, and Wilhelm Weiss, eds, *Der Reichsparteitag der Nationalsozialistischen Deutschen Arbeiterpartei, 19./21. August 1927: Der Verlauf und die Ergebnisse* (Munich: Franz Eher Nachf., 1927)

Ross, Alex, "The Hitler Vortex: How American Racism Influenced Nazi Thought," *The New Yorker* (April 30, 2018): 66–73

Ross, Alex, *The Rest is Noise: Listening to the Twentieth Century* (New York: Farrar, Straus and Giroux, 2007)

Roth, Bert, ed., *Kampf: Lebensdokumente deutscher Jugend von 1914–1934* (Leipzig: Philipp Reclam jun., 1934)

Rothacker, Gottfried, *Das Dorf an der Grenze: Roman* (Munich: Langen Müller, 1936)

Rovit, Rebecca, "Collaboration or Survival, 1933–1938: Reassessing the Role of the *Jüdischer Kulturbund*," in Glen W. Gadberry, ed., *Theatre in the Third Reich, the Prewar Years: Essays on Theatre in Nazi Germany* (Westport: Greenwood, 1995), 141–56

Rovit, Rebecca, "Jewish Theatre: Repertory and Censorship in the Jüdischer Kulturbund, Berlin," in John London, ed., *Theatre under the Nazis* (Manchester: Manchester University Press, 2000), 187–221

Rühmann, Heinz, *Das war's: Erinnerungen* (Frankfurt am Main: ExLibris, 1985)

Ruppelt, Georg, *Schiller im nationalsozialistischen Deutschland: Der Versuch einer Gleichschaltung* (Stuttgart: Metzler, 1979)

Ryding, Erik, and Rebecca Pechefsky, *Bruno Walter: A World Elsewhere* (New Haven: Yale University Press, 2001)

Sachs, Harvey, *Music in Fascist Italy* (London: Weidenfeld & Nicolson, 1987)

Said, Edward W., *Reflections on Exile and Other Essays* (Cambridge, MA: Harvard University Press, 2001)

Salburg, Edith Gräfin, *Der Tag des Ariers: Ein Buch der Zeit* (Berlin: Schlieffen, 1935)

Salburg, Edith Gräfin, *Eine Landflucht: Buch aus der Zeit* (Leipzig: Hase & Koehler, 1939)

Salburg, Edith Gräfin, *Kamerad Susanne: Ein Erleben* (Dresden: Wilhelm Heyne, 1936)

Salomon, Ernst von, *Der Fragebogen* (Hamburg: Rowohlt, 1951)

Salomon, Ernst von, *Die Geächteten: Roman* (Reinbek: Rowohlt, 1968, 1st edn 1929)

Sänger, Fritz, *Politik der Täuschungen: Missbrauch der Presse im Dritten Reich: Weisungen, Informationen, Notizen, 1933–1939* (Vienna: Europaverlag, 1975)

Sänger, Fritz, *Verborgene Fäden: Erinnerungen und Bemerkungen eines Journalisten* (Bonn: Verlag Neue Gesellschaft, 1978)

Sarkowicz, Hans, "'Bis alles in Scherben fällt...': Schriftsteller im Dienst der NS-Diktatur," in Hans Sarkowicz, ed., *Hitlers Künstler: Die Kultur im Dienst des Nationalsozialismus* (Frankfurt am Main: Insel, 2004), 176–209

Sarkowicz, Hans, "Die literarischen Apologeten des Dritten Reiches: Zur Rezeption der vom Nationalsozialismus geförderten Autoren nach 1945," in Jörg Thunecke, ed., *Leid der Worte: Panorama des literarischen Nationalsozialismus* (Bonn: Bouvier Verlag Herbert Grundmann, 1987), 435–59

Sarkowicz, Hans, and Alf Mentzer, *Literatur in Nazi-Deutschland: Ein biografisches Lexikon: Erweiterte Neuausgabe* (Hamburg: Europa, 2002)

Sauder, Gerhard, ed., *Die Bücherverbrennung: Zum 10. Mai 1933*, 2nd edn (Munich: Carl Hanser, 1983)

Saunders, Thomas J., *Hollywood in Berlin: American Cinema and Weimar Germany* (Berkeley: University of California Press, 1994)

Scanzoni, Signe, and Götz Klaus Kende, *Der Prinzipal: Clemens Krauss: Fakten, Vergleiche, Rückschlüsse* (Tutzing: Hans Schneider, 1988)

Schäche, Wolfgang, *Architektur und Städtebau in Berlin zwischen 1933 und 1945: Planen und Bauen unter der Ägide der Stadtverwaltung* (Berlin: Gebr. Mann Verlag, 1991)

Schaenzler, Nicole, *Klaus Mann: Eine Biographie* (Berlin: Aufbau-Taschenbuch, 2001)

Schäfer, Hans Dieter, *Berlin im Zweiten Weltkrieg: Der Untergang der Reichshauptstadt in Augenzeugenberichten* (Munich: Piper, 1985)

Schäferdiek, Willi, *Lebens-Echo: Erinnerungen eines Schriftstellers* (Düsseldorf: Droste, 1985)

Scheding, Florian, "'Problematic Tendencies': Émigré Composers in London, 1933–1945," in Erik Levi, ed., *The Impact of Nazism on Twentieth-Century Music* (Vienna: Böhlau, 2014), 247–71

Schenzinger, Karl Aloys, *Anilin: Roman* (Berlin: Zeitgeschichte-Verlag, 1937)

Schenzinger, Karl Aloys, *Der Hitlerjunge Quex: Roman* (Berlin: Zeitgeschichte-Verlag, 1932)

Schindler, Edgar, "'Blut und Boden': Die Herbstkunstausstellung der Gaudienststelle München-Oberbayern der NS-Kulturgemeinde," *Das Bild* (1935): 369–72

Schindler, Edgar, "Gedanken zur deutschen bildenden Kunst der Zukunft," *Das Bild* (1936): 159–60, 288–92, 317–18, 355–6

Schinköth, Thomas, "Mit Leistung gegen 'undeutsche' Einflüsse – Die 'NS-Kulturgemeinde'," in Matthias Herrmann and Hanns-Werner Heister, eds, *Dresden und die avancierte Musik im 20. Jahrhundert. Teil II: 1933–1966* (Laaber: Laaber, 2002), 63–74

Schinköth, Thomas, "Zwischen Psalm 90 und *Führerworten*: Der Komponist Gottfried Müller," in Matthias Herrmann and Hanns-Werner Heister, eds, *Dresden und die avancierte Musik im 20. Jahrhundert. Teil II: 1933–1966* (Laaber: Laaber, 2002), 305–9

Schirach, Baldur von, *Kantaterede* (Weimar: Gesellschaft der Bibliophilen, 1941)

Schirmbeck, Peter, "Zur Industrie- und Arbeiterdarstellung in der NS-Kunst: Typische Merkmale, Unterdrückung und Weiterführung von Traditionen," in Berthold Hinz et al., eds, *Die Dekoration der Gewalt: Kunst und Medien im Faschismus* (Giessen: Anabas, 1979), 61–74

Schlegel, Werner, *Dichter auf dem Scheiterhaufen: Kampfschrift für deutsche Weltanschauung* (Berlin: Verlag für Kulturpolitik, 1934)

Schlenker, Ines, "Defining National Socialist Art: The First 'Grosse Deutsche Kunstausstellung' in 1937," in Olaf Peters, ed., *Degenerate Art: The Attack on Modern Art in Nazi Germany, 1937* (Munich: Prestel, 2014), 90–105

Schlenker, Ines, *Hitler's Salon: The Grosse Deutsche Kunstausstellung at the Haus der Deutschen Kunst in Munich, 1937–1944* (Bern: Peter Lang, 2007)

Schlösser, Rainer, *Das Volk und seine Bühne: Bemerkungen zum Aufbau des deutschen Theaters* (Berlin: Langen Müller, 1935)

Schlösser, Rainer, "Lebendiges Theater!" *Der Autor* 15, no. 1 (January 1940): 3–4

Schlösser, Rainer, *Politik und Drama* (Berlin: Zeitgeschichte, 1935)

Schlösser, Rainer, *Uns bleibt die heilige deutsche Kunst: Rede des Reichsdramaturgen Obergebietsführer Dr. Rainer Schlösser anlässlich der Kulturtage der Hitler-Jugend des Gebietes Sachsen am 7. November 1943 in der Staatsoper zu Dresden* (n.pl., n.d.)

Schmitz, Eugen, "Oper im Aufbau," *Zeitschrift für Musik* 106, no. 4 (April 1939): 380–2

Schmitz, Eugen, "Zum 70. Geburtstag Paul Graeners," *Zeitschrift für Musik* 109 (January 1942): 1–4

Schnell, Ralf, *Dichtung in finsteren Zeiten: Deutsche Literatur und Faschismus* (Reinbek: rororo, 1998)

Schnell, Ralf, *Geschichte der deutschsprachigen Literatur seit 1945* (Stuttgart: J. B. Metzler, 1993)

Schnell, Ralf, *Literarische Innere Emigration, 1933–1945* (Stuttgart: Metzlerische Verlagsbuchhandlung, 1976)

Schoeps, Karl-Heinz Joachim, *Literatur im Dritten Reich (1933–1945)*, 2nd edn (Berlin: Weidler, 2000)

Scholz, Robert, "'Kunstgötzen stürzen'," *Deutsche Kultur-Wacht* 10 (1933): 5–6

Scholz, Robert, "Kunstpflege und Weltanschauung," *Die Völkische Kunst* 1, no. 6 (1935): 148–9, 176

Scholz, Robert, *Lebensfragen der bildenden Kunst* (Munich: Eher, 1937)

Scholz, Wilhelm von, *Die Gedichte: Gesamtausgabe 1944* (Leipzig: Paul List, 1944)

Schonauer, Franz, *Deutsche Literatur im Dritten Reich: Versuch einer Darstellung in polemisch-didaktischer Absicht* (Olten: Walter, 1961)

Schönberg, Arnold, *Harmonielehre*, 3rd edn (Vienna: Universal Edition, 1922)

Schorer, Georg, *Deutsche Kunstbetrachtung* (Munich: Verlagsgemeinschaft Deutscher Volksverlag, [1939])

Schowalter, August, ed., *Ohm Krüger: Die Lebenserinnerungen des Buren-Präsidenten* (Berlin: Deutscher Verlag, [1941], 1st pr. 1902)

Schramm, Wilhelm von, *Neubau des deutschen Theaters: Ergebnisse und Forderungen* (Berlin: Schlieffen, 1934)

Schubert, Dietrich, *Otto Dix in Selbstzeugnissen und Bilddokumenten* (Reinbek: Rowohlt, 1980)

Schulte-Sasse, Linda, *Entertaining the Third Reich: Illusions of Wholeness in Nazi Cinema* (Durham, NC: Duke University Press, 1996)

Schultze-Naumburg, Paul, *Kampf um die Kunst* (Munich: Eher, 1932)

Schultze-Naumburg, Paul, *Kunst aus Blut und Boden* (Leipzig: A. E. Seemann, 1934)

Schumann, Coco, *The Ghetto Swinger: A Berlin Jazz Legend Remembers* (Los Angeles: DoppelHouse Press, 2016)

Schumann, Gerhard, "Krieg – Bericht und Dichtung," in Rudolf Erckmann, ed., *Dichter und Krieger: Weimarer Reden 1942* (Hamburg: Hanseatische Verlagsanstalt, 1943), 59–71

Schwarz, Birgit, *Geniewahn: Hitler und die Kunst* (Vienna: Böhlau, 2009)

Schwarz, Roswita, *Vom expressionistischen Aufbruch zur Inneren Emigration: Günther Weisenborns weltanschauliche und künstlerische Entwicklung in der Weimarer Republik und im Dritten Reich* (Frankfurt am Main: Peter Lang, 1995)

Schwerter, Werner, "Heerschau und Selektion," in Albrecht Dümling and Peter Girth, eds, *Entartete Musik: Dokumentation und Kommentar zur Düsseldorfer Ausstellung von 1938*, 3rd edn (Düsseldorf: Der Kleine Verlag, 1993), 111–26

Sebald, W. G., *Luftkrieg und Literatur: Mit einem Essay zu Alfred Andersch* (Munich: Carl Hanser, 1999)

Sechs Bekenntnisse zum neuen Deutschland: Rudolf G. Binding, E. G. Kolbenheyer, Die "Kölnische Zeitung," Wilhelm von Scholz, Otto Wirz, Robert Fabre-Luce antworten Romain Rolland (Hamburg: Hanseatische Verlagsanstalt, 1933)

Seghers, Anna, *The Seventh Cross* (Boston: Little, Brown and Company, 1942)

Seghers, Anna, *Transit: Roman* (Reinbek: rororo, 1970; 1st edn 1943)

Sheean, Vincent, *First and Last Love* (Westport: Greenwood, 1979)

Shirakawa, Sam H., *The Devil's Music Master: The Controversial Life and Career of Wilhelm Furtwängler* (New York: Oxford University Press, 1992)

Shirer, William L., *The Rise and Fall of the Third Reich: A History of Nazi Germany* (New York: Simon and Schuster, 1960)

Shorter, Edward, *A Historical Dictionary of Psychiatry* (New York: Oxford University Press, 2005)

Sieburg, Friedrich, *Es werde Deutschland* (Frankfurt am Main: Societäts-Verlag, 1933)

Sieburg, Friedrich, *Neues Portugal: Bildnis eines alten Landes* (Frankfurt am Main: Societäts-Verlag, 1937)

Silex, Karl, *Mit Kommentar: Lebensbericht eines Journalisten* (Frankfurt am Main: S. Fischer, 1968)

Simpson, Christopher, "Elisabeth Noelle-Neumann's 'Spiral of Silence' and the Historical Context of Communication Theory," *Journal of Communication* 46 (1996): 149–73

Siska, Heinz W., ed., *Wunderwelt Film: Künstler und Werkleute einer Weltmacht* (Heidelberg: Verlagsanstalt Hüthig & Co., 1943)

Slansky, Peter, *Filmhochschulen in Deutschland: Geschichte – Typologie – Architektur* (Munich: edition text + kritik, 2011)

Slesina, Horst, *Soldaten gegen Tod und Teufel: Unser Kampf in der Sowjetunion: Eine soldatische Deutung* (Düsseldorf: Völkischer Verlag, [1942])

Slonimsky, Nicolas, *Music Since 1900*, 4th edn (New York: Scribner's, 1971)

Söderbaum, Kristina, *Nichts bleibt immer so: Rückblenden auf ein Leben vor und hinter der Kamera*, 3rd edn (Bayreuth: Hestia, 1984)

Söhnker, Hans, . . . *und kein Tag zuviel* (Hamburg: R. Glöss + Co., 1974)

Sontheimer, Kurt, *Antidemokratisches Denken in der Weimarer Republik: Die politischen Ideen des deutschen Nationalismus zwischen 1918 und 1933*, 4th edn (Munich: Nymphenburger Verlagshandlung, 1962)

Sösemann, Bernd, "Journalismus im Griff der Diktatur: Die 'Frankfurter Zeitung' in der nationalsozialistischen Pressepolitik," in Christoph Studt, ed., *"Diener des Staates" oder "Widerstand zwischen den Zeilen"? Die Rolle der Presse im "Dritten Reich"* (Berlin: LIT VERLAG, 2007), 11–38

Sösemann, Bernd, "Voraussetzungen und Wirkungen publizistischer Opposition im Dritten Reich," *Publizistik* 30 (1985): 195–215

Speer, Albert, *Erinnerungen*, 8th edn (Frankfurt am Main: Propyläen, 1970)

Speer, Albert, "Vorwort," in Rudolf Wolters, *Neue Deutsche Baukunst* (Berlin: Volk und Reich, 1940), 7–14

Spieker, Markus, *Hollywood unterm Hakenkreuz: Der amerikanische Spielfilm im Dritten Reich* (Trier: Wissenschaftlicher Verlag, 1999)

Spoto, Donald, *Blue Angel: The Life of Marlene Dietrich* (New York: Doubleday, 1992)

Spotts, Frederic, *Bayreuth: A History of the Wagner Festival* (New Haven: Yale University Press, 1994)

Spotts, Frederic, *Cursed Legacy: The Tragic Life of Klaus Mann* (New Haven: Yale University Press, 2016)

Spotts, Frederic, *Hitler and the Power of Aesthetics* (Woodstock: Overlook Press, 2003)

Sprengel, Peter, *Abschied von Osmundis: Zwanzig Studien zu Gerhart Hauptmann* (Dresden: Neisse Verlag, 2011)

SS im Einsatz: Eine Dokumentation über die Verbrechen der SS (Berlin: Deutscher Militärverlag, 1967)

Stang, Walter, *Grundlagen nationalsozialistischer Kulturpflege* (Berlin: Junker & Dünnhaupt, 1935)

Stang, Walter, "Nationalsozialismus und Theater: Zur Einführung," *Süddeutsche Monatshefte* 31 (April 1934): 387–91

Stang, Walter, "Weltanschauung und Kulturpflege," *Bausteine zum deutschen Nationaltheater* 2, no. 7 (July/August 1934): 193–200

Stargardt–Wolff, Edith, *Wegbereiter grosser Musiker* (Berlin: Bote und Bock, 1954)

Starr, S. Frederick, *Red and Hot: The Fate of Jazz in the Soviet Union, 1917–1980* (New York: Oxford University Press, 1983)

Statistisches Jahrbuch für das Deutsche Reich 1924/25 (Berlin: Paul Schmidt, 1925)

Statistisches Jahrbuch für das Deutsche Reich 1938 (Berlin: Paul Schmidt, 1938)

Stauffer, Teddy, *Forever is a Hell of a Long Time: An Autobiography* (Chicago: Henry Regnery, 1976)

Stefan Wolpe: Von Berlin nach New York: 14., 15. und 16. September 1988: Sechs Konzerte in der Musikhochschule Köln (Aula), [ed. Westdeutscher Rundfunk Köln] (Saarbrücken: Pfau, 1998)

Stege, Fritz, "Gibt es eine 'deutsche Jazzkapelle'? Die Lehren des Tanzkapellen-Wettbewerbs im Rundfunk," *Zeitschrift für Instrumentenbau* 56 (1936): 251–3

Steguweit, Heinz, *Der Herr Baron fährt ein: Eine Komödie in drei Akten* (Leipzig: Dietzmann-Verlag, 1934)

Steguweit, Heinz, *Heilige Unrast: Roman* (Hamburg: Hanseatische Verlagsanstalt, 1935)

Steguweit, Heinz, *Mit vergnügten Sinnen: Kleine Hauspostille* (Hamburg: Hanseatische Verlagsanstalt, 1938)

Steguweit, Heinz, *Petermann schliesst Frieden oder Das Gleichnis vom deutschen Opfer: Ein Weihnachtsspiel* (Hamburg: Hanseatische Verlagsanstalt, 1933)

Steguweit, Heinz, *Und alles ist Melodie: Verse, Lieder und Balladen* (Hamburg: Hanseatische Verlagsanstalt, 1936)

Stein, Erwin, ed., *Arnold Schoenberg: Letters* (New York: St. Martin's Press, 1965)

Stein, Fritz, "Chorwesen und Volksmusik im neuen Deutschland," *Zeitschrift für Musik* 101 (1934): 281–8

Steinbeck, Dietrich, "Jürgen Fehlings 'Tannhäuser' von 1933," in Gerhard Ahrens, ed., *Das Theater des deutschen Regisseurs Jürgen Fehling* (Berlin: Quadriga Verlag J. Severin, 1985), 134–7

Steinborn, Willi, "Der Erzähler Martin Raschke," *Die Neue Literatur* 41, no. 3 (1940): 61–5

Steiner, Maria, *Paula Wessely: Die verdrängten Jahre* (Vienna: Verlag für Gesellschaftskritik GmbH, 1996)

Steinert, Marlis, *Hitlers Krieg und die Deutschen: Stimmung und Haltung der deutschen Bevölkerung im Zweiten Weltkrieg* (Düsseldorf: Econ, 1970)

Steinkamp, Maike, "Eine wahrhaft deutsche Schöpfung: Der Kampf um Emil Noldes 'Abendmahl' vom Kaiserreich zur frühen DDR," in Uwe Fleckner, ed., *Das verfemte Meisterwerk: Schicksalswege moderner Kunst im "Dritten Reich"* (Berlin: Akademie Verlag, 2009), 283–306

Steinweis, Alan E., "Anti-Semitism and the Arts in Nazi Ideology and Policy," in Jonathan Huener and Francis R. Nicosia, eds, *The Arts in Nazi Germany: Continuity, Conformity, Change* (New York: Berghahn, 2007), 15–30

Steinweis, Alan E., *Art, Ideology, and Economics in Nazi Germany: The Reich Chambers of Music, Theater, and the Visual Arts* (Chapel Hill: The University of North Carolina Press, 1993)

Steinweis, Alan E., "Conservatism, National Socialism, and the Cultural Crisis of the Weimar Republic," in Larry Eugene Jones and James Retallack, eds, *Between Reform, Reaction, and Resistance: Studies in the History of German Conservatism from 1789 to 1945* (Providence: Berg, 1993), 329–46

Steinweis, Alan E., "Weimar Culture and the Rise of National Socialism: The *Kampfbund für deutsche Kultur*," *Central European History* 24 (1991): 402–23

Stelzner, Fritz, *Schicksal SA.: Die Deutung eines grossen Geschehens von einem, der es selbst erlebte* (Munich: Eher, 1936)

Stern, Carola, *Auf den Wassern des Lebens: Gustaf Gründgens und Marianne Hoppe* (Cologne: Kiepenheuer & Witsch, 2005)

Sternburg, Wilhelm von, *"Als wäre alles das letzte Mal": Erich Maria Remarque: Eine Biographie* (Cologne: Kiepenheuer & Witsch, 1998)

Stites, Richard, *Russian Popular Culture: Entertainment and Society since 1900* (Cambridge: Cambridge University Press, 1992)

Stockhorst, Erich, *Fünftausend Köpfe: Wer war was im Dritten Reich* (Velbert: blick + bild Verlag, 1967)

Stollmann, Rainer, "Die krummen Wege zu Hitler: Das Nazi-Selbstbildnis im SA-Roman," in Martin Damus et al., *Kunst und Kultur im deutschen Faschismus* (Stuttgart: Metzler, 1978), 191–215

Stone, Marla Susan, *The Patron State: Culture and Politics in Fascist Italy* (Princeton: Princeton University Press, 1998)

Stöve, Günther, "Über die geschichtliche Dichtung," *Bücherkunde* 7, no. 6 (June 1940): 147–54

Strätz, Hans-Wolfgang, "Die studentische 'Aktion wider den Undeutschen Geist' im Frühjahr 1933," *Vierteljahrshefte für Zeitgeschichte* 16 (1968): 347–72

Strauss, Emil, *Lebenstanz: Roman* (Munich: Langen Müller, 1940)

Streit, Christian, *Keine Kameraden: Die Wehrmacht und die sowjetischen Kriegsgefangenen, 1941–1945*, 2nd edn (Stuttgart: Deutsche Verlags-Anstalt, 1978)

Strobl, Gerwin, *The Swastika and the Stage: German Theatre and Society, 1933–1945* (Cambridge: Cambridge University Press, 2007)

Strobl, Karl Hans, *Dorf im Kaukasus: Roman* (Budweis-Berlin: Verlagsanstalt Moldavia, 1944; first publ. 1936)

Strothmann, Dietrich, *Nationalsozialistische Literaturpolitik: Ein Beitrag zur Publizistik im Dritten Reich*, 3rd edn (Bonn: H. Bouvier, 1968)

Symonette, Lys, and Kim H. Kowalke, eds, *Speak Low (When You Speak Love): The Letters of Kurt Weill and Lotte Lenya* (Berkeley: University of California Press, 1996)

Talbot, George, *Censorship in Fascist Italy, 1922–43* (Houndmills: Palgrave Macmillan, 2007)

Taylor, John Russell, *Strangers in Paradise: The Hollywood Emigrés, 1933–1950* (New York: Holt, Rinehart & Winston, 1983)

Tegel, Susan, *Nazis and the Cinema* (London: Hambledon Continuum, 2007)

Tergit, Gabriele, "Die Exilsituation in England," in Manfred Durzak, ed., *Die deutsche Exilliteratur 1933–1945* (Stuttgart: Philipp Reclam jun., 1973), 135–44

Teut, Anna, ed., *Architektur im Dritten Reich, 1933–1945* (Berlin: Ullstein, 1967)

Thacker, Toby, *Music after Hitler, 1945–1955* (Aldershot: Ashgate, 2007)

Theater von A–Z: Handbuch des deutschen Theaterwesens (Berlin: Theater-Tageblatt GmbH, 1934)

Theweleit, Klaus, *Male Fantasies*, 2 vols (Cambridge: Polity, 2006)

Thies, Jochen, *Hitler's Plans for Global Domination: Nazi Architecture and Ultimate War Aims* (New York: Berghahn, 2012)

Thomae, Otto, *Die Propaganda-Maschinerie: Bildende Kunst und Öffentlichkeitsarbeit im Dritten Reich* (Berlin: Gebr. Mann, 1978)

Thomas Mann, Agnes Meyer: Briefwechsel 1937–1955, ed. Hans Rudolf Vaget (Frankfurt: S. Fischer, 1992)

Tiedt, Yvonne, *Es leuchten die Sterne: Die grosse Zeit des deutschen Films* (Bergisch Gladbach: Lingen, 1995)

Tonietti, Tito M., "Albert Einstein and Arnold Schönberg: Correspondence," *NTM Zeitschrift für Geschichte der Wissenschaften, Technik und Medizin* 5 (1997): 1–22

Traber, Habakuk, and Elmar Weingarten, eds, *Verdrängte Musik: Berliner Komponisten im Exil* (Berlin: Aragon, 1987)

Traub, Hans, *Der Film als politisches Machtmittel* (Munich: Münchener Druck- und Verlagshaus, 1933)

Traub, Hans, *Die UFA* (Berlin: [publisher unknown], 1943)

Tremel-Eggert, Kuni, *Barb: Der Roman einer deutschen Frau* (Munich: Eher, 1935)

Tremel-Eggert, Kuni, *Der Schmied von Hassberg: Roman* (Munich: Eher, 1937)

Trepte, Curt, and Jutta Wardetzky, eds, *Hans Otto: Schauspieler und Revolutionär* (Berlin: Henschelverlag, 1970)

Trommler, Frank, "A Command Performance? The Many Faces of Literature under Nazism," in Jonathan Huener and Francis R. Nicosia, eds, *The Arts in Nazi Germany: Continuity, Conformity, Change* (New York: Berghahn, 2007), 111–33

Trotha, Thilo von, "Rasse und Bühne," *Deutsche Bühnenkorrespondenz* 3, no. 31 (April 21, 1934): 1–2

Trunz, Erich, *Deutsche Dichtung der Gegenwart: Eine Bildnisreihe* (Berlin: Georg Stilke, 1937)

Tschechowa, Olga, *Meine Uhren gehen anders* (Munich: Herbig, 1973)

Türcke, Berthold, "Fortgegangene Klänge: Die Wiener Schule – ihr symbiotisches Verhältnis von Komposition und Interpretation im Exil," in Friedrich Geiger and Thomas Schäfer, eds, *Exilmusik: Komposition während der NS-Zeit* (Hamburg: Von Bockel Verlag, 1999), 20–55

Ullrich, Luise, *Komm auf die Schaukel Luise: Balance eines Lebens*, 2nd edn (Percha: R. S. Schulz, 1973)

Ullrich, Volker, *Hitler: Ascent 1889–1939* (London: The Bodley Head, 2016)

Vaget, Hans Rudolf, "Nazi Cinema and Wagner," *Wagner Journal* 9, no. 2 (2015): 35–54

Vaget, Hans Rudolf, "Schlechtes Wetter, gutes Klima: Thomas Mann und die Schweiz," in *Thomas Mann-Handbuch*, ed. Helmut Koopmann (Stuttgart: Kröner, 1990), 68–77

Vaget, Hans Rudolf, *Seelenzauber: Thomas Mann und die Musik* (Frankfurt am Main: S. Fischer, 2006)

Vaget, Hans Rudolf, *Thomas Mann, der Amerikaner: Leben und Werk im amerikanischen Exil, 1938–1952* (Frankfurt am Main: S. Fischer, 2011)

Vaget, Hans Rudolf, *"Wehvolles Erbe": Richard Wagner in Deutschland: Hitler, Knappertsbusch, Mann* (Frankfurt am Main: S. Fischer, 2017)

Varga, William P., *The Number One Nazi Jew-Baiter: A Political Biography of Julius Streicher, Hitler's Chief Anti-Semitic Propagandist* (New York: Carlton Press, 1981)

Varnay, Astrid, *Fifty-Five Years in Five Acts: My Life in Opera* (Boston: Northeastern University Press, 2000)

Velmede, August Friedrich, ed., *Dem Führer: Worte deutscher Dichter: Zum Geburtstag des Führers 1941: Tournisterschrift des Oberkommandos der Wehrmacht [Abteilung Inland]*, Heft 37 (n.pl., n.d.)

Vesper, Will, *Geschichten von Liebe, Traum und Tod: Gesamtausgabe meiner Novellen* (Munich: Langen Müller, 1937)

Vesper, Will, *Wer? Wen? Ein Lustspiel* (Leipzig: H. Haessel, 1927)

Viertel, Salka, *The Kindness of Strangers* (New York: Holt, Rinehart, and Winston, 1969)

Vogelsang, Konrad, *Filmmusik im Dritten Reich: Die Dokumentation* (Hamburg: Facta Oblita, 1990)

Volck, Herbert, *Rebellen um Ehre: Mein Kampf für die nationale Erhebung 1918–33* (Gütersloh: Bertelsmann, 1939; 1st edn 1932)

Volker, Reimar, *"Von oben sehr erwünscht": Die Filmmusik Herbert Windts im NS-Propagandafilm* (Trier: Wissenschaftlicher Verlag, 2003)

Volz, Hans, *Daten der Geschichte der NSDAP*, 9th edn (Berlin: A. G. Ploetz, 1939)

Volz, Hans, ed., *Von der Grossmacht zur Weltmacht 1937* (Berlin: Junker & Dünnhaupt, 1938)

Vossler, Frank, *Propaganda in die eigene Truppe: Die Truppenbetreuung in der Wehrmacht, 1939–1945* (Paderborn: Schöningh, 2005)

Wagner, Nike, *Wagner Theater* (Frankfurt am Main: Insel, 1998)

Wähler, Martin, "Das politische Kampflied als Volkslied der Gegenwart," *Mitteldeutsche Blätter für Volkskunde* 8, no. 5 (October 1933): 145–56

Waibel, Harry, *Diener vieler Herren: Ehemalige NS-Funktionäre in der SBZ/DDR* (Frankfurt am Main: Peter Lang, 2011)

Walk, Joseph, ed., *Das Sonderrecht für die Juden im NS-Staat: Eine Sammlung der gesetzlichen Massnahmen und Richtlinien – Inhalt und Bedeutung* (Heidelberg: C. F. Müller, 1981)

Walter, Bruno, *Thema und Variationen: Erinnerungen und Gedanken* (Frankfurt am Main: S. Fischer, 1988)

Walter, Hans-Albert, "Deutsche Literatur im Exil: Ein Modellfall für die Zusammenhänge von Literatur und Politik," *Merkur* 25, no. 1 (January 1971): 77–84

Walter, Michael, *Hitler in der Oper: Deutsches Musikleben, 1919–1945* (Stuttgart: J. B. Metzler, 1995)

Walter, Michael, *Richard Strauss und seine Zeit* (Laaber: Laaber, 2000)

Wanderscheck, Hermann, *Deutsche Dramatik der Gegenwart: Eine Einführung mit ausgewählten Textproben* (Berlin: Bong & Co., [1938])

Wapnewski, Peter, *Mit dem anderen Auge: Erinnerungen, 1922–1959* (Berlin: Berlin-Verlag, 2005)

Wardetzky, Jutta, "Ein politischer Schauspieler: Biografie mit zeitgenössischen Dokumenten," in Curt Trepte and Jutta Wardetzky, eds, *Hans Otto: Schauspieler und Revolutionär* (Berlin: Henschelverlag, 1970), 15–75

Wardetzky, Jutta, *Theaterpolitik im faschistischen Deutschland: Studien und Dokumente* (Berlin: Henschelverlag, 1983)

Wasserstein, Bernard, *Britain and the Jews of Europe, 1939–1945* (Oxford: Oxford University Press, 1979)

Weber, Thomas, *Becoming Hitler: The Making of a Nazi* (New York: Basic Books, 2017)

Weber, Thomas, *Hitler's First War: Adolf Hitler, the Men of the List Regiment and the First World War* (Oxford: Oxford University Press, 2010)

Wegner, Matthias, *Exil und Literatur: Deutsche Schriftsteller im Ausland, 1933–1945*, 2nd edn (Frankfurt am Main: Athenäum, 1968)

Wegner, Matthias, *Klabund und Carola Neher: Eine Geschichte von Liebe und Tod* (Berlin: Rowohlt, 1996)

Wehler, Hans-Ulrich, *Deutsche Gesellschaftsgeschichte: Fünfter Band: Bundesrepublik und DDR, 1949–1990* (Munich: C. H. Beck, 2008)

Wehler, Hans-Ulrich, *Deutsche Gesellschaftsgeschichte: Vierter Band: Vom Beginn des Ersten Weltkriegs bis zur Gründung der beiden deutschen Staaten, 1914–1949* (Munich: C. H. Beck, 2003)

Weigert, Hans, *Die Kunst von heute als Spiegel der Zeit* (Leipzig: E. A. Seemann, 1934)

Weimarer Reden des Grossdeutschen Dichtertreffens 1938 (Hamburg: Hanseatische Verlagsanstalt, 1939)

Weinberg, Gerhard L., *A World at Arms: A Global History of World War II* (Cambridge: Cambridge University Press, 1994)

Weise, Georg, "Die Aussprache über das Nordische in der deutschen Kunst," *Zeitschrift für Deutschkunde* 49 (1935): 397–412

Weisenborn, Günther, *Das Mädchen von Fanö: Roman* (Berlin: Gustav Kiepenheuer, 1935)

Weiss, Heinz, ed., *Rundfunk im Aufbruch: Handbuch des deutschen Rundfunks 1934 mit Funkkalender* (Lahr: Moritz Schauenburg, [1934])

Weissler, Sabine, "Bauhaus-Gestaltung in NS-Propaganda-Ausstellungen," in Winfried Nerdinger, ed., *Bauhaus-Moderne im Nationalsozialismus: Zwischen Anbiederung und Verfolgung* (Munich: Prestel, 1993), 48–63

Welch, David, *Propaganda and the German Cinema, 1933–1945* (Oxford: Clarendon Press, 1983)

Weller, Tüdel, *Rabauken! Peter Mönkemann haut sich durch* (Munich: Eher, 1938)

Wendland, Winfried, *Kunst und Nation: Ziel und Wege der Kunst im Neuen Deutschland* (Berlin: Reimar Hobbing, 1934)

Werbick, Peter, "Der faschistische historische Roman in Deutschland," in Martin Damus et al., *Kunst und Kultur im deutschen Faschismus* (Stuttgart: Metzler, 1978), 157–90

Werckmeister, Otto Karl, "Hitler the Artist," *Critical Inquiry* 23 (1997): 270–97

Werkhäuser, Fritz Richard, ed., *150 Jahre Theater der Stadt Koblenz* (Koblenz: Nationalverlag, 1937)

Werner, Ilse, *So wird's nie wieder sein . . .: Ein Leben mit Pfiff*, 5th edn (Bayreuth: Hestia, 1982)

Werr, Sebastian, *Heroische Weltsicht: Hitler und die Musik* (Cologne: Böhlau, 2014)

Werwigk, Sara Eskilsson, "Ein Gemälde geht ins Exil: Auf den Spuren der 'Kreuzabnahme' von Max Beckmann," in Uwe Fleckner, ed., *Das verfemte Meisterwerk: Schicksalswege moderner Kunst im "Dritten Reich"* (Berlin: Akademie Verlag, 2009), 105–36

Westecker, Wilhelm, *Krieg und Kunst: Das Erlebnis des Weltkrieges und des Grossdeutschen Freiheitskrieges* (Vienna: Wiener Verlag, 1944)

Wetzel, Kraft, and Peter A. Hagemann, *Zensur – Verbotene deutsche Filme, 1933–1945* (Berlin: Volker Spiess, 1978)

Wezel, Emil, "Ein kleiner Wunschzettel zur Sonderausgabe von Büchern für die Waffen-SS," *SS-Leitheft* 9 (August 1943): 27–30

Wicclair, Walter, *Von Kreuzburg bis Hollywood* (Berlin: Henschelverlag, 1975)

Wiechert, Ernst, "Brief an einen jungen Dichter," in Heinz Kindermann, ed., *Des deutschen Dichters Sendung in der Gegenwart* (Leipzig: Philipp Reclam jun., 1933), 175–9

Wiechert, Ernst, *Das einfache Leben: Roman* (Munich: Langen Müller, 1939)

Wiechert, Ernst, *Der Totenwolf: Roman* (Berlin: G. Grote'sche Verlagsbuchhandlung, 1935; 1st edn 1924)

Wiechert, Ernst, *Jahre und Zeiten: Erinnerungen* (Erlenbach-Zurich: Eugen Rentsch, 1949)

Wilkens, Josef, "Das Schriftleitergesetz im Urteil des In- und Auslandes," *Zeitungswissenschaft* 8, no. 6 (1933): 361–94

Willett, John, "Die Künste in der Emigration," in Gerhard Hirschfeld, ed., *Exil in Grossbritannien: Zur Emigration aus dem nationalsozialistischen Deutschland* (Stuttgart: Klett, 1983), 183–204

Willett, John, *The New Sobriety, 1917–1933: Art and Politics in the Weimar Period* (London: Thames and Hudson, 1978)

Willrich, Wolfgang, "Eine hohe Aufgabe Deutscher Kunst: Die Darstellung des vollwertigen Germanischen Menschen," *Volk und Rasse* 9 (September 1934): 275–88

Willrich, Wolfgang, *Kunst und Volksgesundheit* (Berlin: Reichsausschuss für Volksgesundheitsdienst, 1935)

Willrich, Wolfgang, *Säuberung des Kunsttempels: Eine kunstpolitische Kampfschrift zur Gesundung deutscher Kunst im Geiste nordischer Art* (Munich: J. F. Lehmanns, 1937)

Wingler, Hans M., *The Bauhaus: Weimar, Dessau, Berlin, Chicago* (Cambridge, MA: MIT University Press, 1986)

Winkler, Heinrich August, "Die deutsche Gesellschaft der Weimarer Republik und der Antisemitismus," in Bernd Martin and Ernst Schulin, eds, *Die Juden als Minderheit in der Geschichte*, 2nd edn (Munich: DTV, 1982), 271–89

Wirsing, Giselher, *Das Zeitalter des Ikaros: Von Gesetz und Grenzen unseres Jahrhunderts* (Jena: Eugen Diederichs, 1944)

Wischmann, Friedrich, *Vogt Boy Fedders: Ein Schauspiel in fünf Akten* (Leipzig: Dietzmann-Verlag, 1935)

Wistrich, Robert, *Who's Who in Nazi Germany* (New York: Macmillan, 1982)

Wolf, Arie, "Stationen des geistigen Wandels des Haifaer Exilanten Arnold Zweig," in Arthur Thilo Alt and Julia Bernhard, eds, *Arnold Zweig: Sein Werk im Kontext der deutschsprachigen Exilliteratur: Akten des IV. Internationalen Arnold-Zweig-Symposiums (Durham [N.C.])* (Bern: Peter Lang, 1999), 212–27

Wühr, Hans, "Graphik: Politische Kunst," *Die Kunst im Dritten Reich* 2, no. 6 (June 1938): 164–8

Wulf, Joseph, ed., *Die bildenden Künste im dritten Reich: Eine Dokumentation* (Gütersloh: Sigbert Mohn, 1963)

Wulf, Joseph, ed., *Literatur und Dichtung im Dritten Reich: Eine Dokumentation* (Frankfurt am Main: Ullstein, 1983)

Wulf, Joseph, ed., *Musik im Dritten Reich: Eine Dokumentation* (Reinbek: rororo, 1966)

Wulf, Joseph, ed., *Presse und Funk im Dritten Reich: Eine Dokumentation* (Reinbek: rororo, 1966)

Wulf, Joseph, ed., *Theater und Film im Dritten Reich: Eine Dokumentation* (Reinbek: rororo, 1968)

Zander, Otto, and Kurt Willimczik, eds, *Reichstheatertage der HJ in Hamburg vom 23. Bis 30. Oktober 1938* (Berlin: Wilhelm Limpert, 1938)

Zeller, Bernhard, ed., *Klassiker in finsteren Zeiten, 1933–1945: Eine Ausstellung des Deutschen Literaturarchivs im Schiller-Nationalmuseum, Marbach am Neckar*, 2nd edn, 2 vols (Marbach: Schiller-Nationalmuseum, 1983)

Zerkaulen, Heinrich, *Hörnerklang der Frühe: Roman* (Berlin: Hochwart-Verlag Junker, 1934)

Zerkaulen, Heinrich, *Jugend von Langemarck: Ein Schauspiel in drei Akten und einem Nachspiel* (Leipzig: Dietzmann-Verlag, 1933)

Ziegler, Hans Severus, *Entartete Musik: Eine Abrechnung* (Düsseldorf: Völkischer Verlag, [1938])

Ziegler, Hans Severus, *Wende und Weg: Kulturpolitische Reden und Aufsätze* (Weimar: Fritz Fink, 1937)

Ziegler, Wilhelm, ed., *Ein Dokumentenwerk über die englische Humanität: Im Auftrage des Reichsministeriums für Volksaufklärung und Propaganda* (Berlin: Deutscher Verlag, [1940])

Ziesel, Kurt, ed., *Krieg und Dichtung: Soldaten werden Dichter – Dichter werden Soldaten: Ein Volksbuch* (Vienna: Luser, 1940)

Zillich, Heinrich, "Die deutsche Dichtung und die Welt der Geschichte: Vortrag, gehalten beim Ersten Grossdeutschen Dichtertreffen in Weimar am 28. Oktober 1938," *Das Innere Reich* (January 1939): 1,179–96

Zimmermann, Peter, "Von der Literatur der Konservativen Revolution zur Gleichschaltung des kulturellen Sektors," in Jan Berg et al., *Sozialgeschichte der deutschen Literatur von 1918 bis zur Gegenwart* (Frankfurt am Main: Fischer Taschenbuch, 1981), 364–416

Zöberlein, Hans, *Der Befehl des Gewissens: Ein Roman von den Wirren der Nachkriegszeit und der ersten Erhebung* (Munich: Eher, 1937)

Zöberlein, Hans, *Der Glaube an Deutschland: in Kriegserleben von Verdun bis zum Umsturz*, 37th edn (Munich: Eher, 1941; 1st edn 1931)

Zuckmayer, Carl, *Als wär's ein Stück von mir: Horen der Freundschaft* (Frankfurt am Main: Fischer-Bücherei, 1971)

Zuckmayer, Carl, *Geheimreport*, ed. Gunther Nickel and Johanna Schrön, 2nd edn (Munich: DTV, 2007)

Zündende Lieder – Verbrannte Musik: Folgen des Nationalsozialismus für Hamburger Musiker und Musikerinnen: Katalog zur Ausstellung in Hamburg im November und Dezember 1988 (Hamburg: VSA-Verlag, 1988)

Zur Mühlen, Patrik von, *Fluchtziel Lateinamerika: Die deutsche Emigration, 1933–1945: Politische Aktivitäten und soziokulturelle Integration* (Bonn: Verlag Neue Gesellschaft, 1988)

Zweig, Arnold, *Insulted and Exiled: The Truth about the German Jews* (London: J. Miles, 1937)

Zweig, Stefan, *Die Welt von Gestern: Erinnerungen eines Europäers* (Berlin: G. B. Fischer, 1965)

Index

Reichskulturkammer (RKK), Berlin xiii, 17,
25–6, 39, 81, 85, 92, 105, 110, 118, 134, 167,
204, 209, 222–3, 306, 322, 330, 336, 339
Reichsmusikkammer (RMK), Berlin 26, 28,
48, 84, 100, 103, 106–7, 123, 169, 209,
211–12, 279, 306, 324
Reichs-Rundfunk-Gesellschaft (RRG),
Berlin 15, 81, 204, 207–8
Reichsrundfunkkammer, Berlin 81–84
Reichsschrifttumkammer (RSK), Berlin 25,
32, 222, 227
Reichstag fire, Berlin, 1933 167
Reichstag Fire Decree, February 1933 11
Reichsverband der Deutschen Presse,
Berlin 26
Reifenberg, Benno 78
Reinecker, Herbert 218
Reinhardt, Gottfried 263–4
Reinhardt, Max 4, 92, 161, 188, 258, 261,
263, 303
Reinhart, Hans 168
Reizenstein, Franz 256
Remarque, Erich Maria 21, 68, 251, 271,
273–5, 281, 283, 287, 302, 382n88
Rentschler, Eric xv, 341n2
Reutter, Hermann 13–14
Revolution of 1848–9 248
Rexroth, H. G. 225–6
Ribbentrop, Joachim von 235, 354n158
Richard II, drama 28
Richard II, King of England 41
Richter, Hans Werner 301
Richter, Ludwig 113
Richthofen Squadron 174
Richthofen, Baron Manfred von 111, 223
Riefenstahl, Leni 8, 88–90, 95, 110, 126,
137, 174, 187, 196, 304, 315, 339,
342n27, 354n181
Riethmüller, Albrecht 107, 355n183
Rilke, Rainer Maria 168
Rio Rita, nightclub, Berlin 3
Ritter, Carl 188
Robert und Bertram, film 166
Robeson, Paul 260
Robinson, Edward G. 261
Rode, Wilhelm 213
Röder, Werner 250
Rodin, Auguste 117
Röhm, Ernst 36
Röhm Putsch, 1934 10, 39, 66, 69, 88, 96,
123, 134, 336
Rökk, Marika 180, 194
Rolland, Romain 160

Roman race laws, 1938 332
Romanisches Café, Berlin 182
Romanticism 60–1, 80, 101–2, 106, 144
Romanych, Marc 362n18
Rommel, Erwin 172, 176, 233, 291
Rönne, novels 30
Roosevelt, Eleanor 312
Roosevelt, Franklin D. 162, 164, 285,
288–9, 295–6
Rosalinda, musical 262
Rosbaud, Hans 214
Rosegger, Peter 76, 123
Rosenberg, Alfred 5–6, 17–20, 24, 26–8,
33, 36–40, 42, 53, 65, 69, 80, 88, 91, 93,
97, 99, 103, 109–10, 112, 120, 123,
125–7, 133, 146, 185, 200, 222, 241,
305–6, 321–3, 334, 346n147, 348n4,
361n323, 376n234, 387n27
Rosenman, Samuel 164, 367n161
Rosenstock, Joseph 144
Rosita Bar, Berlin, nightclub 20, 170
Rosner, Adi 169
Ross, Alex 64, 109, 348n13, 392n8
Rote Fahne, Berlin, newspaper 15
Roth, Joseph 270, 286
Rotholz, Arthur 170
Rotholz, Louis 169
Rothschild, Nathan 155
Rottenberg Ludwig 49, 147
Royal Air Force 182
Royal Opera, Copenhagen 277
Royal Swedish Academy, Stockholm 283
Rubinstein, Helena 239
Ruck, Albert 168
Rühmann, Heinz 136, 315, 363n40
Rumpf, Heinrich 16
Rust, Bernhard 14, 42, 46, 124–5, 306

SA (storm troopers) 9, 11, 21–2, 36, 52, 56,
66, 72, 80, 83, 88, 95, 98, 105, 110–14,
123, 136–7, 139, 149–50, 152, 166–7,
233, 261, 274–5, 310–11, 319
SA-Mann Brand, film 86–8, 315, 354n166
Sachsenhausen, concentration camp 151
Sack of Rome, 410 AD 70
Said, Edward W. 265
Salazar, António de Oliveira 77
Salburg, Edith Gräfin 67, 154
Saliger, Ivo 116
Salome, opera 2
Salomon, Ernst von 389n76
Salzburg Festival 214–15, 230, 240
Satie, Erik 48